# Tolley's Internationa

# Introduction

## Nature of international tax planning

The taxation of UK companies with cross-border activities is complex. It requires consideration of three things:

- aspects of UK tax law which do not generally apply to companies with activities only in the UK, such as the controlled foreign company rules or double tax relief;
- overseas tax law, which may apply to the UK company; and
- the interaction of the UK and overseas tax laws and the use of double tax treaties.

With this complexity, there are also planning opportunities, where it is possible to take advantage of differences in tax treatment and tax rates between jurisdictions.

However, with the advent of the BEPS provisions the possibilities for exploiting mismatches between countries may be significantly reduced. With BEPS seeking to limit more aggressive tax planning, it is more important than ever that UK companies trading overseas get the basics right. Amongst other things, this includes:

- identifying compliance obligations, and minimising them as far as possible;
- ensuring that income is not taxed in more than one jurisdiction, or is taxed at the lowest available rate;
- identifying when a permanent establishment has been created in another jurisdiction so that tax returns can be filed;
- transfer pricing compliance obligations for transactions between companies in different jurisdictions;
- ensuring that overseas trading subsidiaries issue 'ordinary share capital' so that a future disposal qualifies for the substantial shareholding exemption;
- structuring trading activities so that double tax relief is available and overseas tax can be credited against UK corporation tax;
- reducing withholding taxes on cross-border interest, royalties and other payments.

This book focuses on international tax planning for companies. However, it also recognises that all companies have shareholders, to whom anti-avoidance laws may apply as a result of income or gains arising in the company—for example under ITA 2007, s 720 or TCGA 1992, s 13.

## Structure of the book

This book is structured in three parts.

Part A provides a comprehensive discussion of international tax principles and the UK tax laws which apply to cross-border activities. Each chapter includes sections on both basic principles and planning techniques.

The sections on basic principles can act as an introduction to the topic for those who are new to international tax planning and as a reference for specialists.

All sections are supported by the comprehensive index at the end of the book, and there are flowcharts, checklists and tables to assist with the more complex areas.

Part B comprises case studies and practice guides covering the common scenarios where international tax planning is undertaken. These draw together the topics covered in Part A, and each Chapter in Part B closes with a checklist which is cross-referenced to the relevant Chapters in Part A.

Part C provides an overview of some overseas tax systems and the basis of liability to tax. In addition, there are specific chapters on investing in India, China and the US—jurisdictions in which UK companies frequently have activities, and which present practical issues of which an international tax specialist needs to be aware.

## Recent developments

Various sections in this book make reference to the OECD review of base erosion and profit shifting (BEPS) and the development of their 15 point Action Plan to address the fairness and integrity of the global tax system. Further announcements are expected during the next 12 months, and with pressure from the G20, the OECD is timetabled to complete all 15 points in the Action Plan by September 2015.

As this book goes to press, the OECD has just released discussion drafts on two of the BEPS actions. These are on Action 7 (preventing the artificial avoidance of PE status) and Action 10 (low value-adding intra-group services). How each individual country will interpret and adopt the guidelines developed through the Action Plan is, of course, currently unknown as OECD countries are not obliged to fully adopt them. Indeed some of the more significant economies in the world such as India and China, are not full members of the OECD and this could lead to even more of a selective approach as to which of the guidelines they choose to adopt.

The above serves to illustrate not only the extent of the change likely to occur over the next twelve months, but also the current uncertainty inherent within international tax planning. Whilst this book is based on law and practice as at 1 September 2014, international tax advisers must be more aware than ever of the rapidly changing climate in which they advise.

This latest version of the book includes the following new areas:

- Commentary on the potential impact of the OECD Action Plan on Base Erosion and Profits Shifting (BEPS) on international tax planning

- Commentary on how the new UK General Anti-Abuse Rule (GAAR) can impact international tax planning
- A new section providing an overview of Brazil's tax system
- An explanation of important new tax legislation concerning residential property held by non UK residents and revised examples and planning techniques following the introduction of ATED and ATED-related gain
- An update on UK case law as it affects international tax planning and also updates on EU Court of Justice cases
- Restructured content on the taxation of foreign dividends and branches

## Acknowledgements

I would like to thank Robert Langston at Saffery Champness for his help and guidance as Consultant Editor. This book, in its current form, was largely developed by Robert during his time as author and still remains largely his work. The book is a valuable reference tool which is widely used in the industry. My thanks also go to Arthur Munro-Faure of Grant Thornton for his valuable assistance with the book and the National Tax Team at Grant Thornton for their input into some of the new developments.

Chris Mundy

Grant Thornton UK LLP

November 2014

# About the Author

## Chris Mundy Bmus, FCA, CTA

Chris Mundy is a tax partner at Grant Thornton UK LLP. Chris has spent the last 20 years advising on a wide range of international tax matters from full international restructuring and international flotations, to providing hands on assistance to medium-sized enterprises growing their international footprint. Having previously been a member of Grant Thornton's London based International Tax Team, he now leads the Firm's Thames Valley tax practice – serving the highly international Thames Valley community. He is a regular speaker on international tax matters.

## About the Consultant Editor

Robert Langston CTA

Robert Langston is a partner with Saffery Champness where he specialises in advising companies and their shareholders on UK and international tax matters.

Before specialising in international tax, he worked in a number of different areas of tax, including personal and corporate tax compliance and transactions tax.

He may be contacted by email at robertlangston@gmail.com

# Contents

# Contents

# Contents

# Contents

# Contents

# Contents

Contents

Contents

# Contents

Contents

# Contents

**B4 UK companies setting up overseas**

**B5 Supply chain planning**

# Contents

**PART C    OVERVIEW OF SOME OVERSEAS TAX SYSTEMS**

**C1 An overview of some overseas tax systems**

Contents

Contents

# List of abbreviations

## Abbreviations

| | |
|---|---|
| ABA | Agricultural Building Allowance |
| BATR | Business Asset Taper Relief |
| BPR | Business Property Relief |
| CAA 2001 | Capital Allowances Act 2001 |
| CGT | Capital Gains Tax |
| CT | Corporation Tax |
| CTA 2009 | Corporation Tax Act 2009 |
| CTA 2010 | Corporation Tax Act 2010 |
| CTM | Corporation Tax Manual (published by HMRC) |
| CTSA | Corporation Tax Self Assessment |
| DTA | Double Tax Agreement |
| EC | European Community |
| ECJ | European Court of Justice |
| EIS | Enterprise Investment Scheme |
| ESC | Extra-Statutory Concession |
| FA | Finance Act |
| FRS | Financial Reporting Standard |
| GAAP | Generally Accepted Accounting Principles |
| HMRC | Her Majesty's Revenue and Customs |
| IAS | Intenational Accounting Standards |
| IBA | Industrial Buildings Allowance |
| ICAEW | Institute of Chartered Accountants in England and Wales |
| ICTA 1988 | Income and Corporation Taxes Act 1988 |
| IHT | Inheritance Tax |
| IHTA 1984 | Inheritance Tax Act 1984 |

| | |
|---|---|
| ITA 2007 | Income Tax Act 2007 |
| ITEPA 2003 | Income Tax (Earnings and Pensions) Act 2003 |
| ITTOIA 2005 | Income Tax (Trading and Other Income) Act 2005 |
| LLP | Limited Liability Partnership |
| NIC | National Insurance Contribution |
| OECD | Organisation for Economic Co-operation and Development |
| PAYE | Pay As You Earn |
| QCB | Qualifying Corporate Bond |
| REIT | Real Estate Investment Trust |
| s | Section |
| Sch | Schedule |
| SD | Stamp Duty |
| SDLT | Stamp Duty Land Tax |
| SI | Statutory Instrument |
| SIPP | Self-Invested Personal Pension |
| SP | Statement of Practice |
| SSAP | Statement of Standard Accounting Practice |
| SSAS | Small Self Administered Scheme |
| TCGA 1992 | Taxation of Chargeable Gains Act 1992 |
| TIOPA 2010 | Taxation (International and Other Provisions) Act 2010 |
| TOGC | Transfer of a Going Concern |
| UITF | Urgent Issues Task Force |
| VAT | Value Added Tax |
| VATA 1994 | Value Added Tax Act 1994 |
| VCT | Venture Capital Trust |

## References (* denotes current series)

| | |
|---|---|
| AC | * Law Reports, Appeal Cases, (Incorporated Council of Law Reporting for England and Wales, 3 Stone Buildings, Lincoln's Inn, London WC2A 3XN). |
| AD | Appellate Division Reports (South Africa) |
| All ER | * All England Law Reports, (LexisNexis, 35 Chancery |

|          | Lane, London WC2A 1EL.) |
|----------|-------------------------|
| App Cas  | Law Reports, Appeal Cases |
| ATC      | Annotated Tax Cases |
| BTC      | * British Tax Cases |
| CB       | Common Bench Reports |
| Ch       | * Law Reports, Chancery Division |
| Ch App   | Law Reports, Chancery Appeals |
| CLR      | Commonwealth Law Reports (Australia) |
| FCR      | Family Court Reports (Australia) |
| KB       | Law Reports, King's Bench Division |
| LR       | Law Reports (followed by Court abbreviation) |
| NZLR     | New Zealand Law Reports |
| SATC     | South African Tax Cases |
| SC       | * Court of Session Cases (Scotland) |
| Sc LR    | Scottish Law Reporter |
| SLT      | Scots Law Times Reports |
| Sp C     | Special Commissioners |
| STC      | * Simon's Tax Cases (LexisNexis, see All ER above) |
| TC       | * Official Tax Cases, The Stationery Office, 123 Kingsway, London WC2B 6PQ. |

# Table of Statutes

Paragraph references printed in **bold** type indicate where the Statute is set out in part or in full.

# Table of Statutory Instruments

Paragraph references printed in **bold** type indicate where the Statutory Instrument is set out in part or in full.

# Table of Cases

## D

## E

## F

## G

## H

## I

# Part A

# Technical discussion

# A1

# Non-UK resident companies' liability to UK tax

## Introduction

**[A1.1]** This Chapter outlines the liability to UK tax of non-UK resident companies. It provides an overview of the factors and circumstances which can create a liability to UK tax.

It is important to understand these factors and circumstances so that a non-UK company can identify its liability to UK tax—and avoid a liability if possible.

These factors and circumstances are set out in more detail in later chapters. In addition, CHAPTER B1 provides a practical guide to non-UK resident companies establishing businesses in the UK.

## Basic principles—taxation of non-resident companies

### *Definition of non-resident*

**[A1.2]** A non-resident company is one which is not a UK resident company. A company will be resident in the UK if:

(a)     it is incorporated in the UK; or

(b)     its place of central management and control is in the UK.

Where a company has dual or multiple residences, the criterion of 'place of effective management' is used as a 'tie-breaker' in most double taxation agreements (DTAs) negotiated by the UK to determine where a company is resident.

The concept of company residence is explored in more detail in CHAPTER A9.

A non-resident company can be liable to either income tax or corporation tax in the UK.

## Liability to corporation tax

**[A1.3]** Non-resident companies are only subject to UK corporation tax if they are carrying on a trade in the UK through a permanent establishment. The rules used to determine whether a company has a permanent establishment in the UK are explained in detail in CHAPTER A4 but essentially, a company will have a permanent establishment in two circumstances (CTA 2010, s 1141):

(a)     it has a fixed place of business through which the business is wholly or partly carried on; or

(b)     an agent habitually carries on business activities which bind the overseas company.

A fixed place of business specifically includes construction and installation sites, which means that certain property development profits are subject to corporation tax rather than income tax.

Certain DTAs set out activities that do not constitute a permanent establishment and will often overrule the UK domestic rule.

CTA 2009, s 5 sets out the basis of charge to corporation tax for non-resident companies. If a non-resident company is trading through a permanent establishment in the UK, it will be liable to corporation tax on:

(a)     trading income arising directly or indirectly through or from the permanent establishment;

(b)     income from property or rights used by, held by or held for the permanent establishment;

(c)     chargeable gains arising on assets used by the permanent establishment (TCGA 1992, s 10B).

The calculation of the profits of a permanent establishment is considered in more detail in CHAPTER A5.

## Liability to income tax

**[A1.4]** A non-resident company is generally liable to income tax if:

(a)     it is not trading in the UK through a permanent establishment but has income arising in the UK; or

(b)     it is trading in the UK through a permanent establishment but has income arising in the UK which is not connected with the permanent establishment.

Unlike corporation tax, income tax is not restricted to the profits of a permanent establishment. However, there may be territorial restrictions relating to specific items of income. In addition, there is a restriction on the amount of income tax which can arise in respect of certain types of income (see **A1.18** below).

As a result of this restriction, income tax usually arises by way of withholding tax on investment income. However, many anti-avoidance provisions result in a charge to income tax.

ITA 2007, s 11 provides that a non-resident company is subject to income tax at the basic rate of 20% regardless of the level of its income.

### Income from property

**[A1.5]** Income from property may be subject to either income tax or corporation tax.

Construction and development profits may arise from a permanent establishment, and therefore be subject to corporation tax. In the absence of a permanent establishment, profits may subject to income tax under the anti-avoidance provisions of ITA 2007, s 752.

Rental income from UK property is subject to income tax.

### Notification of liability to tax

**[A1.6]** Corporation tax self-assessment applies to non-resident companies trading through a permanent establishment in the UK, and therefore a company which has a permanent establishment is required to notify HMRC of its chargeability to tax, file tax returns and make tax payments (possibly under the quarterly instalment payment regime).

The non-resident company must notify HMRC of its chargeability to UK tax within twelve months of the accounting period in which it became chargeable to tax.

For accounting periods ending before 1 April 2010, the penalty for failure to notify chargeability can be up to 100% of any UK corporation tax outstanding for the period. For accounting periods ending on or after 1 April 2010, the penalty regime in FA 2008, Sch 41 applies. Penalties are only applied if tax is outstanding for more than twelve months—in many cases this will be later than twelve months after the end of the accounting period. If the failure to notify chargeability is not deliberate then the penalty will be between 10% and 30%, and likely to be at the lower end of the range if the failure to notify is disclosed.

A non-resident company may also be required to file accounts at Companies House.

The non-resident company is separately required to provide HMRC with certain information within three months of its first accounting period (for a non-resident company, this will be within three months of becoming subject to UK tax). The penalty for failing to provide this information is £300 plus up to £60 per day (at HMRC's discretion).

### Capital gains of a permanent establishment

**[A1.7]** As for resident companies, a non-resident company with a UK permanent establishment may be liable to UK corporation tax on its chargeable gains.

However, a non-resident company will only be subject to UK corporation tax on the disposal of an asset if:

(a)    the company carries on a trade through a UK permanent establishment at a time when the disposal is made;

(b)    the asset is situated in the UK; and

(c)    the asset is used in or for the purposes of the trade.

Capital gains are explained in more detail in CHAPTER A11.

It should be noted that these are the current rules for capital gains of non-residents. However, the UK government has released a consultation proposing the extension of capital gains tax to the disposal of UK *residential* property by non-residents. This means that non-resident companies may be subject to corporation tax on chargeable gains arising from the disposal of residential property that is not used in or for the purposes of the trade of a UK permanent establishment.

The rules will apply from April 2015. The consultation ended on 31 July 2014, but HMRC had not published their response to the consultation so it is not yet clear exactly how the proposed new rules will be implemented.

### Anti-avoidance provisions

**[A1.8]** The profits and gains of non-resident companies may indirectly be subject to UK tax as a result of UK anti-avoidance provisions:

(a)    profits of a non-resident company may be attributed to corporate shareholders under the controlled foreign company (CFC) rules (see CHAPTER A6);

(b)    profits of a non-resident company may be attributed to individual shareholders (or recipients of untaxed benefits) under ITA 2007, s 720 or s 731 (see CHAPTER A15);

(c)    capital gains of a non-resident company may be attributed to shareholders or other participators under TCGA 1992, s 13 (see CHAPTER A11);

(d)    in the absence of a permanent establishment, profits arising from property development may be subject to income tax under ITA 2007, s 752 (see CHAPTER A8);

### Location through which business is undertaken

**[A1.9]** A2.1 describes how the location of a trade carried on by a UK resident company makes little difference to the taxation of the profits arising from that trade. However, it may be necessary to determine whether a non-resident company is carrying on a business in the UK (for example to determine if it has income which arises through a permanent establishment in the UK—see CHAPTER A4). If there is no business being undertaken through a fixed place in the UK then no permanent establishment can exist.

Case law establishes that simply seeking orders within the UK (directly or indirectly) is not by itself evidence of trading in the UK. In *Grainger v Gough* it was held that trading with a country through seeking orders there is not the same as trading in that country:

> 'In the first place, I think there is a broad distinction between trading with a country, and carrying on a trade within a country. Many merchants and manufacturers export their goods to all parts of the world, yet I do not suppose anyone would dream of saying that they exercise or carry on their trade in every country in which their goods find customers . . . If all that a merchant does in any particular country is to solicit orders, I do not think he can reasonably be said to exercise or carry on his trade in that country'

However, even if contracts are not concluded in the UK, the trade may be carried on in the UK. Whilst the place where contracts are concluded is important, it is not decisive. In the Court of Appeal in *F L Smidth & Co v F Greenwood (Surveyor of Taxes)* (8 TC 193) it was held (without subsequent objection from the House of Lords) that:

> 'There are indications in the case cited and other cases that it is sufficient to consider only where it is that the sale contracts are made which result in a profit. It is obviously a very important element in the enquiry, and, if it is the only element, the assessments are clearly bad. The contracts in this case were made abroad. But I am not prepared to hold that this test is decisive. I can imagine cases where the contract of re-sale is made abroad, and yet the manufacture of the goods, some negotiation of the terms, and complete execution of the contract take place here under such circumstances that the trade was in truth exercised here.'

In summary, the business will be carried on through the fixed place in the UK if it is the location where 'the operations take place from which the profits in substance arise' (*F L Smidth & Co v F Greenwood*).

There is unlikely to be a business carried on 'in' the UK if the activities are restricted to:

(a)     taking orders from UK customers;
(b)     delivering goods to UK customers;
(c)     purchasing goods from UK suppliers.

This is also reflected through the definition of 'preparatory and auxiliary' activities which are not sufficient to create a permanent establishment (see **A4.11**).

Although there is no requirement that contracts actually be concluded in the UK in order for the business to be carried on 'in' the UK or through a fixed place in the UK, this is often the most important factor to consider.

## Basic principles—collection of tax from UK representatives

**[A1.10]** Many non-residents investing or trading in the UK will have a UK representative (a term specifically defined in the legislation), and this UK representative may be liable to tax on behalf of the non-resident. This clearly has an implication for the UK representative, who may wish to obtain indemnity from the non-resident against any tax which arises.

For corporation tax purposes, the provisions are set out in CTA 2010, s 969, and for income tax and capital gains tax purposes they are set out in ITA 2007, Chapters 2B and 2C, Part 14.

### Permanent establishment

**[A1.11]** CTA 2010, s 969 provides that for companies trading in the UK through a permanent establishment (see CHAPTER A4), the permanent establishment itself is the non-resident company's representative. The permanent establishment is liable to corporation tax on behalf of the non-resident company in respect of the permanent establishment's chargeable profits, but only in respect of income which arises from the trade carried on through the permanent establishment. If there is more than one permanent establishment then there may be more than one UK representative.

The permanent establishment is also responsible for ensuring that tax returns etc are filed on behalf of the non-resident company.

A permanent establishment will continue to be treated as the UK representative even after the non-resident company ceases have a permanent establishment in the UK.

As a 'permanent establishment' is a tax concept, it is necessary to consider against whom HMRC can actually take action to collect taxes. INTM268040 sets out that where there is a fixed place of business HMRC will:

- Assess in the name of the non-resident individual or company at the UK business address.
- Send a copy also, for information, to the non-resident's address abroad if known.
- Assess any person who clearly has the capacity of 'UK representative' eg the manager of the UK operations, as 'Mr X as UK representative of XYZ'.

Any individual who works for the permanent establishment, and who has capacity to represent the non-resident company may therefore be liable to the taxes imposed on the non-resident company.

A dependent agent may also create a permanent establishment, and this dependent agent may be liable to the taxes imposed on the non-resident company, even though the dependent agent may have only a limited legal relationship with the non-resident company. Where the UK trade is carried on through a dependent agent, HMRC will:

- Assess in the form 'Mr X as agent for XYZ' sent to the agent's address.

- Send a copy of the assessment on the agent, for information, to the non-resident at their address abroad if known.
- Assess the non-resident individual or company at their address abroad if known.

Independent representatives acting on behalf of a non-resident company in the normal course of their business would not normally create a permanent establishment for the non-resident (see **A4.13**) and would not therefore be a UK representative. Further specific provisions exist to exclude certain investment managers (see **A4.18**), brokers and Lloyd's agents (CTA 2010, s 1142).

In addition, case law establishes that:

- where practical the non-resident company should be assessed in priority to the UK representative (*Tischler & Co v Apthorpe (Surveyor of Taxes)*(1885) 2 TC 89);
- a UK agent can only be a UK representative if they are carrying on a regular agency ie 'not a casual or occasional agency' (*Willson v Hooker* 67 TC 585). However, a regular agency can exist even if there is only a single transaction being undertaken. In *Willson v Hooker*, a UK agent undertook various aspects of a single property transaction, and was held to be liable for the non-resident company's UK corporation tax liability. This case superseded previous case law (*Neilsen Andersen & Co v Collins and Tarn v Scanlan* 13 TC 91) which required that an agent undertake more than 'a transaction or a few transactions' in order to be liable.

When considering the definition of permanent establishment, it will be important to consider the OECD project on Base Erosion and Profit Shifting ('BEPS').

Further details of how this may impact permanent establishments can be found in Chapter **A4**.

## Chargeable gains

**[A1.12]** Any chargeable gains arising to a non-resident company will be subject to corporation tax under TCGA 1992, s 10B. This tax may also be assessed on the UK representative under CTA 2010, s 969.

From 1 April 2013, a non-resident company which owns residential property worth more than £2 million (from 1 April 2015, properties worth more than £1 million and from 1 April 2016, properties worth more than £500,000) may be subject to the Annual Tax on Enveloped Dwellings (ATED). Reliefs are available for certain property development and property rental businesses, as well as properties used by employees, farmhouses, and properties open to the public.

Where the ATED applies, capital gains tax will also apply on the disposal of the property.

As mentioned at **A1.7**, the UK government has announced plans to charge non-residents to capital gains tax on residential property situated in the UK.

Further details on ATED and non-residents capital gains charge can be found in CHAPTER A3.

## Rental income

**[A1.13]** ITA 2007, s 971 applies to rental income from UK property, where the usual place of abode of the person receiving the rental income is outside the UK. Under the Taxation of Income from Land (Non-Residents) Regulations, SI 1995/2902, a UK representative is required to make quarterly and annual returns. The quarterly return is a calculation of basic rate tax due on rent paid for the quarter and is accompanied by payment of the tax withheld from the rental payment payable to the landlord.

In this case, the representative is either the tenant or the letting agent who is liable to withhold the tax.

Under certain circumstances, non-resident landlords may receive rent gross under the non-resident landlord scheme. The details of this scheme are explained in A3.7.

## Other income

**[A1.14]** Apart from the above provisions, the investment income or gains of a non-resident cannot be assessed in the name of a UK resident, unless the income or gain accrues in relation to a permanent establishment.

Withholding tax may arise on such income, and the UK payer may be required to account for the income tax at the time of payment (see **A1.16** below). In most cases the withholding tax will be the only tax on such income.

## Collection of corporation tax from other members of the group

**[A1.15]** Further rules relating to the recovery of tax payable by non-resident companies are in CTA 2010, s 973.

If the corporation tax due from a non-resident company is outstanding for more than six months, then certain other companies can be served a notice requiring them to pay the outstanding tax. A company can be served with a notice if it was:

(a)     a member of the same group as the non-resident company in question;
(b)     a member of a consortium which owns the non-resident company;
(c)     a member of the same group as a consortium member which owns the non-resident company;

at any time during the period beginning twelve months before the start of the accounting period in which the tax became due and ending on the date the tax became due.

For these purposes, a group relationship will exist between companies which are 51% subsidiaries, and a consortium will exist under the normal definition for group relief purposes.

Where tax is recovered from a consortium member, the proportion of the tax recovered cannot exceed the consortium member's proportionate share of the non-resident company.

Any notice must be served within three years of the date on which the liability to corporation tax for the accounting period in question is determined.

## Basic principles—withholding taxes

**[A1.16]** Withholding tax is an amount withheld (as tax) by a payer when making payment to a payee, and then paid to the payer's tax authority. The payer is effectively acting on behalf of the payee in making the tax payment, the purpose of which is to facilitate the collection of tax.

The amount the payer deducts may vary, depending on the nature of the payment. The tax to be withheld (the withholding tax) is/normally computed on the gross amount of any payment.

In the absence of a double tax agreement (DTA), withholding taxes on payments from the UK are as follows:

| | |
|---|---|
| Dividends | nil |
| Royalties (UK source patents and certain copyrights) | 20% |
| Interest | 20% |
| Technical fees | nil |
| Other annual payments | 20% |
| Rental income | 20% |

In many instances, the UK secures basic rate tax from non-residents, by way of withholding tax by the payer.

DTAs may provide for reduced withholding tax rates. A DTA can only reduce the amount of withholding tax and therefore if a DTA provides for a higher rate than rate under UK domestic law, the domestic rate prevails. Withholding taxes and their application to interest, dividends, royalties, technical fees and other annual payments are explained in more detail in CHAPTER A5.

### Precedence of DTAs and EU law

**[A1.17]** The terms of a DTA generally override the UK's domestic tax legislation. In addition, EU case law and directives may affect UK law.

For example, the Interest and Royalties Directive was implemented into UK law from 1 January 2004 and eliminated the withholding tax on interest and royalty payments made between associated companies in different EU Member States. The intended result is that income is taxable only in the country where the recipient is resident.

CHAPTER A7 discusses EU law principles and practice in more detail.

## Basic principles—income not subject to UK tax

**[A1.18]** The basic rule is that non-residents are fully liable to UK tax in respect of their UK income. However, the liability may be restricted in the case of excluded income as defined in ITA 2007, s 811 (for non-UK resident individuals) and in ITA 2007, s 815 (for non-UK resident companies). Excluded income mainly consists of savings and investment income (but not rental income).

ITA 2007, s 815(2) provides that a non-resident company's UK income tax liability is restricted to the sum of:

(a)    the UK tax withheld (or treated as withheld or credited) from 'disregarded company income'; and

(b)    the UK tax due on income which is not 'disregarded company income'.

Disregarded company income is defined in ITA 2007, s 816 as:

(a)    dividends from UK companies (s 825(1)(a) (although, as noted above, there is no UK withholding tax on dividends);

(b)    UK source interest, income from life annuities, unauthorised unit trust distributions or profits from deep discounted bonds (s 825(2));

(c)    UK source royalties and other annual payments (s 826);

(d)    certain income from activities carried out through brokers and investment managers (s 816(1)(e)).

If a non-resident's income is, for example, only interest or royalty income, the UK tax liability cannot exceed the tax withheld. In the absence of anti-avoidance provisions, any UK source trading income (not arising through a permanent establishment and therefore not subject to corporation tax) would not normally be subject to income tax. One of the anti-avoidance provisions being a property dealing transaction carried out by a non-resident which has no permanent establishment in the UK.

ITA 2007, s 815 only applies for income tax purposes, not corporation tax purposes.

It is unusual for ITA 2007, s 815 to affect a non-resident company's UK income tax liability. It is more usual for it to affect a non-resident individual, as personal allowances are not taken into account in calculating the tax due under s 811.

# A2

# UK residents with overseas income—basis of taxation

# Introduction

**[A2.1]** This Chapter considers how UK resident companies are taxed on income which arises outside the UK. It covers the different provisions under which overseas income is taxed, how income is calculated and when income is deemed to arise. Different types of income are considered in this context, including branch profits, partnership profits, dividends, interest and income from intangible assets. The translation of foreign income into sterling is also covered.

The calculation of the trading profits of an overseas permanent establishment is considered in more detail in CHAPTER A5. Following Finance Act 2011, such profits may be exempt from UK corporation tax, and this exemption is considered in CHAPTER A16.

A brief discussion of the taxation of the overseas income of UK resident individuals can be found in CHAPTER A15.

As set out at A1.2, a company is UK resident if it is incorporated in the UK or the central management and control of the business is in the UK. This is also considered further in CHAPTER A9.

## Basic definition of UK and non-UK income

**[A2.2]** CTA 2009, s 5 provides that:

'(1)    A UK resident company is chargeable to corporation tax on all its profits wherever arising.'

Prior to CTA 2009, there was a distinction between income arising in the UK (taxable under Schedule D Case I in the case of trading income) and income arising outside the UK (taxable under Schedule D Case V). ICTA 1988, s 18 defined these Cases as follows:

'(3)    The Cases are—
Case I tax in respect of any trade carried on in the United Kingdom or elsewhere but not contained in Schedule A...

(4)    Case V tax in respect of income arising from possessions out of the United Kingdom not being employment income, pension income or social security income on which tax is charged under ITEPA 2003'

There was no overriding statutory definition of 'possessions out of the United Kingdom', but specific provisions imposed a territorial charge to tax, and the definition has been considered by the courts in a number of cases.

In CTA 2009 there is no distinction drawn between UK and non-UK income, but nor is there a stated change from the previous legislation (as CTA is only a rewrite, any changes should be stated). It could then be assumed that there is no change, and that UK and non-UK income are taxed on a different basis. The case law and interpretation outlined below would therefore continue to be relevant.

The distinction between UK and non-UK income is still made in ITTOIA 2005 and ITA 2007, and remains relevant for individuals. This presents some tax planning opportunities for non-domiciled individuals who are only taxable on the remittance basis in respect of non-UK income (see CHAPTER A15).

These provisions and cases are considered below in the context of different types of income. In some cases (for example loan relationships) there is no distinction between UK and non-UK income.

# Basic principles—difference between UK and non-UK income

### Use of losses

**[A2.3]** Losses of an overseas trade which are carried forward will be relieved against profits of the same trade in the same way as losses of a UK trade under CTA 2010, s 45.

It does not make a difference if part of the trade is carried on in the UK and part is carried on overseas. This is confirmed by the HMRC manuals at INTM167340:

> 'Section [45] provides that a loss incurred in a trade can be carried forward and set off against profits of a subsequent year. If the trade is carried on partly in the United Kingdom and partly abroad, either in one or in several foreign branches, it is not necessary to calculate how much of the loss relates to the trade carried on in the United Kingdom and how much to the trade carried on in each foreign branch. The loss is carried forward in one sum.'

INTM167340 also confirms that the loss can be set against the UK profits in preference to the overseas profits of subsequent periods:

> 'If the profits of the subsequent period include profits from those parts of the trade carried on abroad which have borne foreign taxes, then, for tax credit relief purposes, set off the loss first against the profits of the part of the trade carried on in the United Kingdom and any balance against the profits of the foreign branches so that the maximum tax credit relief is given.'

This will allow more efficient credit for any overseas tax which arises on the overseas profits.

For example, if a company has losses brought forward of 600, UK trading profits of 500 and overseas profits of 500 on which overseas tax of 120 has arisen, the UK tax would be calculated as follows:

|  | Trading profits | Trading profits | Total |
|---|---|---|---|
|  | UK | Overseas |  |
| Profits | 500 | 500 | 1,000 |
| less brought forward losses | (500) | (100) | (600) |
| Taxable profits | – | 400 | 400 |
| UK tax thereon at 21% | – | 84 | 84 |

| | Trading profits | Trading profits | Total |
|---|---|---|---|
| less credit for foreign tax | — | (84) | (84) |
| UK tax payable | – | – | – |

In the absence of this flexibility, losses would be allocated between the profits on a pro rata basis as follows:

| | Trading profits | Trading profits | Total |
|---|---|---|---|
| | UK | Overseas | |
| Profits | 500 | 500 | 1,000 |
| less brought forward losses | (300) | (300) | (600) |
| Taxable profits | 200 | 200 | 400 |
| | | | |
| UK tax thereon at 21% | 42 | 42 | 84 |
| less credit for foreign tax | — | (42) | (462) |
| UK tax payable | 42 | – | 42 |

However, if the losses brought forward are greater than the total of the UK and overseas profits, it is not possible to 'disclaim' the reduction of the overseas profits in order to preserve the losses even where credit for the overseas tax would otherwise be available. Where this problem arises restructuring may be required (see **B4.8**).

## Group relief

**[A2.4]** There is a restriction on group relief (under CTA 2010, s 106) when the losses arise to an overseas branch, and can also be relieved against the profits of an overseas company.

No such restriction exists for UK losses.

## Timing of when income arises

**[A2.5]** Income from UK sources will generally be taxed when it accrues (see below in respect of trading income).

However, income from non-UK sources may only be taxable when it actually 'arises' to the shareholder. This is discussed below in the context of dividends; although the same principles may continue to apply to all types of income from non-UK sources even though the distinction is no longer drawn clearly in CTA 2009.

### Incorporation of an overseas branch

**[A2.6]** On incorporation of an overseas branch, a disposal of UK assets is taking place to a non-UK resident. This may result in a capital gain in the UK company.

In order to claim deferral relief for any gains arising on the incorporation of an overseas branch under TCGA 1992, s 140 (see **A9.37**) there must be:

'  . . . a trade [carried on] outside the UK through a permanent establishment'

When claiming this relief, steps must be taken to ensure that income is derived through the branch, ie it has a non-UK source.

### Goodwill

**[A2.7]** Goodwill which is created or acquired from a third party on or after 1 April 2002 is within the intangible assets rules (at CTA 2009, Pt 8). Any gain on disposal is treated as a profit rather than a chargeable gain, and amortisation may be deductible for corporation tax purposes.

Internally generated goodwill is treated as having been created when the trade commenced.

Where a UK company establishes an overseas branch, the branch may create its own goodwill. If the trade of the branch is considered to be the same as the trade of the UK company, then the goodwill would be created when the UK trade commenced. However, if the trade of the branch is a separate trade, the goodwill would be created at a later date, and potentially fall within the intangible assets rules.

# Basic principles—overseas trading income

**[A2.8]** Case law has established that overseas trades carried on directly by a UK resident company will almost always be treated as arising from a UK source (and before CTA 2009 would have been subject to tax under Schedule D Case I).

### Overview of case law

**[A2.9]** In *San Paulo (Brazilian) Railway Co Ltd v Carter (Surveyor of Taxes)* (1895) 3 TC 407, a UK resident company operated a railway in Brazil which was managed by a local resident. The House of Lords held that the profits were subject to tax under Schedule D Case I because the directors in the UK were ultimately responsible for taking decisions in relation to the trade.

In *Denver Hotel Co Ltd v Andrews (Surveyor of Taxes)* (1895) 3 TC 356, a UK resident company operated a hotel outside the UK which was managed by a local resident. The courts held that the profits were subject to tax under Schedule D Case I.

In *Grove v Elliots and Parkinson* (1896) 3 TC 481, a UK resident company operated oil wells outside the UK. The courts held that the profits were subject to tax under Schedule D Case I.

In *Ogilvie v Kitton (Surveyor of Taxes)* (1908) 5 TC 338, a UK resident individual owned a trading business in Canada which was managed by a local Canadian resident on his behalf. Again the courts held that the 'head and brain of the trading adventure' was located in the UK, even though day to day management was undertaken in Canada. The profits were therefore subject to tax under Schedule D Case I.

Thus even if a company undertakes a trade which is physically located entirely outside the UK, with some element of local management (as in the above cases), it is very likely that the profits will be treated as arising from a UK source.

The exception to this was in *Mitchell (Surveyor of Taxes) v Egyptian Hotels Ltd* 6 TC 542. In this case a company incorporated in the UK owned two hotels in Africa, which were managed by a local board. No decisions were taken in the UK and 'all the Company's affairs and business whatsoever in Egypt and the Sudan [were] under the control of a Local Board, to the exclusion of the Board of Directors of the Company and of all General Meetings of the Company not held in Egypt'. The House of Lords held that no management was undertaken in the UK and therefore it was subject to tax under Schedule D Case V. If this case were heard now it is almost certain that the company would be held to be not resident in the UK because management and control was not exercised here (HMRC previously confirmed this point at ITH343, which is no longer available). The case is therefore distinguished from those above where management and control was in the UK but the trade was outside the UK.

## Calculation of profits

**[A2.10]** A UK company will be subject to tax as income arises under normal UK or international accounting principles (CTA 2009, s 46). Section 46 provides that all trading income must be calculated under accounting principles, and a recalculation will be required if the profits have already been calculated under overseas accounting standards:

> '(1)    The profits of a trade must be calculated in accordance with generally accepted accounting practice, subject to any adjustment required or authorised by law in calculating profits for corporation tax purposes.'

Issues may therefore arise as a result of timing differences in recognising income for UK tax purposes, and recognising income for overseas tax purposes.

## Separate trade

**[A2.11]** It may be necessary to determine if the overseas trade is a separate trade from the UK trade—for example for the purposes of the intangible assets regime as outlined at **A2.7** above.

There is no clear guidance on this point but an overseas trade is likely to be treated as part of the UK trade for tax purposes:

*   The case law outlined at **A2.9** above would indicate that most overseas trades are undertaken in the UK. It would therefore be difficult to argue that they were separate from any other UK trade of the same nature.
*   Losses must be carried forward 'in one sum' (INTM167340) which would indicate that in most cases the losses arise from a single trade.

# Basic principles—partnerships

**[A2.12]** Unlike trading income derived directly, trading income derived by a UK company through a partnership may not be treated as arising from a UK source. Planning opportunities may therefore be available by structuring overseas activities through a partnership rather than a branch (see for instance **A15.33**). However, as noted at **A2.2** this may be more relevant to individuals than companies, as the distinction between income from a UK source and income from a non-UK source is clearer in ITTOIA 2005 and ITA 2007. It would not be prudent for a company to undertake partnership planning solely on the basis that the income will not have a UK source.

### *Colquhoun v Brooks*

**[A2.13]** In *Colquhoun v Brooks* (1890) 54 JP 277, a UK resident individual was a member of an Australian partnership, the activities of which were carried on wholly in Australia. The UK resident individual was not involved in managing the partnership. The House of Lords held that the UK resident individual's share of the profits were subject to tax under Schedule D Case V because the partnership was controlled outside the UK, and its activities were carried on outside the UK.

ICTA 1988, s 112 (now repealed for corporation tax purposes) previously reflected this decision:

> '(1)  Where a trade or business is carried on by two or more persons in partnership, and the control and management of the trade or business is situated abroad, the trade or business shall be deemed to be carried on by persons resident outside the United Kingdom, and the partnership shall be deemed to reside outside the United Kingdom, notwithstanding the fact that some of the members of the partnership are resident in the United Kingdom and that some of its trading operations are conducted within the United Kingdom.'

ICTA 1988, s 112 was repealed for corporation tax purposes when ITTOIA 2005 was introduced. There was no indication in the explanatory notes to ITTOIA that this represented a change in the law.

The 'correct' position should therefore continue to be that under *Colquhoun v Brooks* although, as stated above, in the absence of any positive confirmation from HMRC it would not be prudent to undertake planning solely on this basis.

### Calculation of partnership profits

**[A2.14]** Previously, CTA 2009, s 1259(3) (formerly ICTA 1988, s 114) appeared to contradict s 112 as it treated the partnership as resident in the UK when calculating the profits attributable to a partner which is a company:

'(1)   So long as a trade, profession or business is carried on by persons in partnership, and any of those persons is a company, the profits and losses (including terminal losses) of the trade, profession or business shall be computed for the purposes of corporation tax in like manner, and by reference to the like accounting periods, as if the partnership were a company and, subject to section 115(4), as if that company were resident in the United Kingdom'

However, HMRC previously stated that CTA 2009, s 1259(3) (formerly s 114(1)) is a calculation provision only and does not mean that the source of the income is in the UK where the corporate partner is a UK resident company:

'The troublesome part of the subsection is [sic] the words which say that the Section shall have effect as if the partnership were resident in the United Kingdom. It is sometimes argued that the effect for a resident company is to convert a Case V source into a Case I source.

This view is not accepted. We say that Section 115(4) is machinery legislation only which allows us, for example, to use the specific provisions in Section 114 for assessing company partners rather than, say, the direction in Section 112(2) to assess jointly in respect of any profit from trading in the United Kingdom. It has no effect on the basic charge.' (ITH1650)

### Apportionment of profits

**[A2.15]** It is possible for a single transaction to have both a UK source and a non-UK source, and therefore the profit which arises from the transaction will be apportioned.

The authority for this can be found in *Yates (H M Inspector of Taxes) v GCA International Ltd* [1991] STC 157, 64 TC 37 and the Hong Kong case of *IRC v Hang Seng Bank Ltd* [1991] 1 AC 306, [1990] 3 WLR 1120. In the *GCA International Ltd* case, the High Court summarised and approved the decision in *Hang Seng*:

'  . . .   But Lord Bridge then went on:

"There may, of course, be cases where the gross profits deriving from an individual transaction will have arisen in or derived from different places. Thus, for example, goods sold outside Hong Kong may have been subject to manufacturing and finishing processes which took place partly in Hong Kong and partly overseas. In such a case the absence of a specific provision for apportionment in the Ordinance would not obviate the necessity to apportion the gross profit on sale as having arisen partly in Hong Kong and partly outside Hong Kong. But the present case was a straightforward one where, in their Lordships' judgment, the decision of the Board of Review was fully justified by the primary facts and betrayed no error of law."

So in this judgment Lord Bridge is expressing the opinion, when faced with the need to determine whether profits had arisen in Hong Kong or outside Hong Kong, that, notwithstanding that the profits may arise out of one individual transaction, none the less it is possible to regard them as arising, partly within the territory and partly outside.'

This would support an apportionment, even where there is only a single transaction.

### Residence

**[A2.16]** In order that the profits of a partnership are treated as arising from a source outside the UK, the partnership must be managed and controlled outside the UK. There is no case law on this definition, but HMRC have previously confirmed that the same principles should apply as for company residence:

> 'What determines whether a partnership is within [CTA 2009, Part 17] is the place of control and management of its business. We are concerned with statutory words but there is no judicial guidance on their meaning. This contrasts, somewhat paradoxically, with the control and management aspect of "company residence" work where the words are not statutory but on which there is a good deal of somewhat ancient judicial guidance.

> What then do we do? Generally speaking we follow the thinking on companies and look at the place of the highest level of management rather than day-to-day management. Outside textbooks follow the same line.

> In deciding the location of the control and management of a firm with both United Kingdom and overseas partners, we would usually regard as significant such factors as the comparative seniority of the partners in age and experience (a simple head count will not do of course), the extent of their interests in the firm, the source and control of the finance, the places of decision on policy and major transactions, the places and locations of partners' meetings and what was done at those meetings. The place of meetings incidentally is not a conclusive factor any more than it is—or ought to be—for companies. So the nature of the business done at the meeting is important. Is it really about control and management or just part of a facade to mislead us about the place of actual control and management?' (ITH1612—no longer available)

In *Mark Higgins Rallying (a firm) v Revenue and Customs Comrs* 2011 UK FTT 340 (TC), the Tribunal used the principles of company residence to determine the residence of a partnership.

The residence of a company is considered in CHAPTER A9, and the guidance set out should be followed (with appropriate amendments where necessary) for partnerships.

# Basic principles—interest

### Tax under the loan relationship rules

**[A2.17]** Following the introduction of the loan relationship rules in FA 1996, interest was taxable under Schedule D Case III rather than Schedule D Case V.

ICTA 1988, s 18(3A) previously provided that:

'(3A)   For the purposes of corporation tax subsection (3) above shall have effect as if the following Case were substituted for Cases III and IV, that is to say—

"Case III: tax in respect of—

(a)   profits and gains which, as profits and gains arising from loan relationships, are to be treated as chargeable under this Case by virtue of Chapter II of Part IV of the Finance Act 1996;

(b)   any annuity or other annual payment which—

  (i)   is payable (whether inside or outside the United Kingdom and whether annually or at shorter or longer intervals) in respect of anything other than a loan relationship; and

  (ii)   is not a payment chargeable under Schedule A;

(c)   . . . "

*and as if Case V did not include tax in respect of any income falling within paragraph (a) of the substituted Case III.*' [my emphasis]

The loan relationship rules in CTA 2009, s 299 now confirm that there remains no distinction between UK and non-UK interest:

'(1)   The charge to corporation tax on income applies to any non-trading profits which a company has in respect of its loan relationships.'

Profits are therefore taxable in the same way regardless of the location of the parties to the loan and the source of the interest.

### Timing of receipt of interest

**[A2.18]** Unlike income arising from a foreign source, interest income taxed under the loan relationship rules is calculated on an authorised accounting basis (generally an accruals basis) in accordance with CTA 2009, s 308.

The position for UK resident individuals is different as they are taxed on interest under ITTOIA 2005, s 368. The case law set out under **A2.22** will be relevant.

### Aggregation of non-trading credits

**[A2.19]** In determining the amount of interest income taxable under loan relationship rules, non-trading credits and debits must be aggregated (trading credits and debits are not aggregated). This includes both UK and overseas interest as again there is no distinction of territoriality:

'A company has non-trading profits for an accounting period from its loan relationships if the non-trading credits for the period exceed the non-trading debits for the period or there are no such debits.' (CTA 2009, s 301(4))

This aggregation could cause problems where overseas tax has arisen on interest income. If there is overseas interest income, but UK interest expense, then the net profit will be less that the amount of the overseas interest income. Credit for the overseas tax would be restricted to the UK tax on the net profit (see CHAPTER **A10**).

This problem is dealt with by TIOPA 2010, s 50(2) which allows the disaggregation of non-trading loan relationship profits for the purposes of double tax relief.

The example below illustrates how this would operate.

### Example

A UK company has trading profits of 1,000, overseas interest income of 500 (on which withholding tax of 200 has been suffered) and UK interest expense of 400.

In the absence of s 50(2), the tax would be calculated as follows:

| | Trading profits | Loan relationship profits | Total |
|---|---|---|---|
| | 1,000 | 100 | 1,100 |
| UK corporation tax at 21% | 210 | 21 | 221 |
| less overseas tax suffered (restricted to UK tax) | – | (21) | (221) |
| Tax payable | 210 | – | 210 |
| Unrelieved overseas tax carried forward | | 179 | |

However, as a result of disaggregation under s 50(2), the tax would actually be calculated as follows:

| | Trading profits | Loan relationship profits | | | Total |
|---|---|---|---|---|---|
| | | Overseas | UK | Total | |
| | 1,000 | 500 | (400) | 100 | 1,100 |
| UK corporation tax at 21% | 210 | 105 | (84) | 21 | 231 |
| less overseas tax suffered (restricted to UK tax) | – | (105) | = | (105) | (105) |
| Tax payable | 210 | – | | (82) | 126 |
| Unrelieved overseas tax carried forward | | 95 | | | |

# Basic principles—dividends

## Amount of dividend subject to tax

[A2.20] Where a dividend has suffered either withholding tax, or is eligible for relief from underlying tax (see Chapter A10), TIOPA 2010, s 31 provides that the amount of the dividend subject to corporation tax will be the gross amount (ie the net received plus the withholding tax plus the amount of underlying tax for which relief can be claimed):

'(1)  Where credit for foreign tax falls under any arrangements to be allowed in respect of any income and income tax is payable by reference to the amount received in the United Kingdom, the amount received shall be treated for the purposes of income tax as increased by—

(a)  the amount of the foreign tax in respect of the income, including in the case of a dividend any underlying tax which under the arrangements is to be taken into account in considering whether any and if so what credit is to be allowed in respect of the dividend, and

(b)  the amount of any special withholding tax levied in respect of the income.'

Dividends received after 1 July 2009 will in most cases be exempt for corporation tax purposes (see Chapter A16), but these principles still apply where the exemption is not available and a dividend is taxable.

## Timing of receipt of dividend

[A2.21] As noted above, tax on profits from sources outside the UK was previously due under Schedule D Case V on 'income arising' to a UK resident company. There is now no distinction in CTA 2009, s 933 which merely provides that:

'The charge to corporation tax on income applies to dividends of a non-UK resident company.'

There is no provision dealing with the timing of when tax arises, which may be determined under the previous rule that no tax arises until there is income arising.

There is no case law on how this is defined in respect of dividends received from overseas companies. It is generally understood that the case law (see A2.22) on when interest arises (other than under the loan relationship rules) should also be applied to dividends.

The HMRC manuals summarise the consequence of the case law as follows:

'Interest "arises" when it is received or made available to the recipient. Interest has been made available if it is credited to an account on which the account holder is free to draw.' (SAIM2440)'

In other words, unless a recipient is free to draw on a dividend, it is not subject to tax.

For example, if a dividend is declared but cash is not paid to the recipient shareholder, the shareholder will have a claim against the company paying the dividend. If the company has the cash, then the shareholder would be 'free to draw' on the cash as a result of his claim against the company. However, if the company did not have the cash (for instance it needed to realise assets in order to pay the dividend), then the shareholder would not be 'free to draw' on the cash notwithstanding his claim against the company.

There is authority for this analysis in respect of the date when dividends received by an individual from a UK company were subject to tax. In *Potel v IRC* , [1971] 2 All ER 504, 46 TC 658 the High Court established the following principles:

'(1) If the articles of association of a company contain an article similar to article 80 in the present case, directors who recommend a final dividend have power at the same time to stipulate the date on which such dividend shall be paid . . . (2) If a final dividend is declared by a company without any stipulation as to the date for payment, the declaration of the dividend creates an immediate debt . . . (3) If a final dividend is declared and is expressed as payable at a future date a shareholder has no right to enforce payment until the due date for payment arrives . . . (4) In the case of an interim dividend which a board has resolved to pay, it is open to the board at any time before payment to review its decision and resolve not to pay the dividend . . .

In my view it follows from these principles that, in the case of an interim dividend which the directors resolve shall be paid, they can at or after the time of such resolution decide that the dividend shall be paid at some stipulated future date. If a time for payment is so prescribed, a shareholder has no enforceable right to demand payment prior to the stipulated date.'

Overseas company law may provide that the directors can declare an interim dividend. If the dividend is subject to ratification (for instance by the shareholders at a general meeting) a shareholder may not be 'free to draw' on any payment which is made before that time.

### Overview of case law relating to interest

**[A2.22]** Although there is no longer a distinction between UK and non-UK source interest, the case law on source and when interest is paid is still relevant for determining when:

- a liability to withholding tax arises;
- interest is paid if no deduction is available on the accruals basis;
- other forms of income are paid or received (for example dividends).

In *Dewar v IRC* (1935) 19 TC 561 it was held that interest on which an individual had a claim but which he never requested or received, was not income that had arisen to him and therefore not taxable. Lord Hanworth stated:

'The money is left in this way, that if he were minded to ask for £40,000, or a part of it, it would have been possible for him to have been paid and to have received it. But the fact is he has not done anything at all in respect of that and the money has not been appropriated to his use, it has not been deposited at his direction, and it is not lying under his name, either in the hands of a bank or any other agent.'

In *Parkside Leasing Ltd v Smith Smith (Inspector of Taxes)* [1985] 1 WLR 310, [1985] STC 63 it was held that the date of receipt of money paid by cheque was not the date of receipt of the cheque, but rather the date the funds cleared and became available for the use of the recipient:

' . . . it is well established that for liability to tax to be incurred under Case III receipt of interest is necessary and that receivability of interest is not enough.'

In *IRC v Fisher's Executors* (1926) 10 TC 302 it was held that:

'No doubt, the shareholders got debenture stock which, like the shares in Blott's case, was a valuable thing; but they had no power to call in the stock, which gave them no present right to receive any part of the Company's assets either in money or in money's worth, but only entitled them to a sum to be carved out of those assets if and when the stock was paid off. It is true that debenture stock, unlike shares, creates a debt; but the debt in this case was not presently payable and may never become payable while the Company is in existence. The whole transaction was "bare machinery" for capitalising profits and involved no release of assets either as income or as capital.'

In all these cases, unless the shareholder had the power to call for cash to be paid to him, there was no taxable receipt.

## Funding bonds

[A2.23] The exception to this is where funding bonds (see A5.5) are issued in lieu of interest. ITA 2007, s 939 provides that interest is treated as paid when funding bonds are issued.

There is no territorial distinction in the funding bond rules and it should be assumed that this applies equally to non-UK interest.

## Bonus issue of shares

[A2.24] In some cases, a bonus issue of shares may be made to satisfy a dividend payment, or in lieu of a dividend payment.

The case law on the question of when a dividend arises for the purposes of Schedule D Case V also confirms that a dividend satisfied with a bonus issue of shares does not constitute an income receipt, but is an addition to capital which is not subject to UK tax. This was the decision of the House of Lords in *CIR v Blott* (1921) TC 101, ie that a bonus issue of shares did not constitute income in the hands of the shareholders.

The concluding words of the judgment in *IRC v Coke* (1926) 11 TC 181 set out the transactions undertaken as part of a bonus issue, and confirm that these should not be treated as income, but rather as capital:

'First, capitalisation by the Company of £5,500, part of the accumulated profits; application by the Company of that sum in paying up the liability on the shares issued to Mr. Wright; thirdly, the receipt by Mr. Wright of those shares and nothing else; and, fourthly, retention by the Company of £5,500 under such conditions that it could no longer be distributed in the way of profits. Now, that being the case, in those circumstances, I feel compelled to hold by the decision in Blott's case that what in fact reached the hands of Mr. Wright did not bear the character of income, and that, accordingly, Super-tax was not attracted.'

This can be distinguished from *Parker (Inspector of Taxes) v Chapman* (1928) 13 TC 677 where a shareholder received cash and actively undertook to reinvest in shares of the company. Moreover, there were multiple shareholders in this case and the reinvestment was not therefore simply an addition to the capital of the company as it changed the shareholders' rights with respect to each other.

The HMRC manuals at IM1612 (no longer available) previously supported the position that a bonus issue by an overseas company does not constitute a dividend which is taxable as income:

'Where a foreign company capitalises undivided profits and—

a)    issues to its shareholders the additional capital so created, in the form of its own shares or debentures, in proportion to the number of shares already held by them; or

b)    satisfies a dividend out of such profits by the issue of its own stocks or shares (for example, a 'stock dividend' by a United States company),

such a distribution does not constitute income for Case V purposes in the hands of the shareholder. This principle applies when the distribution is actually made in shares, whether or not an effective option was given to the shareholder to receive cash in place of shares.'

Where a dividend must be paid, for instance for overseas tax or legal reasons, it can be satisfied by way of a bonus issue in order to avoid UK corporation tax (assuming that the dividend exemption is not available).

# Basic principles—royalties

**[A2.25]** Income and gains arising from intangible assets acquired or created after 1 April 2002 are taxed under CTA 2009, Part 8. Such income and gains would include royalty income, as well as any gain arising on the disposal of an intangible asset.

As with the loan relationship rules, Part 8 applies to all intangible assets held by a UK company, whether they are located in the UK or overseas.

This is supported by CTA 2009, ss 712–713 which set out a broad definition of an intangible asset and do not include any requirement that the asset is located in the UK.

## *Timing of receipt of income from intangible assets*

**[A2.26]** Income from intangible assets outside the UK is calculated on the same basis as and will arise at the same time as, the recognition under UK GAAP or IFRS (which will usually be an accruals basis) in accordance with CTA 2009, s 721:

'(2)    The amount of the credit is the same as the amount of the gain recognised by the company for accounting purposes.'

### Aggregation of income from intangible assets

**[A2.27]** As with interest, in determining the amount of taxable income from intangible assets, non-trading credits and debits must be aggregated. Trading credits and debits are not aggregated. This includes both UK and overseas income as again there is no distinction of territoriality (CTA 2009, s 751).

As with interest, this aggregation could cause problems where overseas tax has arisen on overseas income from intangible assets. If there is overseas income, but UK expenses, then the net taxable profit will be lower than the amount of the overseas profit. Credit for the overseas tax would nonetheless be restricted to the UK tax on the net profit (see CHAPTER A10).

This problem is dealt with by TIOPA 2010, s 51 which allows the disaggregation of income from intangible assets for the purposes of double tax relief.

The example above in respect of interest illustrates how this type of disaggregation operates.

# Basic principles—foreign currency

**[A2.28]** A discussion of the UK regime for taxing income arising from foreign exchange is outside the scope of this book. However, when calculating the profits of a company which are subject to UK corporation tax, it may be necessary to translate amounts recognised in non-sterling currencies into sterling.

Outlined below is the basis on which these amounts should be translated.

### Basic rule

**[A2.29]** CTA 2010, s 5 sets out the basic rule that all taxable profits must be computed in sterling:

'(1)    For corporation tax purposes the income and chargeable gains of a company for an accounting period must be computed and expressed in sterling.'

The effects of CTA 2010, ss 6–9 are that accounts prepared in a foreign currency must be converted to sterling before tax is calculated.

Notwithstanding that accounts may be prepared in another currency; all entries on the corporation tax return must always be expressed in sterling.

### Timing of translation of income

**[A2.30]** The point at which an item of income is translated into sterling will depend on the item of income in question, but the general rule in CTA 2010, s 10 is that the average exchange rate for an accounting period is used, unless the amount to be translated relates to a single transaction in which case an appropriate spot rate is used.

For specific types of income the following rules apply:

(a) Where the functional currency is sterling, non-sterling trading income will already be translated in accordance with the accounting policy. IAS21 and FRS23 both provide that either the spot rate for each transaction, or the average rate for the period can be used.

(b) Loan relationships will also be translated in accordance with the accounting policy.

(c) Expenditure on assets qualifying for capital allowances will be translated on the date the expenditure is qualifying expenditure (ie the date on which it becomes unconditional).

(d) Dividends will be translated at the date they are received.

## Presentational and functional currencies

**[A2.31]** A company is free to present its accounts in whatever currency it wishes.

However, CTA 2010, s 6 requires that taxable profits are calculated based on the 'functional currency'. CTA 2010, s 17(4) defines the functional currency as 'the currency of the primary economic environment in which the company operates'. This may not be the same as the currency in which the accounts are presented.

The functional currency will often be the same currency as the currency in which the accounting records are prepared.

If a company changes its functional currency, opening balance may be translated, with any foreign exchange movement recognised in a balance sheet reserve.

This movement may be taxable (as CTA 2009, s 328 includes income recognised in reserves), unless it satisfies the conditions at s 328(4A).

## Timing of translation of foreign tax

**[A2.32]** As outlined in A10.6, foreign tax on income (and gains) is usually translated at the date the tax becomes payable in the overseas jurisdiction, which may not be the same date as actual payment (*Greig v Ashton* 36 TC 581). Underlying tax in respect of dividends will also be translated at the date that it became payable in the overseas jurisdiction.

## Timing of translation of capital gains

**[A2.33]** It was held in *Bentley v Pike* [1981] STC 360 that proceeds and costs must be translated to sterling at the date when they are received or paid respectively. This can result in capital gains tax being paid even where there is no gain in the local currency.

It is not correct to calculate a gain in the foreign currency and then translate the net gain at the date it is realised.

## *Carry forward of losses*

**[A2.34]** CTA 2010, s 13 provides that losses are carried forward in local currency, and not translated until they are utilised. Special rules apply where losses are carried back, or are utilised against profits in a different currency.

Any losses which were brought forward at the start of the first accounting period beginning on or after 29 December 2007 are translated back into local currency at the rate applying on the first day of that accounting period.

If the local currency weakens against sterling, the losses do not gain in value. This may lead to fluctuations in deferred tax balances in statutory accounts which are prepared in sterling.

When these rules were introduced, a company was able to make an election such that:

(a)  the changes did not apply until the accounting period beginning on or after 21 July 2009; and

(b)  any losses brought forward were not translated into sterling and continue to be carried forward in local currency.

Companies may therefore still have losses which are carried forward in non-sterling currencies.

# A3

# Property

# Introduction

**[A3.1]** Property income is almost inevitably subject to tax in the jurisdiction where the property is located. Of all types of income, it arguably has the most obvious source (ie where the property is located).

Double tax agreements (DTAs) (including the OECD Model) typically approve this treatment and allow the source jurisdiction to tax income from land.

In addition to the direct taxes arising, property is often subject to significant indirect taxes, including wealth taxes, transfer taxes and local rates or levies. These taxes are outside the scope of this Chapter, although it will always be important to check whether any additional taxes apply before a company purchases property outside the UK.

The combination of these factors makes it difficult to mitigate taxes completely, and the aim of international property tax planning is often to reduce rather than eliminate tax charges.

This Chapter outlines the UK tax position of overseas companies investing in or developing UK property. It also outlines some issues which should be considered when a UK business acquires or receives income from overseas property.

It should be noted that where residential property is concerned, the Finance Acts of 2012 and 2013 introduced an increased stamp duty land tax rate of 15%, and capital gains tax where such property is held by certain 'non-natural persons', either in the UK or elsewhere. With effect from 1 April 2013, HMRC introduced a new Annual tax on Enveloped Dwellings (ATED). As a result the cost of holding UK property via an offshore structure may be discouraged in certain circumstances. This is discussed further in **A3.15**.

At the time of writing, the UK government had completed a consultation proposing the extension of UK capital gains tax to non-residents disposing of UK residential property. The rules will apply from 1 April 2015. The consultation ended on 31 July 2014, but HMRC had not published their response to the consultation so it is not yet clear exactly how the proposed new rules will be implemented.

# Basic principles—UK investment property

## Liability to tax

**[A3.2]** For a non-resident company, corporation tax only arises in respect of trading profits derived from a permanent establishment in the UK (see **A1.3**). Rental income is unlikely to fall into this category, but a charge to income tax will nevertheless arise.

The charge to tax in respect of UK rental income arises under ITTOIA 2005, s 269:

'(1)    Profits of a UK property business are chargeable to tax under this chapter whether the business is carried on by a UK resident or non-UK resident.

(2)    Profits of an overseas property business are chargeable to tax under this chapter only if the business is carried on by a UK resident.'

A UK property business is one related to generating income from land in the UK (ITTOIA 2005, s 264), which includes rental and other income (s 265), but excludes farming, mining and quarrying (s 267).

In other words, a non-resident is subject to income tax on UK rental income but not on overseas rental income.

## Self-assessment

**[A3.3]** A non-resident (whether an individual, company or other entity) which is subject to income tax as outlined above will also be within the UK income tax self-assessment system.

This means that a non-resident with UK rental income is required to:

(a)    file a tax return by 31 January following the end of the tax year (non-resident landlord tax returns cannot be filed online and are not therefore subject to the earlier online filing deadline);

(b)    notify HMRC of chargeability to income tax by 5 October following the end of the first tax year in which rental income arises;

(c)    pay tax on 31 January following the tax year, and possibly payments on account on 31 January and 31 July.

Compliance with UK filing obligations is a necessary prerequisite for a non-resident to receive rental income free of withholding tax (see below). It is therefore important that a non-resident with UK rental income notifies HMRC of chargeability to UK tax following the first year in which rental income arises.

## Non-Resident Landlords scheme

**[A3.4]** The rental income of most non-residents is subject to withholding tax under the Non-Resident Landlords (NRL) scheme. The relevant provisions of the scheme are set out in ITA 2007, ss 971 and 972, and the Taxation of Income from Land (Non-Residents) Regulations, SI 1995/2902.

HMRC have also issued extensive guidance notes on the operation of the NRL Scheme, which are available on their website (www.hmrc.gov.uk/cnr/nr_land lords.htm).

## Scope of the NRL scheme

**[A3.5]** ITA 2007, s 971 provides that the basic rate of income tax must be withheld from any UK rental income paid to a person whose 'usual place of abode' is outside the UK. The term 'usual place of abode' is not synonymous with 'non-resident'. It is therefore possible (although unlikely) for a UK resident to suffer withholding tax on rental income, or for a non-resident to fall outside the scheme.

For instance, a company which is incorporated in the UK, but centrally managed and controlled outside the UK may be non-resident for tax purposes, but may not have a usual place abode outside the UK if it has no office or place of business outside the UK.

In the case of partnerships, each partner is treated separately as receiving their respective share of the rental income.

The table below provides a general overview of the conditions required for individuals, companies and trustees to be considered as having their 'usual place of abode' outside the UK and therefore subject to withholding tax

| Category | General criteria for classification as non-resident landlords |
|---|---|
| Individuals | usually live outside the UK (but not if this is only temporary ie for less than six months) |
| Companies | incorporated outside the UK, or main office or other place of business outside the UK |
| Trustees | if all the entities that are trustees (based on the criteria above) have a usual place of abode outside the UK then the trustees, when acting as trustees, are regarded as having a usual place of abode outside the UK |

Companies resident in the UK for tax purposes do not have a usual place of abode outside the UK. A UK branch of a non-resident company, where that branch is within the charge to corporation tax, does not have a usual place of abode outside the UK.

If one or more trustees do not have a usual place of abode outside the UK then the trustees, as a whole when acting as trustees, do not have a usual place of abode outside the UK.

## Tax return obligations

**[A3.6]** Even if tax is withheld from a non-resident's rental income, a self-assessment tax return must still be submitted. As noted above, this will be an income tax return rather than a corporation tax return.

Non-resident landlords can set off the tax deducted from their UK rental income under the NRL scheme against their UK tax liability in their UK self-assessment tax return (and claim repayment of any excess tax deducted).

### Clearance to receive rental income with no tax deducted

**[A3.7]** Non-resident landlords may apply to the Centre for Non Residents (CNR) to receive their rental income without tax being deducted, provided:

(a)  their UK tax affairs are up to date; or
(b)  they have never had any UK tax liability; or
(c)  they do not expect to be liable to UK tax for the tax year in which the application is made.

If approval is given to receive rental income gross, the rental income is still subject to tax, and this will be collected through the self-assessment process as outlined above.

CNR are likely to withdraw clearance if tax returns and payments are not made on time.

Receiving rental income gross can provide a cash flow benefit, as tax may not be due until 31 January following the tax year. However, it is important that a non-resident's tax affairs are kept up-to-date to ensure that clearance is not withdrawn.

### Calculation of withholding tax

**[A3.8]** Tax must be withheld from rental income by either the tenant or the letting agent.

Tenants: tenants must operate the NRL Scheme if they:

(a)  pay rent directly to a non-resident landlord; or
(b)  pay rent to a person outside the UK; or
(c)  pay rent to a person who is not a letting agent (see below); or
(d)  receive a notice from HMRC requiring them to operate the scheme.

However, tenants who pay rent to a non-resident landlord of less than £5,200 per annum do not have to operate the scheme. This limit is pro-rated for periods of occupation shorter than a year.

A letting agent: a letting agent is a person:

(a)  whose usual place of abode is in the UK; and
(b)  who acts on behalf of a non-resident landlord in connection with the management or administration of his/her UK rental business; and
(c)  who has the power to receive income of the rental income business, or has control over direction of that income; and
(d)  whose activities are not confined to the provision of legal advice or legal services.

Allowable deductions: both tenants and letting agents must calculate the tax at the basic rate on rental income less allowable deductions. These calculations must be carried out on a quarterly basis and the tax paid to HMRC.

Determining whether an expense is deductible requires the letting agents or tenant to be 'reasonably satisfied' as regards deductibility.

In general terms, expenses are allowable if they are deductible under normal UK principles ie:

(a)   incurred wholly and exclusively for the purposes of the rental business; and

(b)   not of a capital nature.

Letting agents and tenants can only deduct those expenses that they actually pay themselves or (in the case of letting agents but not tenants) which are paid at their direction.

Non-deductible expenses would include:

(a)   expenses which the landlord pays (not at the direction of a letting agent);

(b)   expenses which have accrued in a quarter but which have not been paid in the quarter;

(c)   capital allowances; and

(d)   any personal allowances due to the landlord (this is not likely to be relevant for a company).

## Anti-avoidance provisions

**[A3.9]** The profits of a non-resident's UK property business are calculated on the same basis as trading profits. In particular, this means that:

(a)   any expenses paid to a connected party may be subject to the transfer pricing rules, and will therefore only be deductible to the extent that they are on an arm's-length basis;

(b)   profits from financial instruments relating to the property business (for instance, currency or interest rate swaps) may be taxable;

(c)   there are however some differences in respect of finance costs, as the profits are calculated under income tax principles rather than corporation tax principles

### Controlled foreign companies (CFCs)

**[A3.10]** Where a UK resident company holds shares in a non-resident company which receives UK rental income, the controlled foreign companies (CFC) rules should not apply as the new rules specifically exclude UK property-related income.

### Transfer of assets abroad

**[A3.11]** The provisions of ITA 2007, ss 720, 731 may apply in a similar way to the CFC provisions where a UK ordinarily resident individual is a shareholder, whether directly or indirectly, in a non-resident company which receives UK rental income.

In these circumstances, the individual will have the power to enjoy the income of the non-resident income, and the income may be treated as arising to him directly. The income would then be subject to income tax with credit for any income tax paid by the non-resident company.

These rules are explained in more detail in CHAPTER **A15**.

## Use of debt finance

### Deduction for interest costs

**[A3.12]** Tax relief will be available to a non-resident company on loans to finance the acquisition of investment or rental properties. Interest payable on the loans can be set off against the rental income.

However, HMRC can deny interest relief on normal transfer pricing principles where loans are not provided on arm's length terms or exceed the amount of funding a third party lender would provide. It is therefore essential that any loan funding provided by investors is on arm's length terms.

It should also be noted that the OECD Action Plan on Base Erosion and Profit Shifting ('BEPS') will be considering related party financing transactions under *Action 4 – Limit base erosion via interest deductions and other financial payments.* The outcome of this action is expected in September 2014 and December 2015.

It is therefore recommended that any planning that results in loan balances/funding that results in interest-like payments, considers the BEPS Action Plan.

The outcome of Action 4 will result in recommendations for domestic rules to combat profit shifting through interest and other financial payments, and changes to the OECD Transfer Pricing Guidelines for Multinational Enterprises and Tax Administrations.

The UK currently has robust rules to counteract this type of profit shifting in the form of thin capitalisation provisions and normal transfer pricing rules.

### Deduction for other finance costs

**[A3.13]** The non-resident company may be financed in ways other than by way of a simple loan. The deductibility of financing costs will follow normal income tax (rather than corporation tax) principles.

(a) Deep discounted bonds: specific relief is available in ITTOIA 2005, s 58 for interest, but this excludes a discount on a deep discounted bond. In the absence of any specific relief, the discount on a deep discounted bond is a cost of raising capital and therefore not deductible.

(b) Interest rate swaps: payments under swap contracts are costs of raising loan finance within ITTOIA 2005, s 58 and should therefore be deductible. This is confirmed in the HMRC manuals at PIM2140:

> 'Where a swap is taken out by a non-corporate to hedge interest payments which are deductible in computing the profits or losses of a [property] business, then profits or losses on that contract will normally be taxed or relieved as receipts or deductions of that [property] business.'

### Withholding tax

**[A3.14]** Withholding tax may be due on any interest paid. Steps should to be taken to mitigate this, as outlined in CHAPTER A5. However it may be possible to argue that the loan does not have a UK source so that interest is not subject to withholding tax in the first instance.

Considering the factors identified in the Greek Bank case (see **A5.3**), interest on a loan may not be UK source income if at least one of the following factors applies:

(a)  the loan may be secured on a UK asset (the UK property);

(b)  the debtor (the non-resident landlord) is not resident in the UK;

(c)  the interest will be paid out of cash which may be in an offshore bank account;

(d)  the law under which the loan is enforceable may be non-UK.

A secured loan will therefore always satisfy at least one of the factors, but an unsecured loan may satisfy none of them.

The facts of the recent *Perrin* case (see **A5.4**), reiterate the above factors set out in the Greek Bank case. The *Perrin* case concluded that interest paid from an Isle of Man (IOM) bank account to another IOM bank account, under a loan written up under IOM law was actually UK source as the loan was only enforceable in the UK because this is where Mr Perrin (the debtor) was resident.

It is not usually possible to structure the debt as a deep discounted bond in order to avoid the withholding tax (see **A5.28**), because there is unlikely to be a deduction available for the discount (see **A3.13**). However, it may be possible for a loan to be listed on a recognised stock exchange and qualify for the quoted Eurobond exemption from withholding tax (see **A5.27**).

### The Annual Tax on Enveloped Dwellings (ATED)

**[A3.15]**  As indicated under **A3.1** above, the 2012 Budget saw the Chancellor take a tough stance on perceived tax avoidance by wealthy individuals purchasing high value property. As a result the Finance Act 2012 produced two key changes to SDLT:

- Acquisitions of UK residential property where the consideration is more than £2m (other than those by certain non-natural persons—see below) are now subject to SDLT at a rate of 7% (FA 2012, s 213)

- Where certain non-natural persons acquire UK residential property for consideration exceeding £2m (£1m from 1 April 2015 and £500,000 from 1 April 2016) a new 15% SDLT rate applies.
  Whilst the legislation provides for exemption for property developers, the initial conditions were onerous and it was anticipated that the provisions would affect many businesses and collective investment schemes who may not have been the primary targets.

- There have been refinements to the SDLT provisions in Finance Act 2013. Although these in general were very welcome (for example the removal of the provision that property developers had to be in business for two years) to be outside the scope of the 15% SDLT charge), the effective date was deferred to Royal Assent(ie 17 July 2013), which meant in practice that many transactions were delayed until after this date.

As discussed at **A1.12** above, Budget 2012 also introduced the idea of an annual charge from 2013 on high value residential properties held by non-natural persons and the possibility of a capital gains tax charge on disposal of the property itself. These provisions were enacted in Finance Act 2013 (and subsequently amended by Finance Act 2014) and provide further detail on both the annual charge (known as the Annual Tax on Enveloped Dwelling (ATED) charge) and the capital gains tax charge. The terms of the provisions are set out below:

*Introduction*

**[A3.16]** The provisions in FA 2013 seek to complement and reinforce the new SDLT rate of 15% introduced from 21 March 2012 on single residential dwellings worth over £2m (£1m from 1 April 2015 and £500,000 from 1 April 2016) purchased by 'non-natural persons'. This is to discourage what HMRC refer to as the 'enveloping' of properties within a corporate, or similar, wrapper so that on subsequent transfers SDLT can be avoided or reduced to 0.5% on a share transfer.

Care is needed as the implementation of these provisions are spread across 2012, 2013 and 2014 Finance Acts, with most if not all of the SDLT changes being implemented in 2012, whilst the ATED and capital gains tax charges are implemented from 2013, and subsequent updates were made in 2014. This is then complicated by the announcement in the Autumn 2013 Statement that a capital gains tax charge will be introduced for profits on disposal of UK residential property held by all non-residents, including non-resident individuals and trusts. It is expected that these provisions will overlap with the ATED capital gains tax charge.

*The annual charge (ATED charge)*

**[A3.17]** The original consultation made extensive use the phrase 'non-natural person', but this has now disappeared in favour of the Annual Tax on Enveloped Dwellings (ATED). Finance Act 2013, s 94 now simply talks of the charge and then goes on to define the entities that are affected as:

- companies,
- partnerships one or more of whose members is a company, and
- collective investment vehicles.

However the charge cannot apply to:

- an entity whose entitlement is purely in the capacity of trustee of a settlement or personal representative, or
- an entity whose entitlement is as a beneficiary of a settlement.

Trusts with corporate trustees are therefore not subject to the charge

Taxpayers who may be affected therefore are likely to be companies, partnerships and collective investment vehicles holding UK situs residential property. For example private clients (especially non-domiciled individuals) and trustees who typically hold their UK residential properties through an offshore company for anonymity and capital gains and inheritance tax benefits are likely to be subject to the ATED.

However, extensive exemptions exist from the ATED for example property held for property development, let properties and most farmhouses.

Where the charge applies it will be based on charging bands which will be uprated annually. The 2014/15 proposed charges are:

| Property value | Annual charge | % charge |
|---|---|---|
| £2m–£5m | £15,400 | 0.308%–0.77% |
| £5m–£10m | £35,900 | 0.359%–0.718% |
| £10m–£20m | £71,850 | 0.359%–0.719% |
| £20m+ | £143,750 | 0.719% |

Budget 2014 announced a reduction in the threshold from £2 million to £500,000 to be introduced over two years. The proposed charges are set out below:

| Property value | Annual charge | % charge |
|---|---|---|
| £500k – £1m | £3,500 (applies from April 2016) | 0.35%–0.7% |
| £1m–£2m | £7,000 (applies from April 2015) | 0.35%–0.7% |
| | | |

For the first five years the charge will be based on market value of the property at 1 April 2012 or at the date or acquisition, if later. Revaluations will be made every five years or sooner if certain events occur (eg redevelopment or disposal). Guidance is yet to be released on the appropriate valuation date for properties entering the ATED regime as a result of the reduction in the thresholds to £1 million and £500,000.

*Extension of capital gains tax charge*

**[A3.18]** From 6 April 2013 by virtue of FA 2013, Sch 25 capital gains tax is extended to non-resident persons who have ATED related gains by amending TCGA, s 1 and introducing a new s 2B.

As a result, gains realised by a person chargeable to ATED on the disposal of UK residential property where the consideration for the disposal is more than £2m will be subject to UK capital gains tax, at the rate imposed on individuals, currently up to 28%. Legislation was introduced under the Finance Act 2014 to reduce the threshold at which CGT applies to £1m from 1 April 2015 and to £500,000 from 1 April 2016.

The definition of affected persons here broadly replicates those entities liable to the ATED charge:

- companies and other bodies corporate,
- trustees and personal representatives, and
- collective investment vehicles;

Only the gain arising post 6 April 2013 will be subject to capital gains tax. However it is still possible to make an irrevocable election to subject the whole of the ATED related gain to capital gains tax. This would offer planning possibilities where for example the base cost of the property exceeded the market value at 6 April 2013.

Pre-6 April 2013 gains may remain subject to UK capital gains tax under TCGA 1992, s 13 (see **A15.2**).

For UK resident private clients using these structures there are already significant anti-avoidance provisions which extend the scope of capital gains tax to non-resident companies and trusts. TCGA 1992, s 13 attributes gains of some non-resident companies to UK participators and s 87 can charge beneficiaries of non-resident trusts to the gains accruing to the trustees. Broadly these charges are imposed on UK resident UK doms on capital distributions attributable to the trustees gains, and on UK resident non-doms on a remittance basis. Where the ATED applies, s 13 TCGA 1992 does not apply. In addition TCGA 1992, s 86 applies to settlor interested trusts where the settlor is UK resident and domiciled, such that gains are taxed on an arising basis on the settlor.

Where non-resident, non-natural persons holding residential property are not within these anti-avoidance provisions (usually because there is no settlement or any company is non-close) the liability under the ATED regime will be a new one.

*Reliefs*

**[A3.19]** A number of reliefs are available from the 15% SDLT charge, the ATED and the associated capital gains tax charge.

In principle, property investment business should be entitled to relief where the property purchased is to be rented to third parties and not occupied by 'non-qualifying individuals' as defined by s 136. Equally previously rented properties which are empty prior to a sale should also qualify for relief.

There is a relief for property development businesses where:

* the property is acquired as part of a bona fide property development business, and
* the property was purchased with the intention of re-development and re-sale.

On this basis it is anticipated that most property developers can satisfy the conditions for the exemption. It is noted that the two year qualifying requirement (which was originally required for relief from the 15% SDLT rate) has been removed by Finance Act 2013

There are various other reliefs available, the most significant of which relate to buildings with public access, farmhouses and those occupied by employees holding less than a 10% interest in the company. Reliefs must be claimed via a nil return.

*Planning points: existing structures*

**[A3.20]** For existing structures many taxpayers will want to consider whether and how they may 'de-envelope' properties prior to the lower thresholds coming into force. Some possible solutions are discussed below.

Where property is in a two tier offshore structure (eg owned by an offshore company which is owned by an offshore trust) and it is currently below the thresholds, it should be possible in some cases to 'de-envelope' from the company whilst maintaining the trust holding, without provoking UK tax liabilities (with the exception of SDLT). This would remove the ATED liability. The ATED-related capital gains tax charge will still be an issue in circumstances where the threshold has already been exceeded, but this could be mitigated by the rebasing election if the de-enveloping is undertaken shortly after rebasing (PPR is not available).

Where 'de-enveloping' is being considered, the IHT impact of a property becoming UK property will need to be borne in mind and alternative solutions—such as mortgage to reduce the IHT value—should be considered.

Also, the SDLT impact must be considered. Where a property is removed from a corporate structure and debt is transferred, this is consideration for the purposes of SDLT. If the debt is refinanced prior to the 'de-enveloping' s 75A may apply to disregard the refinancing and result in an SDLT charge. Please see guidance on this at www.hmrc.gov.uk/so/stamps-de-enveloping.htm.

Under the new rebasing legislation there is scope to make an election to ensure that properties that are caught by the ATED-related CGT charge are not unduly penalised.

The most obvious circumstance in which the structures should be maintained might be for a non-domiciled individual in middle age or later for whom annual charges of a maximum of 0.7% would be a reasonable cost to avoid an IHT charge on death of 40%.

*Planning points: new acquisitions*

**[A3.21]** It is unlikely that it will be appropriate to acquire new residential properties into envelope structures at any stage in the future, where the property will not qualify for one of the ATED exemptions. Rather, acquisitions directly by the individual—or possibly by trusts or partnerships—are likely to be more tax efficient in respect of the ATED and related CGT and SDLT charges. In addition, given the extension of the UK capital gains tax on residential property held by non-residents (see below), planning opportunities for UK CGT are fast diminishing. Albeit, where exemption from the ATED can be claimed, offshore company and trust structures may still be advantageous for IHT planning in respect of non doms.

Where properties are being acquired which are already within an existing corporate structure, clients will need to consider the additional tax liabilities these structures involve, (particularly given the reduction in threshold from £2m to £500,000 by 2016) and look at action to wind up the structures as soon as possible post-acquisition.

## Autumn Statement 2013—extension of UK capital gains tax to residential property held by non-residents

**[3.22]** The current UK tax rules do not subject non-residents to UK capital gains tax, unless the gain is in relation to property used in a trade carried on through a UK permanent establishment, or if the ATED rules as set above apply. This means that a non-resident company could own property situated in the UK that does not create a permanent establishment (i.e. a residential property not used in a trade) or with proceeds of less than £2m (£1m from April 2015 and £500k from April 2016), and not be subject to corporation tax on disposal (see planning ideas later in this Chapter). However, the UK government has released a consultation relating to extension of capital gains tax to the disposal of UK residential property by non-residents. The rules will apply from April 2015. The consultation ended on 31 July 2014, however there are complexities and it is not yet clear exactly how the proposed new rules will be implemented. This should be factored in to any planning decisions regarding UK residential property, along with the ATED rules set out above.

## Planning—UK investment property

### *Typical structures*

**[A3.23]** The following examples assume that relief is available from the higher rate of SDLT, the ATED and capital gains tax on properties subject to the ATED. These reliefs are discussed in more detail above.

A typical structure for holding UK property is shown in Diagram 1.

Diagram 1

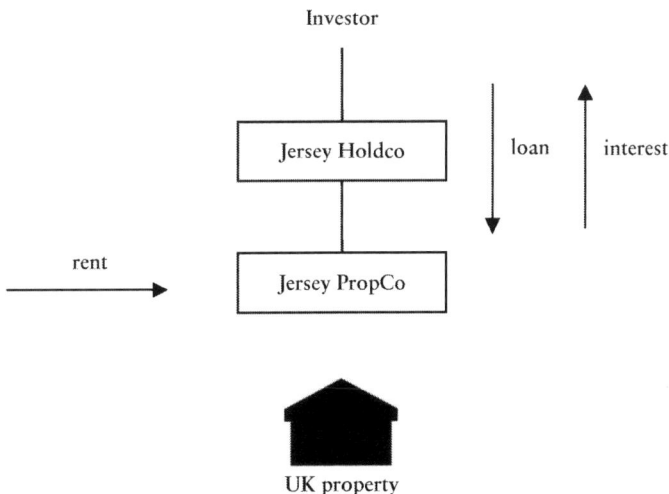

HoldCo and PropCo can be established in any low-tax jurisdiction, but it is important that management and control is not exercised in the UK such that they become UK resident. For that reason Jersey, Guernsey and the Isle of Man are common choices for property investors as they are easily accessible from the UK.

Jersey PropCo is taxed on rental income at a rate of 20%. A deduction will be available for any interest paid on the loan from Jersey HoldCo, subject to the usual rules for deductibility (ie the interest does not exceed an arm's-length rate).

The interest may also be subject to withholding tax if the loan is considered to have a UK source.

If the investor is a UK resident individual, any rental income of Jersey PropCo, or interest and dividend income of Jersey HoldCo may be subject to tax under the anti-avoidance provisions of ITA 2007, ss 720 or 731. A UK resident investor company may be subject to tax under the CFC rules.

### Capital gains tax and Stamp Duty Land Tax (SDLT)

**[A3.24]** Planning for capital gains tax (CGT) and Stamp Duty Land Tax (SDLT) when non-residents hold UK property relies on two basic principles:

(a)   non-UK resident companies are only chargeable to corporation tax on chargeable gains on assets used in a trade carried on through a UK permanent establishment;

(b)   SDLT is only due on actual UK real estate but is not dependent on the residence of the vendor or purchaser. In the following examples care will be needed to remain outside the penal SDLT charges under FA 2012, s 214 referred to above.

The structure shown in Diagram 2 is used to illustrate the planning points discussed below:

**Diagram 2**

```
              Investor
                 │
    ┌────────────────────────┐
    │                        │
    │     Jersey HoldCo      │
    │                        │
    └────────────────────────┘
                 │
    ┌────────────────────────┐
    │                        │
    │     Jersey PropCo      │
    │                        │
    └────────────────────────┘
                 │
           UK Investment
             property
```

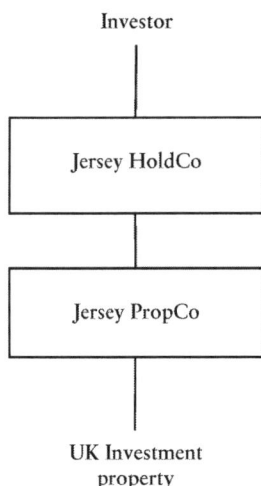

The investor may be a non-resident individual, UK resident individual, non-resident company or resident company.

The use of a non-resident company to hold the property acts as a 'wrapper', to take advantage of the CGT and SDLT restrictions identified above. The capital gains remain subject to the anti-avoidance provisions of s 752, outlined at A3.30.

### Sale of property by Jersey PropCo

**[A3.25]** Jersey PropCo is not within the charge to corporation tax as it does not carry on a trade in the UK through a permanent establishment. No UK tax therefore arises in Jersey PropCo on the disposal of the property.

If Jersey PropCo is a close company, a gain may be treated as arising to any UK resident investor (whether an individual or company) under TCGA 1992, s 13.

SDLT will arise on the disposal of the property as the property is located in the UK.

The distribution of the proceeds of the disposal from Jersey PropCo to Jersey OpCo may also have consequences for any UK residents under the provisions of ITA 2007, ss 720, 731, or the CFC rules.

From April 2015, a new non-resident capital gains tax charge could apply.

### Sale of shares in Jersey PropCo by Jersey HoldCo

**[A3.26]** Jersey HoldCo is not within the charge to corporation tax as it does not carry on a trade through a UK permanent establishment. No UK tax therefore arises in Jersey HoldCo on the disposal of the shares in Jersey PropCo.

If Jersey HoldCo is a close company, a gain may be treated as arising to any UK resident investor (whether an individual or a company) under TCGA 1992, s 13. If the shares in Jersey PropCo are non-UK situs, a non-domiciled individual may only be taxable under s 13 on the remittance basis.

No SDLT will arise on the shares in Jersey PropCo, as they are not UK real estate.

### Sale of shares in Jersey HoldCo

**[A3.27]** If the investor is a UK resident company or individual, the sale of shares in Jersey HoldCo will be subject to CGT.

The substantial shareholding exemption is very unlikely to apply to a corporate investor as Jersey HoldCo will not be a trading company.

If the shares in Jersey HoldCo are non-UK situs, a non-domiciled individual may only be taxable on the remittance basis.

A non-UK resident investor would not be within the charge to UK tax unless the shares in Jersey HoldCo were held for the purpose of trade carried on in the UK through a permanent establishment.

No SDLT will arise on the shares in Jersey HoldCo as they are not UK real estate.

### *Double tax agreements*

**[A3.28]** As noted in the introduction to this chapter, the UK's DTAs generally allow the jurisdiction in which property is located to tax income and capital gains arising from that property. However, there are some specific areas of difference in relation to trading and development profits which are outlined at A3.41 below.

In some cases, the definition of immoveable property in the DTA will extend to shares in companies holding property in that jurisdiction. The jurisdiction in which the property is located could then tax capital gains arising on the sale of shares in the property holding company, and the DTA would provide no relief.

On the basis that non-residents are not subject to capital gains tax on UK property under UK domestic law, a non-resident is not required to rely on a double tax treaty when making a capital gain on a UK situated asset. With reference to the proposed extension of UK capital gains tax to non-residents disposing of UK residential property, most double tax treaties agreed between the UK and other territories state that capital gains on land and buildings are only taxed in the country in which the property is situated. This means that double tax relief should be available to the extent that the non-resident has paid tax on the gain in their home country.

A non-resident may therefore only feel the impact of the new capital gains tax charge to the extent that they are resident in a jurisdiction which has no tax treaty with the UK, or where a treaty exists, the UK capital gains tax rate exceeds that of the home country.

# Basic principles—UK development property

## *Permanent establishment*

**[A3.29]** A non-resident company trading in UK land or property will be subject to UK corporation tax or income only if:

(a)     it is trading in the UK through a permanent establishment; or
(b)     the transaction falls within the anti-avoidance provisions of ITA 2007, s 752.

A non-resident company which simply buys and sells land in the UK, will not usually acquire a UK permanent establishment. The fact that the subject-matter of the transaction is UK land does not necessarily mean that the company has a UK permanent establishment.

It is more likely that the non-resident company will be subject to UK tax by virtue of s 752, subject to relief under a DTA.

A property developer is more likely to acquire a permanent establishment in the UK, as CTA 2010, s 1141 specifically provides that 'a building site or construction or installation project' will constitute a permanent establishment. A DTA would typically follow the same approach.

Given the proposed non-residents capital gains tax charge on residential properties, it will be important to consider the impact of this on any planning.

## *Anti-avoidance provisions—transactions in UK land*

### Overview of legislation

**[A3.30]** Anti-avoidance provisions in ITA 2007, s 752 can apply income tax to development profits even in the absence of a permanent establishment. These provisions will apply where:

(a)     UK tax has been avoided;
(b)     a gain of a capital nature arises from the disposal of the land;
(c)     the land is acquired or developed with the sole or main purpose of realising a gain, or the land is held as trading stock; and
(d)     all, or any part, of the land is located in the UK.

### Avoidance of tax

**[A3.31]** Although it is not explicit in ITA 2007, s 752, HMRC will only seek to apply these anti-avoidance provisions where income tax is otherwise being avoided.

The HMRC Business Income Manual states (in the context of what is now CTA 2010, s 815, but the same principles apply to s 752):

> '[CTA 2010, s 815] cannot be used to catch straightforward transactions of purchase and sale of land that do not amount to a trade, or adventure in the nature of trade.

That is, the Section is not an alternative to [taxation of trading income] in simple transactions of purchase of land by a UK resident person, and its sale by that person to an unconnected person. This is the case even if there has been some construction on, or development of, the land before sale.

[CTA 2010, s 815] is not applicable because the necessary avoidance of tax is not present. In such circumstances we stand or fall on the basic trading principles (see onwards). If they apply we assess any profit [as trading income]. If they do not apply then, by definition, the transaction is not a trading transaction and we cannot argue that [income] tax has been avoided.'

In other words, s 752 should not apply to capital gains made by non-residents on the disposal of investment property, even where this property is developed. s 752 will only apply to a transaction which is in essence a trading transaction which would otherwise not be charged to UK income tax (or corporation tax). This is reflected in the s 756 purpose test (see **A3.33** below).

## Gain of a capital nature

**[A3.32]** A gain of a capital nature is defined in ITA 2007, s 772(1) as a gain that 'does not fall to be included in any calculation of income for income tax purposes.'

Non-UK residents are only subject to income tax in respect of a trade which is carried on wholly or partly in the UK. A non-resident could therefore carry on a trade outside the UK which consists of dealing in, or developing, UK land. As the income is not subject to tax, the profits realised from the trading activity would be a 'gain of a capital nature' for the purposes of s 752.

## Purpose of acquiring or redeveloping the land

**[A3.33]** ITA 2007, s 756(3) provides that ITA 2007, s 752 will only apply where:

'(a)    the land is acquired with the sole or main object of realising a gain from disposing of all or part of the land,

(b)    any property deriving its value from the land is acquired with the sole or main object of realising a gain from disposing of all or part of the land,

(c)    the land is held as trading stock, [or]

(d)    the land is developed with the sole or main object of realising a gain from disposing of all or part of the land when developed.'

It is necessary to consider the intention of the acquisition itself, even if that intention subsequently changes.

The intention behind an investment acquisition should be clearly documented in relevant board minutes, to ensure that HMRC cannot argue that the acquisition was made with the intention of realising a gain.

For example, if a non-resident acquires a property in the UK for investment purposes, but subsequently decides that a greater return would be realised if the property were disposed of in the short-term, s 752 would not apply because the original purpose of the acquisition was for investment. However, if the non-resident actually undertook development of the property, then s 752 may apply to any profit arising from the point that the development began. Section 765 provides that profit is not taxable to the extent that it is attributable to the period before the intention to develop arose.

Where the purpose of holding land or property has changed, the property should not be transferred between group companies. The original intention is still considered when applying s 752. If there is a transfer, the intention of the transferee would then be considered when determining if s 752 applies.

### Definition of land

**[A3.34]** The definition of land for the purposes of ITA 2007, s 752 is very broad, and comprises:

'(a)   any shareholding in a company deriving its value directly or indirectly from land,

(b)   any partnership interest deriving its value directly or indirectly from land,

(c)   any interest in settled property deriving its value directly or indirectly from land, and

(d)   any option, consent or embargo affecting the disposition of land.' (ITA 2007, s 772(2))'

ITA 2007, s 762(2) further provides that 'value may be traced through any number of companies, partnerships and trusts'.

A non-resident company may therefore be subject to s 752 even if it:

(a)   forms a UK subsidiary which acquires the land; and

(b)   sells the shares in the UK subsidiary in order to realise the profit.

### Indirect gains

**[A3.35]** ITA 2007, s 752 also applies to gains which are made indirectly. Section 761 provides a general direction to this effect:

'(1)   For the purposes of this Chapter, account is to be taken of any method, however indirect, by which—

(a)   any property or right is transferred or transmitted, or

(b)   the value of any property or right is enhanced or diminished,'

but more specific provisions are contained within s 756(1)(d), s 757 and s 759(4).

ITA 2007, s 756(1)(d) requires that the gain must be made by the person specified in s 757 ie:

'(1)   . . .

(a)   the person acquiring, holding or developing the land,

(b)   a person connected with a person within paragraph (a), and

(c)   a person who is a party to, or concerned in, an arrangement or scheme within subsection (2).

(2)   An arrangement or scheme is within this subsection if—

(a)   it is effected as respects all or part of the land, and

(b)   it enables a gain to be realised—

(i)   by any indirect method, or

(ii)   by any series of transactions.'

ITA 2007, s 759(4) then provides that the person on whom the income is chargeable under s 752 can include someone other than the person who realises the gain:

'If all or any part of the gain accruing to a person ("A") is derived from value provided directly or indirectly by another person ("B"), the income is B's.'

For example, a non-resident company provides funding to a subsidiary which is not itself subject to tax on the disposal of land, whether under general principles or under s 752. The subsidiary may for example be a UK company with trading losses, or it may be located in a jurisdiction which provides protection under a DTA. The funding may be provided by way of loan or share capital. This is shown in Diagram 3.

When the land is sold, no tax arises. However, when interest or dividends are paid to the non-resident, these are not subject to UK tax, and may therefore constitute 'gains of a capital nature'. The non-resident was 'party to or concerned in an arrangement or scheme' to enable 'a gain to be realised by any indirect method', and may therefore be subject to tax under s 752, even though the land was actually sold by another person.

As an alternative (which would be relevant even if the profits were not distributed) HMRC could seek to assess the non-resident as the value was 'provided directly or indirectly by another person'.

In either case, the transaction would still need to be in the nature of a trade for the non-resident as outlined in **A3.24**.

Diagram 3

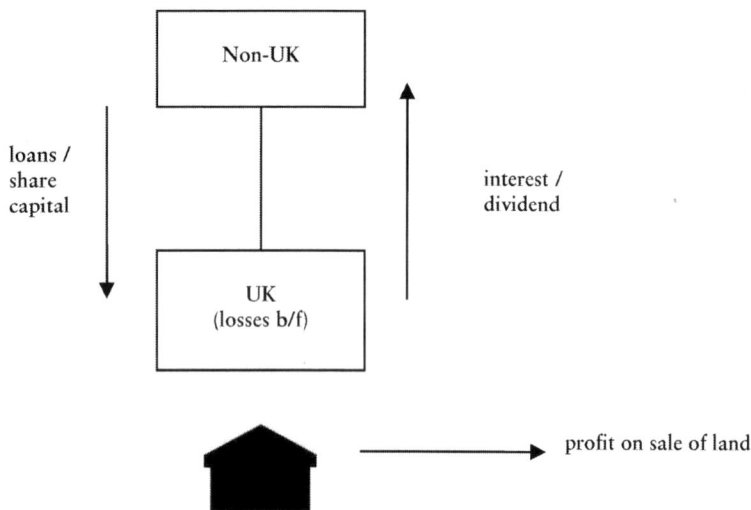

## Exemptions

**[A3.36]** An exemption is available from ITA 2007, s 752 where shares are sold in a company which holds land as trading stock (ITA 2007, s 766). The rationale is that the company itself will be subject to corporation tax or income tax on an eventual disposal of the land.

There is a clearance procedure available to confirm if s 752 will apply to a particular transaction (see CHAPTER **A12**). As noted in CHAPTER **A12**, it would be unusual for clearance to be obtained where s 752 might be relevant.

**Payment of tax**

**[A3.37]** Any tax liability arising under ITA 2007, s 752 is subject to self-assessment. A non-resident would therefore be required to complete a tax return to report any tax arising.

ITA 2007, s 944 allows HMRC to issue a notice to a person making a payment to a non-resident to withhold tax (at the basic rate, currently 20%) from the payment, where the non-resident is subject to s 752.

# Planning—UK development property

## *UK domestic law*

**[A3.38]** Where a non-resident company is developing UK property, a charge to UK tax can be avoided if:

* there is no permanent establishment in the UK (see **A3.21** above); and
* the anti-avoidance provisions of s 752 do not apply.

A non-resident company should therefore ensure that:

* there is no fixed place of business in the UK—the principles outlined under **A3.43** and **A3.21** will be relevant for domestic law as well as for the purposes of a double tax agreement;
* the intention for acquiring the land is clearly documented, and is not to sell the land at a profit (as outlined under **A3.36** above).

Given the proposed non-residents capital gains tax charge on residential properties, it will be important to consider the impact of this on any planning.

## *Double tax agreements*

### Trading v investment

**[A3.39]** A DTA may provide relief where trading profits rather than capital gains are realised from property, for instance from property trading or property development.

Article 7(1) of the UK/US DTA provides that:

'The business profits of an enterprise of a Contracting State shall be taxable only in that State unless the enterprise carries on business in the other Contracting State through a permanent establishment situated therein. If the enterprise carries on business as aforesaid, the business profits of the enterprise may be taxed in the other State but only so much of them as are attributable to that permanent establishment.'

Article 7 does not exclude business profits arising from property activities, and therefore can cover both property trading and property development. The profits of a US company undertaking a property trading activity in the UK should not therefore be subject to UK tax provided there is no permanent establishment in the UK.

Article 6 of the UK/US DTA, which specifically deals with income from real property, only deals with investment income, and not trading income. Article 6(3) provides that:

> 'The provisions of paragraph 1 of this Article shall apply to income derived from the direct use, letting, or use in any other form of real property.'

Article 6 would not therefore apply to property trading or development, and Article 7 would apply to profits arising from these activities.

The provisions of older/non-OECD treaties (for instance those which refer to 'industrial and commercial profits' rather than business profits) apply in the same way.

It is often beneficial for income to fall within the business profits article of a DTA rather than the property article. In order to support the contention that property income falls within the business profits article, the trading intentions should be clearly evidenced.

### Relief under a double tax agreement in respect of s 752

**[A3.40]** A DTA can provide relief from tax under s 752. The OECD business profits article is quite clear that business profits 'shall be taxable only in that State unless the enterprise carries on business in the other Contracting State through a permanent establishment.' In the absence of a permanent establishment, no UK tax can arise, even under the anti-avoidance provisions of s 752, where there is an applicable DTA.

Tax arising under s 752 is actual income tax and should therefore be within the scope of a DTA. This can be contrasted with the position under the CFC anti-avoidance provisions, where it was decided in *Bricom Holdings Ltd v CIR* (1997) 70 TC 272 that the DTA provided no relief as tax arising under the CFC provisions was not corporation tax and therefore not within the scope of the particular DTA.

### Relief under a double tax agreement in respect of development profits

**[A3.41]** Many DTAs offer a specific definition of permanent establishment in respect of construction projects. For example, under the UK/Cyprus DTA a permanent establishment will only be created through 'a building site or construction, installation or assembly project which exists for more than six months'.

In contrast, until recently under the UK/Hungary DTA a permanent establishment could only be created through 'a building site or construction or assembly project which existed for more than twenty-four months'. However, a new DTA was signed with Hungary on 7 September 2011 and with effect from 1 January 2012 the period is reduced to 12 months.

Table 1 at the end of this chapter lists the time for which a building site must exist under UK DTAs in order to create a permanent establishment in the UK. Where 'no specific provision' is noted, the existence of a permanent establishment will be determined by reference to general principles only. Where property transactions are concerned, HMRC are known to use a guideline of six months, although arguably, the absence of a specific time limit may permit treaty protection for a much longer period.

Many DTAs will also specify that a permanent establishment exists where consultancy services are provided in respect of a construction site—typically subject to the same minimum time requirement.

### Non-resident company developing UK land via UK company

**[A3.42]** If it is not possible to restrict the length of a project, it may be possible to ring-fence the development activities in a UK company, as illustrated below.

Diagram 4

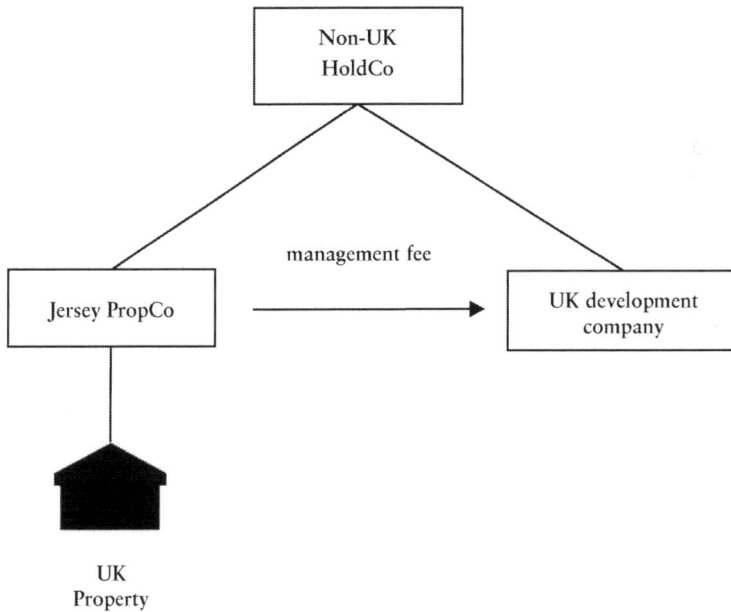

In Diagram 4, Jersey PropCo realises the property development profits, but all development activities are undertaken by the UK development company. Jersey PropCo should not therefore be considered to own a 'building site or construction project' in the UK, as this site belongs to the UK development company. Jersey PropCo has no permanent establishment in the UK, and can therefore rely on the UK/Jersey DTA to avoid tax under ITA 2007, s 752.

The UK development company should receive arm's-length remuneration in order to satisfy the UK transfer pricing requirements. This should also mean that even if there were a permanent establishment, its profits are reduced to nil.

However, HMRC are known to challenge this analysis and to argue that:

•     the offshore company (Jersey PropCo for example) has a permanent establishment in the UK; and

- the profit attributable to the permanent establishment is the full amount of the development profit.

## UK residents and DTAs

**[A3.43]** Until Finance Act 2008, a UK resident individual could establish a non-resident company (or in some cases a non-resident trust or partnership) and avoid tax on UK property trading or development activities. Relief was claimed under the relevant DTA for tax under ITA 2007, s 720.

FA 2008 introduced two new provisions.

TIOPA 2010, s 130 (previously ICTA 1988, s 815AZA) provides that:

'(1)    Subsection (4) applies if double taxation arrangements make the provision, however expressed, mentioned in subsection (2).

(2)    The provision is that the profits of an enterprise within subsection (3) are not to be subject to United Kingdom tax except so far as they are attributable to a permanent establishment of the enterprise in the United Kingdom. [which is essentially a business profits article]

(4)    The provision does not prevent income of a person resident in the United Kingdom being chargeable to income tax or corporation tax.'

And ITTOIA 2005, s 858 was extended by a new subsection (4):

'For the purposes of this section the members of a firm include any person entitled to a share of income of the firm.'

These provisions mean that UK resident shareholders in a non-resident company or partnership which realises profits from UK property trading or development activities cannot claim the benefit of a DTA. This in turn means that anti-avoidance provisions which apply at shareholder level (ITA 2007, ss 720, 754, 731) will apply notwithstanding the existence of a DTA. The company or partnership itself can continue to claim the benefit of a DTA.

## Non-residents and DTAs

**[A3.44]** Non-resident shareholders should be unaffected by the FA 2008 changes, and this structure (shown in Diagram 5) can still be used by non-resident shareholders to obtain protection under a DTA from ITA 2007, s 754.

A resident of a jurisdiction which does not have a DTA with the UK may be subject to tax under ITA 2007, s 754 even if there were no UK permanent establishment. By establishing a company in a jurisdiction with which the UK has an appropriate DTA to undertake the trading or development activity, the relevant DTA should provide relief from a charge under these sections.

ITA 2007, s 754 may still apply to a sale of shares in the Jersey PropCo.

Diagram 5

Investor

Jersey HoldCo

Jersey PropCo

UK Investment
property

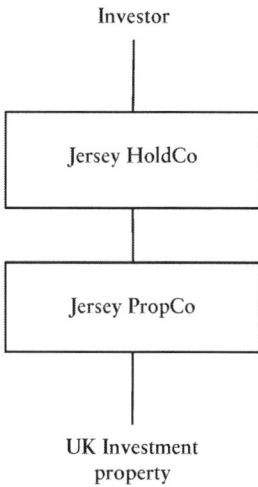

## Planning—overseas investment property

**[A3.45]** As noted in the introduction to this Chapter, almost all jurisdictions look to charge tax on income related to land and property.

CTA 2009, s 5(1) provides that a UK resident company is subject to corporation tax on its profits, wherever they arise. This will include profits from land and property outside the UK, which will be calculated in accordance with CTA 2009, Part 4 on the same basis as profits from land and property in the UK.

It is likely that a UK resident individual or company receiving income or gains from overseas property will therefore be subject to tax in the overseas jurisdiction as well as in the UK. Transfer taxes are likely to be due on the purchase and/or sale of property, and some jurisdictions will also require VAT to be added to property transactions.

Planning to reduce these taxes will depend on the jurisdiction concerned, but may be similar to strategies for overseas companies investing in UK property.

### Leveraging with debt

Diagram 6

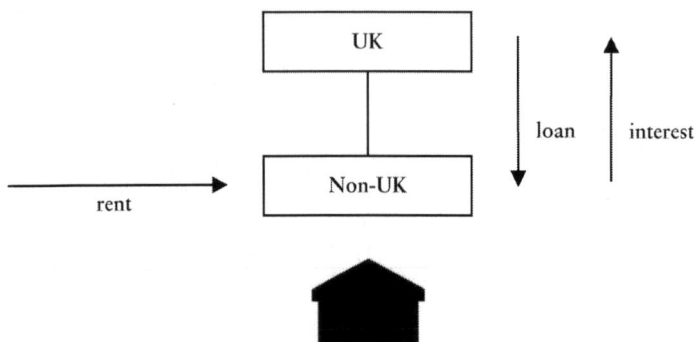

**[A3.46]** As illustrated in Diagram 6, local taxable profits may be reduced by interest payments to the UK.

### Offshore wrapper

Diagram 7

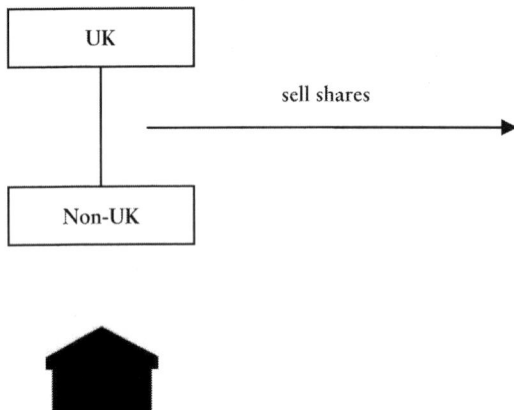

**[A3.47]** As illustrated in Diagram 7, a sale of shares may not be subject to local stamp duty or capital gains tax, even if a sale of the underlying property itself would be.

However, some jurisdictions will treat shares in property in the same way as property itself.

In all cases, local advice should be taken to confirm the consequences of these or other structures.

### Key issues

**[A3.48]** The checklist below identifies the key issues which should be considered when a UK resident is purchasing property overseas:

(a)     Annual taxes based on property value.
   (i)     Annual property taxes may be at differential rates depending on whether the owner of the property is resident in a jurisdiction with a DTA.

(b)     Transfer taxes, stamp duties and fees.
   (i)     Transfer taxes may be collected by the lawyer or notary who undertakes the transaction;
   (ii)    Documents may require notarisation and lawyers' fees will also be due.

(c)     Inheritance/inheritance tax.
   (i)     For non-corporate purchasers, forced heirship rules may apply such that properties pass automatically to certain family members. This may also have inheritance tax consequences;
   (ii)    Local wills may be required to override forced heirship rules;
   (iii)   Property may also be held in corporate structure to avoid forced heirship.

(d)     Benefit in kind.
   (i)     Non-UK property held in a non-UK company will not give rise to a benefit in kind where it is available for the use of any UK directors or shadow directors. Property held by a UK company may, however, give rise to a taxable benefit in kind where it is available for their use.

(e)     Loans to purchase property.
   (i)     Interest on a loan to purchased overseas investment property may reduce the amount of rental profit subject to tax;
   (ii)    Withholding tax may be due on interest.

(f)     Capital gains tax.
   (i)     The disposal of property by a non-resident may be subject to capital gains tax. A DTA will normal allow the overseas jurisdiction to retain taxing rights in respect of local property;
   (ii)    This capital gains tax may be collected by withholding tax from the disposal proceeds;
   (iii)   Capital gains tax may also extend to the disposal of shares in a company which holds local property.

(g)     Permanent establishment.
   (i)     Acquiring a property through which a trading activity is carried on is likely to create a permanent establishment, such that trading profits are taxable in the overseas jurisdiction. Tax registration is likely to be required once a permanent establishment exists;
   (ii)    VAT registration may also be required if an establishment is created.

(h)     Withholding tax on rents paid.
   (i)     If property is leased from a landlord, tax may be required to be withheld from the rental payments and paid to the tax authorities.

(i)  Rental income.
   (i)  Receipt of rental income may be taxable either directly or by way of withholding tax;
   (ii)  Tax registrations and tax returns may be required.

# Planning—overseas development property

### Domestic law

[A3.49] The same principles apply to overseas property development as to UK property development. In other words, the UK company should ensure that:

- there is no fixed place of business—the principles outlined under A3.29 above will be relevant;
- local anti-avoidance rules do not apply even where there is no permanent establishment.

### Double tax agreements

[A3.50] Planning techniques similar to those outlined above can be used by UK residents (individuals or companies) developing or trading in overseas property.

The DTA between the UK and the jurisdiction in question may provide relief from overseas tax on property trading or development profits.

Table 1 will be relevant when determining whether a UK company undertaking development or construction activities outside the UK has a permanent establishment. Where 'no specific provision' is noted, the existence of a permanent establishment will be determined by reference to general principles only.

If no DTA exists, or if the DTA does not provide favourable terms (for instance in respect of the length of time a construction project can exist before it creates a permanent establishment), a company can be established in a third juris-diction which has a more favourable DTA, subject to any limitation of benefit or similar anti-treaty-shopping clauses in the more favourable DTA (see A8.54).

# Table 1—construction sites under UK double tax agreements

| Country | Time for which a construction site must exist in order to create a permanent establishment |
| --- | --- |
| Albania | 6 months |
| Antigua and Barbuda | no specific provision |

| | |
|---|---|
| Argentina | 6 months |
| Armenia | 9 months |
| Australia | 12 months |
| Austria | 12 months |
| Azerbaijan | 12 months |
| Bahrain | 12 months |
| Bangladesh | 183 days |
| Barbados | 9 months |
| Belarus | 24 months |
| Belgium | 12 months |
| Belize | no specific provision |
| Bolivia | 6 months |
| Bosnia-Herzegovina | 12 months |
| Botswana | 6 months |
| Brunei | no specific provision |
| Bulgaria | 12 months |
| Burma | no specific provision |
| Canada | 12 months |
| Chile | 6 months |
| China | 12 months |
| Croatia | 12 months |
| Cyprus | 6 months |
| Czechoslovakia | 12 months |
| Denmark | 12 months |
| | (no minimum for construction or installation of oil or gas pipelines) |
| Egypt | 6 months |
| Estonia | 6 months |
| Ethiopia | 6 months |
| Falkland Islands | 6 months |
| Faroe Islands | 12 months |
| Fiji | 6 months |
| Finland | 12 months |
| France | 12 months |
| Gambia | 6 months |
| Georgia | 12 months |
| Germany | 12 months |
| Ghana | 6 months |
| Greece | no specific provision |
| Grenada | no specific provision |
| Guernsey | no specific provision |
| Guyana | 12 months |

| | |
|---|---|
| Hong Kong | 6 months |
| Hungary | 12 months |
| Iceland | 12 months |
| India | 6 months |
| Indonesia | 183 days |
| Ireland | 6 months |
| Isle of Man | no specific provision |
| Israel | 12 months |
| Italy | 12 months |
| Ivory Coast | 6 months |
| | (no minimum where the fee for construction or installation is more than 10% of a related sale of machinery or equipment) |
| Jamaica | 6 months |
| Japan | 12 months |
| Jersey | no specific provision |
| Jordan | 6 months |
| Kazakhstan | 12 months |
| Kenya | 6 months |
| Kiribati and Tuvalu | no specific provision |
| Korea | 12 months |
| Kuwait | 6 months |
| Latvia | 6 months |
| Lesotho | 6 months |
| Libya | 3 months |
| Lithuania | 6 months |
| Luxembourg | 6 months |
| Macedonia | 12 months |
| Malawi | no specific provision |
| Malaysia | 6 months |
| Malta | 6 months |
| Mauritius | 6 months |
| Mexico | 6 months |
| Moldova | 9 months in any 12 month period |
| Mongolia | 12 months |
| Montenegro & Serbia | 12 months |
| Montserrat | no specific provision |
| Morocco | 183 days |
| Myanmar | no specific provision |
| Namibia | 12 months |
| Netherlands | 12 months |

| | |
|---|---|
| New Zealand | 12 months |
| Nigeria | 3 months |
| | (no minimum where the fee for construction or installation is more than 10% of a related sale of machinery or equipment) |
| Norway | 12 months in any 24 month period |
| Oman | 6 months |
| Pakistan | 6 months |
| Panama | 9 months |
| Papua New Guinea | 183 days in any 365 day period |
| Philippines | 183 days |
| Poland | 12 months |
| Portugal | 12 months |
| Qatar | 6 months in any 12 month period |
| Romania | 12 months |
| Russia | 12 months |
| St Kitts and Nevis | no specific provision |
| Saudi Arabia | 6 months |
| Sierra Leone | no specific provision |
| Singapore | 6 months |
| Slovak Republic | 12 months |
| Slovenia | 12 months |
| Solomon Islands | no specific provision |
| South Africa | 12 months |
| Spain | 12 months |
| Sri Lanka | 183 days |
| Sudan | 12 months |
| Swaziland | 12 months |
| Sweden | 12 months |
| Switzerland | 12 months |
| Taiwan | 6 months |
| Thailand | 6 months |
| Trinidad and Tobago | 3 months |
| Tunisia | 6 months |
| | (no minimum where the fee for construction or installation is more than 10% of a related sale of machinery or equipment) |
| Turkey | 6 months |
| Turkmenistan | 24 months |
| | |
| Uganda | 183 days |

| | |
|---|---|
| Ukraine | 12 months |
| United States | 12 months |
| Uzbekistan | 12 months |
| Venezuela | 12 months |
| Vietnam | 183 days |
| Yugoslavia | 12 months |
| Zambia | 6 months |
| Zimbabwe | 6 months |

# A4

# Permanent establishment

# Introduction

## *Importance in international tax planning*

**[A4.1]** The concept of a permanent establishment is important in international tax planning because it will often determine whether a company is subject to tax in a particular jurisdiction.

For example, CTA 2009, s 5(2) provides that a company that is not resident in the UK will only be subject to UK corporation tax if it carries on a trade in the UK through a permanent establishment. Where it does so, it will be subject to UK corporation tax on all profits that are attributable to the UK permanent establishment.

In many cases planning will focus on a company not creating a permanent establishment, or minimising the profits attributable to that permanent establishment. Chapter B1 gives some further examples of where a permanent establishment is created—and if a permanent establishment is created, whether a subsidiary should instead be established.

In some cases, a company may specifically want to create a permanent establishment. A UK company may want to take advantage of the branch incorporation reliefs (see Chapter A9) or the branch profits exemption (see Chapter A16).

It is therefore important to understand the definition of permanent establishment, and how this applies in particular situations.

This Chapter focuses on the UK definition of permanent establishment, which is itself based on the OECD definition. This Chapter identifies when a non-resident company would have a permanent establishment in the UK, and considers steps which can be taken to mitigate this.

To the extent that another jurisdiction adopts the OECD definition (or similar), these principles are also relevant in determining if a UK company is likely to have a permanent establishment outside the UK, and the steps which can be taken to mitigate this. In any case, if a double tax agreement (DTA) is in place which is based on the OECD model, the OECD definition should override any domestic definition.

## Impact of the OECD Action Plan on Base Erosion and Profit Shifting (BEPS)

**[A4.2]** Whilst the information in this Chapter was up to date at the time of writing this book, it is important to keep up to date on the OECD Action Plan on Base Erosion and Profit Shifting (BEPS). More detail on BEPS can be found on the OECD website www.oecd.org/ctp/beps.htm.

When looking at tax planning around the definition of permanent establishment, it has become very important to keep up to date with the BEPS Action Plan.

The OECD definition of a permanent establishment has not changed since the OECD Model definition in 1963, however the world has changed dramatically with advances in technology and as a result it is quite possible and in fact very common for businesses to generate significant profit from a jurisdiction with no physical presence. The OECD published 15 actions points as part of its plans to tackle the issue of BEPS. The key action points that may impact permanent establishments are as follows:

**Action 1 – the digital economy** This action will examine the ability of a company to derive significant income from a territory due to its digital presence, but having insufficient physical presence/ nexus to be liable to tax in that territory. The expected outcomes of this action point may include changes to the definition of a permanent establishment. It is also important to note that this action point also covers indirect tax implications of the digital economy. The outcome of this action is expected in September 2014.

**Action 7 – Prevent artificial avoidance of PE status** Changes are expected to the definition of a PE so that arrangements such as commissionaire arrangements, and specific activity exemptions are not artificially used to prevent creating a taxable presence (see **A4.23**). The outcome of this action is expected in September 2015.

**Action 13 – Re-examine transfer pricing documentation** As dealings between a head office and its permanent establishment must be conducted on an arm's length basis, and the permanent establishment considered as a separate entity, transfer pricing documentation is also applicable to a permanent establishment. See **A13.2** for further details.

The expected outcome of this action is a common template to be used for documenting all related party transactions and that this is provided to all relevant governments. The time limit for this outcome is September 2014.

### Steps to determine if there is a permanent establishment

**[A4.3]** The steps for determining whether a company has a permanent establishment in the UK are as follows:

*   Is there a fixed place of business in the UK?
*   Is there a dependent agent in the UK?
*   Are the activities undertaken 'preparatory and auxiliary'?
*   If a DTA is in place, does a permanent establishment exist under the provisions of this agreement?

- Is a business carried on through the permanent establishment?

These steps are considered in detail in this Chapter. As noted above, these steps may also be relevant for determining if a UK company has a permanent establishment in another jurisdiction.

# Basic principles—definition of permanent establishment

## UK definition of permanent establishment

**[A4.4]** A permanent establishment is defined in CTA 2010, s 1141 as follows:

'(1)    For the purposes of the Corporation Tax Acts a company has a permanent establishment in a territory if (and only if)—

(a)    it has a fixed place of business there through which the business of the company is wholly or partly carried on, or

(b)    an agent acting on behalf of the company has and habitually exercises there authority to do business on behalf of the company.

This general definition is subject to the following provisions:

(2)    For this purpose a "fixed place of business" includes (without prejudice to the generality of that expression)—

(a)    a place of management;

(b)    a branch;

(c)    an office;

(d)    a factory;

(e)    a workshop;

(f)    an installation or structure for the exploration of natural resources;

(g)    a mine, an oil or gas well, a quarry or any other place of extraction of natural resources;

(h)    a building site or construction or installation project.'

Section 1142 makes provision in relation to independent agents:

'(1)    A company is not regarded as having a permanent establishment in a territory by reason of the fact that it carries on business there through an agent of independent status acting in the ordinary course of his business.'

And s 1143 makes provision in relation to preparatory and auxiliary activities:

'(1)    If the condition in subsection (2) is met, a company is not regarded as having a permanent establishment in a territory by reason of the fact that—

(a)    a fixed place of business is maintained there for the purpose of carrying on activities for the company, or

(b)    an agent carries on activities there for and on behalf of the company,

(2)    The condition is that, in relation to the business of the company as a whole, the activities carried on are only of a preparatory or auxiliary character.

(3)    For this purpose "activities of a preparatory or auxiliary character" include (without prejudice to the generality of that expression)—

(a)    the use of facilities for the purpose of storage, display or delivery of goods or merchandise belonging to the company;

(b)    the maintenance of a stock of goods or merchandise belonging to the company for the purpose of storage, display or delivery;

(c)    the maintenance of a stock of goods or merchandise belonging to the company for the purpose of processing by another person;

(d)     purchasing goods or merchandise, or collecting information, for the company.'

A permanent establishment can therefore exist in two ways:

(a)     a fixed place of business through which the business of the company is carried on (CTA 2010, s 1141(1)(a));

(b)     an agent in the UK acting on behalf of the non-resident habitually exercising authority to do business on behalf of the company (CTA 2010, s 1141(1)(b)).

## Oil and gas activities

**[A4.5]** A company undertaking oil and gas activities in the UK may have a permanent establishment in the UK even if it does not have a permanent establishment within the definition of s 1141. For these purposes, oil and gas activities include supporting activities, such as consulting services.

CTA 2009, s 1313 provides that:

'(1)     Any profits arising to a non-UK resident company—
    (*a*)     from exploration or exploitation activities, or
    (*b*)     from exploration or exploitation rights,
are treated for corporation tax purposes as profits of a trade carried on by the company in the United Kingdom through a permanent establishment in the United Kingdom . . .

(2)     . . . "exploration or exploitation activities" means activities carried on in connection with the exploration or exploitation of so much of the seabed and subsoil and their natural resources as is situated in the United Kingdom or the UK sector of the continental shelf.'

A non-resident company may therefore have a permanent establishment even if there is no fixed place of business—for example, if a project is undertaken for a short period of time which does not have sufficient permanence to be considered 'fixed' under the general definition.

This extended definition of permanent establishment may be overridden by a DTA, but certain DTAs (such as the UK/Canada DTA and the UK/Norway DTA) also contain specific articles dealing with oil and gas activities. For example, Article 27A of the UK/Canada DTA provides that a company undertaking activities connected with:

' . . . the exploration or exploitation of the sea bed and sub-soil and their natural resources situated in that other Contracting State shall . . . be deemed to be carrying on a business in that other Contracting State through a permanent establishment situated therein,'

provided the activities are undertaken for an aggregate of 30 days in any 12 month period.

This form of article would allow the extended definition under UK domestic law to apply.

### Interpretation of UK definition using OECD interpretation

**[A4.6]** The definition of permanent establishment under UK domestic law is based on the definition in the OECD Model Tax Convention. HMRC have confirmed (at INTM264050) that in most cases they will follow the OECD commentary on the permanent establishment article:

> 'Although the Commentary is not imported into UK domestic law the UK has contributed to and agreed the content except in specific instances where the UK has put on record either an observation or a reservation to a specific section of the Commentary. So, where the wording of the UK domestic law P[ermanent] E[stablishment] provisions are the same as those used in the OECD Model Treaty Article 5 then the commentary interpretation on those words will apply to those provisions and this guidance will contain cross-references into the guidance on treaty PE at INTM266000. If the Commentary interpretation of PE were to materially vary through periodic update or amendment the changes would have to be accepted by the UK Parliament before they could be taken to apply also to interpretation of UK domestic law PE.'

The guidance in the OECD commentary is therefore relevant when determining if a company has a permanent establishment in the UK. The current commentary relates to the 2010 Model Convention, which arguably does not 'materially vary' from the previous versions and should be followed by HMRC.

As the outcomes of the OECD BEPS Action Plan come to fruition, this may be crucial in determining whether the OECD commentary/changes to the treaty definition would be taken to apply to the interpretation of UK domestic law PE.

On 19 October 2012, the OECD published a revised discussion draft on the definition of permanent establishment under Article 5 of the 2010 Model Convention. (www.oecd.org/ctp/treaties/PermanentEstablishment.pdf) which proposes certain changes to the commentary. In all, the draft proposes changes in 25 different areas. Some of these are refinements to existing comments, but others are new, not least the consideration of a home office as a permanent establishment. The changes also consider the meaning of 'at the disposal of' under para 4.2, the time required for existence of a permanent establishment under para 6 and the meaning of to 'conclude contracts in the name of the enterprise'. A detailed discussion of the proposed changes is beyond the scope of this book, but they key ones are referred to where relevant to the text.

### Fixed place of business permanent establishment

**[A4.7]** In order that there is a permanent establishment under the fixed place of business, there must be:

(a)    a business;
(b)    a fixed place;
(c)    through which that business is undertaken.

A1.9 sets out the factors to consider when determining whether a business is carried on in the UK for the purposes of (c) above.

**Business**

**[A4.8]** The personnel carrying on the business through the fixed place can be:

(a)    employees of the non-resident company; or

(b)    contractors who are engaged by the non-resident company to act on its behalf.

Either would have the required capacity to carry on the business of the non-resident.

A holding company may have a place of management or an office in the UK, but this is unlikely to create a tax liability in the UK because under CTA 2009, s 5, it will only be subject to corporation tax if it carries on a *trade* through the permanent establishment. However, it could have a trade of providing management services to other group companies.

**Fixed place**

**[A4.9]** CTA 2010, s 1141 (2) sets out a list of what may constitute 'a fixed place of business':

'(a)    a place of management;

(b)    a branch;

(c)    an office;

(d)    a factory;

(e)    a workshop;

(f)    an installation or structure for the exploration of natural resources;

(g)    a mine, an oil or gas well, a quarry or any other place of extraction of natural resources;

(h)    a building site or construction or installation project.'

The list in s 1141(2) is non-exhaustive, and further examples of activities which may constitute a fixed place are outlined later in this chapter.

In order that a non-resident company has a 'fixed' place of business, it must undertake activities through the same place for a period of time. A non-resident company will not generally have a permanent establishment if it merely undertakes a single transaction from a particular location.

The current OECD commentary says:

'1.    Since the place of business must be fixed, it also follows that a permanent establishment can be deemed to exist only if the place of business has a certain degree of permanency, i.e. if it is not of a purely temporary nature. A place of business may, however, constitute a permanent establishment even though it exists, in practice, only for a very short period of time because the nature of the business is such that it will only be carried on for that short period of time. It is sometimes difficult to determine whether this is the case. Whilst the practices followed by Member countries have not been consistent in so far as time requirements are concerned, experience has shown that permanent establishments normally have not been considered to exist in situations where a business had been carried on in a country through a place of business that was maintained for less than six months (conversely, practice shows that there were many cases where a permanent establishment has been considered to exist where the place of business was maintained for a period longer than six months).'

The BIAC (Business and Advisory Committee) of the OECD has suggested that this should be a presumption, but the OECD prefers to refer to 'practices shows' which is less definitive. The proposed new commentary also gives examples of situations where a permanent establishment could exist, even though the non-resident company carries on activities for less than six months. Another exception to this would be where a company undertakes recurrent business in a particular jurisdiction, but does not establish itself there for six consecutive months. Paragraph 6 of the OECD commentary goes on to say:

'One exception has been where the activities were of a recurrent nature; in such cases, each period of time during which the place is used needs to be considered in combination with the number of times during which that place is used (which may extend over a number of years).'

For example, a non-resident company may regularly attend a trade fair at which it makes sales. After a period of years, the attendance would become recurrent and the non-resident company may acquire a permanent establishment. A new section 6.2 is also proposed, governing 'isolated activity' where the business activity is due to its nature of short duration, but takes place entirely and exclusively in the given state, this can create a permanent establishment.

In addition, the OECD commentary says that even where a specified 'fixed place of business' exists, this must also satisfy the general requirements of permanence in order to constitute a fixed place of business:

'it is assumed that the Contracting States interpret the terms listed, "a place of management", "a branch", "an office", etc. in such a way that such places of business constitute permanent establishments only if they meet the requirements of paragraph 1 [the general requirement to be a fixed place]' (paragraph 12 of the Commentary on Article 5).'

### Right to use the place of business

**[A4.10]** The place of business does not have to be rented or owned by the non-resident company itself, but simply has to be available for use by its employees. The OECD commentary confirms this:

Whilst no formal legal right to use a particular place is required for that place to constitute a permanent establishment, the mere presence of an enterprise at a particular location does not necessarily mean that that location is at the disposal of that enterprise. These principles are illustrated by the following examples where representatives of one enterprise are present on the premises of another enterprise. A first example is that of a salesman who regularly visits a major customer to take orders and meets the purchasing director in his office to do so. In that case, the customer's premises are not at the disposal of the enterprise for which the salesman is working and therefore do not constitute a fixed place of business through which the business of that enterprise is carried on

The new proposed commentary on section 4.2 suggests that to qualify as being at the disposal of an enterprise, there is no need of a formal right to use the location, but mere presence is not sufficient. What is needed is 'effective power to use the location' . . . and effectively uses that location for carrying on its own business activities *continuously and during an extended time period'*. There then follows a useful example of an IT trainer contracted to work in another state over an extended time period during which he is given a pass for unrestricted access to the building both to train and prepare. In this example, the building is considered to be at his disposal.

A second example is that of an employee of a company who, for a long period of time, is allowed to use an office in the headquarters of another company (eg a newly acquired subsidiary) in order to ensure that the latter company complies with its obligations under contracts concluded with the former company. In that case, the employee is carrying on activities related to the business of the former company and the office that is at his disposal at the headquarters of the other company will constitute a permanent establishment of his employer, provided that the office is at his disposal for a sufficiently long period of time so as to constitute a "fixed place of business" (see paragraphs 6 to 6.3) and that the activities that are performed there go beyond the activities referred to in paragraph 4 of the Article.

Two conclusions can be drawn from this:

*   an employee who regularly visits a place of business but who does not have a right to freely use that place of business (whether formal or informal) does not create a permanent establishment; and
*   an employee who has a right to use a place of business, but only for a limited period of time (see **A4.9**) does not create a permanent establishment.

## Preparatory and auxiliary activities

**[A4.11]** CTA 2010, s 1143 provides that certain activities carried on through a permanent establishment do not constitute a permanent establishment in the UK. This mirrors in part the case law on whether a trade is carried on in the UK:

'(1    A company is not regarded as having a permanent establishment in a territory by reason of the fact that—

(a)    a fixed place of business is maintained there for the purpose of carrying on activities for the company, or

(b)    an agent carries on activities there for and on behalf of the company, if, in relation to the business of the company as a whole, the activities carried on are only of a preparatory or auxiliary character.

(2)    For this purpose "activities of a preparatory or auxiliary character" include (without prejudice to the generality of that expression)—

(a)    the use of facilities for the purpose of storage, display or delivery of goods or merchandise belonging to the company;

(b)    the maintenance of a stock of goods or merchandise belonging to the company for the purpose of storage, display or delivery;

(c)    the maintenance of a stock of goods or merchandise belonging to the company for the purpose of processing by another person;

(d)    purchasing goods or merchandise, or collecting information, for the company.'

The exemption for preparatory and auxiliary activities in UK domestic law applies both to permanent establishments created as a result of a fixed place of business and a dependent agent.

The activities undertaken in the UK must be preparatory and auxiliary in the context of the company as a whole. Where, for example, the company's business is to provide market research data to its customers then undertaking market research in the UK would not be preparatory and auxiliary. The HMRC Manuals also talk of remoteness from the main profit making apparatus of the business. In practice it is sometimes difficult to draw the line here. Take for example a foreign newspaper journalist operating in London. Historically many journalists have fallen under the collection of information clause under subsection (d) above. However in this day and age it is quite common for journalists to be making live broadcasts from the streets of London on a regular basis. Is this still remote from the profit making apparatus? Some countries take the view that it is part and parcel and therefore a live broadcast on its own can constitute a permanent establishment.

The OECD commentary says:

> '1.    It is often difficult to distinguish between activities which have a preparatory or auxiliary character and those which have not. The decisive criterion is whether or not the activity of the fixed place of business in itself forms an essential and significant part of the activity of the enterprise as a whole.'

Even if some activities carried on in the UK may be preparatory or auxiliary in nature, where other activities are also carried on (eg the negotiation or conclusion of contracts) then the whole of the activities (including those that are in isolation preparatory or auxiliary) will be deemed to create a permanent establishment.

The approach taken in some of the UK's DTAs may be different to this—in particular, it may allow the activities to be considered in isolation and without aggregation.

### Dependent agent

**[A4.12]** A permanent establishment may also exist in the UK if there is a 'dependent agent' in the UK. This is defined within CTA 2010, s 1141 as:

> '(1)    . . .
> (2)    an agent acting on behalf of the company has and habitually exercises there authority to do business on behalf of the company.'

The authority of the agent to conclude contracts may be written, verbal or implied (ie it is implicit by virtue of the non-resident company taking no active involvement in the negotiation or conclusion of contracts). Paragraph 19 of the October 2012 discussion document looks in detail at what is meant by the meaning of 'to conclude contracts in the name of the enterprise' in the context of the recent *Zimmer* (2010) 12 ITLR 739 and *Dell Products (NUF) v Tax East* (2011) 13 ITLR 706 commissionaire cases in France and Norway respectively. The document looks in detail at whether or not one party needs to be legally bound by the activity of the other. There is also an excellent article written by Hans Pijl, a noted authority in this area (Agency Permanent Establishments: in the name of and the Relationship between Article 5(5) and (6)—Part 1 and Part 2, Bulletin for International Taxation 2013 (Part 1: January, p 3–25; Part 2: February, p 62–97)).

### Independent agent

**[A4.13]** Under CTA 2012, s 1142, an independent agent, such as a broker or general commission agent cannot constitute a permanent establishment of a non-resident company provided he is independent of that company, both legally and economically, and acts for the non-resident company in the normal course of business.

In this case the non-resident company would not have the ability to control the agent nor the manner in which the agent carries on his work.

### Nature of contracts

**[A4.14]** The definition of dependent agent specifically refers to agents who conclude contracts with customers. Contracts concluded for the purposes of establishing the business in the UK (for instance a rental agreement to obtain premises) will not fall within this definition. The OECD commentary says:

'1.     The fixed places of business mentioned in paragraph 4 cannot be deemed to constitute permanent establishments so long as their activities are restricted to the functions which are the prerequisite for assuming that the fixed place of business is not a permanent establishment. This will be the case even if the contracts necessary for establishing and carrying on the business are concluded by those in charge of the places of business themselves.'

### Frequency of contracts

**[A4.15]** It is necessary that the agent 'habitually' concludes contracts on behalf of the non-resident company. If occasional contracts are concluded, then this may not give rise to a permanent establishment, as it would not have the necessary degree of permanence. The OECD commentary says:

'2.     The use of the term "permanent establishment" in this context presupposes, of course, that that person makes use of this authority repeatedly and not merely in isolated cases.'

However, best practice would be that no contracts are concluded if possible.

### Negotiation of contracts

**[A4.16]** An agent will be treated as concluding contracts even if he does not actually sign the contract. The negotiation and agreement of key contractual terms will constitute 'conclusion' under the OECD definition:

'3.     . . . A person who is authorised to negotiate all elements and details of a contract in a way binding on the enterprise can be said to exercise this authority "in that State", even if the contract is signed by another person in the State in which the enterprise is situated or if the first person has not formally been given a power of representation.'

Some of the UK's older DTAs contain a different definition of dependent agent, which requires that the agent 'negotiates and concludes' the contract—conclusion of a contract in this case would arguably not include the negotiation as it is separately identified. This wording is discussed in more detail in **A8.29**.

This should be contrasted with the situation where some terms of a contract are negotiated in the UK, but the majority of the contractual terms are negotiated outside the UK. The OECD commentary says:

'4.    . . . The mere fact, however, that a person has attended or even participated in negotiations in a State between an enterprise and a client will not be sufficient, by itself, to conclude that the person has exercised in that State an authority to conclude contracts in the name of the enterprise.'

Employees of a non-resident company can therefore attend occasional meetings in the UK to discuss contractual terms without necessarily creating a permanent establishment in the UK. Best practice would suggest that this should happen only where it is not possible to do otherwise.

### Subsidiary company as dependent agent

**[A4.17]** The existence of a subsidiary company in a particular jurisdiction does not necessarily create a permanent establishment for a parent company. However, nor does it preclude a permanent establishment from existing. If the subsidiary company habitually concludes contracts on behalf of the parent company, it may create a permanent establishment by virtue of being a dependent agent.

This is recognised by the commentary on Article 5 of the OECD model tax convention:

'1.    A subsidiary may be authorized to conclude contracts on behalf of the parent company. A PE is constituted if all of the conditions under the agency clause are satisfied. Clearly, such authority to act on behalf of the parent company may also be based on the circumstance that the subsidiary habitually acts on behalf of the parent even if a contract between the two companies does not exist  . . . The subsidiary may, for example, conclude contracts in its own name and buy the commodities from the parent company. In many cases the commercial benefits of the foreign business activities of the two companies as a group may be exactly identical, although the tax situation is different.'

A subsidiary should therefore conclude contracts in its own name, and not have the authority to conclude contracts in the name of its parent company.

### Investment manager exemption

**[A4.18]** A specific exemption (CTA 2010, s 1146) is available for UK resident investment managers who manage investments on behalf of non-resident companies. This would be relevant where an offshore company is regularly trading in shares or other investments, such that it has a trading activity. In the absence of the exemption, the investment manager could be treated as a dependent agent of the non-resident company such that the non-resident company has a permanent establishment in the UK.

The exemption is subject to a number of conditions, which require *inter alia* that the investment manager is not connected with the non-resident company.

## Differences between UK and OECD definitions of permanent establishment

### Preparatory and auxiliary activities

**[A4.19]** The UK domestic definition of preparatory and auxiliary activities is narrower than the OECD model (and most DTAs). Where the benefit of such a DTA is available, a non-resident company may be able to rely on this to support that it is undertaking only preparatory and auxiliary activities in the UK, even where its activities would fall outside the definition based on CTA 2010, s 1143 alone.

Preparatory and auxiliary activities are defined in the OECD model as follows:

'2. Notwithstanding the preceding provisions of this Article, the term "permanent establishment" shall be deemed not to include:
   (a) the use of facilities solely for the purpose of storage, display or delivery of goods or merchandise belonging to the enterprise;
   (b) the maintenance of a stock of goods or merchandise belonging to the enterprise solely for the purpose of storage, display or delivery;
   (c) the maintenance of a stock of goods or merchandise belonging to the enterprise solely for the purpose of processing by another enterprise;
   (d) the maintenance of a fixed place of business solely for the purpose of purchasing goods or merchandise or of collecting information, for the enterprise;
   (e) the maintenance of a fixed place of business solely for the purpose of carrying on, for the enterprise, any other activity of a preparatory or auxiliary character;
   (f) the maintenance of a fixed place of business solely for any combination of activities mentioned in subparagraphs a) to e), provided that the overall activity of the fixed place of business resulting from this combination is of a preparatory or auxiliary character.'

(e) and (f) are not included in the UK definition, which does not require an 'aggregation' of preparatory and auxiliary activities (see **A4.11**), nor include an overriding general definition of preparatory and auxiliary activities as at (e).

Examples of activities which may be preparatory and auxiliary include:

(a) preparing company management profiles;
(b) maintaining industry information databases;
(c) assisting with financial analysis;
(d) monitoring industries/companies;
(e) researching market data;
(f) providing information and analysis; and
(g) maintaining client contact database (addresses, profiles etc).

In addition, the exemption in the OECD model only applies to permanent establishments created as a result of a fixed place of business and not a dependent agent. In practice, however, a dependent agent (who concludes contracts) will not be undertaking only preparatory and auxiliary activities.

## Construction and installation activities

**[A4.20]** The OECD model states that a permanent establishment will only exist if a construction or installation site exists for at least six months.

Different time periods may be specified in the UK's DTAs—see **A3.41**.

### *Permanent establishment outside the UK*

#### Overseas definition of permanent establishment

**[A4.21]** Where a country follows the OECD definition, the principles outlined in this Chapter will apply to determine if a UK company has a permanent establishment outside the UK.

However, many jurisdictions do not follow the OECD definition. For example:

* A permanent establishment will exist in France if a 'commercial cycle' is undertaken there. A commercial cycle is the purchase, processing and onward sale of goods.
* A permanent establishment will exist in India if services are performed in India, even if no fixed place of business exists.
* A taxable presence will exist in China if a representative office is registered, even if there is no permanent establishment.

In these cases, it will be necessary to consider whether a DTA provides relief, and determines that there is in fact no permanent establishment.

#### Double tax agreement override

**[A4.22]** A DTA will normally set out a definition of 'permanent establishment' which applies when a resident of one contracting state undertakes activities in the other contracting state. This may be different from the definitions under the domestic law of the contacting states.

The DTA may therefore provide relief where the activities would be treated as creating a permanent establishment under domestic law, but not under the DTA.

A DTA only provides relief from double taxation (ie where a tax liability would otherwise exist). Of course, if no tax liability exists there is usually no benefit in considering the DTA.

Most DTAs concluded by the UK follow the OECD model tax convention (and therefore the principles outlined in this chapter). However, there may be differences which need to be considered, and some examples are outlined in **A8.28**.

# Planning—specific situations

**[A4.23]** As discussed in **A4.2**, the OECD Action Plan on BEPS is looking to tackle artificial avoidance of permanent establishment status. The specific planning situations set out in this Chapter are based on current definitions of permanent establishment and should be considered in light of the outcomes of the BEPS Action Plan.

## Commissionaires and commission agents

**[A4.24]** A commission agent (see **A13.47**) makes sales to customers on behalf and in the name of its disclosed principal. Because it is entering into sales contracts in the name of the principal, it is very likely to create a permanent establishment for the principal.

A commissionaire (see **A13.48**) on the other hand makes sales in its own name albeit for the benefit of its undisclosed principal. All economic risks are borne by the principal.

In a civil law jurisdiction, no permanent establishment is created because the commissionaire does not enter into sales contracts in the name of the principal. In common law jurisdictions such as the UK, a commissionaire will be treated the same as a commission agent, with the same risk of creating a permanent establishment. Most European countries are civil law jurisdictions rather than common law and so distinguish between commission agents and commissionaires.

The profit attributed to any permanent establishment would in any case be reduced by any commissions paid to the commission agent or commissionaire (see **A4.43**).

However, if not structured correctly, a commissionaire in a civil law jurisdiction can create a permanent establishment for its principal. In the French case of *Zimmer Ltd* (31 March 2010 Case No 304715), the French Conseil d'Etat (Supreme Court) held that a commissionaire which was properly structured under French civil law could not directly bind the principal, and it could not therefore create a dependent agency permanent establishment.

However, the French court did state that a commissionaire could create a permanent establishment for the principal if for example the principal is bound by contracts concluded by the commissionaire. It is therefore important that there are distinct contracts—one between the principal and the commissionaire, and one between the commissionaire and the customer.

In the *Dell [2 March 2011 Oslo Court of Appeals]* case, the Norwegian court stated that the substance of the arrangements should be considered rather than the legal form. In this case, the commissionaire did create a permanent establishment for its principal because:

*   the commissionaire relied on the name of the principal when making sales;
*   customers would believe that the group as a whole (and therefore the principal) would fulfil the contract;

- the principal did not in fact refuse any contracts;
- the principal set the terms of the contract between the commissionaire and the customer, and the commissionaire was not allowed to make amendments;
- the commissionaire and the principal had an integrated accounting system.

The *Dell* decision was subsequently overturned in the Norwegian Supreme Court on 2 December 2011 (HR-2011-02245-A)). The key element of the decision was that under civil law the commissionaire could not bind its principal. There was nothing in the OECD Model Treaty or other sources of law which gave a different result. In line with the *Zimmer* case the Court held that something extra was required over and above a normal commissionaire arrangement in order to create a permanent establishment. The court also has regard to the fact that in 15 other countries in Europe a commissionaire arrangement did not create a permanent establishment.

It was hoped that the *Dell* case would give a clear position on permanent establishments in Europe in general but this was followed by an adverse judgements in the *Roche* (actually a business restructuring case) (12 January Spanish supreme court) (STS January 12, 2012). In Roche the judgment of the Spanish authorities seemed to be coloured by the change in role of a Spanish fully fledged manufacturer to a contract manufacturer and it was held that the Swiss parent had both a fixed place of business and a dependent agency permanent establishment.

However, in the case of *Boston Scientific* theItalian Supreme Court, Tax Section, n 3769 of 9 March, 2012 gave some hope in finding that the legal arrangements of a commissionaire arrangement could not be overturned by a substance over form argument.

It should be noted that much of the debate revolves around precise wording of local rules and the wording of double tax agreements so great care needs to be exercised when concluding such arrangements in continental Europe.

Although these cases are specific to civil law jurisdictions, some general principles can be deduced:

- it should be clear to customers (for example in advertising material) that they are contracting with the commissionaire—and not the group;
- there should clearly be two separate contracts—one between the commissionaire and the customer, and one between the commissionaire and the principal;
- the commissionaire and the principal should have separate accounting systems.

## Concession agreements

[A4.25] Some shops (in particular department stores) enter into concession agreements, which allow companies to sell their products through a branded area or 'concession' within the shop.

The terms of such concession agreements vary, but typically cover matters such as staffing, ownership of stock, responsibility for maintenance, and processing customer transactions.

In some cases, these terms can create a permanent establishment for a non-resident company. For example, if the non-resident company is responsible for providing staff, maintaining the concession, and taking payment from customers, this is likely to constitute a fixed place of business through which its business is carried on.

However, if the concession is run by staff employed by the shop, who also take payment from customers (with a payment subsequently made to the non-resident company after deduction of a commission), this is unlikely to constitute a fixed place of business, because the non-resident company is not undertaking business there (notwithstanding that it provides the branding and the product).

### *Automatic equipment*

**[A4.26]** The OECD recognises that automatic equipment (such as gaming or vending machines) may also have the capacity to undertake the business of a non-resident company. This will only be the case if the company receives the income arising from the equipment. The OECD commentary says:

'1      . . . a permanent establishment may nevertheless exist if the business of the enterprise is carried on mainly through automatic equipment, the activities of the personnel being restricted to setting up, operating, controlling and maintaining such equipment. Whether or not gaming and vending machines and the like set up by an enterprise of a State in the other State constitute a permanent establishment thus depends on whether or not the enterprise carries on a business activity besides the initial setting up of the machines. A permanent establishment does not exist if the enterprise merely sets up the machines and then leases the machines to other enterprises. A permanent establishment may exist, however, if the enterprise which sets up the machines also operates and maintains them for its own account. This also applies if the machines are operated and maintained by an agent dependent on the enterprise.'

Automatic equipment may be located in another company's premises, and operated and maintained by their employees. If the non-resident company continues to receive all of the income from the equipment, a permanent establishment may nonetheless exist because the equipment is still operated and maintained 'for its own account'.

However, if the non-resident company receives a payment from the local company which is characterised as rent for the use of the equipment, and from which the local company retains an amount to reflect its share of the profits derived from the equipment, it may not have a permanent establishment.

### E-commerce

**[A4.27]** Another form of automated equipment can exist where a company is engaged in selling goods or services over the internet ('e-commerce'). The server through which the sale is made may constitute a fixed place of business, as it is:

- a fixed piece of hardware;
- through which the business is carried on;
- which the company is entitled to use.

An internet website is a combination of software and electronic data and as such does not constitute tangible property that is capable of having a location that could constitute a place of business. The server on which the website is stored and through which it is accessed is a physical piece of equipment that will have a physical location and hence may constitute a fixed place of business for the enterprise that operates the server.

### UK view

**[A4.28]** In the UK, HMRC take the view that a server alone or together with a website does not on its own create a permanent establishment for a company that is making sales and has no other presence in the UK. This view is taken regardless of whether the server is owned, rented or otherwise at the disposal of the business (*HMRC Press Release* published on 11 April 2000).

Following recent press controversy in the UK in this area relating to the tax affairs of Amazon and Google (amongst others) it is likely that the taxation affairs of internet companies will be revisited. Much of this will be done by the BEPS project (see preface) but other countries such as France have looked at alternate methods already—notably the Collin and Colin report published on 18 January 2013 which looked at taxing internet companies based on data or number of users.

### OECD view

**[A4.29]** The OECD consider that a company which makes sales through a website may have a permanent establishment where the website servers are located:

'1    . . . A different example is that of an enterprise (sometimes referred to as an "e-tailer") that carries on the business of selling products through the Internet . . . If . . . the typical functions related to a sale are performed at that location (for example, the conclusion of the contract with the customer, the processing of the payment and the delivery of the products are performed automatically through the equipment located there), these activities cannot be considered to be merely preparatory or auxiliary.'

A website may be used simply to advertise goods or services or to gather market research and data for the enterprise. These activities would likely be preparatory or auxiliary in nature such that a permanent establishment would not be created.

Before hosting a website on a server located in another jurisdiction, a non-resident company should confirm whether this server will constitute a permanent establishment. The treatment of a server may differ significantly between jurisdictions, and should be confirmed in every case.

Historically non-resident internet companies operating in the UK have been able to benefit from a benign regime which allowed them to have substantial sales and presence in the UK and yet pay little or no corporate tax. A typical structure would have had staff performing a support role in the UK with costs recharged on a cost plus basis to a group company based in say Ireland or Luxembourg. At the same time activity in any UK warehouses would be able to rely on the there being no permanent establishment because only a warehouse was maintained in the UK.

Given the press storm created by such structures in the last 12 months, I think it is safe to say that even if the UK does not go down the line of the Collin and Colin report in France, there will in future be greater enforcement in this area going forward, with closer examination of the overall business cycle, particularly as the UK has signed up to the BEPS action plan referred to at A4.2.

### Internet service providers (ISPs)

**[A4.30]** Both the UK and the OECD consider that an Internet Service Provider (ISP)—whose business includes operating web hosting servers which they own or lease to other companies—will likely have a permanent establishment where the servers are located. The OECD commentary says:

'1      . . . some ISPs are in the business of operating their own servers for the purpose of hosting web sites or other applications for other enterprises. For these ISPs, the operation of their servers in order to provide services to customers is an essential part of their commercial activity and cannot be considered preparatory or auxiliary.'

The same concept is likely to apply to companies who own or lease servers which are the main part of their business, rather than the medium through which they conduct sales of other products or services. This could include data warehouses, electronically delivered service providers, and online gambling operators.

### *Partnerships and Limited Liability Partnerships (LLPs)*

**[A4.31]** By virtue of CTA 2009, s 1273(1)(a), a member of a limited liability partnership (LLP) is deemed to carry on the activities of LLP. If the activities of the LLP are sufficient to constitute a permanent establishment in the UK, then a non-resident company which is a member of the LLP will have a permanent establishment in the UK. It would then be subject to UK corporation tax (subject to the application of a double tax agreement).

The position of a general partnership is not as clear, but s 1259(4)(a) requires that the profits of a non-resident partner are 'the amount of the profits of the trade chargeable to corporation tax for that period if a non-UK resident company carried on the trade'. Because a non-resident company would only be subject to corporation tax if it had a permanent establishment in the UK, the non-resident partner would only be taxable if the partnership had a permanent establishment. This is also confirmed by HMRC at INTM261000.

The mere existence of a partnership or an LLP is not sufficient to create a permanent establishment in the UK—it must actually carry on activities which create a permanent establishment. As a consequence it is perfectly possible for two non-resident companies to create a UK LLP for a trade that does not have a permanent establishment in the UK and as a result they would not pay UK tax on the profits. For countries that treat a UK LLP as an opaque entity, this may create planning possibilities.

### Property development

**[A4.32]** A non-UK company which develops property in the UK may have a permanent establishment in the UK if it has a construction site here.

This is considered in detail at A3.29.

# Planning—practical guidance

### Steps to avoid creating a permanent establishment

**[A4.33]** The following steps should be followed to avoid creating a permanent establishment in the UK. Similar steps can be followed to avoid creating a permanent establishment outside the UK where the OECD definition of permanent establishment is used.

Fixed place of business:

(1)  The non-resident company should not have a lease or rental agreement, and should not own property in the UK.
(2)  The non-resident company should not have the right to use any premises in the UK—for example, premises which are owned by another group company, or an employee. Access to any such premises should be limited—for example, employees of the non-resident company should not be issued entry passes, and should be treated as visitors.
(3)  The non-resident company should not regularly use the same premises, for example a stand at a trade fair or a particular hotel room.
(4)  Employees of the non-resident company should not have business cards showing a UK address.
(5)  The website of the non-resident company should not advertise a UK address (although a group website could show a UK address as belonging to a subsidiary).
(6)  Any advertisements or stationery of the non-resident company should not show a UK address.

Dependent agent:

(1) All prices should be determined outside the UK, including any bulk discounts. Prices should only be communicated in the UK.
(2) Any price negotiation should take place outside the UK.
(3) Other contractual terms should be determined or negotiated outside the UK.
(4) Contracts with customers should not be signed in the UK. A permanent establishment should only be created if contracts are 'habitually' concluded in the UK, and employees of the non-resident company may therefore attend occasional meetings in the UK to discuss contractual terms without necessarily creating a permanent establishment in the UK. However, best practice would suggest that this should happen only where it is not possible to do otherwise.

Preparatory and auxiliary activities:

(1) Where a fixed place of business or a dependent agent is unavoidable, the activities undertaken in the UK should be preparatory and auxiliary to the main trading activities of the non-resident company.

Again, all of these steps should be considered in light of the BEPS Action Plan.

## Documentation

**[A4.34]** If a non-resident company has an employee based in the UK, the employee should not be given authority to negotiate or conclude contracts, otherwise a permanent establishment will be created. This restriction can be written specifically into the employment contract, and followed in practice.

Similar restrictions can be written into inter-company agreements if there is a risk that a subsidiary could be a dependent agent.

## Splitting activities

**[A4.35]** A company may undertake different activities in a particular jurisdiction, only some of which are sufficient to create a permanent establishment. However, once a permanent establishment is created, the profits of all the activities may be subject to tax as part of the permanent establishment. This is known as the 'force of attraction' principle and may not apply in every case.

The activities can therefore be split between two companies—one of which has a permanent establishment, and the other which does not.

Diagram 1 shows a UK group which sells and installs equipment in another jurisdiction. The installation activity is sufficient to create a permanent establishment, but the sales activity by itself would not be. However, if the same company both sold and installed the equipment, there is a risk that the profit on the sales activity could be attributed to the permanent establishment. The group has therefore established a separate company to undertake the installation activity, to ensure that the profit on the sales activity is not attributed to the permanent establishment.

Diagram 1

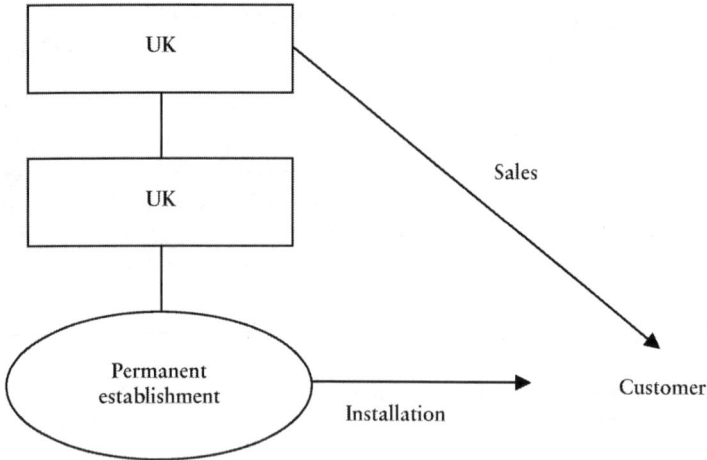

This analysis was upheld in the Indian case of *Ericsson Radio Systems A.B. v Deputy C.I.T* (2005) 96 TTJ Delhi 1. A Swedish company sold telecommunications equipment to a customer in India, and the Indian branch of another group company installed the equipment under a separate contract. The sale of the equipment was not taxable in India, even though a permanent establishment existed as a result of the installation.

However, care must be taken that a permanent establishment is not created under general principles in such circumstances. In the linked cases of *Motorola Inc. And Nokia Networks Oy v Deputy C.I.T*, (2005) 96 TTJ Delhi 1, the non-resident companies making the sale had a permanent establishment in India because they had access to the offices of Indian group companies. The sale of equipment was therefore taxable in India, because the company making the sale had a fixed place of business in India.

### Steps to create a permanent establishment outside the UK

**[A4.36]** As noted in the introduction to this Chapter, there are circumstances where it might be beneficial for a company to have a permanent establishment outside the UK:

- a permanent establishment must exist in order to the incorporate a branch under the provisions of TCGA 1992, s 140 or CTA 2009, s 827;
- an exemption is available for branch profits where a permanent establishment exists outside the UK.

In order to deliberately create a permanent establishment in a particular jurisdiction, a company could for example:

- acquire premises;
- conclude contracts in the jurisdiction;
- have employees who are permanently based in the jurisdiction;
- register a branch;

- open a bank account;
- enter into contracts with customers and suppliers in the name of the branch.

These would need to exist for a period of time (perhaps as long as six months) in order to have the permanence necessary for a fixed place of business to exist.

# Basic principles—other issues

## Attribution of profits and losses

**[A4.37]** CTA 2009, ss 19–32 set out how the profits of a permanent establishment in the UK are calculated.

The permanent establishment should recognise profits equal to the profit it would have expected to make had it been:

(a)     a company separate from the non-resident company;
(b)     engaging in the same (or similar) activities;
(c)     under the same (or similar) conditions,

as if it had been dealing with an independent non-resident company.

In effect, non-resident companies are required to follow the arm's length principle (using transfer pricing principles and methodologies—see CHAPTER A13) to calculate the profits of a UK permanent establishment.

In the calculation of the taxable profits of the permanent establishment allowance will be given for expenditure incurred, including administrative expenses, as would be deductible for a UK resident company.

A charge to UK taxation will also arise on gains arising from the disposal of assets used in or for the purposes of the trade of the permanent establishment (see CHAPTER A11).

## Equity and capital requirements

**[A4.38]** The transfer pricing rules should be considered to establish the appropriate level of equity and loan capital which should be attributed to the permanent establishment, and therefore the amount of interest which is deductible.

The amount of capital required will depend on the size and nature of the activities of the permanent establishment and requires, in simple terms, a hypothetical balance sheet to be created including any tangible and intangible fixed assets, with the liabilities being represented by the loan capital and equity. Transfer pricing rules are used to determine how much of that liability should be represented by interest bearing loan capital and how much by non-interest bearing capital or equity.

One must, therefore, consider the types of capital structure that other companies have of a similar size and undertaking similar activities in the UK.

Retained profits can be included as equity where the funds have been retained in the UK and not remitted to the overseas company.

### Profits of overseas permanent establishment

**[A4.39]** A UK company will need to be able to calculate the profits attributable to an overseas permanent establishment for a number of reasons:

- calculating the overseas tax due;
- determining the profits which are exempt from UK corporation tax as a result of the branch exemption (see **A16.27**);
- if the branch exemption does not apply, determining the profits against which double tax relief can be claimed (see **A10.17**).

In the first instance, the profits attributable to the permanent establishment will be determined under the relevant overseas tax system. This may then be overridden by a DTA—see below.

### Royalties paid to the parent company

**[A4.40]** Under CTA 2009, s 31, no deduction is available in respect of royalties which are paid by the permanent establishment to its parent company.

Royalties will only be deductible where the non-resident parent company has made actual payments to a third party and some or all of those payments relate directly to the permanent establishment. For example, the parent company may pay royalties in respect of software which is used by the permanent establishment. In this case, the part of the royalty payments relating to the permanent establishment can be attributed to the permanent establishment, and deducted for corporation tax purposes.

As a consequence, the royalty may acquire a UK source such that it is subject to UK withholding tax (see **A5.12**).

### Interest paid to the parent company

**[A4.41]** Similarly, no deduction is available in respect of interest or other finance costs which are paid by the permanent establishment to its parent company (CTA 2009, s 32).

Interest will only be deductible where the non-resident parent company has made actual payments and some or all of those payments relate directly to the permanent establishment. For example, the parent company may have taken out a loan which is used by the permanent establishment to purchase assets. In this case, the part of the interest relating to the permanent establishment can be attributed to the permanent establishment, and deducted for corporation tax purposes.

As a consequence, the interest may acquire a UK source such that it is subject to UK withholding tax (see **A5.3**).

In both of these instances, royalties and interest will normally be deductible (subject to the arm's length principle) when paid to a different group company.

### Allocation of parent company expenses

**[A4.42]** Expenses may be attributed to the permanent establishment where the expenses were incurred by the non-resident company for the purposes of the permanent establishment. An attribution may be made regardless of whether the permanent establishment reimburses the non-resident company. This is supported by CTA 2009, s 29, although in practice such management charges charged by the parent are often challenged by HMRC both in principle and quantum.

### Payment of arm's-length fees for local activities

**[A4.43]** Where a permanent establishment is created by the activity of another person—for example a third party contractor who undertakes work on a construction site—an arm's-length fee paid to the other person should reduce the taxable profits of the permanent establishment to nil.

Best practice would be to file a tax return nonetheless, showing no profit attributable to the permanent establishment.

In the Indian case of *BBC Worldwide Ltd v DDIT* (ITA No 1188/Del/06) (15 January 2010, unreported), the UK company's Indian subsidiary earned a commission on advertising sales. The Tribunal held that even if the UK company had a permanent establishment in India (by virtue of the subsidiary being a dependent agent) the commission payment would be deductible, and no profits would remain assessable.

### Double tax agreements

**[A4.44]** The 2010 update to the OECD Model Tax Convention made a number of changes to the method by which the profits of a permanent establishment should be calculated. In many cases, the profits of a permanent establishment will be lower under a DTA than under UK domestic law. In particular:

- interest charged by the parent company is deductible by the permanent establishment, provided sufficient capital is allocated to the permanent establishment;
- royalties charged by the parent company are deductible, provided sufficient capital is allocated to the permanent establishment;
- services provided by the parent company can be charged to the permanent establishment at cost plus a mark up, irrespective of whether similar services are also provided to third parties.

An overseas company with a permanent establishment in the UK may therefore reduce the profits chargeable to corporation tax by following the DTA rather than UK domestic law.

### Disclosure of Information

**[A4.45]** Depending on local regulations, a non-resident company may be required to file its accounts in the overseas jurisdiction as a result of having a business presence there (even if this business presence does not constitute a permanent establishment).

In the UK a non-resident company must file accounts or other information with Companies House (where they are on public record) if it has either a branch or a place of business in the UK.

As a result, the non-resident company may wish to establish a new subsidiary which undertakes no activity other than the permanent establishment (see Diagram 2). The accounts filed would then only reflect the activities of the permanent establishment.

Where a non-resident company establishes a subsidiary specifically to hold a UK branch, and this subsidiary does not undertake any other activity, then the activities undertaken in the UK will not constitute preparatory and auxiliary activities, even if they are performed for another group company. The subsidiary does not carry on a business in relation to which the UK activities could be preparatory and auxiliary. The UK activities are the only activities of the subsidiary.

Diagram 2

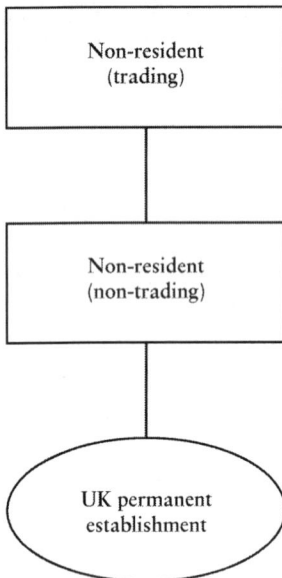

### Filing tax returns

**[A4.46]** A permanent establishment is likely to be required to file tax returns and pay tax.

Interest and penalties may become due in some jurisdictions if a permanent establishment exists but no tax returns are filed. In addition, the company may be required to notify the local tax authorities of the existence of a permanent establishment.

In the UK, non-residents subject to UK corporation tax are required to:

(a)    notify HMRC that the company is subject to corporation tax;

(b)    file corporation tax self-assessment returns; and

(c)    pay tax on the profits of the permanent establishment, possibly through the quarterly instalment payment regime if the thresholds are met.

Failure to do so may attract penalties. A1.9 outlines the notification requirements in more detail.

## Ease of establishment

**[A4.47]** If the overseas activities are new, the non-resident company may not be certain as to their success. The company may therefore prefer to commence operations as a permanent establishment as this may be quicker, easier and cheaper than incorporating a subsidiary.

If the operations are successful the permanent establishment could subsequently be incorporated into at a later date although consideration would need to be given to the tax implications both in the jurisdiction in which the company is resident and the jurisdiction in which the permanent establishment exists.

The incorporation of a UK permanent establishment of a non-resident company should be free from UK tax by virtue of TCGA 1992, s 171, and the incorporation of an overseas permanent establishment should be exempt from tax by virtue of TCGA 1992, s 140. These provisions are outlined in more detail in CHAPTER A9 and CHAPTER A11.

If the activities are unsuccessful it is may be significantly easier to cease operations of a permanent establishment than to liquidate a subsidiary.

In practice, however, many inbound UK investors choose to incorporate from the outset for reasons of liability. This also affords a (cosmetic) degree of protection against transfer pricing enquiries as it is generally thought easier to ring fence profits in a subsidiary.

## Other taxes

**[A4.48]** In addition to corporation tax, other taxes may arise if an overseas company has a presence in the UK (or if a UK company has a permanent establishment outside the UK). For example:

•    VAT (or sales tax outside the UK);

•    employment tax if there are employees;

•    other indirect taxes such as gambling duties or customs duty.

It should be noted that HMRC has introduced new 'place of consumption' rules for gaming duties (under the old rules, duties were applied on a 'place of supply' basis). This means that remote gaming machines in the UK (whether or not they create a permanent establishment) may be subject to UK gaming duties.

# A5

# Withholding tax

**[A5.1]** Withholding tax is an important aspect of international tax planning and can have a significant impact on the cost of cross border transactions, not least because it is a tax on gross income, and not on profits.

This Chapter highlights the key withholding tax implications for payments made by a UK company and the methods for obtaining relief from overseas withholding tax.

This Chapter also provides guidance on structuring cross-border transactions to minimise the impact of both UK and overseas withholding tax.

# Basic principles—interest

**[A5.2]** ITA 2007, s 874 requires that where a payment of yearly interest arising in the UK is made by:

(a)     a company;
(b)     a partnership of which a company is a member; or
(c)     any other person to another person whose usual place of abode is outside the UK,

tax at the basic rate (20%) must be withheld from the interest and paid to HMRC.

Place of abode is not always the same as residence, and is discussed further at A3.5.

### Source of interest

**[A5.3]** Interest is treated as arising in the UK if it has a source in the UK.

The source of interest does not follow the residence of the payer. This may sometimes cause difficulties as a non-UK payer of interest may be obliged to withhold UK tax if the interest has a UK source. For instance, a non-resident company with a loan secured on UK property, or with a UK permanent establishment, may be required to withhold tax on interest.

The correct approach was considered in the House of Lords case *Westminster Bank Executor and Trustee Co (Channel Islands) Ltd v National Bank of Greece SA* [1971] AC 945, [1971] 1 All ER 233 (which is commonly referred to as the 'Greek Bank' case).

In this case the following factors were considered relevant in deciding that income did not have a UK source:

(a)     there was an obligation undertaken by a principal debtor which was a foreign company;
(b)     the obligation was guaranteed by another foreign company with no place of business in the UK;
(c)     the obligation was secured on lands and public revenues outside the UK;
(d)     funds used for payment by the debtor of principal or interest to residents outside Greece would have been provided either by a remittance from Greece or funds remitted by debtors from abroad (even though a cheque might be drawn in London).

In the Greek Bank case Lord Hailsham placed much emphasis on the fact that neither the debtor nor the creditor had a place of business in the UK. He focused on the residence of the guarantor. Even though the successors of the rights had a branch in the UK, this did not change the fact that the interest was sourced outside the UK as this was the residence of the original debtor and creditor involved. This emphasis on residence continues throughout the case and Lord Hailsham stated that it would be outside the scope of the UK tax system to charge income of residents outside the UK. His conclusion emphasised that the obligation was undertaken by a principal debtor which was a foreign company and therefore the interest did not have a UK source.

Following on from the Greek Bank case, HMRC outlined in Tax Bulletin 9 that they view the following as the key factors:

(a)     the place in which the debt will be enforced—which may also require a consideration of the law under which the loan agreement is drawn up, but will often be the residence of the debtor;

(b)     the source from which interest is paid;

(c)     where the interest is paid; and

(d)     the nature and location of the security for the debt.

If all of these are located in the UK then HMRC are likely to consider that the interest has a UK source. Their wider view on source is now set out in SAIM9090, which further says:

•     they consider the residence of the debtor to be the most important factor; and

•     EU rules on jurisdiction may affect where the debt will be enforced.

In the recent case of *Perrin v Revenue and Customs Comrs*(TC03363) [2014] UKFTT 223 (TC), [2014] All ER (D) 08 (Apr), [2014] SFTD 919, the court held that interest paid from an Isle of Man (IOM) bank account, to an IOM bank account, under the terms of a loan written under the laws of IOM was in fact UK source interest on the basis that the debtor (Mr Perrin) was UK resident and this is the only place where the loan could be enforced.

This reiterates the point above that HMRC consider residence of the debtor to be the most important factor. The tribunal found that the fact that the agreement was under IOM law and paid to and from an IOM bank account, although relevant, carried little weight.

Another recent case considering the source of interest was the *Ardmore Construction Ltd v Revenue and Customs Comrs*[2014] UKFTT 453 (TC), and in this case the FTT held that the source of interest should be determined based on a multi-factoral test as set out in (a)–(d) above.

Similar case law exists in other jurisdictions, for example:

•     *IRC v Philips Gloeilampenfabrieken* 10 ATD 435 [1955] NZLR 868 (New Zealand);

•     *Studebaker Corporation of Australasia v Commissioner of Taxation for New South Wales* [1921] 29 CLR 225 (Australia);;

•     *Commissioner of Taxation v Spotless Services Ltd* [1995] 62 FCR 244 (Australia);

- *IRC v Lever Bros and Unilever Ltd* [1946] AD 441, 14 SATC 1 (South Africa);
- *IRC v Hang Seng Bank Ltd* [1990] STC 733 (Hong Kong);
- *IRC v Orion Caribbean Ltd (in voluntary liquidation)* [1997] STC 923 (Hong Kong).

This case law is useful when specifically considering interest paid in these jurisdictions and also supports some general principles about the source of interest.

## Timing of withholding tax

**[A5.4]** ITA 2007, s 874 provides that withholding tax is due when 'a payment of yearly interest arising in the United Kingdom is made'. No obligation to withhold tax arises if interest is only accrued—the obligation arises when the interest is actually paid.

Interest will be considered to be paid when the recipient is free to draw upon the interest. HMRC consider (CTM51790) that a book entry (for instance an increase in an inter-company balance reflecting that interest is due) will constitute payment of interest only where the paying company has sufficient funds to pay the interest, and the recipient would be able to call on these funds to satisfy the intercompany balance.

The concept of payment was considered in *Paton (as Fenton's trustee) v CIR* (1938) 21 TC 625 and *Minsham Properties v Price* (1990) STC 718, where an increase in a loan to reflect interest accrued did not constitute payment.

## Funding bonds

**[A5.5]** Even where interest is not paid in cash, withholding tax may still arise under ITA 2007, s 939 where funding bonds are used to pay interest. Payment in kind (or PIK) loan notes are a type of funding bond, and are typically used where there will be insufficient cash to pay interest, and further loan notes are instead issued.

Funding bonds are defined broadly to include 'any bonds, stocks, shares, securities or certificates of indebtedness' (ITA 2007, s 939(6)). There is no requirement that it is intended from the outset that the interest will be paid by issuing shares.

The rules will also apply where interest has been accrued because insufficient cash is available to pay the interest, and the borrower satisfies the accrued interest by issuing shares. This 'capitalisation of interest' payable to an overseas lender will therefore require tax to be withheld.

ITA 2007, s 939(2) requires that the payer of the interest:

> 'must retain bonds the value of which is, at the time of their issue, equal to income tax on the deemed interest at the basic rate in force for the tax year in which the bonds are issued.'

The value for these purposes will be the market value, not the face value, of the bond or shares.

ITA 2007, s 939(4) then provides that the payer can pass the bonds withheld to HMRC in order to satisfy the payment of tax withheld.

This is only a permissive requirement (s 939(4) says that the payer 'may' tender the bonds, rather than that they 'must'), and the payer can instead choose to account for the withholding tax in cash. From a practical perspective, this may be more beneficial as a borrower may not want HMRC to acquire rights over the company by virtue of being a shareholder or loan note holder.

If the recipient is entitled to a refund of the tax withheld, HMRC can satisfy this repayment using any funding bonds which the payer of interest has used to pay the withholding tax.

### Gross-up clause

**[A5.6]** It is customary to include a payment clause in a loan document along the lines of:

> 'All payments made by the Borrower under this Agreement shall be made free and clear of, and without deduction or withholding for or on account of, any present or future income, stamp or other taxes, levies, imposts, duties, charges, fees, deductions or withholdings, now or hereafter imposed, levied, collected, withheld or assessed by any governmental authority.'

The effect of this clause is that the borrower suffers the burden of any withholding taxes on interest. There is a commitment under the agreement to pay an amount of interest, and (as a result of the clause) this amount must be net of any withholding taxes.

The clause is therefore commonly referred to as a 'gross-up clause'.

If a borrower is required to pay 10% interest on a loan of 1,000, but under domestic law (in the UK for instance) is required to withhold 20% tax, then he must actually pay 125 in order for the lender to receive the 100 which is due. The remaining 25 is paid to the tax authorities.

This gross-up can significantly increase the cost of borrowing, and minimising withholding tax is often a key aspect of tax advice on financing arrangements.

Where a gross-up clause is in effect, a clause should also be included to the effect that any repayment of withholding tax obtained by the lender is returned to the borrower.

Although HMRC now believe this approach to be incorrect—see INTM413220.

### Exceptions from the obligation to withhold tax

**[A5.7]** Not all interest payments are subject to withholding tax under UK domestic law even if they have a UK source. The exceptions relevant to cross-border payments of interest are:

(a)     'Banking' exemptions;
(b)     Quoted Eurobonds (see below under Planning—interest);

(c)     Payments between UK companies;
(d)     Discounts or premiums (see below under Planning—interest);
(e)     Interest paid where a treaty or Directive clearance is in place (see below).

## Banks

**[A5.8]**  A bank may pay interest gross where the interest is paid in the ordinary course of its business. Interest paid to a bank will also be free of withholding tax, provided the bank is subject to UK corporation tax on the receipt.

Where a UK company is borrowing from an overseas bank, it should seek to do so through the UK branch of the bank in order to avoid withholding tax on the interest. For these purposes a bank is defined in ITA 2007, s 991, (broadly) as an entity which is authorised to act as a bank under FSMA 2000.

However, banks and other 'deposit takers' may be subject to additional withholding tax requirements under ITA 2007, s 850. A deposit-taker for these purposes is (broadly) an entity which is authorised under FSMA 2000 to take deposits. A discussion of these provisions is outside the scope of this book.

## Payments between UK companies

**[A5.9]**  There is no obligation to withhold tax from payments of interest between companies where, the company making the payment has a 'reasonable belief' that the recipient company is within the charge to UK corporation tax. The recipient may be a UK resident company (ITA 2007, s 933) or a non-resident company with a UK permanent establishment which is subject to tax on the interest (ITA 2007, s 934). The recipient company must be beneficially entitled to the interest (see below for the definition of beneficial ownership).

## Partnerships

**[A5.10]**  As noted above, the basic principle is that a payment of interest to a partnership will be subject to withholding tax if any partner in the partnership is a company.

The exemption for payments between companies will only apply to payments to a partnership if every member of the partnership satisfies the exemption. A payment of interest to a partnership comprising both UK resident and non-UK resident companies would therefore be subject to withholding tax.

The partners in the partnership must then obtain relief (for example under a double tax agreement (DTA)) in their own name.

This can be an onerous process, particularly where there are a significant number of partners in the partnership. For US partnerships, HMRC offer a concessionary treatment whereby the partnership itself can make an application on behalf of its partners.

The same principles may apply where a UK company is a member of a partnership which receives (interest) income from overseas.

# Basic principles—royalties

**[A5.11]** ITA 2007, s 898 provides that income tax at the basic rate (20%) must be withheld from:

(a)    royalties and other sums paid in respect of the use of patents;
(b)    qualifying annual payments;
(c)    payments in respect of 'relevant intellectual property' made to a person whose place of usual abode is outside the UK,

if the payment 'arises' in the UK.

Qualifying annual payments include those received by a non-resident company which would be subject to tax under ITTOIA 2005, s 579(2), ie royalties and other income in respect of:

'(*a*)    any patent, trade mark, registered design, copyright, design right, performer's right or plant breeder's right,
(*b*)    any rights under the law of any part of the United Kingdom which are similar to rights within paragraph (*a*),
(*c*)    any rights under the law of any territory outside the United Kingdom which correspond or are similar to rights within paragraph (*a*), and
(*d*)    any idea, information or technique not protected by a right within paragraph (*a*), (*b*) or (*c*).'

'Relevant intellectual property rights' include (ITA 2007, ss 907, 909(3)):

(a)    a copyright (but not copyright in a film or video recording nor the soundtrack of such a recording, unless it is separately marketed);
(b)    a design right (as defined by Copyright, Designs and Patents Act 1988, s 213) or a right in a design registered under the Registered Designs Act 1949; or
(c)    the public lending right in respect of a book (as created by the Public Lending Right Act 1979, s 1).

Taken together, these impose a withholding tax requirement on almost all payments for the use of intellectual property.

## Source of royalties

**[A5.12]** Although no case law on the point exists, if the source of the royalty is in the UK (determined under the principles outlined above in respect of interest) it should be deemed to arise in the UK.

## Exceptions from UK withholding tax

**[A5.13]** The requirement to withhold basic rate tax does not apply to:

(a)    Payments made in respect of copies of works, or articles, which have been exported from the United Kingdom for distribution outside the United Kingdom (ITA 2007, s 906(4)).
(b)    Royalties paid where a DTA or Directive applies (see below).

# Basic principles—dividends

### Reclaiming the notional UK tax credit

[A5.14] UK domestic law does not impose a withholding tax on dividend payments to non-residents. Instead dividends are paid net of a notional 'tax credit' (10% of the gross dividend).

UK resident shareholders receiving dividends from a UK resident company are entitled to offset the tax credit against tax due on the dividend, but there is no provision for the repayment of tax credits where they exceed the tax liability.

The ability to claim a repayment of tax credits is retained for non-residents under certain DTAs.

Some of the UK's DTAs provide that a non-resident shareholder is entitled to a tax credit on a dividend from a UK-resident company but this is only payable to the extent that it exceeds the amount of tax to which the UK is entitled under the terms of the agreement.

The DTAs with Belgium, Italy, Luxembourg, the Netherlands, Norway, Sweden and Switzerland allow a company resident in those jurisdictions to claim a credit if they hold at least 10% of the shares in the UK company paying the dividend.

For example the UK/Netherlands DTA provides that (subject to certain conditions) a Dutch company holding at least 10% of a UK company is entitled to a tax credit equal to half that which a UK resident individual would be entitled (Article 10(3)(*c*)). However, the UK is entitled to charge 5% tax on the gross amount under the DTA, so the repayment due to a Dutch company would be calculated as follows:

| | |
|---|---|
| Dividend | 100 |
| Tax credit | 11.11 |
| Repayment of half tax credit | (5.55) |
| Taxable under DTA | 105.55 |
| Tax at 5% | 5.27 |
| Less repayment | (5.55) |
| Net refund | 0.28 |

### EU Parent/Subsidiary Directive

[A5.15] In 1990 the EU issued Council Directive 90/435/EEC (the Parent/Subsidiary Directive). The Directive aims to eliminate withholding tax on dividends paid between companies in the EU. It is therefore of considerable use when structuring European groups which will distribute dividends. Even where the ultimate parent is outside the EU a sub-holding company can be established in the EU in order to take advantage of the directive. The Directive also applies to companies resident in Switzerland (see **A7.8**).

Although not relevant to a UK company paying dividends (as there is no withholding tax on dividends paid by a UK company), the Directive is relevant to the extent that a UK company receives dividends from a subsidiary in another Member State. For this reason, the UK is a common jurisdiction in which to establish a European holding company, as it can receive dividends free of withholding tax, and then distribute them without any further withholding tax arising.

Dividends paid by a subsidiary company to its parent company in a different EU Member State are exempt from withholding tax, provided the parent company:

(a)    is resident for tax purposes in an EU Member State;

(b)    has one of the legal forms listed in the Annex to the Directive;

(c)    is subject to one of the taxes listed in the Annex to the Directive, without the possibility of benefiting from an exemption, unless temporarily or territorially limited; and

(d)    holds at least 10% of the shares in the subsidiary.

It is important to check that (b) and (c) are satisfied.

As with the Interest and Royalties Directive, Member States are required to implement the Parent/Subsidiary Directive in domestic law. Some Member States have relaxed the conditions above, for instance in relation to the minimum shareholding requirement. However, a Member State is not permitted to introduce more onerous requirements, although certain states (for example Germany where there are specific anti-avoidance rules) deny the application of the Parent/Subsidiary Directive in the case of a pure UK holding company with little substance.

In June 2014, the Council of the EU reached political agreement on a revised version of the Parent/Subsidiary Directive containing measures to combat the use of hybrid loans.

The changes are specifically aimed at arrangements that utilise the Parent/Subsidiary Directive to secure double non-taxation through the use of hybrid loans. For example, where a lender in one Member State advances a sum of money to a borrower in another Member State. The amount is treated as equity in the lender state, but as debt in the borrower state. This would result in a deduction in the borrower state for interest paid, and income being exempt in the lender state.

The changes aim to prevent this abuse by ensuring that payments will no longer be exempt in the state that treats the income as a distribution.

All Member States will be required to implement the anti-hybrid rules by 31 December 2015.

## Basic principles—double tax agreements

**[A5.16]** Rates of withholding tax on interests and royalties (and other amounts) may be reduced under the terms of a relevant DTA. The typical provisions of the UK's DTAs are discussed in detail in CHAPTER A8.

The procedure for claiming relief from overseas withholding tax may be similar to claiming relief from UK withholding tax, but may require a certificate of residence to be obtained. This is discussed at A12.11.

It should also be noted that some countries (Switzerland and Qatar, for example) operate a refund only system so that payments must always be subject to withholding tax and relief will be given by way of refund rather than relief at source.

### Royalties

**[A5.17]** Approval is not required from HMRC to apply a reduced rate of withholding tax on royalty payments. The responsibility for ensuring that the reduced rate applies is on the payer.

In order to apply a reduced rate under a double tax agreement, the payer should have a 'reasonable' belief that the conditions are satisfied (ITA 2007, s 911). If the conditions are in fact not satisfied, the payer will be liable for the tax, plus any interest or penalties arising as a result of late payment. A similar provision exists under ITA 2007, s 914 relating to the EU Interest and Royalties Directive.

### Interest

**[A5.18]** The payment of interest to a person overseas must not be made at the reduced treaty rate, until clearance to apply the treaty rate is obtained from HMRC.

In order to obtain relief under a DTA (or the EU Interest and Royalties Directive), firstly the lender must file a clearance form with the relevant overseas tax authority (specific forms are available for certain jurisdictions, and a generic form can be used for others; these are currently available on the HMRC website at www.hmrc.gov.uk/cnr/dtcompany.pdf). Next, the overseas tax authority will confirm that the lender is entitled to benefit under the treaty and pass the form to HMRC. Finally, HMRC will review the form and advise the borrower if clearance is given to pay interest under the reduced withholding rate.

Given the time which can be required for this process, it is important that clearance is obtained as early as possible. This is particularly important given the principle in *Tenbry Investments Ltd v Peugeot Talbot Motor Company Ltd*. Whilst this case related to rental income relating to the former ICTA 1988, s 349(1) it established the principle that a payer cannot deduct withholding tax from future payments which it failed to deduct previously.

Treaty clearance should be obtained as part of the financing process itself and, given the onus on the lender to make the application, it is usual to include a contractual term in the finance documents to the effect that they will do so.

INTM574040 sets out some small relaxations to this process:

- Once the overseas tax authority has passed the application to HMRC, and subject to the agreement of the borrower's Inspector of Taxes, interest can be paid gross in advance of clearance actually being given. This relaxation will often make little difference to the overall process, as it still requires that the lender submits the form, and that the overseas tax authority confirms entitlement to treaty benefits.
- If interest is paid gross without a clearance in place, and clearance is subsequently given, strictly speaking an obligation still exists for tax to be withheld. However, HMRC will accept contract settlement of the interest on the withholding tax (from the date when the interest was paid to the date that the clearance was given), and not require that the withholding tax itself is actually paid.

The liability to pay withholding tax may give rise to a liability which must be recognised on the borrower's balance sheet. As any repayment of the withholding tax will be to the lender, the borrower cannot recognise a corresponding asset even where the withholding tax will be repayable. The borrower should therefore obtain a written confirmation from the lender that any repayment will be passed back to the borrower. This could alternatively be confirmed in the loan agreement. Such confirmation may allow the borrower to recognise an asset in its balance sheet equal to the withholding tax liability.

### Interest under the business profits article

**[A5.19]** Withholding tax will normally be reduced under the interest article in a particular DTA. However, a company which undertakes a financial business may treat interest as business profits.

The OECD model tax convention specifically excludes income from the business profits article if it is dealt with under another article. In these cases, relief could not be obtained under the business profits article for interest received by a non-resident company.

However, some DTAs do not follow the OECD model. The UK/Jersey DTA for example does not exclude interest from the business profits article. Where a company in Jersey undertakes a financial business and receives interest from the UK, it may obtain relief under the business profits article. This means that it will be not be subject to UK (withholding) tax if it does not have a permanent establishment in the UK.

HMRC accept that (for example) Jersey banks can obtain relief in this way, but may challenge relief claimed by other companies—see the HMRC International Manual at INTM355225.

### Syndicated Loan Scheme

**[A5.20]** A further relaxation is found with the Syndicated Loan Scheme (previously called the Provision Treaty Relief Scheme).

Under the Scheme, a group of borrowers is able to apply directly to HMRC for provisional clearance to withhold tax at a reduced rate. This application can be made even before the overseas tax authority has received the treaty clearance form from the lenders. Any clearance given under the Scheme is only provisional, and the lender must subsequently file the clearance form in the normal way.

A loan may fall within the Scheme where the loan is made by a syndicate, of which there is a syndicate manager. Where there is only a single lender, the Passport Scheme (see below) must be applied instead of the Syndicated Loan Scheme.

The Scheme requires one of the syndicate members to be responsible for the clearance process on behalf of the other lenders, and many lenders are reluctant to do this.

### Double Taxation Treaty Passport Scheme

[A5.21] From 1 September 2010, HMRC introduced a 'Passport Scheme'. Under this Scheme a company which is entitled to benefit under a DTA may obtain clearance from HMRC in relation to all future loans it may make.

If HMRC issue a passport (ie give clearance), the lender's details will be entered onto a publicly available register. A UK borrower can then rely on this to pay interest without deduction of withholding tax. The UK borrower must provide details of the loan to HMRC within 30 days of it being made, following which HMRC will issue a formal Direction.

The existing clearance arrangements and the Syndicated Loan Scheme continue to run alongside the Passport Scheme.

This Scheme would appear to reduce complexities for borrowers, as they can now have clarity on the withholding tax position, and will not have to rely on the overseas lender (or the overseas tax authority) to obtain a reduced rate.

However, there are a number of requirements of which a lender should beware:

- its details will be available on a publicly accessible database;
- any changes in these details must be notified to HMRC;
- it must 'enter into a loan making use of the DTTP only where (to its certain knowledge and belief) all conditions for relief under the relevant double taxation arrangements are present'—this would include for example confirming that the lender has beneficial ownership of any interest income.

### EU Interest and Royalties Directive

[A5.22] EU Directive 2003/49/EC (the Interest and Royalties Directive) requires that EU Member States exempt payments of interest and royalties between associated companies resident in EU states from withholding tax. The Directive also applies to companies resident in Switzerland (see A7.8) and to payments made by permanent establishments in the EU.

The Directive has been implemented in UK domestic law by ITTOIA 2005, s 757.

In the UK, the exemption is subject to the following conditions: (ITTOIA 2005, s 758):

(a)     The payer must be a UK resident company or a UK permanent establishment of an EU resident company.
(b)     The beneficial owner of the royalties must be an EU resident company, but not a permanent establishment of an EU resident company situated in the UK or in any non-EU country. Beneficial ownership is discussed at **A8.54.**
(c)     The payer and the beneficial owner must be associated by virtue of one holding 25% or more of the share capital or voting rights of the other, or a third company holding 25% or more of the share capital or voting rights of both.

Under current rules, the shareholder must have a direct relationship, so whilst the payment in Diagram 1(a) may qualify for exemption, the payment in Diagram 1(b) will not.

On 11 November 2011, the European Commission published a proposal to revise the Interest and Royalties Directive which should, if enacted, go some way towards addressing this issue. In particular it will address the following points;

(1)     widening the definition of eligible companies.
(2)     reducing the minimum holding from 25% to 10%
(3)     broadening the definition of associated company to include indirect holdings
(4)     introducing a subject to tax requirement in the recipient jurisdiction

At the time of writing (August 2013) enquiries of HMRC suggest that the changes are unlikely to be adopted in the near future.

**Diagram 1(a)**

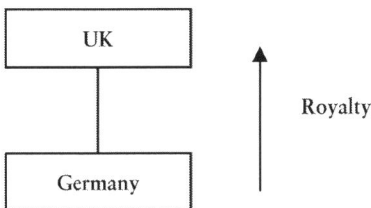

Diagram 1(b)

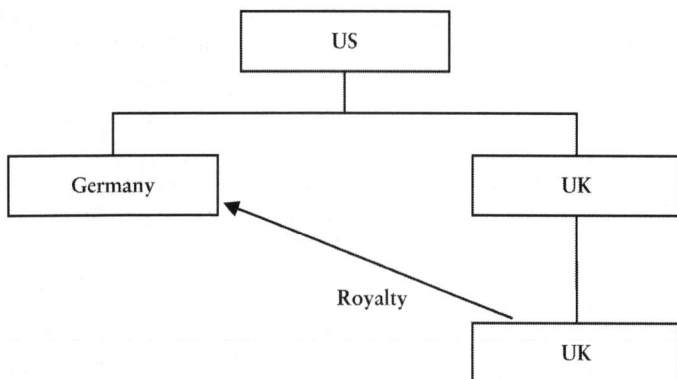

Where a 'special relationship' exists between the payer and the beneficial owner, (ie where they are connected as defined in TIOPA 2010, s 131 for interest and s 132 for royalties), the exemption will only apply to the extent that payments are made on an arm's length basis. Any excess will be subject to withholding under the normal domestic or treaty rates, although this point is rarely taken in practice by HMRC.

**Anti-avoidance**

**[A5.23]** The exemption does not apply to payments under an agreement if the main purpose, or one of the main purposes, for the creation of the agreement was to take advantage of the exemption.

In Diagram 2 if Jersey Co transfers the intellectual property to Luxembourg Co, the benefit of ITA 2007, s 757 may not be available unless the transfer were undertaken for commercial purposes.

If Luxembourg Co had acquired the intellectual property directly from a third party then it may be easier to demonstrate that this was an acquisition for commercial purposes.

Diagram 2

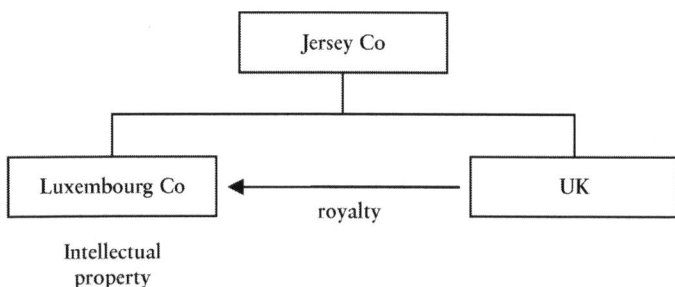

As this anti-avoidance provision is not typically present in the UK's DTAs, it may be preferable to obtain relief from withholding tax under a DTA rather than under the Directive where this anti-avoidance provision is potentially relevant.

### Royalties

**[A5.24]** Approval is not required from HMRC to obtain exemption from withholding tax on royalty payments and the responsibility for ensuring that the exemption applies is on the payer.

In order to apply the exemption, the payer should have a 'reasonable' belief that the conditions are satisfied (ITA 2007, s 914). If the conditions are in fact not satisfied, the payer will be liable for the tax, plus any interest or penalties arising as a result of late payment.

### Interest

**[A5.25]** Clearance is required from HMRC to obtain exemption from withholding tax on interest. The procedure is generally the same as a claim under a DTA which is discussed below. A clearance application must be made by the recipient rather than the payer of the interest. The Passport Scheme is however not available in respect of the Interest and Royalties Directive.

# Planning—interest

### Source

**[A5.26]** As noted at A5.3 above, interest will only be subject to withholding tax if it has a source in the UK. It may be possible to avoid a source in the UK if most or all of the following conditions are satisfied:

(a)     The loan is not secured on an asset in the UK.
(b)     The loan is not drawn up under English (or Scottish) law.
(c)     The debtor and creditor are both resident outside the UK.
(d)     Interest is paid from income which arises outside the UK.
(e)     The interest is paid from a non-UK bank account of the debtor to a non-UK bank account of the creditor.

The planning points set out in **A5.27–A5.29** were considered by HMRC in 2013 and they issued a consultation to abolish these exemptions. Following the consultation, it was decided that the exemptions would remain.

### Quoted Eurobonds

**[A5.27]** ITA 2007, s 882 provides that payments of interest on a 'quoted Eurobond' are excluded from the general requirement to deduct income tax.

For these purposes, a 'quoted Eurobond' is defined (ITA 2007, s 987) as any security that:

(a)     is issued by a company;
(b)     is listed on a recognised stock exchange; and
(c)     carries a right to interest.

There is no requirement that the bond be denominated in Euro, or actively traded on the exchange.

The costs of listing a loan on a small exchange such as the Channel Islands Stock Exchange may be lower than the costs of withholding tax.

### Discounts

**[A5.28]** Withholding tax is not due on payments which are not interest.

Where a loan is advanced at a discount, the payment of the discounted amount on redemption is not treated as a payment of interest. Such loans are commonly called 'deep discounted bonds' (DDBs) because they are issued at a significant discount.

For instance, a loan of 100 could be advanced, with a face value of 120 repayable in four years' time. The payment of the 20 would not be treated as a payment of interest and therefore not subject to withholding tax. However, the economic return to the lender would be the same as if a loan had been made at interest.

A practical disadvantage of a discounted loan is that no cash is paid until the end of its term. If payments are made earlier, during the term of the loan, they may be characterised as interest.

The First Tier Tribunal case of *Pike v Revenue and Customs Comrs* [2011] UKFTT 289 (TC) summarises the case law on what is treated as interest (rather than a discount) for tax purposes. It concludes that interest is:

> 'a sum of money calculated by reference to an underlying debt which is payment by time for the use of money borrowed and which accrues from day to day, whether or not it is paid periodically.'

When structuring a loan as a DDB the discount should not therefore be calculated by reference to the amount of the underlying loan or the period of the loan. In addition, early redemption should not trigger the discount on a pro-rated basis, as this would imply interest is accruing from day-to-day.

For accounting purposes, the discount will usually be accrued over the term of the loan in the same way as the equivalent interest amount. The discount will then be deductible for corporation tax purposes.

In certain situations, the discount may not be deductible until it is actually paid. However, unlike interest on a loan, the payment of the discount will not crystallise a withholding tax obligation, and the tax deduction can be claimed without the withholding tax cost.

On 2 October 2012 the government announced that they would be bringing forward rules to address withholding tax on returns that were economically equivalent to interest. This was subsequently enacted as FA 2013, Sch 12, which introduced a new ITTOIA 2005, s 381A, which provides as follows:

'381A Charge to tax on disguised interest.

(1)     This Chapter applies where a person is party to an arrangement which produces for the person a return in relation to any amount which is economically equivalent to interest.

(2)     Income tax is charged on the return if the return is not charged to income tax under or as a result of any other provision of this Act or any other Act.

(3)     Subsection (2) does not apply to a return that would be charged to income tax under or as a result of another provision but for an exemption.

(4)     For the purposes of this Chapter a return produced for a person by an arrangement in relation to any amount is "economically equivalent to interest" if (and only if)—

(a)     it is reasonable to assume that it is a return by reference to the time value of that amount of money,

(b)     it is at a rate reasonably comparable to what is (in all the circumstances) a commercial rate of interest, and

(c)     at the relevant time there is no practical likelihood that it will cease to be produced in accordance with the arrangement unless the person by whom it falls to be produced is prevented (by reason of insolvency or otherwise) from producing it.

(5)     In subsection (4)(c) "the relevant time" means the time when the person becomes party to the arrangement or, if later, when the arrangement begins to produce a return for the person.

(6)     In this Chapter "arrangement" includes any agreement, understanding, scheme, transaction or series of transactions (whether or not legally enforceable).'

As part of the responses to the consultation HMRC made it clear that instruments caught by existing legislation (for example DDBs) would not be caught by these new proposals.

### Short interest

**[A5.29]** ITA 2007, s 874 only applies to payments of 'yearly interest'. If interest is paid on a loan which has a fixed term of less than a year then it will generally not be yearly interest.

However, if a series of loans are made subsequent to each other, and each for a term of less than a year, HMRC will look to construe it as a single loan with a term of more than a year (INTM542010). Where there is no fixed term, the intention of the parties will be considered when determining whether the loan has a term of more than a year (see *Cairns v MacDiarmid (Inspector of Taxes)* [1983] STC 178).

# Planning—specific royalty situations

## Computer software

**[A5.30]** Although the 'purchase' of computer software usually takes the form of a limited licence to install and use that software, HMRC do not regard the payment for the licence as being a royalty for the use of the software (INTM 342630).

A software distributor may operate in broadly two ways:

(a)    it may acquire a 'boxed product' where the software has already been written to a computer disc or similar media. The software distributor then sells the physical product to the customer; or

(b)    it may acquire an intangible asset (the software or source code) from which it produces the 'boxed product' by writing to a computer disc or similar media.

The distributor may be remunerated by way of a commission, a profit on the sale of the product or by taking a share of revenues. However, the form of this remuneration should not affect the analysis of the rights acquired by the distributor.

Paragraph 14.4 of the commentary on Article 12 the OECD model tax convention provides that the payment by the software distributor for the second of these is likely to be a royalty, but payment for the first is more likely to fall within the business profits article:

> '14.4 Arrangements between a software copyright holder and a distribution intermediary frequently will grant to the distribution intermediary the right to distribute copies of the program without the right to reproduce that program. In these transactions, the rights acquired in relation to the copyright are limited to those necessary for the commercial intermediary to distribute copies of the software program. In such transactions, distributors are paying only for the acquisition of the software copies and not to exploit any right in the software copyrights. Thus, in a transaction where a distributor makes payments to acquire and distribute software copies (without the right to reproduce the software), the rights in relation to these acts of distribution should be disregarded in analysing the character of the transaction for tax purposes. Payments in these types of transactions would be dealt with as business profits in accordance with Article 7. This would be the case regardless of whether the copies being distributed are delivered on tangible media or are distributed electronically (without the distributor having the right to reproduce the software), or whether the software is subject to minor customisation for the purposes of its installation.'

Where possible therefore, a software distributor should acquire a 'boxed product' from the developer, rather than the right to duplicate or produce the software from the underlying intangible asset (source code).

Where product is distributed electronically—for example, as a download from the internet—similar principles will apply as it is the sale of a copy of the copyright material. However, if the product is downloaded from the distributor the distributor will likely be treated as 'duplicating' the software for each sale, which could give rise to a withholding obligation as the duplication of copyright material is an intellectual property transaction. The download should therefore be directly from the developer rather than the distributor and arrangements put in place which replicate the distribution of a tangible 'boxed product'—for example, the distributor requires separate product key from the developer for each download.

**Case law**

**[A5.31]** Some recent Indian cases also illustrate these principles:

(a)    In *Infrasoft Ltd v ADIT (International Tax)* (ITA No 847/Del/2008) (22 June 2010, unreported), a UK company licensed software to customers in India via its Indian branch. The licenses imposed limitations on the customers' rights to copy, sell and use the software. The Indian Income Tax Appellate Tribunal (ITAT) held that the payments made by customers under the licenses were business profits rather than royalties as the limitations meant that the customers did not obtain any rights over the intellectual property contained in the software.

(b)    In *Lucent Technologies International Inc v DCIT* (ITA No 161/Del/2009), a US company sold hardware and licensed software to customers in India. The licenses prevented customers from making copies of the software other than for of backup purposes. The ITAT held that the payments made by customers under the licenses were not royalties because the customers did not acquire any rights to copy the software.

(c)    A similar principle was followed in *Kansai Nerolac Paints Ltd v ADIT* (ITA No 155/Mum/2010) and *DDIT v TII Team Telecom International Ltd* (ITA No 62/Mum/2010), where the licensee obtained a limited, exclusive right to use the software, the payment for which was not considered a royalty.

(d)    A different conclusion was reached in *Microsoft Corpn v ADIT* (ITA No 1331–1336/Del/2008), as the court determined that the licensee obtained a non-exclusive right to use the software (ie they were able to exploit it other than for their own use). This case is considered to be an exception rather than the rule.

These cases are also important because India is not a member of the OECD and does not consider itself bound by OECD guidelines in all cases. It should also be noted that Indian Court decisions on this are inconsistent and in practice the Indian Tax Authorities often attempt to impose a withholding tax on shrink-wrapped software sales. In fact, in view of several conflicting decisions, it is now proposed to retrospectively amend the definition of a royalty from 1976, which means that henceforth all software purchases could be subject to withholding tax.

### Sale of rights

**[A5.32]** Some sales of computer software may also be an outright sale of rights, as discussed below under **A5.37**. For example, the Russian tax authorities (in Guidance Letter 03-08-05) have confirmed that the sale by a Czech company to a Russian company of exclusive rights to computer software does not constitute a royalty.

### Software as part of a service

**[A5.33]** A further type of transaction is where a customer is given the right to use computer software as part of a wider service which is provided. If the customer merely has the right to use the software for a limited purpose (and not to reproduce it for example) then the whole payment should be characterised as a payment for the service, and not a royalty for the use of the software. The Argentinian tax court followed this principle in the case of

*Austral Líneas Aéreas Cielos del Sur S.A.* (Tax Court, Tribunal 'A', 02/06/07) which concerned the payment of a fee by an Argentinian company to a Spanish company for the use of a hotel booking system.

### Dependent agent

**[A5.34]** Care must be taken that a software distributor does not sell software as agent for the manufacturer, as this may create a permanent establishment under the dependent agent principles (see **A4.12**).

### *Franchise fees*

**[A5.35]** If a payment is made for a number of services, including the use of intangible assets, then it may not be a royalty payment.

This is typical of many franchise arrangements where the franchisee pays the franchisor for:

(a)    use of a brand name;
(b)    training;
(c)    access to suppliers and possibly financing;
(d)    IT and sales support.

Under these circumstances, the payment is not a royalty as the payment is made for a number of services, and cannot be characterised as a payment for the use of the brand name or other intangibles alone.

However, if the payment can be 'unbundled' then part of it may be treated as a royalty payment, and potentially subject to withholding tax.

Payments should therefore be expressed and calculated on a total basis. For example, it is better to have:

(a)    a franchise fee equal to 10% of sales; rather than
(b)    a franchise fee equal to 4% of sales for the use of the brand name and a further fee equal to 6% of sales for access to training and support.

### *The golf cases*

**[A5.36]** Two recent US Tax cases in involving the golfers Sergio Garcia and Retief Goosen have underlined the importance of distinguishing between what constitutes a royalty and what constitutes income for services. In the case of Garcia, he paid normal US income tax rates on income from services performed in the US, but as a resident of Switzerland royalties for his image rights and his endorsement income were able to benefit from the US/Swiss treaty to obtain a zero rate of withholding tax. The image rights royalties and endorsement income were determined by the US courts to represent 65 per cent of his US source income. This can be contrasted with the earlier case of Pierre Boulez, the famous conductor (*Boulez v Revenue and Customs Comrs* 83 TC 584 (1984)) where all of the earnings from M Boulez performances were held to be personal service income.

It should be noted that in the UK, HMRC do not take this approach, and the income of sportsmen and entertainers which is subject to UK tax is calculated on a different basis.

### *Sale of limited rights*

**[A5.37]** As noted above under **A5.11**, withholding tax is due on payments 'for the use of' patents, and on 'royalties and other income from intellectual property'.

Consideration for a complete sale of intellectual property rights is not a payment 'for the use of' or income arising 'from' intellectual property, because the seller no longer owns those rights.

In *Evans Medical Supplies Ltd v Moriarty (Inspector of Taxes)* [1957] 1 All ER 336, a UK company sold intellectual property relating to the manufacturing of pharmaceuticals to an overseas government. The effect of this was to permanently reduce the sales by the UK company in the overseas jurisdiction, and was therefore treated as capital rather than income. The UK company permanently disposed of an asset, being the right to make sales in that jurisdiction.

This would be the case even if the rights sold are limited, for instance a sale of the right to use an intangible asset for a limited time or the right to use an intangible asset in a particular geographical area.

Paragraph 8.2 of the commentary on Article 12 of the OECD model tax convention also supports the argument that a payment for the purchase of limited rights (either time-limited or geographically-limited) is not a royalty:

'Where a payment is in consideration for the transfer of the full ownership of an element of property referred to in the definition, the payment is not in consideration—for the use of, or the right to use that property and cannot therefore represent a royalty. As noted in paragraphs 15 and 16 below as regards software, difficulties can arise in the case of a transfer of rights that could be considered to form part of an element of property referred to in the definition where these rights are transferred in a way that is presented as an alienation. For example, this could involve the exclusive granting of all rights to an intellectual property for a limited period or all rights to the property in a limited geographical area in a transaction structured as a sale. Each case will depend on its particular facts and will need to be examined in the light of the national intellectual property law applicable to the relevant type of property and the national law rules as regards what constitutes an alienation but in general, if the payment is in consideration for the alienation of rights that constitute distinct and specific property (which is more likely in the case of geographically-limited than time-limited rights), such payments are likely to be business profits within Article 7 or a capital gain within Article 13 rather than royalties within Article 12. That follows from the fact that where the ownership of rights has been alienated, the consideration cannot be for the use of the rights. The essential character of the transaction as an alienation cannot be altered by the form of the consideration, the payment of the consideration in instalments or, in the view of most countries, by the fact that the payments are related to a contingency.'

For example, Company A is resident in Australia and grants a licence to Company B which is resident in the UK, to use its trademark in the UK. This licence expires after three years, and Company A retains all rights to the trademark for its duration. Any payments under the licence are likely to be royalties under both UK domestic law and under the UK/Australia DTA, and therefore potentially subject to withholding tax.

Instead Company A could sell to Company B the exclusive right to use the trademark in the UK for three years. A single payment would be made for the sale (although it could perhaps be paid in instalments). Under the UK/Australia DTA this payment may be business profits or a capital gain rather than a royalty, and therefore not subject to withholding tax unless Company A has a permanent establishment in the UK.

HMRC will follow the OECD commentary in most cases (see **A8.18**), and these principles should apply in the UK.

The legal position would also need to be considered to confirm that a separate right can be created.

### Payments for distribution rights

**[A5.38]** Similar to paragraph 8.2 in relation to the sale of limited rights, paragraph 10.1 of the commentary on the OECD model tax convention provides that a payment made to obtain exclusive distribution rights is not a royalty:

> 'Payments that are solely made in consideration for obtaining the exclusive distribution rights of a product or service in a given territory do not constitute royalties as they are not made in consideration for the use of, or the right to use, an element of property included in the definition. These payments, which are best viewed as being made to increase sales receipts, would rather fall under Article 7. An example of such a payment would be that of a distributor of clothes resident in one Contracting State who pays a certain sum of money to a manufacturer of branded shirts, who is a resident of the other Contracting State, as consideration for the exclusive right to sell in the first State the branded shirts manufactured abroad by that manufacturer. In that example, the resident distributor does not pay for the right to use the trade name or trade mark under which the shirts are sold; he merely obtains the exclusive right to sell in his State of residence shirts that he will buy from the manufacturer.'

The example given replaces a payment to use a trademark (which may be subject to withholding tax) with a payment for exclusive distribution rights (which would not be subject to withholding tax). The distributor may operate in the same way, but with a different legal agreement supporting the operations.

### Customer lists

**[A5.39]** Paragraph 11.4 of the commentary on the OECD model tax convention provides that a payment for a customer list, which is prepared from public information, for instance by a market research company, is not a royalty. This is contrasted with a payment for a customer list which is prepared from private information, which may be a royalty:

> '11.4 . . . payments for a list of potential customers, when such a list is developed specifically for the payer out of generally available information (a payment for the confidential list of customers to which the payee has provided a particular product or service would, however, constitute a payment for know-how as it would relate to the commercial experience of the payee in dealing with these customers).'

# Planning—double tax agreements

**[A5.40]** DTA structures are often used to reduce withholding taxes on interest and royalties.

For example, in Diagram 3(a), interest on the loan from Jersey to the UK would be subject to withholding tax at 20%. The UK/Jersey DTA would not reduce this and, as there is no tax in Jersey against which the withholding tax could be relieved, the withholding tax represents an absolute cost to the group.

However, in Diagram 3(b), interest is paid from the UK to Luxembourg. Subject to the anti-avoidance rules outlined below, the withholding tax on the interest should be reduced under the UK/Luxembourg DTA. Alternatively, and subject to the anti-avoidance rules outlined under **A5.23**, the withholding tax may be reduced under ITTOIA 2005, s 757 (the Interest and Royalties Directive).

There is no withholding tax under Luxembourg domestic law on the interest paid from Luxembourg to Jersey.

Diagram 3

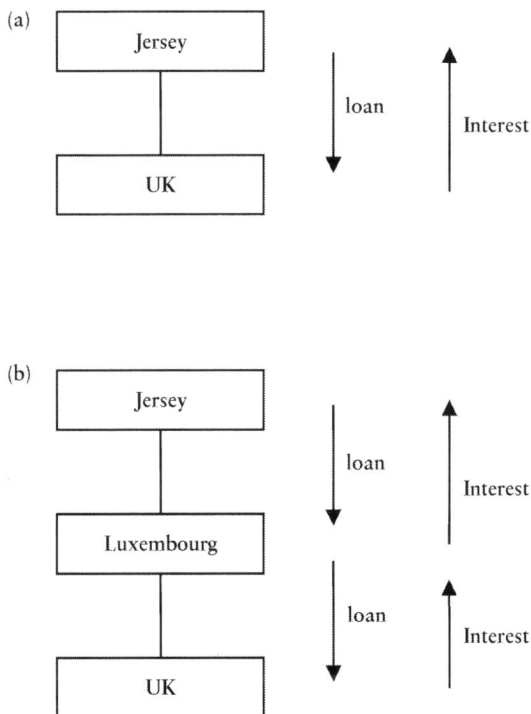

### *Anti-avoidance*

[A5.41] In order to prevent groups from taking advantage of DTAs as outlined above, anti-avoidance provisions are increasingly being included in DTAs.

The three most common and relevant to withholding taxes are outlined below:

(a)    beneficial ownership requirements;
(b)    limitation on benefits articles;
(c)    anti-conduit requirements.

These provisions are considered in detail at **A8.54.**

# A6

# Controlled Foreign Companies

## Introduction

**[A6.1]** Many UK companies will establish subsidiaries in low tax jurisdictions. This may for example be as a result of establishing financing and transfer pricing planning structures (see CHAPTER B5 and CHAPTER B7).

The Controlled Foreign Company (CFC) rules may cause the profits of such subsidiaries to be subject to UK corporation tax.

This Chapter outlines when the CFC rules apply, and the exemptions which are available from the rules. It is important to understand the exemptions, so that activities can be properly structured to fall outside the CFC rules, subject to not falling foul of various targeted anti-avoidance rules.

Following the changes to the CFC rules in FA 2011 as part of the wider reform of the taxation of foreign profits, consultation was undertaken on the further reform of the CFC rules from 2012 which resulted in the new Finance Act

2012, Sch 20 (FA 2012, Sch 20). The new regime made substantial changes and improvements, but with it (perhaps inevitably) some extra degree of complexity. It will take some time operating under the new rules before we understand how these will apply in practice. Given this uncertainty, clearances under the non-statutory clearance facility should be considered.

# Reform of the CFC rules from 2013

**[A6.2]** FA 2012, Sch 20 introduced a new TIOPA 2010, Part 9A. Some concepts are carried forward from the previous CFC regime, and capital gains continue to be excluded. In addition, profits arising from property are also excluded from scope. It is important to note that there is no real transition from the old rules and that for example any CFC losses brought forward may well be lost in the new regime. However several familiar features disappear, and there are many new features. The overall thrust of the proposals is to limit the scope of tax to those profits which have been artificially diverted from the UK.

Under the new rules, all non-UK companies 'controlled' from the UK will be 'CFCs' (s 371AA(3))—including those under a new accounting control test (s 371RE). The default presumption will no longer be that all of a CFC's profits are 'bad' unless an exemption applies. Rather, 'bad' profits will be defined by the so called 'Gateway' test, so the presumption is all profits are excluded unless they are included. Thus, if profits do not pass through the Gateway, the CFC's profits will not normally be included on the relevant UK Corporate Tax Self-Assessment (CTSA) tax return. However, it is not an all or nothing approach—some of a CFC's profits could be caught, with others exempt. The Gateway test is a new concept in terms of approach, and it will remain to be seen how practical it will be to apply. Many of the new provisions contain a high degree of transfer pricing analysis, which will create extra costs and complexity for taxpayers as well as rather a high degree of subjectivity. Draft guidance updated on 31 May 2013 is available on HMRC's website.

The grace period for acquired CFC's previously exempted such profits is 24 months after the end of the accounting period in which the acquisition took place. This has now been replaced by a straight 12 month period under s 371JB which, subject to agreement, may be extended by HMRC. However, this exemption is not at all straightforward, with detailed conditions to be met which may catch the unwary.

In addition to the 'Gateway' itself, there is an initial Gateway, which acts as a filter to the main Gateway, Gateway 'safe harbours' and entity based exemptions. Groups can rely on any of the exemptions and/or Gateway, and in any order. In some cases a combination of exemptions may be relevant. The use of a main purpose test is prevalent throughout, as is the right of HMRC to apply a just and reasonable outcome where the rules do not work as they intended. The new rules apply to accounting periods beginning on or after 1 January 2013. Thus for the two most common accounting dates, the first periods to which the new rules will apply will be the years ending 31 December 2013 or 31 March 2014. The previous rules continue to apply for earlier accounting periods.

# Details

## *What is a CFC under the new regime?*

**[A6.3]** A CFC is a non-UK resident company under the control of UK residents. The control test under Chapter 18 is similar to the previous rules, so any non-resident company that is controlled by a UK person at any time during its accounting period by holding more than 50% of the shares, plus 40% joint ventures. It is important to note that the 75% lower level of tax test is no longer retained as part of the definition of a CFC. However, it is replicated as the basis of the tax exemption under Chapter 14. In practice most UK groups' CFCs will therefore be all the direct or indirect non-UK resident subsidiaries (ss 371RA–371RE). In addition, if a company is treated as the parent under FRS2, it will be treated as controlling any foreign subsidiary for CFC purposes, regardless of whether or not there is a requirement to consolidate the entity. As mentioned above, some companies have sought to exploit the control test in the past by using protected cell companies, but each cell will now be treated as if it is a separate company. Exempt foreign branches are also brought within the provisions. It is important to note that in contrast to the previous provisions, dual resident companies (those that are UK incorporated but non-UK resident by treaty) are no longer considered UK resident for the new CFC rules.

## *Who suffers apportionment of a CFCs profits?*

**[A6.4]** Profits of CFCs which cannot be excluded through the Initial Gateway, Main Gateway or other exemptions/safe harbours will need to be self-assessed by UK corporate shareholders ('Chargeable companies') who own at least a 25% interest in the CFC (s 371BD). Therefore, all UK groups with foreign companies meeting the control test will need to consider this.

## *Which profits are apportioned?*

**[A6.5]** The objective of the CFC reforms is largely to restrict the application of the CFC apportionment to those profits which have been artificially diverted from the UK. This is the purpose of the new Gateway test under s 371BB—it defines circumstances where there is an artificial diversion of profits. The Initial Gateway (Chapter 3) then determines which, if any, of the Main Gateways Chapters 4–8 apply for the accounting period. The Gateway itself is essentially split into two distinct areas: finance profits and business profits; each defining those profits which are within the scope of an apportionment. Thus, if profits do not pass through the Gateway, they are exempt from the CFC rules. This partial assessment of profits is a clear move away from historic entity based apportionment to a territorial system. As a result, applying the Gateway in practice will be complex—hence the driving force for offering groups safe harbours and entity based exemptions as simpler alternatives to excluding profits of companies.

## Entity based exemptions

**[A6.6]** In practice, given the complexity of the Gateway approach, most groups will look to see if they are able to use the entity exemptions first as these provide for an exclusion of the entire profits of the CFC rather than a proportion.

Indeed, the previous CFC regime historically operated through entity based exemptions, so the new entity exemptions have a familiar feel even though they have been somewhat recast. It is important to note that the motive test is not replicated as an entity based exemption but instead as Condition A of the Initial Gateway, which asks whether the CFC holds any asset or risks which have a main purpose of reducing the UK tax liability of any person.

Each entity based exemption is summarised in turn below. Some are relatively easy to apply. Some that at first sight may appear simple will require considerable work.

Note there is no significance in the order in which they are set out—the legislation does not set any priority or ranking of any of the entity exemptions and therefore it is open to the taxpayer which to choose.

### The low profits exemption (ss 371LA et seq)

**[A6.7]** Section 371LB specifies four distinct circumstances where the low profits exemption applies:

- where the CFC's accounting profits are no more than £50,000, or
- where the CFC's assumed total taxable profits are no more than £50,000, or
- where the CFC's accounting profits are no more than £500,000 and the non-trading element is less than £50,000, or
- where the CFC's assumed total taxable profits in accordance with UK tax rules are no more than £500,000 and the non-trading element is less than £50,000.

As one might expect the terms accounting profits and assumed total taxable profits are tightly defined under Chapter 22 and contain all the usual provisions relating to UK GAAP and calculation according to UK tax rules, including of course transfer pricing. Capital gains and losses are excluded from both accounting profits and assumed total taxable profits. Accounting profits also exclude distributions which would be exempt if the CFC was UK resident (for example dividends) and also property profits and losses. The profits are also then subject to a transfer pricing check under s 371VD (unless the adjustment would be less than £50,000). This could create problems for example if the CFC is making outbound interest free loans.

Assumed total taxable profits are profits defined by CTA 2010, s 4(2), omitting chargeable gains.

The continued exclusion of capital gains from both the definition of accounting profits and taxable profits is welcome. Equally the exclusion of property profits also makes sense on the basis that most countries adopt a territorial system for the basis of taxing property transactions.

Tempting as it may seem to split profits between group companies to take advantage of the thresholds, there is a targeted anti-avoidance rule (TAAR) at s 371LC which seeks to address this where the following conditions are met:

- an arrangement is entered into with a main purpose to secure the low profits exemption where it would otherwise have not been due,
- a UK resident individual provides services in the UK under an obligation to a client and the contract for these services is between the client and the CFC, or
- in computing the CFC's equivalent taxable profits, group mismatch scheme rules exclude an amount from being brought into tax.

The first of these is clearly designed to prevent the artificial division of profits between group companies to fall under the threshold. However it could also apply for example if a group were to attempt to shelter significant amounts of non-trading income by the use of losses.

It is thought that the £50,000 limit is also retained for a similar reason. If for example a CFC has more than £50,000 of investment income it may fail the '500 and 50' test. The retention of the £50,000 limit would therefore address the position where say £80,000 of investment income might be covered by £40,000 of losses.

In conclusion the low profits exemption will be helpful in two ways. Firstly by reducing the compliance burden for larger groups by rendering a more detailed analysis unnecessary. Secondly for smaller UK businesses with subsidiaries in lower tax jurisdictions such as Dubai or Switzerland, it offers the possibility of deferral of tax on up to £500,000 of the profits concerned and even the possibility of tax free repatriation if the UK dividend exemption applies. This is of course subject to a robust transfer pricing support for the level of profits concerned.

## The low profit margin exemption (ss 371MA et seq)

**[A6.8]** This excludes a CFC with 'adjusted accounting profits' of no more than 10% of its 'relevant operating expenditure'. Accounting profits for this purpose are adjusted for exempt distributions, property business profits, capital profits, transfer pricing adjustments and interest expense (but not income).

It is important to note that relevant operating expenditure excludes:

- The cost of goods purchased by the CFC (other than those used by the CFC in the territory in which it is resident), and
- Related party expenditure (defined as expenditure which directly or indirectly is income in the hands of a related person, UK or otherwise).

The cost of goods condition will therefore exclude goods not delivered into the CFC's territory of residence and is clearly aimed at reinvoicing companies. The historical practice of routing goods via a Swiss principal company with a short stop in Geneva may well continue.

In the same way, the second condition is designed to stop intra-group service companies benefitting from the exemption. However in practice it will be attractive to low value added service providers such as call centres and back office support as well as toll manufacturers.

There is also a main purpose test to exclude artificial arrangements. Nevertheless for low margin businesses with some commercial substance this could prove to be a worthwhile exemption.

### The excluded territories exemption (ss 371KA et seq)

**[A6.9]** This is similar to the previous excluded countries exemption and will apply to countries where the headline rate of tax is greater than 75% of the UK main corporation tax rate. There are two main differences. The new rules are much more detailed, but unlike the old list in SI 1998/3081 there are no explicit exclusions of some types of companies, with the exception of Luxembourg insurance companies. The excluded territories are listed in SI 2012/3024, and predictably territories that do not impose tax on trading profits are absent from the proposed list. However the UK's main trading partners (Australia, Canada, The US, France, Germany and Japan) are given a near blanket exemption, provided the CFCs profits are actually taxed in that territory. Other than that, the excluded territories are set out below:

| | | |
|---|---|---|
| Afghanistan | Fiji | Papa New Guinea |
| Algeria | France | Peru |
| Angola | Falkland Islands | Philippines |
| Argentina | Faroe Islands | Poland |
| Armenia | Gabon | Portugal |
| Aruba | Gambia | Puerto Rico |
| Australia | Germany | Republic of Korea |
| Austria | Ghana | Russia |
| Azerbaijan | Greece | Saudi Arabia |
| Bangladesh | Honduras | Senegal |
| Barbados | Iceland | Sierra Leone |
| Belarus | India | Slovakia |
| Belgium | Indonesia | Slovenia |
| Belize | Iran | Solomon Islands |
| Benin | Israel | South Africa |
| Bolivia | Jamaica | Spain |
| Botswana | Japan | Sri Lanka |
| Brazil | Kenya | Swaziland |
| Brunei | Lesotho | Sweden |
| Burundi | Libya | Tanzania |
| Cameroon | Luxembourg | Thailand |
| Canada | Malawi | Trinidad and Tobago |
| China | Malaysia | Tunisia |
| Colombia | Malta | Turkey |

| Croatia | Mexico | Uganda |
|---|---|---|
| Cuba | Monaco | Ukraine |
| Czech Republic | Morocco | United State of America |
| Democratic Republic of the Congo | Namibia | Uruguay |
| Denmark | Netherlands | Venezuela |
| Dominican Republic | New Zealand | Vietnam |
| Ecuador | Nigeria | Zambia |
| Egypt | Norway | Zimbabwe |
| El Salvador | Pakistan | |
| Finland | Panama | |

The absence of Ireland and Singapore from the list is notable.

Outside of this, to meet the excluded territories exemption requires detailed analysis of the income and profits of the CFC to show that all the CFC's income and profits are, one might say, 'good'. This is aimed at excluding any type of income which is low taxed, and there are a number of categories (eg a local tax incentive, income sheltered in a corporate partnership, low taxed non local source income for example). The conditions are set out below:

- In the first instance, a CFC on the list will only qualify if the persons with the interest on the CFC are taxed in that territory on the CFC's income. For example a US LLC will only qualify if the LLC or its members are taxable in the US on the income. This is clearly designed to address the historic use of US LLCs as pass through vehicles with non-resident members not subject to US tax.
- The total amount of the CFC's 'bad' income must not exceed the greater of 10% of:
  - the CFC's accounting profits as defined by ss 371VC and 371VD (excluding transfer pricing adjustments)—broadly these are profits determined by GAAP but excluding amounts that would be exempt distributions if the CFC were a UK resident company, property business profits and capital profits and losses, or
  - £50k if greater.
  'Bad' income comprises four categories of income that is subject to a reduced rate:
  (A) s 371KE exempt income (apart from distributions), income taxed at a reduced rate under an investment incentive, or tax paid by a CFC and then repaid to any person;
  (B) s 371KG investment income received from outside the CFC's territory which benefits from a 'notional' interest deduction (such as that available in The Netherlands and Luxembourg. This means that a finance company established in one of these territories which makes use of the notional deduction to minimise local tax is unlikely to qualify for the excluded territories exemption (ETE));

    (C)    s 371KH profits arising as partnership profits which are not included in a CFC's accounting profits or amounts that accrue to a settlement of which the CFC is settlor/beneficiary;

    (D)    s 371KI 'unilateral' transfer pricing adjustments or tax rate reductions agreed by a governmental authority in the CFC's territory (ie where no corresponding increase elsewhere. An example of the sort of situation caught is Dutch informal capital rulings which reduce the profits of a Dutch company to an arm's length result.)

- The intellectual property (IP) condition (s 371KJ—this definition mirrors that in the trading profits safe harbour)—the ETE is met *unless*:
  - the CFC's assumed taxable profits include amounts from IP, and
  - all or parts of the IP was transferred to the CFC by a UK related person at any time in the relevant period (as defined in s 371KJ(5)) or the previous 6 accounting periods (or it was derived out of IP held by a UK related person at *any time* during that period), and
  - as a result of the transfer there was a significant reduction in the value of the IP held by the related person(s) in the UK, and
  - if only part of the IP was transferred/otherwise derives from the UK where the significance condition is met. The significance condition is met if the IP transferred or otherwise derived from the UK:
    - forms a significant part of the CFC's total IP;
    - the transfer results in the CFC having significantly higher profits than they would otherwise have been.
- The final condition is a TAAR at s 371KB(1)(d) to deny the exemption if the CFC is involved in an arrangement, where the purpose was to obtain a tax advantage. HMRC's draft guidance gives examples of two arrangements which may be caught (see paragraph 45, Chapter 11).

The definition of IP in s 371VA appears quite tight and relates to specific IP such as licences, rights etc. However broader IP such as customer lists do not appear to be included.

It will be noted that there are some low tax jurisdictions, eg Switzerland, on the list. However it is expected that where for example a ruling has been obtained in Switzerland leading to a low effective tax rate, the use of the ETE would be excluded by condition D above.

The modified ETE for major trading partners drops the bad income condition and the IP condition, but still retains the subject to tax clause with the exclusion of dividends. The CFC should also not itself have had a foreign permanent establishment (PE) during the period concerned. Therefore, if a CFC in one of the major trading partners does have a PE, it would be necessary to see if it could be exempted instead under the main ETE.

On balance therefore the compliance burden for subsidiaries in those countries should be less. Furthermore, CFCs which meet the ETE do not need to be reported on the CT600B return.

## The tax exemption (ss 371NA et seq)

[A6.10]  Under the old rules, for a company to be a CFC it must be subject to a lower level of taxation—broadly the tax it pays is less than 75% of the UK tax that would be paid were the company UK resident (ignoring capital gains and losses). This has been recast as one of the exemptions from apportionment. The computational rules are similar to those in ICTA, ss 750 and 750A. The provisions relating to anti-designer rate regimes have also been retained.

Section 371 TB provides for a series of tests to ensure that a CFC is effectively managed in the territory in which it is resident. If effective management is carried out in two countries, the test then looks at where most of the assets are situated.

It could be argued that with the decline in UK corporate tax rates this provision will cause more CFCs to fall out of the net. The practical issue will be the need to prepare a UK tax computation for the CFC to see whether the test is met.

## Exempt period exemption (ss 371 JA et seq)

[A6.11]  The final entity based exemption applies where a non-UK resident company comes under UK control (for example following an acquisition). A grace period of 12 months is permitted subject to the application of anti-avoidance rules relating to shifting profit into the newly acquired company or shortening an accounting period.

The exempt period exemption is not as straightforward as the grace period which used to be allowed in the past as various conditions need to be met.

There is an initial condition, which requires, inter alia, that the CFC existed immediately before that time, so newly formed companies will not usually qualify, other than acquisition vehicles.

Furthermore, the exemption is only given on a provisional basis. The subsequent period condition requires the CFC to continue as a CFC for at least one accounting period beginning after the exempt period and for the CFC to be exempt in that period, either because there are no chargeable profits or because the CFC qualifies for an entity exemption. Thus, it is necessary to restructure the CFC to avoid a CFC charge in the first full accounting period after the 12 month exemption. Another effect of the subsequent period condition is that the exemption is denied if there is no accounting period after the end of the exempt period (eg because the CFC ceases to trade or where it is sold to non-UK persons). HMRC may grant an extension if it can be demonstrated that it has not been possible to restructure the CFC because of circumstances outside the group's control.

Note that because the CFC must be exempt in first full accounting period following the exempt period, the group has a maximum possible period of 24 months in which to effect any necessary reorganisation (the maximum 24 months would arise where the CFC's accounting period starts the day before the 12 month exempt period comes to an end). The period between the 12 month exempt period and the start of the first full accounting period after the 12 month exempt period is the 'bridging' period. It is important to realise that the 'bridging' period is subject to the full CFC rules—so it is possible for companies to take longer to reorganise the CFC's business than 12 months, but the problem in taking longer is this may result in a CFC charge arising in the bridging period.

The chargeable company condition requires that throughout the 'relevant period' (from immediately after the exempt period begins to the end of the first full accounting period after the exempt period) there is a chargeable company. This can either be the company that acquired the CFC or one connected with it.

As to be expected, there is a TAAR, which prevents the exemption applying where arrangements are entered into to take advantage of it (eg shifting 'mobile' profits into the CFC during its exempt period in an attempt to shelter them or shortening the length of an accounting period to less than 12 months to ensure the subsequent period condition is met).

Where none of the entity exemptions apply, it is then necessary to go on to consider the Initial Gateway, the Gateway, safe harbours and the Main Gateway in order to calculate whether all or a proportion of the profits may be exempted. This by its very nature is more subjective and more complicated to operate in practice, as can be seen below. Companies would normally look to use the Initial Gateway or safe harbour Gateways first as in principle they are easier to satisfy.

## The Initial Gateway—business profits (Chapter 3)

**[A6.12]** Section 371CA states that profits attributable to UK activities will pass through to the Main gateway unless conditions A, B, C or D are met. If one of conditions A–C is met, then it is not necessary to apply the detailed testing under the Main Gateway. (Condition D excludes property and non-trade finance profits)

Condition A is akin to a motive test based on the assets held and risks borne by the CFC at any time in the accounting period where the main purpose (or one of the main purposes) is to reduce UK tax as a result of which the CFC becomes more profitable. This is allied to an expectation test which suggests that the arrangement might not have been entered into but for the tax reduction.

Condition B is ostensibly simpler; that at no time during the accounting period does the CFC have any UK managed assets or bear any UK managed risks during the accounting period.

Condition C is essentially an independence test to establish whether the CFC could still function, in the same business operating at the same scale, if UK management in respect of its assets and risk were withdrawn. Essentially this seeks to test whether the UK activities are capable of being replaced by similar arrangements with third parties.

Condition D also provides for non-trading finance profits and property business profits to fall outside the Gateway where these comprise the company's entire profits.

Tests A–C are summarised in the following flowcharts:

Condition A: Purpose of arrangements

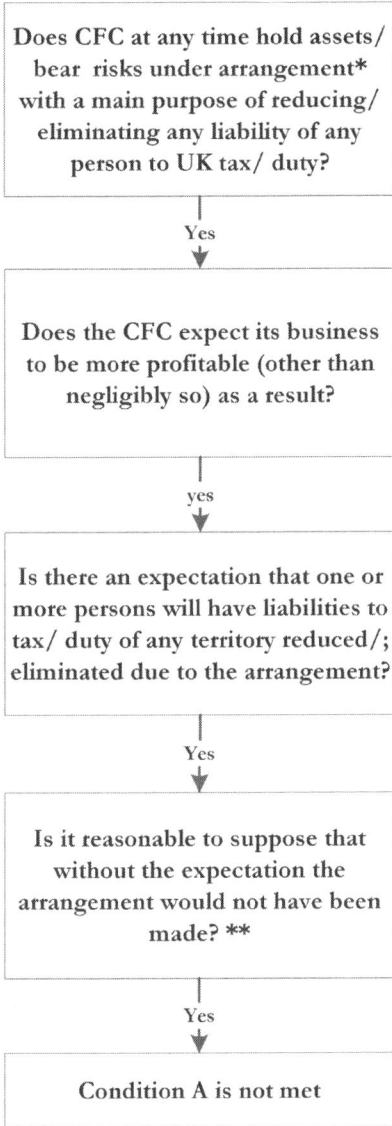

```
┌─────────────────────────────────┐
│ Does CFC at any time hold assets/│
│ bear  risks under arrangement*   │
│ with a main purpose of reducing/ │
│ eliminating any liability of any │
│ person to UK tax/ duty?          │
└─────────────────────────────────┘
              │
             Yes
              ▼
┌─────────────────────────────────┐
│ Does the CFC expect its business │
│ to be more profitable (other than│
│ negligibly so) as a result?      │
└─────────────────────────────────┘
              │
             yes
              ▼
┌─────────────────────────────────┐
│ Is there an expectation that one or│
│ more persons will have liabilities to│
│ tax/ duty of any territory reduced/;│
│ eliminated due to the arrangement?│
└─────────────────────────────────┘
              │
             Yes
              ▼
┌─────────────────────────────────┐
│ Is it reasonable to suppose that │
│ without the expectation the      │
│ arrangement would not have been  │
│ made? **                         │
└─────────────────────────────────┘
              │
             Yes
              ▼
┌─────────────────────────────────┐
│ Condition A is not met           │
└─────────────────────────────────┘
```

*'Arrangements' defined at s371VA- any agreement, scheme or transaction or understanding, whether legally enforceable or not*

**Are the non-tax reasons clearly sufficient on their own to justify the arrangements?*

Condition B: CFC must have no UK managed asset or risk

> Are there any UK managed assets or risks? Ignore (a) activities carried on by CFC through a UK PE and (b) group wide activities of UK parent as shareholder. The activities must be directed at the CFC.

*An asset or risk is UK managed if (a) the acquisition, development, creation or exploitation of asset, or (b) the taking on or bearing of risk, is controlled or managed to significant extent by UK activities. Provided active decision-making in respect of assets/ risks does not take place in UK, the fact that the CFC's activities are in-line with general parameters set by UK is not 'UK managed'.*

Yes

> Are those UK activities carried on in UK by the CFC itself (other than a UK PE of the CFC) or by connected companies under arrangements that unconnected persons would not enter into?

*Is there evidence that similar arrangements actually exist between unconnected companies? If one company's profits depend on decisions of the other, the presumption is this is not the case.*

Yes

> Condition B is not met

Yes

> Go to Condition C

Condition C: Is the CFC itself capable commercially?

Despite failing Condition B, does the CFC have the capability throughout the AP to ensure its business would be commercially effective if those assets or risks were no longer UK managed?

*Could support services be outsourced instead with third parties under commonly found business arrangements?*

Could the CFC do this without making significant changes to nature or scale of its business to adapt to withdrawal of UK management or control activities?

*Synergies that would be lost as a result of not working other group companies do not mean the CFC is not commercially effective.*

Yes

Can the CFC do this without relying on a connected person at any time (because the activities are of a type that can be obtained on a commercial basis at arm's length)?

Yes

Does the CFC have the necessary capability to select appropriate providers and manage its transactions with them?

Yes

Condition C is not met

# The Initial Gateway—non-trading finance profits (Chapter 3)

**[A6.13]** There are helpful exemptions for non-trading finance profits. Section 371CB(3) excludes non-trading finance profits which arise from cash retained by a trading CFC to fund its working capital requirements (provided no profits from the trade itself pass through the Gateway). Section 371CB(4) exempts profits arising from the investment of funds held for a UK or overseas property business.

Profits arising on non-trading profits are excluded by s 371CB(6) and (7) if there is a temporary restriction on paying dividends but only where the intention is to make a distribution within 12 months of the accounting period.

The exclusions at s 371CB(3) and (4) do not apply to non-trading finance profits arising from funds held:

- where there is a prohibition on the payment of dividends whether by local law, the CFC's articles, or where upstream loans are made to UK instead of paying dividends,
- because they have been rolled up rather than paying dividends within 12 months of the end of the accounting period,
- with a view to acquiring shares in any company or making capital contribution,
- with a view to acquiring, investing or developing land more than 12 months after the end of the accounting period,
- only or mainly as contingency fund
- only or mainly to reduce or eliminate tax or duty of any territory for any person.

# Safe harbours

## Trading profits safe harbour

**[A6.14]** The trading income of a CFC will be excluded if the conditions of ss 371DF et seq are all met. This is clearly targeted at testing whether businesses have substance in the overseas jurisdictions concerned and the extent to which it is operating independently. The conditions are as follows. All of them need to be met to be able to benefit from the trading profits safe harbour.

(1) The business premises test—s 371DG. Business premises must be used with a reasonable degree of permanence—in practice at least 12 months, or intended to be used this way. They should also be the main place of business of the CFC in its territory of residence.

(2) The income test—s 371DH. UK derived income must be less than 20% of the CFC's total relevant trading income which excludes UK income from the sale of goods produced in the CFC's territory of residence. In

practice this will provide an exclusion for income arising from the actual production of goods in the territory where the CFC is present where these are sold to the UK.

(3) The management expenditure test—s 371DI. The management expenditure condition is met if the UK related management expenditure is no more than 20% of the total related management expenditure. This is based on the costs in the accounts of staff carrying our relevant management functions. The latter is defined as any staff carrying out the management of relevant risks and assets. Where the CFC does not meet the 20% test, if less than 50% of the relevant management expenditure on an individual asset or risk basis is UK related and all the other trading profits safe harbour conditions are met, then the test is not failed.

(4) The intellectual property test—s 371DJ. If the CFC's profits derive to a significant extent from IP transferred from related parties in the UK in the last six years prior to the accounting period and the profits of the transferor have been significantly reduced, then if the profits of the CFC are significantly higher than they would have been without the transfer then the test will be failed. There is however a further test which allows CFC's to escape if the IP transferred did not lead to a significant increase in the CFC's profit. HMRC guidance suggests that significant means 10% or more.

(5) The export of goods test—s 371DK. This introduces an exclusion if not more than 20% of the CFC's trading income arises from good exported from the UK, excluding goods exported into the CFC's territory of residence. Note that it is not necessary for the goods to come from a related party. Again this appears to be targeted at reinvoicing companies and principal type structures and adds a presumption that such profits are more likely to have been supported by UK activity.

In practice the trading profit safe harbour seems to offer some opportunities for planning but business will need substantive presence in the CFC jurisdiction. In addition the IP test and the test for UK links will mean that supply chain planning with a previous or future UK connection will be more difficult, perhaps restricting opportunities to non-UK IP and non-UK transactions.

Again, there is a TAAR at s 371DL to prevent manipulation of the above conditions.

## Property safe harbour

**[A6.15]** All property income is excluded from the CFC rules.

## Incidental non-trading finance profits safe harbour

**[A6.16]** Where a CFC is a trader or has a property business, incidental non-trading finance profits will be exempt provided they do not exceed 5% of PBIT(s 371CC). If this threshold is failed, it is still possible for non-trading/property income to be excluded provided it arises from funds held for the purposes of that business (s 371CB(3) and (4)) so long as none of the business profits themselves pass through the Gateway. The legislation also specifies circumstances where CFCs will not be able to rely on this exclusion at s 373CB(5).

This exclusion will also be useful for holding companies as they will be able to exclude non-trade finance profits provided they do not exceed 5% of exempt distribution income (ie dividends that would qualify for the dividend exemption in the UK). However, the need to incorporate the finance income of sub-holdcos could be problematic. Mixed activity companies can exclude non-trade finance profits if they do not exceed 5% of the total of their trading/property business plus exempt distribution income, provided a substantial part of their business is holding 51% subsidiaries (as defined). If that test is failed, there is a fall-back at s 371CD.

## The Main Gateway—business profits (Chapter 4)

**[A6.17]** The Main Gateway will in practice only be considered where none of the entity exemptions apply and the CFC is not able to benefit from either the Initial Gateway test or the safe harbour Test. From hereon the whole process becomes much more complex to operate in practice with a strong transfer pricing element to the analysis. Profits only have to pass through one of the Main Gateways to be chargeable profits.

- The key issue is whether there is a separation of key assets and risks from the management activity (or 'significant people functions' (SPFs)). In practice SPFs refer to active decision making or strategic functions, such as acceptance or management of risks and assets, rather than routine activities. They become UK SPFs if they are habitually performed in the UK. If there are no UK SPFs, then there are no chargeable profits to pass through the Gateway.
- If there are UK SPFs then the question becomes whether in reality the CFC could have existed on its own as an independent entity without support (s 371DE). Unless the trading profits safe harbour applies (see A6.5) it is necessary to follow an eight step process specified by s 371DB. The purpose of this is to allow a comparison to be made between the profits the CFC actually makes (based on the actual allocation of assets ad risks) and those it would have made if the principles of the OECD's 2010 Report on the Attribution of Profits to Permanent Establishments had been followed. It follows that if there are no UK SPFs, there are no chargeable profits. If there are UK SPFs, the chargeable profits identified can still be reduced or eliminated via a transfer pricing exercise.
- Step 6 also provides a helpful exclusion for profits relating to those assets or risks where UK SPFs do not contribute to at least 50% of the CFC's income in respect of those assets or risks (s 371DC).
- Step 8 may eliminate further profits through the independent arrangements exclusion (s 371DE) or the economic value exclusion (s 371DD), where the non-tax value resulting from the CFC holding the asset or

bearing the risk concerned is 'substantial'. HMRC's draft guidance on Chapter 4 indicates that 20% of the economic value would be regarded as 'substantial'.

## The Gateway—finance profits

**[A6.18]** Chapters 5 and 6 define which non-trading and trading finance profits will pass through the Gateway. In broad terms, these will be caught if they arise from any of the following categories:

Under Chapter 5 non-trading finance profits will normally pass through the gateway to the extent that they arise from relevant UK Funds or other assets, although a hypothetical deduction is given for a fee which an independent entity might have charged to manage the activity concerned. There are also provisions to tax profits arising on upstream loans as an alternative to dividends and where the CFC provides a finance lease to a UK company or connected party. In order to be exempt, non-trade finance profits must not pass through the Gateway under any of the tests under ss 371EB, EC, ED and EE. These are as follows:

- The UK activities test—s 371EB. If there is active decision making relating to the acceptance of risk and ongoing management of loans, such as decisions about the overall tax efficiency of the loan arrangements or how the funds of the group are employed. This basically re-runs the tests under s 371DB, omitting the helpful exclusions under step 6 and 8 referred to above. This seems to suggest that only modest UK involvement would mean that the test is failed and all of the profits pass through the Gateway.
- Capital investment from the UK—s 371EC. In broad terms, if profits arising in the CFC arise from the use of UK funds or other assets there will be chargeable profits even if there are no SPFs in the UK. UK funds are widely defined and in order to fall outside of this provision a UK parent will need to carefully track the source and history of funds used to finance CFC's. If the profits pass through the Gateway then there is a deduction available under s 371EC(2) for the cost of managing the loan. The finance company partial exemption detailed later provides a 75% exemption for these loans without the need to undertake this tracking.
- Arrangements in lieu of dividends—s 371ED. Where an upstream loan is made but it can be proved for example that the main purpose of the loan is a non-tax purpose—for example a dividend block—then the profits should not pass through the Gateway, provided there isn't another reason which is tax-related.
- Finance lease—s 371EE. Where there is a finance lease arrangement with a connected UK person there is a main reason test similar to the one in s 371 ED, ie where it can be proved that the arrangements did not have a UK tax motive, the CFC profits will not pass through the Gateway.

It should be borne in mind that even if non-trade finance profits pass through the Gateway, companies may still be able to avail themselves of the finance company exemption under Chapter 9. (see **A6.11** below). However it is important to note that the exemption under Chapter 9 is not available for non-trade finance profits unless they arise from money debts which are also Qualifying Loan Relationships or QLRs. Therefore substantial non-trade finance income could still be subject to tax—for example bank deposits, profits from finance leases, upstream loans and, importantly, loans to UK companies or UK PEs.

Chapter 6, relating to trading finance profits, requires some rather detailed economic analysis to determine whether the CFC is 'overcapitalised' as a result of either direct or indirect UK capital contributions from a UK connected company in order to ascertain the elements that pass through the Gateway. Essentially this treats the CFC as if it were an independent company with its own capital and ignores the support of the parent. The chargeable profits are calculated under a 3 step process set out in s 371FA and seek to calculate the amount of profit that would arise if the CFC had its own free capital. This element would then not pass through the Gateway. There are specific exclusions for banking and insurance businesses.

Outside of this, the main application would appear to be group treasury companies, where their activities relate to trading. However a group treasury company can also give notice that it wishes to treat such income as non-trade finance profits in order that it may benefit from the finance company exemption, although it should be noted that unless the full exemption applies, 25% of the profits will remain in charge.

The basic rule under s 371GA also brings in profits from captive insurance businesses where there is a contract of insurance with a UK company or connected party. Where the captive is resident in the EEA, profits will be caught if they derive from UK connected companies or PEs without a significant non-tax reason for entering into the arrangements. However, for captives outside the EEA, all profits with a UK connection will be caught.

As noted above, the Gateway defines what 'bad' profits are. Thus if a CFC's profits do not fall within the Gateway, the profits do not need to be self-assessed. However, given its complexity (in assessing the significant people or Key Entrepreneurial Risk Taker (KERT) functions), the Gateway may be difficult to apply in practice. Therefore, for businesses which prefer mechanically based tests, it would be preferable to use the Gateway, safe harbours and entity based exemptions if possible. Groups are completely free to choose which combination of exemptions, safe harbours or Gateway they use in arriving at their self-assessment.

### Calculation of tax due

**[A6.19]** The rules are lengthy and complex. In the publicity on the new rules much has been made by HM Treasury and HMRC of the Gateway test (the provisions that set out how to compute apportionable income (ss 371QA et seq)).

However as currently drafted, the steps required to prove the profits do not fall into the Gateway are onerous. As such this is likely to be one of the more contentious areas of the new legislation, although the policy intention is welcome. A detailed transfer pricing functional analysis will often be required to calculate the profits to pass through the Gateway. The 'basic rule' is that the CFC's profits are to be the profits that would be determined applying the OECD's Report on the Attribution of Profits to Permanent Establishments of June 2010 (s 371DA). As discussed previously, the basic thrust is to identify situations where there are any people in the UK (not just UK based employees) and referred to as significant people functions who are generating profits which are realised overseas. In other words, are UK profits commensurate with activity? This raises a whole series of questions about the roles of UK based management and their oversight of a potential CFC, both during the accounting period concerned and either side of it. The sort of management activity relevant here is active decision making in respect of the CFC's assets and risks rather than the general governance of a CFC.

If the activities of the CFC have no connection with the UK, it should have no profits that will be apportioned—even if these profits arise in a territory where there is no corporate tax on profits. One could say that this 'Gateway' replicates in a much more formalised way the current motive test.

For CFCs that cannot be excluded by any of the exemptions there could be considerable work in computing apportionable profits which could require considerable input from transfer pricing specialists which in turn will increase compliance cost.

## Finance company exemption

**[A6.20]**   Chapter 9 introduces a new s 371IA which has attracted a great deal of press attention and is designed to provide an attractive tax environment for group treasury companies, although in principle it is open to any company which meets the conditions in a straightforward intra-group lending scenario. It is also appealing to those companies which might otherwise fail the entity exemptions or Gateway test. For example, it removes the need for groups to trace the source of funding used to finance the CFC which would otherwise be required by s 371EC. In addition to this, the exemption could also be considered in the context of plans to make an acquisition of an overseas company.

Upon a claim, the CFC's qualifying loan relationship profits only pass through the Gateway to the extent that they do not benefit from what was originally termed the new exemption. The main new exclusion from CFC apportionment is therefore the exemption for offshore group finance companies (finance company partial exemption). In essence 75% of the profits from a qualifying loan relationship (QLR) will be exempt. The QLR definition is designed to encourage the treasury company to lend on to other non-UK companies and discourage the lending of such funds back to the UK or any entity with UK source profits which might otherwise receive a tax deduction for the interest payable.

In essence, then, a QLR is a loan relationship where:

- the CFC is the lender, and
- the ultimate debtor (ie the borrowing company) is a qualifying company which is a connected company controlled by the same UK person that controls the CFC; and
- section 371IH does not apply to treat the loan as non-qualifying. In broad terms this operates to deny relief where the foreign company might have UK source income (ie rents) against which it was claiming a UK tax deduction or the debit is taken into account elsewhere resulting in a reduction in UK tax.

There are also a further series of anti-avoidance provisions under s 371IH which target arrangements which increase a UK interest expense as part of the arrangements. Additional exclusions were added to s 371H by FA 2014.

The ultimate debtor rule in s 371IG(2) and (3) also operates to act as a look through mechanism to enable loans to qualify where they would not otherwise do so as long as the ultimate debtor is under the control of the UK person that controls the CFC. Typically this would apply in cases where there are back to back loans.

QLR profits themselves are broadly credits from QLRs included in non-trading finance profits, as adjusted for relevant debits or credits from any associated hedging and a 'just and reasonable' apportionment of any loan relationship debits included in non-trading finance profits. Therefore in principle, foreign exchange differences would also qualify. Loan relationship profits which are ancillary to an exempt trade or property businesses are excluded as they are already exempted by s 371CB.

The treasury company will also need to have business premises at its disposal (in broad terms applying the same test as that for the trading profits safe harbour), perhaps not every day but available for use and actually used.

In practice the regime will not apply to:

- loans to UK resident connected persons (which would otherwise create a UK tax deduction followed by a lowly taxed receipt in the CFC),
- loans to unconnected persons—this is to counter the simple diversion of profits which would otherwise accrue to the UK,
- loans to connected persons where the loan has been sourced from a UK resident person with a banking or insurance business,
- arrangements where loans are moved from overseas to the UK to create a tax saving.

In order to benefit from the provisions, a claim must be made within 12 months of the filing date for each UK company with a stake of 25% or more.

The net result of this is that from 1 April 2014 the rate of UK tax payable on such profits would be only 5.25%, falling to 5% from 1 April 2015.

# Full exemption

**[A6.21]**  In limited circumstances a full exemption may be available where the loans are funded either entirely out of qualifying resources or by using the matched interest rule.

Qualifying resources are defined by s 371IB—in essence they are locally sourced lending profits from loans and local dividends as well as funds acquired by a new share issue by the ultimate parent. Where a claim is made for the full exemption for a given QLR, the partial exemption will not apply (s 371ID). Given that the full exemption is only given in respect of the specified proportion of a QLR out of qualifying resources, the partial exemption may give a better result in some situations, and has the advantage of simplicity. For example, a QLR which is only 60% out of qualifying resources will be 100% exempt on 60% of the loan (ie 60%)—whereas the partial exemption would have resulted in 75% exemption instead.

It is, however, possible to claim the full exemption in respect of some QLRs and the partial exemption on the others (s 371ID).

# Matched interest rule

**[A6.22]**  The matched interest rule under s 371IE applies where there are non-trading finance profits which remain chargeable after the full or partial finance company exemptions have been claimed. These 'leftover' profits should be exempt insofar as they exceed the net UK interest deduction. The test borrows terminology from the worldwide debt cap, referring to the tested income amount and tested expense amount. The overall effect is that if a group has no net UK debt, non-trading finance profits arising in a CFC will be fully exempt.

# Tax planning with the new finance company exemption

**[A6.23]**  The tax efficiency of this idea flows from the UK's relatively generous corporation tax relief for interest expense. There is no suggestion of any further restrictions to the deductibility of interest expense for the purposes of UK corporation tax. Thus, provided setting up the offshore finance company can be justified on commercial grounds (ie not solely or mainly motivated by the tax saving) this new exemption may enable the group to have UK tax relief on the full amount of the interest expense on its external financing whilst most of the intra-group receipts of the offshore finance subsidiary will be excluded from UK tax. The proposed partial CFC exemption will apply to income received by the group's international finance company.

To benefit, UK groups will set up the finance company in a suitable offshore jurisdiction. The location will normally vary depending on the group's profile. The first requirement is that there is no (or minimal) local tax on finance income, the second that the finance company should receive the interest gross—requiring examination of the withholding arrangements between the finance company jurisdiction and that of each of the other non-UK members of the group that will be borrowing funds. To benefit from the finance company partial exemption, the finance company must meet all the requirements, including in particular as regards its capital structure.

Profits of the international finance company may be transferred to the UK by way of dividend to its parent, which should be exempt from UK corporation tax on the receipt under the UK's distribution exemption.

As mentioned above, the full finance company exemption test is more onerous as it requires that the QLR is funded by qualifying resources. Therefore although this achieves 100% exemption as opposed to 75%, tax payers may find that the 75% exemption is easier to operate in practice and gives more certainty of outcome in the absence of certainty over the source of funds (and indeed having to monitor them). In summary, assuming the finance company is located in a jurisdiction that does not subject the company's profits to tax, the combined effect of the partial exemption from the CFC regime and the UK dividends received exemption will cause the return on equity invested in the finance company to carry little tax cost.

## Summary structure

**[A6.24]** A simplified structure showing the entities involved in this idea, may be illustrated diagrammatically as follows:

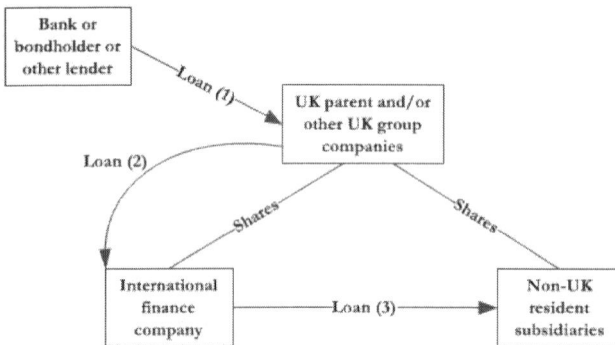

Notes:

**Loan (1)** from external sources is not a requirement for the structure. However subject to meeting existing rules, there will be no further restriction in tax relief for interest expense on the external borrowings. A cash rich group could use its own resources to provide working capital to the international finance company with the UK lending company including the loan interest income in its UK taxable profits.

**Loan (2)** on balance the UK parent is likely to fund the Finance Company via equity where possible in order not to generate excess deductions for interest at a low tax rate and the corresponding income being taxed at UK rates.

Whilst the international finance company could borrow externally, the loan is likely to be from the UK group as commercially the finance company would not have the necessary standing to borrow directly or, if it did, its loan would be on less favourable terms than a comparable third party borrowing by a UK group member.

**Loan (3)** is to non-UK members of the group only. The CFC exemption for international finance companies will not be available if loans are made by the non-UK company to UK members of the group.

The ultimate impact of this structure is an effective UK tax rate of 5.25% from 1 April 2014, which caused some degree of debate in the passage of the Finance Bill through parliament. The fact that it survived intact gives a clear statement of intent from the government in their attempts to attract and maintain the presence of large corporate businesses in the UK.

# A7

# EU law principles and practice

# Introduction

**[A7.1]** This Chapter considers how European Union (EU) law is relevant for direct tax purposes. EU law is important because it can override UK domestic law, and provide relief from UK tax based on the principles of EU law rather than the statutory wording on UK domestic law.

UK tax provisions which may be affected in this way are listed later in the Chapter, as well as relevant cases which have been decided by the UK or European courts.

Where HMRC challenge a company's tax position it is important to consider whether EU law provides any relief from the UK domestic position. Many UK tax provisions may be contrary to EU law, including the controlled foreign company rules, group relief and the taxation of foreign dividends.

Although tax planning is rarely undertaken on the basis of EU law alone, it can provide further protection to HMRC challenge against planning which has been undertaken on other bases.

# Basic principles—the European Union and the fundamental freedoms

### History of the European Union

**[A7.2]** The EU was created in the 1950s with six member countries: France, Germany, Italy, Belgium, the Netherlands and Luxembourg. The timeline below illustrates the expansion of the EU, and the signature of Treaties establishing the key principles of the EU.

1951   Treaty of Paris establishing the European Coal and Steel Community (ECSC) signed by France, Germany, Italy, Belgium, Netherlands and Luxembourg

1957   Treaty of Rome (also known as the EEC Treaty) establishing the European Economic Community (EEC)

1973   The United Kingdom, Ireland and Denmark join the EEC

1981   Greece joins the EEC

1986    Portugal and Spain join the EEC

1986    Single European Act the objective of which was to complete the internal market being an area without internal frontiers in which 'the free movement of goods, persons, services and capital is ensured'

1992    Treaty on European Union (the 'Maastricht Treaty' or the EU Treaty)—this treaty formed the 'European Union' (EU) by establishing the political infrastructure of the EU. The EEC Treaty was at the same time officially renamed the EC Treaty, and the EEC was renamed the EC.

1995    Austria, Finland and Sweden join the EU

1996    Treaty of Amsterdam which amended the EC Treaty and the EU Treaty.

2001    Treaty of Nice which dealt with reforming the institutions of the EU and amended the EC Treaty and the EU Treaty.

2004    Cyprus, the Czech Republic, Estonia, Hungary, Latvia, Lithuania, Malta, Poland, the Slovak Republic and Slovenia join the EU

2007    Bulgaria and Romania join the EU

2009    The Treaty of Lisbon is ratified by all Member States and on 1 December 2009 the Treaty of Lisbon came into effect. The EC Treaty was amended and renamed as the Treaty of the Functioning of the European Union (TFEU–hereafter referred to as the Treaty).

## Membership of the European Union

**[A7.3]** The EU is now composed of 28 Member States, with Croatia having joined on 1 July 2013.

| | | |
|---|---|---|
| Austria | Hungary | Netherlands |
| Belgium | Ireland | Poland |
| Bulgaria | Italy | Portugal |
| Croatia | Germany | Romania |
| Cyprus | | |
| Czech Republic | Greece | Slovakia |
| Denmark | Latvia | Slovenia |
| Estonia | Lithuania | Spain |
| Finland | Luxembourg | Sweden |
| France | Malta | UK |

## Overseas territories including the Isle of Man, Channel Isles and Gibraltar

**[A7.4]** The EC Treaty specifically excludes the Channel Isles (which include Jersey and Guernsey) and the Isle of Man except in relation to certain very limited matters. Protocol 3 to the UK's Act of Accession to the EU in 1973

confirmed that residents of the Channel Islands and the Isle of Man do not benefit from the Treaty freedoms other than the free movement of goods as they are part of the EU for customs duty purposes only.

Gibraltar is the only British Overseas Territory which is a member of the EU having joined by virtue of the 1973 Act of Accession. However, Gibraltar is not within the EU for VAT or customs duty purposes. The other British Overseas Territories (including the British Virgin Islands, the Cayman Islands and Bermuda) are not part of the EU although they are required to be party to certain of the EU treaties for administrative purposes only. The case of *Prunus SARL v Polonium SA* (C-384/09) confirmed that companies established in the British Virgin Islands and other overseas territories cannot benefit from the freedoms in the TFEU.

The UK and the Isle of Man have separately enacted the Customs and Excise Agreement 1979 to make the Isle of Man part of the UK, and therefore the EU, for VAT purposes.

When considering a zero tax jurisdiction which is close to the UK, there is often a choice between the Isle of Man and the Channel Isles. If it is important that the company can register for VAT, or recover VAT in another member state, the Isle of Man is therefore preferred to the Channel Isles.

Historically there has been pressure from the UK and the EU for the Channel Isles and the Isle of Man to abolish the 0% corporate tax rate. However in December 2012 the EU Code of Conduct group announced that it was happy that Guernsey had removed the harmful features from its 'Zero/Ten' regime and as a result is now compliant with the principles of the EU code of conduct for business taxation. This follows the earlier approval of the Isle of Man and Jersey tax regimes on a similar basis.

### Accession states

**[A7.5]** In addition other countries are looking at fulfilling the conditions for entry into the EU. Since the accession of Bulgaria and Romania on 1 January 2007, and of Croatia on 1 July 2013, there are currently no acceding countries. Any decision on the accession of a country has to be taken unanimously by all Member States.

The current candidates for entry, and an estimate of when they may become Member States, are as set out below. It is important to take into account potential future EU law protections when advising groups investing in these jurisdictions.

### Formal candidate countries

**[A7.6]** These countries have begun the formal process for entry into the EU:

(a)     Serbia

(b)     Iceland;

(c)     Former Yugoslav Republic of Macedonia;

(d)     Turkey;

(e)     Albania; and

(f)     Montenegro.

## Potential candidate countries

[A7.7] These countries are identified as future candidate countries by the EU's enlargement policy:

(a)     Bosnia; and
(b)     Kosovo.

## Non-EU countries

[A7.8] The European Economic Agreement came into force on 1 January 2004.

This Agreement effectively unites the EU Member States with Norway, Iceland and Liechtenstein (the European Free Trade Area (EFTA) states). It ensures *inter alia* that primary and secondary European legislation such as Treaty freedoms (see below for further details) applies to these countries as well.

In 2004, Switzerland became a party to the Savings Directive and the benefit of the Parent/Subsidiary Directive and the Interest and Royalties Directive were extended at the same time. The agreements are currently available at: eur-lex.europa.eu/JOHtml.do?uri=OJ:L:2004:385:SOM:en:HTML          as 2004/911/EC and 2004/912/EC.

## Objectives of EU law

### Nature of EU law

[A7.9] EU law comprises a number of different aspects:

(a)     'Primary law', which includes the various treaties noted above, starting with the Treaty of Rome (as amended by the subsequent treaties) and which is now known as the Treaty of the Functioning of the European Union (TFEU or the Treaty).
(b)     'Secondary law', which includes directives and regulations made pursuant to the TFEU. These are submitted to and approved by the European Council.
(c)     The Court of Justice, created under the terms of the Treaty. The primary role of the Court is to adjudicate on matters dealing with the interpretation of Community law. The role of the Court is discussed further below. On 1 December 2009 (the day the Lisbon Treaty came into effect), the European Court of Justice (ECJ) was renamed the Court of Justice.

### Aims of the Treaty

[A7.10] One of the aims of the Treaty is to establish an 'internal market'. Article 26(2) of the Treaty provides that:

' . . . The internal market shall comprise an area without internal frontiers in which the free movement of goods, persons, services and capital is ensured in accordance with the provisions of the Treaties.'

The Court of Justice has confirmed that:

'although direct taxation is a matter for the Member States they must nevertheless exercise their direct taxation powers consistently with Community law' (*ICI plc v Colmer (Inspector of Taxes)* C-264/96).'

The *Hughes de Lasteyrie du Saillant* (C-9/02) confirms that a restriction is prohibited even if it is of limited scope or minor importance.

In subsequent cases the Court of Justice has held that domestic rules which impede, restrict or hinder rights under the Treaty should be disapplied except in the case of artificial arrangements which amount to tax evasion, or unless the rules are required to maintain the balanced allocation of taxing rights between Member States and the scope of the rules is limited to that which is required to achieve such balanced allocation (see, for example, the *Société de Gestion Industrielle SA (SGI) v Etat belge* (C-311/08)).

However, the Treaty itself makes little reference to direct taxation. Article 115 provides that Directives can be issued in order to ensure the proper functioning of the common market and several tax directives have been issued as a result, for example the Parent/Subsidiary Directive.

## Fundamental freedoms

**[A7.11]** Article 18 of the Treaty prohibits discrimination on grounds of nationality. However most of the direct tax cases which have come before the Court of Justice are based on specific prohibitions ie they have asserted that one of the four fundamental freedoms enshrined in the Treaty has been breached:

(a)    free movement of goods (Articles 34–37);
(b)    free movement of services (Articles 56–62);
(c)    free movement of people or establishment (Articles 45–55);
(d)    free movement of capital (Articles 63–66).

In a direct tax context, the freedom of establishment is often of most relevance but the free movement of capital and the freedom to provide services may also be relevant. The text of these articles is reproduced below.

## Discrimination

**[A7.12]** The principle has been established that a domestic tax law may be overridden by the EU if it breaches one of the freedoms.

None of these articles refer to tax but all are designed to prevent discrimination. In *Italy v EEC Commission* (C-13/63) the Court of Justice interpreted the concept of discrimination as meaning different treatment of subjects in comparable situations or the same treatment of subjects in different situations.

The key question in many cases is therefore determining whether a non-resident is in a comparable situation to a resident (ie when exercising one of the freedoms).

## Freedom of establishment

**[A7.13]** Article 43 of the Treaty provides that:

'Within the framework of the provisions set out below, restrictions on the freedom of establishment of nationals of a Member State in a territory of another Member State shall be prohibited. Such prohibition shall also apply to restrictions on the setting-up of agencies, branches or subsidiaries by nationals of any Member State established in the territory of any Member State.

Freedom of establishment shall include the right to take up and pursue activities as self-employed persons and to set up and manage undertakings, in particular companies or firms within the meaning of the second paragraph of Article 48, under the conditions laid down for its own nationals by the law of the country where such establishment is effected, subject to the provisions of the Chapter relating to capital.'

Article 48 of the Treaty confirms that the freedom of establishment applies to companies formed under a Member State with a registered office, central administration or principal place of business within the European Union.

The Court of Justice has confirmed in cases such as *R v IRC, ex p Commerzbank AG*: (C-330/91) [1993] 4 All ER 37 and *CARTESIO Oktato es Szolgaltato bt* (C-210/06) [2009] Ch 354, [2008] ECR I-9641, that for companies the legal seat serves as the connecting factor with the legal system of a particular state, just like nationality in the case of natural persons. Therefore a company can claim the freedom to establish either its legal seat or registered office in a particular Member State. This may mean that exit charges arising on migration or redomiciliation may be in breach of the freedom of establishment (see **A7.43** and **A7.44**).

## Free movement of capital

**[A7.14]** Article 63 of the Treaty provides that:

'1. Within the framework of the provisions set out in this Chapter, all restrictions on the movement of capital between Member States and between Member States and third countries shall be prohibited.
2. Within the framework of the provisions set out in this Chapter, all restrictions on payments between Member States and between Member States and third countries shall be prohibited.'

## Free movement of services

**[A7.15]** Article 56 of the Treaty provides that:

'Within the framework of the provisions set out below, restrictions on freedom to provide services within the Union shall be prohibited in respect of nationals of Member States who are established in a Member State other than that of the person for whom the services are intended.'

## Justification for breaching the freedoms

**[A7.16]** Even if a taxpayer can prove that there has been discrimination arising from a breach of one of the freedoms, the Treaty specifically allows some justifications for this discrimination. The Court of Justice has accepted for example that tax provisions may be justified if they are in place to:

- combat tax evasion;
- ensure fiscal supervision; or
- protect the balanced allocation of taxing powers.

On the other hand, the Court of Justice has not accepted that discrimination is justified by the potential loss of tax revenue, or by economic aims such as promoting investment in domestic companies.

Even if the Court of Justice accepts a justification for a breach of a fundamental freedom, the rules must still be proportionate, ie the discriminatory measures must be appropriate and necessary in order to attain the objectives pursued by the legislation (*Fedesa* case C-331/88).

## The Court of Justice

**[A7.17]** As noted above, the primary role of the Court is to adjudicate on matters dealing with the interpretation of EU law. Individuals and companies within the EU can rely on the provisions of EU law and via the Court of Justice can seek to have a national law disapplied if it is contrary to EU law.

### Composition of the Court of Justice

**[A7.18]** The Court of Justice is composed of 27 Judges and eight Advocates General, who are lawyers appointed collectively by the Member States.

The Court of Justice sits:

(a)    as a full court in certain specified circumstances or where a case is considered to be of exceptional importance; or

(b)    as a Grand Chamber of 13 Judges if a Member State so requests, and in particularly complex or important cases; or

(c)    as a Chamber of either three or five Judges.

### References for preliminary rulings

**[A7.19]** The Court of Justice may hear a number of different types of case and requests for rulings, but the 'reference for preliminary ruling' is relevant to most tax matters.

Courts of Member States may, and sometimes must, refer to the Court of Justice and ask it to pass judgment on the interpretation of EU law. This will allow the court to determine, for example, if their domestic legislation is in compliance. The court will be bound by the judgment of the Court of Justice, both in respect of the current case and future similar cases which arise.

Individuals and companies cannot take cases directly to the Court of Justice, and therefore must first of all take their case to the court of the relevant Member State.

### Procedure

**[A7.20]** The procedure for hearing a case before the Court of Justice depends on the type of case heard, but is typically as follows.

The court of the Member State submits its questions about the interpretation of EU law. These will be translated and circulated to all EU Member States. A notice will be published in the Official Journal of the European Union identifying the parties to the case and the questions asked.

Written observations are then normally submitted (by the parties to the case or Member States) to the Court of Justice within two months of the notice being published in the Official Journal.

A public hearing is arranged, and the case is presented before the Judges and the Advocate General. If necessary, preparatory enquiries are undertaken by the Court of Justice prior to the hearing.

Subsequently (often after six months), the Advocate General delivers an Opinion analysing the legal detail of the case, and his view on the correct interpretation of the EU law in question. This Opinion is prepared to assist with the judgment, but is not a binding judgment itself.

The Judges deliberate and agree a judgment by majority vote. The judgment is pronounced in public court, and is made available on the same day via the Court of Justice website (curia.europa.eu/en/actu/communiques/communiq ue.htm for current cases or curia.europa.eu/en/content/juris/index.htm for an archive of historic cases). The judgment will be subsequently published in the European Court Reports.

The court of the Member State will then decide the case before it based on the judgment of the Court of Justice.

# Planning—use of the fundamental freedoms in tax planning

### UK provisions which breach the freedoms

**[A7.21]** There are a number of provisions in UK domestic law which arguably breach the fundamental freedoms, and could therefore be overridden by EU law. In addition to those provisions which are the subject of decided or ongoing cases (see below), affected provisions may include:

(a)  TCGA 1992, s 13: gains of non-resident companies are attributed to UK resident and domiciled participators of the company if the company would be a close company if it were resident in the UK. This provision is arguably contrary to the freedom of establishment.

(b)  CTA 2010, s 18: non-resident companies may only benefit from the starting or small companies' rate of corporation tax if they are resident in a territory which has a double tax treaty with the UK containing a non-discrimination article.

    The fact that the position is corrected through the UK's treaty network is no defence for the domestic law being discriminatory *(Commission v France)*.

(c)  ITA 2007, s 971: the non-resident landlord scheme does not apply to UK resident companies or individuals receiving rental income.

(d)    ITA 2007, s 714: the 'transfer of assets abroad' anti-avoidance legislation only applies where income arises to a non-UK incorporated company.

(e)    TCGA 1992, s 171 no gain no loss rules do not apply to transfers to companies established in other EU Member States.

Where possible, a company should be established in the EU when undertaking tax planning as the company may then rely on EU law principles in order to fall outside of certain UK anti-avoidance provisions such as the CFC rules, TCGA 1992, s 13 or ITA 2007, s 720 (provided the company has genuine substance etc).

In February 2011, the ECJ filed a formal request with the UK government to amend TCGA 1992, s 13, ITA 2007, s 714, and the controlled foreign company rules to remedy the relevant breaches Following a consultation in 2012, the government included provisions in FA 2013, s 62 and Sch 10 designed to remedy the relevant breaches under TCGA 1992, s 13 and ITA 2007, s 714. In broad terms these introduced an exemption for 'genuine transactions'. These measures are dealt with in further detail under **A11.30** and **A15.5** respectively.

### UK process for making EU claims

**[A7.22]** In 2005 the House of Lords gave its decision in Re Claimants under Loss Relief Group Litigation Order and *Autologic Holdings plc v IRC* [2004] EWCA Civ 680, [2004] 3 All ER 957. The question before the House of Lords was one of jurisdiction ie:

(a)    could a claim under EU law be made directly at the High Court; or

(b)    must a taxpayer make a claim by way of tax return and then appeal any refusal in the normal way to Special Commissioners (now the First Tier Tax Tribunal).

In its judgment the House of Lords held that claims under EU law (for group relief in this case) must be made in the tax return in accordance with the prescribed statutory procedure.

However claims for periods which are closed can be made at the High Court where the company has sought to make a late claim via its tax return but HMRC has refused to exercise its discretion to allow late claims.

Following this decision, EU claims should in the first instance be made through the prescribed tax procedures—in most cases via the tax return. Where however the relief sought cannot be awarded by the First Tier Tribunal a claim should be pursued at the Upper Tribunal.

### Time limits

**[A7.23]** In October 2006, the UK House of Lords considered the case of *Deutsche Morgan Grenfell Group plc v IRC* [2006] UKHL 49, [2007] 1 AC 558, which concerned the time limit for making claims to repayment of tax under EU law principles.

The House of Lords held that although there is normally a six year period within which claims needed to be made, where those claims involve recovery of tax paid under a mistake of law (such as where UK law does not comply with EU law) then the six year period does not begin until the mistake is known.

However, 'blocking legislation' was introduced in FA 2004, s 320 such that claims are restricted to a six year time limit when a mistake of law arises in a tax case. This restriction applies to all claims made after September 2003 and claims which, although made before this date, are amended after November 2003.

FA 2007 introduced a further restriction such that the six year time limit also applies to claims brought before 8 September 2003.

It is widely believed that these changes themselves are in breach of EU law because they do not include appropriate transitional provisions. Therefore further developments are likely.

In *Test Claimants in the FII Group Litigation v Revenue and Customs Comrs* [2010] EWCA Civ 103, claimants challenged the limitation of claims for recovery of Advance Corporation Tax (ACT) paid but not due, arguing that recent changes to the legislation were contrary to the European Union (EU) law principles of effectiveness, legal certainty and the protection of legitimate expectations.

Prior to the legislation change, HMRC allowed two remedies for claimants for recovery of ACT payments made in breach of EU law:

(1)     Recovery of sums unlawfully levied, within six years of the date the cause of the action arose (usually the tax payment).

(2)     Recovery of sums paid under a mistake of law, within the remit of the Limitations Act (1980), thereby allowing a period of six years from the date on which the claimant discovered the mistake of law or could with reasonable diligence have discovered it.

HMRC introduced legislation in the FA 2004 (s 320), enacted on 24 June 2004 but retroactively in force from 8 September 2003 – the date the claimants issued proceedings – providing that remedy (2) did not apply when the action related to a taxation matter under the care and management of the Commissioners.

HMRC contended that under EU law there need only be an effective remedy for enforcing rights under EU law, which remained satisfied by the existence of remedy (1).

The Court of Justice held that national legislation curtailing, retroactively and without any transitional arrangements, the period within which repayment could be sought of sums collected in breach of EU law was incompatible with the principle of effectiveness. The Court of Justice also held that it was irrelevant whether at the time the taxpayer issued its claim, the availability of the cause of action affording the longer limitation period had been recognised only recently by a lower court and was not definitively confirmed by the highest judicial authority until later.

### Cases involving UK provisions

**[A7.24]** Outlined below are some significant UK Court of Justice cases which considered, or which are due to consider, UK tax provisions. These cases may support claims in respect of other aspects of the UK tax system.

### Losses

*ICI v Colmer (C-264/96)*

**[A7.25]** The *ICI v Colmer* case involved a claim to consortium relief by ICI, which at the time was not available where more than half of a consortium member's business consisted of holding shares in non-UK resident subsidiaries.

The Court of Justice held that the UK group relief rules at the time imposed a restriction on the right of UK companies to establish subsidiaries in other Member States of the European Union contrary to EU law.

As a result of the Court of Justice decision, the UK group and consortium relief rules were changed such that:

(a)   for group relief purposes a group exists broadly where one UK company owns 75% of the other UK company or a third company (wherever resident) owns 75% of both of them;

(b)   for consortium relief purposes the UK subsidiary residency requirement was removed.

These changes went beyond those strictly required by the Court of Justice decision in that they extended beyond the EU, and aimed to ensure that these other provisions were compliant with EU law.

*Felixstowe Dock & Railway Company v HMRC (TC/2010/04962)*

**[A7.26]** In *Felixstowe Dock and Railway Co Ltd v Revenue and Customs Comrs* (TC/2010/04962) [2011] UKFTT 838 (TC), UK resident companies with a Hong Kong resident parent claimed consortium relief for losses in a UK resident joint venture, where the link company was resident in Luxembourg. HMRC refused relief under the legislation applying at the time, as the 'link company' was not resident in the UK and did not carry on a trade in the UK through a permanent establishment. From 2010, new legislation applies, under which the link company is permitted to be resident in the EEA, rather than the UK, but only if it is under common 75% control with the surrendering or claimant company, without the involvement of non EEA companies.

Aspects of the case were referred to the EU Court of Justice, which ruled that the 'link company' should not be required to be UK resident in these circumstances, and moreover that the status of the link company was not affected by the presence of non-EEA companies in the chain, including the ultimate parent in Hong Kong. Consortium relief should be available for structures with an EEA link company under the same conditions as for a UK-resident link company.

*Marks & Spencer plc vHalsey (Inspector of Taxes) (C-446/03)*

**[A7.27]** In this case, Marks and Spencer plc claimed group relief for losses arising in its European subsidiaries, as illustrated in Diagram 1. At the time, UK law did not allow a UK company to claim losses from a non-resident company except where the non-resident carried on a trade in the UK through a permanent establishment.

Diagram 1

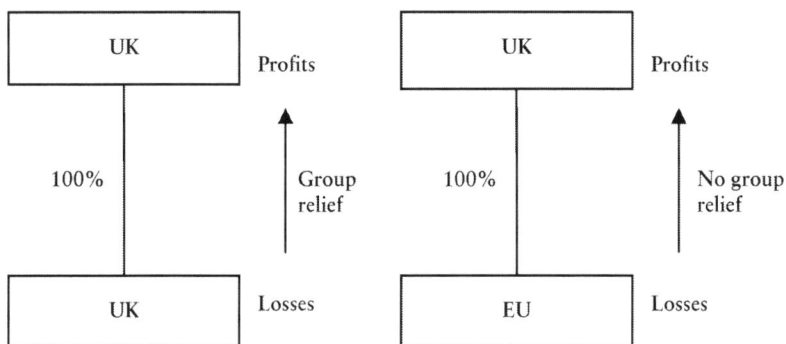

The Court of Justice held that the exclusion of loss relief for losses of a foreign subsidiary is a breach of the freedom of establishment since its deters UK companies from setting up subsidiaries in other Member States. However the Court of Justice held that the restriction in the UK group relief rules would be justified in certain circumstances:

(a)     To prevent companies obtaining double relief for losses.

(b)     To prevent companies from avoiding tax by choosing to relieve losses against profits which are subject to the highest rate of tax.

(c)     To maintain the 'balanced allocation of the power to impose taxes between Member States'.

The Court of Justice went on to note that the UK rules went beyond what was necessary in certain circumstances, specifically where it can be demonstrated that:

'the non-resident subsidiary has exhausted the possibilities available in its state of residence of having the losses taken into account for the accounting period concerned by the claim for relief and also for previous accounting periods, if necessary by transferring those losses to a third party or by offsetting the losses against the profits made by the subsidiary in previous periods'; and

'there is no possibility for the foreign subsidiary's losses to be taken into account in its state of residence for future periods either by the subsidiary itself or by a third party, in particular where the subsidiary has been sold to that third party.'

Since the Court of Justice judgment the case has been referred back to the UK Courts and has been heard by the High Court, Court of Appeal and most recently the First Tier Tribunal. The Courts have now agreed that:

(1)    the 'no possibility' test means having regard to the recognised legal possibilities available there is no possibility to use the losses. The Courts held it was not enough to show that the company had stopped trading if the losses could still be carried forward. The Tax First-tier Tribunal considered that a company in liquidation which was no longer able to trade passed the no possibilities test; and

(2)    the 'no possibilities' test must be assessed at the point a claim for group relief is made, and not at the end of the accounting period (which is the view of HMRC).

During 2014, the timing of the 'no possibilities' test was heard by the Supreme Court. HMRC argued that a 'no possibilities' test had to be applied on the day after the end of the accounting period in which the losses arose. M&S argued that the test should be met at the date the claim for loss relief was made. The Supreme Court agreed unanimously with M&S

*Finance Act 2006*

**[A7.28]** Following the decision in the *Marks and Spencer* case, the group relief rules were amended by Finance Act 2006.

In particular, CTA 2010, Chapter 3 Part 5 (previously ICTA 1988, s 403F) was introduced for accounting periods of UK claimant companies beginning on or after 1 April 2006. Pursuant to these rules the non-UK losses of an EEA resident company may be claimed if certain conditions are met:

(a)    s 114: the equivalence condition. The loss must be of a kind which would be available for surrender by way of group relief by a UK resident company.

(b)    s 115: the EEA tax loss condition. There must be a loss for overseas tax purposes, although these are further specific rules where the overseas company is not a resident in the EEA but carries on a trade in a EEA country through a permanent establishment.

(c)    s 117: the qualifying loss condition. Loss relief is denied where relief has been obtained in any territory outside the UK for the losses (in current or past periods) or where the losses can be carried forward and relief obtained. For this purpose that the determination of whether the losses can be carried forward and relief obtained should be made immediately after the end of the current period. Even if the overseas company has subsequently ceased trading, this cannot therefore be taken into account.

(d)    s 121: the precedence condition. Relief for the losses must not otherwise be available overseas in the defined circumstances.

There are also anti-avoidance rules contained in CTA 2010, s 127 which prevent the losses being utilised in the UK where arrangements have been entered into specifically to claim the group relief.

Marks and Spencer's position was that the losses incurred by their EU subsidiaries could not be utilised because the subsidiaries had ceased trading.

Where a company is in an equivalent position to Marks and Spencer, the company may wish to consider a claim for the losses under EU law even if the conditions of CTA 2010, Part 5 Chapter 3 are not strictly met.

*Further European action*

**[A7.29]** In September 2008 the European Commission sent the UK a formal request to properly implement properly its judgment in this case. The Commission considered that the conditions imposed on cross-border group relief made it virtually impossible for taxpayers to benefit from the relief.

Although CTA 2010, Part 5 Chapter 3 was introduced to give effect to the Court of Justice ruling, the Commission considered the following conditions too restrictive:

(a)    the UK's interpretation of the restriction that there should be no possibility of using the loss in the state of the subsidiary (s 119(2));

(b)    the date for determining whether that condition is met is set immediately after the end of the accounting period in which the loss arises (s 119(4));

(c)    the time limit for claiming the relief is set at twelve months after the filing date for the tax return of the claimant company (FA 1998, Sch 18 para 74); and

(d)    the application of the legislation only to losses incurred after 1 April 2006 (FA 2006, Sch 1 Pt 3).

Accordingly, the Commission considered the legislation to be incompatible with the freedom of establishment (Articles 43 and 48 of the EC Treaty (now Articles 49 and 54 TFEU) and Articles 31 and 34 of the EEA Agreement).

The formal request was in the form of a 'reasoned opinion' under Article 226 of the EC Treaty (now Article 258 TFEU), and the UK was required to make a satisfactory reply within two months. In October 2009 the Commission referred the matter to the Court of Justice as it considered that no satisfactory reply had been received.

The principles outlined above have been back through the UK court system and following the victory of M&S in the Court of Appeal in 2011, such claims should in principle be easier to conclude. However on a day-to-day basis the 'no possibilities test' tends to be very stringently operated by HMRC.

*Philips Electronics UK Ltd v Revenue and Customs Comrs [2009]*

**[A7.30]** This case, brought by Philips Electronics UK Limited, concerned a claim for consortium relief by a UK company in respect of losses incurred by a UK branch of a Dutch company.

HMRC rejected the claims on the grounds that the requirements of the UK consortium relief rules were not met. They two key issues, which the taxpayer argued were both infringements of EU law, were:

(a)    the requirement of that a link company for consortium relief purposes must be within the charge to corporation tax; and

(b)    the requirement of that group relief is only available if no part of the loss of the UK branch is deductible from or otherwise allowable against non-UK profits of the overseas Head Office.

The Tax First-tier Tribunal decided that it could consider EU law without referring the case to the Court of Justice and held that both these requirements were unjustified restrictions. However the Tribunal went on to say that if they are wrong and TA 1988, s 403D(1)(c) can be justified, it considered that s 403D(1)(c) should be interpreted as to be in conformity with the 'no possibilities' test in *Marks & Spencer*.

This decision was subsequently appealed by HMRC and the Upper Tribunal asked the CJEU for a ruling. On 6 September 2012 the ECJ has provided a judgment which upholds the claims which should encourage claims for losses incurred by the UK permanent establishment of any EEA resident member. The case also has potentially wider implications for sister company claims along M&S lines, although again in practice HMRC are strongly resisting such claims.

HMRC responded to the judgment by introducing an amended CTA 2010, s 107 in the Finance Act 2013 with regard to losses arising after 1 April 2013. The HMRC press release on Budget day (www.gov.uk/government/uploads/s ystem/uploads/attachment_data/file/179247/loss_surrenderable_by_non-UK_ resident_established_in_EEA_state.pdf.pdf) rather underplays its significance. In essence if groups have previously been unable to make consortium relief claims due the presence of a link company in the EEA there is a good case for filing claims now, subject of course to the extra test relating to the losses not being used twice.

### Controlled foreign companies

*Cadbury Schweppes plc v Revenue and Customs Comrs (C-196/04)*

**[A7.31]** In *Cadbury Schweppes plc and Cadbury Schweppes Overseas Ltd v Commissioners of Inland Revenue* Cadbury challenged the UK Controlled Foreign Company (CFC) rules, arguing that they were in breach of the freedom of establishment.

Cadbury Schweppes plc indirectly held 100% of the shares of two Irish companies. The business of the Irish companies was to raise finance and to provide that finance to other group companies. They were subject to a 10% tax rate under a special tax regime in Dublin (now phased out under the EU Code of Conduct). The UK tax authorities sought to tax Cadbury in the UK on the profits of the Irish companies.

The Court of Justice confirmed that the UK CFC rules restrict the freedom of establishment. However, the Court of Justice held that such rules can be justified as pursuing a legitimate objective of countering tax avoidance to the extent that they only counter 'wholly artificial arrangements'. In this regard the Court of Justice held that as well as considering the subjective intentions of a tax payer (for instance the intention of obtaining a tax advantage by establishing itself in another Member State), tax authorities must also take account of objective criteria which are ascertainable by third parties (for instance the extent to which a company has genuine substance in terms of premises, staff and equipment).

The Court of Justice concluded that it is for the UK courts to determine whether the UK CFC rules support an interpretation which takes account of such objective criteria. The case has been awaiting the outcome of the *Vodafone 2* case (see below) before it will be heard by the UK courts.

Following the Court of Justice decision, clauses amending the CFC rules were published in December 2006 which provide that profits of a subsidiary resident in the EEA are not subject to attribution under the CFC rules, provided they arise from 'genuine economic activity'.

HMRC appear to be satisfied that the new CFC rules introduced from 1 January 2013 onward (see CHAPTER **A6**) are EU compatible. If remains to be seen if over time there are further challenges once the new rules bed in.

*Test Claimants in the CFC and Dividend Group Litigation v Revenue and Customs Comrs (C-201/05)*

**[A7.32]** In April 2008, the Court of Justice reinforced the point that the UK CFC rules must allow companies to demonstrate that there is 'genuine economic activity' and to be exempt from the CFC rules as a result. In *Test Claimants in the CFC and Dividend Group Litigation* (C-201/05) it was held that:

'Articles 43 EC and 48 EC [now Articles 49 and 54 of the TFEU] must be interpreted as precluding the inclusion in the tax base of a resident company established in a Member State of profits made by a controlled foreign company in another Member State, where those profits are subject in that State to a lower level of taxation than that applicable in the first State, unless such inclusion relates only to wholly artificial arrangements intended to escape the national tax normally payable.

Accordingly, such a tax measure must not be applied where it is proven, on the basis of objective factors which are ascertainable by third parties, that despite the existence of tax motives, that controlled foreign company is actually established in the host Member State and carries on genuine economic activities there.'

*Vodafone 2 v Revenue and Customs Comrs [2009]*

**[A7.33]** This case considered whether the CFC rules should apply to a Luxembourg subsidiary of a UK company.

HMRC argued that income earned by a Luxembourg holding company should be taxed in the UK as a result of the UK CFC rules. Vodafone however contended that the CFC legislation did not apply for several reasons, one being that paying UK tax in respect of the Luxembourg company's profits would constitute an unlawful restriction on the UK company's freedom of establishment.

The High Court agreed with Vodafone and ordered the disapplication of the CFC rules. It decided that the CFC legislation was not compatible with the Treaty in light of the Court of Justice decision in the Cadbury Schweppes case.

HMRC appealed and the Court of Appeal upheld their appeal, finding that it was possible to adequately protect the Treaty rights of the UK company without disapplying the CFC rules. It judged that the CFC rules should be interpreted as if they had a new additional exception, with retrospective effect. The CFC rules should not therefore apply to companies which:

- are 'actually established' in another Member State of the EEA; and
- carry on 'genuine economic activities' there.

The Court of Appeal held that the normal CFC rules still apply to companies operating outside the EEA and to EEA companies without genuine economic activities. One point of discussion in the judgment was whether the above change was a permissible interpretation of the statute, which is within the Court's remit, or the creation of a new legislation, which is not within the Court's remit. It was held that it was an interpretation of the current laws and therefore permissible.

In December 2009 the House of Lords refused Vodafone's request for permission to appeal. This refusal means that the Court of Appeal's interpretation of the law will stand. The case was subsequently settled with HMRC, although not without controversy over the amount concerned. However, on 14 June 2012 the NAO announced that it had reviewed the settlement and that it represented fair value for tax payers.

### Thin capitalisation

*Thin Cap Group Litigation (Test Claimants in the) v IRC (C-524/04)*

**[A7.34]** In December 2002 the Court of Justice held in the *Lankhorst-Hohorst* case (C-324/00) that the German thin capitalisation rules were contrary to EU law. Following this, a group litigation order (GLO) was formed to challenge the UK thin capitalisation rules. In broad terms a GLO is similar to US 'class action' where similar cases are grouped together, a test case is heard by the court and the judgment is then binding on all companies in the group action.

Before 1 April 2004, the UK thin capitalisation (and transfer pricing) rules only applied to transactions between a UK company and a non-UK company. Therefore in some cases an interest deduction was denied for interest paid by UK companies on loans from non-UK group companies.

The group litigation was headed by the Lafarge and Volvo groups (with a parent company in France and Sweden, respectively) and Caterpillar and PepsiCo groups (with a parent company in the US ie a non-Member State).

The Court of Justice gave its decision on 13 March 2007 and held that the UK thin capitalisation rules were a restriction on the freedom of establishment since they resulted in a difference in treatment according to the place in which the lending company was a resident.

However the Court of Justice commented that the restriction could be justified where the rules applied to 'wholly artificial arrangements' and were targeted at tax avoidance. In this regard the 'arm's length test' would provide a valid starting point for determining whether or not a loan is a 'wholly artificial arrangement'. However, if the arm's length test were not satisfied the taxpayer must be given an opportunity to support the commerciality of the loans. The Court of Justice held that it is for the UK domestic courts to determine whether the UK thin capitalisation rules allowed companies to provide such evidence of the commercial reasons. The Court of Justice rejected outright the claims made by the groups with US parent companies (ie those resident in third countries). Such third country claims are considered further later in this Chapter.

## ACT claims

**[A7.35]** Although the Advance Corporation Tax (ACT) rules were repealed in 1999, the cases below are important because they established relevant principles of EU law.

*Metallgesellschaft Ltd (C-397/98) and Hoechst AG v IRC (C-410/98)*

**[A7.36]** The joined cases of *Hoechst* and *Metallgesellschaft* concerned the inability of a UK company to enter into an ACT group income election with a non-UK company. This is shown in Diagram 2.

The Court of Justice held that this led to a cash flow disadvantage to UK companies which were held by EEA parent companies as they had to make an advance payment of corporate tax compared to UK subsidiaries of UK parent companies which could avoid paying ACT by entering into a group income election. As a result of the decision many UK subsidiaries of EU parent companies made similar claims and received repayments from HMRC to compensate them for the loss of the use of the money (calculated from the date that the ACT was paid until it was utilised against the mainstream corporate tax liability). In cases where the ACT was still surplus this has been repaid as well.

Diagram 2

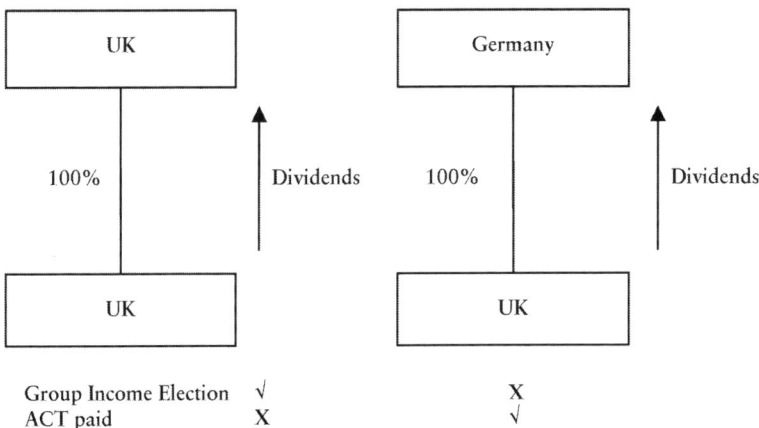

|  | |  | |
|---|---|---|---|
| Group Income Election | √ | X | |
| ACT paid | X | √ | |

*Group litigation order*

**[A7.37]** Due to the very large number of claims which were made in the UK High Court following the success of *Hoechst* and *Metallgesellschaft*, the UK courts agreed to a GLO covering all claims.

While *Hoechst* and *Metallgesellschaft* were successful in their claims, other members of the GLO with different fact patterns were less successful. For example:

(a)    non-EU parented groups have not been able to benefit;

(b)    other EU parented groups, where the double tax treaty with the UK provided for a partial tax credit repayment to the overseas parent company have had only limited success since the UK courts have held that account has to be taken of the tax credit received by the overseas parent; in many cases this eliminates any compensation which may be payable.

## Dividends

*Test Claimants in the FII Group Litigation v IRC (C-446/04)*

**[A7.38]** On 12 December 2006 the Court of Justice handed down its decision in this case, concerning the UK rules for taxing overseas dividends. The difference in tax treatment between UK and overseas dividends is shown in Diagram 3 below.

Where a UK company received a dividend from another UK company before 1 July 2009, it was not subject to corporation tax. However, where a UK company received a dividend from a non-UK company, it was subject to corporation tax, with credit for any underlying tax provided the UK company held at least 10% of the shares in the non-UK company.

Diagram 3

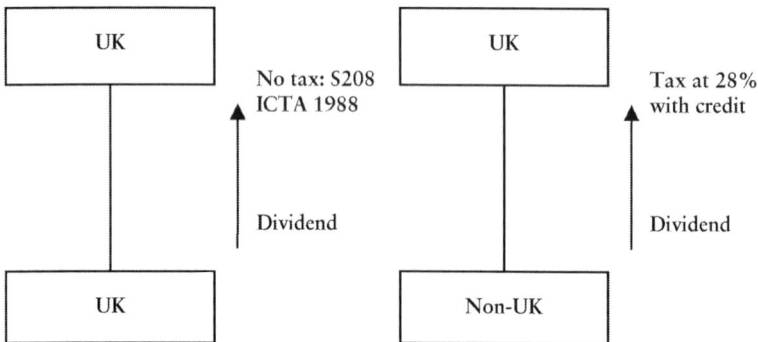

In its judgment the Court of Justice held that it is not incompatible with the freedom of establishment for the UK to treat domestic dividends as exempt from corporation tax while taxing foreign source dividends (with a tax credit) provided that:

•    foreign sourced dividends are not subject to a higher rate of tax than domestic dividends; and

- the tax credit on EEA dividends is at least equal to the amount of tax paid in the Member State of the distributing subsidiary (up to the limit of the amount of corporation tax for which the UK company receiving the dividends is liable).

The Court of Justice referred the case back to the UK courts to consider whether in fact the tax rates are the same in relation to both foreign and domestic dividends.

The case was heard by the High Court in 2008, and on 27 November 2008 the High Court gave its judgment. The High Court ruled that UK taxation on dividends received by UK companies with holdings of 10% of more in companies resident in the EU or EEA infringes EU law. The Court of Justice had already confirmed this for shareholdings under 10% (see next section below for details).

Both parties appealed aspects of the judgment and the case was heard by the Court of Appeal in October 2009 with the judgment issued in February 2010 (*Test Claimants in the FII Group Litigation v Revenue and Customs Comrs* [2010] EWCA Civ 103, (2010) STC 1251).

The Court of Appeal decided that the taxation of foreign dividends received from companies resident in the EU should be re-referred to the Court of Justice for clarification on its previous judgment. In particular clarification was requested on whether the reference to a higher rate of tax by the Court of Justice was a reference to the nominal rate (ie the then headline corporate tax rate—30%) or effective rate (the actual rate paid is in many cases lower than the applicable nominal rate because of the availability of reliefs).

However the Court of Appeal did confirm that claims for repayments could only go back six years and closed the door on claims going back any further, overturning the High Court judgment on this point.

As mentioned earlier under **A7.23**, the Supreme Court ultimately ruled that the claims were valid.

*Test Claimants in the CFC and Dividend Group Litigation v Revenue and Customs Comrs (C-201/05)*

**[A7.39]** This case (discussed above in relation to the CFC rules) also confirmed that restricting the grant of a credit for underlying tax to dividends where the UK recipient holds at least 10% of the shares in the non-UK company may constitute a breach of EU law:

> 'Article 56 EC [now Article 63 TFEU] is, furthermore, to be interpreted as meaning that it precludes legislation of a Member State which exempts from corporation tax dividends which a resident company receives from another resident company, where that State levies corporation tax on dividends which a resident company receives from a non-resident company in which it holds less than 10% of the voting rights, without granting the company receiving the dividends a tax credit for the tax actually paid by the company making the distribution in the State in which the latter is resident.'

*Prudential Assurance Co Ltd v Revenue and Customs Comrs [2013]*

**[7.40]** This case relates to a class of taxpayers who have brought claims regarding the taxation of dividends from foreign shareholdings of less than 10% (known as 'portfolio holdings').

Before the UK foreign dividend exemption was introduced in July 2009, dividends received from foreign portfolio holdings were taxed, whilst dividends received from UK portfolio holdings were exempt from corporation tax. This difference in treatment has already been found to be contrary to EU law as it contravened the principle of freedom of establishment.

This case considered the application of the Court of Justice of the European Union's (CJEU) rulings to UK domestic law. The key issues discussed were:

- Should foreign dividend income be regarded as exempt to correspond with the treatment of income from UK residents; or
- Should the income be accorded an enhanced credit, taking account of the nominal rate of the foreign jurisdiction (capped at the UK's rate), rather than just the tax paid on the underlying profits

The court ruled in favour of the latter, with the credit being the higher of the tax actually paid on the underlying profits or the nominal rate of tax (being capped at the UK rate in either case).

Taxpayers will now have to wait and see if HMRC appeals the judgment.

## Cases involving other countries

**[A7.41]** The cases outlined above have specific application to UK tax provisions.

However, Court of Justice cases may find that provisions in other jurisdictions are in breach of EU law, and these provisions may have equivalents in the UK. This would imply that the UK provisions were also in breach, and could successfully be challenged.

Some examples are given below in the context of exit charges and group restructuring. A number of cases are currently proceeding through the Court of Justice in relation to exit taxes. As a result of these, and the decided cases below, it would be surprising if there were not some impact on the group transfer provisions (TCGA 1992, s 171) and the business migration rules (TCGA 1992, ss 140 and 185).

### Hughes de Lasteyrie du Saillant v Ministère de l'Économie, des Finances et de l'Industrie (C-9/02)

**[A7.42]** In this case, a French resident (M de Lasteyrie) ceased to be French tax resident and became Belgian tax resident. He was deemed to have disposed of a substantial shareholding that he held in a French company, and subject to French tax on the gain arising. It was possible to defer this gain, but this required the filing of annual tax return, the provision of security and the appointment of a fiscal representative in France.

The Court of Justice held that this provision was a restriction on M de Lasteyrie's freedom of establishment, and that the deferral mechanism was administratively too burdensome to represent an adequate relief.

### N v Inspecteur van de Belastingdienst Oost/kantoor Almelo (C-470/04)

**[A7.43]** This case followed the de Lasteyrie case, and was similar in many ways. A Dutch resident (N) ceased to be Dutch tax resident and became UK tax resident. He was deemed to have disposed of shareholdings in three Netherlands Antilles companies, and was subject to Dutch tax on the gain arising. It was possible to defer this gain if security were provided.

As with the case of M de Lasteyrie, the Court of Justice held that this provision was a restriction on N's freedom of establishment, and that the deferral mechanism was administratively too burdensome to represent an adequate relief.

These cases cast doubt on the validity of the UK exit charge under TCGA 1992, s 185, where deferral of a liability is restricted to certain assets, and requires a UK resident parent company to effectively provide a guarantee against the liability.

### *X Holding BV v Staatssecretaris van Financien* (C-337/08)

**[A7.44]** In this case X Holding BV, a Dutch company with a subsidiary in Belgium, argued that the Dutch fiscal unity rules, which do not allow subsidiaries from other Member States to be included, constitute a breach of the freedom of establishment. The Court of Justice has ruled that although the Dutch fiscal unity rules do constitute a restriction on the freedom of establishment they can be justified by the need to safeguard the allocation of the power to impose taxes between Member States.

### *National Grid Indus BV (NGI)* (C-371/10)

**[A7.45]** NGI was a Dutch incorporated and tax resident company which moved its effective management to the UK. As a result it became UK resident under the Netherlands/UK Tax Treaty. The Dutch tax authorities demanded immediate payment of tax on NGI's unrealised capital gains. NGI contested the decision as contrary to the freedom of establishment.

The CJEU found that:

*   NGI was disadvantaged compared with a Dutch company retaining its place of effective management in the Netherlands
*   This was contrary to the freedom of establishment. Such a restriction could only be justified if it was necessary to preserve the balance of taxing rights between Member States, and also proportionate.
*   Establishing the amount of tax due at the point of migration was proportionate. In other words, Member States were entitled to charge tax on unrealised gains which arose during the period the company was tax resident.

- However, the requirement for the immediate payment of tax is not proportionate and a deferral option must be offered. The Court recognised that in some cases the deferral route would cause administrative problems in tracing the gains on particular assets. For that reason, Member States should offer migrating companies the following choice:
- Immediate payment of tax (which will be attractive where the administrative burden outweighs the cash flow disadvantage); or
- Deferral of the tax liability, subject to the tax authority being entitled to charge interest and require security of the tax (e.g. a bank guarantee).

**The UK position**

**[A7.46]** The UK position is considered in detail at **A9.43**. Broadly, the UK grants a deferral option in limited circumstances

**Planning**

**[A7.47]** Affected companies which do not meet the terms of the new legislation should consider filing on the basis that the UK exit charge is in breach of EU law in those circumstances when it cannot be deferred, or the tax has been deferred but is then triggered by an event other than the disposal of the assets concerned (eg where the subsidiary cases to be a 75% subsidiary of a UK parent). It is understood that The EU Commission would also support the non-taxation of single asset transfers within The EU as part of this, although HMRC are known the strongly resist this.

**Extending EU law principles beyond the EU**

**[A7.48]** Some non-EU groups have sought to claim the benefits of EU law. They have put forward two arguments to support their claims:

(a)     the free movement of capital provision in Articles 56–60 of the EC Treaty;

(b)     the non-discrimination article in a relevant double tax agreement (DTA).

**Free movement of capital under Article 63**

**[A7.49]** This freedom may be relevant because it is the only fundamental freedom which specifically states that it applies to 'third countries' (ie non-Member States).

The recent *Glaxo* case (C-182/08) is the first time that the Court of Justice has accepted that the free movement of capital is the primary freedom which is breached in a third country situation where usually it considers the freedom of establishment also applies. The Court of Justice had previously rejected cases because the free movement of capital was not the primary freedom which had been breached. Instead, another freedom, which does not extend to non-Member States, was the primary freedom which in the Court's view had been breached, and the breach of the free movement of capital was therefore construed as an indirect consequence of the primary breach.

However in the Glaxo case the application of the legislation in question applied to minority shareholdings and therefore the breach of the freedom of establishment was only an indirect consequence of the breach of the free movement of capital.

In addition, the Court of Justice has confirmed in the *Thin Capitalisation GLO* that the freedom of establishment can apply to a transaction between a UK company and its sister company resident in a non-EEA country where both companies have a common EEA parent. Specifically the Court held that restrictions of loan interest deductions on loans to a UK company from a third country where both companies have the same EEA parent breaches the freedom of establishment.

This was confirmed by the High Court in its further judgment in the *Thin Cap GLO*, where when commenting on whether Treaty freedoms are engaged where third countries are involved, the High Court held that the freedom of establishment can apply where there is a transaction between a non-EEA company and a UK company under the control of a common EEA parent.

This judgment is a shift in the thinking of the Courts and should hopefully enable third countries to benefit from Treaty rights in more circumstances.

Groups making portfolio investments to and from third countries may be able to rely on the EC Treaty under the free movement of capital as long as another freedom such as services is not in point. This was confirmed by the High Court in the *Test Claimants in the FII Group Litigation* case (see **A7.39**).

### Pre-31 December 1993 rules

**[A7.50]** In some cases, there is a further restriction on the application of the free movement of capital and third countries. Article 64 of the Treaty excludes rules which may prejudice the free movement of capital where those rules were in place on 31 December 1993.

In the Austrian *Holbock v Finanzamt Salzburg-Lan* (C-157/05) [2007] ECR I-4051, the Court of Justice held that any rules adopted after 31 December 1993 may also be protected by the deadline where the new provisions:

(a)     are in substance identical to legislation in force at that date; or
(b)     are put in place to reduce or eliminate an obstacle to the exercise of community rights and freedoms in earlier legislation.

The Court of Justice held that Austrian legislation which was amended in 1996 should be regarded as having existed on 31 December 1993 and therefore protected under Article 64.

### DTA non-discrimination articles

**[A7.51]** Many UK DTAs include a non-discrimination Article which is typically drafted as follows:

'Enterprises of a contracting state, the capital of which is wholly or partly owned or controlled, directly or indirectly, by one of more residents of the other contracting state, shall not be subjected in the first-mentioned contracting state to any taxation or any requirement connected therewith which is other or more burdensome than the taxation and connected requirements to which other similar enterprise of that first-mentioned state are or may be subjected.' (Article 25(3) of the UK/Japan treaty)'

It could therefore be argued that any domestic provision which discriminates against a non-resident company is contrary to the non-discrimination Article in the DTA, in a similar way to the discrimination principle inherent in the fundamental freedoms of the EC Treaty.

The application of the non-discrimination Article was considered by the House of Lords in the *Boake Allen Ltd v Revenue and Customs Comrs (sub nom NEC Semi-Conductors Ltd v Revenue and Customs Comrs)* [2007] UKHL 25(2007) 3 All ER 605 case where judgment was delivered on 23 May 2007.

UK subsidiaries of US and Japanese parent companies sought to obtain compensation for having to pay ACT since they were unable to enter into a group income election. As noted above, following the Court of Justice decision in the *Hoechst* case, UK subsidiaries of EU parent companies were entitled to receive repayments from HMRC as the UK group income election rules were deemed to be in breach of the freedom of establishment.

The House of Lords rejected the claims on the basis that there was no discrimination due to the existence of a foreign parent company, but held that the difference arose because the parent company was not itself liable to ACT.

## Basic principles—Directives and other EU measures

**[A7.52]** Directives are issued by the EU, and require Member States to enact them into their domestic legislation. They are not effective unless the Member State has enacted them, but action can be taken by the EU against a Member State for failing to implement a Directive within the prescribed time. Even if it is not enacted, a taxpayer may nonetheless be able to rely on a Directive where its meaning is clear and unambiguous.

Where minimum conditions are specified in a Directive (for instance the minimum shareholding requirements of the Parent/Subsidiary Directive), a Member State is permitted to introduce more lenient conditions, but cannot apply more onerous conditions.

Because these Directives apply in all Member States, tax planning which relies on their principles should also work in all Member States. For instance, it can generally be assumed that dividends can be paid by a company in any Member State, to a parent company in another Member State without being subject to withholding tax. However, some countries have transitional arrangements and may delay implementation.

### Parent/Subsidiary Directive (90/435)

**[A7.53]** The Parent/Subsidiary Directive provides for a reduction in withholding tax on dividends paid by companies to their parent companies within the EU/EEA.

When the Directive was implemented it originally required a minimum 25% shareholding but this was reduced to 20% (from February 2004), to 15% from 1 January 2007, and 10% from 1 January 2009.

In addition, the parent company must be a type of company falling within the list in the Directive.

The Directive also provides that Member States must apply an exemption or a method of credit when such dividends are received by a parent company. In the UK little legislative change was needed to enact the directive as the UK does not levy a dividend withholding tax and already provided for credit for withholding tax and foreign underlying taxes.

As noted in **A7.8**, measures have been introduced to allow Swiss companies to benefit from the Parent/Subsidiary Directive as well.

Non-EU companies therefore commonly invest into Europe via the UK—there is no withholding tax on dividends paid by the European subsidiaries to the UK (because of the Parent/Subsidiary Directive), and there is no withholding tax on dividends from the UK under UK domestic law.

It should be noted however that the Parent Subsidiary Directive still permits local countries to impose their domestic anti-abuse legislation to prevent its application. Whilst this is relatively rare, some countries, for example The Netherlands, are increasingly looking at substance in superior holding company structures in receipt of dividends from the Netherlands with a view to determining whether or not the directive might be applied.

As discussed in **A5.15**, the Council of the EU recently agreed on changes to the Parent Subsidiary Directive in order to prevent abuse through hybrid loan arrangements. These changes should be implemented by Member States no later than 31 December 2015.

### Interest and Royalties Directive (03/49)

**[A7.54]** The Interest and Royalties Directive provides for the abolition of withholding tax on interest and royalty payments between companies resident in EU Member States.

The companies must be 'associated' ie one company directly holds 25% of the other company, or a third company directly holds 25% of both the payer and the recipient of the royalties. In addition, the companies must be of a type of company falling within the list in the Directive.

Some Member States have a transitional period before implementing complete exemption from withholding tax, during which period specific rates of withholding tax are provided.

In the UK, the Directive is now implemented by ITTOIA 2005, s 758. This provision is discussed in **A5.22**.

As noted in **A7.8**, measures have been introduced to allow Swiss companies to benefit from the Interest and Royalties Directive as well.

## Merger Directive (90/434)

**[A7.55]** The Merger Directive provides for gains arising on the cross-border transfer of assets within the EU undertaken as part of a restructuring to be deferred until disposal of the assets.

Restructuring includes the incorporation of branches, full or partial demergers, transfers of assets and exchanges of shares.

In the UK, various changes were made to the capital gains rules (mainly the introduction of TCGA 1992, s 140A and subsequent sections—see **A11.18**) to implement the Merger Directive, and to extend the existing UK deferral rules to transactions included in the Directive.

## Savings Directive (03/48)

**[A7.56]** The Savings Directive requires Member States to collect and share information on interest payments which are made to individuals resident in other Member States.

The Directive has also been extended to Switzerland, Andorra, Monaco, San Marino and Liechtenstein.

Similar measures have been agreed with dependent territories, including the Isle of Man and the Channel Islands.

Some Member States (including Luxembourg, Austria and Belgium) and dependent territories had a transitional period (which ended on 30 June 2011) before implementing full information reporting, within which time they were required to withhold tax from interest payments, and share this with the member state in which the recipient of the interest was resident.

TMA 1970, ss 18B–18E (formerly FA 2003 s 199) was introduced to implement the Directive in the UK. This requires certain payers of interest to individuals in other EU Member States to report the interest payments to HMRC. Unlike the reporting requirements under TMA 1970, ss 17, 18, the reporting requirements under TMA 1970, ss 18B–18E are mandatory and do not require notice from HMRC.

## Arbitration Convention (90/436)

**[A7.57]** The Arbitration Convention is effectively a multi-lateral treaty that provides for resolution of transfer pricing disputes within the EU. It provides a right for taxpayers to initiate a procedure and a negotiation process between the competent authorities (HMRC in the case of the UK) in the event of double taxation as a result of transfer pricing adjustments between associated enterprises.

The Convention lays down an arbitration procedure and sets a deadline of two years for the negotiation process within which competent authorities must agree on how to resolve a case.

The Convention entered into force on 1 January 1995 with an initial application period of five years. Before this period expired, the European Council adopted a Protocol that provides for an automatic extension of the Convention for successive five year periods unless any Member State objects. New Member States have two years from their accession into the EU in which to ratify the Arbitration Convention.

The Arbitration Convention supplements provisions in DTAs which provide for a mutual agreement procedure between the competent authorities of the contracting states. However, unlike the Arbitration Convention, there is no obligation on contracting states to come to agreement under mutual agreement procedures. The Arbitration Convention goes further as it provides that an independent arbitrator will be appointed if Member States cannot come to agreement within the two year period.

## Common Consolidated Corporate Tax Base (CCCTB)

**[A7.58]** In March 2011, the European Commission reintroduced proposals for the CCCTB. The proposals had originally been issued in 2007, but then dropped in 2008 due to political opposition.

The proposals would introduce a consolidated tax base for companies operating in Europe. In other words, groups would consolidate their profits and losses arising from all their operations within the EU. The consolidated profit would then be allocated between the member states in which the group operates and subject to tax at the relevant rate.

A number of member states (including the UK) have formally rejected the proposals, and it is unlikely that they will be implemented in the short-term. At the time of writing, nine Member States have expressed concerns over the proposal, which falls short of the threshold of 18 which would oblige the commission to review its proposal.

### Method of allocation

**[A7.59]** It is proposed that profits will be allocated between member states based on a number of weighted factors:

(a)    sales by destination (one third);
(b)    location of tangible assets (one third);
(c)    payroll costs (one sixth);
(d)    employee numbers (one sixth).

A formulaic profit allocation (as currently operated in the US at State level) is clearly contrary to transfer pricing principles, and many DTAs would need to be amended to take account of this.

# A8

# Double taxation agreements

# Introduction

**[A8.1]** A double taxation agreement (DTA, known alternatively as a double taxation treaty or convention) is a key tool of international tax planning as it allows UK and foreign tax to be reduced or eliminated on cross border transactions. Specific planning using DTAs is discussed elsewhere in this book, for example in relation to capital gains (**A11.10**) and withholding taxes (**A5.40**).

This Chapter explains why DTAs exist and how they can be used. It discusses the interpretation and scope of DTAs, and provides an overview of the key articles in the OECD Model Convention (see **A8.17**) which apply to companies. Although some general principles usually apply, the precise wording of the relevant DTA should always be confirmed.

It also highlights anti-avoidance provisions of DTAs, such as the inclusion of limitation on benefits articles.

For a more detailed discussion of DTAs, Jonathan Schwarz's *Tax Treaties* and Phillip Baker's *Double Taxation Conventions* are recommended. The HMRC Double Tax Relief manual also provides information on the interpretation of specific DTAs, including taxes covered and the documentation which must be completed in order to obtain benefits.

This chapter also covers the recent 'Inter-Governmental Agreements' (IGAs) entered into between tax authorities, specifically covering the US regulations on the Foreign Account Tax Compliance Act.

# Basic principles—purpose, implementation and scope of double taxation agreements

## *Double taxation*

**[A8.2]** In the absence of a DTA, there are two ways in which double taxation may arise.

Firstly, UK residents are generally subject to tax in the UK on their worldwide income. As income arising outside the UK may also suffer foreign taxation (on the source basis) it is likely that the income of a UK resident will be subject to taxation in two jurisdictions. This is known as 'juridical double taxation'.

The second way in which double taxation can arise is through 'economic double taxation'. This will arise where the same income suffers tax in two locations, in the hands of different taxpayers. For example, if a UK company has a subsidiary in Denmark, the subsidiary will pay Danish tax on its profits. If those profits are remitted to the UK parent, by way of dividend they may be taxed again in the hands of the UK company if the dividend exemption does not apply.

## *Objectives of a DTA*

**[A8.3]** The objectives of a DTA are reflected in the title of the DTA. The UK/US DTA for instance is titled:

> 'Convention between the government of the United Kingdom of Great Britain and Northern Ireland and the government of the United States of America for the avoidance of double taxation and the prevention of fiscal evasion with respect to taxes on income and on capital gains.'

The objectives of a DTA are therefore typically twofold:

- avoidance of double taxation; and
- prevention of fiscal evasion.

## Avoidance of double taxation

**[A8.4]** The first objective of a DTA is to relieve juridical (and occasionally economic) double taxation as described above. This is important as it allows businesses to conduct international trade with a degree of certainty to where and how they will be taxed and without incurring disproportionate tax liabilities.

A reduction in taxation will encourage cross-border trade between jurisdictions, and encourage inward investment. For example, the current Mauritius/India DTA provides that capital gains on the sale of shares in an Indian resident company are only taxable in Mauritius. The DTA can therefore help to mitigate against Indian capital gains tax and encourages investment from Mauritius (see **A11.14**). It should be noted that India has been attempting to renegotiate the treaty for many years and relaunched its efforts in early 2013.

The provisions of a DTA also clarify the taxing rights of each jurisdiction. This can provide a stable environment for international trade. Countries with higher tax rates will not usually enter into DTAs with low tax countries (such as the Cayman Islands or British Virgin Islands) as there is no incentive to divide taxing rights with them.

## Prevention of fiscal evasion

**[A8.5]** From the perspective of the territories which are party to a DTA, the prevention of fiscal evasion is the second objective. This is particularly apparent from the provisions of the DTA that allow countries to exchange information on taxpayers. For example, HMRC are frequently using the provisions of DTAs to obtain access to details of funds held by UK residents in overseas bank accounts.

HMRC are known in practice to adopt a purposive integration of double tax agreements. For example where the application of a DTA results in double non-taxation, they have been known to resist its application on the basis that that could never have been the intention when the treaty was drafted. It can be expected that with effect from Royal Assent 2013, the new General Anti-Avoidance Rule (GAAR) will be used to counter uses of tax treaties which might be considered to be abusive.

## *Domestic law implementing double taxation agreements*

**[A8.6]** Under the law of some jurisdictions, a DTA becomes effective automatically when the DTA comes into force. Other jurisdictions require parliamentary or other approval before the DTA becomes part of domestic law.

## Implementation under UK law

**[A8.7]** In the UK, DTAs become law by virtue of TIOPA 2010, s 2 (and TCGA 1992, s 277 for capital gains tax purposes) and an Order-In-Council.

## Precedence of domestic law over treaty

**[A8.8]** A DTA cannot impose a UK tax charge if one does not exist under domestic law. For example, if an Indian company undertakes services in the UK which would constitute a permanent establishment under the terms of the UK/India DTA, but not under UK domestic law, there is no permanent establishment. Unless tax arises under UK domestic law, there is generally no need to consider the DTA. This reflects the stated objective of a DTA as the 'avoidance of double taxation'—if there is no double taxation then a DTA is not relevant.

However, overseas jurisdictions may use the DTA as the basis for imposing a charge to tax. For instance, in some jurisdictions a permanent establishment will exist if the activity meets the definition of a permanent establishment within the definition of a relevant DTA.

Notwithstanding that domestic law should be normally considered before the DTA, if no tax arises under a DTA then (subject to any domestic anti-avoidance rules), no tax should arise. In some cases, it may not be necessary to consider the domestic rules if a company is able to benefit from the DTA and this can be a shortcut when advising companies expanding overseas. However, it may still be necessary to file tax returns or the claims to relief under the DTA.

## *Scope of a double taxation agreement*

**[A8.9]** There are a number of questions which must be considered before a company can take advantage of a DTA, in order to confirm that its scope covers the transaction or income in question.

### Jurisdiction

**[A8.10]** DTAs generally only apply to the territories (each usually referred to as the Contracting State) which have signed the agreement.

In the case of countries which cease to exist, the DTA may remain in force and cover the new country or countries which come into existence as a result. For example:

(a)     SP3/92 and SP4/01 provide that the DTA with the former USSR will continue to apply to the former states of the USSR with which new DTAs have not yet been negotiated. In cases where the former state does not itself apply the former DTA, the UK generally does not apply the treaty either.

(b)     SP3/04 provides that the DTA with the former Yugoslavia will continue to apply to the former states of Yugoslavia with which new DTAs have not yet been negotiated (ie Bosnia-Herzegovina, Croatia, Montenegro, Serbia and Slovenia).

(c)     SP5/93 provides that the former DTA with Czechoslovakia will continue to apply to the Czech Republic and Slovakia.

## Dates in force

[A8.11] DTAs will apply from a particular date, which is generally set out in the 'Entry into force' article. This may be subject to specific processes in one or both of the Contracting States, for example parliamentary approval.

In addition, territories may terminate DTAs such that they no longer apply. In some cases, DTAs can be terminated unilaterally, but others (for instance the India/Mauritius DTA) require both jurisdictions to agree to amendment or termination.

Territories may conclude a new treaty which supersedes an existing treaty, or may simply issue a Protocol which amends an existing treaty.

## Taxes covered

[A8.12] A DTA will 'outline' the taxes which are covered. Not all taxes are covered, in particular, inheritance tax is not generally covered by the UK's DTAs (separate DTAs are usually concluded to deal with inheritance tax, of which there are comparatively few).

For example, Article 2(3) of the UK/US DTA provides that:

'The existing taxes to which this Convention shall apply are:
(a)     in the case of the United States:
(i)     the Federal income taxes imposed by the Internal Revenue Code (but excluding social security taxes); and
(ii)     the Federal excise taxes imposed on insurance policies issued by foreign insurers and with respect to private foundations;
(b)     in the case of the United Kingdom:
(i)     the income tax;
(ii)     the capital gains tax;
(iii)     the corporation tax; and
(iv)     the petroleum revenue tax.'

The DTA does not therefore cover state taxes, although these may qualify for unilateral relief in the UK (see A10.15).

Article 2(4) UK/US DTA goes on to provide that:

'This Convention shall apply also to any identical or substantially similar taxes that are imposed after the date of signature of this Convention in addition to, or in place of, the existing taxes. The competent authorities of the Contracting States shall notify each other of any changes that have been made in their respective taxation or other laws that significantly affect their obligations under this Convention.'

This clause allows the parties to a treaty to introduce new taxes without amending the treaty. For example, DTAs concluded by the UK prior to the introduction of corporation tax would nonetheless apply to corporation tax as this is a 'substantially similar' tax to income tax which previously applied to companies.

## Residence

[A8.13] The benefit of a DTA can normally only be claimed by a resident of one of the Contracting States. Article 1 of the DTA normally confirms this in the manner of:

'This Convention shall apply to persons who are residents of one or both of the States.'

The DTA will define who is a resident for these purposes (see below).

### Relevant article of the treaty

**[A8.14]** Some items of income may be covered by more than one Article of a treaty. For example, royalties received may be treated as business income if derived through a permanent establishment, technical service fees if related to the provision of technical services (if the DTA includes such an Article), or royalties falling within the royalty Article. The relevant Article of the specific DTA will normally set out which applies in priority to the others.

### General anti-avoidance provisions

**[A8.15]** The DTA may include general anti-avoidance provisions which restrict its application. These are typically limitations on benefit provisions, which if not satisfied will prevent the DTA from applying to any income.

Some jurisdictions (such as Germany and China) will also challenge the application of DTAs under domestic law—see **A8.68**.

### Specific anti-avoidance provisions

**[A8.16]** Specific anti-avoidance provisions may be included in the Articles of a DTA, which prevent that particular Article from applying to a transaction or item of income, although do not affect the application of that DTA more generally. These include beneficial ownership requirements and anti-conduit rules.

## *Interpretation of DTAs*

### Model tax agreements

**[A8.17]** The first model DTAs were created by the League of Nations in 1921. Since then the OECD has worked to further standardise the content of DTAs. The work of the OECD has led to the publication of a number of Model Tax Conventions, and the most recent update was published on 23 July 2010, which also included an update to the commentary to the Convention.

The Model Convention aim to standardise and harmonise DTAs between members of the OECD and therefore help to eliminate double taxation and provide certainty to taxpayers. Most of the UK's DTAs follow the OECD standard, even with territories which are not themselves members of the OECD.

The OECD has also published commentaries to the model conventions and these are a useful tool in interpreting a DTA.

There is sometimes flexibility on interpreting certain Articles of the model, and some jurisdictions have published 'reservations' to the interpretation contained in the commentary, which set out their position.

There are other model DTAs besides that of the OECD, most notably the UN model and the US model.

The UN Model Tax Convention was first drafted in 1980. This Model is typically used where developing countries are entering into a double tax agreement with a developed country. A common theme is the preservation of a greater level of source country taxation rights than is found in the OECD Model Tax Convention. This relates to its focus on the needs of developing countries, thereby enabling them to retain a greater level of the taxation rights to be levied on particular income profits or gains made in the source company.

This chapter focuses on the OECD interpretation of the Model Tax Treaty. Where relevant, a comparison of how the 2011 UN Model Treaty differs to the 2010–2012 OECD Model Treaties is given after each section.

Many of the UK's early DTAs (before the agreement of the OECD Model) follow a very different pattern to the OECD Model. These are typically with former colonies, and are often referred to as the 'colonial' treaties, although there are still some non-OECD Model DTAs with jurisdictions elsewhere, including Europe.

## OECD Commentary

**[A8.18]** HMRC have confirmed that they will follow the OECD Commentary in most cases, although the author is aware of instances where this has not been the case:

> 'Where a provision in a double taxation agreement is in the same terms in all relevant respects as the corresponding provision in the OECD Model, the Commentary on the OECD Model may be used as an aid to the interpretation of that provision. The exception is where the United Kingdom has entered an Observation or Reservation on the relevant part of the Commentary. These are reproduced at the end of the comments on the Article in question.

> The United Kingdom courts have indicated their willingness to consider the Commentary as an aid to interpretation. Vinelott J stated in *Sun Life Assurance Co of Canada v Pearson* that the OECD Commentary 'can and indeed must be referred to as a guide to the interpretation of the treaty' 59TC page 310, also page 331).

> As far as possible the latest Commentary should be used to interpret a double taxation agreement, even if an older version was current when it was negotiated (Model Convention introduction, paragraph 33).' (INTM159015)'

It is interesting to note that the latest OECD Commentary should be followed, even where the DTA was agreed at an earlier date. Thus the updates made to the Commentary in 2010 apply automatically to all pre-existing treaties.

## Case law

**[A8.19]** There have been a few tax cases which deal with the interpretation of DTAs, most importantly *Union Texas Petroleum Corpn v Critchley (Inspector of Taxes)* (1990) 63 TC 244, *Sun Life Company of Canada v Pearson* (1986) 59 TC 250 and *CIR v Commerzbank AG* (1990) 63 TC 218.

The principles established in *IRC v Commerzbank AG [1990] STC 285* (1990) 63 TC 218 were summarised in *Memec plc v IRC* (1998) 71 TC 77 as follows:

'(1)    the approach should be purposive;
(2)    it should be international, not exclusively English;
(3)    it should have regard to Article 31(1) of the Vienna Convention;
(4)    recourse may be had to supplementary means of interpretation such as travaux preparatoires [the record of negotiations of a treaty];
(5)    subsequent commentaries and decisions of foreign courts have persuasive value only;
(6)    recourse to travaux preparatoires, international case law and the writings of jurists in discretionary, not mandatory. The Court of Appeal has recognised the official commentaries on successive versions of the OECD Model Convention as supplementary means of interpretation: see *Sun Life Assurance Co. of Canada v. Pearson*'.'

This approach has been confirmed in subsequent cases, including *Smallwood (trustees of The Trevor Smallwood Trust) v Revenue and Customs Comrs* [2008] STC (SCD) 629 and FCE Bank plc [2010] UKFTT 136 (TC).

### Other aids to interpretation

**[A8.20]** Many DTAs are accompanied by an Exchange of Notes which clarifies the application of certain aspects of the DTA.

Tax authorities may publish their own interpretation of a DTA. For example, HMRC published a Manual on the 2003 UK/USA DTA (www.hmrc.gov.uk/ manuals/dtmanual/DT19850.htm), and the US Treasury published a Technical Interpretation (www.treasury.gov/resource-center/tax-policy/treaties/Docume nts/teus-uk.pdf). The DTA was also accompanied by an Exchange of Notes (www.treasury.gov/resource-center/tax-policy/treaties/Documents/teus-uk.pdf ).

Where changes are made to a DTA, this may either be by way of a new DTA, or issuing a Protocol to an existing treaty. The Protocol will state the date from which it applies, but it will amend the effect of an existing DTA. There is, for example, a Protocol to the 2001 UK/USA DTA (www.treasury.gov/resource-c enter/tax-policy/treaties/Documents/ukprotoc.pdf).

# Residence

**[A8.21]** This Article defines who is a resident for the purpose of a DTA, and therefore who can benefit from that DTA.

## OECD Model

**[A8.22]** Article 4 of the UK/France DTA provides a typical definition of residence, and reflects the wording of the OECD Model Convention:

'1.    For the purposes of this Convention, the term 'resident of a Contracting State' means any person who, under the laws of that State, is liable to tax therein by reason of his domicile, residence, place of management or any other criterion of a similar nature. But this term does not include any person who is liable to tax in that State in respect only of income from sources in that State.

[2 . . . .]

3.    Where by reason of the provisions of paragraph 1 a person other than an individual is a resident of both Contracting States, then it shall be deemed to be a resident of the Contracting State in which its place of effective management is situated.'

In other words:

(a)    a company which is treated as a UK resident under UK domestic law will be treated as a UK resident for the purposes of the DTA;

(b)    if a company is treated as a resident of both the UK and France under their respective domestic law, for the purposes of the DTA, it will be treated as resident in the jurisdiction where its effective management is located.

The operation of the effective management 'tie breaker' clause in the context of UK residence is discussed further in **A9.18**. A list of the DTAs which contain tie breaker clauses (current at 1 December 2009) is in the HMRC International Manual at INTM120070.

## UK/US DTA

**[A8.23]** The 'tie breaker' clause in Article 4 of the UK/US DTA is less useful:

'1.    Where by reason of the provisions of paragraph 1 of this Article a person other than an individual is a resident of both Contracting States, the competent authorities of the Contracting States shall endeavour to determine by mutual agreement the mode of application of this Convention to that person. If the competent authorities do not reach such an agreement, that person shall not be entitled to claim any benefit provided by this Convention, except those provided by paragraph 4 of Article 24 (Relief from double taxation), Article 25 (Non-discrimination) and Article 26 (Mutual agreement procedure).'

There is no objective test to determine where a dual resident company should be treated as resident for the purposes of the DTA, and no obligation on the tax authorities to reach an agreement if one is sought.

## Colonial DTAs

**[A8.24]** Similar problems may arise under the wording in the 'colonial' DTAs which pre-date the OECD Model Convention. Article 2 of the UK/Jersey DTA defines a resident as follows:

'1.    the terms "resident of the United Kingdom" and "resident of Guernsey" mean respectively any person who is resident in the United Kingdom for the purposes of United Kingdom tax and not resident in Guernsey for the purposes of Guernsey tax and any person who is resident in Guernsey for the purposes of Guernsey tax and not resident in the United Kingdom for the purposes of United Kingdom tax; and a company shall be regarded as resident in the United Kingdom if its business is managed and controlled in the United Kingdom and as resident in Guernsey if its business is managed and controlled in Guernsey;'

This provides for mutual exclusivity of residence rather than a tie breaker. A company will only be treated as a UK resident for the purposes of the DTA if it is treated as UK resident under UK domestic law, but not treated as Guernsey resident under Guernsey domestic law.

A company which is a resident of *both* the UK and Guernsey cannot therefore benefit from the DTA.

### Fiscally transparent entities

**[A8.25]**  Where an entity is treated as transparent (such as certain partnerships and trusts), the definition of residence can be problematic. It can be unclear as to whether the entity itself, or its partners or beneficiaries, should be considered as residents when determining entitlement to benefits under a DTA and it is known that many EU countries adopt conflicting approaches in this respect.

A discussion of partnerships and trusts is outside the scope of this book. However, it should be noted that some DTAs specifically deal with this problem. For example, Article 1(8) of the UK/US DTA specifically provides that:

> 'An item of income, profit or gain derived through a person that is fiscally transparent under the laws of either Contracting State shall be considered to be derived by a resident of a Contracting State to the extent that the item is treated for the purposes of the taxation law of such Contracting State as the income, profit or gain of a resident.'

Diagram 1

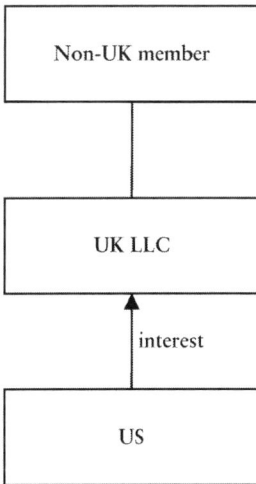

In Diagram 1, the UK company pays interest to a US LLC which is treated as a transparent for US tax purposes. Although the LLC would usually be treated as a US company under UK tax principles, the DTA requires consideration of the position under US tax principles. And as the US treat the LLC as transparent, for the purposes of the DTA the interest is not treated as paid to a US resident company, and therefore the benefit of the DTA would not be available to the LLC.

Similarly, in Diagram 2, the benefit of the DTA would not be available because the LLP is transparent for UK tax purposes. The treatment for US tax purposes is not relevant.

Diagram 2

```
┌─────────────────────────┐
│     Non-UK member       │
└─────────────────────────┘
           │
┌─────────────────────────┐
│        UK LLP           │
└─────────────────────────┘
           ▲
        interest
┌─────────────────────────┐
│          US             │
└─────────────────────────┘
```

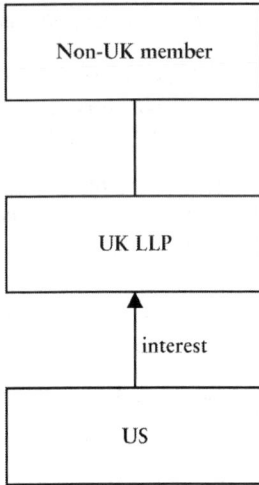

A partnership or other fiscally transparent entity therefore faces a considerable administrative burden when making a claim for relief under a DTA, because it is the partners who are eligible for relief under that DTA and who must make the claim. This may involve a number of different DTAs where the partners are resident in different jurisdictions.

The 2010 OECD Model Commentary recognises this burden in the context of collective investment vehicles, and allows contracting states to make specific provisions under which such vehicles can qualify for benefits in their own right. However, this is subject to such provisions being actually included in the relevant DTA—the OECD Commentary does not apply automatically.

In respect of the UK/US DTA only, there is a relaxation of the process outlined in the Centre for Non-Residents Guidance Note 3 (currently available at www.hmrc.gov.uk/cnr/cnr_dt_guidance_notes_3_final.htm). Partnerships and LLCs which would be fiscally transparent entities are able to make an application for relief under the DTA where all the members would also qualify for relief under the UK/US DTA. The partnership or LLC must then monitor its membership to ensure that this remains the case if relief is claimed for future payments.

## *Branches*

**[A8.26]** A branch is not a 'person' and therefore cannot claim the benefit of a DTA.

In Diagram 3, interest is paid to the UK branch of a Jersey company. The UK branch is not a person, and would not be treated as a resident of the UK under the UK/US double tax agreement. The payment would be treated as paid from the US to Jersey, and the UK/US DTA would not apply.

In addition, the branch is not beneficially entitled to the income it receives, as it legally belongs to the UK parent company.

Diagram 3

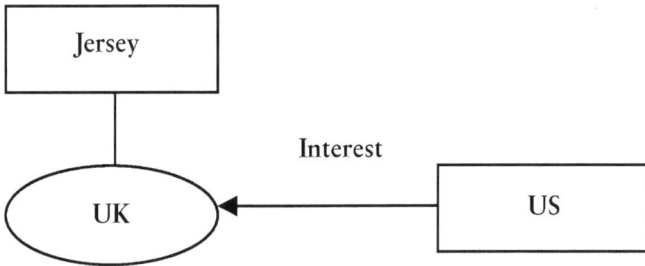

## *Subject to tax requirement*

**[A8.27]** The residence Article in the OECD Model (and other) DTAs also contains a requirement that a person is subject to tax in a jurisdiction in order to be treated as resident there. The UK/France DTA for instance provides that a resident is:

> ' . . . any person who, under the laws of that State, *is liable to tax therein by reason of his domicile, residence, place of management or any other criterion of a similar nature.* But this term does not include any person who is liable to tax in that State in respect only of income from sources in that State.' [my emphasis]'

If a company is not liable to tax in a particular jurisdiction, for instance because it is exempt from tax, it may not be treated as a resident for the purposes of a DTA and will not be able to claim relief under that DTA.

The Commentary on Article 4 provides some useful examples of where an entity may be liable to tax and therefore not treated as a resident for the purposes of a DTA:

(a)    a company which is only subject to tax on income sourced in a jurisdiction under a territorial tax system (for instance Hong Kong) should not be prevented from qualifying as a resident of that jurisdiction;

(b)    a company which is incorporated in Country A but resident in Country B by virtue of the tie breaker in the DTA between Country A and Country B will be not be subject to tax in Country A and therefore not a resident of Country A;

(c)     charities, pension funds and other similar organisations may be exempt from tax but depending on the rules of the jurisdiction concerned, may nonetheless be 'liable to tax' absent the exemption;

(d)     a partnership or other fiscally transparent entity may not be subject to tax in its own right (see also **A8.25** above).

Particular care is required with sovereign wealth funds. Such funds may be exempt from tax, but may nonetheless qualify for benefits under a DTA. For example:

•     they may be specifically included in the list of persons qualifying under the DTA

•     they may be part of the contracting state itself

•     they may be banks for which specific provision in made in the interest article of the DTA.

# Basic principles—overview of key articles

### Permanent establishment

**[A8.28]** This Article provides a definition of a permanent establishment for the purposes of a DTA. The business profits Article of a treaty will normally only allow a jurisdiction to tax the business profits of a non-resident if a permanent establishment exists.

In most UK DTAs, the definition of permanent establishment follows the OECD definition and is discussed in more detail in CHAPTER **A4**. There may be variations in specific DTAs, for instance in relation to:

(a)     the duration of a construction or installation project that constitutes a permanent establishment;

(b)     whether preparatory or auxiliary activities can be considered separately when determining if a permanent establishment exists, or whether they must still be preparatory and auxiliary when taken together.

These are also considered in CHAPTER **A4**. There may however be other variations in this Article which are discussed below.

Article 5(3)(a) of the UN Model Convention has a six-month duration test for building sites, as opposed to twelve months given in the OECD Model Convention.

### Colonial DTAs

**[A8.29]** Some of the UK's older DTAs contain a definition of permanent establishment which is different to the OECD definition.

Article 2(1)(j) of the UK/Jersey DTA defines a permanent establishment as follows:

'the term 'permanent establishment', when used with respect to an enterprise of one of the territories, means a branch, management or other fixed place of business, but does not include an agency unless the agent has, and habitually exercises, a general authority to negotiate and conclude contracts on behalf of such enterprise or has a stock of merchandise from which he regularly fills orders on its behalf. An enterprise of one of the territories shall not be deemed to have a permanent establishment in the other territory merely because it carries on business dealings in that other territory through a bona fide broker or general commission agent acting in the ordinary course of his business as such. The fact that an enterprise of one of the territories maintains in the other territory a fixed place of business exclusively for the purchase of goods or merchandise shall not of itself constitute that fixed place of business a permanent establishment of the enterprise. The fact that a company which is a resident of one of the territories has a subsidiary company which is a resident of the other territory or which is engaged in trade or business in that other territory (whether through a permanent establishment or otherwise) shall not of itself constitute that subsidiary company a permanent establishment of its parent company.'

In many cases, this will have the same effect as the OECD definition (ie that a fixed place of business will constitute a permanent establishment).

There is however an important distinction in what constitutes a permanent establishment under the dependent agent rules (see CHAPTER **A4**). Under the UK/Jersey DTA a permanent establishment may only exist if an agent has 'a general authority to negotiate and conclude contracts . . . ' The OECD definition only requires that the agent 'concludes' contracts, and the commentary to the model convention sets out that this can include either negotiation of a contract or the actual act of conclusion. The UK/Jersey DTA on the other hand makes it clear that both negotiation *and* conclusion are required for a dependent agent to create a permanent establishment. If the agent only negotiates the contract, but does not conclude it, then no permanent establishment is created.

### Services-related permanent establishment

**[A8.30]** The UK/India DTA provides that a permanent establishment may exist where services are performed in India (similar provisions exist in Indian domestic law). Article 5(2) provides that a permanent establishment includes:

'(a)    the furnishing of services including managerial services, other than those taxable under Article 13 (Royalties and fees for technical services), within a Contracting State by an enterprise through employees or other personnel, but only if:

   (i)    activities of that nature continue within that State for a period or periods aggregating more than 90 days within any twelve-month period; or

   (ii)    services are performed within that State for an enterprise within the meaning of paragraph 1 of Article 10 (Associated enterprises) and continue for a period or periods aggregating more than 30 days within any twelve-month period.'

Thus under the UK/India DTA a permanent establishment may exist even in the absence of a fixed place of business or dependent agent.

The UN Model Treaty contains special provisions for 'services permanent establishments', whilst in the OECD treaty services are treated as the provision of goods. Services permanent establishments are considered created if the services provided 'continue within a Contracting State for a period or periods aggregating more than 183 days in any 12-month period'..

## Profit attribution

**[A8.31]** The business profits Article of a DTA will normally provide that the profits attributable to a permanent establishment are to be calculated as if the permanent establishment were a separate entity dealing on arm's length terms with its parent company, ie a similar basis to that set out in UK domestic law (see CHAPTER A4).

Article 7 of the UK/US DTA for instance provides that:

'1.    Subject to the provisions of paragraph 3 of this Article, where an enterprise of a Contracting State carries on business in the other Contracting State through a permanent establishment situated therein, there shall in each Contracting State be attributed to that permanent establishment the business profits that it might be expected to make if it were a distinct and separate enterprise engaged in the same or similar activities under the same or similar conditions and dealing wholly independently with the enterprise of which it is a permanent establishment. For this purpose, the business profits to be attributed to the permanent establishment shall include only the profits derived from the assets used, risks assumed and activities performed by the permanent establishment.

2.    In determining the business profits of a permanent establishment, there shall be allowed as deductions expenses that are incurred for the purposes of the permanent establishment, including executive and general administrative expenses so incurred, whether in the State in which the permanent establishment is situated or elsewhere.'

However, there may be variations on this and it is important to check the terms of the specific DTA. Article 7 of the UK/India DTA for instance provides that profits can be attributed to the permanent establishment using a formulaic apportionment method (a similar provision exists in Indian domestic law):

'3.    Where a permanent establishment takes an active part in negotiating, concluding or fulfilling contracts entered into by the enterprise, then, notwithstanding that other parts of the enterprise have also participated in those transactions, that proportion of profits of the enterprise arising out of those contracts which the contribution of the permanent establishment to those transactions bears to that of the enterprise as a whole shall be treated for the purposes of paragraph 1 of this Article as being the profits indirectly attributable to that permanent establishment.

4.    Insofar as it has been customary in a Contracting State according to its law to determine the profits to be attributed to a permanent establishment on the basis of an apportionment of the total profits of the enterprise to its various parts, nothing in paragraphs 1 and 2 of this Article shall preclude that Contracting State from determining the profits to be taxed by such an apportionment as may be necessary; the method of apportionment adopted shall, however, be such that the result shall be in accordance with the principles laid down in this Article.'

The Commentary to the 2010 OECD Model Convention makes it clear that the profits attributable to a permanent establishment must be calculated in accordance with transfer pricing principles. Significant changes were made in the 2010 Commentary on this point, as outlined in the OECD's 'Report on Attribution of Profits to Permanent Establishments'.

Only profits directly arising from the activities carried on through the permanent establishment can be attributed. For example, if a permanent establishment sells a product that is manufactured elsewhere by the head office, only the profits arising from the sales activity will be attributable to the permanent establishment. Any profit arising from the manufacture of the product will not be attributed to the permanent establishment.

The UN Model Treaty contains a limited 'force of attraction' rule which allows taxation of certain profits not actually attributable to the PE under normal rules, but which relate to other business activities carried on by the enterprise in that jurisdiction. In practice, this force of attraction rule is often not used in bilateral treaties as it can lead to uncertainty and act as a disincentive to investment.

### Technical services

**[A8.32]** Some DTAs permit tax to be imposed on fees paid to a non-resident for technical services. This essentially imposes a tax charge on business profits even where the non-resident has no permanent establishment.

Article 13 of the UK/Malaysia DTA for instance provides:

'1.    Technical fees derived from one of the Contracting States by a resident of the other Contracting State who is the beneficial owner thereof and is subject to tax in that other State in respect thereof may be taxed in the first-mentioned Contracting State at a rate not exceeding 8 per cent of the gross amount of the technical fees.

2.    The term "technical fees" as used in this Article means payments of any kind to any person, other than to an employee of the person making the payments, in consideration for any services of a technical, managerial or consultancy nature.

3.    The provisions of paragraph 1 of this Article shall not apply if the beneficial owner of the technical fees, being a resident of a Contracting State, carries on business in the other Contracting State in which the technical fees arise through a permanent establishment situated therein, or performs in that other State independent personal services from a fixed base situated therein, and the technical fees are effectively connected with such permanent establishment or fixed base. In such case, the provisions of Article 7 or Article 15, as the case may be, shall apply.'

Withholding tax can therefore be charged on a technical fee paid by a Malaysian company to a UK company even if the UK company does not have a permanent establishment in Malaysia. In practice this can create problems in the UK where the tax is effectively withheld on gross income, whereas HMRC will normally only give relief for taxes paid on profits (*Yates (H M Inspector of Taxes) v GCA International Ltd* (1991) STC 157).

The UK/China DTA has similar language to the UK/Malaysia DTA. However, the Chinese tax authorities have issued a notice (Public Announcement [2011] No 19) confirming that notwithstanding this article, technical fees will normally fall under the business profits article and therefore not subject to tax in China unless a permanent establishment exists.

In other DTAs, for instance the UK/India DTA, technical fees may be included in the definition of royalties (see below) with similar results.

### Shipping and international air transport

**[A8.33]** Most DTAs (including the OECD Model Convention) include separate provisions dealing with the business profits of companies undertaking shipping and air transport activities. As a general rule, profits tend to be taxable only the place of effective management or residence. This therefore often creates a situation where profits are not taxed in the source country even if there is a permanent establishment. It is important to consider which profits are included for this purpose. For example they would normally include leasing fully equipped vessels, but bareboat charters are normally taxed under Article 7 in the case of a permanent establishment.

### Associated enterprises

**[A8.34]** The associated enterprises Article essentially imposes transfer pricing adjustments on profits which may be taxed under a DTA.

Article 8 of the UK/France DTA provides that:

'Where:

(a)     an enterprise of a Contracting State participates directly or indirectly in the management, control or capital of an enterprise of the other Contracting State; or

(b)     the same persons participate directly or indirectly in the management, control or capital of an enterprise of a Contracting State and an enterprise of the other Contracting State;

and in either case conditions are made or imposed between the two enterprises in their commercial or financial relations which differ from those which would be made between independent enterprises, then any profits which would, but for those conditions, have accrued to one of the enterprises, but, by reason of those conditions, have not so accrued, may be included in the profits of that enterprise and taxed accordingly.'

This will allow one jurisdiction to make an adjustment to profits under its domestic law, and for this adjustment to be respected by the DTA. Otherwise, a company could claim that the DTA did not allow the transfer pricing adjustment to be taxed as it did not constitute actual income earned by the company in question.

### Compensating adjustment

**[A8.35]** Some DTAs will also allow a company to claim a compensating adjustment where a transfer pricing adjustment is made (see **A13.22**).

Article 9 of the UK/Canada DTA for instance provides for an automatic adjustment if the affected company makes a claim:

'1.    Where a Contracting State includes in the profits of an enterprise of that State-and taxes accordingly – profits on which an enterprise of the other Contracting State has been charged to tax in that other State and the profits so included are profits which would have accrued to the enterprise of the first-mentioned State if the conditions made between the two enterprises had been those which would have been made between independent enterprises, then, subject to the provisions of paragraph 3 of this Article, *that other State shall* (notwithstanding any time limits in the domestic law of that other State) *make an appropriate adjustment to the amount of tax charged* therein on the profits. In determining such adjustment, due regard shall be had to the other provisions of this Convention and the competent authorities of the Contracting States shall if necessary consult each other.'

On the other hand, Article 9 of the UK/US DTA (and indeed the UK/France DTA quoted above) only provides for a compensating adjustment if the relevant tax authority expressly agrees.

'2.    Where a Contracting State includes in the profits of an enterprise of that State, and taxes accordingly, profits on which an enterprise of the other Contracting State has been charged to tax in that other State, *and the other Contracting State agrees that the* profits so included are profits that would have accrued to the enterprise of the first-mentioned State if the conditions made between the two enterprises had been those that would have been made between independent enterprises, then that other State shall make an appropriate adjustment to the amount of the tax charged therein on those profits. In determining such adjustment, due regard shall be paid to the other provisions of this Convention and the competent authorities of the Contracting States shall if necessary consult each other.' [my emphasis]'

### *Dividends*

**[A8.36]** Whilst there is no withholding tax on dividends paid by a UK company, the dividends Article of a DTA may provide for a reduced rate of tax on dividends paid by a non-resident company to a UK resident. This tax would normally be charged by way of a withholding tax.

Often, the reduced rate of withholding tax will depend on the shareholding which the UK resident has in the overseas company.

For example, Article 10(2) of the UK/Canada DTA provides that the rate of withholding tax will be:

'(a)    5 per cent of the gross amount of the dividends if the beneficial owner is a company which controls, directly or indirectly, at least 10 per cent of the voting power in the company paying the dividends;

(b)    15 per cent of the gross amount of the dividends in all other cases.'

In the UK/US DTA, the precise paragraph of the Limitation on Benefits Article under which a UK company qualifies will determine the rate of withholding tax imposed by the US.

Whilst the OECD Model Treaty gives values up to a maximum of the percentages described in the above UK/Canada DTA example, the UN Model Treaty does not specify a maximum dividend withholding rate of tax. This is left subject to negotiation between treaty partners, and often leads to higher maximum rates than the OECD Model prescribes, as a fairer outcome for countries that are net capital importers.

## UK tax credit

**[A8.37]** The dividends Article may also allow a non-resident to reclaim a tax credit on dividends paid by a UK company. This is discussed at **A5.14**.

## Definition

**[A8.38]** The Article will only apply to 'dividends' as defined for the purposes of the Article. Article 6(4) of the UK/Germany DTA for instance defines dividends as:

> 'income from shares, jouissance shares or jouissance rights, mining shares, founders' shares or other rights, not being debt-claims, participating in profits, as well as income from other corporate rights assimilated to income from shares by the taxation law of the territory of which the company making the distribution is a resident; in the case of the United Kingdom, the term includes any item (other than interest or royalties exempt from United Kingdom tax under the provisions of Article VII of this Convention) which under the law of the United Kingdom is treated as a distribution of a company; in the case of the Federal Republic the term includes income arising from participation in the capital and profits of a company resident in the Federal Republic, and the income derived by a sleeping partner from his participation as such.'

In the *Memec* (1998) 71 TC 77 case (see **A14.6**), it was held by the High Court that this definition of dividends only applied for the purposes of Article 6 of the UK/Germany DTA, and not for the purposes of any other Article.

## Subject to tax requirement

**[A8.39]** Some DTAs (although not the OECD Model) require that the recipient is subject to tax on the dividends in order to benefit from a reduced rate of tax in the jurisdiction of the payer.

Article 11 of the UK/Kenya DTA for instance provides that:

> '(1)    Dividends derived from a company which is a resident of Kenya by a resident of the United Kingdom may be taxed in the United Kingdom. Such dividends may also be taxed in Kenya but the tax so charged shall not exceed 15 per cent of the gross amount of the dividends *if the recipient of the dividends is subject to tax* on them in the United Kingdom.' (my emphasis)'

This form of Article should be considered when establishing a holding company in a jurisdiction which exempts dividends (for instance the participation exemptions common in many jurisdictions including France, Cyprus and the Netherlands).

It is possible for a UK company to make an election that a particular dividend is not subject to the dividend exemption, which should ensure that the requirements of this form of Article are met (see **A16.7**).

## Interest

**[A8.40]** The interest Article in a DTA usually provides that the rate of tax charged on interest received by a resident of one jurisdiction from the other jurisdiction is subject to tax at a reduced rate, or not at all. This tax would normally be charged by way of withholding tax.

Withholding tax rates are subject to negotiation between treaty partners in the UN Model Treaty, whilst the OECD gives a maximum withholding tax rate of 10% of the gross amount of the interest.

Article 11 of the UK/Canada DTA for instance provides that:

'1.    However, such interest may be taxed in the Contracting State in which it arises, and according to the law of that State; but if the recipient is the beneficial owner of the interest, the tax so charged shall not exceed 10 per cent of the gross amount of the interest.'

The beneficial ownership requirement is discussed later in this Chapter.

It is usually necessary for the recipient to obtain clearance from the tax authority in the jurisdiction where the interest arises before the reduced rate of withholding can be obtained. This procedure is discussed in **A5.18** and **A12.11**.

### Source

**[A8.41]** The Article will only apply to interest which 'arises' in one of the jurisdictions.

This is generally defined as including:

(a)    interest paid by a resident of that jurisdiction;
(b)    interest paid by a permanent establishment located in that jurisdiction.

Article 11 of the UK/Canada DTA for instance provides that:

'1.    Interest shall be deemed to arise in a Contracting State when the payer is that State itself, a political subdivision, a local authority or a resident of that State. Where, however, the person paying the interest, whether he is a resident of a Contracting State or not, has in a Contracting State a permanent establishment in connection with which the indebtedness on which the interest is paid was incurred, and that interest is borne by that permanent establishment, then such interest shall be deemed to arise in the Contracting State in which the permanent establishment is situated.'

This definition may be narrower than the definition under the domestic law of the jurisdiction in question. The UK, for instance, considers that interest can have a source in the UK even if the payer is not located in the UK under the principles established in the *Westminster Bank Executor and Trustee Co (Channel Islands) Ltd v National Bank of Greece SA* [1971] AC 945, [1971] 1 All ER 233 case (see **A5.3**). However, a DTA may only permit the UK to tax an interest payment if the payer is a UK resident.

### Definition

**[A8.42]** The Article will only apply to 'interest' as defined for the purposes of the article. Article 11 of the UK/Canada DTA defines interest as:

'1.      . . . income from debt-claims of every kind, whether or not secured by mortgage, and whether or not carrying a right to participate in the debtor's profits, and in particular, income from government securities and income from bonds or debentures, including premiums and prizes attaching to bonds or debentures, as well as income assimilated to income from money lent by the taxation law of the State in which the income arises. However, the term 'interest' does not include income dealt with in Article 10 [Dividends].'

The definition of interest for the purposes of the DTA may be different from the definition of interest under domestic law. It is therefore possible that withholding tax would be charged on interest, and no relief would be available under the DTA if the payment did not constitute interest as defined in the interest Article.

## Special relationship

**[A8.43]** Where a 'special relationship' exists between the payer and the recipient of interest, the benefit of the interest Article will be restricted to the arm's length amount of any interest. The excess amount would remain subject to tax without any relief under the DTA.

Article 11 of the UK/France DTA for instance provides that:

'1.      Where, by reason of a special relationship between the payer and the beneficial owner or between both of them and some other person, the amount of the interest paid exceeds, for whatever reason, the amount which would have been agreed upon by the payer and the beneficial owner in the absence of such relationship, the provisions of this Article shall apply only to the last-mentioned amount of interest. In such case, the excess part of the payments shall remain taxable according to the laws of each Contracting State, due regard being had to the other provisions of this Convention.'

The OECD Model provides slightly different wording which is for example reflected in Article 11 of the UK/Kenya DTA:

'2.      Where, owing to a special relationship between the payer and the recipient or between both of them and some other person, the amount of the interest paid, having regard to the debt-claim for which it is paid, exceeds the amount which would have been agreed upon by the payer and the recipient in the absence of such relationship, the provisions of this article shall apply only to the last-mentioned amount. In that case, the excess part of the payments shall remain taxable according to the law of each Contracting State, due regard being had to the other provisions of this Agreement.'

There is no definition of 'special relationship', but it is generally considered to be broader than the definition of 'associated enterprise'.

The HMRC manuals at DT1917 state:

'A special relationship exists not only where the parties are associated (parent and subsidiary companies or companies under common control), but also where there is any community of interests as distinct from the legal relationship giving rise to the payment of the royalty.'

The OECD Commentary on the interest Article states that a special relationship not only includes situations where one party directly or indirectly controls the other, but also where there is 'any community of interests as distinct from the legal relationship giving rise to the payment of the interest.' (paragraph 34 of the commentary on Article 9).

### Thin capitalisation and special relationship

**[A8.44]** The OECD Model (as reflected in the UK/Kenya DTA article reproduced above) only requires consideration of the rate of interest charged, rather than the amount of the loan itself. It would therefore be possible for a foreign lender to thinly capitalise a UK subsidiary, and still obtain withholding tax relief on the full amount of the interest. Most UK DTAs therefore modify the OECD Model to require consideration of the amount of the loan as well. This is reflected in the UK/France DTA by the requirement to consider 'the amount of the interest paid exceeds, *for whatever reason*, the amount which would have been agreed upon  . . . '

HMRC consider (the guidance was previously at ITH1229) that this gives more adequate coverage of thinly capitalised structures. However, this distinction is now largely irrelevant because withholding tax relief will be available under UK domestic law if the recipient makes a claim under TIOPA 2010, s 181 (see **A13.75**) where interest is disallowed under transfer pricing provisions. HMRC have also confirmed (see **A13.76**) that interest which is reclassified as a distribution will not be subject to withholding tax under domestic law.

Some DTAs have specific provisions which prevent the UK from disallowing interest under transfer pricing or thin capitalisation principles. Article VII of the UK/Germany DTA for instance provides that:

'(1)   Any provision in the law of either of the territories which relates only to interest paid to a non-resident company or only to royalties so paid shall not operate so as to require interest or royalties paid to a company which is a resident of the other territory to be left out of account as a deduction in computing the taxable profits of the company paying the interest or royalties, unless the debt-claim in respect of which the interest is paid, or the right or property giving rise to the royalties, as the case may be, was created or assigned mainly for the purpose of taking advantage of this paragraph and not for bona fide commercial reasons.'

These provisions are also now largely irrelevant as the UK thin capitalisation and transfer pricing rules apply equally to UK residents and non-residents.

It has been suggested that the interest Article by itself may prevent a transfer pricing adjustment from being made because it would result in double taxation if the paying company were denied a deduction for the interest but the recipient company were still taxed. However, this does not appear correct, as it is not the same income which is being taxed in both companies. The interest is taxed in the recipient company, but it is the income of the paying company (for instance business profits) which is taxed, albeit without a deduction for the interest. There may be economic double taxation but there is no juridical double taxation and a DTA will not therefore provide any relief other than by allowing a corresponding adjustment under the associated enterprises Article (**A8.35** above).

## Subject to tax requirement

**[A8.45]** Some DTAs (although not the OECD Model) require that the recipient is subject to tax on the interest in order to benefit from a reduced rate of tax in the jurisdiction of the payer.

Article 12 of the UK/Kenya DTA for instance provides that:

> '(1)   However, such interest may be taxed in the Contracting State in which it arises, and according to the law of that State; but where such interest is paid to a resident of the other Contracting State *who is subject to tax there in respect thereof* the tax so charged in the Contracting State in which the interest arises shall not exceed 15 per cent of the gross amount of the interest.'

This form of Article should be considered when establishing a holding company in a jurisdiction which exempts interest from tax (for instance as part of a participation exemption).

### Royalties

**[A8.46]** The royalties Article usually provides that the rate of tax charged on a royalty received by a resident of one jurisdiction from the other jurisdiction is subject to tax a reduced rate, or not at all. This tax would normally be charged by way of withholding tax.

The UN Model Treaty provides for the taxation of royalties in the contracting state in which they arise, at a rate negotiated between the treaty partners. The OECD Model Treaty does not provide for the source country taxation of royalties, but in practice most treaties do tax royalties at source.

Article 12 of the UK/France DTA for instance provides that:

> '1.   Royalties arising in a Contracting State and paid to a resident of the other Contracting State shall be taxable only in that other State if that resident is the beneficial owner of the royalties.'

The beneficial ownership requirement is discussed later in this Chapter.

It may be necessary for the recipient to obtain clearance from the tax authority in the jurisdiction where the royalty arises before the reduced rate of withholding can be obtained. This procedure is discussed in **A5.17** and **A12.9**.

However, a UK resident company which pays a royalty to a non-resident may apply the terms of the relevant DTA if it has a 'reasonable belief' that the DTA will apply.

### Source

**[A8.47]** As with interest, the Article will only apply to royalties which 'arise' in one of the jurisdictions.

This is generally defined as including:

(a)   royalties paid by a resident of that jurisdiction;
(b)   royalties paid by a permanent establishment located in that jurisdiction.

## Definition

**[A8.48]** The Article will only apply to 'royalties' as defined for the purposes of the Article. Article 12 of the UK/France DTA defines royalties as:

> 'payments of any kind received as a consideration for the use of, or the right to use, any copyright of literary, artistic or scientific work (including cinematograph films and films or tapes for radio or television broadcasting), any patent, trade mark, design or model, plan, secret formula or process, or for the use of, or the right to use, industrial, commercial or scientific equipment, or for information concerning industrial, commercial or scientific experience and shall include gains derived from the sale or exchange of any rights or property giving rise to such royalties.'

The definition of royalties for the purposes of a DTA may be different from the definition of royalties under domestic law. It is therefore possible that withholding tax would be charged on royalties, and no relief would be available under that DTA if the payment did not constitute royalties as defined in the royalties Article.

The definition of royalties under the OECD Model is considered further in **A5.30**. There are a number of planning opportunities available if a payment can be classified as something other than a royalty (for instance business profits), and therefore not subject to withholding tax under either domestic law or a relevant DTA.

## Special relationship

**[A8.49]** As with interest, where a 'special relationship' exists between the payer and the recipient of interest, the benefit of the royalties Article will be restricted to the arm's length amount of any royalties. The excess amount would remain subject to tax without any relief under the relevant DTA.

## Subject to tax requirement

**[A8.50]** Some DTAs (although not the OECD Model) require that the recipient is subject to tax on the royalties in order to benefit from a reduced rate of tax in the jurisdiction of the payer.

Article 13 of the UK/Kenya DTA for instance provides that:

> '(1)    However, such royalties may be taxed in the Contracting State in which they arise, and according to the law of that State; but where such royalties are paid to a resident of the other Contracting State who is subject to tax there in respect thereof the tax so charged in the Contracting State in which the royalties arise shall not exceed 15 per cent of the gross amount of the royalties.'

This form of Article should be considered when establishing a holding company in a jurisdiction which exempts royalties from tax.

## *Capital gains*

**[A8.51]** This Article, and associated planning opportunities, is discussed in more detail in CHAPTER **A11**.

In most UK DTAs, the effect of this Article is to:

(a)    exempt most gains from tax in the jurisdiction where the asset is located (for example Article 13(3) in the UK/France DTA below);

(b)    allow both jurisdictions to tax gains on assets used for the purposes of a permanent establishment (for example Article 13(2) in the UK/France DTA below);

(c)    allow both jurisdictions to tax gains on real estate (for example Article 13(1) in the UK/France DTA below).

Article 13 of the UK/France DTA provides that:

'1.    Gains derived by a resident of a Contracting State from the alienation of immovable property, as defined in paragraph 2 of Article 5, which is situated in the other State may be taxed in that other State. For the purposes of this provision the second sentence of paragraph 2(b) [shares in a company which holds immovable property] of Article 5 shall not apply.

2.     Gains from the alienation of movable property forming part of the business property of a permanent establishment which an enterprise of a Contracting State has in the other Contracting State or of movable property pertaining to a fixed base available to a resident of a Contracting State in the other Contracting State for the purposes of performing professional services, including such gains from the alienation of such a permanent establishment (alone or together with the whole enterprise) or of such a fixed base, may be taxed in the other State,

3.     Gains from the alienation of any property other than that referred to in paragraphs 1 and 2 shall be taxable only in the Contracting State in which the alienator is resident.'

## Relief for double taxation

**[A8.52]** This Article of a DTA generally provides that credit will be given against the tax liability of a company which is resident in one jurisdiction for any tax suffered in the other jurisdiction. In the case of dividends, it may also provide for an underlying tax credit in the same way as the UK double tax relief rules.

An alternative version of the Article provides that any income which is taxed in one jurisdiction will be exempt in the other jurisdiction. The OECD Model Convention provides for either the credit or the exemption Article to be used.

Historically, the UK's DTAs follow the credit model, but DTAs between other jurisdictions may follow the exemption model. The combination of the exemption method and a low or zero tax rate in the source country can often lead to significant tax planning opportunities.

## Tax sparing

**[A8.53]** In DTAs with developing countries, the UK has sometimes included a 'tax sparing' Article.

Article 21(3) of the UK/Indonesia DTA for instance provides that:

'Indonesian tax payable' shall be deemed to include any amount which would have been payable as Indonesian tax for any year but for an exemption or reduction of tax granted for the year or any part thereof under Article 15(5) and Article 16(1) and (2) of Law No. 1 of 1967 of Indonesia to the extent that these provisions continue in force by virtue of Article 33(2)(a) of Act No. 7 of 1983 of Indonesia.

Provided that relief from United Kingdom tax shall not be given by virtue of this paragraph in respect of income from any source if the income arises in a period starting more than 10 years after the exemption from, or reduction of, Indonesian tax was first granted in respect of that source.'

Where a company has obtained the specific exemptions from Indonesian tax which are listed (usually these exemptions are to encourage investment in particular sectors), it is deemed nonetheless to have paid the tax which it would otherwise have paid, which enables it to receive the full benefit of the original tax incentive.

This Article also applies for the purposes of determining the amount of credit available for underlying tax (if the dividend exemption is not available).

For example, in Diagram 4, the UK company will be entitled to credit for the 10% withholding tax on the dividend, and the 30% Indonesian tax which would have been paid were it not for the exemption.

At a policy level, it is known that the UK government is keen to eliminate tax sparing clauses from DTAs as and when they are renegotiated.

Diagram 4

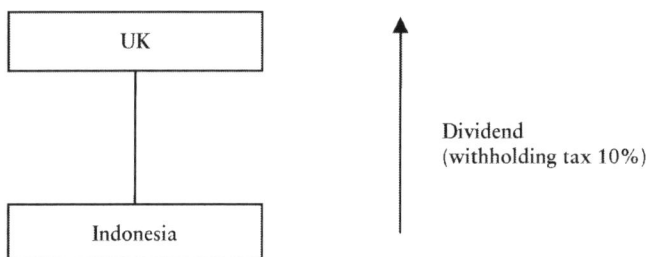

Dividend
(withholding tax 10%)

Tax paid £nil due to relevant tax exemption
(normal tax rate 30%)

# Planning—anti-avoidance provisions

[A8.54] DTAs are often used in international tax planning to reduce withholding taxes or capital gains taxes on cross border payments (see A5.16 and A11.10). It is therefore important to understand what limitations there are on the application of DTAs and ensure that all relevant conditions are satisfied.

Modern DTAs may contain three key anti-avoidance provisions:

(a)     a requirement that the recipient of income (such as interest or royalties) has beneficial ownership of that income;

(b)     a Limitation on Benefits Article, which restricts the benefit of the treaty to persons who satisfy certain conditions;

(c)     anti-conduit provisions which prevent a company from receiving income and immediately paying it out to another company which cannot itself benefit from the DTA.

Specific Articles may contain also anti-avoidance provisions. For instance, Article 12 of the UK/France DTA provides that in relation to royalties

'1.      The provisions of this Article shall not apply if the right or property giving rise to the royalties was created or assigned mainly for the purposes of taking advantage of this Article and not for bona fide commercial reasons.'

Such a provision is similar to the anti-avoidance provision in the Interest and Royalties Directive (see **A5.23**).

## Beneficial ownership

**[A8.55]** In order to benefit from a reduced rate of withholding tax under the interest, dividends or royalty article of a DTA, the recipient is typically required to have 'beneficial ownership' of the income.

Article 10(2) of the UK/Netherlands DTA sets out the requirement as follows:

'(a)      . . . if the *beneficial owner of the dividends* is a resident of the other Contracting State, the tax so charged shall not exceed:

(i)      10 per cent of the gross amount of the dividends, except as provided in sub-paragraph a) (ii);

(ii)     15 per cent of the gross amount of the dividends where those dividends are paid out of income or gains derived directly or indirectly from immovable property within the meaning of Article 6 by an investment vehicle which distributes most of this income annually and whose income from such immovable property is exempted from tax.' (my emphasis)'

The *Indofood* case (see below) established the principle that beneficial ownership is 'the sole and unfettered right to use, enjoy or dispose of' an item of income. This right must be unfettered legally, economically and practically.

Paragraph 12.1 of the commentary on Article 9 of the OECD Model Treaty also confirms this:

' . . . a conduit company cannot normally be regarded as the beneficial owner if, though the formal owner, it has, as a practical matter, very narrow powers which render it, in relation to the income concerned, a mere fiduciary or administrator acting on account of the interested parties.'

Changes have been proposed to this part of the commentary which gives further detail on the rights which a beneficial owner would be expected to have. These are broadly in line with the case law discussed below.

In Diagram 5, the UK company immediately pays all the interest it receives from the Netherlands as interest to its Hong Kong parent company. The terms of the loan are the same, and the interest payment dates are the same. The UK company has no other sources of funds, and therefore cannot pay the interest to Hong Kong otherwise than by using the interest it receives from the Netherlands. The UK company is very unlikely to satisfy the beneficial ownership requirement as a result.

Diagram 5

```
┌──────────────────┐
│    Hong Kong     │
└────────┬─────────┘
         │
         │          loan £1,000,000      interest £100,000
         │                 ↓                   ↑
┌────────┴─────────┐       │                   │
│       UK         │       ↓                   │
└────────┬─────────┘
         │          loan £1,000,000      interest £100,000
         │                 ↓                   ↑
┌────────┴─────────┐       │                   │
│   Netherlands    │       ↓                   │
└──────────────────┘
```

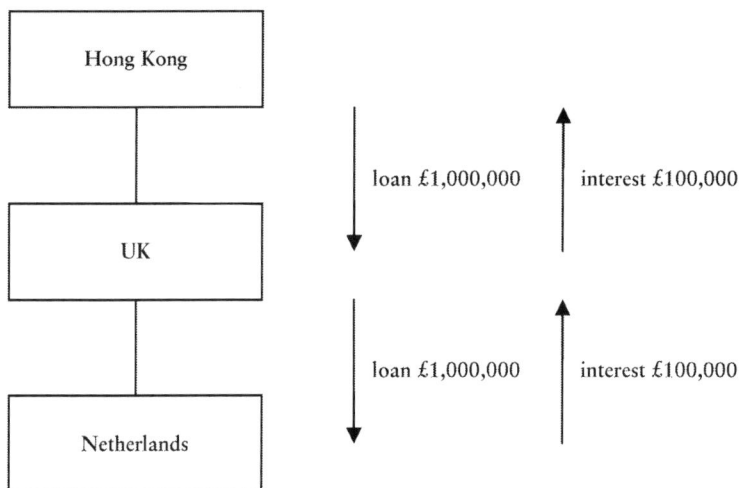

In order to establish beneficial ownership, an intermediate company should not be required, either economically or legally to pay out all the income it receives in substantially the same form as it receives it.

For instance, a company which receives interest income and pays a dividend is more likely to have beneficial ownership of that interest income because the directors must actively vote a dividend, and would be free to choose not to. The company should also have other sources of funds so that it was not economically required to use the interest received to make dividend payments,

## DTAs with no beneficial ownership requirement

**[A8.56]** Only a few DTAs do not include beneficial ownership conditions. For example, the royalties Article of the UK/Barbados DTA is drafted as follows (the interest Article is very similar):

'Any royalties derived from sources within a Contracting State by a resident of the other Contracting State who is subject to tax in the other State in respect thereof, shall be exempt from tax in that first-mentioned Contracting State . . . '

This provides a planning opportunity as a UK company can pay royalties or interest to a Barbados trust (which would not typically have beneficial ownership if it holds assets for the benefit of its beneficiaries). A Barbados trust is subject to tax on its income, with a deduction for any distributions made to beneficiaries. This should satisfy the requirement in the DTA that the recipient is subject to tax on the royalties or interest, but should not result in a material tax liability in Barbados if most of the income is distributed to beneficiaries.

In Diagram 6, if the UK company paid royalties directly to Jersey they would be subject to withholding tax of 20%. If they are instead paid to a Barbados trust of which the Jersey company is a beneficiary, the withholding tax is reduced to 0% under the UK/Barbados DTA. Most of the royalties are then distributed to the Jersey company, and tax only arises in Barbados on a small profit.

Diagram 6

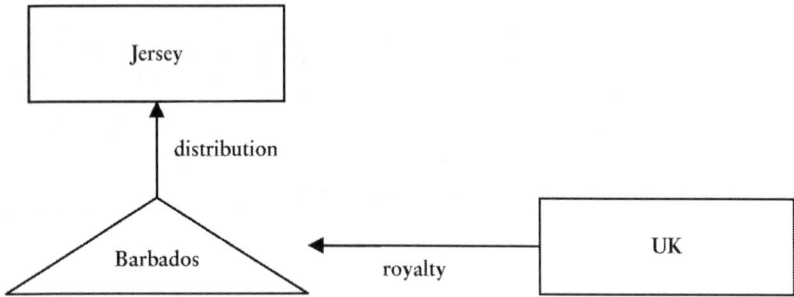

*Indofood International Finance Ltd v JP Morgan Chase Bank NA* **[2006] EWCA Civ 158**

[A8.57] In this case, a Mauritius company borrowed money from an Indonesian bank, interest on which was subject to a reduced rate of withholding tax under the Indonesia-Mauritius DTA. The Mauritius company then lent the money on to its Indonesian parent company, interest on which was due at the same rate and at the same time as the interest paid to the Indonesian bank.

The Indonesia/Mauritius DTA was subsequently terminated, and the loan agreement with the bank required the bank to take all reasonable steps to minimise withholding tax on the loan, otherwise the loan could be repaid early. The Indonesian bank (which did not want the loan repaid due to prevailing interest rates) argued that this included the bank establishing a subsidiary in the Netherlands through which to make the loan, in order to benefit from the Indonesia/Netherlands DTA.

The loan agreement was drafted under English law and was therefore heard in the English courts. The Court of Appeal held that the Netherlands company would not have beneficial ownership of the interest because:

(a)     the terms of loan documentation would require the Netherlands company to make a payment of interest of exactly the same amount and at exactly the same time as the interest it received;

(b)     the Netherlands company had no other source of income out of which it could pay the interest.

HMRC produced guidance following the case (currently located at www.hmrc.gov.uk/manuals/intmanual/INTM332040.htm) which sets out their view of its impact on the definition. Two particular examples are relevant to international tax planning:

'Example 7: Access to group-sourced funding from a Non treaty country using Luxembourg conduit company

A claim is made under the UK/Luxembourg DTA for relief from UK withholding tax in respect of a loan from a Luxembourg resident company (LuxCo) to a UK group borrower.

- LuxCo was set up (or has been maintained in the group) specifically to deal with this intra group loan and is taxed on a small "turn" for administering loans;
- the source of the loan is an affiliate in a territory with which the UK has no DTA (NoA Co)
- the NoA Co/LuxCo loan agreement shows that this interest bearing loan was predetermined to be lent onward to the UK
- similarly, the interest payable by the UK on its loan from LuxCo is predetermined to be passed on to NoA Co.

The conduit company is not beneficial owner of the relevant income within the 'international fiscal meaning', because it has clear obligations to forward the interest to NoA Co.

The terms and conditions of the loan agreements show that the flow of income out of the UK is predestined to be passed on to NoA Co. It is clear that one of the main purposes of the Luxembourg company is to avoid the withholding tax which would be due on payments of interest to NoA Co. The interest will not benefit from the Luxembourg/UK treaty and tax will be withheld.

Example 8: Access to group-sourced funding from a Treaty country using Luxembourg conduit company

The facts are as in example 7 except that this time the source of the funds is a US taxpayer who receives interest directly from the Lux Company. If the interest had gone directly to the US recipient, it would have qualified for exemption under the US/UK treaty. Although the Lux Company will not satisfy the international fiscal meaning, this is irrelevant as its imposition into the arrangement does not affect the withholding tax position. The same conclusion could not be drawn if the US taxpayer had passed funds to a non-treaty intermediary, which then lent the funds to the Lux Co.'

In order to satisfy HMRC's test of beneficial ownership, it would therefore be necessary to demonstrate that the recipient was not 'pre-destined' to pass on its income to LuxCo, as outlined under **A8.55**.

### *Prevost Car Inc v R* **[2008] TCC 231, 10 ITLR 736**

**[A8.58]** A UK company and a Swedish company together established a holding company in the Netherlands, which held shares in a Canadian company (Prevost).

The shareholders' agreement between the UK company and the Swedish company provided that the income of the Netherlands company would be distributed by way of dividend.

The Canadian subsidiary claimed a reduced rate of withholding tax under the Canada/Netherlands DTA on dividends paid to the Netherlands company. The Canadian tax authorities argued that the treaty did not apply because the Netherlands company did not have beneficial ownership of the dividend.

The Canadian Federal Court of Appeal held that a company would have beneficial ownership of income 'unless the corporation . . . has absolutely no discretion as to the use or application of funds put through it as conduit'. This is similar to the test established in *Indofood*.

In the present case, the Federal Court held that the Netherlands company did have beneficial ownership of the dividends because (*inter alia*):

(a)     the Netherlands company was not a party to the shareholders agreement, and the UK and Swedish companies could not therefore take action against it for not distributing a dividend;

(b)     the deed of incorporation of the Netherlands company did not require it to pay a dividend;

(c)     the Netherlands company was properly constituted and managed under Netherlands law, which had to be followed when paying the dividend;

(d)     any dividends received by the Netherlands company remained its property until a dividend was declared.

This was a Canadian case, but it considered the international meaning of the term 'beneficial ownership' in the same way as the *Indofood* case. In addition, decisions of the Canadian court (as a Commonwealth court) may be taken into account by the UK courts.

### *Velcro Canada Inc v R* 2012 TCC 57

**[A8.59]** The *Velcro* case extended the principles in the *Prevost* case. In this instance, Velcro Canada Inc paid royalties to Velcro Industries BV (VIBV), a resident of the Netherlands, based on net sales. In 1995, VIBV became a resident of the Netherlands Antilles, and assigned its rights under the royalty agreement to a subsidiary, Velcro Holdings BV (VHBV), which was resident in The Netherlands. In exchange for the assignment, VHBV agreed to pay to VIBV a royalty based on an arm's-length percentage of net sales of the licensed products within 30 days of receiving royalty payments from VCI. Under an agreement with the Dutch tax authorities, this amounted t to 90% of the royalties received from VCI.

Canada has no tax treaty with the Netherlands Antilles, and if royalties were paid by VCI to VIBV, or VIBV were the beneficial owner of royalties paid to VHBV, the royalties would have been subject to a 25% withholding tax, rather than the 10% rate under the Canada-Netherlands treaty which was subsequently reduced to zero in 1998)

The Canada Revenue Agency took the position that VHBV was not the beneficial owner of the royalties, as required by Article 12 of the treaty, and reassessed VCI for not withholding tax at the 25% rate.

The Court applied the following comments from the decision in *Prévost*:

' . . . the "beneficial owner" of dividends is the person who receives the dividends for his or her own use and enjoyment and assumes the risk and control of the dividend he or she received . . . .When an agency or mandate exists or the property is in the name of a nominee, one looks to find on whose behalf the agent or mandatory is acting . . . When corporate entities are concerned, one does not pierce the corporate veil unless the corporation is a conduit for another person and has absolutely no discretion as to the use or application of the funds put through it as a conduit, or has agreed to act on someone else's behalf pursuant to that person's instructions without any right to do other than what the person instructs it . . . '

The Court held that, similar to the finding in *Prévost*, there was no 'pre-determined flow of funds' from VCI to VIBV, despite the contractual obligation between VHBV and VIBV. VHBV had possession, use, risk and control of the income in its bank account. The funds were also fully exposed to currency risk and interest receipts.

To quote the judge, in the case: 'It is quite obvious that though there might be limited discretion, VHBV does have discretion'.

The key message from this appears to be that providing the recipient is able to independently manage its incoming resources and pay on at its own discretion, then the corporate veil will not be pierced.

The *Indofood*, *Prevost* and *Velcro* cases give useful guidance on what steps must be undertaken to ensure that companies have beneficial ownership of income or assets in international tax planning arrangements.

## Limitation on benefits

**[A8.60]** The UK's DTAs with the US and Japan contain Limitation on Benefit (or 'LOB') Articles. The UK/US Article is reproduced below under **A8.61**. The specific paragraph of the LOB Article under which a company qualifies for benefits also determines the rate of withholding tax under the dividend Article of the UK/USA DTA (see above).

In the absence of the Limitation on Benefits Article, a company in a jurisdiction which does not have a DTA with the US could establish a UK company through which it receives income, as illustrated in Diagram 7. In this case, the UK company would not satisfy the shareholding conditions in Article 23(2) and Article 23(3) as the Jersey company does not fall into any of the categories of shareholder listed.

However, the UK company may satisfy the 'substantial business' test in Article 23(4), or the competent authorities may agree that the structure was not established for tax avoidance purposes. This ensures that the UK company will only qualify for benefits under the DTA if it has a genuine business in the UK.

Some common structures which qualify for benefits under the Limitation on Benefits Article in the UK/US DTA are:

(a)    A UK company which is listed, or which is a subsidiary of a UK listed company. Both HMRC and the IRS have confirmed privately that a company listed on AIM will be treated as listed for these purposes. (Article 23(2)(*c*)).

(b)    A UK company which is owned at least 50% by UK residents and which satisfies a 'base erosion' test (Article 23(2)(*f*)). The base erosion test in Article 23(2)(f)(ii) requires that the UK company does not make substantial tax deductible payments to other jurisdictions.

(c) A UK company which is part of a group which carries on 'substantial business' in both the UK and the US (Article 23(4)). The definition of 'substantial business' is outlined in the US Treasury Technical Interpretation to the UK/US DTA (www.ustreas.gov/offices/tax-policy/library/teus-uk.pdf).

Diagram 7

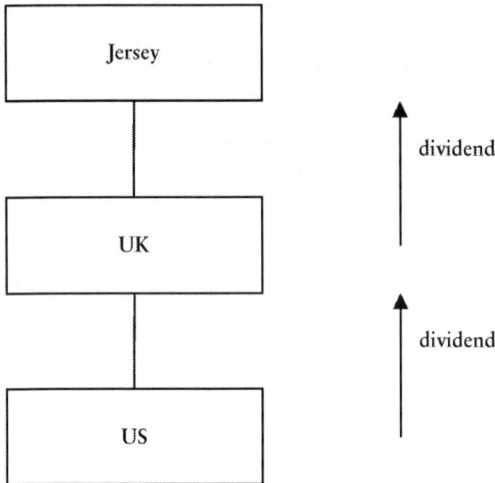

### Limitation on benefits article in the UK/USA DTA

**[A8.61]** The full text of the limitation on benefits article is reproduced below. It is important to work through this article in a logical order, and determine precisely which condition is satisfied as this will affect the application of other articles in the treaty, including the rate of withholding tax on dividends.

'Article 23 Limitation on benefits

1. Except as otherwise provided in this Article, a resident of a Contracting State that derives income, profits or gains from the other Contracting State shall be entitled to all the benefits of this Convention otherwise accorded to residents of a Contracting State only if such resident is a 'qualified person' as defined in paragraph 2 of this Article and satisfies any other specified conditions for the obtaining of such benefits.

2. A resident of a Contracting State is a qualified person for a taxable or chargeable period only if such resident is either:
   (a) an individual;
   (b) a qualified governmental entity;
   (c) a company, if:
       (i) the principal class of its shares is listed or admitted to dealings on a recognized stock exchange specified in clauses (i) or (ii) of sub-paragraph (a) of paragraph 7 of this Article and is regularly traded on one or more recognized stock exchanges, or

      (ii)      shares representing at least 50 per cent of the aggregate voting power and value of the company are owned directly or indirectly by five or fewer companies entitled to benefits under clause (i) of this sub-paragraph, provided that, in the case of indirect ownership, each intermediate owner is a resident of either Contracting State;

(d)     a person other than an individual or a company, if:

      (i)      the principal class of units in that person is listed or admitted to dealings on a recognized stock exchange specified in clauses (i) or (ii) of sub-paragraph (a) of paragraph 7 of this Article and is regularly traded on one or more recognized stock exchanges, or

      (ii)      the direct or indirect owners of at least 50 per cent of the beneficial interests in that person are qualified persons by reason of clause (i) of sub-paragraph (c) or clause (i) of this sub-paragraph;

(e)     a person described in sub-paragraph (a), (b) or (c) of paragraph 3 of Article 4 (Residence) of this Convention, provided that, in the case of a person described in sub-paragraph (a) or (b) of that paragraph, more than 50 per cent of the person's beneficiaries, members or participants are individuals who are residents of either Contracting State;

(f)     a person other than an individual, if:

      (i)      on at least half the days of the taxable or chargeable period persons that are qualified persons by reason of sub-paragraphs (a), (b), clause (i) of sub-paragraph (c), clause (i) of sub-paragraph (d), or sub-paragraph (e) of this paragraph own, directly or indirectly, shares or other beneficial interests representing at least 50 per cent of the aggregate voting power and value of the person, and

      (ii)      less than 50 per cent of the person's gross income for that taxable or chargeable period is paid or accrued, directly or indirectly, to persons who are not residents of either Contracting State in the form of payments that are deductible for the purposes of the taxes covered by this Convention in the State of which the person is a resident (but not including arm's length payments in the ordinary course of business for services or tangible property and payments in respect of financial obligations to a bank, provided that where such a bank is not a resident of a Contracting State such payment is attributable to a permanent establishment of that bank located in one of the Contracting States); or

(g)     a trust or trustee of a trust in their capacity as such if at least 50 per cent of the beneficial interest in the trust is held by persons who are either:

      (i)      qualified persons by reason of sub-paragraphs (a), (b), clause (i) of sub-paragraph (c), clause (i) of sub-paragraph (d), or sub-paragraph (e) of this paragraph; or

      (ii)      equivalent beneficiaries,

provided that less than 50 per cent of the gross income arising to such trust or trustee in their capacity as such for the taxable or chargeable period is paid or accrued, directly or indirectly, to persons who are not residents of either Contracting State in the form of payments that are deductible for the purposes of the taxes covered by this Convention in the Contracting State of which that trust or trustee is a resident (but not including arm's length payments in the ordinary course of business for services or tangible property and payments in respect of financial obligations to a bank, provided that where such a bank is not a resident of a Contracting State such payment is attributable to a permanent establishment of that bank located in one of the Contracting States).

3.    Notwithstanding that a company that is a resident of a Contracting State may not be a qualified person, it shall be entitled to the benefits of this Convention otherwise accorded to residents of a Contracting State with respect to an item of income, profit or gain if it satisfies any other specified conditions for the obtaining of such benefits and:

    (a)    shares representing at least 95 per cent of the aggregate voting power and value of the company are owned, directly or indirectly, by seven or fewer persons who are equivalent beneficiaries; and

    (b)    less than 50 per cent of the company's gross income for the taxable or chargeable period in which the item of income, profit or gain arises is paid or accrued, directly or indirectly, to persons who are not equivalent beneficiaries, in the form of payments that are deductible for the purposes of the taxes covered by this Convention in the State of which the company is a resident (but not including arm's length payments in the ordinary course of business for services or tangible property and payments in respect of financial obligations to a bank, provided that where such a bank is not a resident of a Contracting State such payment is attributable to a permanent establishment of that bank located in one of the Contracting States).

4.

    (a)    Notwithstanding that a resident of a Contracting State may not be a qualified person, it shall be entitled to the benefits of this Convention with respect to an item of income, profit or gain derived from the other Contracting State, if the resident is engaged in the active conduct of a trade or business in the first-mentioned State (other than the business of making or managing investments for the resident's own account, unless these activities are banking, insurance or securities activities carried on by a bank, insurance company or registered securities dealer), the income, profit or gain derived from the other Contracting State is derived in connection with, or is incidental to, that trade or business and that resident satisfies any other specified conditions for the obtaining of such benefits.

    (b)    If a resident of a Contracting State or any of its associated enterprises carries on a trade or business activity in the other Contracting State which gives rise to an item of income, profit or gain, sub-paragraph (a) of this paragraph shall apply to such item only if the trade or business activity in the first-mentioned State is substantial in relation to the trade or business activity in the other State. Whether a trade or business activity is substantial for the purposes of this paragraph shall be determined on the basis of all the facts and circumstances.

    (c)    In determining whether a person is engaged in the active conduct of a trade or business in a Contracting State under sub-paragraph (a) of this paragraph, activities conducted by a partnership in which that person is a partner and activities conducted by persons connected to such person shall be deemed to be conducted by such person. A person shall be connected to another if one possesses at least 50 per cent of the beneficial interest in the other (or, in the case of a company, shares representing at least 50 per cent of the aggregate voting power and value of the company or of the beneficial equity interest in the company) or another person possesses, directly or indirectly, at least 50 per cent of the beneficial interest (or, in the case of a company, shares representing at least 50 per cent of the aggregate voting power and value of the company or of the beneficial equity interest in the company) in each person. In any case, a person shall be considered to be connected to another if, on the basis of all the facts and circumstances, one has control of the other or both are under the control of the same person or persons.

5.      Notwithstanding the preceding provisions of this Article, if a company that is a resident of a Contracting State, or a company that controls such a company, has outstanding a class of shares:

    (a)     which is subject to terms or other arrangements which entitle its holders to a portion of the income, profit or gain of the company derived from the other Contracting State that is larger than the portion such holders would receive in the absence of such terms or arrangements; and

    (b)     50 per cent or more of the voting power and value of which is owned by persons who are not equivalent beneficiaries,

the benefits of this Convention shall apply only to that proportion of the income which those holders would have received in the absence of those terms or arrangements.

6.      A resident of a Contracting State that is neither a qualified person nor entitled to benefits with respect to an item of income, profit or gain under paragraph 3 or 4 of this Article shall, nevertheless, be granted benefits of this Convention with respect to such item if the competent authority of the other Contracting State determines that the establishment, acquisition or maintenance of such resident and the conduct of its operations did not have as one of its principal purposes the obtaining of benefits under this Convention.

The competent authority of the other Contracting State shall consult with the competent authority of the first-mentioned State before refusing to grant benefits of this Convention under this paragraph.'

## Anti-conduit provisions

**[A8.62]** In addition to the requirement that the recipient of income has beneficial ownership, there may also be a requirement that the income is not paid as part of a 'conduit arrangement'.

Article 11(7) of the UK/US DTA provides for instance that:

'The provisions of this Article shall not apply in respect of any interest paid under, or as part of, a conduit arrangement.'

A 'conduit arrangement' is defined in Article 3(1)(n) as follows:

'(a)     the term 'conduit arrangement' means a transaction or series of transactions:

    (i)     which is structured in such a way that a resident of a Contracting State entitled to the benefits of this Convention receives an item of income arising in the other Contracting State but that resident pays, directly or indirectly, all or substantially all of that income (at any time or in any form) to another person who is not a resident of either Contracting State and who, if it received that item of income direct from the other Contracting State, would not be entitled under a convention for the avoidance of double taxation between the state in which that other person is resident and the Contracting State in which the income arises, or otherwise, to benefits with respect to that item of income which are equivalent to, or more favourable than, those available under this Convention to a resident of a Contracting State; and

(ii)    which has as its main purpose, or one of its main purposes, obtaining such increased benefits as are available under this Convention;'

In other words, the anti-conduit provisions will apply if:

(a)    the UK company which receives interest from the US company;
(b)    pays this interest to a company resident in a third jurisdiction;
(c)    under the DTA between the US and this third jurisdiction, the ultimate recipient would not be entitled to the same reduced rate of withholding tax as the UK company.

This is similar to the beneficial ownership requirement, but differs in two important respects:

(a)    the income paid to the ultimate beneficiary must only be 'substantially all' of the income received;
(b)    the provisions will only apply to artificial arrangements specifically put in place to take advantage of the treaty.

It is therefore possible that treaty benefits would not be available in respect of the structure shown in Diagram 8. Although the UK company may be entitled to a 0% rate of withholding tax under the UK/US DTA, there is no DTA between the US and Hong Kong, and the Hong Kong company would therefore not be entitled to a 0% rate of withholding tax.

Diagram 8

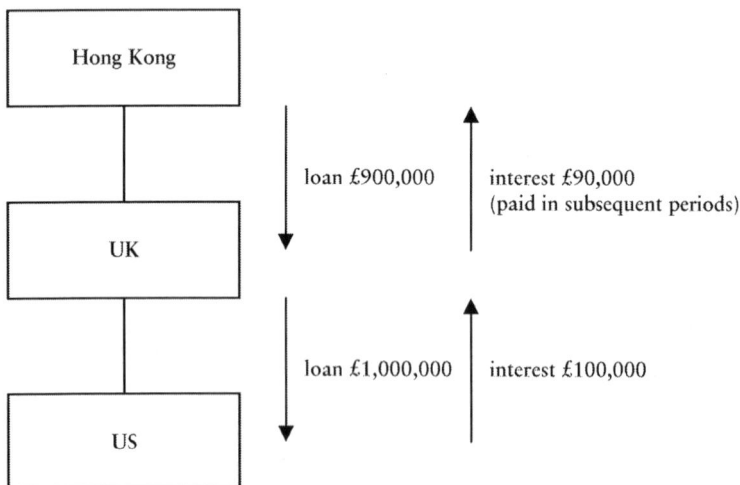

## Black listed territories

**[A8.63]** Some jurisdictions maintain a 'black list' of jurisdictions which may be treated less favourably for tax purposes. These jurisdictions are generally tax havens, and those jurisdictions with which the jurisdiction in question does not have a DTA. For example in Italy, amounts paid to black-listed jurisdictions (even as part of a trading transaction) may not be deductible for tax purposes.

An example of this in the UK is the exemption from transfer pricing for small and medium sized enterprises. The exemption does not apply unless the transaction in question is with a jurisdiction which is a 'qualifying territory'. A 'qualifying territory' is defined in TIOPA 2010, s 173 as one with which the UK has a DTA which includes a non-discrimination article

## Provisions which override a DTA

**[A8.64]** There are a number of anti-avoidance provisions in UK law which prevent a DTA from applying in specific circumstances.

### Trusts and TCGA 1992, s 13

**[A8.65]** TCGA 1992, s 79B provides that a trust is not entitled to benefit from a DTA in respect of gains arising under TCGA 1992, s 13 (see CHAPTER **A11**):

'(1)   This section applies where the trustees of a settlement are participators—
   (*a*)   in a close company, or
   (*b*)   in a company that is not resident in the United Kingdom but would be a close company if it were resident in the United Kingdom.
For this purpose 'participator' has the same meaning as in section 13.
(2)   Where this section applies, nothing in any double taxation relief arrangements shall be read as preventing a charge to tax arising by virtue of the attribution to the trustees under section 13, by reason of their participation in the company mentioned in subsection (1) above, of any part of a chargeable gain accruing to a company that is not resident in the United Kingdom.'

This means that gains can be attributed to non-UK resident trusts, and then to beneficiaries under the anti-avoidance provisions of TCGA 1992, ss 86 and 87.

### UK residents and business profits

**[A8.66]** ITTOIA 2005, s 858 provides that a UK resident partner in an overseas partnership cannot rely on benefits under a DTA which may be available to the partnership:

'(1)   This section applies if—
   (*a*)   a UK resident ('the partner') is a member of a firm which—
      (i)   resides outside the United Kingdom, or
      (ii)   carries on a trade the control and management of which is outside the United Kingdom, and
   (*b*)   by virtue of any arrangements having effect under ICTA 1988 s 788 ('the arrangements') any of the income of the firm is relieved from income tax in the United Kingdom.

(2)     The partner is liable to income tax on the partner's share of the income of the firm despite the arrangements.

(3)     If the partner's share of the income of the firm consists of or includes a share in a qualifying distribution—

(a)     made by a UK resident company, and

(b)     chargeable to tax under Chapter 3 of Part 4,

the partner (and not the firm) is, despite the arrangements, entitled to the share of the tax credit which corresponds to the partner's share of the distribution.'

ITTOIA 2005, s 858 was extended by Finance Act 2008 to include UK residents who have an indirect interest in a partnership. In addition, TIOPA 2010, s 131 provides that UK residents cannot take advantage of the business profits article of a DTA if the business in question is carried on by a non-resident (for example if the UK resident is subject to tax as a result of anti-avoidance provisions under which the profits are attributed).

The effect of this change was to prevent UK residents from realising business profits in overseas companies, and claiming relief under a DTA against the charge under ITA 2007, s 720—see **A3.44** for an example of this type of structure.

The retrospective application of this change was upheld in R *(on the application of Huitson) v Revenue and Customs Comrs [2010] EWHC 97 (Admin)* [2011] QB 174, [2010] 3 WLR 1015.

## Controlled foreign companies

**[A8.67]** Although not explicit, tax arising under the controlled foreign company (CFC) rules (see CHAPTER **A6**) does not constitute 'corporation tax' for the purposes of UK DTA, and therefore is not eligible for relief. This was confirmed in *Bricom Holdings Ltd v IRC* [1997] STC 1179, 70 TC 272.

Tax arising under other anti-avoidance provisions, for instance ITA 2007, s 729 or ITA 2007, s 754 should be unaffected by the *Bricom* decision, although this has not been tested by the courts. However, ITTOIA 2005, ss 858 and 815AZA would still need to be considered.

## *WT Ramsay Ltd v IRC and Furniss v Dawson*

**[A8.68]** There are no specific DTA anti-avoidance rules in UK domestic legislation. However, UK case law has established certain fundamental anti-avoidance principles.

*WT Ramsay Ltd v Inland Revenue Commissioners* [1981] 1 All ER 865 involved a number of pre-ordained steps whereby a company sought to reduce a substantial capital gains tax liability through the use of a series of transactions. It was held in the House of Lords that where a transaction has pre-arranged artificial steps which serve no commercial purpose other than to save tax, the proper approach is to tax the effect of the transaction as a whole.

*Furniss (Inspector of Taxes) v Dawson and related appeals* [1984] 1 All ER 530 was heard three years later and applied the same principles as those established in *Ramsay*.

These cases highlight the risk that HMRC may seek to disregard the effect of an inserted step such as the use of a company in a transaction solely to obtain benefits under a DTA.

Diagram 9

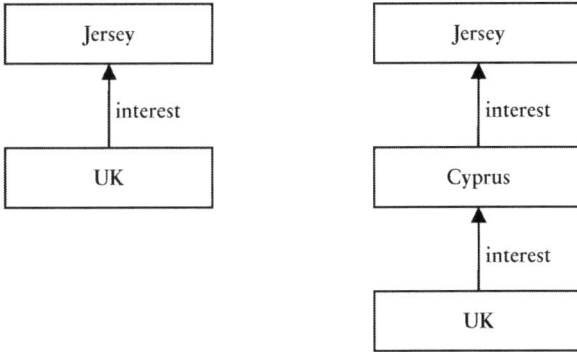

In Diagram 9 the UK company would be required to withhold 20% tax from the interest paid to the Jersey company. If the UK company paid interest instead to a Cyprus company the withholding tax may be reduced under either the Interest and Royalties Directive or the UK/Cyprus DTA. The Cyprus company would then pay interest to the Jersey company from which no tax would be withheld under Cyprus domestic law.

In addition to the anti-avoidance provisions in the Interest and Royalties Directive and the UK/Cyprus DTA, HMRC could argue that the use of the Cyprus company was an artificial step, and that interest was pre-ordained to be paid to the Jersey company. The interest payment would then be treated as paid directly by the UK company to the Jersey company and therefore subject to withholding tax.

If the Cyprus company had genuine economic substance, similar to the substance necessary to establish beneficial ownership (see **A8.55**), it would be more difficult for HMRC to argue that the use of the Cyprus company was an 'artificial' step.

## Domestic anti-avoidance in other jurisdictions

### Germany

**[A8.69]** In 2007, Germany extended its DTA anti-avoidance rule in s 50(d)(3) of the Income Tax Act. Section 50(d)(3) provides that the benefit of a DTA will not be available to a parent company receiving dividends from a German subsidiary:

(a)  if its own immediate shareholder(s) would not qualify for benefit under a DTA; and

(b)  there are no economic or other relevant business reasons for the interposition of the parent company; or

(c)     the parent company generates less than 10% of its income from trading activities;

(d)     the parent company does not have sufficient substance to undertake its trading activities.

A parent company must show that *none* of the above three criteria are met, which may be difficult in many cases. For instance, the second criterion will only be avoided if the parent company is a trading company rather than a holding company. This can be problematic when using a UK holding company to invest in Germany.

There is an exception from the rules for companies which are listed, which should include companies listed on AIM. A subsidiary of a listed company would therefore also qualify for treaty benefits because its own shareholder would qualify. This is shown in Diagram 10.

Therefore, when establishing a German subsidiary the treaty anti-avoidance rule will not apply if:

(a)     dividends are paid directly to an operating company;

(b)     dividends are paid directly to a listed holding company, and not via a sub-holding company;

Diagram 10

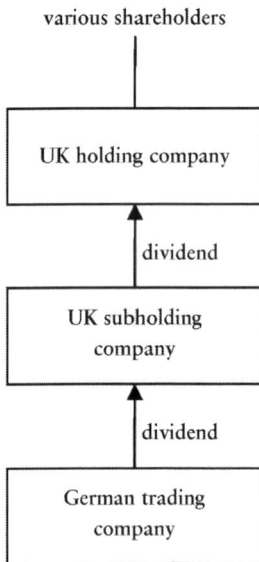

**China**

**[A8.70]** Most of the DTAs concluded by China require that the recipient of interest, royalties or dividends is the beneficial owner in order to obtain benefit under the DTA. On 27 October 2009, the State Administration of Taxation

(SAT) issued Circular Guoshuihan [2009] No 601 (Circular 601) which provides guidelines on how 'beneficial ownership' should be interpreted. This is narrower than the interpretation in *Indofood*, *Prevost*, and adopted by other countries.

A 'substance over form' approach is adopted, but a number of factors are outlined which would indicate that the recipient does not have beneficial ownership:

(1)   The recipient is obligated to pay or distribute at least 60% of the income to residents of a third country or region within a prescribed time frame;

(2)   Except for holding the rights or assets deriving the income, the recipient has no or almost no business activities;

(3)   The recipient is a company whose assets, activities and staff are not commensurate with the level of its income;

(4)   The recipient has no or almost no control its income or the rights or assets from which the income is derived;

(5)   The recipient is not subject to tax on the income, or the effective tax rate is very low;

(6)   A lender is also a borrower under a loan agreement on similar terms (eg amount, interest rate, and contract date);

(7)   A licensor of copyrights, patents, or other intellectual property has another contract with a third party on the similar terms.

The Circular specifies that a 'conduit company' cannot be a beneficial owner, and defines this as a company which is established for the purposes of avoiding or reducing tax. Such a company will only have the necessary legal form and does not carry on substantive business activities such as manufacturing, trading or management.

## Australia

**[A8.71]** The Australian General Anti-Avoidance Rule (GAAR) can apply to structures to take advantage of DTAs.

This is confirmed in Taxation Determination TD 2010/20 which gives the following example. A company in the Cayman Islands establishes a subsidiary in the Netherlands to acquire an Australian group. The Netherlands company disposes of the Australian group within a short period of time, such that the gain arising is treated as business profits and therefore taxable under Australian domestic law. The Australia/Netherlands DTA would provide relief, but does not apply because the Netherlands company was not established for a commercial reason.

## UK General Anti-Abuse Rule ('GAAR')

**[A8.72]** The introduction of the UK GAAR arguably draws a line in the sand for many types of international tax planning. The legislation has been a long time coming following a report by Graham Aaronson QC and an extensive consultation period. In many ways the GAAR looks to bring an end to evolutionary incremental tax planning where tax planners have often sought to interpret the letter of the law rather than its original intention, often developing different versions of the same planning to combat specific anti-avoidance legislation. The impact of the GAAR in international tax planning remains to be seen and indeed the operation of such a rule in other countries such as Canada and Australia has not always been successful. However it is fair to say that from now on the potential application of the GAAR will need to be considered in all kinds of tax planning. No doubt over time views will evolve over which transactions are or are not 'GAARable', but in the meantime all we have to rely on is the legislation and HMRC guidance. Whether the transaction falls under the new rules should therefore be considered in every international tax planning assignment.

In essence, the GAAR applies from 17 July 2013 to taxes listed in FA 2013, s 206(3) and to NICs from 31 March 2014 (date of Royal Assent of the National Insurance Contributions Act 2014).

HMRC has issued detailed guidance on the GAAR see (www.hmrc.gov.uk/av oidance/gaar.htm) including an expanded set of examples of arrangements that will or will not, in their view, be caught. The guidance is important because it must be taken into account by a court or tribunal (FA 2013, s 211(2)) and as such it has a quasi-legal status. References to this guidance are therefore provided where relevant. The examples given provide some useful references and benchmarks, including some unusual exemptions for long held practices. On the other hand there are clear steers on mismatches in accounting treatment which might lead to a one sided tax deduction.

Notwithstanding HMRC's guidance, the GAAR will create uncertainty in assessing whether some tax planning is abusive or not. The basic test is whether the arrangements can be 'reasonably regarded as a reasonable course of action in relation to the relevant tax provisions, having regard to all the circumstances . . . '. A test requiring a view to be taken on 'reasonableness' is by its nature subjective rather than objective—thus creating uncertainty as different people have different views on what is reasonable. However, provided there is a reasonably held view that the tax arrangements taken as a whole are a reasonable course of action the GAAR should not apply.

The scope of the GAAR as enacted in FA 2013 appears wider than the 'egregious' schemes as envisaged in the Aaronson report. Furthermore, there is no clearance mechanism to provide any comfort, which creates a high degree of uncertainty.

As the GAAR falls within self-assessment, its possible application must be considered at an early stage in any tax planning.

Any arrangement assessed to fall the wrong side of the dividing line is self-defeating—the tax advantage must be self-assessed out. Where the taxpayer does not consider the GAAR applies, it is then a matter for HMRC to invoke the GAAR to challenge (and counteract on a just and reasonable basis) arrangements they consider to be abusive. However, there is an important safeguard for taxpayers: an Advisory Panel, which HMRC must consult before issuing a counteraction notice. The taxpayer is entitled to make representations to the Panel. The Advisory Panel will provide an opinion on whether the arrangements in question are or are not abusive—but HMRC is not bound by their opinion.

Where HMRC counteract arrangements, there is further uncertainty over what is 'just and reasonable' because the counteraction must be based on a judgment by HMRC of what would have happened absent the abusive tax purpose (FA 2013, s 209(2), see also **C2.5**). This is cited as being the transaction the taxpayer would most likely have carried out (following the approach in the Hong Kong case of *Tai Hing Cotton Mill Ltd v Liu Chong Hing Bank Ltd (No 2)* [1986] AC 519, [1986] 1 All ER 897, PC) and might not necessarily be that which gives rise to the highest additional tax liability. It nevertheless inserts a degree of fiction which is unwelcome.

*Tax arrangements*

**[A8.73]** The GAAR applies to 'tax arrangements' which are 'abusive', with arrangements being defined as follows:

Tax arrangement—any arrangement which, viewed objectively having regard to all the circumstances, it is reasonable to conclude has obtaining a tax advantage as its main purpose or one of its main purposes (FA 2013, s 207(1) and **C3.2**). This is a relatively low threshold, so many arrangements will fall to be 'tax arrangements' but these will only then be susceptible to counteraction if they then pass the higher threshold of being 'abusive' under the double reasonableness test (see **C3.9**).

Points to note from HMRC's guidance are:

- C3.3: in determining if it is 'reasonable to conclude' that obtaining a tax advantage is the main purpose/one of the main purposes of the arrangements, 'it is neither necessary nor appropriate to enquire whether any particular person (eg the taxpayer, or a promoter) actually had that intention'. However, usually the participants will have had that aim where there is a tax advantage.
- C4.1: 'arrangements' includes any agreement, understanding, scheme, transaction or series of transactions (whether or not legally enforceable). Something relatively simple like converting a limited company to an unlimited company potentially therefore falls under this wide definition (C4.2).
- C4.3:'arrangements can be viewed both narrowly and widely, so the GAAR can be applied to an arrangement that is part of a wider arrangement or to the wider arrangement as a whole. This prevents the weighting of purposes from being manipulated, such as combining a tax scheme with a commercial transaction'.

Tax advantage is defined in s 208 as including (but not limited to):

- relief or increased relief from tax;
- repayment or increased repayment of tax;
- avoidance or a reduction of a charge to tax or an assessment to tax;
- avoidance of a possible assessment to tax;
- deferral of a payment of tax or an advancement of a repayment of tax; and
- avoidance of an obligation to deduct or account for tax.

Clearly this could affect many international tax planning techniques, such as double dips, and one sided tax deductions.

'Tax' is the taxes to which the GAAR applies (IT, CT, CGT, IHT, PRT, SDLT, ATED and any amounts chargeable as if they were CT so for example it would cover a CFC charge).

In terms of further interpretation, HMRC have suggested that:

- 'it will usually be clear whether trying to obtain a tax advantage is the main purpose of a particular arrangement'. For example where the arrangement would not have been carried out at all if it were not for the tax advantage, or where a non-tax objective is secondary to obtaining the tax advantage; and secondly
- 'determining whether obtaining a tax advantage is one of the main purposes can be more difficult'. This looks at whether the arrangements have been reshaped in some way to significantly change the tax result, eg changing the terms and conditions, changing an accounting period

*Meaning of 'abusive'*

**[A8.74]** Only those tax arrangements which are abusive will be within the scope of the GAAR. The meaning of 'abusive' is given at FA 2013, s 207(2)-(6). This is the core part of the GAAR legislation. Part D of HMRC's guidance states at D1.1 that 'it is important to remember a key policy objective of the GAAR—that it is targeted at abusive tax avoidance schemes' and goes on to say that planning can nevertheless be challenged under other anti-avoidance provisions where it falls outside the GAAR.

Section 207(2) states that '[t]ax arrangements are 'abusive' if they are arrangements the entering into or carrying out of which cannot reasonably be regarded as a reasonable course of action in relation to the relevant tax provisions, having regard to all the circumstances . . . '. This is the famous double reasonableness test which introduces a high degree of subjectivity—reasonable in whose opinion—the man on the Clapham Omnibus?

Amongst the examples given as not reasonable is structuring to overcome the intended purpose of the legislation. Does this mean for example that if HMRC maintain that double non-taxation was ever intended under a Tax Treaty then any transaction which results in that outcome is not reasonable? This remains to be seen.

The GAAR also rejects the premise from old case law that taxpayers are at liberty to use their ingenuity to reduce their tax bills by any lawful means.

The guidance also states that consideration of the relevant tax provisions and the policy objectives of those provisions is important:

- 'in most cases the relevant principles and policy objectives will be apparent from the legislative provisions concerned, read together with any non-legislative material (such as Parliamentary debates or press releases)' FA 2013, s 211(3) states that a court or tribunal may take into account:
  - guidance, statements or other material (HMRC, Minister or 'anyone else') that was in public domain at time arrangements were entered into;

- evidence of established practice at that time.
- Even with recurrent recourse to Hansard, it may be difficult to discern the original underlying policy objectives. Amendments to legislation (eg specific anti-avoidance rules) 'might make it possible to see what types of arrangements were intended to excluded from certain tax benefits'. Where this happens, later arrangements attempting to circumvent that anti-avoidance will thus be inconsistent with those 'updated' policy objectives.

Contrived or abnormal steps:

- Examples given to illustrate what steps might count as contrived are temporarily breaking a group structure or temporarily transferring property to a foreign nominee to exploit a loophole.

Arrangements intended to exploit shortcomings in tax provisions:

- Legislation may give rise to unintended opportunities.
- D2.7.1 makes it clear that if 'keep off the grass warnings' such as TAARs to prevent certain behaviour are not heeded, arrangements intended to exploit any shortcomings in the TAAR will fall within the GAAR.

The double reasonableness test—whether the arrangements 'cannot reasonably be regarded as a reasonable course of action'

- The guidance states that this does not mean whether the arrangements are reasonable in relation to the tax provisions. Instead, it is whether, taken as a whole, there can be a reasonably held view that the tax arrangements were a reasonable course of action.
- C5.10.2: in an appeal to a tribunal or court, a judge would need to consider the range of reasonable views that could be held in relation to the arrangements. This could for example include counsel's opinion that the tax arrangements are a reasonable course of action (provided of course that all relevant information has been made available to counsel, assuming it is in itself a reasonably held view.
- According to HMRC, a 'commonly held view' is that if the Parliamentary draftsman fails to get legislation right that there is nothing wrong with the defects being exploited. The Guidance refutes this as wholly inconsistent with the basic purpose of the GAAR, and such a view will not be regarded as reasonable.

*Conclusion*

**[A8.75]** The GAAR applies to tax arrangements entered into on or after the date of Royal Assent (17 July 2013). It does not apply to arrangements entered into before 17 July. However, if arrangements span the date of Royal Assent, transactions prior to Royal Assent can be taken into account if they help show that the arrangements after Royal Assent are not abusive. HMRC cannot, however, do the opposite and refer back to transactions pre-dating Royal Assent to show that later arrangements are abusive. So, arrangements will only be caught by the GAAR if elements of larger arrangements after Royal Assent are themselves abusive.

It is reassuring that the guidance does not aim to interfere with the allocation of taxing rights between countries as a result of the application of double tax treaties. In particular at B5 the guidance states:

'There is a network of treaties between states setting out rules that govern the taxation of investment and business activities involving more than one state. These treaties (which are typically based on an OECD model treaty) are usually referred to as 'double tax treaties', and their purpose is to avoid subjecting such investments or activities to tax in more than one state and to prevent tax evasion. The UK has entered into over 100 such treaties, and they are given effect in domestic tax law.

'Many of the established rules of international taxation are set out in double taxation treaties. These cover, for example, the attribution of profits to branches or between group companies of multi-national enterprises, and the allocation of taxing rights to the different states where such enterprises operate. The mere fact that arrangements benefit from these rules does not mean that the arrangements amount to abuse, and so the GAAR cannot be applied to them. Accordingly, many cases of the sort which have generated a great deal of media and parliamentary debate in the months leading up to the enactment of the GAAR cannot be dealt with by the GAAR . . .

. . . However, where there are abusive arrangements which try to exploit particular provisions in a double tax treaty, or the way in which such provisions interact with other provisions of UK tax law, then the GAAR can be applied to counteract the abusive arrangements.'

In the view of HMRC then this would therefore seem to offer a contrast between the kind of arrangements that have made the press for the likes of Amazon and Google and more extreme international tax planning techniques. In that instance we can expect the GAAR to target the more aggressive planning, whilst leaving the more 'vanilla' arrangements to be dealt with under the BEPS proposals.

As mentioned earlier, in theory GAARable arrangements are to be self-assessed. If they are not (and it is unlikely that taxpayers will self-assess in the negative). The onus is therefore on HMRC to demonstrate that the arrangements could not be 'reasonably regarded as a reasonable course of action in relation to the relevant tax provisions'. If we look at the way in which this has been attempted in other countries, tax authorities have met with mixed results. In France the principle has been established for many years and one could argue that it has on balance approved to be an effective weapon (not least as the French Tax Code is 10% of the size of the UK one). By implication one could therefore contend that it obviates the need for more prescriptive legislation. In other countries such as Canada and Australia, it has met with more mixed success, with one recent success for the taxpayer in Canada (*Birchcliff Energy Ltd v The Queen* (2012-1087(IT))) as the CRA had failed to demonstrate or disclose the policy statement that the abuse was going against. On the other hand, Australia has recently taken steps to strengthen its current GAAR rules (which incidentally have been around for nearly 100 years) and even the EU Commission has sought to introduce a European GAAR. One thing is for certain. With the combination of the GAAR and the BEPS action plan, the world of international tax planning will not be the same again.

# Recent double tax agreement updates with the UK

## UK/USSR Double Taxation Convention no longer applies to Tajikistan

**[A8.76]** Tajikistan does not consider the UK/USSR convention to have effect in Tajikistan. Therefore, the UK will not be applying the terms of the convention for residents of Tajikistan for profits arising on or after 1 April 2014 (for companies) or income and gains arising on or after 6 April 2014 (for individuals). Claims to unilateral relief are still available in respect of Tajik taxes levied on profits, income or gains arising in Tajikistan.

A UK-Tajikistan Double Taxation Agreement was signed on 1 July 2014, and will enter into force after legislative procedures have been completed.

## Other new double tax agreements

**[A8.77]** The Double Taxation Convention between the UK and Spain, which was signed in London on 14 March 2013 will enter into force on 12 June 2014.

The Double Taxation Agreement between the UK and Albania, which was signed in Tirana on 26 March 2013, entered into force on 30 December 2013.

The Double Taxation Convention between the UK and Norway, which was signed in London on 14 March 2013, entered into force on 17 December 2013.

A new comprehensive Double Taxation Agreement between the United Kingdom and the Republic of Zambia was signed in Lusaka on 4 February 2014 by James Thornton, British High Commissioner to Zambia, and Alexander Bwalya Chikwanda, Zambian Finance Minister.

The Double Taxation Agreement between the UK and China, which was signed in London on 27 June 2011, and the Protocol signed in Beijing on 27 February 2013, entered into force on 13 December 2013.

The UK/Panama Double Taxation Convention entered into force on 12 December 2013

# Foreign Account Tax Compliance Act ('FATCA')

**[A8.78]** The purpose of this Act is to ensure the Internal Revenue Service (IRS) can identify and collect the appropriate tax from US persons holding financial assets outside the US and is intended to prevent tax evasion by US persons through foreign bank or financial accounts, as well as shell entities.

The rules seek to obtain information about US account holders or US owners from certain foreign entities, particularly foreign financial institutions (FFIs) and some non-financial foreign entities (NFFEs) FATCA compels these foreign entities to disclose information by imposing a 30% penalty withholding tax against entities not in compliance.

FATCA will place a significantly increased burden on any non-US FFI and certain NFFEs who must identify, document and report on US persons. FFIs include institutions such as:

- Banks
- Funds
- Brokers
- Custodians
- Asset managers
- Insurance companies

NFFEs that are most likely to be impacted by the regulations are trusts.

The UK tax authorities entered into the FATCA Inter-Governmental Agreement (IGA) in September 2012 and withholding obligations began on 1 January 2014.

## Non-US IGAs with the UK tax authorities

**[A8.79]** The UK has entered into a number of IGAs to improve international tax compliance through the exchange of information. The UK has entered into such agreements with the following countries to date:

- Guernsey
- Jersey
- Gibraltar
- Isle of Man
- Cayman Islands
- Bermuda
- Montserrat
- Turks and Caicos
- British Virgin Islands
- Anguilla

The IGAs signed with the Crown Dependencies are reciprocal, meaning that UK financial institutions also have reporting obligations under the terms of the agreements. The overseas territories IGAs are non-reciprocal, so that the UK financial institutions do not have reporting obligations under the terms of the agreements.

# A9

# Residence of companies

**[A9.1]** This Chapter deals with the residence of companies. The concept of residence is important because it typically determines where a company is subject to tax. In the UK, corporation tax is chargeable on the worldwide profits of any company which is resident in the UK. CTA 2009, s 5 provides that:

'(1) A UK resident company is chargeable to corporation tax on all its profits wherever arising.

(2) A non-UK resident company is within the charge to corporation tax only if it carries on a trade in the United Kingdom through a permanent establishment in the United Kingdom.'

Other jurisdictions will often make a similar distinction between the taxability of resident and non-resident companies. Understanding the residence of a company is therefore fundamental to determining its tax liability in the UK and elsewhere.

International tax planning in relation to residence typically involves consideration of the following issues:

- Determining if a company is resident in the UK, and therefore subject to tax in the UK. Similar principles may apply to determine if a company is resident elsewhere and this Chapter briefly considers the residence tests in Australia, China, Hong Kong, Ireland, India, South Africa and the US.
- Taking steps to avoid a company becoming resident in the UK.
- Where a company is resident in the UK and another jurisdiction, considering whether a double tax agreement (DTA) determines in which jurisdiction it is resident. In the absence of such an agreement, certain UK tax reliefs may not apply to dual resident investing companies.
- Migrating the residence of a company to or from the UK, and planning to mitigate the tax consequences of doing so.
- Incorporating an overseas branch of a UK company, or a UK branch of an overseas company.

# Basic principles—UK residence

## *Statutory definition*

**[A9.2]** Although legislation provides that UK resident companies are subject to corporation tax, it does not give the term residence an exhaustive definition. The only legislative provisions that define residence for corporation tax purposes are CTA 2009, s 14 and CTA 2009, s 18.

## CTA 2009, s 14

**[A9.3]** CTA 2009, s 14 states that a company incorporated in the United Kingdom is treated as resident in the UK. This effectively renders irrelevant the management and control test for companies incorporated in the UK, as they are presumed to be UK tax resident regardless of where they are managed and controlled.

## CTA 2009, s 18

**[A9.4]** The exception to the rule in CTA 2009, s 14 is in CTA 2009, s 18, which provides that where a UK incorporated company is resident outside the UK under the terms of a DTA, this takes precedence over s 14. This establishes the general principle that the DTA overrides domestic law in respect of a company's residence.

However, it is necessary that the DTA applies in the first instance. DTAs apply to avoid double taxation, and do not normally apply otherwise. If a company would be considered resident both in another jurisdiction (under resident domestic law) and in the UK, then a DTA may apply to determine in which jurisdiction the company in actually resident.

A company may be resident in two countries in the following circumstances:

(a)     a UK incorporated company that is managed and controlled in another jurisdiction;
(b)     an overseas incorporated company that is managed and controlled in the UK;
(c)     a company that is managed and controlled in two jurisdictions.

In these cases CTA 2009, s 18 provides that if:

(a)     a tax treaty exists between the two jurisdictions in question; and
(b)     the tax treaty determines tax residence to be with one jurisdiction,

then that determination will apply under UK tax law as well.

The provision in tax treaties that deals with this is commonly referred to as the 'tie breaker' provision. This provision typically provides that where a company is resident in two countries, it will be considered to be resident for tax purposes where its place of 'effective management' is situated.

The distinction between 'management and control' and 'effective management' is subtle but significant in this context. This is discussed further at **A9.20**. It must also be noted that not all tax treaties have the residence 'tie breaker' clause and in such cases a company will be unable to rely on CTA 2009, s 18 to avoid UK tax residence.

CTA 2009, s 18 will not apply to treat a UK incorporated company as resident outside the UK unless a relevant tax treaty applies. When looking at establishing tax residence outside the UK for a UK-incorporated company, one should look at jurisdictions that have a DTA with the UK with a tie breaker clause that awards tax residence definitively to one jurisdiction.

For instance the UK's DTAs with the Jersey, Guernsey and the Isle of Man do not have tie breaker clauses. A company which is incorporated in the Isle of Man but managed and controlled in the UK would therefore be considered to be resident in both the Isle of Man and the UK.

If a company is likely to be managed and controlled in a jurisdiction with which the UK does not have a relevant DTA, it should be incorporated there rather than in the UK so that residence does not remain in the UK even if management and control is exercised outside the UK.

## Case law definition

**[A9.5]** The statutory definitions of residence are inclusive rather than exclusive. Therefore, when considering residence, the courts have been forced to give it a broader meaning.

Early views on the concept of residence ranged from regarding a company as resident where it was incorporated, to a purely factual test which sought to regard residence as the place where the company itself, as a legal entity, could be said to act.

The test eventually established by case law is that a company is treated as resident in the UK if its 'central management and control' is exercised in the UK.

### De Beers Consolidated Mines Ltd v Howe [1905] 5 TC 198

**[A9.6]** The management and control test for determining a company's residence was first set down in *De Beers Consolidated Mines v Howe* [1905] 5TC198. The De Beers company was established in South Africa and its main mining business was carried on there. However, the controlling board of directors exercised its powers in the UK. The company was determined to be resident in the UK and it was held that ' . . . a company resides where its real business is carried on . . . and the real business is carried on where the **central management and control** actually abides' (my emphasis).

### Unit Construction Co Ltd v Bullock [1959] 3 All ER 831

**[A9.7]** This case involved companies operating in East Africa. The constitution of each company gave control to the board of directors, who were required to hold their meetings outside the UK. However, as a question of fact, it was found that real control was being exercised by the directors of the parent company in the UK, even though this was unconstitutional. The UK directors had usurped the central management and control from the board. Accordingly, the company was held to be resident in the UK for tax purposes.

This emphasises the importance of the activities of the directors, rather than what they are legally able or required to do.

The principle established in *Unit Construction* does not apply where the board of directors continues to meet but under the influence of a shareholder or parent company. It is entirely proper for a shareholder to be concerned with the affairs of a company in which he has invested. However, a dominant UK shareholder must take care not to go beyond influence and exercise central management and control.

The risk of this may be reduced if a non-UK resident acts as the immediate shareholder of the company in question. For instance, a UK resident individual may establish a non-resident trust to hold his shares in a non-resident company. The influence of the shareholder of the company is then the influence of non-resident trustees. They must exercise their influence in favour of the UK resident individual, but he cannot exercise influence directly, and therefore he is not in a position to usurp central management and control from the board so easily.

### Untelrab Ltd v McGregor [1996] STC (SCD) 1

**[A9.8]** A Jersey subsidiary of a UK group previously had a board comprising Bermuda residents. It was held that when the composition of the board changed to one comprising UK residents who exercised central management and control in the UK, the company became resident in the UK from that time.

Assessments to UK tax for earlier years raised by HMRC were not upheld on the grounds that the directors at that time were resident in Bermuda and the company was not resident in the UK.

### Wood v Holden [2006] STC 443

**[A9.9]** The taxpayer appealed against a decision that a non-resident company which existed for the purposes of a tax planning scheme should be regarded as UK resident. The appeal was successful on the basis that the board made independent decisions outside the UK and that these decision making powers had not been bypassed by others resident in the UK. The fact that there may have been an external influence of the shareholder and his tax advisers was not relevant in that a decision still had to be made and was still made independently.

Although the non-resident company only took part in a single transaction, the conduct of this single transaction was sufficient to evidence that management and control was exercised outside the UK. It was not necessary that further board meetings were held to discuss other matters.

This case also emphasises the need for directors to properly consider matters on which they are making decisions. The directors in this case were professional directors employed by ABN Amro, and the court agreed that they had an additional professional responsibility to properly consider matters. In other situations, however, directors should ensure that they discuss and consider all matters and briefing materials which are before them, and evidence this if necessary. It is not sufficient that board minutes are drafted and approved without the directors actually meeting.

### News Datacom Ltd v Atkinson [2006] STC 732

**[A9.10]** In this case, in 1992 a company incorporated in Hong Kong transferred its business to another group company which was resident in the UK, and which subsequently left the group. If the transferor company were resident in the UK then the transfer would have been within TCGA 1992, s 171 and a degrouping charge would arise under TCGA 1992, s 179 when the transferee company left the group.

The transferor company held no board meetings in the UK between 1988 and 1991, and no board meetings anywhere between 1991 and 1992. However, a board meeting was held in the UK in 1992 to register a transfer of the company's shares, and to amend the articles insofar as they related to the quorum for board meetings.

The Special Commissioners held that:

(a)    as there had been no usurpation of the board's authority, central management and control was located where the board meetings were held;
(b)    the board meeting held in the UK was of 'a purely ministerial or housekeeping nature and was to be disregarded as not being an exercise of central management and control'.

In the decision, the Special Commissioners referred to the existence of an Executive Committee which was appointed by the board to carry out its decisions. The Commissioners did not consider that the carrying out of decisions constituted central management and control.

This decision provides some comfort and flexibility to groups who want to carry out certain activities in the UK without prejudicing the location of central management and control.

However, the decision also emphasises the importance of maintaining clear records of who participated in board meetings, and where they were located even if they participated via telephone. The Commissioners considered these records in some detail.

### Laerstate BV v HM Revenue and Customs Comrs (2009) TC 00162

**[A9.11]** A former director (and sole shareholder) of a company incorporated in the Netherlands continued to exercise significant control over the company. He took decisions in the UK, and these were executed by the remaining director of the company who did not consider them himself.

As in the *Unit Construction* case, it was not relevant that the former director did not have legal authority to take these decisions.

This case highlighted the importance of appropriate procedures being followed:

•    the directors must properly consider decisions and not simply execute decisions which have been made elsewhere;
•    the directors must be informed of matters affecting the company, and this must be evidenced by correspondence;

- the directors must be suitably qualified to take decisions, and not be over-reliant on advice.

## Role of directors

**[A9.12]** The importance attached to the role of the directors in the *De Beers* case stems from the fact that under English company law, the board of directors are responsible for managing and controlling the affairs of a company on behalf of its shareholders. The focus on the activities of the directors is also important in noting the distinction between the day-to-day conduct of the business and the vital, decision making functions which represent the central functions of a business.

Some jurisdictions permit (such as France) or require (such as German in the case of AGs and larger GmbHs, and the Netherlands) a two-tier board structure—a supervisory board and a management board. The supervisory board will generally be responsible for monitoring and advising the management board, which includes appointing its members. However, it does not take (or have the power to take) decisions.

HMRC consider that the management and control rests with the management board rather than the supervisory board, as all decisions are generally taken by the management board. Even if the supervisory board must approve decisions, the *Unit Construction* decision (see **A9.7**) requires consideration of where the decisions are actually taken (even if subject to negative approval).

In some jurisdictions, greater authority may be reserved to the shareholders than in the UK. For instance, in a German GmbH the shareholders can instruct management directly. However, under the principle established in *Unit Construction* it is again still necessary to consider where decisions are actually taken. Unless the shareholders actually do take decisions affecting the company, central management and control will remain with the directors.

## UK resident directors

**[A9.13]** Where there are a majority of UK resident directors, the risk of management and control being exercised in the UK is increased, because decisions are likely to be taken in the UK without a formal board meeting.

The HMRC view of this risk is summarised in INTM120210, which reproduces the previous text of ITH334 (now withdrawn):

> 'It has been said that the management and control test is bad because it leads to the nonsense of directors flying to Jersey for board meetings. That device is no longer of use to a United Kingdom incorporated company which is resident here anyway. But it is quite easy for a company operating here to incorporate in Jersey and claim to be managed and controlled there with only a minimal tax cost in Jersey provided the shareholders are not resident there. So the criticism is still relevant.

> On the face of it the point is a valid one. But criticism of that kind is concerned as much with questions of fact as of concept and the two things must be kept separate in our minds. There is, in principle at any rate, no reason why a business which is visibly in this country should not be managed and controlled from, let us say, Jersey.

But if the directors of that company are working in this country on a regular basis and probably living here as well, it may be highly unlikely that they will be doing anything more in Jersey than reaffirming decisions already taken here. If that is so the mere fact of having board meetings in the Channel Islands is irrelevant. The question is, where do the people concerned exercise management and control. If they really do it in this country and go through a meaningless form of words in Jersey, that will achieve nothing for them but, of course, it leaves the Revenue with the difficult burden of proof.

It may help to put the problem into a context which is very familiar. A small grocery store is run by a man A and his son A junior. There is a grandfather, once sole proprietor, who no longer takes an active part in the business but owns the property and makes his views known on important matters. A company is formed with A as chairman and managing director, the son as sales director and grandfather as a mere shareholder. Every year A and his son spend holidays in Jersey. It is very unlikely that any body of Commissioners would accept that by holding their only board meetings when they are in Jersey they had made the company resident outside the United Kingdom. Both level two and level three management are exercised by A and his son and they are clearly based in the United Kingdom.

But an alternative scenario has grandfather as both major shareholder and chairman with A and his son as full-time working directors. Grandfather takes no part in the day-to-day running of the business but takes a keen interest in its success and his word on important matters carries great weight. Here level three management emerges as something quite distinct from level two which remains with A and his son. Level three may be found either with grandfather alone or with grandfather and his sons acting as a board depending on the extent of grandfather's real power. If grandfather moves to Jersey, level three management may genuinely move with him, either because he alone exercises central management and control from Jersey or because the board meetings, at which he plays an important part, are held there. Grandfather's move to Jersey may, however, have Jersey tax consequences for the company if he retains his shares because some tax advantages may be lost if the company is owned by Jersey residents.'

As HMRC consider where the directors actually exercise their powers, the board of an offshore company should not include a majority of UK residents. This reduces the risk of central management and control being inadvertently exercised in the UK.

### HMRC view of residence—SP1/90

**[A9.14]** The view of HMRC on tax residence and 'management and control' is set out in the Statement of Practice 1/90, and reflects the cases discussed above.

HMRC acknowledge that the place of management and control is a question of fact which refers to the highest level of control of the business and the place of strategic management. Their view is that although commonly a company's strategic decisions will be made by directors in board meetings, this is not always the case. The place of directors' meetings is significant only insofar as those meetings constitute the medium through which central management and control is exercised. If, for example, the directors of a company were engaged together actively in the UK in the complete running of a business which was wholly in the UK, the company would not be regarded as resident outside the UK merely because the directors held formal board meetings outside the UK.

In summary, HMRC's approach is:

(a)    To look at the facts and decide whether the directors of a company in fact exercise central management and control.

(b)    Where the directors do exercise management and control, HMRC will look at where this power is exercised. The place where the directors formally meet will not necessarily be where management and control takes place.

(c)    Where the directors do not exercise management and control, HMRC then look to establish where and by whom it is exercised. This may be a majority shareholder where the power of the board has been usurped. Care should therefore be taken when a non-UK shareholder is replaced with a UK shareholder. The risk of a HMRC challenge to residence may increase, and it becomes more important that the directors are properly exercising their powers outside the UK.

In addition to the decisions taken at board meetings, it is critical that the board of directors is provided with appropriate information and documentation to make the decisions at board meetings. For example, the board cannot decide to approve a major contract without detailed information—a feasibility/ profitability report etc.

### *Liquidations and administrations*

**[A9.15]** The activities of a liquidator or administrator of a company incorporated outside the UK may lead to central management and control being located in the UK.

In order to reduce the risk that HMRC argue that central management and control is located in the UK, the following steps should be taken:

•    A majority of non-UK residents are appointed eg two non-resident liquidators and one resident liquidator.

•    Any strategic decisions are taken outside the UK, and documentation is prepared to support this—for instance minutes of meetings, and travel documentation showing that any UK resident participants were not in the UK at the time. Strategic decisions could include decisions relating to the sale of assets or the terms of any agreement with creditors. Creditors meetings can however take place in the UK.

In some cases, the relevant insolvency law will not give the liquidator or administrator sufficient authority to exercise central management and control.

## Planning checklist to determine residence

**[A9.16]** The following summary illustrates some of the practical steps that could be taken by an offshore company to ensure that it is not regarded as UK resident by virtue of management and control being exercised in the UK.

For the purposes of establishing central management and control, the distinction between executive and non-executive directors is not usually relevant as they are both equally empowered to take decisions.

| | |
|---|---|
| Company documenta-tion | The company's articles of association (or equivalent) should lawfully empower the directors to control and manage the company. |
| | Directors must do what they are legally empowered to do and this should be appropriately evidenced. |
| | Directors should take planning and policy decisions and this should be appropriately evidenced. |
| | Major planning and policy decisions should be made outside the UK. |
| | Minutes of board meetings should be available and must document the actual decisions made by the directors. |
| | The company's articles of association can require that requirements relating to the directors are complied with, for instance: |
| | – Directors' meetings must be held outside the UK, and (if possible) UK residents must not attend by way of telephone. |
| | – Where this is not expected to be possible, a majority of attendees must be resident outside the UK. |
| | – A majority of directors must be resident outside the UK. |
| Location of board meet-ings | Board meetings and management meetings should be held outside the UK and should be formally documented. |
| | Attendance by telephone or video-conference should be infrequent, and only where it is unavoidable that some directors attend the meeting from outside the offshore jurisdiction. When telephone meetings or video conferences are used, the chairman should be present and significantly more directors should be present in the offshore jurisdiction where the meeting takes place than in any other country. |
| Personnel | Only non-UK resident managers/directors should have the authority to hire or dismiss senior staff. |
| | The board of directors should set remuneration levels for senior staff. |
| | Powers, duties and responsibilities of all senior staff must be defined and documented to mitigate the risk that they are able to exercise central management and control in place of the directors. |

Directors    A majority of the directors should be resident outside the UK. Ideally, the chairman should be resident outside the UK, particularly if he is to use a casting vote.

A majority of the directors present at each board meeting should be resident outside the UK.

Board meetings must be held regularly (depending on business requirements and the scale and nature of the business).

Major contracts should be entered into following specific approval at board meetings. Where this cannot be done, they should be entered into on the authority of a non-UK resident director or manager.

Discussions must take place on major issues and there should be no 'rubber-stamping' of significant decisions made outside the meeting.

A UK resident director should not have the power to, and should not in practice, make binding decisions without reference to the board.

### Key decisions

**[A9.17]** The above summary emphasises the need for the board of directors to make all key decisions affecting the company, such as:

(a)    approval of the financial statements of the company;
(b)    dividend policy of the company;
(c)    approval of annual budgets, profit forecasts, cash flow forecasts and similar projections;
(d)    changes in capital structure;
(e)    funding of the company and arranging financial facilities;
(f)    pension policies;
(g)    product service lines;
(h)    management changes;
(i)    major new capital projects
(j)    significant changes in marketing strategy, pension policies and employee relations.

# Basic principles—dual residence and DTAs

### Dual tax residence

**[A9.18]** It is possible for a company to be regarded as tax resident in more than one jurisdiction. This could arise because of the different criteria for tax residence in different parts of the world. For example, a company could be incorporated in the UK and therefore considered by virtue of CTA 2009, s 14 to be tax resident in the UK. At the same time, that company could have its management and control exercised in India and therefore deemed to be tax resident in India as well.

### Resolution provided by DTAs

**[A9.19]** The above example of dual residence indicates the importance of a DTA which assists in resolving such conflicts. However, DTAs have to overcome the fact that the test of residence differs in each jurisdiction. Article 4 of the OECD Model Convention (see CHAPTER **A8**) attempts to resolve this problem by including a 'tie breaker' clause which states that where:

> 'a person other than an individual is a resident of both contracting States, then it shall be deemed to be a resident of the State in which its place of effective management is situated.'

A list of the DTAs which contain tie-breaker clauses (current at 1 December 2009) is in the HMRC International Manual at INTM120070.

CTA 2009, s 18 provides that a company is resident in another jurisdiction if that is the position under the relevant DTA. Accordingly from a UK perspective, where two jurisdictions claim taxing rights by virtue of a company's residence, the following scenarios are possible:

(a)     no DTA is in place between the two countries;
(b)     a DTA is in place and contains a tie breaker clause in the residence article;
(c)     a DTA is in place but does not contain a tie breaker clause.

The implications for a dual resident company in each of these scenarios is discussed below.

### Effective management

**[A9.20]** This 'effective management' test which is provided for in many DTAs is similar (but not the same) as the concept of central management and control discussed earlier. In seeking to define the term, the Commentary to Article 4 of the OECD Model Convention says that effective management is:

> 'the place where key management and commercial decisions that are necessary for the conduct of the entity's business are in substance made. The place of effective management will ordinarily be the place where the most senior person or group of persons . . . makes its decisions, the place where the actions to be taken by the entity as a whole are determined; . . . An entity may have more than one place of management, but it can only have one place of effective management at any one time.'

In a Swiss Case in May 2013 (2C_1086/2012, 2C_1087/2012), the Federal Supreme Court ruled on the definition of the place of effective management in the context of an offshore finance company. A Swiss holding company had established a financing subsidiary in Guernsey, granting loans to fellow subsidiaries of the group. In considering whether the effective management of the Guernsey company was in Switzerland, the Federal Supreme Court decided that 'place of effective management' was the economic and effective centre of a company. In essence this was the management of daily business activities and the place of board meetings or the general assembly was to be disregarded. The court concluded that the key business decisions were taken by the Swiss holding company and, that the Guernsey company was subject to tax in Switzerland.

As with central management and control, the place of effective management will be a question of fact.

The view was once held in the UK that both these tests meant the same thing, but it is now understood that there is a distinction between the two tests. Effective management will broadly be located where the head office is and where company operations are directed from, whereas central management and control can be exercised away from this head office. The place where the managing director, finance director and sales director operate from is an example of a head office. The place of effective management ie the head office, would not be altered if the directors held board meetings in a different jurisdiction, but there is a risk that central management and control may shift to this jurisdiction as a result of the meetings.

However, the two tests are in many ways similar and therefore central management and control and effective management will often be located in the same place.

In SP1/90, HMRC confirms this approach as follows:

'It is now considered that effective management may, in some cases, be found at a place different from the place of central management and control. This could happen, for example, where a company is run by executives based abroad, but the final directing power rests with non-executive directors who meet in the UK. In such circumstances the company's place of effective management might well be abroad but, depending on the precise powers of the non-executive directors, it might be centrally managed and controlled (and therefore resident) in the UK.' (para 22)'

### *Revenue and Customs Comrs v Smallwood* [2007] EWCA Civ 462

**[A9.21]** The decision in *HMRC Commissioners v Smallwood 78 TC 560* considered the definition of 'effective management' in the UK/Mauritius DTA. Although the case concerned a trust, the principles established will also be relevant when determining the effective management of a company.

Mr Smallwood—a UK resident individual—settled a trust for the benefit of himself and his family, the assets of which included shares standing at a substantial gain. The initial trustees were resident in Jersey. Following advice given by UK tax advisers, the Jersey trustees were replaced with a Mauritius trustee company, after which the shares were sold. The trustee company was a wholly owned subsidiary of the UK tax advisers' affiliated firm in Mauritius, and was recommended by the UK tax advisers. The shares held by the trust were sold, and in the same tax year, UK resident trustees (being Mr Smallwood and his wife) were appointed.

TCGA 1992, s 77 provided that the gain would be taxed on Mr Smallwood as the settlor of the trust. He argued that he was entitled to relief under Article 13(4) of the UK/Mauritius DTA, which provided that 'capital gains from the alienation of any property  . . .   shall be taxable only in the Contracting State of which the alienator is a resident'.

Under the definition in Article 4(1) of this DTA, the trust would be treated as resident in both the UK and Mauritius, as UK trustees had been appointed during the tax year. It was therefore necessary to consider Article 4(3) which provided that:

'Where by reason of the provisions of paragraph 1 of this Article a person other than an individual is a resident of both Contracting States, then it shall be deemed to be a resident of the Contracting State in which its place of effective management is situated.'

Mr Smallwood argued that the effective management of the trust was in Mauritius and therefore it should be treated as a resident of Mauritius and not the UK.

In considering the definition of 'place of effective management', the Special Commissioners referred to the concept established in *Wensleydale's Settlement Trustees v IRC* [1996] STC (SCD) 241 that effective management was 'realistic, positive management'. They also considered the commentary on the OECD Model Tax Convention, that the place of effective management is the place where 'key management and commercial decisions' are made.

The Special Commissioners found that although the decision to sell the shares was taken in Mauritius by the directors of the trustee company, this was a 'low level management decision'. The real management decision of the trust was to dispose of the shares in a tax efficient way, and the UK tax advisers took this decision in the UK. The place of effective management was therefore located in the UK.

In arriving at this conclusion, the Special Commissioners considered that the following facts were particularly relevant:

(a) The trustee was approached by the UK tax advisers. The tax planning proposals and the expectation that the shares would be sold were set out in an email, which also referred to the appointment of the trustees being made 'on that basis'.

(b) All parties were informed by the UK tax advisers of the planning exercise and the expectation that the trustees would instruct for the shares to be sold.

(c) The UK tax advisers prompted the trustees to instruct that the shares be sold.

(d) An employee of the trustee company sought advice from the UK tax advisers in the absence of the directors of the trustee company.

The HMRC appeal in the *Smallwood* case was subsequently heard by the High Court in January 2009 and the Court of Appeal in July 2010, but the effective management point was not considered. The courts decided in favour of HMRC based on the technical interpretation of s 77 alone.

### Central management and control in *Smallwood*

**[A9.22]** If the *Smallwood* case had turned on central management and control (rather than effective management), it is possible that it would have been decided in favour of the taxpayer. Professional trustees had been appointed, and had genuinely undertaken the transactions required of them.

This is similar to the situation in *Wood v Holden (Inspector of Taxes)* [2006] EWCA Civ 26, [2006] 1 WLR 1393 where it was held that the directors had exercised central management and control, as they were required to under local company law, even though they closely followed the guidance given by professional advisers in the UK.

However, in *Wood v Holden*, Chadwick LJ commented that the place of effective management in that case was the same as where central management and control was exercised. This would appear to indicate that the guidance given by professional advisers etc did not prevent the directors from exercising effective management.

Unfortunately this distinction was not considered on appeal in *Smallwood*.

### Planning for effective management following *Smallwood*

**[A9.23]** The principles established by the *Smallwood* case are only relevant to the definition of 'effective management'. *Wood v Holden (Inspector of Taxes)* [2006] EWCA Civ 26, [2006] 1 WLR 1393 and other recent cases remain relevant to the definition of 'central management and control', and arguably impose less onerous requirements on offshore directors. Where possible therefore, dual resident companies should be avoided in order that it is not necessary to rely on the 'effective management' tie breaker clause in a DTA.

For example, a company which is incorporated in France but centrally managed and controlled in the UK would need to rely on its effective management being undertaken in France in order to be treated as not resident in the UK for tax purposes. It may be easier for the company to ensure that central management and control is undertaken outside the UK.

However, where it is necessary to rely on 'effective management' being undertaken in a particular jurisdiction, a number of planning points can be taken from the *Smallwood* case:

(a)    Parties involved in transactions should not be given the expectation of a particular outcome.

(b)    Significant freedom must be given to offshore directors in undertaking transactions.

(c)    Where advice is sought from advisers this must not constitute guidance as to how a particular transaction should be undertaken. The directors should consider any advice received as part of their wider deliberations, and not be guided only by the advice. The directors should clearly document this.

(d)    Offshore directors must be appointed on genuine terms; there must be no expectation of what transactions they will undertake once appointed, and they must not be appointed on the basis that they are bound to undertake particular transactions.

(e)    Shareholders should be given a choice of potential directors to appoint, and should appoint directors without undue influence from their advisers.

### OECD Model Tax Convention

**[A9.24]** In the 2008 update to the OECD Model Tax Convention, the guidance on the definition of 'place of effective management' was made more general, leaving it open to interpretation on a case by case basis. The guidance used to read:

'1.    . . .    The place of effective management is the place where key management and commercial decisions that are necessary for the conduct of the entity's business are in substance made. The place of effective management will ordinarily be the place where the most senior person or group of persons (for example a board of directors) makes its decisions, the place where the actions to be taken by the entity as a whole are determined; however, no definitive rule can be given and all relevant facts and circumstances must be examined to determine the place of effective management.'

It now reads:

'2.     . . .   The place of effective management is the place where key management and commercial decisions that are necessary for the conduct of the entity's business as a whole are in substance made. All relevant facts and circumstances must be examined to determine the place of effective management.'

In other words, the guidance no longer specifically refers to 'the place where the most senior person or group of persons (for example a board of directors) makes its decisions'. This should allow greater regard to be taken of where operational staff undertake their activities when determining where effective management is located.

## No DTA

**[A9.25]** Where there is no DTA between two jurisdictions, there is no agreement between them for the avoidance of double taxation. A company faced with this position may therefore be subject to tax in both jurisdictions.

It is possible that the domestic law provides some measure of relief from double taxation. For example, in the UK, there is unilateral relief available in certain circumstances, whereby credit is given in the UK for tax suffered overseas. However, this is not always as beneficial as the relief that may be provided under a treaty. For example, the unilateral relief in the UK is subject to a limit of 26% (the main rate of corporation tax) and therefore, if tax is suffered overseas, at say 40%, the company is still effectively paying tax at a rate of 40%.

Although double tax relief is available (and therefore double taxation avoided), the income is still taxable in both jurisdictions—unlike where a DTA is in place, where the income may not be taxable in one jurisdiction.

## DTA exists with a tie breaker clause

**[A9.26]** Where a company is regarded as tax resident in two jurisdictions and a DTA exists, the DTA must be considered to determine which of the two jurisdictions has taxing rights.

The UK domestic tax position on dual residence is set at in CTA 2009, s 18. This provides that a UK dual resident company will be treated as non UK resident where there is a DTA between the UK and the other jurisdictions which contains a 'tie breaker' clause under which the company is resident in the other jurisdiction.

For example, the UK/Belgium DTA has such a tie breaker clause that grants tax residence to the jurisdiction in which the place of effective management is situated. Accordingly, if effective management is situated in Belgium, the company will be considered to be not resident for UK tax purposes.

### DTA without a tie breaker clause

**[A9.27]** The existence of a DTA without a tie breaker clause to determine tax residence leaves a company outside CTA 2009, s 18. For residence purposes at least, a company is in the same position as if there were no DTA in place.

### Alternative tie breaker clauses

**[A9.28]** Not all DTAs contain an 'effective management' tie breaker.

For example, the UK/USA DTA provides that the tax residence of a dual resident company will be determined by the competent authorities of the two jurisdictions (ie HMRC and the IRS) reaching an agreement. Until the competent authorities have reached agreement, CTA 2009, s 18 will not apply and the company will remain dual resident.

A competent authority ruling of this kind is costly and time-consuming, and therefore very rare.

### Anomalous provisions

**[A9.29]** There are two important UK tax provisions which do not follow the rule set out in CTA 2009, s 18:

(a)     A UK incorporated company which is resident outside the UK by virtue of s 18 remains subject to the Controlled Foreign Companies (CFC) rules.

(b)     A non-UK incorporated company which is resident in the UK by virtue of its central management and control being exercised in the UK is treated as an 'overseas person' for the purpose of ITA 2007, ss 720, 731. Income arising to such a company may therefore be attributed to UK resident shareholders under these provisions.

### Dual resident investing companies (CTA 2010, s 109)

**[A9.30]** Although there are disadvantages to a company being regarded as dual resident, such a company could also take advantage of domestic tax reliefs in each of the jurisdictions in which it is considered resident. For example, a company that is resident in the UK and USA (and hence dual resident absent competent authority agreement) could relieve its losses against the profits of both a UK group and a US group. As a result, anti-avoidance legislation exists in the UK (and elsewhere) to address these issues.

CTA 2010, s 109 prevents certain dual resident companies from surrendering their losses by way of group relief. The legislation was introduced to deal with dual resident companies that were used to exploit group relief provisions such as illustrated in Diagram 1 below.

Diagram 1

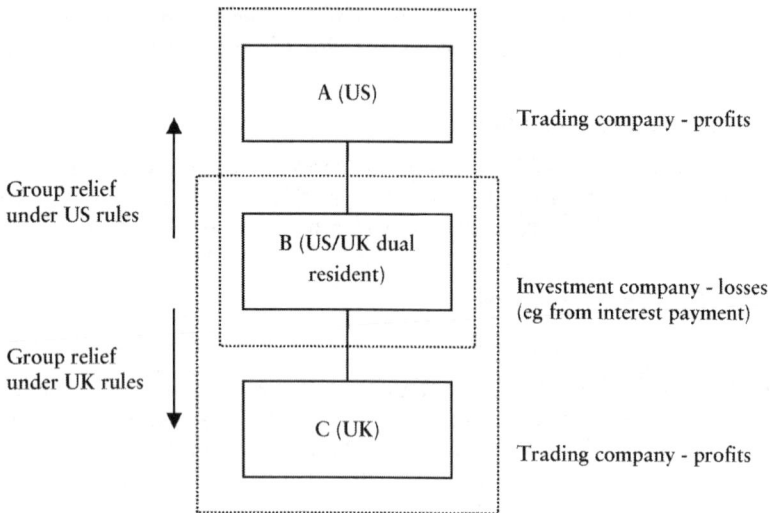

## Dual residence for CTA 2010, s 109 purposes

**[A9.31]** For the purposes of CTA 2010, s 109, a dual resident company is a company which is UK resident and also within the charge to tax in another jurisdiction by virtue of:

(a)     incorporation there; or
(b)     having a place of management there; or
(c)     local laws providing it is resident there for any other reason.

It should be noted that 'territory' is a wider term than 'country' and encompasses a state or other political sub-division (for instance Hong Kong).

HMRC's view is that most dual resident companies within the scope of CTA 2010, s 109 would be incorporated in the United States.

## Effect of CTA 2010, s 109

**[A9.32]** Section 109 prevents certain dual resident companies from surrendering their losses by way of group relief. The effect of s 109 is that no loss or other amount can be surrendered if the surrendering company is a dual resident investing company. CTA 2010, Pt 22, Ch 1 also applies to prevent a dual resident investing company obtaining double relief for its losses by some other means.

Section 109 only applies to a dual resident **investing** company. The definition of an 'investing' company is a company:

(a)     that is not mainly or wholly of trading throughout the accounting period; or
(b)     whose activities are mainly financial activities as defined in s 109(4).

Examples would include:

(a) group financial services companies;
(b) holding companies;
(c) former trading companies whose activities have ceased in a given accounting period (as they would not be trading throughout the period).

## Example

As illustrated in Diagram 1, A and B are members of a US group and B and C are members of a UK group. On the basis that B has incurred losses and A and C are profitable, B could surrender its losses against both A's profits and C's profits and therefore gain double relief. However, s 109 prevents B's losses from being available for surrender against C's profits as B is a dual resident investing company.

## Capital gains

**[A9.33]** Similar provisions exist under TCGA 1992, s 171 in order to prevent the avoidance of tax on capital gains. Absent these provisions, a company could transfer an asset in respect of which a capital gain has accrued to a dual resident investing company at no gain/no loss. The recipient company could then realise the capital gain by disposing of the asset to a third party.

An intra-group transfer to a dual resident investing company does not fall within the no gain/no loss rules of TCGA 1992, s 171, and a chargeable gain may therefore arise on such a transfer.

## Migration

**[A9.34]** Migration refers to the transfer by a company of its tax residence from one jurisdiction to another. This may be done for a number of reasons. Historically, many companies migrated overseas as a way of escaping the burden of UK taxation and taking advantage of lower tax rates. Alternatively, commercial factors may require a company to be incorporated in the UK but be tax resident in another country, for example due to all the directors being resident in that country. Whatever the reasons for a company's migration, there will be a need to consider and address the issue of dual residence to ensure that there is certainty around the tax residence position (ie to ensure that the company is only resident in one jurisdiction).

This is discussed further above, but should be considered before migration occurs so that there is no ambiguity in the tax treatment for a company after its supposed migration.

## Redomiciliation

**[A9.35]** The company law of some jurisdictions (although not the UK) will allow a company to disincorporate there and reincorporate in another jurisdiction, constituting a migration for both legal and tax purposes.

The tax consequences of a redomiciliation will typically be the same as a migration. A UK resident shareholder in a company which is redomiciled will typically (applying the test in *Rae (Inspector of Taxes) v Lazard Investment Co Ltd* [1963] 1 WLR 555, 41 TC 1, HL — see **A14.8**) not be treated as having made a disposal of his shares, as no such disposal has taken place for legal purposes in the overseas jurisdictions.

Jurisdictions where a redomiciliation is possible include Luxembourg, Cyprus, Malta, the Isle of Man and Jersey.

**No DTA**

**[A9.36]** In the absence of a DTA, a successful migration to or from the UK will depend on the domestic rules of the country from which a company is trying to migrate.

Where a company is trying to migrate out of the UK and it is UK incorporated, the transfer of central management and control out of the UK will not mean that it ceases to be UK resident (due to the incorporation test set out in FA 1988, s 66).

However, if the company is not UK incorporated, the transfer of its central management and control to another country would normally cause it to cease UK residence.

**DTA with tie breaker clause**

**[A9.37]** The existence of a DTA with a residence tie breaker clause can support the migration.

Where a UK resident company is seeking to migrate to another jurisdiction with which the UK has a DTA with a residency tie breaker clause, it can do so without UK incorporation prejudicing its position if the tie breaker so allows. This is because CTA 2009, s 18 allows a UK incorporated company to be treated as non UK resident for treaty and domestic law purposes if it satisfies a relevant tie-breaker.

**No tie breaker clause**

**[A9.38]** As with the normal rules on residency, a DTA without a tie breaker clause will mean that a company is in the same position as if no DTA were in place.

# Planning—outward migration

**[A9.39]** A company may wish to move its residence ie migrate outside the UK for a number of reasons, but the most usual reason is so that it ceases to be subject to UK corporation tax.

There are broadly two ways in which a company can migrate its business from the UK:

- The company itself ceases to be resident in the UK.
- The company transfers assets (for example of an overseas branch) to a company outside the UK (ie it incorporates the branch).

As noted above at **A9.35**, it is not possible to reincorporate or redomicile a UK company.

The broader issues arising from a migration are considered in CHAPTER **B8**.

### Ceasing residence in the UK

**[A9.40]** It is necessary under TMA 1970, s 109B for a company to give notice of its intention to cease to be resident in the UK. This notice alerts HMRC that a migration is intended and for them to approve arrangements by the company for the payment of any outstanding tax liabilities.

As discussed above, a UK incorporated company does not cease to be UK tax resident simply by transferring its central management and control outside the UK unless a relevant DTA exists and CTA 2009, s 18 applies. However, a non-UK incorporated company can cease to be UK tax resident on this basis.

In any event, a migration of a UK company may lead to tax liabilities arising, and these are outlined below.

### End of accounting period

**[A9.41]** It is likely that a migrating company will cease to be within the charge to corporation tax and therefore be treated as ceasing to trade. This could lead to:

(a)     balancing charges or allowances arising on plant and machinery;
(b)     deemed receipt of income from trading stock;
(c)     the end of an accounting period.

It is also necessary to consider TCGA 1992, s 185 which may trigger an exit charge. This point is considered in more detail at **A9.43**.

### Notification

**[A9.42]** TMA 1970, s 109B ensures that a UK company migrating overseas does not leave behind any outstanding tax liabilities which HMRC consider would be difficult to collect following migration. The legislation requires that a company intending to migrate:

(a)     notifies HMRC of its intention to cease to be UK tax resident;
(b)     provides a statement of its tax liabilities;
(c)     makes arrangements to ensure that these liabilities are settled; and
(d)     obtains the approval of HMRC of these arrangements.

In practice, HMRC will also require:

(a)     confirmation from the local Inspector of any outstanding liabilities;
(b)     appointment of an individual in the UK under a power of attorney to act as the company's representative;

(c)     a guarantee against possible liabilities from a bank or a UK group company which is financially sound.

If a company ceases to be resident without giving notice making the arrangements, it is liable to a penalty of up to 100% of any tax which is unpaid as at the date of migration. This includes tax in respect of the current and preceding periods and includes PAYE and certain other taxes as well as corporation tax.

It would also include any corporation tax arising as a result of exit charges.

The penalty for failure to notify falls primarily on the company. However, if HMRC are unable to recover the penalty from the company, they can seek to recover this from a related company which has been a member of the same group in the twelve month period before migration, or from controlling directors of the company (or of a company which controls it).

Companies should take steps to pay any outstanding liabilities prior to migration. If a company is unable to obtain HMRC approval under TMA 1970, s 109B, this should enable migration to occur nevertheless, without any penalties arising.

Detailed guidance notes for companies wishing to migrate from the UK are set out in Statement of Practice 2/90 which includes the details that should be provided to HMRC.

**Exit charge**

**[A9.43]** In addition to the administrative requirements associated with the migration of a UK company, it is also necessary to consider any tax liabilities that may arise directly as a result of the migration.

TCGA 1992, s 185 imposes a charge on the unrealised capital gains of a company which migrates from the UK. This 'exit charge' deems a company to have disposed of and reacquired all of its assets at market value immediately before it ceases to be UK tax resident. This may result in a capital gain arising, which is subject to UK corporation tax.

In many cases, a company's most valuable assets will be goodwill and other intangible assets, which may not be recognised on its balance sheet.

For intangible assets acquired or created after 1 April 2002 (and which therefore fall outside TCGA 1992), equivalent provisions to s 185 exist within CTA 2009.

Where a company has significant unrealised gains, the exit charge under s 185 may make a migration prohibitively expensive.

If the company continues to be within the scope of UK corporation tax (for instance if it continues trading in the UK through a permanent establishment) the assets which are still within the charge to corporation tax fall outside of s 185. Although this presents a way of avoiding the charge, the assets concerned would still be within the charge to UK tax. Depending on the circumstances, this may defeat the objective of the migration. Section 185 has recently been brought into focus by the case of *National Grid Indus* and the subsequent introduction by HMRC of TMA 1970, Sch 3ZB by FA 2013—see **A7.45** for further details.

**[A9.44]** A recent EU case regarding exit charges (C-164/12 (*DMC Beteiligungsgesellschaft mbH v Finanzamt Hamburg-Mitte*: C-164/12 [2014] 2 CMLR 1391) was heard by the Court of Justice. The facts of the case were two Austrian corporate partners in a German limited partnership exchanged their partnership interests with a German company in return for shares in the latter. The German tax authorities argued that the reorganisation was equivalent to a migration and an exit charge should apply based on the market value of the interest in the partnership (not the book value, which was the amount received by the partners). The partners argued that this was against the freedom of establishment. The Court of Justice agreed with the German tax authority approach.

It was also held that the German tax authorities decision to allow deferral of the exit charge over a five year period was reasonable on the basis that a period of any longer would increase the risk of non-recovery.

## Postponement of exit charge

**[A9.45]** When a UK company migrates from the UK by moving the location of its effective management and control, it is taxable on the deemed disposal of its assets at market value. Following the decision in *National Grid*, this charge would be punitive as it arises on unrealised gains on chargeable assets (eg land and buildings and shares), loan relationships and derivatives and intangibles – notwithstanding that a loss may arise on individual assets on their eventual sale. Where SSE is available, this mitigates the charge that would otherwise arise on shares in trading companies. However, the exit charge still applies to the disposal of subsidiaries which do not qualify for SSE, and other assets held by the company (including goodwill and land and buildings).

The UK currently grants a deferral option in limited circumstances (essentially where the migrating company is a 75%+ subsidiary of a UK parent and both companies make a joint election within two years of migration).

Due to the rulings made in recent EU cases, Schedule 49 of Finance Act 2013 has been introduced to deal with the exit charge on chargeable assets (TCGA 1992, ss 185–187). This schedule provides that where a company that is incorporated in the UK or another EEA territory becomes a resident of, and carries on a business in, another Member State of the EU (or EEA), it has two deferral options to manage corporation tax exit charges that arise under any of the following: TCGA 1992, ss 185 and 187, CTA 2009, ss 859–860, CTA 2009, s 609 and CTA 2009, s 333.

Both of these new options allow companies to defer the time at which they must settle some or all of the tax they are due to pay under current tax rules. The standard instalment method involves a calculation of the tax due at the time of migration, with staged payments of the tax attributable to exit charges then made in six equal annual instalments starting with the first payment due after 9 months. This option allows all assets to be taken together, without distinguishing between different classes, and without the need for them to be tracked individually after migration.

The realisation method is more directly related to the economic life of assets. It involves a calculation of the tax due at the time of exit, with the tax attributable to exit charges allocated on an asset by asset basis. Companies are obliged to provide HMRC with an annual statement identifying the realisations of assets in that period, and the tax would become payable in respect of those realisations. For intangible assets, derivative contracts and loan relationship profits, the useful economic life of each asset would be determined at the point of migration. Tax would then be payable in equal annual instalments over the useful life of the asset. Tax related to exit charges on any other assets may be deferred for up a maximum of ten years, or until the disposal of the asset if sooner.

The amounts deferred under either of the above options will be subject to interest.

It is generally considered that the new rules do not go far enough to match the precedent in the NGI decision. It is therefore possible that exit charges could be still be challenged on this basis.

The NGI case was further endorsed by the decision in *European Commission v Portuguese Republic*: C-38/10 [2013] 1 CMLR 273, ECJ delivered on 6 September 2012.

### Example

A Limited is a UK incorporated company which owns 100% of the ordinary share capital of B Limited, as shown in Diagram 2.

Diagram 2

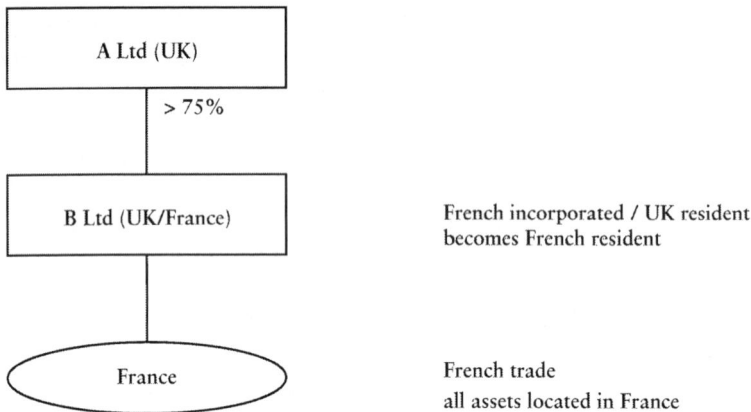

A Ltd (UK)

> 75%

B Ltd (UK/France) — French incorporated / UK resident becomes French resident

France — French trade / all assets located in France

B Limited is a French incorporated company which has assets in France which it uses for its trade, but is regarded as UK tax resident under the central management and control test.

B Limited transfers its central management and control wholly to France and therefore ceases to be UK tax resident and makes a joint election under s 187 with A Limited to postpone the s 185 charge.

The deemed disposal of B Limited's assets results in the following gains and losses:

| Asset 1 | £20,000 gain |
|---------|--------------|
| Asset 2 | £40,000 gain |
| Asset 3 | £80,000 gain |
| Asset 4 | £60,000 loss |
| Net | £80,000 gain |

An appropriate proportion of the net postponed £80,000 gain becomes chargeable if:

(a)     an asset is disposed of by B Limited within six years of it ceasing to be UK resident;

(b)     A Limited disposes of ordinary shares in B Limited which result in it holding less than a 75% shareholding; or

(c)     A Limited itself ceases to be UK resident.

### Incorporation of overseas branch

**[A9.46]** Gains may also be deferred on the incorporation of an overseas branch. TCGA 1992, s 140 provides for a deferral of any chargeable gain that accrues where part or all of a non-UK trade is transferred to an overseas company.

TCGA 1992, s 140 will apply where:

(a)     a UK company carries on a trade outside the UK through a permanent establishment;

(b)     the transfer of the trade is wholly in exchange for shares or shares and loan stock issued by the transferee company to the transferor company;

(c)     the shares issued (together with any other shares already held by the transferor company) amount to at least 25% of the ordinary share capital of the transferee company.

The deferred gain will be subject to tax when the shares or loan stock are subsequently disposed of. This includes a disposal of qualifying corporate bonds the gain on which would otherwise be exempt.

As shares are issued as part of a branch incorporation, it may be necessary to consider if notification is required under the International Movement of Capital provisions (see CHAPTER **A12**).

Section 140 can be used as an alternative to migration whereby a company simply transfers its non-UK trade as opposed to formally migrating. The relief under s 140 operates by deferring the gain until the point at which either:

(a)     the assets transferred are sold within six years of transfer;

(b)     or the shares which are given in consideration for the transfer of assets are themselves sold.

Where a company is looking to physically relocate its business abroad, s 140 may provide a tax-free method of achieving this. A migration of a company itself would result on gains which could not be deferred unless the conditions of s 187 are satisfied—which would not be if for instance there were no UK parent company. If the assets are first transferred to an overseas branch, then the branch can be incorporated tax-free under s 140.

This is shown in Diagram 3.

**Diagram 3**

Step 1

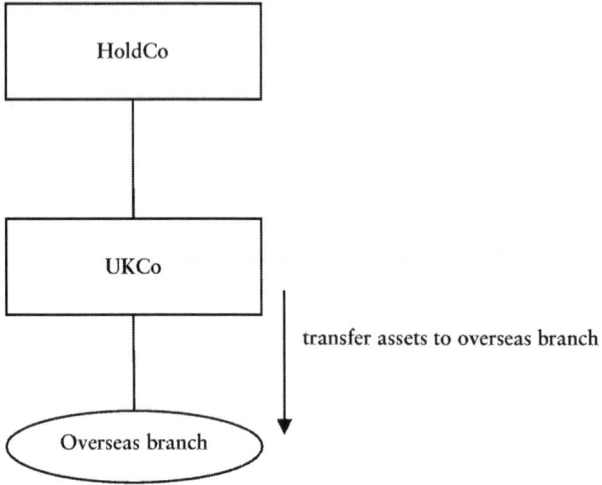

There is no disposal of any assets by the UK company at this stage because it still owns all the assets.

and the assets are still within the charge to UK corporation tax

Step 2

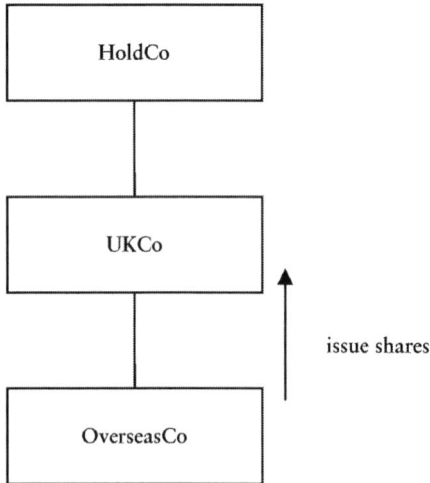

Any gain that might arise on the transfer of the business out of the UK company is deferred per s140 TCGA 1992.

It is not necessary that the branch is incorporated into a company established in the same jurisdiction as the branch itself. A UK company could therefore transfer the assets of a branch in (say) Jersey to a company in Ireland and qualify for relief under TCGA 1992, s 140.

## Intangible assets

**[A9.47]** Similar provisions exist in CTA 2009, s 827 for intangible assets created or acquired after 1 April 2002. An important difference is that s 827 requires that the branch incorporation is undertaken for bona fide commercial reasons. Clearance can be obtained from HMRC that this condition is satisfied.

Some intangible assets (including goodwill) may fall within TCGA 1992, s 140 and some within s 827. Where a branch has been established as a result of a UK trade expanding overseas, any goodwill may be treated as having been created when the UK trade commenced (and therefore within s 140 if this was before 1 April 2002). Where a branch is entirely separate from an existing UK trade, any goodwill may be treated as having been created when the branch was established.

The full list of conditions for s 140 and s 827 can be summarised as follows:

| TCGA 1992, s 140 | CTA 2009, s 827 |
| --- | --- |
| Applies to all chargeable assets except those within CTA 2009, Part 8 | Applies to intangible assets acquired or created after 1 April 2002 |
| All assets used for the trade (or part trade) which is incorporated (except cash) must be transferred | All assets used for the trade (or part trade) which is incorporated (except cash) must be transferred |
| The transfer must be wholly or partly in exchange for shares and loan stock | The transfer must be wholly or partly in exchange for shares and loan stock |
| The transferor must hold at least 25% of the ordinary share capital in the new subsidiary | The transferor must hold at least 25% of the ordinary share capital in the new subsidiary |
| The aggregate gain on the transfer of the assets to the new subsidiary is calculated and deferred. | The gain on each asset transferred to the new subsidiary is calculated separately and deferred. |
| No claim can be made if a claim is made under the EU Mergers Directive (TCGA 1992, s 140C) | No claim can be made if a claim is made under the EU Mergers Directive (TIOPA 2010, s 116) |
| No requirement that incorporation is for bona fide commercial purposes | Incorporation must be for bona fide commercial purposes |

## Practical issues

**[A9.48]** Some practical issues which arise when considering a branch incorporation include:

- Not all overseas companies can issue ordinary share capital and specific steps may need to be taken to ensure that the parent company satisfies the requirement to hold at least 25% of ordinary share capital in the new subsidiary. HMRC Business Brief 87/09 outlines what constitutes ordinary share capital of an overseas company.
- Relief is only available where the UK parent company carries on a trade through a permanent establishment, and relief is not therefore available for non-trading branches, or for assets not used in the trade of the branch.
- All of the assets used for the trade of the branch must be transferred, and it is important that the UK parent company identifies them in advance of the incorporation so that they can be included in any transfer documentation.

The incorporation will also result in the cessation of the branch's trade for UK corporation tax purposes, as it is no longer carried on by the UK parent company. This will have a particular impact on losses and unutilised foreign tax.

If the branch activity was considered part of another trade of the UK parent company, any losses may be carried forward against future profits of this trade (CTA 2010, s 45). However, if the branch was considered a separate trade, any losses would be extinguished.

Any utilised foreign tax which arose in respect of the branch cannot be carried forward, even if another branch is subsequently established in the same jurisdiction (TIOPA 2010, s 76).

### Incorporation of EU branch—Mergers Directive

**[A9.49]** The Mergers Directive aims to ensure that companies can transfer trades between EU Member States on a tax-free basis. It may therefore be relevant when considering the incorporation of a UK branch of a company in another Member State, or the incorporation of a branch in another member state which is held by a UK parent company.

The Directive has been implemented in the UK as TCGA 1992, s 140A (for the transfer of UK trades) and TCGA 1992, s 140C (for the transfer of non-UK trades). As an EC Directive, it should also be implemented in other member states, although the precise mechanics and the conditions do vary from one EU country to another. In particular some EU countries are known to apply the Mergers Directive in a more generous way than the UK.

In the UK, both s 140A and s 140C are subject to the following conditions:

- the parent company of the branch and the transferee company must be tax resident in an EU Member State;
- the transfer must be wholly in exchange for shares or securities of the transferee company;
- the transfer must take place for bona fide commercial reasons.

Under s140A, the transfer of a UK branch will take place at no gain/no loss provided that the assets of branch continue to be within the charge to UK corporation tax ie the transferee company continues to have a permanent establishment in the UK as a result of the branch activities. This would be the case if the UK branch is incorporated into a new UK subsidiary.

Similar provisions apply for capital allowances purposes (CAA 2001, s 561), and to intangible assets (CTA 2009, s 819).

The operation of s 140C is slightly more complicated. Where a UK parent company transfers the assets of an overseas branch, a chargeable gain arises and corporation tax is calculated in the normal way. However, a tax credit is given for the tax which would have been payable in the EU Member State where the branch is located, but for relief under the Mergers Directive in that Member State. It is therefore necessary to calculate what the tax would have been on the branch incorporation, and confirm that the Mergers Directive (and not some other relief) applies to relieve this tax. This is illustrated in the example below.

Similar provisions apply to intangible assets and loan relationships (TIOPA 2010, s 116).

### Example

**[A9.50]** A Ltd is a UK company which has a branch in Ireland. A Ltd transfers the assets of the branch to a company established in this Member State in exchange for preference shares. All of the ordinary shares are held by another group company.

The chargeable assets of the branch (including local premises and goodwill) have a base cost of €100k and a current market value of €600k. The local tax rate is 22% but relief can be claimed under the local implementation of the Mergers Directive. The calculation of the capital gain for local tax purposes is the same as in the UK.

A Ltd has a UK corporation tax liability of €120k (€500k x 24%) against which it can claim a notional tax credit of €110k (€500k x 22%) by virtue of TCGA 1992, s 140C. Relief under TCGA 1992, s 140 is not available because A Ltd does not hold 25% of the ordinary share capital in subsidiary following the incorporation.

# Planning—inward migration

**[A9.51]** A company can also migrate to the UK from another jurisdiction. A company may wish to be resident in the UK to:

(a)   take advantage of a UK DTA;
(b)   avoid the attribution of a gain under TCGA 1992, s 13 (which only applies to non-resident companies);
(c)   prevent a company being treated as resident of another jurisdiction with a higher effective tax rate than the UK.

There is no specific UK legislation to deal with inward migrations except the fact that the profits of the company would now be chargeable to UK taxes. The practical guidelines outlined at **A9.16** equally apply when seeking to establish or maintain tax residence in the UK.

A CT41G form will need to be sent to HMRC within three months of the company becoming subject to UK tax. This should also satisfy the requirement to notify chargeability to UK tax within twelve months of the end of the period.

However, the way in which a company effects its migration to the UK—the practical steps it takes to become UK tax resident—are extremely important. It is not uncommon for a company to implement steps that seek to inward migrate but which are ineffective.

The company should be able to clearly identify the date on which it last was resident outside the UK and demonstrate a change in its central management and control which changes this position. An example of this could be a board meeting called to effect the migration ie the appointment of UK resident directors with existing non UK resident directors resigning. Although this is one example, and central management and control is a question of fact, such steps would help to show that there is a shift of decision making powers from overseas to the UK and this should further be supported by facts that indicate that such powers have actually been exercised from the UK since that date.

If board meetings have previously taken place in the UK, there is a risk that HMRC may challenge whether central management and control had actually been exercised outside the UK at all and therefore argue that the company was always tax resident in the UK.

An overseas company may have significant accumulated profits or gains that it wishes to repatriate to its UK resident parent company. If the overseas company is resident in a non-qualifying jurisdiction the payment of a dividend would not be exempt in the hands of a small UK company (see Chapter **A16**). A possible solution would be to migrate the company to the UK and then declare a dividend. This dividend should then be exempt in the hands of a small UK company.

## Incorporation of a UK branch

**[A9.52]** The tax consequences of incorporating a UK branch are relatively straightforward.

Trading losses and capital allowances balances are transferred from the branch to the new subsidiary, provided the parent company (or its group) owns at least 75% of the new subsidiary immediately after the transfer (CTA 2010, Pt 22, Ch 1). There is no requirement that the transferor company is UK resident—merely that it is subject to corporation tax, which would be the case if it had a UK branch.

If the 75% test is not met, the losses are not carried forward into the new subsidiary, and for capital allowances purposes assets are treated as having been sold and reacquired for market value.

For chargeable gains purposes, the transfer of assets from the branch to the new subsidiary will take place at no gain/no loss (TCGA 1992, s 171) provided the parent company and the new subsidiary are in the same group (although the EC Mergers Directive may apply where the companies are not in same group). Again, there is no requirement that the transferee company is UK resident—merely that it is subject to corporation tax.

The parent company and the new subsidiary will be in the same group if parent company (or its group) owns at least 75% of the new subsidiary at the time of the transfer. It is therefore important that the new subsidiary is part of the group immediately prior to the transfer of the branch assets—if the subscriber shares are held by a lawyer or local director, this condition will not be satisfied.

If the parent company and the subsidiary are not in the same group, the assets of the branch will be treated as sold to the new subsidiary for their market value (TCGA 1992, s 17). Any resulting gain will be within the charge to UK corporation tax by virtue of TCGA 1992, s 10B.

Where s 171 applies on the branch incorporation, a sale of the new subsidiary within six years will result in a degrouping charge will arise under TCGA 1992, s 179. If this is anticipated, the incorporation could be structured as a taxable transaction, for example by holding the new subsidiary outside the group prior to the incorporation. Section 171 would not then apply, and a gain would be calculated based on asset values at the time of incorporation rather than at the time of disposal.

These reliefs are only relevant if the overseas company carries on a trade in the UK through the branch. However, there should be no UK tax if a non-resident company disposes of other assets—for example investments—even where these assets are located in the UK. TCGA 1992, s 10B restricts the charge to UK tax to those assets used in a trade carried on through a UK permanent establishment.

# Basic principles—overseas concepts of tax residence

**[A9.53]** Similar principles to those outlined above may apply when looking to establish, or avoid, residence in other jurisdictions.

## *Australia*

**[A9.54]** A company which is not incorporated in Australia will be treated as resident in Australia if it carries on a business in Australia and:

(a)     its central management and control is undertaken in Australia; or
(b)     it has resident shareholders controlling the voting power.

The definition of central management and control follows the definition established by early UK case law in *De Beers* and *Unit Construction*.

## US

**[A9.55]** There is no distinction between resident and non-resident companies in the US. A company which is not incorporated in the US will only be subject to US tax on income that is 'effectively connected' to the conduct of a trade or business in the US. This is not the same definition as a permanent establishment, although a DTA is likely to provide that profits can only be taxed to the extent that they relate to a permanent establishment in the US.

### Ireland

**[A9.56]** A company which is not incorporated in Ireland will be treated as resident in Ireland if its central management and control is undertaken in Ireland. The definition of central management and control follows the definition established by the UK case law.

### South Africa

**[A9.57]** A company which is not incorporated in South Africa will be treated as resident in South Africa if its place of effective management is located in South Africa. The place of effective management is defined as where the day-to-day operational management is undertaken.

### India

**[A9.58]** A company which is not incorporated in India will be treated as resident in India only if its management and control is undertaken wholly in India. If any decisions are made outside India, or board meetings are held outside India, then management and control will not be undertaken wholly in India, and the company will not be treated as resident in India.

As part of the reform to the Direct Taxes Code which is expected to become effective in 2014, it has been proposed that this test will be changed so that a company not incorporated in India will also be resident in India if management and control is undertaken partly in India.

### China

**[A9.59]** A company which is not incorporated in China will be treated as resident in China if its place of effective management is located in China. Guidance provides that the place of effective management will be in China if:

(a)     the primary location of day to day operational management is in China;
(b)     decisions relating to staff or financial matters are taken or approved in China;
(c)     assets, accounting records, company seals etc are located in China; and
(d)     at least of the 50% directors and senior executives are resident in China.

## *Hong Kong*

**[A9.60]** Hong Kong operates a territorial tax system, under which all profits derived in Hong Kong are subject to Hong Kong tax. There is no distinction between resident and non-resident companies.

# A10

# Double tax relief

# Introduction

**[A10.1]** Income and gains arising in another jurisdiction to UK residents may be subject to tax both overseas and in the UK. UK residents may also be subject to UK tax on dividends received from subsidiaries which have paid tax overseas.

In order to mitigate this, the UK has entered into a large number of double taxation agreements (DTAs) to reduce the incidence of double taxation. DTAs are covered in CHAPTER A8. In addition, the UK has legislation to provide unilateral double taxation relief in certain situations where no DTA relief is available. The double taxation relief rules (for both DTA and unilateral relief) are in TIOPA 2010, Part 2. Double tax relief is extended to capital gains tax by virtue of TIOPA 2010, s 9(2). Although it has no legal force, there is also guidance to be found in the HMRC International Manual at INTM160000 onwards.

The rules in respect of double tax relief for dividends have become less relevant following the introduction of the dividend exemption for dividends paid after 1 July 2009. However, the rules will remain relevant for non-exempt dividends.

In relation to double tax relief, the objectives of international tax planning are typically:

- identify the amount of overseas tax which is creditable under a DTA or as unilateral relief;
- identify the amount of UK tax against which the overseas can be credited, and also the income on which these arise;
- maximise relief by efficient utilisation of losses.

# Basic principles—what relief can be claimed?

### Overview

**[A10.2]** The basic rules are common to unilateral and DTA relief. Credit is claimed for tax which is charged by the country in which the income or gain arose. The credit is claimed against the UK tax on the foreign income or gain by reference to which the foreign tax was charged, and is limited to the lower of the foreign tax and the UK tax on the same income or gain. Finally, the foreign tax must be one which is broadly comparable to income tax, capital gains tax or corporation tax and allowed as such by HMRC.

### DTA relief

**[A10.3]** A DTA will normally provide relief from double taxation with respect to certain types of income and gains by specifying that the source jurisdiction will not tax, or will tax at a reduced rate, the amounts in question. The source jurisdiction is the one in which the income has a source, and the residence jurisdiction is the one in which the recipient is resident.

Additionally, a DTA may provide that the jurisdiction of residence will allow credit, against the tax arising in that jurisdiction, for overseas tax which is not relieved at source. Some DTAs also provide for the jurisdiction of residence to exempt certain types of overseas income, but this is not found in the UK's DTAs.

It should be noted that some DTAs provide for double tax relief at source. However, countries such as Switzerland and Qatar do not allow this and a refund must be applied for in order to obtain the treaty rate of withholding tax.

### Unilateral relief

**[A10.4]** Where no DTA applies, the UK may grant unilateral relief under TIOPA 2010, s 9 from double taxation by allowing credit for foreign tax suffered on overseas income against the UK liability on the same income.

HMRC guidance at INTM 170040 set out the anti-avoidance provisions in relation to unilateral credit relief. Broadly, the following circumstances can result in anti-avoidance provisions preventing relief and can be found in TIOPA 2010, ss 84 to 88:

- The foreign tax is not properly attributable to the source from which the income or gain is derived.
- The payer of the foreign tax, taken together with all other parties to the scheme or arrangement, has not suffered the full economic cost of the foreign tax against the income or gain against which relief is claimed.
- The payer of the deemed foreign tax has not suffered the full economic cost of the foreign tax against the income or gain against which relief is claimed.
- A claim, election or other arrangement could have been made by any person which would have reduced the amount of credit for foreign tax. Alternatively, a claim, election or arrangement was made that had the effect of increasing the amount of credit for foreign tax.
- The foreign tax credit given as a result of the scheme or arrangement reduces the amount of tax payable to an amount less than would have been payable if the transactions making up the scheme had never taken place.
- A source of income subject to foreign tax has been acquired wholly or partly as consideration for a tax-deductible payment.

### Residence

**[A10.5]** TIOPA 2010, s 26 provides that double tax credit relief is normally available only to UK residents. Exceptionally, unilateral relief for UK tax is also given to:

(a)    companies and individuals resident in the Isle of Man and Channel Islands with respect to tax paid under the laws of those territories;

(b)    a resident of another jurisdiction with respect to income from an employment performed wholly or mainly in that jurisdiction where the income is taxable under ITEPA 2003;

(c) a UK permanent establishment of a non-resident company, where the jurisdiction in which the tax arises is not one in which the person is liable to tax by reason of domicile, residence or place of management (provided that the relief may not exceed the amount which would be allowed to a UK resident with the same income or gains).

Most DTAs allow relief only to residents of one or other of the parties to the DTA, with residence defined in the DTA.

Subject to the above, relief for foreign tax is only available against UK tax if the recipient of the income is resident in the UK. If UK tax arises to a non-resident because the source of income is in the UK, relief must be claimed for the UK tax in the non-resident's jurisdiction of residence, and not the other way round.

## Foreign currency translation of tax and income

### Income

**[A10.6]** As outlined in **A2.30**, profits and other income will normally be translated in accordance with the company's accounting policy.

### Tax on income

**[A10.7]** INTM162160 sets out that foreign tax on income should be translated at the date the tax becomes payable. Withholding tax becomes payable at the same time the income is received. Where tax is suffered by direct assessment (rather than withholding), for instance on branch profits, this may not be the same as the date on which the tax is actually paid.

However, INTM162160 also sets out that HMRC will generally accept the date of payment as the relevant translation date unless a company requests otherwise.

Where the foreign tax is significant and there have been large exchange rate movements, it will be beneficial to calculate translation at both the date of payment and the payable date, and request translation at the payable date if this is more favourable.

### Dividends and underlying tax

**[A10.8]** Underlying tax will also be translated at the date that it became payable in the overseas jurisdiction, which again may not be the date it was actually paid (see **A2.32**).

When determining the amount of relevant of profits (see **A10.32**) out of which a dividend is paid, it is not necessary to translate the underlying profits. The dividend will be matched against profits in local currency, before translating both the dividend and the amount of the underlying tax.

For example, a UK company receives a dividend of $1,000,000 from a US subsidiary at a time when the exchange rate is $1.50:£1. The profits from the latest accounting period were $2,000,000, and tax of $800,000 was paid on the due date when the exchange rate was $1.40:£1. The dividend in dollars is compared to the relevant profits in dollars, such that 50% of the underlying tax is eligible for relief. 50% of the underlying tax is $400,000 and this is translated at $1.40:£1. The dividend is translated at $1.50:£1. It is not necessary to translate the relevant profits.

## Source

**[A10.9]** Unilateral credit relief will be given for income or gains which are treated (under UK law) as arising in a foreign jurisdiction. Income or gains derived from property or rights which are located in a jurisdiction are usually treated as arising there. The source of other types of income is considered in CHAPTER A2.

DTAs may provide for source to be determined on a more generous basis. Under many DTAs, any profits, income or capital gains earned by a resident of the UK which are taxable in the overseas country under the terms of the DTA are deemed to have their source in the foreign country. Accordingly, the DTA requires the UK to give relief for the foreign taxes charged on those profits, income or gains.

### Personal and professional services

**[A10.10]** In order to allow double tax relief to be claimed in respect of foreign taxes suffered on the profits of certain trades which are carried on partly in the UK and partly overseas, TIOPA 2010, s 9(3) deems income arising from personal or professional services to arise in the territory where the services are performed. In the absence of this rule, the source of the income would be in the UK.

In *Yates (H M Inspector of Taxes) v GCA International Ltd*, 1991 STC 157, a UK company suffered Venezuelan tax on a contract which was performed partly in the UK and partly in Venezuela. The court held that unilateral relief was available only for the proportion of the foreign tax which related to the work performed in Venezuela.

Where a UK resident carries on a trade in a country with which the UK has a DTA, the overseas country will normally only have the right to tax the profits if the UK resident has a permanent establishment there. The DTA will also typically provide that, as a consequence of the foreign country having taxing rights, such income will be deemed to arise for credit relief purposes in the foreign country.

### Interest

**[A10.11]** Determination of the country in which interest arises may be complex, depending on factors such as the residence of the borrower, the law under which the debt can be enforced and the location of any security for the debt. Under the OECD Model Tax Convention, interest is deemed to arise in the country where the payer is resident or, in some circumstances, where it has a permanent establishment. This is followed by many of the UK's DTAs.

Under UK domestic law, and for the purpose of unilateral relief, the decision in the *Westminster Bank Executor and Trustee Co (Channel Islands) Ltd v National Bank of Greece SA* [1971] AC 945, [1971] 1 All ER 233 case will determine the source of the interest (see **A5.3**).

### Intellectual property

**[A10.12]** Royalties and other amounts received by a UK resident from a non-resident for the use of copyrights, trademarks, patents, know-how and similar property may have a UK source if, for example, the right is registered in the UK. Under ESC B8, such income may be treated for double tax relief purposes as arising overseas where the recipient carries on a trade in the UK and the payments do not represent consideration for services rendered in the UK. Where the recipient does not carry on a trade, the income may be regarded as arising in the country where the right is enforceable.

### US disregarded entities

**[A10.13]** In *Bayfine UK v Revenue and Customs Comrs* [2011] EWCA Civ 304, a UK subsidiary of a US parent company was treated as a disregarded entity for US tax purposes (see **A14.13**). The US parent company therefore paid US tax on the profits of the UK subsidiary.

The profits of the UK subsidiary had a US source as they arose from financial transactions executed in the US.

The Court of Appeal held that no double tax relief was available under the UK/US DTA. The DTA made clear that the US was able to tax the US parent company in accordance with its own law, and give credit for any UK tax paid. The UK therefore had primary taxing rights and therefore should not give credit for foreign tax.

In addition, unilateral relief was not available because such relief was only intended to apply where a DTA did not. In this case, the DTA applied to determine the taxing rights, and unilateral relief was therefore not relevant.

### Tax sparing

**[A10.14]** Some developing countries offer tax holidays and other incentives to foreign investors undertaking certain businesses or activities. The incentive for a UK resident would clearly be negated if the tax spared in the foreign country was paid instead in the UK on repatriating the income.

TIOPA 2010, s 4 therefore allows for relief to preserve the incentive in respect of certain foreign taxes if specified in the relevant DTA. Accordingly, the foreign tax which would have been due but for a tax relief is treated as if it had been paid.

Credit relief is allowed for the amount treated as paid, subject to the normal rules except that the income received is not grossed up for the tax notionally paid.

If the tax spared arises on interest or royalties, the relief given is limited to the withholding tax rates specified in the interest or royalty article of the applicable DTA (see Chapter **A8**).

## Nature of creditable tax

**[A10.15]** The foreign tax must be one which is specifically admissible under the terms of the applicable DTA or which has been accepted as admissible by HMRC for the purposes of unilateral relief. In addition, the DTA may specify that other taxes which are 'similar' to those listed are also admissible.

The HMRC Double Taxation Relief Manual sets out a list of admissible and inadmissible taxes, both unilateral and under the terms of treaties, for a large number of countries at DT2100 onwards.

TIOPA 2010, s 8 provides that tax is only creditable for unilateral relief purposes if it is calculated by reference to income:

'(1)      . . . references to tax payable or paid under the law of a territory outside the United Kingdom include only—

(a)      taxes which are charged on income and which correspond to income tax,

(b)      taxes which are charged on income or chargeable gains and which correspond to corporation tax, and

(c)      taxes which are charged on capital gains and which correspond to capital gains tax.

(2)      For the purposes of subsection (2), tax may correspond to income tax, corporation tax or capital gains tax even though it—

(a)      is payable under the law of a province, state or other part of a country, or

(b)      is levied by or on behalf of a municipality or other local body.'

This would therefore exclude taxes which are calculated by reference to turnover or assets. It is this basis on which HMRC's list of admissible taxes is prepared.

Following the decision in *Yates (H M Inspector of Taxes) v GCA International Ltd* (1991) 64 TC 37, HMRC published SP7/91 which states that any tax will be creditable if 'it serves the same function as income and corporation tax serve in the UK in relation to the profits of the business'. In that case, a Venezuelan tax calculated as 25% of 90% of gross receipts was held to be creditable. The tax had been introduced in Venezuela to replace a profits tax, and was intended to raise an equivalent amount.

Where an overseas tax is charged on some basis other than profits (eg on receipts as with the Venezuelan tax), it is important to understand the nature of the tax and how it was introduced, as it may serve the same function as a tax on profits and therefore be creditable.

Some taxes may not be covered by a relevant DTA (see **A8.12**), but be creditable nonetheless because they are taxes on profits—for instance most US state taxes. Some US states charge a franchise tax, which is equivalent to a fee rather than a tax on profits, and such a franchise tax is not creditable. HMRC provide a list at DT19855 of the state taxes which they consider to be creditable. To be creditable the UK tax due must be charged by reference to income upon which the foreign tax had been paid (*Wimpey (George) International Ltd v Rolfe (Inspector of Taxes)* [1989] STC 609, 62 TC 597).

# Planning—maximising relief

[A10.16] Relief is given against the UK tax on the same income or gains on which the foreign tax is paid. The relief cannot exceed the UK tax on the income or gains, and it is therefore necessary to establish how the income and gains (and therefore the UK tax) should be measured.

TIOPA 2010, s 31 provides that, the relevant income is generally:

(a)   the net amount received;
(b)   plus any direct foreign taxes suffered (whether by withholding or direct assessment);
(c)   plus (in the case of non-exempt dividends) underlying foreign taxes.

However, this is subject to modification for certain types of income as set out below.

Once the measure of the income has been computed then, in accordance with s 31, the UK tax payable on it is the difference between the tax charged on the total income for the year and the tax charged on total income excluding the foreign income. Where there is more than one source of foreign income in the year, this computation is repeated for each one, but excluding each time the item(s) taken into account in the previous iteration.

## Trading income

[A10.17] For trading income, TIOPA 2010, s 44 provides that the measure of the income is to be found by calculating the equivalent UK trading profits.

This means that the gross income is reduced by the allowable deductions, charges and expenses which would be allowable in calculating the UK tax liability on that income.

Where such deductions or expenses relate partly to that income and partly to other matters, a just and reasonable apportionment is to be made. In addition, any expenses of a connected company which are 'reasonably attributable' to the income or gain are also to be brought into the computation. For further context see *Legal & General Assurance Society Ltd v Thomas* Spc 492. By virtue of TIOPA 2010, s 42 (3), the company may choose to allocate deductions such as management expenses and non-trading loan relationship deficits to UK source income in priority to foreign source income, for the purposes of calculating the amount of the foreign source income chargeable to corporation tax. The UK corporation tax payable on the net foreign source income is then determined as the rate of corporation tax payable by the company on its profits for the accounting period.

For longer term contracts, where for example there is a mismatch with UK and overseas accounting treatment, HMRC will generally permit the aggregation of tax payable over the accounting periods during which UK tax arises.

## Example

In the year ended 31 March 2014, A Ltd had UK trading profits, branch income from the US which had suffered tax at 40% and interest from Australia which had been subject to deduction of tax at 10%. Group relief and non-trading loan relationship deficits are available to A Ltd.

| | UK | US | Australia | Total |
|---|---|---|---|---|
| Foreign tax rate | | 40% | 10% | |
| | £ | £ | £ | £ |
| Income | 100,000 | 250,000 | 50,000 | 400,000 |
| NTLR deficits | (10,000) | 0 | 0 | (10,000) |
| Group relief | (90,000) | 0 | (10,000) | (100,000) |
| PCTCT | 0 | 250,000 | 40,000 | 290,000 |
| Corporation tax at 23% | 0 | 57,500 | 9,200 | 66,700 |
| Double tax relief limited to 23% | ¯ | (57,5 00) | (5,000) | (62,500) |
| Corporation tax due | 0 | 0 | 4,20000 | 4,200 |

## Loan relationships and intangible assets

**[A10.18]** There are specific rules in TIOPA 2010, ss 50 and 51 with respect to the allocation of deficits on UK loan relationships and intangible assets respectively.

Under the basic computational rules for non-trading loan relationships, all debits and credits are aggregated to form a single amount which is brought into the corporation tax computation. There are similar provisions for debits and credits arising on intangibles not held for the purposes of a trade.

However, for double tax relief purposes only, a company is allowed flexibility to treat the non-trading debits as set off first against other income of the accounting period, prior to being set against non-trading credits, in order to maximise the double tax relief for any foreign taxes suffered on those credits.

There is an example of this in **A2.19**.

This flexibility allows a company to maximise the amount of taxable income, and therefore the amount of relief which can be claimed for foreign tax.

INTM168060 sets out two further relaxations when calculating the amount of income from intangibles against which the foreign tax can be offset.

Firstly, there is no requirement to allocate indirect expenses, for instance overheads, against income from intangibles which are held for the purposes of a trade:

'Where the royalties are not pure income profit of the United Kingdom resident recipient, because they are trading receipts (for example, a United Kingdom concern licenses foreign residents to use its patents in return for royalties) credit can nevertheless be given for the foreign tax against the United Kingdom tax charged on the profits to which the royalties give rise, that is after deduction of an appropriate amount of expenses, whether incurred in the foreign country or elsewhere, and capital allowances attributable to the royalty income (see INTM168010). Only expenses directly attributable to the earning of the income should be taken into account, not indirect or general overhead expenses.'

Secondly, income from different assets can be disaggregated, even though CTA 2009, Part 8 would normally require income from all intangible assets to be aggregated:

'All foreign royalties derived from the same intangible asset are treated as a single item of foreign income with a single tax payment. Royalties originating from different assets should be considered separately for the purpose of calculating the maximum credit available for tax paid on the royalties, unless it is reasonable to suppose that further aggregation does not materially alter the outcome of the calculation of maximum credit.'

This does not affect the normal rule that foreign tax can only be credited against the UK corporation tax on the same income—it is not possible to aggregate income from intangibles from different jurisdictions when calculating the UK corporation tax.

## Minimisation of foreign tax

[A10.19] Under TIOPA 2010, s 33, the creditable foreign tax cannot exceed the amount which would have been suffered if all reasonable steps had been taken under the laws of the foreign country, or under any applicable DTA, to minimise the amount of tax payable there. This requires making claims or elections for available reliefs, deductions, reductions or allowances under both the local law and any relevant DTA. This applies to both withholding taxes and underlying taxes.

If, therefore, tax is deducted at source from the payment of a royalty but the recipient is entitled to reclaim it from the overseas tax authority under the applicable DTA, there can be no claim for double tax relief in the UK. The exception to this may be where a claim was so onerous that the costs of making the claim would outweigh the tax at stake. When s 33 was introduced (as ICTA 1988, s 795A), guidance was given by the Paymaster General at Committee Stage:

'Subsection (3) of the new section refers to what a taxpayer might reasonably be expected to have done if he had not been able to obtain credit for the tax in the United Kingdom. In such cases, the taxpayer might have tried to keep his foreign tax bill down, having regard to the amount of time, effort and expense involved in discussing his case with the foreign tax authorities on the one hand and the amount of the expected reduction on the other.'

### Underlying tax on dividends

[A10.20] At INTM164140, HMRC give the following examples of where they consider s 33 could apply to restrict a claim to underlying tax on dividends:

(a)     where an estimated tax assessment has been made which is likely to be too high;

(b)     not claiming relief for capital allowances or losses;

(c)     where the local law provides for different bases of taxation, not following the basis which would result in the lower tax.

They do not consider that s 33 would apply to underlying tax where a shareholder cannot influence the company which is paying the dividend.

### Reasonable steps taken by other companies

**[A10.21]** In *Hill Samuel Investments Ltd v Revenue and Customs Comrs* [2009] STC (SCD) 315, a UK company invested into a US partnership which was treated as a company for US tax purposes, and was therefore subject to US tax. The UK company claimed relief for the US tax which had been paid on its share of the partnership income. HMRC argued that under s 33 relief was not available because the US tax could have been reduced if the UK company had made a loan rather than invested in a partnership. The Special Commissioners held that it was not reasonable for the UK company to enter into a different transaction in order to minimise foreign tax:

'1.     Applying that interpretation to the facts of this case, we decide that the steps that might reasonably be taken do not include the entering into a completely different transaction, whether or not it has a similar economic effect. While the transaction entered into may have economic similarities to a loan it is not a loan but an investment in a US partnership, as it purports to be. There are no other reasonable steps open to the Appellant that would reduce the amount of US tax. Accordingly [s 33] does not restrict the Appellant's ability to claim relief.'

The Special Commissioners also confirmed that the UK company must be in a position to influence the amount of tax paid:

' . . . while the person taking the steps may include persons other than the taxpayer claiming relief, the steps must be those that the taxpayer is in a position to influence.'

This was reinforced by *Bayfine UK v Revenue and Customs Comrs* [2010] EWHC 609 (Ch), where it was held that:

' . . . Suppose hypothetically that a tax liability could be reduced by a subsidiary of the taxpayer serving a notice of doing some other act within its power. It seems to me plain that the taxpayer which controls the subsidiary would be in a position to compel it to do something and must do so, so as to reduce its tax liability.'

A UK company should ensure that it makes all claims possible to reduce withholding tax on overseas income, however onerous this may be. Otherwise, it will not be able to obtain relief in the UK for the overseas tax.

The only exception would be if it could demonstrate that the costs of making a claim would outweigh the tax.

# Planning—excess foreign taxes

**[A10.22]** Where the foreign tax exceeds the amount which can be relieved by credit (for example, where the foreign tax has been charged at a higher rate than in the UK), the excess cannot normally be carried forward. However, there are exceptions to that rule with respect to permanent establishments of UK companies and certain dividends received.

## *Unrelieved foreign tax of overseas branch*

**[A10.23]** Under TIOPA 2010, s 72, unrelieved foreign tax in respect of a UK company's foreign permanent establishment may be carried forward to a subsequent accounting period and relieved as a credit against UK corporation tax on income from the same source. Alternatively, the unrelieved foreign tax may be carried back to earlier accounting periods beginning not more than three years before the accounting period in which it arises.

If a UK company which owns a branch has losses, there will either be a timing disadvantage as it cannot immediately utilise all of the foreign tax suffered by the branch, or an absolute cost because it can never utilise the foreign tax.

As far as possible, a profitable foreign branch should be held by a UK company which does not have UK losses in order to avoid this problem—there is an example of this in **B4.8**. To that end, in order to maximise foreign tax relief, taxpayers may consider ring fencing overseas branches in separate UK SPVs.

If a company ceases to have a permanent establishment in a particular jurisdiction, any unrelieved foreign tax cannot be carried forward, even if a new permanent establishment is subsequently created in the same jurisdiction (TIOPA 2010, s 76).

Credit for foreign tax will not be relevant if a company has elected for its foreign branches to be exempt—see CHAPTER **A16**.

## *Relief by deduction*

**[A10.24]** There may be circumstances where a company cannot benefit from credit relief—for example where there is a loss or relief from another source which reduces taxable income to nil. Where credit relief is not claimed, TIOPA 2010, s 112 permits the foreign tax to be treated as a deduction from income instead. No separate claim for deduction is required—it applies automatically where a claim for credit is not made.

Relief is not available by deduction where a claim for credit relief is made but not all the foreign tax can be so relieved. It is therefore not possible to claim relief by both credit and deduction on the same tax. This is made clear by TIOPA 2010, s 31(2)(a) which provides that 'no deduction is to be made for foreign tax . . . whether in respect of the same or any other income or gain'.

In some cases it will be necessary to calculate whether it is better to claim relief by way of credit (and lose any tax which cannot be credited), or by way of deduction (and effectively only obtain relief for 21% of the foreign tax).

TIOPA 2010, s 112 gives a deduction for taxes which would otherwise be admissible for credit relief, but only if they are actually 'paid'. This therefore excludes a deduction for spared taxes (see **A10.14**).

In addition, a deduction may be available under general principles for taxes which would not otherwise be admissible for credit relief. For example, it will be possible to obtain a deduction for an inadmissible tax suffered by an overseas branch (such as an irrecoverable sales tax) if it can be demonstrated that it was incurred wholly and exclusively for the purposes of the trade for the purposes of CTA 2009, s 54.

On a similar basis, TIOPA 2010, s 113 allows a deduction for foreign taxes in the computation of chargeable gains where it is not possible to benefit from credit relief.

An amount can be claimed by way of deduction within six years of when 'all material determinations have been made' whether in the UK or elsewhere. This means that if adjustments are made to foreign taxes (for example following an enquiry), the relief for deduction can be adjusted as well. HMRC must be notified within twelve months of any claim for deduction becoming excessive.

# Basic principles—other types of income and gains

## *Chargeable gains*

**[A10.25]** The fundamental principles which govern double tax relief for income apply also to chargeable gains. However, disparities between the UK and foreign tax systems in terms of measuring the quantum of the taxable amount, or the taxpayer on whom the liability falls, may be encountered more frequently when dealing with chargeable gains.

The calculation of a capital gain under a DTA may differ from the calculation of a gain for UK or the relevant overseas tax purposes. This may mean that:

(a)  credit cannot be obtained for all the overseas tax suffered because the gain as calculated for overseas tax purposes is less than calculated for UK tax purposes (and part of the overseas tax is suffered on a gain which does not crystallise for UK tax purposes); or

(b)  relief cannot be obtained from overseas capital gains tax because the gain as calculated for overseas tax purposes is greater than calculated under the DTA.

### Allocation of losses

**[A10.26]** Where a taxpayer has chargeable gains in an accounting period or year of assessment with respect to disposals of both foreign assets and UK assets, any capital losses (and, for individuals and trustees, the annual exemption) may be set against UK gains first to maximise tax credit relief.

**Timing**

**[A10.27]** There are a number of circumstances in which a gain may be treated as accruing for UK tax purposes at a different time than for foreign purposes. Similarly, the gain may be treated as accruing to a different person for UK purposes than for foreign purposes. This does not necessarily prevent the UK resident who is liable to tax from claiming double tax relief: the legislation requires that relief is given only with respect to the 'same gain'. HMRC have issued SP 6/88 which sets out certain circumstances where they will allow credit relief:

(a) overseas tax is due on a disposal which gives rise to neither a gain nor a loss under TCGA 1992, s 171, and a subsequent disposal gives rise to a UK liability;

(b) a gain is deferred under TCGA 1992, s 140 on incorporation of a foreign branch, but taxed at that time in the foreign country, and within six years a UK charge arises, either on the disposal of the shares in the foreign subsidiary or on the disposal of those assets by the subsidiary;

(c) a foreign jurisdiction charges tax on unrealised increases in value of an asset, and there is a disposal of it in a subsequent period which gives rise to a UK chargeable gain;

(d) a foreign jurisdiction treats capital gains as income.

**Rolled over gains**

**[A10.28]** SP 6/88 makes it clear that credit relief is conditional on the subject matter of the overseas tax being the same as on which the UK tax liability arises. Thus, where rollover relief is claimed on disposal of one asset, any overseas tax paid on that disposal will not be eligible for relief on a disposal of the second asset into which the gain is rolled over, no matter how much of the gain chargeable on the second disposal is in fact referable to the first.

*Dividends*

**[A10.29]** Most dividends received by a UK company from an overseas subsidiary are exempt from corporation tax (See **A16.2**). However, where the exemption is not available, and dividends are therefore taxable, double tax relief is available in respect of:

• withholding taxes imposed on the payment of the dividend;

• underlying tax suffered on the profits out of which the subsidiary pays a dividend, provided the UK company hold at least 10% of the subsidiary.

Companies with an interest below 10%, as well as other UK residents, are not allowed relief for underlying tax and can claim relief only for the withholding taxes imposed on the dividend itself. In some cases, a corporate tax liability is triggered when a dividend is paid—for example the Secondary Tax on Companies (STC) in South Africa, and the Dividend Distribution Tax (DDT) in India. These are underlying taxes rather than withholding taxes.

## Underlying tax relief—DTAs

**[A10.30]** Most UK DTAs provide for credit to be claimed in respect of underlying tax. The typical requirement is for the UK company to directly or indirectly control at least 10% of the voting power in the company paying the dividend. There are only a small number of DTAs where the threshold is lower (eg the treaties with Myanmar and St Kitts & Nevis).

## Underlying tax relief—unilateral relief

**[A10.31]** For corporation tax purposes, TIOPA 2010, s 12 provides for unilateral relief in respect of underlying tax on dividends which are not exempt from tax in the UK. The basic requirement is for the UK company to directly or indirectly control at least 10% of the voting power in the company paying the dividend.

The basic rule is extended by TIOPA 2010, ss 13–17. By virtue of TIOPA 2010, s 63, relief is extended to tax suffered both in the UK and in countries other than the territory of residence of the payer. Additionally, where the overseas company has received a dividend from a third company, to which it is related, tax relief is available in respect of the underlying tax suffered by that third company. Relief is thus available for a 'chain' of companies, provided broadly that each is related to the next, which requires 10% voting control.

Under TIOPA 2010, s 57, there is a cap on the foreign tax which may be relieved, which effectively means that the rate of underlying tax on the dividend cannot exceed the UK corporation tax.

## Underlying tax and relevant profits

**[A10.32]** Underlying tax is the foreign tax paid on the proportion of the relevant profits of the company represented by the dividend paid by it. Under TIOPA 2010, s 59(8), the relevant profits are the profits available for distribution, as shown in the accounts drawn up under company law in its country and making no provision for reserves, bad debts, impairment losses or contingencies except as required under that law.

In *Bowater Paper Corpn v Murgatroyd (Inspector of Taxes)* [1969] 3 All ER 111, HL, the UK company received a dividend from a US subsidiary. The profits shown in the accounts were substantially lower than the profits subject to US tax, because of depreciation. The company argued that the relevant profits were the profits which were subject to tax, but the House of Lords held that the relevant profits were those shown in the accounts, notwithstanding that the taxable profits may be different.

The relevant profits out of which a dividend is paid are:

(a)    if the dividend is paid for a specified period, the profits of the period;
(b)    if the dividend is not paid for a specified period, the profits of the last period for which accounts were made up which ended before the dividend became payable.

It is not possible to specify that a dividend is paid out of specified profits of a particular type. If a dividend is paid before accounts are drawn up for this period (even though the period may have ended) then the dividend will be matched the preceding accounting period (or periods). This may be beneficial where the underlying tax paid for the latest period is low.

Under the motive test dividend exemption (see **A16.5**), where no other exemption is satisfied, dividends are treated as first paid out of profits which have been diverted from the UK. Such a dividend is taxable, and is treated as having been paid out of these profits when calculating the amount of underlying tax.

### Foreign tax groups and mergers

**[A10.33]** Under TIOPA 2010, s 71, where a foreign company is a member of a consolidated tax group, underlying tax relief on non-exempt dividends is to be determined as if the companies were a single entity.

Where a merger (or similar transaction) has taken place, profits originally earned by one company may be recognised as belonging to another legal entity. In such cases, by virtue of TIOPA 2010, s 69 the second company is treated as if it had paid the tax suffered by the first company, provided that the underlying tax available as a result shall not exceed the amount which would have been available if the first company had paid a dividend equal to the amount of those profits to the second.

### Deductible dividends

**[A10.34]** Under TIOPA 2010, s 57(3), no underlying tax is available in respect of a deductible dividend. This means a dividend by reference to which an amount is determined which is allowed as a deduction for tax purposes to a resident of an overseas territory.

For example, where dividends are paid by an Australian company in respect of preference shares, they may be deductible against the profits of the Australian company.

### Shares as loan relationships

**[A10.35]** Certain shares may be recharacterised as debt under CTA 2009, s 523. Dividends declared on such shares are accordingly treated as profits arising on a loan relationship and it appears to follow that no underlying tax relief is intended to be available in respect of such dividends.

### Unremittable foreign earnings

**[A10.36]** A UK resident company may claim relief under CTA 2009, s 1274 for income which cannot be remitted to the UK by reason of:

(a)     the law of the country in which it arose;
(b)     executive action of the government of that country; or
(c)     the impossibility of obtaining foreign currency there.

If it is subsequently possible to remit the income, it will be treated for UK tax purposes as arising at that time.

## Controlled Foreign Companies (CFCs)

**[A10.37]** Following changes to the CFC rules from 1 January 2013, there are provisions in TIOPA, s 371BC and Chapter 16 of the same Act to provide for double tax relief for tax suffered by a Controlled Foreign Company (CFC). where an apportionment is made to a UK company with a relevant interest in the CFC. This is referred to as 'creditable tax' and is the aggregate of:

(a)   foreign taxes suffered by the CFC, computed in accordance with the double tax relief rules of TIOPA 2010, Part 2 as if it were a UK resident company;
(b)   UK income tax deducted at source from payments received by the CFC;
(c)   UK corporation or income tax charged on the profits of the company (eg with respect to a UK permanent establishment).

Once computed, the creditable tax is attributed to any UK resident company with a relevant interest in the company on the same basis as the chargeable profits are attributed. The creditable tax reduces the tax chargeable on the attributed profits.

## Anti-avoidance

**[A10.38]** Anti-avoidance provisions at TIOPA 2010, s 81 restrict the availability of double tax relief. This section applies where four conditions are met:

(a)   Condition A is that there is in respect of income or gains an amount of foreign tax for which, under any arrangements, credit is allowable against United Kingdom tax;
(b)   Condition B is that there is a scheme or arrangement the main purpose, or one of the main purposes, of which is to cause an amount of foreign tax to be taken into account;
(c)   Condition C is that the scheme or arrangement is a prescribed scheme or arrangement;
(d)   Condition D is that the amount is more than a minimal amount.

With reference to Condition C, a prescribed scheme or arrangement is one where:

(a)   the foreign tax is not properly attributable to the source from which the income or gain is derived;
(b)   the payer of the foreign tax, taken together with all other parties to the scheme or arrangement, has not suffered the full economic cost of the foreign tax against the income or gain against which relief is claimed;
(c)   a claim, election or other arrangement could have been made by any person under the law of any other territory or under any arrangements made in relation to any other territory, which would have reduced the amount of credit for foreign tax, or, alternatively, a claim, election or arrangement was made that had the effect of increasing the amount of credit for foreign tax;

(d)   the foreign tax credit given as a result of the scheme or arrangement reduces the amount of tax payable to an amount less than would have been payable if the transactions making up the scheme had never taken place; or

(e)   a source of income subject to foreign tax has been acquired wholly or partly as consideration for a tax-deductible payment.

# A11

# Capital gains

## Introduction

**[A11.1]** A UK resident is generally subject to UK tax on capital gains arising on assets wherever they are located.

The objective of most international tax planning for UK residents is therefore to:

(a)    minimise overseas capital gains taxes;

(b)    avoid deemed gains on which tax arises without an actual disposal of an asset or receipt of proceeds;

(c)    take advantage of UK tax reliefs such as the substantial shareholding exemption or the reorganisation provisions;

(d)    ensure that a double tax agreement (DTA) applies.

A non-UK resident, on the other hand, is only subject to tax on the disposal of certain assets. The objective of planning for non-residents is therefore to ensure that assets are, as far as possible, kept outside the scope of UK tax.

Whilst this type of tax planning is currently relevant, it should be noted that due to the recent introduction of the Annual Tax on Enveloped Dwellings, and the proposed introduction of a capital gains tax charge on residential property held by non-residents, these planning ideas may be short lived.

## Basic principles—disposal of a UK asset

**[A11.2]** Non-residents are generally only subject to tax in respect of gains arising on assets used for the purposes of a UK trade. The non-resident charging provisions for companies are found in TCGA 1992, s 10B. A company will only be subject to UK corporation tax on a capital gain arising from the disposal of an asset if:

(a)    the company carries on a trade through a UK permanent establishment at a time when the disposal is made;

(b)    the asset is situated in the UK; and

(c)    the asset is used in or for the purposes of the trade, or acquired for use by the permanent establishment.

Where such a gain is subject to tax, the provisions of TCGA 1992, s 190 allow the tax to be collected from other group companies, directors, or directors of parent companies of the company which makes the gain.

The non-resident charging provisions for individuals are found in TCGA 1992, s 10 and are broadly similar to those in s 10B.

In addition to actual disposals, a deemed disposal will arise if:

(a)    an asset used for the purposes of a permanent establishment becomes situated (ie is physically transferred) outside the UK; or

(b)    a trade ceases to be carried on through the permanent establishment.

In these cases, the asset is deemed to disposed of for its market value. Certain reliefs (in particular under TCGA 1992, s 140) may be available to mitigate the gain arising on the cessation of trade in the UK, or the transfer of assets outside the UK.

If a trade ceases to be carried on through a permanent establishment and assets are transferred abroad at the same time, only a single charge to tax will arise (TCGA 1992, s 25(2)(a)).

It is possible to split the ownership of assets from the ownership of a permanent establishment. Diagram 1 shows a common structure for property which is owned by a non-resident group trading in the UK. OffshoreOpCo has a UK permanent establishment, and the disposal of any assets by Offshore-OpCo which are used by the permanent establishment would be subject to tax under s 10B.

OffshorePropCo does not have a UK permanent establishment so a disposal of the property by OffshorePropCo should not be subject to UK tax.

Diagram 1

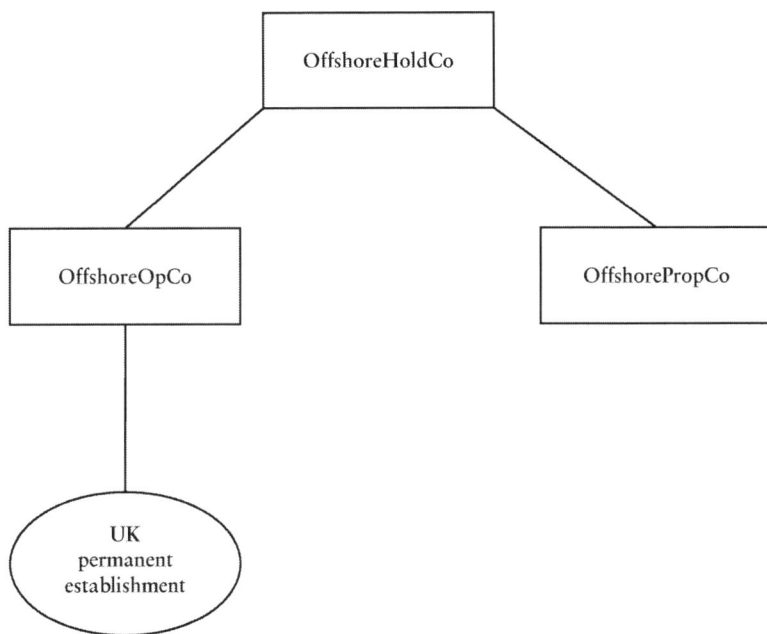

## Basic principles—disposal of an overseas asset

### *Overseas capital gains taxes*

**[A11.3]** When a UK company or individual disposes of an overseas asset, it is possible that capital gains tax will arise in the jurisdiction where the asset is located.

For instance, many jurisdictions impose tax on property transactions undertaken by non-residents, even if they do not have a permanent establishment. Some jurisdictions (for example India) require that tax is withheld by the purchaser from the consideration.

The relevant DTA may provide relief to a non-resident investor, although as noted below taxing rights are often retained by a jurisdiction in which real estate is located. In addition, credit should be available against the UK corporation tax liability arising on a gain for any overseas capital gains tax.

However, it is not possible to claim credit for the overseas tax arising on a particular gain against the tax arising on another gain. Nor is it possible to carry forward unrelieved tax against UK tax arising on future gains. There are exceptions for certain timing differences such as where relief is available in the UK under TCGA 1992, s 171 or s 140 and a gain only later becomes chargeable (see **A10.27**).

Problems in utilising overseas tax will therefore arise if the gain is not subject to tax in the UK. For instance, the substantial shareholding exemption may apply, or brought forward capital losses may be available. Any overseas tax will, in these cases, be an absolute cost to the group.

As noted below, credit against the UK tax arising on a chargeable gain will also be unavailable if the overseas tax is paid by a different entity.

### Nature of asset

**[A11.4]** Where a UK company disposes of an overseas asset (or vice versa), it will be necessary to consider the application of both the UK and the overseas tax system. In some cases, they will treat the transaction differently.

The sale of an overseas company may not be classified as a disposal of 'share capital' (or a disposal of 'ordinary share capital') for UK purposes such that the conditions of the substantial shareholding exemption or another relief are not satisfied. This is discussed further in **A14.21**.

### Transactions treated as disposals

**[A11.5]** Transactions other than disposals may give rise to capital gains. For instance, certain jurisdictions allow a company to pay a capital dividend or undertake a partial liquidation which may be characterised as a capital gain rather than an income distribution for UK tax purposes. This is discussed further in **A14.22**.

### Capital contributions

**[A11.6]** Capital contributions are commonly used outside the UK to provide funding to a subsidiary company.

No specific provisions exist in UK tax law to deal with capital contributions, and they must therefore be analysed under general principles to determine how they should be treated for UK tax purposes.

(a) If the capital contribution is repayable to the contributor, then it will be treated as a loan relationship.

(b) If the capital contribution is not repayable, then it will be treated as a capital item. This may increase the base cost of the shares under TCGA 1992, s 38. However, in *Fenston Will Trusts (Trustees of) v Revenue and Customs Comrs* (SpC 589) [2007] SWTI 556, SCD it was ruled that a capital contribution was not 'reflected in the state or nature of the asset' as required by s 38(1)(b) and did not therefore increase the base cost.

Where capital contributions are made to an overseas entity, new shares (or their equivalent) should be issued in consideration to ensure that the contribution is treated as a reorganisation, and the base cost is increased by virtue of TCGA 1992, s 128.

(c)     A parent company contributes to specific costs of its overseas subsidiary. Such a contribution may be deductible as an expense of the trade if it can be shown that it directly benefits the parent company's trade (*Robinson (Inspector of Taxes) v Scott Bader Co. Ltd* [1981] 2 All ER – see **A13.60**).

### Entity classification

**[A11.7]** As outlined in Chapter **A14**, an overseas entity may be treated as opaque for UK tax purposes but transparent for the purposes of an overseas tax (or vice versa). This can cause difficulties when claiming credit for overseas taxes, including capital gains taxes, as illustrated in the example below.

### Example

A US LLC (treated as a transparent entity in the US) has UK resident members.

The LLC makes a capital gain, which for US tax purposes is treated as arising to the members who pay the tax on the gain. However, for UK tax purposes, the gain is deemed to arise in the LLC as HMRC usually considers an LLC to be an opaque entity similar to a company, and so for UK tax purposes the members are treated as receiving a dividend on a distribution of profits.

For a member who is an individual, there would be no tax credit available for any capital gains tax imposed on the member by the US. For a member which is a company, any tax imposed by the US on that member in respect of the gain may be available for credit as underlying tax.

If a capital gain realised by a non-resident entity is subject to tax under TCGA 1992, s 13, then credit for this tax will be available against a subsequent distribution. In Example 1 above, the UK resident members of the LLC may be attributed part of the gain under TCGA 1992, s 13. Credit would be given for any overseas tax paid on the gain arising under s 13, and credit would be given for any tax paid under s 13 on a subsequent distribution of the gain. Economically, the LLC has been treated in the same way as if it were a transparent entity for UK tax purposes.

However, it would need to be confirmed that:

(a)     the conditions of s 13 were satisfied;
(b)     the relevant DTA did not prevent the gain from being taxed in the UK.

Where capital gains are anticipated, an entity should be used which is treated the same for both UK and overseas tax purposes, in order that UK and overseas taxes are realised by the same entity.

If the disposal proceeds are to be distributed to shareholders then an entity which is transparent for the purposes of UK and overseas taxes may be most tax efficient. This will usually ensure that only a single level of tax arises, and credit can be obtained against the UK tax liability for the overseas tax.

## Foreign exchange

**[A11.8]** As outlined in A2.33, it was held in *Bentley v Pike (Inspector of Taxes)* [1981] STC 360 that proceeds and costs must be translated to sterling at the date when they are received or paid respectively. This can result in capital gains tax being paid even where there is no gain in the local currency.

Foreign tax on gains is usually translated at the date the tax becomes payable in the overseas jurisdiction.

## Trading profits

**[A11.9]** Some jurisdictions may recharacterise certain gains as trading profits, which are then subject to tax.

For example, in Australia, capital gains made by a non-resident on shares are not generally subject to Australian tax. However, Taxation Determination TD2010/21 sets out that:

> ' . . . shares in an Australian company acquired for the purpose of profit-making by sale in a commercial transaction (such as a LBO [Leveraged Buy Out] with a short to medium term time frame) will constitute ordinary income.'

Such gains would then be subject to Australian tax, subject to relief under a DTA.

# Planning—DTAs

**[A11.10]** Where both UK and non-UK tax may arise on a capital gain, a DTA may provide relief from double taxation.

Where a DTA does not provide relief, unilateral relief may be available, by virtue of which credit is given against the UK tax liability for any overseas tax suffered on the gain. This is considered further in A10.4.

## *Typical Articles in UK DTAs*

**[A11.11]** The capital gains Article in UK DTAs typically follows the OECD model. The relevant provisions (ignoring aircraft, shipping, oil and gas) of the OECD model treaty read as follows:

'1.    Gains derived by a resident of a Contracting State from the alienation of immovable property referred to in Article 6 and situated in the other Contracting State may be taxed in that other State.

2.    Gains from the alienation of movable property forming part of the business property of a permanent establishment which an enterprise of a Contracting State has in the other Contracting State, including such gains

from the alienation of such a permanent establishment (alone or with the whole enterprise), may be taxed in that other State.

3.      . . .

4.      Gains derived by a resident of a Contracting State from the alienation of shares deriving more than 50 per cent of their value directly or indirectly from immovable property situated in the other Contracting State may be taxed in that other State.

5.      Gains from the alienation of any property, other than that referred to in paragraphs 1, 2, 3 and 4, shall be taxable only in the Contracting State of which the alienator is a resident.'

Where a non-resident company holds UK assets, the effect of this Article is to:

(a)     exempt most gains from UK tax (as the residence jurisdiction has taxing rights);

(b)     allow both the UK and the residence jurisdiction to tax gains on assets used for the purposes of a permanent establishment in the UK;

(c)     allow both the UK and the residence jurisdiction to tax gains on real estate. For overseas companies, UK tax could arise under either TCGA 1992, s 10B or ITA 2007, s 752.

Real estate is generally defined by reference to the jurisdiction in which the real estate is located.

### No capital gains Article

**[A11.12]** Certain UK DTAs (generally the older DTAs) may not include a capital gains Article, for example Jersey, Isle of Man and Greece.

There are also some major jurisdictions with which the UK does not have a DTA, for example Brazil (and many other South American jurisdictions), Iran, and Saudi Arabia.

The UK also does not have DTAs with many 'tax havens', for example the Cayman Islands or the British Virgin Islands.

Where companies in these jurisdictions realise gains in the UK the tax implications may be limited. The UK domestic provisions would generally only tax assets used for the purposes of a permanent establishment (TCGA 1992, s 10B) and real estate (ITA 2007, s 752).

However, the absence of a DTA may expose a UK company to capital gains tax in the overseas jurisdiction, and planning may be required using an intermediate holding company—see **A11.14** below.

### Real estate

**[A11.13]** Where possible (subject to other tax and commercial considerations), property should be held by an offshore property holding company. The shares in this offshore property holding company can be sold rather than the property itself.

There may also be stamp duty or other transfer tax benefits from this structure.

Some jurisdictions may tax any gain arising on the disposal of the shares in the property holding company, but in some cases this will be restricted to structures where the property company is incorporated in the same jurisdiction where the property is located.

As noted above, the disposal of real estate tends to remain taxable under UK DTAs. The definition of 'real estate' in the DTA, can also include shares in property holding companies, certain mining rights, and shares in companies that hold mining rights.

Diagram 2 shows a typical holding structure for property where this would be relevant—as there is no DTA between the UK and Brazil which would relieve capital gains tax on a direct disposal of shares in the Brazilian company.

**Diagram 2**

Brazilian Property

## *Intermediate holding company/India*

**[A11.14]** Where a UK DTA does not provide relief from the overseas capital gains tax, an intermediate holding company can be established to take advantage of a more beneficial DTA.

As noted in **A8.55** it is important that an intermediate holding company has sufficient substance to be eligible for benefits under a DTA, and has beneficial ownership of the underlying assets.

The DTA between the UK and India allows India to charge tax on UK residents disposing of Indian assets. Other Indian DTAs (for instance those with Mauritius and Cyprus) do not allow India to charge tax on the non-resident company making the disposal.

A UK parent company may therefore establish an intermediate holding company in Mauritius, which in turn establishes a subsidiary in India. When the Mauritius company sells shares in the Indian company, any gain will not be subject to tax under the terms of the Mauritius/India DTA. This structure is illustrated in Diagram 3.

In order for a company to be treated as resident in Mauritius for the purposes of the DTA, it is sufficient that it obtains a residence certificate from the Mauritius tax authorities. This was confirmed in *Union of India v Azadi Bachao Andolan* (2003) 6 ITLR 233, Ind SC.

A similar analysis has been confirmed under the India/Cyprus DTA and the India/Netherlands DTA (the latter in the ruling in *VNU International B. V., AAR* No 871 of 2010).

**Diagram 3**

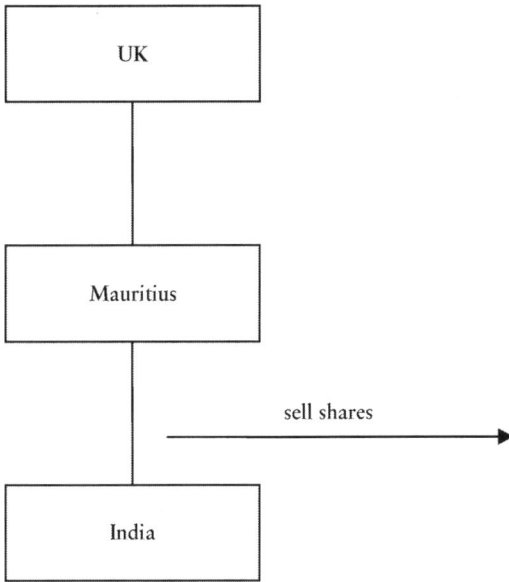

If the UK parent company in Diagram 3 instead sold the shares in the intermediate holding company, any gain arising may also not be subject to tax in India, as it is not the disposal of an Indian asset. This structure is often used where there is no DTA available to reduce the non-resident capital gains tax.

However, in India this analysis is frequently challenged. In the *Vodafone International Holdings BV v Union of India* (2010) 13 ITLR 59, Ind HC case, a Cayman company sold shares in another Cayman company to a Dutch subsidiary of Vodafone. The second subsidiary owned an Indian telecoms group. The Indian tax authorities were arguing before the courts that the value of the shares in the intermediate holding company represents an underlying Indian asset, and the disposal is within the charge to Indian tax. Vodafone (as purchaser) was assessed because it should have collected tax on behalf of the vendor by way of withholding tax. A similar approach was followed in *Richter Holding Ltd v ADIT* (W.P No 7716 of 2011) (TII-14-HC-KAR-INTL) (24 March 2011, unreported). However, in an Indian Supreme Court ruling in January 2012 the decision was overturned.

Following this, the Indian Government amended the relevant legislation with retrospective effect from 1 April 1962, to consider that 'an asset or capital asset being any share or interest in a company or entity registered or incorporated outside India shall be deemed to be and shall always be deemed to have been situated in India, if the share or interest derives, directly or indirectly, its value substantially from assets located in India'. The definition of 'property' was amended with the same retrospective effect to include 'any rights in an Indian company including rights of management or control or any rights whatsoever'.

To make sure everything was covered, the term 'transfer' was also amended with retrospective effect to include 'disposing of or parting with an asset or any interest, directly or indirectly, absolutely or conditionally, voluntarily or involuntarily, by way of an agreement (whether entered into in India or outside) notwithstanding that such transfer of rights has been characterized as being effected or dependent upon or flowing from the transfer of a share or shares of a company registered or incorporated outside India'.

This, together with the introduction of a new GAAR in India will effectively ensure that such transactions are taxed in future in India. It remains to be seen the extent to which the provisions will be enforced retrospectively.

In addition, the Indian government is putting significant pressure on Mauritius to amend the India/Mauritius DTA to remove the favourable capital gains treatment for Mauritius companies.

## Planning—overseas reorganisations

**[A11.15]** Overseas jurisdictions may provide for tax-free reorganisations which may also satisfy the conditions to be tax-free under UK reorganisation provisions.

For example, the reorganisation shown in Diagram 4 may qualify as a non-divisive Type D Reorganisation which would be tax-free for US tax purposes. It may also meet the conditions of TCGA 1992, s 136 and also be tax-free for UK tax purposes (clearance may be advisable under TCGA 1992, s 137(1)).

Diagram 4

```
                    ┌──────────────┐
                    │      UK      │  ◄──────── issue of shares
                    └──────────────┘
                      │          │
        ┌──────────────┐        ┌──────────────┐
        │   US1 Inc.   │ ──────►│   US2 Inc.   │
        └──────────────┘        └──────────────┘
              transfer of assets
```

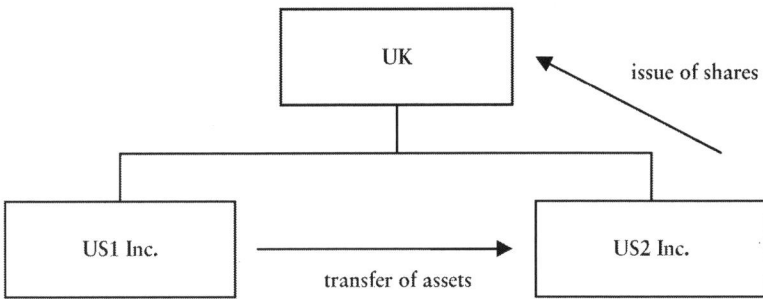

However, there are some circumstances where overseas reorganisations would not satisfy the relevant UK conditions.

Diagram 5 shows another reorganisation which may qualify as a non-divisive Type D Reorganisation for US tax purposes. For UK tax purposes, a reorganisation must be a 'scheme of reconstruction' in order to fall within TCGA 1992, s 136, which requires (*inter alia*) that ordinary share capital is issued (TCGA 1992, Sch 5AA, para 2).

Depending on the terms of the LLC agreement, members' interests in a US LLC may not constitute 'ordinary share capital', and therefore the reorganisation would not satisfy the conditions of s 136.

Diagram 5

```
                    ┌──────────────┐
                    │      UK      │
                    └──────────────┘
                      │          │
        ┌──────────────┐        ┌──────────────┐
        │   US1 LLC    │ ──────►│   US2 LLC    │
        └──────────────┘        └──────────────┘
              transfer of assets
```

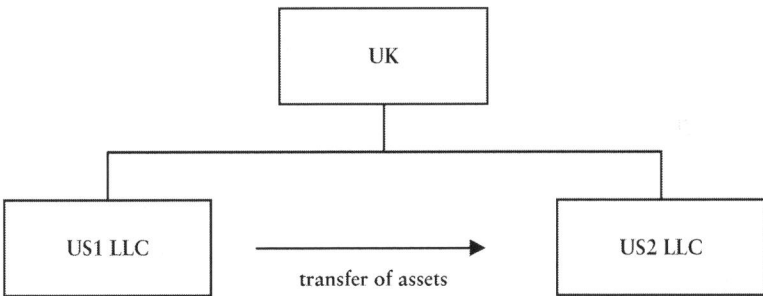

Diagram 6 shows a reorganisation which may qualify as a triangular Type D Reorganisation for US tax purposes. The UK tax rules in respect of a 'scheme of reconstruction' require that the successor company (US2 Inc) issues shares to the shareholders of the predecessor company (US1 Inc.). As BVI issues the shares, this requirement is not met, and therefore the reorganisation would not satisfy the conditions of s 136.

Diagram 6

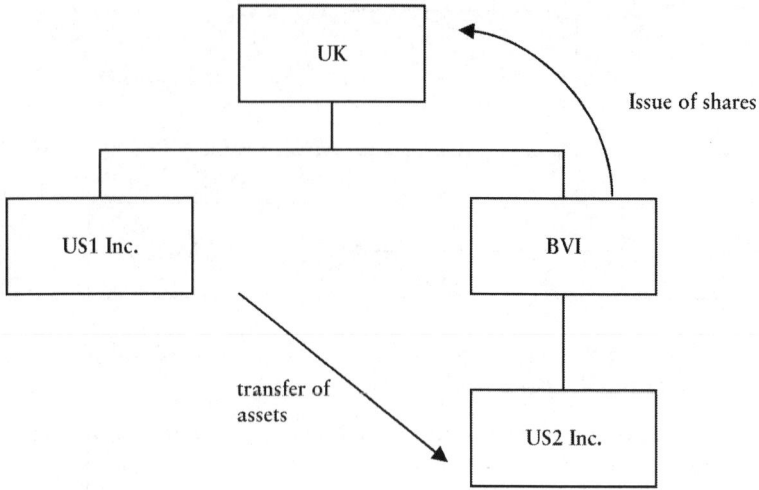

In order for the reorganisation shown in the diagram above to meet the requirement of issuing share capital in the successor company, it would be necessary to undertake the reorganisation as shown in Diagram 7. The assets could subsequently be transferred from BVI to US2 Inc, and the reorganisation may still be tax-free for US tax purposes.

Diagram 7

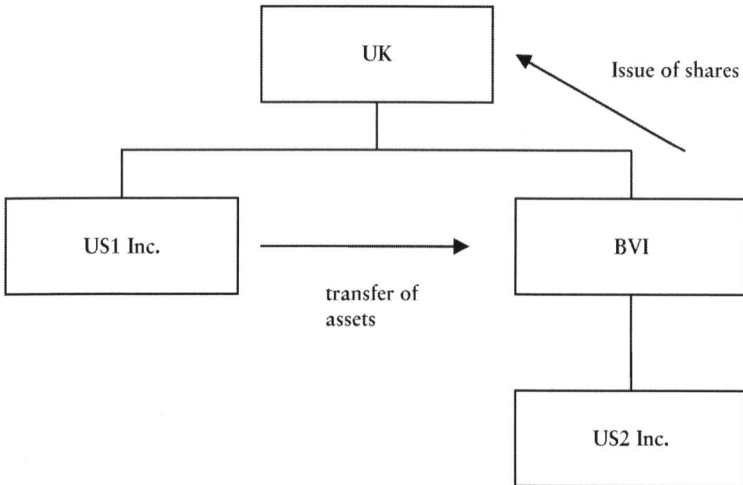

### Substantial shareholding exemption

**[A11.16]** The substantial shareholding exemption (TCGA 1992, Sch 7AC) provides that gains made by UK companies on the disposal of subsidiaries are exempt from tax, subject to meeting certain conditions. These conditions are, broadly, that:

(a)    the investing company has held at least 10% of the ordinary share capital of the investee company for twelve months out of the previous two years;

(b)    the investing company is a trading company or the member of a trading group both from the beginning of the twelve month period to the date of disposal, and immediately after the disposal;

(c)    the investee company is a trading company or the holding company of a trading (sub-)group both from the beginning of the twelve month period to the date of disposal, and immediately after the disposal.

There is no requirement that the investee company is resident in the UK or has a permanent establishment in the UK—Sch 7AC, para 18 merely requires that the company is trading.

A gain realised by a UK company on disposal of an overseas subsidiary may therefore be exempt provided the conditions are satisfied (see **A11.4** in relation to the ordinary share capital requirement).

Diagram 8

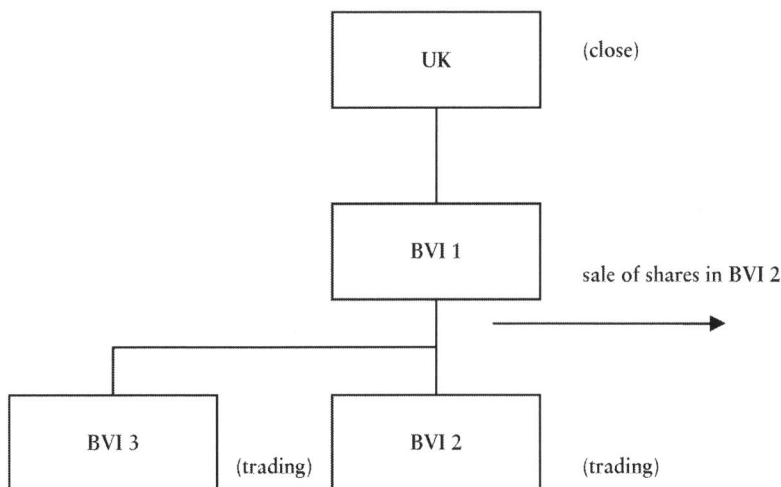

Equally, the substantial shareholding exemption can apply to gains attributed to shareholders under TCGA 1992, s 13.

As outlined in Diagram 8, the gain realised by BVI1 on disposal of the shares in BVI2 could be attributed to UK under s 13. The opening words of s 13 provide that 'this section applies as respects *chargeable gains* accruing to a company' (my emphasis). Schedule 7AC provides that 'a gain accruing to a company . . . is not a chargeable gain'. A gain which is not a chargeable gain by virtue of Sch 7AC does not therefore fall within s 13.

However, an issue arises in the situation shown in Diagram 9. Following the disposal of BVI2, BVI1 has no other trading activity and cannot satisfy the conditions of the main exemption (TCGA 1992, Sch7AC, para 1).

If the investing company is liquidated immediately following the disposal, HMRC accept that the trading activity condition is satisfied for the subsidiary exemption (TCGA 1992, Sch 7AC, para 3) by virtue of sub-paragraph 3. However, the subsidiary exemption requires that that the investing company is resident in the UK. As BVI1 is not resident in the UK it does not meet this requirement, and the disposal does not qualify for either the main or the subsidiary exemption. A chargeable gain therefore arises, which can be attributed to UK under s 13.

BVI1 would need to reinvest the disposal proceeds in a qualifying trading activity in order to be a 'trading company' following the disposal, and therefore satisfy the conditions of the main exemption. There is no requirement in the main exemption that the investing company is UK resident.

**Diagram 9**

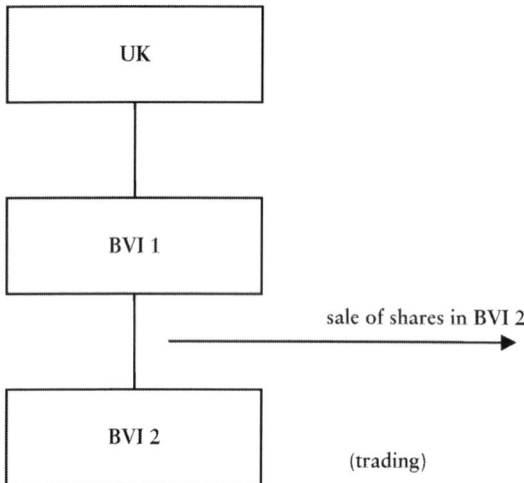

The substantial shareholding exemption should be reviewed even where a disposal is made by a non-UK company, if an attribution under s 13 may be in point.

If the conditions of the subsidiary exemption would be satisfied if the investing company were UK resident, then the company could be made UK resident prior to the disposal (see A9.51). The conditions of the substantial shareholding exemption would then be satisfied and the disposal made tax free. No attribution would be required under s 13 because the company would be UK resident.

## Incorporation of overseas branch

**[A11.17]** Gains arising on the incorporation of a foreign branch may be held over against the base cost of the shares in the new subsidiary. This is discussed in **A9.46**.

**A9.46** also outlines the planning possibilities which arise from this.

### EU Merger Directive

**[A11.18]** TCGA 1992, s 140C enacted the provisions of the EU Merger Directive in UK law. The effect of the Directive is that where a UK company has a permanent establishment in another EU Member State, that permanent establishment can be incorporated in that Member State in exchange for the issue of shares or securities to the UK company without a charge to tax in the other Member State. The UK may tax the transfer of assets, but must give relief for the overseas tax which would have been charged but for the Directive. Whilst there may be circumstances where a transfer of the assets of a permanent establishment in an overseas EU state could be relieved under either TCGA 1992, ss 140 or 140C, a claim may not be made under both with respect to the same transfer.

There is a similar provision in s 140F in relation to the transfer of assets of an overseas permanent establishment on the merger of a UK company into a European *Societas Europaea*.

Branch incorporation using s 140C is also discussed in **A9.49**.

# Intangible assets

**[A11.19]** For corporation tax purposes, intangible assets created after 1 April 2002, or acquired after 1 April 2002 from an unconnected party, fall to be treated under CTA 2009, Part 8 rather than TCGA.

Part 8 applies broadly similar provisions to intangible assets as those applied by TCGA to capital assets. These are noted below as they are relevant to international structures, and important differences are highlighted.

|  | TCGA 1992 | CTA 2009 Part 8 |
|---|---|---|
| Value shifting | s 29, s 30 | no provision |
| Incorporation of foreign branch | s 140 | s 827 |
|  |  | (clearance required under s 831) |
| Group relief | s 170 ff | s 774 ff |
| Reorganisation | s 135 ff | s 818 |
| Taxation of assets held for UK permanent establishment | s 10B | ss 741 and 745 |

| | TCGA 1992 | CTA 2009 Part 8 |
|---|---|---|
| Attribution of gains to participators | s 13 | within Controlled Foreign Company (CFC) rules ICTA 1988, s 747 ff |
| Deemed gain on migration | s 185 | s 859 |
| Uplift in base cost on inward migration | no provision | s 863 |

## Basic principles—attribution of gains to resident shareholders

[A11.20] If a company which is resident outside the UK, but which would be close if it were UK resident makes a chargeable gain, part of this gain may be attributed to UK participators under TCGA 1992, s 13.

Diagram 10 sets out a flowchart which summarises the circumstances under which s 13 will apply. The main restrictions to its application are that:

(a)    it only applies to 'close' companies and groups as defined in CTA 2010, s 439, which means that in practice it applies to privately held groups rather than large groups with many shareholders.

(b)    gains are only attributed to 'participators' (as defined in CTA 2010, s 454) with an interest of more than 25% (increased from 10% by Finance Act 2013).

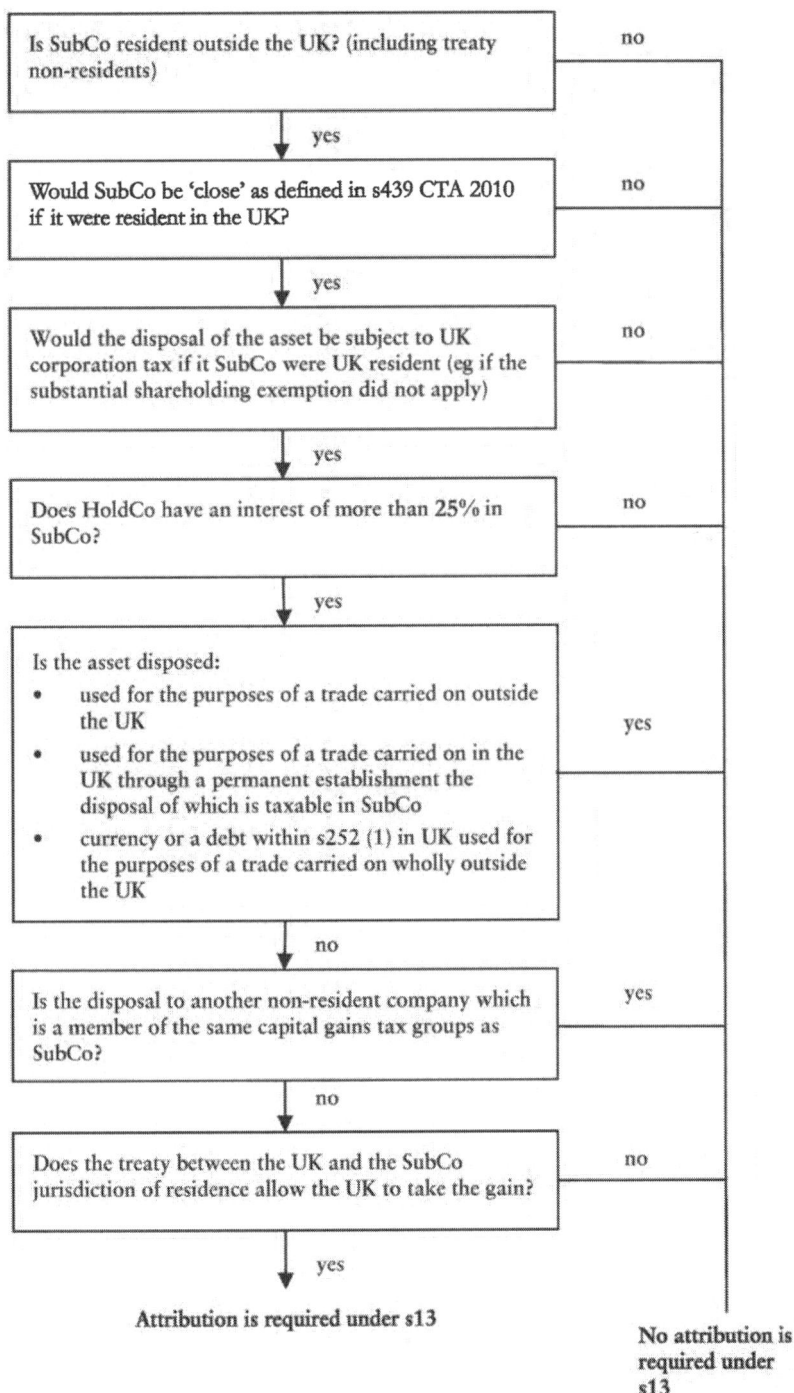

Diagram 10

| | |
|---|---|
| Is SubCo resident outside the UK? (including treaty non-residents) | no |

↓ yes

| | |
|---|---|
| Would SubCo be 'close' as defined in s439 CTA 2010 if it were resident in the UK? | no |

↓ yes

| | |
|---|---|
| Would the disposal of the asset be subject to UK corporation tax if it SubCo were UK resident (eg if the substantial shareholding exemption did not apply) | no |

↓ yes

| | |
|---|---|
| Does HoldCo have an interest of more than 25% in SubCo? | no |

↓ yes

| | |
|---|---|
| Is the asset disposed: <br> • used for the purposes of a trade carried on outside the UK <br> • used for the purposes of a trade carried on in the UK through a permanent establishment the disposal of which is taxable in SubCo <br> • currency or a debt within s252 (1) in UK used for the purposes of a trade carried on wholly outside the UK | yes |

↓ no

| | |
|---|---|
| Is the disposal to another non-resident company which is a member of the same capital gains tax groups as SubCo? | yes |

↓ no

| | |
|---|---|
| Does the treaty between the UK and the SubCo jurisdiction of residence allow the UK to take the gain? | no |

↓ yes

**Attribution is required under s13**

**No attribution is required under s13**

Diagram 11 shows a structure under which s 13 may apply.

**Diagram 11**

```
┌─────────────────────┐
│                     │     (close)
│         UK          │
│                     │
└──────────┬──────────┘
           │
┌──────────┴──────────┐
│                     │
│         BVI         │
│                     │
└─────────────────────┘

        ──────────────────────▶
             sells assets
```

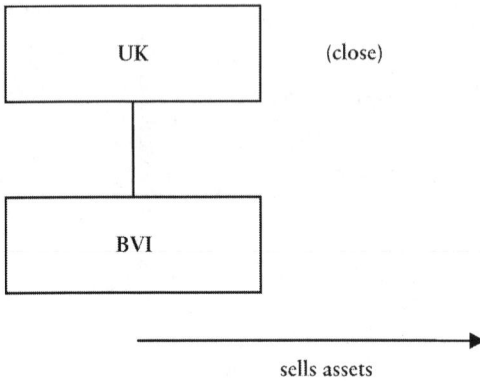

No attribution is required under s 13 if either:

• a company in the intermediate overseas holding structure is not close, because attribution through the holding structure under s 13(9) is only possible if every company in the holding structure is close;
• the company realising the gain is not close.

A company will not be close if it has a large number of shareholders. In certain offshore jurisdictions it is possible to establish a 'protected cell company'. A protected cell company has a number of unrelated shareholders, each of whom can hold shares in a separate cell. Each cell is operated as if it were a standalone company, but for legal purposes there is only one company—it is this which must be considered for s 13 purposes. However, this is an aggressive structure which would very likely to be challenged by HMRC.

Although restructuring can be undertaken prior to realisation of a gain it is better to ensure that the holding structure is not close when it is first established.

The FA 2013, s 62 made a number of changes to TCGA 1992, s 13. The main impact of which was to introduce a motive test but also to raise the de-minimis exemption in TCGA 1992, s 13.

### Attribution of gain

**[A11.21]** When attributing the gain any intermediate non-UK companies are looked through in order to attribute this gain to the ultimate UK participator (s 13(9)).

The exception to this is where non-resident trustees are participators. In this case, the gain is attributed to the non-resident trustees. Other anti-avoidance legislation (TCGA 1992, ss 86 and 87) exists to ensure that gains arising to the trustees are taxable on UK resident individual beneficiaries or settlors.

The part of the gain treated as accruing to the participator is that which corresponds to his 'interest as a participator' (s 13(3)). This requires that all factors which can make a person a participator are taken into account and the gain is then divided on a 'just and reasonable basis' (s 13(13)(b)). This is illustrated in Example 1 and Example 2.

## Example 1

Shareholder 1 and Shareholder 2 each hold a 50% shareholding in OffshoreCo which is resident outside the UK, and Shareholder 2 has made an interest-free loan of EUR2m to OffshoreCo. OffshoreCo has net assets of EUR10m. On a winding up, Shareholder 1 would receive EUR4m and Shareholder 2 EUR6m (because of his loan). OffshoreCo is a close company because five or fewer participators would receive the majority of the assets on a winding up.

If OffshoreCo makes a chargeable gain, on a just and reasonable basis, 40% would be treated as accruing to Shareholder 1, and 60% to Shareholder 2.

## Example 2

Example 1 would be unchanged if there were an intermediate non-UK holding company between the shareholders and OffshoreCo. If instead there were an intermediate UK holding company, the entire gain would be treated as accruing to UKCo as it is the only participator in OffshoreCo.

HMRC consider (CG57260) that loans which are made on normal commercial terms are disregarded when considering a participator's interest. In Example 1, if interest had been charged at an arm's length rate on the loan by Shareholder 1, it may be possible to argue that Shareholder 1's interest as a participator is only 50%. Only 50% of the chargeable gain would therefore, on a just and reasonable basis, be treated as accruing to Shareholder 1.

It may be more difficult to determine the just and reasonable apportionment in more complicated circumstances. For example, in a protected cell company, a shareholder may hold 100% of the shares in a particular cell, but only (say) 25% of the shares in the entire company. If the cell makes a gain, the shareholder is entitled to 100% of this gain—his interest in the entire company is not relevant. On a just and reasonable basis, 100% of the gain would be treated as accruing to Shareholder 1.

No attribution is required under s 13 if the UK shareholder is not a participator at the time the gain is realised. For example:

- the shares could be repurchased by the company prior to the gain being made;
- the shares could be sold to another shareholder—this could be on deferred terms which the other shareholder could satisfy by receiving a dividend from the overseas company once the gain has been realised.

However, it is important that the UK shareholder does not inadvertently remain a participator, for example, if the consideration for a share repurchase is left outstanding as a loan, the UK shareholder will still be entitled to participate in the profits of the company and therefore will remain a participator.

*Calculation of gain*

**[A11.22]** The chargeable gain of the overseas company which is deemed to accrue to the UK resident participators must be calculated on a UK corporation tax basis (s 13(11A)).

This can create particular issues where no gain has been recognised in the overseas jurisdiction, but would be recognised under UK principles, as it may not be immediately apparent that a charge under s 13 may arise.

**Liquidation**

**[A11.23]** On the liquidation of a company, any distributions are normally treated as a disposal by the company receiving the distribution. In Diagram 12, the BVI company will be treated as realising a chargeable gain under UK principles, and this will be attributed to the UK resident participators.

Diagram 12

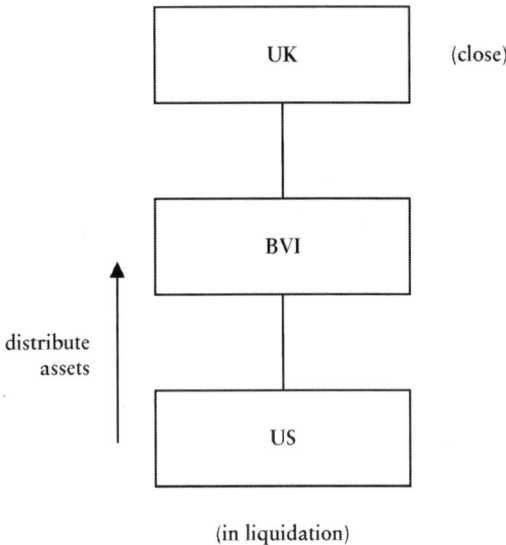

**Value shifting**

**[A11.24]** In Diagram 13, OffshoreCo1 exercises its control (via its shareholding) such that BVI2 issues shares to another shareholder at undervalue. This results in value passing out of OffshoreCo1's shareholding into the third party's shareholding, such that BVI1 is deemed by virtue of s 29 to crystallise a capital gain. This capital gain would be attributed to the UK resident participators under s 13.

Diagram 13

```
┌──────────────┐
│      UK      │        (close)
└──────────────┘
        │
        │
┌──────────────┐                    third party
│    BVI 1     │                          ↗
└──────────────┘                       ↗
        │                           ↗
        │                        ↗
┌──────────────┐              ↗
│    BVI 2     │───────────↗
└──────────────┘
                    issue of shares for
                    less than MV
```

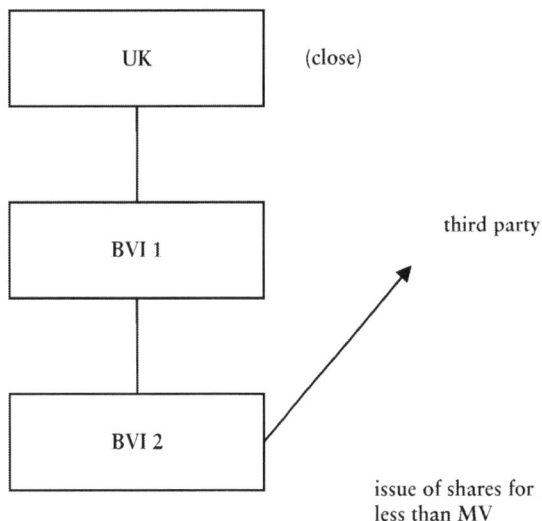

## Substantial shareholding exemption

**[A11.25]** The substantial shareholding exemption will in some cases provide exemption from s 13, as noted above under **A11.16**.

## Intra-group transfers

**[A11.26]** Section 13 specifically imports the TCGA 1992, s 171 relief for intra-group transfers between non-resident companies (TCGA 1992, s 14). This will generally mean that an intra-group transfer of assets will not give rise to a capital gain when calculated on a corporation tax basis, and therefore no gain can be deemed to accrue under s 13.

However, the relief is withdrawn if the transferee company leaves the group within six years of the transfer, and the clawback of this relief will give rise to a capital gain which can be deemed to accrue to the participator under s 13.

In addition, s 14 does not provide relief where a transfer is made from a non-resident company to a UK resident company.

## Diagram 14

Step 1

```
                    ┌─────────────────────┐
                    │  Offshore VendorCo  │
                    └──────────┬──────────┘
                               │
                    ┌──────────┴──────────┐
                    │  Offshore HoldCo    │
                    └──────────┬──────────┘
              ┌────────────────┴────────────────┐
    ┌─────────┴─────────┐            ┌───────────┴─────────┐
    │   Offshore Sub1   │            │   Offshore Sub2     │
    └───────────────────┘            └─────────────────────┘
```

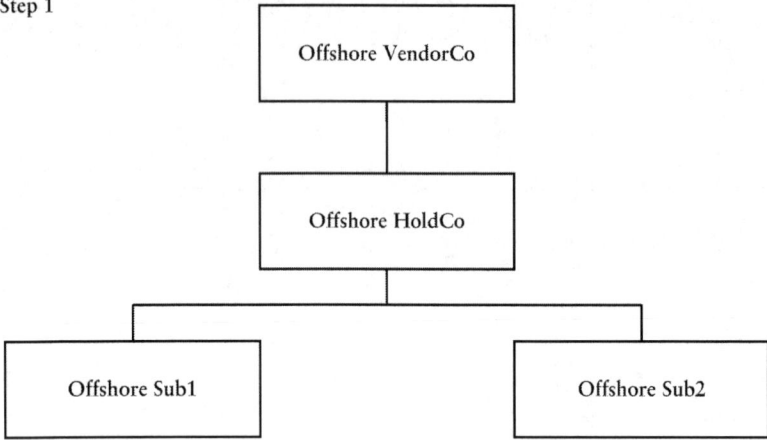

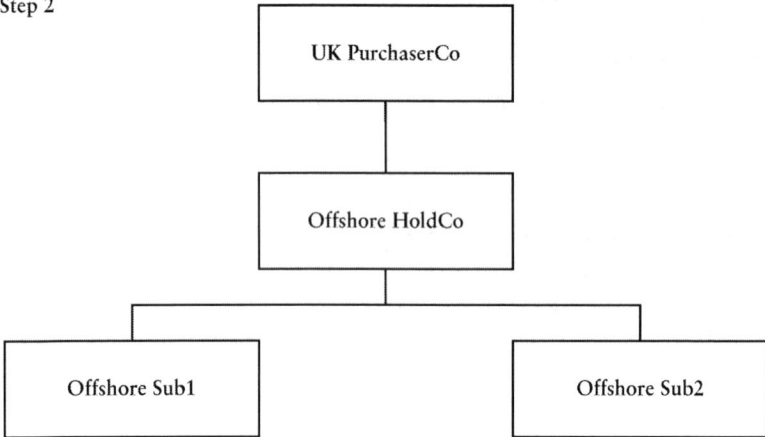

Asset
base cost 100        ─────────transfer────────►
                     transfer
                     market value 500

Step 2

```
                    ┌─────────────────────┐
                    │   UK PurchaserCo    │
                    └──────────┬──────────┘
                               │
                    ┌──────────┴──────────┐
                    │  Offshore HoldCo    │
                    └──────────┬──────────┘
              ┌────────────────┴────────────────┐
    ┌─────────┴─────────┐            ┌───────────┴─────────┐
    │   Offshore Sub1   │            │   Offshore Sub2     │
    └───────────────────┘            └─────────────────────┘
```

Asset
base cost 100

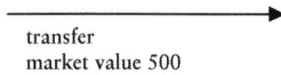

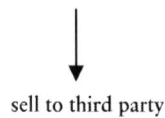

↓

sell to third party

## Diagram 15

Step 1

```
                    ┌─────────────────────┐
                    │  Offshore VendorCo  │
                    └─────────────────────┘
                              │
                    ┌─────────────────────┐
                    │   Offshore HoldCo   │
                    └─────────────────────┘
                              │                    no ordinary share capital
          ┌───────────────────┴───────────────────────┐
┌─────────────────────┐                    ┌─────────────────────────┐
│                     │                    │      Offshore Sub2      │
│   Offshore Sub1     │                    │   (guarantee company)   │
└─────────────────────┘                    └─────────────────────────┘
```

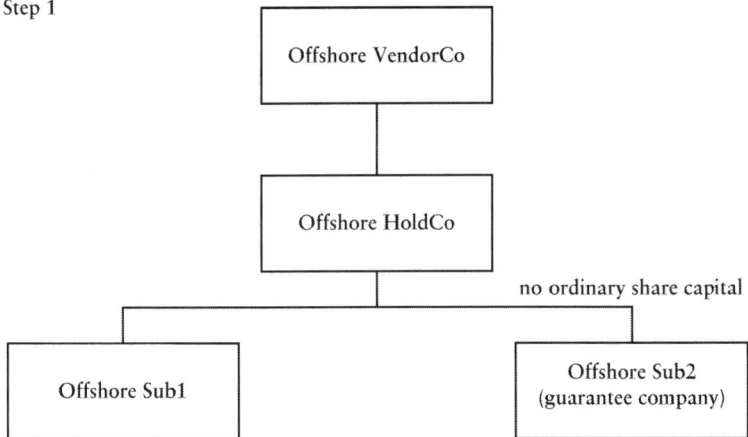

Asset
base cost 100

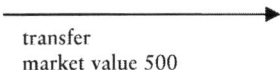

transfer
market value 500

Step 2

```
                    ┌─────────────────────┐
                    │   UK PurchaserCo    │
                    └─────────────────────┘
                              │
                    ┌─────────────────────┐
                    │   Offshore HoldCo   │
                    └─────────────────────┘
                              │                    no ordinary share capital
          ┌───────────────────┴───────────────────────┐
┌─────────────────────┐                    ┌─────────────────────────┐
│                     │                    │      Offshore Sub2      │
│   Offshore Sub1     │                    │   (guarantee company)   │
└─────────────────────┘                    └─────────────────────────┘
```

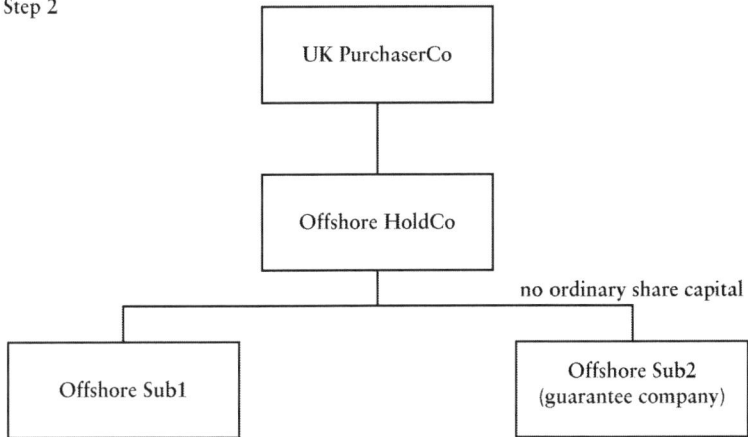

Asset
base cost 500

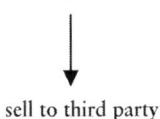

sell to third party

Section 14(1) provides that '[t]his section has effect for the purposes of section 13'. There is no requirement that there would be otherwise be an attribution under s 13. Section 14 could therefore apply to an intra-group transfer even when there are no UK participators. In this case, the base cost under s 13 would be determined in accordance with s 14, which would have 'effect for the purposes of section 13'.

In Diagram 14, the UK Purchaser Co acquires the shares in Offshore HoldCo following an intra-group transfer of an asset from Offshore Sub1 to Offshore Sub2. The gain attributed to UK Purchaser Co on a subsequent disposal of the asset will be calculated by reference to the original base cost to Offshore Sub1, because the original transfer of the asset would fall within s 14.

Section 14 will not apply where the transferor and transferee companies are not members of the same group, as defined for capital gains tax purposes. A company will not be a member of a group if it does not have ordinary share capital.

The structure in Diagram 15 is the same as in Diagram 14, but Offshore Sub2 is a company limited by guarantee, which does not have share capital, and is therefore not a member of the same group as Offshore Sub1. The original transfer of the asset from Offshore Sub1 to Offshore Sub2 will not fall within s 14. On a subsequent disposal of the asset, the gain attributed to UK Purchaser Co under s 13 will be calculated by reference to a base cost equal to market value at the time of the transfer from Offshore Sub1 (by virtue of TCGA 1992, s 17 will apply).

## Rate of tax

**[A11.27]** Although the gain is calculated on a UK corporation tax basis, the tax charged will depend on the nature of the participator to whom it is deemed to accrue. A UK company will pay corporation tax of up to 21%.

Any overseas tax paid by the company in fact making the disposal will reduce the amount of UK tax due on the shareholder.

In addition, if the gain is distributed (either by way of dividend or capital distribution) within four years from the date the gain accrues, or (if earlier) within three years of the accounting period in which the gain accrues, the tax paid by the shareholder under s 13 will reduce the subsequent tax paid (s 13(5A)).

## Exemptions

**[A11.28]** Section 13 does not apply to gains realised on:

(a)     assets used by a UK permanent establishment of the asset-holding company (which would in any case be subject to UK tax on gains under s 10B) (s 13(5)(d));

(b)     assets used for the purposes of a trade carried on by the asset-holding company outside the UK (s 13(5)(b));

(c)     trading currency and debts (s 13(5)(c)).

These exemptions require that the company making the disposal itself carries on the relevant trade. Relief is not therefore available where one group company owns an asset which is used by another company in the group.

### Relief under DTAs

**[A11.29]** HMRC have confirmed that relief under a DTA is available in respect of s 13 if there is a properly drafted capital gains article in the DTA which provides that the transferor is not taxable in the UK (CCAB TR500 10/3/83 Consultative Committee of Accounting Bodies).

However, some of the UK's newer DTAs specifically exclude relief for certain capital gains, including s 13 gains. The capital gains article of the UK/Mauritius DTA for instance provides that:

'(1)    The provisions of this Article shall not affect the right of a Contracting State to levy according to its law a tax chargeable in respect of gains from the alienation of any property on a person who is a resident of that State at any time during the fiscal year in which the property is alienated . . . '

The UK therefore retains taxing rights over any gains which arise to a UK resident, including gains which are deemed to arise under s 13. The DTA in this case only provides relief from tax in Mauritius for gains arising on certain assets.

This wording can be contrasted with the capital gains article of the UK/Ireland DTA for instance, which provides that:

'(2)    The provisions of paragraph 5 shall not affect the right of a Contracting State to levy according to its law a tax chargeable in respect of gains from the alienation of any property derived by an individual who is a resident of the other Contracting State . . . '

The UK therefore only retains taxing rights over gains which are derived by an individual who is an Irish resident (which is relevant to the taxation of gains realised by temporary non-residents). Paragraph 6 does not apply to gains realised by a company, and the DTA would provide relief where gains are deemed to arise under s 13.

Most UK DTAs still follow the latter model and provide relief in respect of s 13. However, the more recent DTAs with France, Slovenia, Netherlands and Mauritius follow the former model, and do not provide relief from tax on gains which are deemed to arise under s 13. There is a risk that as other DTAs are renegotiated they will be amended to follow this model.

In addition, as noted above, the UK is likely to retain taxing rights over real estate located in the UK, and therefore s 13 is likely to apply to gains realised on UK property notwithstanding the existence of a DTA.

Where there is no DTA in place between the UK and the jurisdiction in which a subsidiary is resident, it may be possible to transfer an asset to another subsidiary which is resident in a jurisdiction which does have a DTA with the UK prior to the asset being sold.

In Diagram 16, any gain on the disposal of the asset by the Jersey subsidiary will be attributed to the UK parent company under s 13.

In Diagram 17, the asset is transferred to a Luxembourg subsidiary prior to disposal. The transfer will take place under TCGA 1992, s 14 as both companies are members of the same group, and no gain will arise. The subsequent disposal of the asset by the Luxembourg subsidiary will not result in an exit charge under s 14, and any gain arising will be subject to relief under the UK/Luxembourg DTA.

It is of course necessary to transfer the asset to a subsidiary which is resident in a jurisdiction which will not itself subject the gain to tax, or at least subject it to tax at a lower rate than it would be in the UK.

As an alternative to the structure in Diagram 17 of the Jersey company could be made resident in another jurisdiction by virtue of being redomiciled there or by its management and control being transferred there if that is effective for the purposes of the relevant domestic law and DTA.

**Diagram 16**

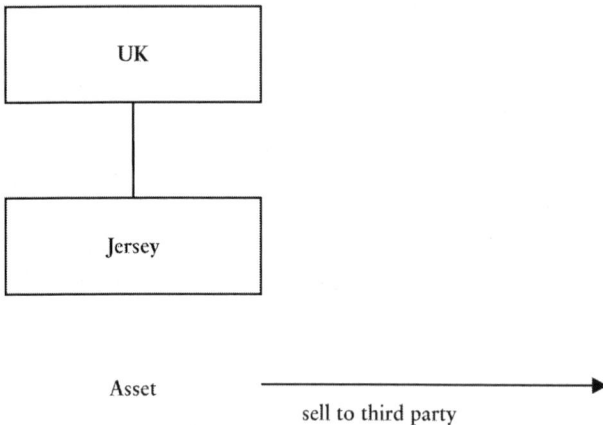

**Diagram 17**

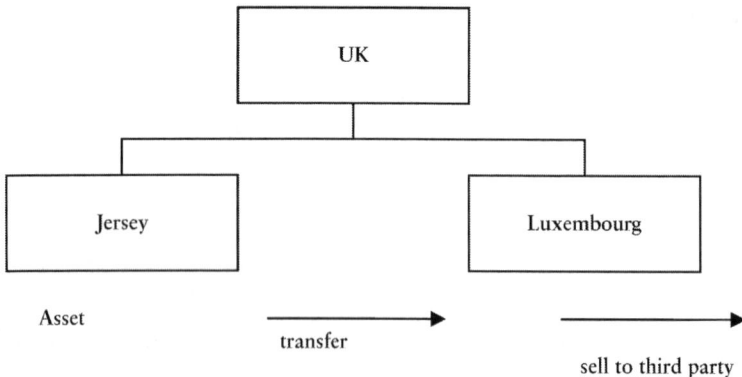

## European law

**[A11.30]** Section 13 does not apply to gains made by companies which are resident in the UK, and is therefore a clear breach of the freedom of establishment in the Treaty of the Functioning of the European Union (TFEU). In February 2011, the European Commission filed a formal request with the UK government to amend s 13 and remedy the breach.

In response to this on 30 July 2012 HMRC issued a consultation document on the reform of s 13 which proposed to include a motive test for the first time, as well as expanding the categories of assets that would be excluded from the charge. This was subsequently enacted by Finance Act 2013, s 62 which amended s 13 with effect from 5 April 2013. In broad terms, the new version provides for three main changes:

(1)    Gains will only be attributed to participators owning more than 25% of the company;
(2)    Gains will be excluded from charge under s 13 where the asset was used, and used only, for the purposes of 'economically significant' activities carried on outside the UK by the company through a business establishment in a territory outside the UK; and
(3)    Participators will not be assessable on gains of the company on a disposal of an asset where neither:
(a)    the disposal by the company, nor
(b)    the acquisition or holding of the asset by the company
formed part of a CGT or CT avoidance scheme or arrangements.

## Economically significant activities

**[A11.31]** The new s 13(5A), (4)–(6) defines the test of economically significant activities.

This depends on the company having a 'business establishment' in a country outside the UK but that does not need to be the country where it is resident. The test of 'business establishment' is the permanent establishment test set out in CTA 2010, ss 1141–1144.

As well as the company having a permanent establishment, it must, through that permanent establishment, carry on economically significant activities which are:

'activities which consist of the provision by the company of goods or services to others on a commercial basis and involve:

a    the use of staff in numbers, and with competence and authority,
b    the use of premises and equipment, and
c    the addition of economic value, by the company, to those to whom the goods or services are provided,

commensurate with the size and nature of those activities.'

The intention is that the exclusion should be denied to companies that are mere wrappers and the test is biased towards trading or quasi-trading activities. Although what must be borne in mind is that the EU law test of proportionality in domestic legislation is that anti-abuse provisions should only counter 'wholly artificial' arrangements. The changes enacted are themselves not immune to future challenge on the grounds that the amended provisions still conflict with EU law.

## No avoidance purpose

**[A11.32]** The motive test in s 13(5)(cb) uses well-known terminology, requiring that:

'neither:

(i)    the disposal of the asset by the company, nor
(ii)   the acquisition or holding of the asset by the company,

formed part of a scheme or arrangements of which the main purpose, or one of the main purposes, was avoidance of liability to capital gains tax or corporation tax . . .'

Given the restrictive nature of the other tests this is likely to be used in many cases where there is an overriding commercial purpose. It is likely to be better to rely on the other exemptions first wherever they apply, simply as a matter of good practice and relative ease of persuading HMRC. However, failure to meet any one of the criteria for exemption in s 13 will not mean that the others cannot be applied. Often, more than one may apply.

The changes to the provisions will hopefully mean that s 13 can be discounted at an early stage in 'genuine' commercial transactions.

See CHAPTER A7 for further discussion on EU law principles.

# A12

# Clearances

## Introduction

[**A12.1**] There are two types of clearance in UK tax law—those which are required to be obtained before a transaction can be undertaken, and those which allow the taxpayer to clarify the application of a particular provision. These are in addition to the normal tax reporting requirements for a company which is subject to UK tax—see **A1.6**.

These latter clearances can provide clarity, certainty and speed of resolution of complex issues to enable businesses to undertake transactions and self assess their tax liabilities with some degree of accuracy.

It is important to understand clearance requirements when undertaking international tax planning as failure to obtain clearances may render a structure open to challenge.

This Chapter considers the clearances which are of particular relevance to international planning. These can be summarised as follows:

| Mandatory clearances | Where relevant |
|---|---|
| Notification of International Movements of Capital | Issue or transfer of shares or securities over £100m |
| Notification of migration | Company ceases to be resident in the UK |
| Double Tax Agreements | Obtain reduced rates of withholding tax |
| Interest and Royalties Directive | Obtain reduced rates of withholding tax |
| Optional clearances | |
| Non statutory clearance service | Many transactions—for example to confirm if the dividend exemption applies, if an overseas company has issued ordinary share capital, or entity classification issues |
| Advance Pricing Agreements (APAs) | Significant transactions with connected parties |
| Advance Thin Capitalisation Agreements (ATCAs) | Lending from connected parties |
| Transactions in land | Sale of UK land which has been developed or acquired with a view to selling at a profit |
| Transfer of intangible assets to an overseas company | Transfer of intangible assets on incorporation of a branch |

In addition, UK domestic provisions such as share exchanges (TCGA 1992, s 135) and transactions in securities (CTA 2010, Part 15) may provide for clearance procedures when undertaking cross-border restructuring.

# Notification of International Movements of Capital (FA 2009, Sch 17)

## *Reporting requirement*

**[A12.2]** Transactions must be reported within six months of being undertaken. The information which must be included in the report is set out in the International Movement of Capital (Required Information) Regulations SI 2009/2192.

The requirement falls within TMA 1970, s 98, and therefore the penalty for failure to report will be up to £300 and potentially a daily penalty of up to £60.

The requirement applies to all transactions with a value over £100m. The regulations set out how the value of the transaction is to be calculated. It should be noted that a 'series of transactions' must be aggregated when calculating their value.

## Scope of rules

**[A12.3]** The reporting requirement applies to:

(a)    a body corporate (which would include an LLP);
(b)    which is resident in the UK;
(c)    which controls one or more bodies corporate not resident in the UK (which would include a non-resident LLP); and
(d)    which is not controlled by another UK body corporate (this effectively imposes the notification requirement on the ultimate parent company of a group, rather than on its UK subsidiaries).

For example, if a UK LLP owns 100% of a UK company, which in turn owns 100% of an overseas subsidiary, the notification requirement will fall on the LLP.

Control for these purposes is defined by reference to the CFC rules (s 755D— see **A6.3**).

Where a group has a non-UK holding company, which in turn has more than one UK sub-holding company, one of the UK sub-holding companies may be nominated to be responsible for the reporting requirement for the whole group, including the subgroups controlled by the other UK sub-holding companies. For example, in Diagram 1, either UK1 or UK2 could be nominated. In the absence of a nomination, both UK1 and UK2 would be responsible for reporting any relevant transactions.

Diagram 1

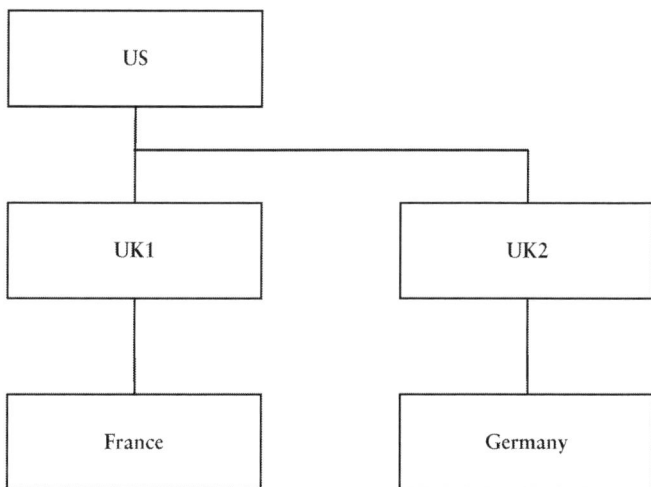

A body corporate will only fall within the notification requirement if it controls non-resident bodies corporate. A group with only UK subsidiaries will never therefore fall within the notification requirement.

### Reportable transactions

**[A12.4]** Reportable transactions are as follows:

(1)     An issue of shares or debentures by a foreign subsidiary. A subsidiary is a body corporate which is controlled by the UK body corporate, as defined by reference to the Controlled Foreign Companies (CFC) rules. The value of this transaction is the market value of the shares or debentures.

(2)     A transfer by the reporting entity, or a transfer caused or permitted by the reporting entity, of shares or debentures of a foreign subsidiary in which the reporting entity has an interest. Where the reporting entity is the nominated entity for a group with a non-UK parent company (see above), this includes transfers caused or permitted by other UK sub-holding companies in the group. The value of this transaction is the market value of the shares or debentures.

(3)     A transaction which results in a foreign subsidiary becoming a controlling partner in a partnership. Control for these purposes means the right to share in more than 50% of the assets or more than 50% of the income of the partnership. The value of this transaction is the market value of the share in the partnership held by the subsidiary either immediately after it becomes a partner, or immediately before it ceases to be a partner. Diagram 2 illustrates a reportable transaction of this type. There is no requirement that the partnership itself is a non-UK partnership.

Diagram 2

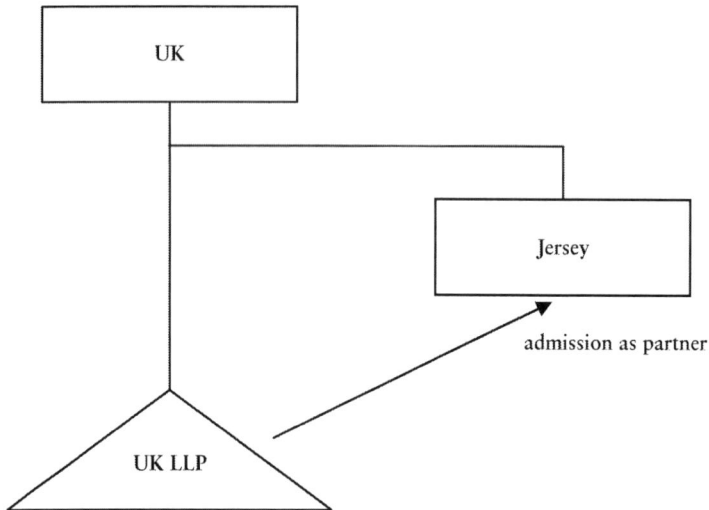

For these purposes, a debenture takes its ordinary meaning (ie any evidence in writing of a debt). It may be possible in some circumstances to make a loan without issuing a debenture.

Regulations may specify further reportable transactions, but none have yet been specified.

## Exclusions

**[A12.5]** There are exclusions from the notification requirement for certain transactions. Excluded transactions are:

(a)    transactions carried out in ordinary course of a trade (for instance share dealers); or

(b)    transactions where all parties to the transaction are resident in the same territory; or

(c)    transactions carried out for the purpose of giving security to a bank or an insurance company.

Diagram 3 shows a structure which may qualify under the second of these exclusions, as both the transferor and transferee companies are in the same jurisdiction. The subsidiary whose shares are transferred is not resident in the same jurisdiction, but should not be considered a 'party' to the transaction.

This should be contrasted with Diagram 4 where the issuer of the shares may be considered a 'party' to the transaction, and therefore the exclusion may not apply.

Diagram 3

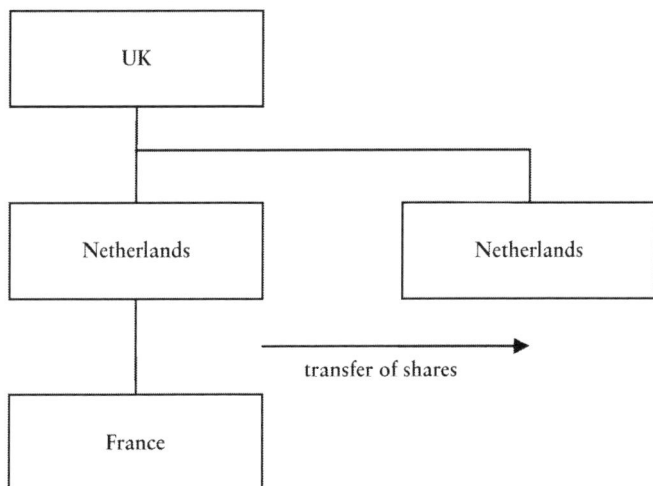

Diagram 4

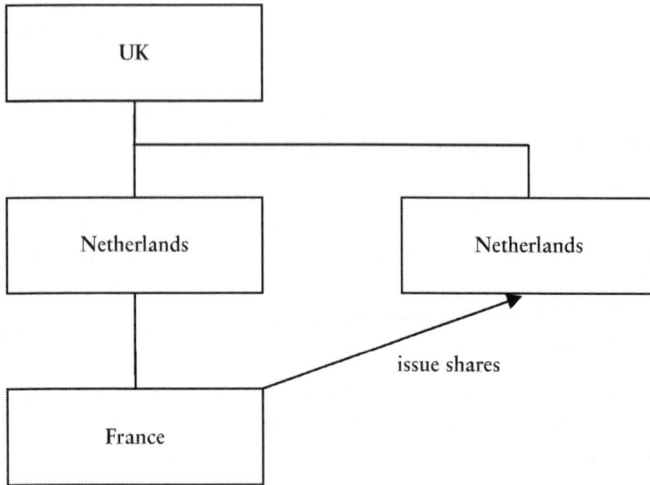

The International Movement of Capital (Required Information) Regulations 2009, SI 2009/2192 specify further exclusions. There is no reporting requirement where:

(1)     Non-redeemable shares are issued to the UK parent or another company within the 51% group. The transaction must take place for full consideration paid in cash to the non-resident company, or in payment for any business undertaking or property acquired by the non-resident company for full consideration.

(2)     Redeemable or non-redeemable shares, or debentures, are issued to a person not connected with the UK parent. The transaction must take place for full consideration but there is no requirement that this is paid in cash. In addition, there must be no arrangements under which the UK parent or a connected person may become entitled to the shares or debentures.

(3)     Redeemable or non-redeemable shares are issued to all existing shareholders of the non-UK resident company in proportion to their shareholding. Shares may only be redeemable if there are no UK resident shareholders, and the transaction takes place for full consideration paid in cash.

(4)     Debentures are issued to the UK parent or another company within the 51% group. The issue must not be part of arrangements under which a loan is made by a non-UK resident company to a UK resident company (whether or not the same amount as the loan which is secured by the debenture).

(5)     Redeemable or non-redeemable shares, or debentures, are transferred by the UK parent or a non-resident company, to a person not connected with the UK parent. The transaction must take place for full consider-

ation but there is no requirement that this is paid in cash. In addition, there must be no arrangements under which the UK parent or a connected person may become entitled to the shares or debentures.

These exclusions should usually enable groups to restructure without the need to report the transaction to HMRC. However, there are certain restructuring transactions where the conditions would not be met.

Diagram 5

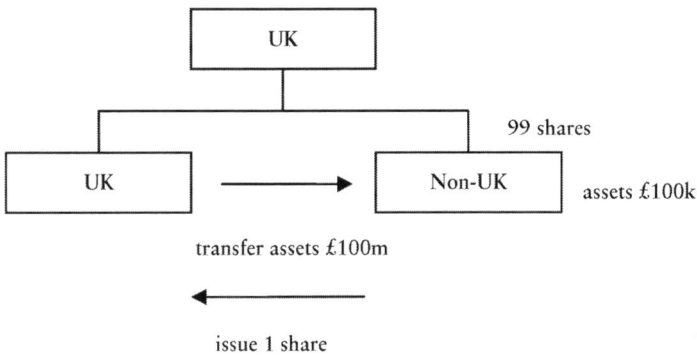

A common transaction is shown in Diagram 5. The UK transferor does not receive 'full consideration' for the transfer of the assets as the value of the shares issued is:

$1\% \times (£100,000,000 + £100,000) = £1,001,000$.

# Notification of migration

**[A12.6]** TCGA 1992, s 185 imposes an 'exit charge' such that assets are deemed to have been disposed of and immediately reacquired at their market value (see **A9.43**), although see **A7.45** above for potential EU challenges to this and new deferral rules under TMA 1970, Sch 3ZB introduced by FA 2013. In addition, TMA 1970, s 109B requires that a company intending to migrate from the UK must first notify HMRC and make acceptable arrangements for payment of all tax due for periods up to the date of the proposed migration.

Tax for these purposes includes:

(a) corporation tax (including any corporation tax which arises as a result of capital gains on the migration);
(b) income tax;
(c) PAYE, and other income tax withheld such as under the construction industry scheme.

Statement of Practice SP2/90 sets out the information which must be provided to HMRC in the notification:

(a) the name of the company, its address in the UK and its place of incorporation;

(b)     its tax district and reference number;

(c)     a copy of the latest available accounts;

(d)     a detailed statement of all tax liabilities which are or will be due for periods commencing before the date of migration. The statement should cover corporation tax, PAYE and income tax any accrued interest on tax. It should also include any charges which arise as a consequence of the migration itself;

(e)     the company's proposals for securing the payment of tax liabilities;

(f)     the intended date of migration;

(g)     the proposed method of payment of tax liabilities.

SP2/90 also sets out what arrangements for payment of tax are likely to be acceptable to HMRC. Typically they will require:

(a)     a guarantee from a UK bank against anticipated liabilities. SP2/90 also refers to a UK company acting as guarantor, but where this is a group company HMRC may not accept the strength of the guarantee;

(b)     a power of attorney appointing an individual in the UK as the company's formal representative. SP2/90 refers to a professional person (a lawyer or accountant) being appointed but in practice HMRC may also accept that a UK resident director or employee of the company can be appointed.

The company's local tax district will be consulted to confirm that anticipated liabilities have been correctly identified. Otherwise, an unlimited guarantee will be required—which an unconnected company or bank may be unlikely to give.

There may be a requirement to agree the valuation of assets being transferred which can increase the length of time it takes to get approval unless an unlimited guarantee is agreed, in which case approval should take less than two months of giving notice. Companies should take this into account to ensure that approval is requested early enough in the process.

### Failure to comply

**[A12.7]** Where a company migrates without meeting the requirements of s 109B the company may be liable for penalties (up to the amount of tax due) and any unpaid tax liabilities may be recovered from directors or certain other group companies.

Where it is not possible to obtain approval before migration takes place, payment of all outstanding tax liabilities should ensure that no penalty arises.

# DTA and Directive withholding tax clearances

### Payments by UK resident companies

**[A12.8]** A UK company may be required to withhold tax from payments of interest and royalties to a non-resident (see **A5.1** and **A5.11**).

The terms of a double tax agreement (DTA) between the UK and the overseas jurisdiction may provide for a reduced rate of withholding tax. For payments to EU residents, the EU Interest and Royalties Directive (enacted in UK law as ITTOIA 2005, s 754 ff) may provide for a reduced rate.

In the case of royalties, a UK company may apply the reduced rate if it has a 'reasonable belief' that the recipient is entitled to it. However, in the case of interest it is necessary to obtain clearance from HMRC before the reduced rate is applied.

### Applications for clearance

**[A12.9]** It is important to note that applications for treaty clearance are made by the recipient, not the payer. All forms are signed by and in the name of the recipient.

In order to apply for clearance, the recipient must first of all be satisfied that the relevant conditions of the treaty or Directive are satisfied, for instance in relation to beneficial ownership or anti-avoidance provisions.

The process is then as follows:

(a)   The form must then be submitted to the tax authority in the jurisdiction where the recipient is resident, in order for them to certify that the recipient is resident there.

(b)   The overseas tax authority passes the form to HMRC Centre for Non-Residents (CNR).

(c)   If CNR are satisfied with the form, they will issue a clearance letter to the payer confirming that the reduced rate of withholding tax to be applied.

Specific treaty clearance forms are available for certain jurisdictions, but a generic form is also available. Forms are (at the time of writing) available at www.hmrc.gov.uk/cnr/app_dtt.htm. Where a claim is made under the Interest and Royalties Directive, the form is available at www.hmrc.gov.uk/cnr/eu-cla im-form.pdf.

If withholding tax has already been suffered by the recipient, then the treaty clearance form also acts as a request for a refund.

The liability to withhold tax arises to the payer of the interest. If interest is paid before clearance is obtained then HMRC will charge interest on the unpaid withholding tax from the date the interest was paid to the date that clearance is given (INTM574040).

If clearance has been submitted and received by CNR before the interest is paid (but clearance not yet given), then interest will arise, but there will be no requirement to pay the withholding tax itself.

In all other cases, even if the application has been submitted to the overseas tax authority, the payer of the interest will be required to pay the withholding tax, and the recipient to recover it. However in practice, HMRC may be prepared to adopt a more concessionary treatment.

It is common for loan agreements to include a 'gross up' clause, such that a UK payer of interest must pay a certain net amount to the recipient. If the recipient has not obtained a treaty clearance for a reduced rate of withholding tax, the payer must gross up the interest payment, account for the withholding tax and pay the correct net amount to the recipient.

This gross up increases the interest cost to the payer, and it is therefore important to ensure that:

(a)     loan agreements commit the lender to obtaining a treaty clearance;

(b)     any refund of withholding tax as a result of obtaining clearance after a gross up has occurred is passed to the payer.

## Income from outside the UK

**[A12.10]** Where a UK company is receiving income from another jurisdiction (whether interest, royalties, dividends or fees) it may be subject to withholding tax. If the DTA between the UK and the other jurisdiction provides for a reduced rate of withholding tax, this may usually be obtained by:

(a)     providing a certificate of residence to the payer or the overseas tax authority; or

(b)     completing a treaty clearance form which is filed with the overseas tax authority; or

(c)     providing confirmation to the payer that the provisions of the DTA apply.

### Certificates of residence

**[A12.11]** In order to obtain a certificate of residence to confirm that the recipient is resident in the UK, an application must be made to HMRC by way of letter. HMRC will typically require the following information:

(a)     the name and address of the payer;

(b)     the purpose for which the certificate is required;

(c)     confirmation that the recipient is the beneficial owner of the income;

(d)     confirmation that the recipient is subject to UK corporation tax;

(e)     where the recipient has overseas permanent establishments;

(f)     where the recipient carries on its trade;

(g)     confirmation that the recipient is centrally managed and controlled in the UK;

(h)     the names and addresses of the directors;

(i)     details of other group members.

Where the UK recipient is a transparent entity (eg a partnership or a trust), the entity itself is not entitled to treaty benefits, and cannot normally complete the relevant forms or obtain a certificate of residence. However, HMRC will usually provide such assurance as they are able about the tax status of the partners themselves.

The entitlement of fiscally transparent entities to relief under a DTA is considered at **A8.25**.

# Non-Statutory Clearances Service

**[A12.12]** The Clearances Service allows businesses to seek clarification from HMRC and receive advance clearance in respect of uncertainties about the tax treatment of a particular transaction.

The commercial significance of the transaction must be demonstrated, and this will be considered in the context of the business making the application. What is commercially significant for a small business may not be significant for a larger business.

Typical international tax planning issues on which HMRC's view may be sought are:

(a)    whether an overseas entity is transparent or opaque, and if it has issued ordinary share capital (which clearances should be addressed to the specific team as outlined in INTM180020);
(b)    if underlying tax is creditable on payment of a non-exempt dividend;
(c)    if the substantial shareholding exemption applies to the disposal of an overseas subsidiary;
(d)    the application of the CFC rules (which clearances should be addressed to the specific team as outlined at www.hmrc.gov.uk/cap).

## *Uncertainty*

**[A12.13]** It should be noted that clearance may only be obtained where there is a genuine uncertainty as to the interpretation of the law and will not be available where it can be determined with certainty as to how a transaction will be subject to tax.

When clearance applications are submitted, the analysis should reflect genuine uncertainty, and not merely provide a single interpretation for HMRC to confirm or not.

## *Application process*

**[A12.14]** Requests for clarification and rulings should be made in writing setting out all of the relevant facts and issues including any questions of interpretation of the law relating to the point on which advice is required. HMRC aim to respond within 28 days unless the matter is difficult or complex in which case HMRC should notify the taxpayer that a response will take longer.

The request should contain the following information:

### Information about the applicant and the application

**[A12.15]** The following information about the company should be provided:

(a)    Name and address of the person carrying on the business (and name of the business if different) and relevant identification number in full, eg Unique Taxpayer Reference, VAT Registration Number;

(b)     Agent's contact details (if relevant) and authority to act for the client where it has not yet been submitted;

(c)     A brief indication of the subject of the application. Fuller details should be provided under the appropriate headings below.

## Information about the transaction(s)

**[A12.16]** The following information about the proposed transactions should be provided:

(a)     The details of which tax(es) the application refers to;

(b)     The reasons why the business is undertaking the transaction;

(c)     The relevant facts about the transaction, set out chronologically as transaction steps, so that HMRC have enough information to provide the clearance response eg what was supplied, price, contact terms etc;

(d)     Analysis of the tax consequences of the transaction and the issues HMRC are required to consider;

(e)     The proposed date of the transaction if it has not yet happened, and supporting information, such as a draft contract where available;

(f)     Any details that are contingent, eg on future events or the consent of others.

## Information about commercial background

**[A12.17]** The following information about the commercial rationale for the transaction should be provided:

(a)     The significance of the tax result in achieving the desired outcome;

(b)     Why this form of transaction was chosen over another that could achieve the same commercial result, where alternative forms have been considered;

(c)     Details of how the transaction will be accounted for (If relevant to the tax consequences);

(d)     Details of any related clearances (both statutory and non-statutory) including the relevant clearance references where known;

(e)     For queries which relate to direct tax legislation that is older than four Finance Acts, details of the commercial significance to the business of the issue.

## Information about legal points

**[A12.18]** The following information about the technical points should be provided:

(a)     The specific legislation at issue;

(b)     Details of why the application of the legislation is open to possible different interpretations, summary of those different interpretations, and why the tax consequences are uncertain, including reference to published HMRC guidance or to case law;

(c)     Any legal advice already received;

(d)     Details of any relevant previous advice received from HMRC;

(e)     Details of how it is intended that the clearance will be used, such as for public documents.

Such clearances are usually considered binding unless based on information provided that was incomplete or incorrect. HMRC will not withdraw the clearance if the interpretation of the law subsequently changes (eg following a Court decision) but it may be subject to change if the underlying law to which the transaction is subject is changed by Parliament. However, where there is a change of legislation or interpretation before the tax return enquiry window has closed then a Court decision may render an earlier clearance invalid.

Once a clearance has been given it cannot be appealed against but it does not have to be accepted by the company. It will, however, draw HMRC's attention to the transaction and the tax return for the period in which the transaction took place may subsequently be subject to enquiry.

# Advance Pricing Agreements (APAs)

**[A12.19]**  TIOPA 2010, s 218 enables UK companies to agree in advance with HMRC that their transfer pricing is on arm's length terms for a pre-determined period of time. Overseas tax authorities may offer similar advance pricing agreements.

HMRC guidance however, makes it clear that APAs are designed to assist taxpayers with 'complex' issues—generally only where there is significant doubt as to the manner in which the arm's length principle should be applied or where there is difficulty in establishing a market comparable.

In practice, APAs in the UK are rarely given to all but the largest businesses.

In their consultation response document '2006 review of links with large business' (October 2007), HMRC indicated that they are prepared to advise taxpayers on the risk status of their transfer pricing transactions in advance of submitting a return. Again, this approach will only apply to businesses sufficiently large and complex to be dealt with by HMRC's Large Business Service.

To give an idea of the anticipated complexity of APAs, HMRC state that their 'aim is to complete APA agreements within 18–21 months from receipt of the application' (INTM469030).

In 2010 HMRC issued a statement of practice (SoP 2/10) on APAs which amongst other things encouraged real time working and early stage engagement on approval of methodology. The statement of practice also updates their guidance on cost contribution agreements and their commercial rationale, together with revisions to practice on share options.

# Advance Thin Capitalisation Agreements (ATCAs)

**[A12.20]** Thin capitalisation is considered in more detail at A13.62 onwards. To summarise, a company may be thinly capitalised if the level of debt is considered unsustainable and unlikely to be obtainable from third party sources. The legislation aims to prevent companies from obtaining excessive interest deductions through related party borrowing.

This section considers the process for agreeing in advance with HMRC on the thin capitalisation position of a company.

Thin capitalisation can impact on withholding tax obligations, as the borrower is only required to withhold tax on the amount of interest which is actually allowable as a tax deduction (TIOPA 2010, s 187). As such, HMRC historically considered the thin capitalisation position of the borrower at the same time as considering an application for treaty relief from withholding tax.

However, Statement of Practice 04/07 separated the thin capitalisation clearance from the withholding tax analysis . At the time of making an application for withholding tax relief under a treaty, HMRC will not review the thin capitalisation position of the borrower. Any enquiries will be raised into the corporation tax return under the self assessment process. The Financial Transfer Pricing team at HMRC will also consider clearances under CTA 2009, s 441 (unallowable purpose), arbitrage and worldwide debt cap provisions.

ATCAs under SP04/07 will fall within TIOPA 2010, s 218 in the same way as APAs. However, unlike APAs, ATCAs can be obtained by all taxpayers regardless of the size of the transaction.

HMRC state that they generally encourage a less formal approach to ATCAs than to APAs, but applications will still need to include the information specifically required by TIOPA 2010, s 218:

'(a)    the taxpayer's understanding of what would, in his case, be the effect, in the absence of any agreement, of the provisions in relation to which clarification is sought;

(b)    the respects in which it appears to the taxpayer that clarification is required in relation to those provisions; and

(c)    how the taxpayer proposes that matters should be clarified in a manner consistent with the understanding mentioned in paragraph (a) above.'

In other words, the taxpayer must identify the likely impact of the thin capitalisation rules.

HMRC suggest that applications for an ATCA should include:

(a)    a statement that agreement under s 218 is being sought;

(b)    the proposed treatment of the interest under the loan ie the proposed terms of the ATCA;

(c)    the group structure at the time the loan was put in place;

(d)    background information on the business of the group and/or company in question.

ATCAs will generally apply for between three and five years, although this will depend on the terms agreed with HMRC.

As thin capitalisation may have a material impact on both withholding tax obligations and corporation tax liability, ATCAs should where possible be obtained before interest is paid, and before corporation tax returns are submitted. Whilst the intention of an ATCA is to apply to periods for which no return has been filed, it is possible for them to apply retrospectively as a 'roll back' or they may apply to settle an open enquiry for periods that have ended.

HMRC issued updated thin capitalisation guidance on 11 April 2014 (INTM510000). A summary of the key changes is as follows:

(1)    An option to extend an ATCA if funding is likely to be refinanced within 18 months of the expiry of an ATCA .

(2)    In the case of smaller transactions, a Transfer Pricing Panel approval is not always required for ATCAs.

(3)    HMRC recommends that an initial meeting should be held with a taxpayer prior to entering into detailed correspondence on ATCAs.

(4)    New guidance on netting of debt when considering debt:equity ratios.

Guidance on the process for agreeing an ATCA with HMRC can be found at INTM512000.

## Transfer of intangible assets to non-resident company

**[A12.21]** As noted in CHAPTER A9, CTA 2009, s 827 provides that no gain arises on the disposal of intangible assets where:

(a)    a UK company carries on a trade outside the UK;

(b)    the UK company transfers all or part of that trade to a non-resident company;

(c)    the non-resident company issues shares to the UK company such that the UK company holds at least 25% of the shares in the non-resident company;

(d)    the transfer is undertaken for bona fide commercial reasons; and

(e)    the transfer does not form part of a scheme or arrangements of which the main purpose, or one of the main purposes, is avoidance of tax.

A clearance can be obtained under CTA 2009, s 831 that the last two conditions are satisfied in relation to a particular transfer.

These clearance provisions are similar to others in that the application must be made in writing, and HMRC must reply within 30 days with an acceptance, a refusal, or a request for further information. Provided full disclosure is made, the clearance is binding on HMRC.

There is no requirement in the equivalent capital gains provision (TCGA 1992, s 140) that the transaction is undertaken for bona fide commercial purposes, and hence no clearance provision exists for capital gains purposes.

However, many transfers of branches to non-resident companies will include both capital gains and CTA 2009 intangible assets, and a clearance may be required in respect of some assets being transferred.

## Transactions in land

**[A12.22]** It is possible to obtain a clearance under ITA 2007, s 770 that the anti-avoidance provisions of s 752 will not apply to a transaction.

In practice, it is unusual for such clearance applications to be made. By making a clearance application a transaction will be drawn to the attention of HMRC where it might otherwise have gone unnoticed. Full disclosure should obviously be made on the self-assessment tax return, but a taxpayer who makes a clearance application will also be conceding that the land is being held for the purposes of realising a non-investment gain. A taxpayer who is simply realising an investment gain is clearly outside the scope of s 752 and has no need to make a clearance application.

HMRC guidance on clearance applications states that:

'A clearance should be given if:
- you are the appropriate Inspector, that is the Inspector to whom the applicant makes his returns;
- you are given all the necessary background information;
- you are satisfied that the transaction is not a disguised land trading deal and that no tax will be deliberately or unwittingly avoided.'

Even if 'unwitting' tax avoidance is present, a clearance is therefore likely to be refused.

# A13

# Transfer pricing

# Introduction

**[A13.1]** Transfer pricing refers to the pricing of goods, services, funds and tangible and intangible assets transferred within a group, and between connected parties. Since the prices are set with the mutual agreement of the parties, they are not subject to normal market pressures that establish prices for similar transactions between third parties.

Transfer pricing rules in the UK and elsewhere require that transactions between connected parties should be recognised for tax purposes by applying the amount of profit that would have arisen if the same transaction had been carried out by unconnected parties. This is referred to as the 'arm's length principle'. The arm's length principle is endorsed by the OECD (Organisation for Economic Co-operation and Development) and enshrined in the Associated Enterprises Article of the OECD Model Tax Convention.

Most countries (other than the United States and some developing countries) enforce transfer pricing laws and guidelines based on the arm's length principle as defined in the OECD's publication Transfer Pricing Guidelines for Multinational Enterprises and Tax Administrations (OECD Guidelines) published in July 1995 and updated subsequently. The United States sets out its rules for the pricing and reporting of transactions between related parties in s 482 of the Internal Revenue Code and the regulations thereunder.

In recent years there has been increased focus on transfer pricing by tax authorities, and a number of cases have been heard by the courts—including *DSG Retail Ltd v Revenue and Customs Comrs* [2009] UKFTT 31 (TC) in the UK, *Glaxosmithkline Inc v R* (2008) TCC 324 and *GE Capital Canada Incv The Queen* (2009) TCC 563 in Canada and *Société Man Camions et Bus* (2009) in France.

Although transfer pricing is usually a compliance issue it also offers planning opportunities. It is possible for a group to adopt transfer pricing policies that not only comply with the rules and guidelines, but also recognise profits in low-tax, rather than high tax jurisdictions.

The arm's length profits earned by a company will depend on the functions it performs, the risks it holds, and the assets it owns. Companies undertaking activities which add little value, and carry no risk, will not usually earn significant profits. The objective of transfer pricing planning is therefore to ensure that functions, risks and assets are as far as possible held by companies in low tax jurisdictions. This can be achieved in large part by ensuring that companies in the group are characterised appropriately for transfer pricing purposes (see **A13.39**).

This Chapter considers the transfer pricing rules in the UK which determine when the arm's length principle must be applied. It also considers how the transfer pricing apply to specific transactions such as share options and financing. Finally, it considers how activities can be characterised to reduce or increase profits in line with the arm's length principle.

# Impact of the OECD Action Plan on Base Erosion and Profit Shifting (BEPS)

**[A13.2]** Whilst the information in this Chapter was up to date at the time of writing this book, it is important to keep up to date on the OECD Action Plan on Base Erosion and Profit Shifting (BEPS). More detail on BEPS can be found on the OECD website www.oecd.org/ctp/beps.htm.

Before considering any transfer pricing planning, taxpayers should review the potential application of BEPS. The key Actions that are likely to have an impact for transfer pricing purposes are set out below:

Action 8 – IntangiblesThe aim of this action is to develop rules to prevent BEPS by moving intangibles among group members. The expected outcome is a new definition of intangibles which aims to ensure that taxation of the intangible is closely linked with the location of value creation.

This outcome is expected in two phases, phase one to be completed by September 2014 and phase two by September 2015

**Action 9 – Risks and capital** The aim of this action is to develop rules to prevent BEPS by transferring risks among, or allocating excessive capital to, group members. This will involve transfer pricing rules/ special measures to ensure that inappropriate returns will not accrue to an entity solely because it has contractually assumed risks or has provided capital.

This outcome is expected in September 2015.

**Action 10 – Other high-risk transactions** The aim of this action is to develop rules to prevent BEPS by engaging in transactions which would not, or would only very rarely, occur between third parties. This will involve adopting transfer pricing rules or special measures to clarify when transactions can be characterised and provide protection against common methods of base erosion, such as management fees and head office expenses.

This outcome is expected in September 2015.

**Action 13 – Re-examine transfer pricing documentation** The aim of this action is to enhance transparency for tax administrations through the use of documentation. The OECD has stated in its action plan that the compliance cost for business will be taken in to consideration as part of this.

The expected outcome of this action is a common template to be used for documenting all related party transactions and that this is provided to all relevant governments. The time limit for this outcome is September 2014.

# Basic principles—scope of UK transfer pricing rules

**[A13.3]** The UK transfer pricing legislation is set out in TIOPA 2010, Part 4. TIOPA 2010, s 164 incorporates into UK law the OECD Guidelines. This legislation applies to accounting periods ending on or after 1 July 1999 and (for income tax purposes) years of assessment from 1999/2000 onwards. FA 2004 expanded the original legislation to cover transactions between UK companies from 1 April 2004.

The legislation allows for the adjustment of income by HMRC where a provision is made or imposed between connected parties, which departs from the arm's length principle and has created a potential UK tax advantage. Essentially, it obliges companies to apply the arm's length principle when computing taxable profits.

The legislation defines an arm's length price as the price which might have been expected if the parties to the transaction had been independent persons dealing at arm's length.

## Entities subject to UK transfer pricing

**[A13.4]** The transfer pricing rules apply to transactions between 'persons'—and are not therefore limited to transactions between companies. Persons potentially include companies, partnerships, individuals, trusts and permanent establishments of overseas companies.

The OECD Guidelines only apply to transactions between enterprises, and it can be argued that where one of the parties to a transaction is not an enterprise, the transfer pricing rules cannot apply. HMRC do not necessarily accept this argument.

### Individuals

**[A13.5]** Discrete transactions between a company and its shareholders (for instance a shareholder loan) should not be subject to the transfer pricing rules as the individual would not be acting as an enterprise. If the individual were undertaking a series of loans, or were making a loan as part of a broader commercial transaction (for instance a management buy out) then such a loan may be subject to the rules as he would be acting as an enterprise.

In their response to the consultation comments on the rewrite of the transfer pricing legislation (currently available at www.hmrc.gov.uk/rewrite/exposure/081222-rd.pdf), HMRC have indicated that they may seek to apply the transfer pricing rules even where one of the parties is not an enterprise:

'1.    The wording of paragraph 1 of Schedule 28AA [the predecessor to Part 4] only requires the provision to be compared with the provision that would have been made between independent enterprises. In principle the provision may be applied between persons who are not enterprises (although this would be unusual) and this is the position we wish to retain.

2.    International Manual 432090 states that the requirement in paragraph 2 of Schedule 28AA that the Schedule should be construed in accordance with the OECD model treaty suggests that the Schedule should be applied only where both parties are enterprises. This would be the normal application of Schedule 28AA but it is not the strict legal position.'

This view is also reflected in INTM431060.

### Partnerships

**[A13.6]** It is not clear whether a partnership can be treated as a 'person' in its own right. This point was to have been tested by the courts in the *Hozelock* case, but this case was settled by HMRC before it reached the courts, the terms of which settlement are not known.

As a direct result of the *Hozelock*, the provisions in TIOPA 2010, s 161 were introduced, so that financing provided by a number of persons (whether in partnership or not) 'acting together' was within the transfer pricing rules.

### *Terminology*

**[A13.7]** In the UK legislation, the company whose tax position is improved as a result of non-arm's length prices is referred to as the 'advantaged person'. The other party to the transaction is the 'disadvantaged person'.

## Diagram 1

**Does the entity fall within the UK's transfer pricing rules?**

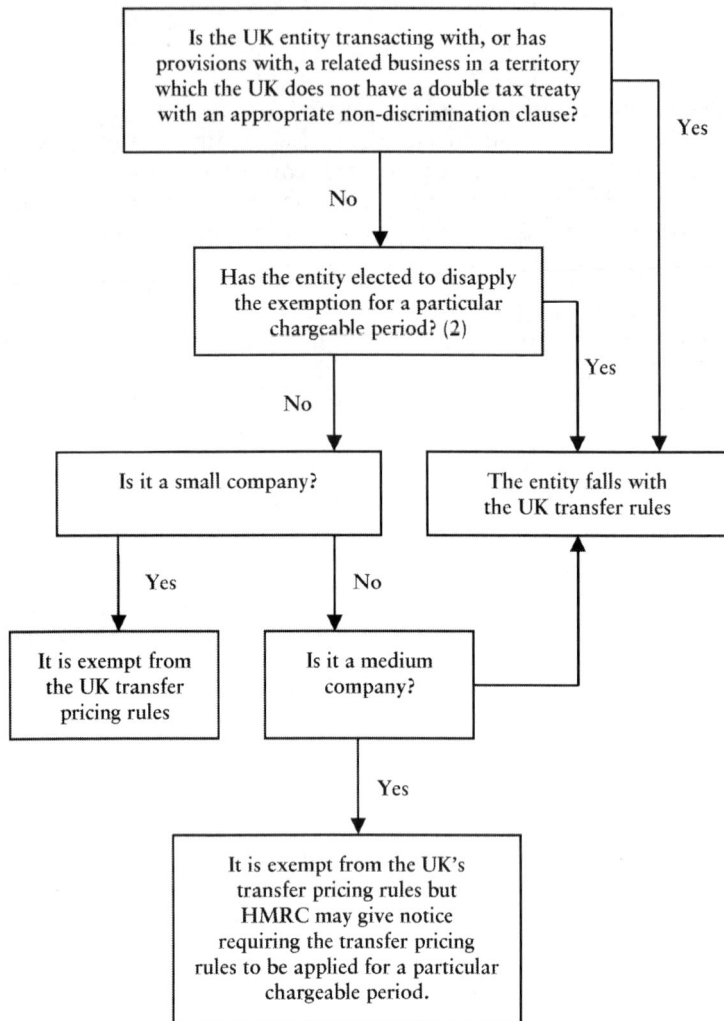

Is the UK entity transacting with, or has provisions with, a related business in a territory which the UK does not have a double tax treaty with an appropriate non-discrimination clause?

Yes

No

Has the entity elected to disapply the exemption for a particular chargeable period? (2)

Yes

No

Is it a small company?

The entity falls with the UK transfer rules

Yes

No

It is exempt from the UK transfer pricing rules

Is it a medium company?

Yes

It is exempt from the UK's transfer pricing rules but HMRC may give notice requiring the transfer pricing rules to be applied for a particular chargeable period.

(1) An appropriate non-discrimination clause is one that ensures a resident of a contracting state may not be less favourably treated in the other contracting state than a resident of the latter state in the same circumstances.

(2) An entity wishing to make an election to remain subject to the transfer pricing rules should do so in its tax return.

Diagram 2

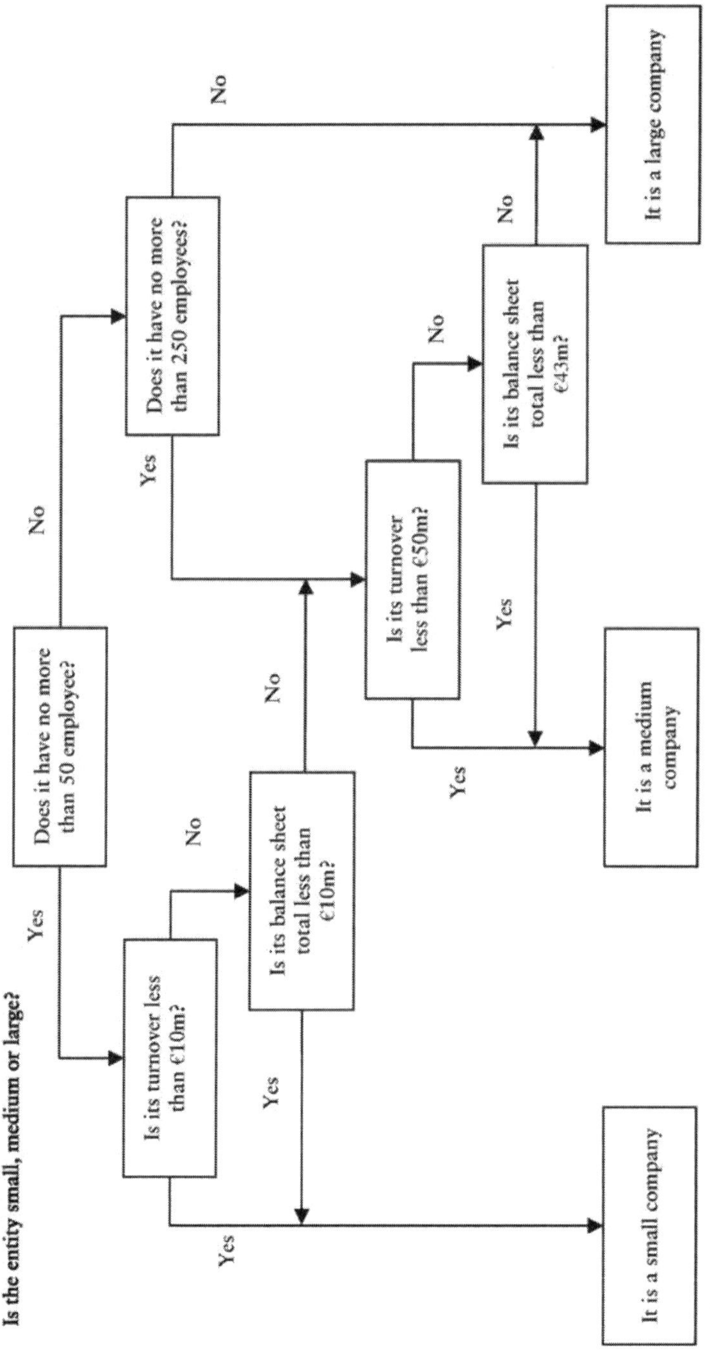

**Is the entity small, medium or large?**

Does it have no more than 50 employee?

Is its turnover less than €10m?

Is its balance sheet total less than €10m?

It is a small company

Does it have no more than 250 employees?

Is its turnover less than €50m?

Is its balance sheet total less than €43m?

It is a medium company

It is a large company

(1) Part-time employees are counted as fractions

(2) Balance sheet total means total assets (eg as calculated for the purpose of s 382 Companies Act 2006) before deducting any liabilities.

## *Exemptions for small and medium sized enterprises*

**[A13.8]** There are exemptions from the UK transfer pricing rules for small and medium sized enterprises, and also for transactions with dormant companies. The definitions (subject to modification) follow the EU definitions in 2003/361/EC.

Small enterprises are those with fewer than 50 employees and either turnover or gross assets of less than €10m. Medium sized enterprises are those that are not small but have fewer than 250 employees and have either turnover of less than €50m or gross assets of less than €43m. It is important to note that for these purposes the employees, turnover and assets of the consolidated *world-wide* group are taken into account (if accounts are prepared on a consolidated basis)—in addition to the data of linked and partner enterprises (see **A13.9** below).

Diagrams 1 and 2 outline whether an entity falls within the rules or not. Because the size limits are denominated in euros, the turnover and balance sheet tests should be reviewed annually to reflect exchange rate differentials.

The exemption for small and medium sized enterprises is within the UK legislation (and not the OECD Guidelines), so an overseas counterparty to a transaction may not benefit from a similar exemption.

The exemption for small and medium sized enterprises does not apply to any transactions which take place with an entity in a 'non-qualifying territory'. A qualifying territory is one with which the UK has a double tax agreement (DTA) which contains a non-discrimination article (a list of which is in the HMRC International Manual at INTM432112).

The exemption also provides HMRC with the power to give notice to medium sized enterprises requiring them to compute profits/losses for a particular period of assessment in accordance with arm's length provisions, but only after a notice of enquiry has been raised.

This effectively means that medium sized companies can only be certain that the exemption applies once the enquiry window for a particular accounting period has closed.

Qualification as small or medium sized will be determined solely by reference to the accounting period for which a return is being made. This differs from the EU definitions which are by reference to the latest accounting period for which accounts are drawn up. In addition, a company will cease to be small or medium sized in the first period when it breaches the limits. This differs from the EU definitions under which a company will only cease to be small or medium sized if it breaches the conditions for two consecutive accounting periods.

A small or medium sized entity can make an election that the exemption will not apply. This may, for instance, allow a corresponding adjustment to be claimed in another jurisdiction which has a higher tax rate than the UK.

Because the exemptions do not apply to non-qualifying territories, jurisdictions with which the UK has a DTA may provide greater tax planning possibilities for small or medium sized enterprises. Although it has to be said that in practice, HMRC will simply find different ways of attacking the arrangements.

For example, a small UK company may sell goods at a non arm's-length price to a distribution subsidiary in Ireland, but would be required to recognise an arm's-length profit on sales to a subsidiary in Jersey.

As set out in **A13.32** one of the Actions arising from the OECD's work on Base Erosion and Profit Shifting is a Country by Country reporting template for transfer pricing purposes. It should be noted that the OECD has proposed that there should not be exemptions for SMEs from the country by country reporting requirement, and that reports should be submitted alongside tax returns for all companies. If this is followed in the UK it will represent a significant compliance burden for SMEs

### Linked and partner enterprises

**[A13.9]** When calculating the size of a company or group, the data of associated companies must be included.

Associated enterprises include both parent companies and subsidiary companies. They are classified into two types.

(a)    Linked enterprises are those which hold more than 50% of the voting rights or control of the company or group, or in which the company or group holds such an interest.
All the employee and financial data of linked enterprises are added to the data of the company or group.

(b)    Partner enterprises are those which hold more than 25%, but not more than 50% of the voting rights, or capital of the company or group, or in which the company or group holds such an interest.
The appropriate percentage of the employee and financial data of partner enterprises are added to the data of the company or group.

The data of linked enterprises include the data of any linked or partner enterprises of that linked enterprise. However, the data of partner enterprises only includes the data of any linked enterprises of that partner enterprise.

Certain investors are excluded from being considered linked or partner enterprises, such as:

(a)    universities and not-for-profit research centres;
(b)    institutional investors such as regional development funds;
(c)    venture capital companies and business angels investing less than €1,250,000 in a company.

Individuals will only be considered to be partner or linked enterprises if they are themselves in the same business as the company or group under consideration.

The European Union has published guidance on these definitions in the guidance on the definition of small or medium sized enterprises, which can be found at: ec.europa.eu/enterprise/enterprise_policy/sme_definition/sme_user_g uide.pdf.

### Dormant companies

**[A13.10]** Dormant companies are exempt from the transfer pricing rules, if:

(a)     they were dormant for the whole of the accounting period ending on 31 March 2004, or the three months prior to 31 March 2004; and
(b)     they have continued to be dormant since then.

A dormant company which satisfied these conditions could own intangible assets used by the group, or it might have made interest-free loans to other group companies, and would not be required to recognise arm's length royalties or interest income.

The counter-party to the transaction with the dormant company will, however, remain subject to the transfer pricing rules.

Because a company must remain dormant from 1 April 2004 in order to remain outside the transfer pricing regime, if a group company was dormant on 31 March 2004 it should not become active subsequently in order to preserve its exemption.

## Transactions affected by the legislation

### Provisions

**[A13.11]** The legislation refers to a 'provision' made between connected persons by means of a transaction or series of transactions. This can include situations in which no charge has been made and where transactions are unrecorded in the accounts or not recognised by the company, for instance:

(a)     use of brand names by subsidiaries;
(b)     management services provided by a parent company.

These unrecognised transactions can provide both compliance and planning issues.

In *DSG Retail Ltd v Revenue and Customs Comrs* [2009] UKFTT 31 (TC), there was held to be a provision between the UK company and its Isle of Man subsidiary which provided insurance to customers. Payments were made directly by customers to the subsidiary, and no payments were made by the UK company itself, but the courts held that the subsidiary only received the payments because of the activities of the UK company. The case is worthy of note as it is the only real UK transfer pricing case in the last 50 years and makes it clear that amongst other things, interposing a third party between group members is not a panacea. Equally in spite of the fact that *Dixons* had gone to some length to demonstrate the prices were arm's length via extensive comparables, these were largely dismissed by the Tribunal.

### Connected companies

**[A13.12]** The transfer pricing rules apply where:

•     a provision has been made or imposed between two persons;
•     by means of a transaction or series of transactions; and
•     at the time of making the provision one of the affected persons was directly or indirectly participating in the management, control or capital of the other; or

- the same person(s) was or were directly or indirectly participating in the management, control or capital of the affected persons.

Control of a company is taken to be where:

- a person is able to exercise, or is entitled to exercise or acquire, direct or indirect control (as defined in CTA 2010, s 1124) over the company's affairs; or
- a person possesses, or is entitled to acquire the greater part of the ordinary share capital or voting rights of the company; or
- a person possesses, or is entitled to acquire a part of the share capital which would give him the greater part of a distribution, or rights to receive the greater part of the company's assets on winding up.

Ordinary share capital is defined as all issued share capital other than share capital which carries only a right to a dividend at a fixed rate.

Indirect control arises where a person would control a company or partnership if certain rights were attributed to him. These rights include:

(a) rights which may be acquired at a later date (for instance if the first person holds an option to acquire further shares, or holds a special class of shares which will acquire greater rights at a later date);
(b) rights which may be exercised for the benefit of, or under the direction of the first person (for instance this may include rights which are held by subsidiary companies);
(c) rights of connected persons.

In the context of a company, the definition of connected person includes a trust which has been settled by the company. For instance, an employee benefit trust (EBT) which holds shares would be a connected person, and the rights attaching to those shares would be attributed to the company which had settled the EBT.

Indirect control will also arise where a person is a major participant in a company or partnership. A person can be a major participant when two people taken together control the company and each has rights amounting to at least 40% of the rights in the company. The 40% test is satisfied where two persons *each* have interests, rights and powers representing at least 40% of the holding, rights and powers in the joint venture entity.

### Example—purchase of a call option over shares

A Ltd is a UK incorporated company and has entered into a call option over shares in B Ltd, another UK company. A Ltd needs to determine if it is connected with B Ltd under the UK's transfer pricing legislation due to the existence of the option arrangement. A Ltd and B Ltd are 'large' companies and are otherwise unconnected.

The important provision of the legislation is the term 'entitled to acquire'. Currently, A Ltd has an option over the shares of B Ltd, which will vest on the conclusion of certain events, therefore A Ltd is entitled to acquire shares in B Ltd once the vesting conditions have been satisfied. A Ltd is therefore connected with B Ltd and transactions between A Ltd and B Ltd should be recognised at arm's length.

Diagram 3 outlines some structures under which companies will be connected.

**Diagram 3**

(a)

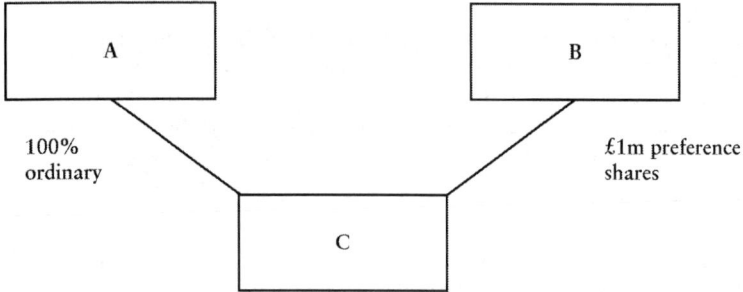

(b)

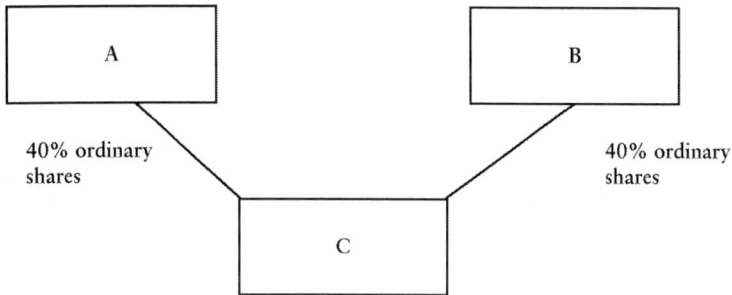

(c)

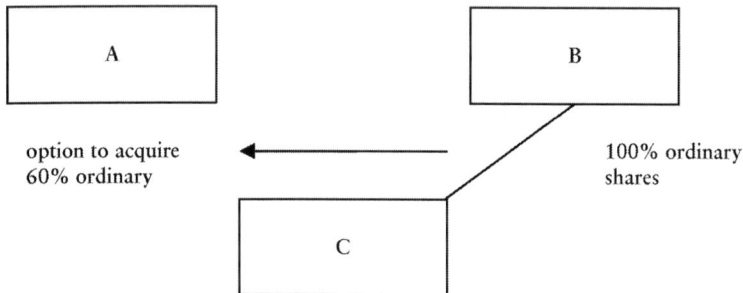

In Diagram 3(a), A will be a direct participant in C because the ordinary share rights give A control of C under the definition in CTA 2010, s 1124. The existence of the preference shares do not affect this. In Diagram 3(b), A will be an indirect participant in C, because A and B taken together control C, and both A and B hold at least 40% of the rights in C. A will not be a direct or an indirect participant in B.

In Diagram 3(c), A will be an indirect participant in C as outlined in the example above.

# Basic principles—arm's length principle

**[A13.13]** The OECD Guidelines focus on the application of the arm's length principle. The arm's length principle is generally applied by comparing the conditions in a controlled transaction (ie the transaction between the connected parties) with the conditions in transactions between independent enterprises based on the 'economically relevant characteristics of the situations being compared'.

The transfer pricing methods presented in the OECD Guidelines and used to apply the arm's length principle are categorised into two groups:

(a)  Traditional transactional methods—these include:
  (i)  comparable uncontrolled price (CUP) method;
  (ii)  the resale price method;
  (iii)  the cost plus method.
(b)  Transactional profit methods—these include:
  (i)  the profit split method;
  (ii)  the transactional net margin method (TNMM).

Although UK law does not prescribe any order of preference for the methods set out in the OECD Guidelines, the Guidelines themselves dictate that the objective is to select the most appropriate method, that which provides the best estimate of an arm's length price. The Guidelines previously established a hierarchy in which the methods should be considered, preferring the CUP method, but this preference and hierarchy were removed in the 2010 update to the Guidelines, published in July 2010. All methods should now be considered and the most appropriate selected.

The process of selecting which method to apply involves assessing which of the methods can be implemented with the most accuracy to support a particular pricing strategy.

Other countries may accept different methods of calculating a transfer price. For instance, Japan requires that the three traditional methods, outlined below, be systematically discounted before allowing the use of alternative methods.

## *Traditional transactional methods*

### Comparable uncontrolled price (CUP) method

**[A13.14]** The CUP method compares the price charged for property or services transferred in a controlled transaction to the price charged for the same goods or services in an uncontrolled transaction in comparable circumstances.

When addressing comparability, a company should review functionality, risk and the ownership of intangibles, but also address the contractual terms supporting the transactions which are being compared.

At its most basic level, the CUP method would require consideration of:

(a)    goods sold to both third parties and other group companies;
(b)    similar goods sold by third parties to other third parties.

The CUP method was not followed in *DSG Retail and others v HMRC (TC00001)*, because the courts decided that there were no sufficiently comparable transactions as the Jersey subsidiary had significantly less bargaining power than comparable insurance companies. A residual profit split method (see **A13.19**) was therefore followed instead.

## Resale price method (RPM)

**[A13.15]** Under the RPM, an arm's length price for goods is determined by subtracting an appropriate profit margin from the price at which the goods are subsequently sold to third parties.

The RPM compensates a reseller or distributor of goods for costs incurred and provides an appropriate profit for functions performed, tangible and intangible assets employed and risks borne. The RPM can be calculated from the price charged by the same reseller on items purchased and sold in uncontrolled transactions, or from the retail price of an unrelated party engaged in comparable uncontrolled transactions.

The RPM is generally applicable to selling or distribution operations.

The RPM is not considered to be as accurate as other methods if the reseller adds substantially to the value of the product (through functions or intangibles) or incorporates the product into another product.

## Cost plus method

**[A13.16]** This method is most useful for the sale of semi-finished goods, long-term 'buy-and-supply' arrangements (buy-and-supply arrangements involve an agreement to purchase all of the output produced by a seller or to supply the entire product needed by a purchaser) and for the provision of services.

HMRC have issued guidance on the application of the cost plus method to certain services (INTM463050).

The costs incurred by the supplier of goods or services are increased by a percentage, and this is the charge made for the supply.

Under the RPM or the cost plus method fewer adjustments are needed to account for product differences than under the CUP method, because minor product differences are less likely to have a material effect on profit margins than on price.

HMRC typically accept a mark up in the range of 5% to 10% for the remuneration of routine, low commercial risk services. Mark ups significantly in excess of 10% may be challenged by HRMC who might argue that the service remunerated at this level is not actually routine in nature, and that a cost plus method is therefore inappropriate. To be confident about the arm's length nature of the cost plus mark up applied, benchmarking analysis should be undertaken to demonstrate that a company's chosen cost plus mark up falls within an arm's length range.

## *Transactional profit methods*

### Profit split method

**[A13.17]** Where a number of transactions are very interrelated it may be difficult to evaluate them separately, so a form of profit split might be agreed.

The profit split method determines the division of profits that independent enterprises would be expected to realise from engaging in the transactions under review. The profit split method calculates the total consolidated profit of all associated companies and splits those profits based on the economic contribution of each company to the transaction. The contribution of each company is determined by performing a functional analysis and valued, to the extent possible, by external market data.

Profit can be split either on a contribution analysis and/or on a residual basis. Generally the profit to be split is operating profit.

*Contribution analysis*

**[A13.18]** Profit (or loss) is allocated to each company in order to provide a basic return for the transactions in which it is engaged (ordinarily a market return based on the returns of independent entities) based on its economic contributions.

*Residual profit*

**[A13.19]** Any residual profit (or loss) is allocated based on how it would be divided between independent companies. The parties' contributions to intangible property and their relative bargaining positions are useful indicators for allocating residual profit. The company acting as the entrepreneur of the group, or a company bearing the ultimate risk, may be allocated all, or more, residual profits accordingly.

### Transactional net margin method (TNMM)

**[A13.20]** The TNMM examines the net profit margin relative to an appropriate base (for example costs, sales or assets). Ideally, the net margin should be established by reference to net margins earned by the same taxpayer in comparable uncontrolled transactions. If that is not possible, the TNMM is calculated by reference to comparable transactions between independent entities.

Adjustments must be made to account for material differences between the controlled and uncontrolled transactions. Use of an arm's length range of profitability, rather than a single price, can further reduce the effect of differences between the controlled and uncontrolled transactions.

The TNMM should consider only the profits of the controlled entity that are attributable to the transactions under review. The application of the TNMM on a company-wide basis is inappropriate if the company engages in a variety of different controlled transactions that cannot be compared on an aggregate basis with those of an uncontrolled comparable company.

TNMM is often used for limited risk distribution and sales entities.

## Basic principles—UK compliance requirements

### Transfer pricing adjustments

**[A13.21]** A transfer pricing adjustment is only made for tax calculation purposes. Companies can charge what they wish in their accounts (subject to local accounting practices). However, where a compensating adjustment is not available, companies may wish to make actual charges which are reflected in their accounts.

A tax adjustment will only be made where there is a UK tax advantage conferred as a result of a non-arm's length provision. TIOPA 2010, s 155 provides that there is a potential advantage in relation to UK taxation where a smaller amount of profits is chargeable to tax or larger amounts of losses are available than would otherwise be under arm's length pricing terms.

No adjustment will normally therefore be made by HMRC to reduce profits, nor can a company make an adjustment to reduce profits. As HMRC are often fond of saying, transfer pricing is a one way street, so great care is needed to make sure transactions with overseas affiliates are not conducted at over value.

A UK tax advantage can arise where both parties are UK residents, for example if one company has brought forward losses which can reduce its taxable income. Prior to 1 April 2004, an advantage could only arise in respect of transactions between a UK resident and a non-UK resident.

### Compensating adjustments

**[A13.22]** If an adjustment is made and the other party is UK tax resident and subject to UK income or corporation tax, the disadvantaged person can generally make a compensating (or corresponding) adjustment to its taxable profits under s 174. Adjustments are not available for overseas entities unless a relevant clause exists in the DTA between the UK and the overseas jurisdiction (see **A8.35**).

HMRC introduced legislation under FA 2014 to prevent compensating adjustments being claimed under certain arrangements. One of these arrangements was where large partnerships that employed staff through a service company were under-remunerating the service company for the provision of staff. A transfer pricing adjustment would then be required so that the service company was taxed on the correct arm's length rate. This would then result in the partners being able to claim a compensating adjustment for the difference between the actual payment and the arm's length provision.

The new legislation at s 174A applies to all transactions from 25 October 2013 as follows:

'A claim under section 174 may not be made if

(a)     the disadvantaged person is a person (other than a company) within the charge to income tax in respect of profits arising from the relevant activities, and

(b)     the advantaged person is a company.'

Instead of being allowed a compensating adjustment, the partners will instead be treated as receiving a qualifying distribution equal to the amount of the transfer pricing adjustment. Under s 187A, the new legislation covers finance payments (such as interest) that fall under s174A and recharacterises them as a dividend.

Whilst this amended legislation was aimed at two particular arrangements (see **A13.70**), it will apply in many more scenarios and should be considered where the disadvantaged person to a transaction is an individual.

A balancing payment can be made between the parties where an adjustment has been made (but there is no obligation to make one). This can be made without any UK tax consequences provided that the payment does not exceed the reduction made to the taxable profits of the disadvantaged person in consequence of a claim for a compensating adjustment. No notification needs to be made to HMRC that a balancing payment has been made.

### Controlled Foreign Companies (CFC)

**[A13.23]** With the advent of the new Controlled Foreign Company (CFC) provisions from 1 January 2013 the role of transfer pricing in allocating profits for these purposes has become much more prevalent, as only profits which are attributable to UK functions will pass through the Gateway. Changes have now been made to TIOPA 2010, s 179 to allow a compensating adjustment claim under the UK transfer pricing rules when the 'advantaged person' is a CFC. The amendments ensure that s 179 now refers to the new CFC rules at TIOPA 2010, Part 9A and require that the CFC in question has chargeable profits which are increased by virtue of the application of the UK transfer pricing rules.

### Enquiries

**[A13.24]** HMRC normally carry out a transfer pricing risk assessment and have produced guidance on the factors that will be considered when deciding whether to enquire into a company's transfer pricing arrangements:

(a)     a large amount of tax is at stake;

(b)     there is a significant difference in the marginal tax rates borne of the companies that are transacting, or the UK company is loss making;

(c)     income received by the UK company from an overseas associate appears to be small or payments made to that overseas entity appear large by reference to the relationship;

(d)   non-tax factors exist which might provide an incentive for price manipulation, such as customs duty, valuations, exchange controls or price;

(e)   intellectual property has been acquired, enhanced or created in the UK that is used by other group members;

(f)   a cost sharing agreement is in place with future income streams that are not obviously commensurate with the obligation to share costs;

(g)   there are cash flow incentives within a group affecting where profit is reported or how dividends are financed.

### Dealing with transfer pricing enquiries

**[A13.25]** There are a number of important points to note when dealing with transfer pricing enquiries:

(a)   an experienced transfer pricing adviser should identify potential challenges so that they can be addressed at the outset and advice obtained from specialist HMRC enquiry specialists where appropriate;

(b)   more emphasis should be placed on the functional analysis than the benchmarking which may carry less weight in an enquiry, particularly where a company is loss-making;

(c)   the functional analysis should explain the transfer pricing situation clearly;

(d)   evidence should be produced that the transfer pricing strategy made sense at the time it was implemented by producing contemporaneous financial forecasts; and if it did not, prove that this was a result of unexpected market developments;

Arguments that may be successful in influencing transfer pricing disputes include:

(a)   the pricing is in within an arm's length range, and supported by an economic benchmarking study, although following the *Dixons* case the importance of having strong comparables is more vital than ever;

(b)   if not, the profits were strongly influenced by the state of the market;

(c)   there were offsetting transactions (especially in the context of funding arrangements).

In addition, the cost (and opportunity cost) of management time in dealing with the enquiry should be considered when deciding the depth of argument to present to HMRC.

### Disputes between tax authorities

**[A13.26]** Article 9 of the OECD Model Tax Convention deals with double taxation of business profits. Many DTAs include a mutual agreement procedure which allows a taxpayer which considers that it has suffered double taxation and has not been taxed in accordance with the DTA, to present its case to the competent authority of the state of which it is resident (which is normally the tax authority).

The DTA may empower that competent authority to consider the point and give corresponding relief to resolve the case without contacting the competent authority of the other state. If the case cannot be resolved unilaterally, the competent authorities of both states can consult to resolve issues by mutual agreement. However, there is often no obligation on the tax authorities to reach agreement.

This is a consultation process between the competent authorities and the taxpayer is not party to the process. This is often a lengthy procedure which should be carefully considered before pursuing. Should the taxpayer opt for this dispute resolution procedure experienced transfer pricing advisers should be consulted and engaged.

Where the dispute involves EU jurisdictions only, the EU Arbitration Convention may apply. Under this convention there is a specified time limit for resolution of disputes and the taxpayer may be involved in the process. This is considered in more detail in A7.57.

## Penalties for non-compliance

**[A13.27]** The general self-assessment rules relating to the imposition of penalties for incorrect returns apply to errors in a return that relate to transfer pricing. Where a return is incorrect due to 'deliberate and concealed' under-statement of tax, a penalty of up to 100% of any further tax due may be payable.

HMRC has issued guidance on the circumstances in which they will apply these penalty provisions specifying that penalties will not be imposed where the taxpayer has made an 'honest and reasonable' attempt to comply with the arm's length standard. The examples that HMRC use in the guidance indicate that this would involve finding third party comparables and 'seeking professional help where they know they need it'.

In addition to the tax-geared penalty, HMRC may impose a fixed penalty of £3,000 a year for each company, for failure to maintain adequate transfer pricing documentation.

## Penalties for loss making companies

**[A13.28]** A new penalties regime applies for periods ending on or after 1 April 2008. This provides for penalties of up to 100% of 10% of any adjustment which HMRC may make to a taxpayer's losses. The penalty percentage will increase from zero to 100% depending on whether the misstatement of the loss was deliberate or concealed. This new penalty will create a new exposure to tax-geared penalties for taxpayers who otherwise would have been protected by their losses.

## Advance Pricing Agreements (APAs) and Advance Thin Capitalisation Agreements (ATCAs)

**[A13.29]** It is possible to obtain confirmation from HMRC that a particular price will be accepted as arm's length under an APA or (for loans) an ATCA—see **A12.19** and **A12.20**.

## Transfer pricing documentation

**[A13.30]** Evidence to demonstrate arm's length transfer prices need only be produced upon HMRC request, but the documentation should be contemporaneous. The mere existence of an inter-company agreement covering the transaction in question is not sufficient—transfer pricing documentation must describe and justify how the price has been calculated.

The rules on documentation requirements differ across jurisdictions, and documentation prepared to satisfy overseas requirements may not necessarily satisfy UK requirements (and vice versa).

Where arrangements continue in force for more than one accounting period (eg a distribution agreement lasting several years), there is no need to prepare fresh documentation for each period, provided that the original documentation is sufficient to demonstrate that a complete and correct return has been made. Any significant changes in the nature or terms of the transaction or transactions in question should be recorded and the documentation updated or amended. However, economic benchmarking studies should be updated for new financial data at least every three years, assuming three years' financial data was utilised for the purposes of calculating the original margins.

HRMC issued guidance in October 1998 on its interpretation of the corporation tax self-assessment (CTSA) record keeping requirements for transfer pricing purposes (*Tax Bulletin 37*).

### EU master file

**[A13.31]** A common EU-wide approach on documentation requirements has been developed under an approach called 'EU Transfer Pricing Documentation' (EU TPD) which was adopted by the European Commission on 27 June 2006 and provides guidelines for standardised and partially centralised transfer pricing documentation for EU entities. EU TPD consists of two main parts: one set of standardised information relevant for all EU entities ('master file') together with sets of non-standardised documentation containing 'country-specific information' for each entity. Companies opting into EU TPD have a standardised and consistent set of documentation (the master file) supplemented by the country specific documentation at local entity level.

Use of EU TPD is optional for taxpayers and the relevant tax authority should be notified if an entity opts into the EU TPD agreement.

### Documentation and BEPS

**[A13.32]** As part of the OECD BEPS project, changes have been proposed to the documentation requirements in the Transfer Pricing Guidelines. These changes are expected (according to the published OECD timetable) to be effective from September 2014. As the UK documentation automatically follows the Guidelines, the new documentation requirements are expected to apply in the UK. Groups considering their transfer pricing documentation now may wish to delay any updates until the new rules are in place: see www.oecd .org/ctp/transfer-pricing/discussion-draft-transfer-pricing-documentation.pdf

*Two tier documentation*

**[13.33]** A two-tier documentation structure has been proposed, consisting of:

- a master file containing standard information relevant for all members of the group; and
- a local file referring specifically to material transactions of the local taxpayer.

Annex I of the consultation document sets out the proposed content of the master file which will cover:

- The group organisational structure
- Description of the group's business
- Intangibles held by the group
- Intercompany financial transactions
- Financial and tax positions of group members

Annex II of the consultation document sets out the proposed content of the local file which will cover the specific transfer pricing analysis of the companies located in that country. This will include

- Functional analysis
- Comparability analysis
- Selection of the most appropriate transfer pricing method
- Benchmarking

This two-tier documentation structure is similar to the master file which is used currently within the EU.

*Country by country reporting*

**[13.34]** The master file will include country by country (CbC) reporting of financial and tax information split between the countries in which the group operates. This information will include:

- Profits
- Taxes paid
- Location of assets, employees etc
- Capital
- Accumulated earnings

Annex III of the consultation document sets out the proposed format of the country by country reporting template. It is expected that the country by country reporting will assist tax authorities in their transfer pricing risk assessment. The OECD has proposed that there should not be exemptions for SMEs from the country by country reporting requirement, and that reports should be submitted alongside tax returns for all companies. If this is followed in the UK it will represent a significant compliance burden for SMEs.

## Functional analysis

**[A13.35]** A functional analysis sets out the activities and responsibilities undertaken or to be undertaken by the associated companies. It outlines the functions performed, risks borne and tangible and intangible assets used in order to identify how these are divided between the companies and transactions involved. A functional analysis assists with the development of transfer pricing policies for the companies under review by evaluating their relative contribution to profit.

The functions, risks and assets used in a company's business will have an effect on its profitability. The functional analysis provides the information necessary to characterise the entities to identify transactions under review and determine the appropriate method of pricing inter-company transactions.

The functional analysis is also required when undertaking tax planning as it will identify what functions, risks and assets may be transferred to low tax jurisdictions.

## Content of documentation

**[A13.36]** The information which is included in transfer pricing documentation will depend upon the functions of the company. The detail of the documentation will depend on the size of the company (or the group) and the type and number of transactions under review.

However, documentation will typically include the following:

(a)　Introduction, executive summary and scope of the documentation;
(b)　Industry analysis and background (optional);
(c)　Overview of the group:
　　(i)　Organisational, legal and operational structure, business overview, history and background, details of solutions, products, competitors, suppliers, customers, distributors, etc and possibly a brief (high level) financial summary;
　　(ii)　Country overview (optional) containing a brief description of the functional roles of relevant group companies;
(d)　Transactions under review:
　　Description of the inter-company transactions within the group concerning intellectual property, products, services and funding. These may be depicted diagrammatically;
(e)　Functional Analysis:
　　(i)　Description of the functions performed by the entities which may include research and development, (of product, processes and intangibles), manufacturing, purchasing, product strategy and design, quality control, marketing, advertising, sales, distribution, strategic, tactical and general marketing, pricing, warranty support, strategic and general management, planning, accounting and controllership, treasury, compliance, legal and regulatory, training, HR, administration, IT support, etc;
　　(ii)　Ownership of intangibles, including trademarks, patents, secret know-how, rights in software, design rights, databases, manufacturing know-how, etc;

(iii)    Ownership of tangible fixed assets;

(f)    Risks:

These may include:

(i)    Market risks. The risk of adverse sales conditions or demand, input/output price fluctuations, development of new markets, product positioning, competitive influences etc;

(ii)    Product liability risk. The risk of products failing to perform at accepted or advertised standards, products causing harm or failing etc;

(iii)    Customer credit risk. Consider the entity's bad debt profile over several years and any concentrated customer dependence;

(iv)    Employee risk. Consider staff turnover levels and the risk of losing key personnel, how difficult is it to replace staff?;

(v)    Financial risks such as foreign exchange risk, interest rate variability and the ability to obtain credit;

(vi)    Stock risk. Consider stock turnover rates and the existence of obsolescent or perishable stock;

Risks should be characterised as high, medium, low or even non-existent. An overall conclusion should be given of risk and comments on any future or contingent risks arising;

(g)    Characterisation:

The characterisation of the entity is important. The functional analysis forms the basis for characterisation and examples are detailed further below under the trading models and entity classification section (see **A13.39**);

(h)    Transfer pricing policy:

This details the methods selected and transfer pricing policies commensurate to each transaction;

(i)    Economic benchmarking studies (if applicable);

(j)    Signed inter-company agreements;

(k)    It may be beneficial to include an overview of each country's transfer pricing law;

(l)    If an economic benchmarking study is not undertaken then details of anecdotal evidence, CUP analysis or relevant hourly rate, etc workings may be included.

## Benchmarking

**[A13.37]** Transfer pricing documentation frequently includes benchmarking studies to support arm's length profits. This is an economic, rather than a tax assessment.

A benchmarking study will identify other businesses undertaking similar functions to the function being tested, to determine the range within which profits typically fall, or the range within which transactions are priced. The 2010 OECD Transfer Pricing Guidelines outlines a nine step process for undertaking benchmarking of comparables:

'Step 1: Determination of years to be covered.

Step 2: Broad-based analysis of the taxpayer's circumstances.

Step 3: Understanding the controlled transaction(s) under examination, based in particular on a functional analysis, in order to choose the tested party (where needed), the most appropriate transfer pricing method to the circumstances of the case, the financial indicator that will be tested (in the case of a transactional profit method), and to identify the significant comparability factors that should be taken into account.

Step 4: Review of existing internal comparables, if any.

Step 5: Determination of available sources of information on external comparables where such external comparables are needed taking into account their relative reliability.

Step 6: Selection of the most appropriate transfer pricing method and, depending on the method, determination of the relevant financial indicator (eg determination of the relevant net profit indicator in case of a transactional net margin method).

Step 7: Identification of potential comparables: determining the key characteristics to be met by any uncontrolled transaction in order to be regarded as potentially comparable, based on the relevant factors identified in Step 3 and in accordance with the comparability factors set forth [in the Guidance].

Step 8: Determination of and making comparability adjustments where appropriate.

Step 9: Interpretation and use of data collected, determination of the arm's length remuneration.'

The Guidelines also recommend ongoing review of the prices determined as a result of this process.

Databases are available which can assist with identification of similar businesses, and the ranges of profits/prices.

It is useful for inter-company agreements to include a price comparability clause whereby the supplier agrees to alter the inter-company pricing structure if the buyer of the services/products bring to the attention of the supplier a comparable but substantially different pricing structure provided by a third party, or if the supplier supplies products or services to third parties on a substantially different basis to other customers.

A clause should also be included to the effect that the parties reserve the right to reduce the basis of charging should severe market failure arise.

### Deadlines for the preparation of documentation

**[A13.38]** Evidence to demonstrate arm's length prices need only be produced upon HMRC request, although such requests are frequently accompanied by deadlines of thirty days of the date of the enquiry letter. In practice, therefore, it is advisable to maintain documentation that is contemporaneous with the transactions concerned and documentation should be in place by the time a company submits its tax return.

Documentation may also be required to support the entries on a tax return.

# Planning—trading models and entity characterisation

**[A13.39]** Entity characterisation determines the method of reward for an enterprise. By establishing the functions, risks and assets employed by the 'tested party' through the functional analysis it is possible to ascertain, using the OECD Guidelines, the characterisation which should apply to an entity. This will assist with applying the appropriate transfer pricing method.

When undertaking transfer pricing planning, the objective is often to characterise entities in high tax jurisdictions as low risk, and therefore entitled to lower levels of profits. Functions of companies in the group can therefore be structured by reference to this principle and the characterisations below.

This can be done by identifying what activities are undertaken and ensuring that these are undertaken in the appropriate jurisdiction.

Two Indian transfer pricing cases highlight the importance of correctly determining the functions, assets and risks of the entity.

*In Gap International Sourcing (India) Pvt Ltd*, the Delhi Income Tax Appellate Tribunal held that cost-plus was the most appropriate method for calculating the profits of a procurement service provider. The facts in this case were distinguished from the earlier case of *Li & Fung India Pvt Ltd* where the Tribunal held that a commission based remuneration was the most appropriate method. In the latter case, the company had greater risks and undertook wider functions than just those of a routine service provider.

## Manufacturing entity characterisations

**[A13.40]** There are three key manufacturer characterisations: fully-fledged manufacturer, contract manufacturer and consignment or toll manufacturer. The expected return earned by each characterisation is related to the entity's functions, assets and risks which are different for each characterisation. This is illustrated in Diagram 4, although it should be noted that the higher the potential for profit, the greater the potential that an entity can make a loss. An entity which has a low profit potential may continue to make a small level of profit even if supply chain as a whole makes a loss.

The typical functions, assets and risks of each characterisation are summarised in the table below.

| Functions, assets and risks | Fully fledged manufacturer | Contract manufacturer | Consignment manufacturer |
|---|---|---|---|
| Design of production processes | Yes | No | No |
| Development of product specifications | Yes | No | No |
| Product research and development | Yes | No | No |
| Process research and development | Yes | No | No |

| Functions, assets and risks | Fully fledged manufacturer | Contract manufacturer | Consignment manufacturer |
|---|---|---|---|
| Development of purchasing policies and materials specifications | Yes | No | No |
| Planning inventory | Yes | No | No |
| Determination of corporate manufacturing strategy | Yes | No | No |
| Product and process intangibles | Yes | Some | Some |
| Trademark / trade name | Yes | No | No |
| Reputation | Yes | Some | No |
| Production scheduling | Yes | Some | Some |
| Sourcing raw materials | Yes | No | No |
| Owns materials, work in progress | Yes | Yes | No |
| Owns finished goods | Yes | No | No |
| Shipping | Yes | Some | No |
| Manufacturing and assembly | Yes | Yes | Yes |
| Packaging and labelling | Yes | Maybe | Maybe |
| Quality control and quality assurance procedures | Yes | Some | Some |
| Inventory risk | Yes | No | No |
| Market risk | Yes | No | No |
| Warranty risk | Yes | No | No |

## Fully-fledged manufacturer

**[A13.41]** A fully-fledged manufacturer typically undertakes all the entrepreneurial and operational activities, including:

(a)    production scheduling;
(b)    design of production processes;
(c)    development of product specifications;
(d)    quality control and quality assurance procedures;
(e)    product and process research and development;
(f)    development of purchasing policies and materials specifications;
(g)    planning inventory of raw materials, work in process and finished product;
(h)    determination of corporate strategy;
(i)    sourcing raw materials.

A fully-fledged manufacturer typically incurs risks typically associated with these activities such as inventory, market and warranty risks. It typically develops product and process intangibles, trademark/trade name and the reputation for quality.

Operational functions include the manufacturing or assembly activities necessary to manufacture the product, packaging and labelling, and the daily administrative tasks required to maintain a viable production facility.

## Contract manufacturer

**[A13.42]**  A contract manufacturer typically undertakes the operational functions required to manufacture a product on behalf of a principal, but transfers title of the finished goods to the principal immediately.

Contract manufacturers do not typically carry out significant entrepreneurial activities which would result in risk-bearing or intangible asset development. Intangible assets are typically limited to customer relationships and some process technology. Production scheduling is organised by the requirements of the principal. The contract manufacturer may utilise production technology, product specifications, quality assurance and quality control procedures established by the principal or its end customer.

Operational functions undertaken include manufacturing and/or assembly activities and the daily administrative tasks required to maintain a viable production facility. As production is conducted solely to order for a principal, the contract manufacturer faces no market risk because its sales are guaranteed, nor does it face inventory or warranty risk.

A contract manufacturer may be remunerated on a cost plus, price per unit, or a service fee basis. A contract manufacturer faces less risk and earns, on average, lower returns than a fully fledged manufacturer operating in the same industry and markets.

## Consignment manufacturer

**[A13.43]**  A consignment manufacturer is functionally similar to the contract manufacturer, but it processes goods belonging to the principal and never takes title to the raw materials or components, work in progress or finished product. It has no inventory or warranty risks and holds no intangible assets.

It assumes less risk and receives a lower return than a contract manufacturer and its remuneration usually takes the form of cost plus or service fee.

## *Sales entity characterisations*

**[A13.44]**  Sales entities may be classified as commission agents, commissionaires, fully-fledged distributors or limited risk distributors. Sales entities' profitability is related to the functions, assets and risks associated with their activities. Consequently, as the functionality decreases and risks diminish, so does the return. This is illustrated in Diagram 4, although again it should be noted that the higher the potential for profit, the greater the potential that an entity can make a loss. An entity which has a low profit potential may continue to make a small level of profit even if supply chain as a whole makes a loss.

Diagram 4

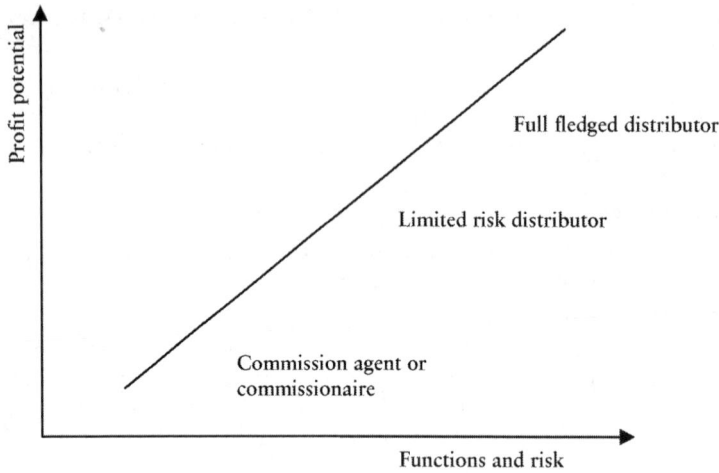

The typical functions, assets and risks of each characterisation are summarised in the table below.

|  | Fully fledged distributor | Limited risk distributor | Commission agent/ commissionaire |
|---|---|---|---|
| Setting marketing strategy | Yes | No | No |
| Setting marketing budget | Yes | No | No |
| Setting prices | Yes | No | No |
| Setting credit terms | Yes | Maybe | No |
| Market research | Yes | Maybe | Maybe |
| Preparing sales forecasts | Yes | Some | Some |
| Sales training | Yes | No | No |
| Marketing intangibles (brand awareness etc) | Yes | No | No |
| Customer list | Yes | Yes | Some |
| Advertising and promotional campaigns and attending trade shows | Yes | Yes | No |
| Identifying customers and making sales calls | Yes | Yes | Yes |
| Taking customer orders | Yes | Yes | Yes |
| Arranging delivery | Yes | Maybe | Maybe |

|  | Fully fledged distributor | Limited risk distributor | Commission agent/ commissionaire |
|---|---|---|---|
| Invoicing and receiving payment | Yes | Yes | Maybe |
| After-sales service | Yes | Yes | Some |
| Maintaining customer relationships | Yes | Some | Some |
| Inventory risk | Yes | Some | No |
| Warranty risk | Yes | No | No |
| Credit risk | Yes | Maybe | No |

## Fully fledged distributor

**[A13.45]** A fully fledged distributor may have some commercial management and investment functions and is also likely to be responsible for design. It may provide global brand and global customer/supplier contractual support. It will hold inventory and sell to customers as principal, undertaking normal selling functions, such as taking and processing customer orders and enquiries, negotiating sales, invoicing and collecting payments, satisfying statutory regulations, and monitoring market demand.

It will typically have significant authority to discount prices from the price list (although broad limits may be set with respect to volumes and price levels). It will take title to the product and will be responsible for forecasting and scheduling inventory shipments. The fully-fledged distributor has bad debt and inventory risks and may hold or share warranty risk.

It undertakes strategic marketing activities and its resulting brand awareness may represent a significant intangible asset, in addition to the ownership of other intangibles such as customer lists and customer relationships. The fully-fledged distributor usually performs more extensive customer service activities than the limited risk distributor.

## Limited risk distributor

**[A13.46]** A limited risk distributor sells to customers but buys product from a principal, either on a sale or return basis or upon receipt of a customer order. It therefore has little or no inventory risk. The principal may be either the manufacturer or a master (super) distributor. The distributor undertakes no strategic marketing activities and does not develop any marketing intangibles. The principal is responsible for approving its sales forecast and marketing budget and for establishing a price list. Any discount in selling price beyond a certain level must be approved by the principal. The principal generally funds marketing expenses and may undertake market research.

The limited risk distributor may undertake a variety of tactical marketing tasks, including:

(a)  conducting advertising and promotional campaigns and attending trade shows;

(b)    building sales forecasts;

(c)    identifying customers and making sales calls;

(d)    taking customer orders;

(e)    setting credit terms and assuming credit risk (although, ideally, this should be the responsibility of the principal);

(f)    invoicing the customer;

(g)    receiving payment, performing after-sales service and maintaining customer relationships.

The limited risk distributor may be responsible for arranging transport to the customer for products, although this activity may be undertaken by the principal. Sales force training is also generally carried out by the principal.

The limited risk distributor takes title to the products it distributes but has limited inventory risk since it sells very shortly after purchase (this is sometimes known as 'flash title') or buys goods from the principal on a sale or return basis. Warranty risk is borne by the principal.

The profits earned by a limited risk distributor are lower than those earned by a full distributor.

### Commission agent

**[A13.47]** A commission agent is a service provider and generally operates as a sales representative, arranging the sale of goods to customers on behalf and in the name of its disclosed principal. A UK commission agent of a foreign corporation will usually create a permanent establishment of the overseas entity in the UK, (see **A4.24**). Even in the absence of a permanent establishment, tax authorities may seek to challenge the profits of the commission agent under transfer pricing principles. A commission agent does not purchase products for resale, but receives a commission on the sale of products to customers made on behalf of its principal which is generally a manufacturing or distribution entity. It is responsible for functions such as identifying potential customers, calling on active and potential customers, introducing new products, taking customer orders, maintaining customer relations and providing limited technical assistance within its territory.

The commission agent undertakes a more limited range of operational activities than a full distributor and is typically not involved in any strategic marketing activities. Its only intangible asset is typically a customer list or customer relationships and, since the commission agent does not take title to the product, it has no accounts receivable nor inventory risk.

As mentioned above, a commission agent receives a commission on sales, but may need to be remunerated on the cost plus basis initially, whilst in a market penetration period.

### Commissionaire

**[A13.48]** The commissionaire sells to customers in its own name but for the benefit and risk of an undisclosed principal. Its risk is limited and it earns a lower return than a full distributor. It has certain advantages over the use of a commission agent, but in common law jurisdictions (such as the UK) it will be treated in broadly the same way as a commission agent.

If not structured correctly, a commissionaire can also create a permanent establishment for its principal (see **A4.24**). Even in the absence of a permanent establishment, tax authorities may seek to challenge the profits of the commissionaire under transfer pricing principles.

Where a UK principal has a foreign commissionaire it is important to address VAT issues and to ensure that invoicing procedures are correct and in line with the commissionaire structure ie that goods are sold from the principal to the commissionaire, and then to the customer. The group's accounting systems must also deal with the unique invoicing structure which applies to commissionaires.

The commissionaire has similar functions and risks as a commission agent and also earns a commission on sales.

### Service provider

**[A13.49]** A service provider may carry out similar functions and has similarly low risks as a commission agent but may also carry out market liaison, back office, financial, administrative and research and development functions. Service providers are commonly remunerated on a cost plus basis. They may also be characterised as shared service centres when supplying several services within a group. A shared services centre may also be party to a cost contribution agreement.

A company may be both a commissionaire (for instance) and a service provider. It would then be remunerated to take into account both its sales functions, and the other support services provided.

### *Cost contribution transaction model*

**[A13.50]** Cost sharing or cost contribution agreements are contractual arrangements under which the costs of developing, producing or obtaining assets, services or rights are shared between the participants. The costs are shared between participants, in proportion to the anticipated benefits that they will receive.

A cost contribution agreement is a contractual relationship—it is specifically recognised for instance in the US regulations that cost contributions agreements do not constitute a partnership between the participants.

Tax planning opportunities may arise where cost contribution agreements are used for the development of intellectual property.

In Diagram 5, the UK parent company undertakes development of intellectual property and then charges a royalty to other group companies. Two tax problems arise from this arrangement:

(a)     The royalty must be at arm's length, and is very likely to represent a profit over the original cost of development by the UK company. Although the subsidiaries may be entitled to a deduction for the royalty, they may not be able to use it efficiently because of losses or because they pay a lower tax rate than in the UK.

(b)    The royalty would be subject to withholding tax (although this could potentially be reduced under the EU Interest and Royalties Directive or a relevant DTA).

Diagram 5

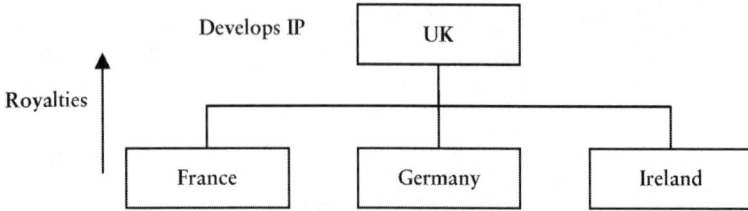

These problems may be avoided if a cost contribution agreement is used.

In Diagram 6, the UK parent company and the subsidiaries enter into a cost contribution agreement under which the costs of developing the intellectual property, and the benefits arising from it, are shared. Each participant is entitled to use the intellectual property.

(1)    The payments made by the subsidiaries to develop the intellectual property should be business expenses rather than royalties, and therefore not subject to withholding tax.

(2)    There are no inter-company charges for development or use of the intellectual property, to which transfer pricing rules or withholding tax could apply.

Diagram 6

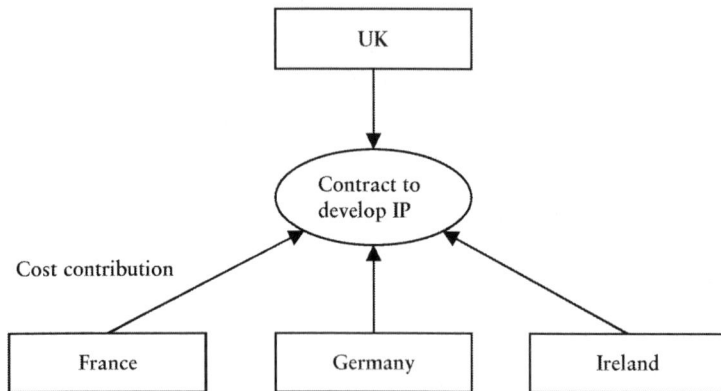

When companies join or leave a cost contribution agreement, they may acquire or dispose of any accrued benefits (for instance intellectual property which has been developed under the agreement), for which an arm's length payment would need to be recognised.

Cost contribution agreements are recognised by both the OECD and US transfer pricing guidelines. However, HMRC believe that in most cases cost contribution agreements will not be arm's length because they are not generally entered into between independent parties.

INTM463090 gives the example of a recharge of marketing costs by a UK parent company at no mark up, in proportion to the turnover of its subsidiaries. This would not be an arm's length recharge because the UK company retains the risks associated with providing these benefits. In order for a cost contribution agreement to exist, there must be a genuine pooling of risks and benefits under the agreement.

## 'Hub and spoke' transaction model

[A13.51] B5.3 outlines a transaction structure where one group company (the hub) makes all sales to customers. Other group companies (the spokes) provide services to the hub company, such as manufacturing, sales, management services, distribution.

Each of the spoke companies are characterised as outlined above, with the residual profit being recognised in the hub company.

This provides a significant tax planning opportunity as the hub company can be located in a low-tax (or in some cases low-VAT) jurisdiction. The spoke companies can be established in higher-tax jurisdictions, where employees or customers may be located, and are subject to a higher rate of tax but on lower profits than are recognised in the hub company.

Typical jurisdictions for a hub company are outlined below.

### Jersey or Guernsey (or Isle of Man)

[A13.52] These jurisdictions offer a 0% tax rate on profits. However, given their geographical location and limited infrastructure, it may be difficult to establish functions, risks and assets there.

In addition, these jurisdictions have very limited DTA networks and withholding taxes may arise on payments of interest or royalties, and in some cases other payments (where for instance they are 'black listed' in the paying jurisdiction as tax havens).

When considering a 0% tax jurisdiction which is close to the UK, there is often a choice between the Isle of Man and Jersey or Guernsey. If it is important that the company can register for VAT, or recover VAT in another Member State, the Isle of Man may be preferred to Jersey or Guernsey.

However, locating a company in a jurisdiction outside the EU for VAT purposes may provide planning opportunities to reduce VAT or customs duty, where goods can be sold directly to customers and take advantage of reliefs such as the low value consignment relief.

### Ireland

**[A13.53]** Ireland offers a 12.5% tax rate on trading profits, but 25% on non-trading profits. It is important therefore that sufficient trading substance is established, and the Irish tax authorities have published a list of decisions which been made on whether companies are trading or non-trading (www.re venue.ie/en/about/publications/submitted-cases.html).

A number of companies (including US companies distributing software and other products in Europe) have relocated staff and functions to Ireland.

Ireland is a member of the EU and therefore interest and royalties received from other EU group companies should be free of withholding taxes.

### Malta

**[A13.54]** Although the corporate tax rate in Malta is 35% much of this is refunded when dividends are paid to shareholders, resulting in an effective tax rate of approximately 4% to 7% depending on the nature of the income from which the dividends are paid.

Malta is a member of the EU and therefore interest and royalties received from other EU group companies should be free of withholding taxes.

### Cyprus

**[A13.55]** The corporate tax rate in Cyprus is 12.5%, and there is no withholding tax on dividends paid to shareholders.

However, Cyprus is a considerable distance from the UK and other Western European countries and it may be difficult to undertake central management and control there. It may also be difficult to persuade staff to relocate there.

Cyprus is a member of the EU and therefore interest and royalties received from other EU group companies should be free of withholding taxes.

### Switzerland

**[A13.56]** The effective tax rate in Switzerland depends on the canton in which a company is located and the activity undertaken. It may be possible to obtain a rate as low as 12%.

Although Switzerland is not a member of the EU, it does benefit from many of the EU Directives, and therefore interest and royalties received from EU group companies should be free of withholding taxes.

Locating a company in a jurisdiction outside the EU for VAT purposes may provide planning opportunities to reduce VAT or customs duty, where goods can be sold directly to customers and take advantage of reliefs such as the low value consignment relief.

# Planning—specific situations

## *Share options*

Diagram 7

**[A13.57]**

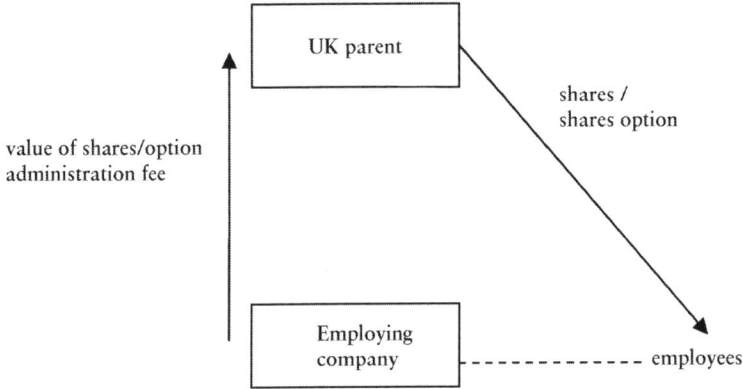

The provision of shares (for instance under an option scheme) in a company to employees of other group companies is a transaction which may fall within the transfer pricing regime. This principle was established in the case of *Waterloo plc v IRC* [2002] STC (SCD) 95.

There are two aspects to this from a UK perspective.

In Diagram 7, a UK parent company issues shares, or share options to employees of its subsidiaries. For tax purposes:

(a)     The UK parent has provided its shares for the benefit of the subsidiary, and should be remunerated for this. If the cost of the shares is not recognised as an expense in the profit and loss account, HMRC consider that any transfer pricing adjustment will not be taxable.

(b)     However, if a payment is made by the subsidiary in excess of fair value, HMRC consider that the whole payment may be taxable under the anti-arbitrage rules (TIOPA 2010, s 249), if the subsidiary is able to obtain a deduction for payment. This would not be the case with a UK subsidiary where the deduction would be limited by CTA 2009, Pt, 12 Ch 2 and the transfer pricing rules.

(c)     The UK parent may also have provided an administration service for the share scheme, for which it should be remunerated.

Diagram 8

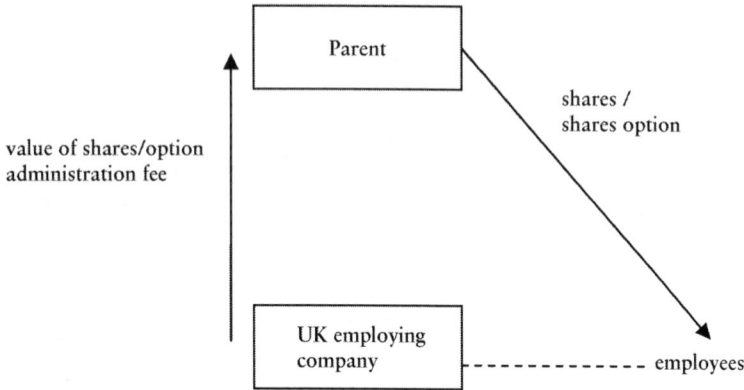

In Diagram 8, a UK subsidiary company has shares or share options provided to its employees. For tax purposes:

(a)     Any payment (or corresponding adjustment) for the cost of the shares or share options will be disallowed if a deduction is also available under CTA 2009, Pt 12, Ch 2.

(b)     Provided it can be distinguished, any payment (or corresponding adjustment) for administration services should be deductible.

HMRC have published guidance on these principles, and on more complex situations such as cash-settled options, invested options and employee benefit trusts. This guidance can be found (at the time of writing) at www.hmrc.gov .uk/international/new-share-plan-guidance.pdf.

## Business restructuring

**[A13.58]** Transfer pricing planning often involves restructuring existing inter-company relationships, so that functions, assets and risks are transferred to low-tax jurisdictions.

Greater profits are then recognised in the low-tax jurisdiction.

However, transferring these tangible assets may crystallise capital gains in the company which previously held these functions, assets and risks. This gain may be realised in respect of identifiable assets such as customer lists, or less identifiable assets such as goodwill.

In 2008, the OECD released a discussion draft of its paper 'Transfer Pricing Aspects of Business Restructurings', currently available at www.oecd.org/data oecd/59/40/41346644.pdf

Following the comments received in 2009 and 2010, a new Chapter IX was included in the OECD guidelines on 22 July 2012. The Chapter addresses four main issues covering:

(a)     the allocation of risks between related parties;

(b)     transfer pricing of the actual restructuring;

(c)     transfer pricing of transactions following the restructuring;

(d)     exceptional circumstances where a business restructuring can be disregarded by tax authorities.

As the UK transfer pricing rules are required to follow the OECD Transfer Pricing Guidelines these issues will impact on business restructuring which involves UK companies. At present, any restructuring will be considered in the UK under general principles (see **B5.25** and **B5.26**).

Other jurisdictions (such as the US and Germany see **B5.27** and **B5.28**) already have specific rules dealing with business restructuring.

The discussion draft sets out a number of points which will support business restructuring. It sets out that business restructuring can be effective, even if undertaken for tax reasons. It also sets out that transactions should be recognised following the restructuring as if they had been in place from outset.

However, the discussion draft also outlines ways in which business restructuring will not be effective for tax purposes, for instance:

(a)     there should be greater scrutiny of profit allocation following a restructuring;

(b)     while a business restructuring is not itself a taxable event, valuable intangibles may be transferred as part of a restructuring.

Once the draft is adopted, a UK member of a group undertaking a business restructuring will need to have regard to these more specific guidelines.

## Interaction with customs duty, VAT and expatriate tax issues

**[A13.59]** The focus of transfer pricing has traditionally been on direct taxation, but in the past decade, the customs duty and VAT dimensions of transfer pricing have become more prominent and are increasingly attracting the attention of tax authorities seeking to protect their revenues. The following issues should therefore be considered when undertaking business restructuring:

(a)     transactions should be addressed separately for VAT purposes where they have been netted off;

(b)     the place of supply rules which will affect the supply of services and recharging of costs;

(c)     transfer pricing adjustments do not result in a corresponding adjustment to customs duties;

(d)     new rules are being considered in relation to customs duty payable on trademark royalties.

Expatriate tax issues should also be considered when altering secondment arrangements etc, to ensure that recharges do not create any personal tax issues for the secondees or permanent establishment risk for any group entities.

## Payments on behalf of subsidiaries

**[A13.60]** In order that a payment is deductible for UK tax purposes, it must be made 'wholly and exclusively' for the purposes of the trade of the company which makes the payment (CTA 2009, s 54).

Where a parent company makes a payment on behalf of a foreign subsidiary, HMRC will argue that it benefits the subsidiary rather than the parent company. It will therefore not be deductible for UK tax purposes by the parent company.

However, it is possible to argue that a payment actually benefits the wider business of the parent company. In *Robinson (Inspector of Taxes) v Scott Bader Co Ltd* [1981] 2 All ER 116, a UK parent company seconded an employee to a French subsidiary, but continued to pay his salary and expenses. The Court of Appeal held that the payments were made to further the parent company's own business in Europe by ensuring that the subsidiary could continue to supply products which were sold by the parent company. The payments were therefore deductible for UK tax purposes.

Where a parent company does make payments which provide a benefit to a subsidiary, an arm's length charge may need to be recognised under transfer pricing principles. However, if no deduction is allowed for the payment by the parent company, it is unlikely that a transfer pricing adjustment would also be required (this is for example clear in the case of share options—see **A13.57**).

In any case, the benefit to the trade of the parent company (rather than the subsidiary) should be clearly documented and evidenced. It is also important (and this point was fundamental in *Robinson v Scott Bader Co Ltd* [1981] 54 TC 757) that there is not a dual purpose to the payments. The intention behind such payments must be to benefit the parent company only, even if there is a consequential benefit to the subsidiary. If the intention is to benefit both the subsidiary and the parent company then the payment will not be *exclusively* for the benefit of the parent company. It was held in the *Scott Bader* case that intention is subjective, and contemporaneous evidence will therefore be valuable in defending against an HMRC challenge.

From an accounting perspective, a payment on behalf of a subsidiary may create an inter-company loan. This would not result in an expense in the profit and loss account, and therefore no tax deduction would be available.

If significant payments are made on behalf of a subsidiary, the overseas jurisdiction may treat the payments as a capital contribution by the parent company to the subsidiary, and this may in turn have tax consequences.

## Joint ventures

**[A13.61]** Joint venture companies can frequently cause problems, as the parties to the joint venture will view their commercial return as being through dividends and increased value of their shares. Transactions with the joint venture may therefore not be undertaken on an arm's length basis.

However, the transfer pricing rules will likely require an adjustment to the profits of the joint venture partner providing the goods or services even where the joint venture partner does not have 50% control over the joint venture company (see the major interest rules outlined at **A13.12**).

The joint venture agreement should set out how any corresponding adjustment should be dealt with, as it will likely arise as a result of only one of the joint venture parties being disadvantaged

In Diagram 9 below, Companies A and B create a JV company. Company A provides services in exchange for shares and Company B provides cash for shares. In order to avoid a transfer pricing adjustment, the shares should be issued to Company A initially as unpaid, and the services invoiced to the JV company on a commercial basis. Instead of paying Company A cash for the service, the JV offsets the cash owed for services against the share capital debtor.

**Diagram 9**

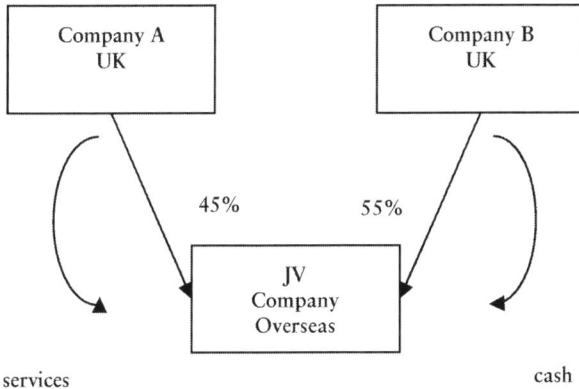

services                                                    cash

# Basic principles—thin capitalisation and interest deductibility

**[A13.62]** Loans between associated companies where one of those companies controls the other, or where both are under common control, will be subject to the transfer pricing legislation by virtue of TIOPA 2010, s 152.

Where a loan exceeds the amount which the borrower would or could have borrowed from an independent lender, or where the other terms of the loan differ from those that would have been agreed with such a lender, a company will be considered to be 'thinly capitalised' ie it does not have enough capital to support the debt. In this case, the interest on the excessive part of the loan will be disallowed as a deduction in arriving at the assessable profits or allowable losses of the borrower.

In addition, the transfer pricing rules may apply to the rate of interest charged on a loan if this rate is higher than would have been charged by an independent lender.

HMRC consider that a company is thinly capitalised where the level of debt is higher than would be made available to the company in an arm's length relationship. In the absence of the transfer pricing rules, this would mean that thinly capitalised businesses could claim a higher tax deduction for interest paid on their loans than would be possible under an arm's length level of gearing.

Thin capitalisation enquiries are typically raised by HMRC in respect of trading groups where a significant level of funding is provided by related parties. Financing arrangements between two related UK parties and also in some cases borrowings from a third party are also caught by the rules.

Legislation was introduced in March 2005 under which certain lenders could be considered to be connected to the company to which it provides its finance even if the lender does not itself control the borrowing company (see **A13.77**).

The effect of the transfer pricing rules is generally the denial of tax relief for interest payments on the amount of debt deemed excessive on loans made to the company, or the imposition of interest income in respect of loans made by the company. The rules also apply to situations where one connected party has guaranteed the borrowing of another entity.

Where adjustments are required it is possible to claim a compensating adjustment by or on behalf of the lender in some situations, so the lender is taxed as if it had received only the arm's length amount of interest (see **A13.74**).

## Loans between connected companies

**[A13.63]** The principal transfer pricing rules relating to loans are found in TIOPA 2010, s 152. These rules apply where both of the affected persons are companies and a provision has been made or imposed by means of a transaction or series of transactions in relation to a security and that provision is not on arm's length terms, resulting in a UK tax advantage for one of the affected persons.

Prior to 1 April 2004, thin capitalisation rules were included in ICTA 1988, s 209, under which interest was reclassified as a dividend which was not deductible for corporation tax purposes. In some circumstances, s 209 (now CTA 2010, s 1000) may still be relevant—see **A13.76** below.

## Special relationship

**[A13.64]** For the transfer pricing rules under s 152 to apply there has to be a 'special relationship' between the companies concerned. A special relationship is defined in s 154 (3) and s 148 as a relationship where at the time of the making of the provision one of the affected persons was directly or indirectly participating in the management, control or capital of the other, or the same person, or the other persons was or were directly or indirectly participating in the management, control or capital of each of the affected persons. These definitions are the same as apply to other transactions, and are discussed at **A13.12**.

If there is a special relationship, it is necessary to consider whether the provision between the companies is at arm's length. s 152 (2) states that account should be taken of all factors, including but not limited to:

(a)  whether the loan would have been made at all in the absence of the special relationship;

(b)  the amount which the loan would have been in the absence of the special relationship; and

(c)  the rate of interest and other terms which would have been agreed in the absence of the special relationship.

When considering whether or not a loan would have been made in the absence of the special relationship the fact that the lender is not in the business of making loans is generally disregarded.

Section 154 (7) extends the application of s 152 to circumstances where no security is issued but money is advanced in return for interest payments or other consideration.

### Separate entity rules

**[A13.65]** Section 152(5) requires a borrower to be considered in isolation from its parent group for the purposes of determining the maximum amount it would have borrowed from an independent lender.

When making this determination it is necessary to ignore any 'guarantee' given by any company with which the borrower has a 'participatory relationship'. Two companies have such a relationship if one controls the other or both are controlled by the same person or persons. The term guarantee is very widely defined in s 154(4). This extends beyond the provision of a formal, written guarantee to any situation where the lender has a reasonable expectation that, if the borrower defaults on the loan, he will be paid by another company or companies. However, where a guarantee is provided it is necessary to consider the special rules relating to guarantees (see **A13.66**).

### Guarantees

**[A13.66]** Thin capitalisation may arise in circumstances other than a straight-forward loan from one company to a connected company and it may arise where there is a series of transactions, such as where one company provides a guarantee to a lender in respect of a loan to another company. Where there is such a guarantee between connected companies, the transfer pricing rules will apply to the loan even if it is from an independent lender. (TIOPA 2010, s 153)

Where a loan has been made to a company and a guarantee has been provided by an associated company, in deciding whether an adjustment needs to be made for excessive interest regard should be made as to whether, in the absence of a special relationship:

(a)     a guarantee would have been provided;

(b)     the loan under scrutiny would have been guaranteed; and,

(c)     the amount of consideration that would have been required for the guarantee and what other terms would have been agreed.

As with the rules for excessive interest, no account is to be taken of the fact that the provider of the guarantee is not in the business of providing guarantees. And again the borrowing company must be looked at in isolation from the rest of the group.

The effect of s 153 is to disallow interest deductions where a loan is guaranteed by a connected party, to the extent that the loan would not have been provided in the absence of the guarantee. The guarantor may be entitled to a compensating adjustment (see **A13.74**).

If a guarantee reduces the interest cost to the borrower, this may imply that the guarantor has an increased risk. The guarantor would then be required to recognise an arm's length profit in respect of providing the guarantee (although the borrower may then be entitled to a corresponding adjustment).

An example of s 153 and a compensating adjustment is at **A13.74**.

The Canadian case of *GE Capital Canada Inc v R* (2009 TCC 563) provides an interesting insight into the transfer pricing of guarantees and in particular the concept of implicit support from a parent to a subsidiary.

### Advance Thin Capitalisation Agreements (ATCAs)

**[A13.67]** In November 2007 HMRC issued a revised Advance Thin Capitalisation Agreement (ATCA) template and an accompanying Statement of Practice, since updated by HMRC Brief 01/09. This procedure is available to all companies seeking certainty on the future tax treatment of loans but also as a means of resolving outstanding thin capitalisation enquiries.

The ATCA process is outlined in more detail at **A12.20**.

### Thin capitalisation defences

**[A13.68]** The following points should be considered when defending thin capitalisation enquiries, agreeing arm's length financial ratios with HMRC, or defending breaches of financial covenants which have previously been agreed with HMRC.

(1)     Although HMRC takes a separate entity approach, where a company has no income it should be possible to reflect the market value of its subsidiaries when calculating its equity by including the profit and loss account reserve balances of its direct subsidiaries.
This should be acceptable to HMRC because these balances could be paid up to the holding company as dividends, should they be required. A similar exercise can be undertaken where a subsidiary owns property which is included in the accounts at book value, which is then re-valued at market value and included in the equity calculation.

(2)    Certain breaches of acceptable or agreed debt/equity ratios may be ignored, such as catastrophic events and other matters which are generally included in the force majeure clause of an inter-company agreement. It may be possible to treat, as an unusual event, a large acquisition requiring exceptional costs for reconstruction and redundancies as long as this event was not being considered when the agreement was being drawn up.

Where an acquisition is being considered which would temporarily affect the covenants and the company can show an improvement in the position through financial budgets over an acceptable period, then it should be possible to agree a temporary breach of covenant (similar to agreeing higher debt equity or other financial ratios in a new start up situation).

There could therefore be scope to amend the debt/equity ratios for future acquisitions. Additionally, an unexpected event, such as a one-off accountancy provision, which does not affect the ability to service the debt, should also be an acceptable breach.

Market demise, or a one-off commercial problem could also be an acceptable defence.

(3)    If the borrowings are from an overseas third party bank, currency fluctuations may have affected the terms and amount of debt and equity.

(4)    There may have been a change in the term of lending (ie when negotiating original covenants, the borrowing was long term, but the borrower itself made an onward loan which was short term). This may have changed in the intervening years to long term borrowing and long term lending, which could in turn change the acceptable debt/equity ratios.

(5)    Long term borrowing could mean that market trading conditions have changed and the underlying business has been affected. A change in the business model could create an argument for a change in the debt/equity ratio.

(6)    It should be acceptable to offset cash balances against debt, as long as these are not earmarked for particular expenditure, such as the payment of a dividend or capital expenditure. The cash must be available to pay down the debt and the debt should not be fixed term nor attract penalties for early redemption.

(7)    Where a company borrows from a third party bank and lends on to a connected company where there is a low risk of default, it may be possible to agree a low margin should be taxed in the original borrower.

(8)    If the bad debt profile of the UK group is fairly constant over a period of time, but then increased, there is an argument for the bad debt differential to be added back to the profit and loss account reserve, although this is unlikely to have a large impact, unless a substantial debt is written off.

Evidence from third party banks stating that they would have made the current loan without a guarantee can be a powerful demonstration of a UK company's borrowing capability. However, where such evidence is available, it is useful to have on file the associated banking covenants and third party banking review procedure, including an idea of the capital requirements to support the loan.

The HMRC guidance on undertaking a thin capitalisation transfer pricing enquiry can be found in their manuals at INTM513000.

There is useful guidance in INTM518000 on HMRC's views on lending against asset values). This also highlights their practice of using third party data such as the De Montfort Report to challenge property based lending.

### Conduit finance and treasury companies

**[A13.69]** Many larger groups have treasury companies, whose main purpose is to borrow in order to lend funds on to the wider group. These companies typically have very little equity funding and their borrowing may be supported by a guarantee provided by one or more other group companies.

A margin is generally earned on the difference between interest received and interest paid to reflect the conduit company's role in procuring finance for the group. The spread will depend on the nature and extent of its activities. The overall profit attributed to a conduit company should be proportionate to the functions it undertakes and the risks it retains.

### Quasi-equity

**[A13.70]** A loan or cash transfer made by a UK company to a related party could be considered as 'quasi-equity' (ie the loan performs the function of share capital and interest is therefore not payable). Structuring cash transfers in this way may be particularly relevant to

- companies that have operations in countries with high geo-political risks;
- companies engaged in mining, oil, gas and other international mineral extraction activities; or
- where there are onerous regulatory provisions in place in regard to cash movements or exchange controls.

It is important to ensure that the capitalisation is correctly documented from the outset. The existence of a loan agreement or other written documentation characterising the transaction as a loan could make it difficult for the lender to argue otherwise.

Points to note when documenting and defending quasi-equity arrangements are:

(a)   board minutes should document the provision of cash and explain the rationale for treating it as quasi-entity, rather than loan finance;

(b)   the board minutes of the lender should document that the lender neither expects repayment nor interest receipts from the cash transfer, explaining the amount will be treated as equity;

(c)   an inter-company agreement between the 'lender' and the 'borrower' should be drafted documenting the provision;

(d) relevant economic evidence should be available to demonstrate that (*i*) the borrower could not have obtained funding from a third party lender independently and (*ii*) evidence of geo-political or regulatory risk thus preventing the 'lender' from making a direct capital investment in the subsidiary;

(e) accounting advice should be sought on the appropriate treatment of the capital payment for the purposes of the statutory accounts, of both the borrower and the lender.

If the above guidance is not followed, problems may arise where companies need to justify their position under enquiry several years after the 'loan' was first made. In such circumstances there is often little contemporaneous evidence available to demonstrate that the 'loan' was always intended to be 'quasi-equity'.

As a matter of practice, HMRC are known to accept the quasi equity argument only for downstream loans (ie parent to subsidiary) and not vice versa. HMRC have also been known to accept that only a proportion of the funding made could be considered as 'quasi-equity'.

### Arm's length interest rates

**[A13.71]** Inter-company interest rates are often based on LIBOR (London Interbank Offered Rate) plus a percentage (or basis point) up-lift. Loan terms may be fixed or variable. The equivalent EURIBOR (Euro Interbank Offered Rate) can be used for loans dominated in Euro. The margin on the LIBOR/EURIBOR rate will be dependent on risk or default, the amount loaned, term of the loans, and whether the debt is secured or guaranteed.

### Inter-company accounts

**[A13.72]** Where a company has a long outstanding inter-company trading balance due to it, HMRC may argue that there is effectively a loan and seek interest thereon.

### Debt/equity ratios

**[A13.73]** When determining an appropriate amount of debt, the debt/equity ratio of the borrowing company is usually considered, and compared with debt/equity ratios of comparable businesses.

For these purposes, HMRC accept (INTM517030) that equity includes:

(a) share capital;
(b) share premium;
(c) capital redemption reserve;
(d) profit and loss reserve;
(e) revaluation reserve where audited or supported by a valuation;
(f) other reserves where audited or supported by a valuation.

HMRC consider (INTM517020) that debt includes all loans (both inter-company and third party) and also:

(a)  liabilities under debt factoring arrangements;
(b)  liabilities under guarantees or indemnities, but not product warranties;
(c)  net liabilities under foreign exchange or interest derivative contracts;
(d)  liabilities for deferred payments over 90 days;
(e)  the finance element of finance leases;
(f)  tax creditors (if material).

Trade creditors and accrued income that do not bear significant interest can be excluded from the calculation of debt.

Ratios on an EBITDA (earnings before interest, tax, depreciation and amortisation) basis may be calculated, but an EBIT (earnings before interest and tax) ratio may be more consistent with third party terms.

It may be possible to argue a higher debt/equity ratio for an entity in a start up position for up to (say) the first three years of trading. However, budgets should be available to support future profitability and the ability to repay the debt and any accrued interest. Long term contracts showing a defined income stream, economic forecasts and budgets can also be used to support higher debt/equity and interest cover ratios, especially if they have been presented to a bank in support of the loan or even audited. However, letters of credit from banks may be heavily caveated and may not be robust enough to support a more aggressive debt/equity position.

HMRC historically accepted 'rule of thumb' debt/equity ratios and interest cover ratios, but this is no longer the case. Other jurisdictions may have statutory safe harbours, within which a company will automatically not be considered to be thinly capitalised.

## Compensating adjustments for interest

**[A13.74]** Where interest payments are subject to a transfer pricing adjustment, a claim may be made for a compensating adjustment under TIOPA 2010, s 174. This compensating adjustment will reduce the profits of the lender that are subject to UK corporation tax. DTAs may also provide for a compensating adjustment to be claimed where one of the parties in not resident in the UK (see **A8.35**).

HMRC introduced legislation under FA 2014 to prevent compensating adjustments in certain situations. One of these situations was where an individual lends money to a connected company and the company is thinly capitalised. In this example, the company would likely be subject to a transfer pricing adjustment so that it did no claim excessive interest deductions. The individual as the 'disadvantaged person' was prior to October 2013, entitled to claim a compensating adjustment under TIOPA 2010, s 174.

The new legislation at s 174A applies to all transactions from 25 October 2013 as follows:

'A claim under section 174 may not be made if

(a)  the disadvantaged person is a person (other than a company) within the charge to income tax in respect of profits arising from the relevant activities, and

(b)    the advantaged person is a company.'

Instead of being allowed a compensating adjustment, the individual will instead be treated as receiving a qualifying distribution equal to the amount of excessive interest. This means that the individual will be taxed on the excessive interest at dividend tax rates, rather than paying no tax at all.

Under s 187A, the new legislation covers finance payments (such as interest) that fall under s 174A and recharacterises them as a dividend.

Whilst the amended legislation was aimed at two particular arrangements, the October 2013 draft legislation also made reference to transactions between partnerships and their wholly controlled service companies. It is possible that a compensating adjustment may not be available in situations, for example, where an individual has provided services to a related company.

A claim for a compensating adjustment can also be made by the guarantor of a loan (subject to the new legislation introduced as set out above). A claim can only be made where the guarantee has caused the transfer pricing adjustment. The claim is limited to restriction on interest deductibility as a result of the guarantee that has been taken into account in determining the borrower's lending capacity.

Effectively, the guarantor makes a claim to be treated as if it had paid the interest which was disallowed, and this gives the guarantor the right to an interest deduction. In cases where there is more than one guarantor, the amount is split amongst them.

If the lender also makes a claim for a compensating adjustment because it is connected to the borrower, then any claim by the lender must take account of a claim made by the guarantor that has already been made. A claim by the guarantor cannot be made where a claim has already been made by the lender. The guarantor needs the financial capacity to be allowed the interest deduction in its own right.

A guarantor can make a balancing payment to a borrower to take account of the transfer of the interest deduction to him without a tax effect, but there is no obligation to make such a payment.

A claim for a compensating adjustment by a guarantor can be made by either the guarantor or the borrower, but a claim by the borrower will be taken to have been made on behalf of the guarantor.

For example, in Diagram 10 the subsidiary pays interest of £500,000 per annum to the bank. In the absence of the guarantee from the parent company, the bank would only have been prepared to lend £8m, and at an interest rate of 7%.

Under s 153, the guarantee from the parent company must be disregarded when establishing how much the subsidiary could have borrowed. As it could have borrowed only £8m, 20% of the interest will be disallowed. If the parent company were resident in the UK then it would be entitled to claim a tax deduction of this disallowed amount as a compensating adjustment.

In addition, the parent company has provided a guarantee to the subsidiary which is a provision in its own right. The arm's length price for the guarantee is likely to be the amount by which the interest rate has been reduced (ie 2%

x £10m = £200,000). If the parent were resident in the UK then its profits would be increased by £200,000 and the subsidiary would be entitled to claim a compensating adjustment for the same amount.

Diagram 10

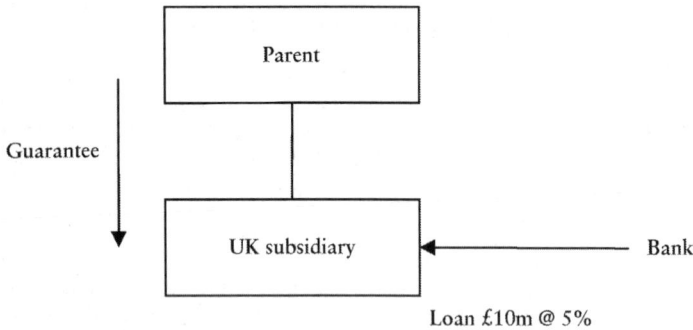

Loan £10m @ 5%

Per TIOPA 2010, s 175, it should be noted that no compensating adjustment is available where the lender and borrower are connected through the 'acting together' rules (see **A13.76**) and there is a guarantor in place with whom the borrower has a 'participatory relationship'.

## Withholding tax

**[A13.75]** Where a transfer pricing adjustment is made in respect of interest, denying a deduction for the borrower, the lender will not be treated as receiving interest income (s 187 (6)) provided that a claim for a compensating adjustment is made under s 174 or s 182. This means that in the case of an overseas lender, withholding tax does not need to be deducted if a claim is made.

## Interest reclassified as a distribution

**[A13.76]** Interest may also be recharacterised as a dividend under CTA 2010, s 1000 (1)(E)(b), where it represents:

'Any interest or other distribution out of assets of the company in respect of securities of the company, where they are securities under which the consideration given by the company which are non-commercial securities, except . . . however much (if any) of the distribution represents a reasonable commercial return for the use of the principal.'

Dividends are not deductible for tax purposes, and recharacterisation therefore means that there is no deduction for the interest. Withholding tax is not due where interest is recharacterised as a dividend under s 1000, which is confirmed by HMRC in Business Brief 47/2008. It is not necessary for either the borrower or the lender to make a claim for the interest to be free of withholding tax.

As mentioned in **A13.74** above, the excessive interest may also be classified as a distribution where the disadvantaged person is an individual and the advantaged person a company.

### 'Acting together'

**[A13.77]** TIOPA 2010, s 161 provides that where a lender 'and other persons acted together in relation to the financing arrangement', the rights of those other persons will be attributed to the lender when determining if it controls the borrower.'

This means that even though a lender may not control the borrower, a loan will fall within the transfer pricing rules if other (controlling) shareholders were involved in arranging the loan.

Section 161 only applies to financing arrangements—the transfer pricing rules will not apply to other transactions between a lender and borrower who are only connected by virtue of the acting together provisions in s 161.

# A14

# Foreign entity classification

## Introduction

**[A14.1]** It is necessary to characterise overseas entities for UK tax purposes, as this will determine how they are taxed. Broadly speaking, an entity may be:

- transparent, such that the profits and gains are taxed on the owners/members/beneficiaries of the entity;
- opaque, such that the profits and gains are taxed on the entity itself;
- if opaque, with or without ordinary share capital (certain reliefs are dependent on ordinary share capital).

It is also necessary to characterise distributions received from an opaque entity (as either income or capital) as this will determine how they are taxed in the hands of a UK recipient.

This Chapter outlines the factors which are relevant to determine:

- how an overseas entity is characterised for UK tax purposes;
- if a distribution is income or capital;
- if an entity has issued ordinary share capital.

Planning opportunities may also arise from entity characterisation. These may be straightforward structures—for example, the profits of a transparent entity may be taxed as they arise, but the profits of an opaque entity may not be taxed until they are distributed. Or they may be more complex structures which rely on a mismatch in the characterisation of entities between two jurisdictions (hybrid entities) to achieve a tax deduction without a corresponding taxable receipt.

## Impact of the OECD Action Plan on Base Erosion and Profit Shifting (BEPS)

**[A14.2]** Whilst the information in this Chapter was up to date at the time of writing this book, it is important to keep up to date on the OECD Action Plan on Base Erosion and Profit Shifting (BEPS). More detail on BEPS can be found on the OECD website www.oecd.org/ctp/beps.htm.

Before considering any international tax planning using hybrid entities, taxpayers should review the potential application of BEPS. The key Actions that are likely to have an impact for planning around entity characterisation are set out below:

**Action 2 – neutralise the effects of hybrid mismatch arrangements** Hybrid mismatch arrangements can be used to obtain unintended double non-taxation or long-term deferral. This action aims to develop model treaty provisions and recommendations for domestic law in order to neutralise the effect of the arrangements.

The expected outcome of this action is September 2014.

# Basic principles—UK classification of a foreign entity

**[A14.3]** UK statute provides little guidance on whether a foreign entity is to be treated as transparent or opaque for UK tax purposes.

A 'company' is defined by CTA 2010, s 1121 to mean:

'any body corporate or unincorporated association but does not include a partnership, a local authority or a local authority association.'

The terms 'body corporate' and 'unincorporated association' are not further defined in the statute, but the UK courts have considered whether a foreign entity should be treated as a company or a partnership on several occasions.

### Dreyfus v IRC (French Societe en Nom Collectif)

**[A14.4]** In *Dreyfus v IRC* (1929) 14 TC 560 the Court of Appeal considered whether a French société en nom collectif (SNC) should be treated as a company or a partnership. If it were a partnership then super-tax would have been due from its members/shareholders.

It was held that the SNC should be treated as a company because the SNC had a separate legal personality and carried on business in its own name. The members were not liable for the debts of the SNC, and it could not contract in its name. This was distinguished from a partnership, where the business was carried on in the name of the partners.

HMRC have subsequently confirmed (in INTM180030) that they consider that an SNC should be regarded as a partnership for UK tax purposes. This is contrary to the decision in *Dreyfus*.

However, the case itself is noteworthy because it established the principle that it is the foreign law under which it is established which should be considered to determine whether an entity is transparent or opaque for UK tax purposes. Lord Hanworth stated:

'We must respect the foreign entity established, because it is not a mere matter of the *lex fori*; it is a matter of the status which an entity brings over here with it.'

### Ryall v The Du Bois Company (German GmbH)

**[A14.5]** The *Dreyfus* case was followed by *Ryall v The Du Bois Company Ltd* (1933) 18 TC 431. The Court of Appeal considered the status of a German GmbH and held that it was to be treated as a company for UK tax purposes. In his judgment in the High Court (the decision of which was later affirmed by the Court of Appeal) Finlay J said:

'The first thing to be noted, of course, is that this is a case relating to foreign income, and I do not think that it is useful to look at the precise technicalities of English law. There must, of course, be differences between English law and foreign law, and it is useless to attempt to restrict words in a case relating to foreign income to what would be considered income from shares if the company were an English company . . .'

Essentially, he applied the principle established by *Dreyfus*, that it is the foreign law that should be considered to determine the status of a foreign entity. Finlay J also went on to make further helpful comments by listing those features of the GmbH which he considered to contain the essential elements of a company:

> '[The GmbH] contains the essential elements of a company. You have the persons who have interests or shares in the company, and then you have, as a separate entity, the company itself, and the company, and not the shareholders, or interest holders, . . . own the property. The assets are the property of the company, and what those who own those shares get is such dividend . . . as a result of the trading as it is thought proper to divide.'

This was confirmed in the Court of Appeal which found that a GmbH was analogous to an English company (it had separate legal personality, share capital etc) other than the fact that a member could be liable for unpaid capital of other members. This was not considered to be significant because it was possible under English law for shareholders to agree between themselves that they will have a liability in addition to their own unpaid capital.

### *Memec plc v CIR (German silent partnership)*

**[A14.6]** The next significant decision of the UK courts in this area was *Memec plc v IRC* [1998] STC 754, 71 TC 77, CA. It was also a Court of Appeal decision and the court held that a German silent partnership (stille gesellschaft) was 'not transparent' for UK tax purposes.

In this case, a UK company made a capital contribution to a German company, as a result of which it became a member of a silent partnership with the German company. Under the terms of the silent partnership, the UK company had a contractual right to receive the majority of the income of the partnership, which consisted of dividends from subsidiaries. Under German law, the Germany company remained the owner of the subsidiaries, but the UK company had access to information about the subsidiaries.

The Court of Appeal held that the income received by the UK company was received as a result of a contract with the German company, and the UK company was not therefore entitled to underlying tax on the dividends paid to the German company.

The *Memec* case distinguished the features of a German silent partnership with those of an English or Scottish partnership. In particular:

(a)     the silent partnership did not carry on a business with a view to a profit, unlike an English or Scottish partnership;

(b)     the partners in the silent partnership had no rights to the assets of the partnership, unlike an English or Scottish partnership;

(c)     the partners in the silent partnership were not jointly and severally liable, again unlike partners in an English or Scottish partnership.

A German silent partnership (stille gesellschaft) is therefore regarded as 'opaque' for UK tax purposes. The word 'opaque' was not used in the judgment, but it did consider whether it was 'transparent' and held that it was not. 'Opaque' is now the word used by HMRC to describe an foreign entity that is not transparent for UK tax purposes.

Until *Memec* the issue normally addressed was whether an entity was to be treated as a company or a partnership for UK tax purposes. This case introduced the concept of a 'transparent' entity and this caused HMRC to subsequently issue Tax Bulletins 39, 50 & 83 which now follow the approach of the Court of Appeal in this case and classifies entities as either 'transparent' or 'opaque' for UK tax purposes.

### Anson v Revenue and Customs Commissioners FTC/39/2010 (US LLC)

**[A14.7]** This case was heard before the First Tier Tribunal as *Revenue and Customs Comrs* [2010] UKFTT 88 (TC), where it was held that a US limited liability corporation (LLC) incorporated in Delaware was transparent. The UK resident individual member of the LLC was treated as having received the income of the LLC personally, and therefore entitled to double tax relief for the US tax that he had paid on the income as a result of being a US citizen.

However, the Upper Tribunal reversed this decision and held that the LLC was opaque. This decision was on the basis that the members of the LLC do not have 'an interest in the profits of the LLC in any meaningful sense'. This confirms HMRC's previous practice, and the US LLC remains on the entity classification list at INTM180030 as an opaque entity.

A separate appeal was made on whether the transfer of assets abroad rules (see **A15.5**) could apply so that the underlying income is taxed on the member, therefore giving credit available for the US tax. The appeal was heard by the Upper Tribunal early in 2012 and it was held that as an anti-avoidance provision s 720 could not be invoked to claim relief for the US tax paid.

The taxpayer appealed further and the Court of Appeal delivered its decision on 12 February 2013 (*Revenue and Customs Comrs v Anson* [2013] STC 557 at 558), upholding the tests in *Memec* (1998) STC 754. On the facts, the profits of the LLC did not belong to its members. The members were not entitled to the profits as they arose; they were not entitled to the profits from the beginning. The profits arose from the LLC trading as principal, and the deductions that could be made from the profits before they were allocated were indications that confirmed that the profits did not belong to the members from the moment of their creation. The amount allocated to members was a residual amount. What the members obtained was a distribution out of the LLC's profits. As a result double tax relief was not available.

The taxpayer has appealed this case again and HMRC are taking a narrow view of entity characterisation until the appeal is heard.

### HMRC's interpretation and views

**[A14.8]** The view of HMRC (for instance in respect of the classification of a French SNC) does not always follow case law. Although HMRC's approach is useful, a review of the features highlighted by the case law will be the final arbiter of any dispute.

Following the decision in the *Memec* case, HMRC issued guidance on the factors to be considered in classifying a foreign entity for UK tax purposes. The guidance was initially issues in Tax Bulletins 39, 50 & 83 but is now included in the International Tax Manual at INTM180010–30. The factors which it considers relevant are as follows (those marked here with a 'T' would be indicative of transparency, while those marked with 'O' would be indicative of opacity):

(a)     Whether the foreign entity has a legal existence separate from that of the persons who have an interest in it (O);

(b)     If the entity issues share capital or something else which serves the same function as share capital (O);

(c)     If the business is carried on by the entity itself (O) or jointly by the persons who have an interest in it that is separate and distinct from the entity (T);

(d)     Whether the persons who have an interest in the entity are entitled to share in its profits as they arise (T); or whether the amount of profits to which they are entitled depend on a decision of the entity or its members, after the period in which the profits have arisen, to make a distribution of its profits (O);

(e)     Whether the entity (O) or the persons who have an interest in it (T) are responsible for debts incurred as a result of the carrying on of the business;

(f)     Whether the assets used for carrying on the business belong beneficially to the entity (O) or to the persons who have an interest in it (T).

HMRC comment that some of the above factors may point in one direction and some may point in another. An overall conclusion is therefore reached from looking at all the factors together, though some have more significance than others. Particular attention is, however, paid to factors (c) and (d).

HMRC further state that in considering the above factors they look at the foreign law under which the entity is formed and at the internal constitution of the entity. This approach, of looking at the law of the jurisdiction under which the foreign entity is formed, is consistent with the approach adopted by *Dreyfus v IRC* (1929) 14 TC 560, as referred to above and as further confirmed in *Rae (Inspector of Taxes) v Lazard Investment Co Ltd* [1963] 1 WLR 555, (1963) 41 TC 1. How the entity is classified for tax purposes in any other country is not relevant.

A list of classifications of certain foreign entities for UK tax purposes is published in HMRC's International Tax Manual at INTM180030. This list is reproduced in the Appendix to this Chapter. These classifications reflect previous cases where HMRC have provided a view to taxpayers. Where an entity does not appear on the list, it is likely that:

(a)     HMRC have never been asked for a view on that particular entity; or

(b)     the entity may either be transparent or opaque, depending on the precise terms of its constitution.

Where an entity does not appear in the entity classification list, care must be taken to review the terms its constitution and legal characteristics.

## *Taxation of foreign entities*

**[A14.9]** If an entity is transparent, then UK resident members (shareholders, beneficiaries, partners etc) will be subject to the tax as profits or gains arise in the entity. It is also these members who must normally claim benefit under a DTA (see **A8.25**).

If an entity is opaque, then (subject to anti-avoidance rules such as Controlled Foreign Companies (CFC) or ITA 2007, ss 720, 731) UK resident shareholders (or beneficiaries, partners etc) will not be taxable until they receive a return (eg a dividend) from the entity.

Depending on the position of the investing company, it may want either an income or a capital return. An income return may carry tax credits to reduce the UK tax liability, or losses may be available to reduce the taxable amount.

On the other hand, a capital return may be eligible for a participation exemption (eg the substantial shareholding exemption), or capital losses may be available.

Investment into an overseas company can be made in such a way as to secure such a return. For instance, interest on a loan will likely be treated as income, whereas the redemption of shares at a premium will likely be treated as capital. The overseas company law may provide great flexibility in structuring a return to be either income or capital. The nature of the return is considered under **A14.15**.

Alternatively, if the company invests in a transparent entity, its return will be the same as that received by the entity. For example, if a UK company is a member of a partnership which makes a capital gain, the UK company will also make a capital gain.

# Basic principles—overseas tax authorities' views

**[A14.10]** Overseas tax authorities also need to determine whether foreign entities are fiscally 'transparent' or 'opaque'. Briefly outlined below is the approach taken by the Revenue Authorities in Australia, Canada and the United States, and how this approach has evolved.

Broadly, Australia now follows the overseas tax characterisation, Canada follows the overseas commercial law characterisation and the US allows the taxpayer to decide by making the so-called 'check-the-box' election.

### *Australia*

**[A14.11]** In Australia, the tax law relating to foreign hybrids was changed from the start of the financial year 2003–04. Previously a 'foreign hybrid' was an entity that had been taxed as a corporation in Australia but was taxed overseas as a partnership. They included foreign limited liability companies (LLPs) and US limited liability companies (LLCs).

Under the new laws, foreign hybrids are now taxed as partnerships in Australia, thereby taking their foreign tax forms.

## Canada

**[A14.12]** Canada Revenue Agency (CRA) issued an Interpretation Bulletin IT-343R on 26 September 1977 (at the 2006 Canadian Tax Foundation annual conference, the CRA stated that it had no plans to update IT-343R) to define the meaning of the term 'Corporation'. The Bulletin is very short and includes the following statement:

> 'A corporation is an entity created by law having a legal personality and existence separate and distinct from the personality and existence of those who caused its creation or those who own it. A corporation possesses its own capacity to acquire rights and to assume liabilities, and any rights acquired or liabilities assumed by it are not the rights or liabilities of those who control or own it. As long as an entity has such separate identity and existence, the Department will consider such entity to be a corporation even though under some circumstances or for some purposes the law may ignore some facet of its separate existence or identity.'

The approach of the CRA is therefore very similar in principle to the approach adopted in the UK.

## United States

**[A14.13]** Until 1996, the US classified a foreign entity as a corporation or as a partnership on the basis of six characteristics specified in US Treasury Regulations. The six characteristics were: associates; an objective to carry on business and divide gains therefrom; continuity of life; centralisation of management; limited liability; and free transferability of interests. The last four listed characteristics were the distinguishing features as the first two are common to both partnerships and corporations.

However, the 'check-the-box' regulations were issued in 1996 and took effect from 1 January 1997. The new regulations replaced the former classification rules with 'a much simpler approach that generally is elective'.

Under the rules, any foreign or domestic 'eligible' entity which has two or more owners can elect to be treated as a corporation or a partnership. Where there is a single owner the entity can elect to be treated as a corporation or to be disregarded and treated as a sole proprietorship, branch or division of its owner. The regulations also provide for 'default' classifications for entities that fail to make an election.

The Classification Regulations were introduced by Treasury Decision 8697 and the entity classification election may be made on IRS Form 8832. This forms requires a box to be ticked to determine the classification, and it is from this that the term 'check-the-box' derives.

Certain entities (for instance UK plcs) are not 'eligible' entities and will always be treated as corporation.

Unless an election is made on incorporation of entity, there may be tax consequences if an election is subsequently made. For instance, an election to treat as a branch a company that was previously treated as a corporation could be treated (for US tax purposes) as a liquidation.

A check-the-box election is only relevant for US tax purposes—it does not affect the treatment of an entity for UK tax purposes. Double tax relief may however be available for any tax which is paid in the US as a result of the election being made.

### Double tax agreement (DTA) recognition of trusts and partnerships

**[A14.14]** UK partnerships are not liable to UK tax and as such cannot be treated as resident in the UK for purposes of the UK's double tax agreements (DTAs). A UK partnership cannot, therefore, claim benefits under a DTA, but its UK resident partners may be able to do so.

Problems may therefore arise if a partnership has members resident in different jurisdictions, as multiple DTA claims will be required for a single item of income, and DTAs may not be in place for all members.

Similarly, trusts are not themselves liable to UK tax but the trustees on behalf of the trusts may be so liable. However, there are some UK DTAs that specifically include trusts within the definition of a 'resident of a contracting state' and so the definitions within relevant DTAs will need to be reviewed. For example, the UK/US DTA includes an employee benefit trust within the definition of a resident and the UK/Japan DTA includes charitable (and other) 'organisations' that are exempt from tax.

The UK/US DTA also contains specific provisions which deal with hybrid entities. Article 1(8) provides that the status of an entity will be determined under the law of the jurisdiction in which the entity is resident:

> 'An item of income, profit or gain derived through a person that is fiscally transparent under the laws of either Contracting State shall be considered to be derived by a resident of a Contracting State to the extent that the item is treated for the purposes of the taxation law of such Contracting State as the income, profit or gain of a resident.'

A UK LLP which holds shares in a US company will therefore be treated as transparent for the purposes of the DTA, because it is transparent for UK tax purposes, even if a check-the-box election has been made to treat the LLP as a company rather than a partnership for US tax purposes. The members of the LLP would then have to claim benefits under the treaty if they are able.

A US LLC which receives interest from a UK company will be treated as transparent in the US unless it has made a check-the-box election to be treated as a company (and therefore opaque) for US tax purposes. The status of the LLC as a company (and therefore opaque) for UK tax purposes is not relevant. The LLC would therefore also be treated as transparent for the purposes of the DTA.

# Basic principles—taxation of distributions from foreign entities

**[A14.15]** Having determined that an entity is opaque, the next issue that needs to be addressed is the character of that return from the entity.

The entity may be permitted by local company law to return income or capital to shareholders in ways which do not have equivalents in UK company law. Essentially, if a payment is received in respect of the shares in an overseas entity, it must be determined whether it is a dividend or a return of capital/capital gain. This is important because:

- UK resident individuals are subject to income tax under ITTOIA 2005, s 402 on dividends (but not other distributions) from a non-UK resident company provided they are not 'dividends of a capital nature'.
- UK resident individuals are subject to income tax under ITTOIA 2005, s 687 on '*income* from any source' which is not otherwise subject to income tax, and subject to capital gains tax on capital receipts.
- UK resident companies are subject to corporation tax under CTA 2009, s 979 on *income* which is not otherwise subject to corporation tax. Companies are separately subject to corporation tax on chargeable gains.

It may also be important to determine if an amount received is a 'dividend or other distribution' within the definition of CTA 2010, s 1000, which is subject to tax under CTA 2009, s 931A, or which may be exempt under the distribution exemption—see **A16.2**.

There have been a several UK tax cases on whether amounts received from overseas companies are taxable as income.

### CIR v Reid's Trustees

**[A14.16]** In *IRC v Reid's Trustees* HL 1949, 30 TC 431, the trustees received a dividend from a South African company which was described as 'payable from capital profits' and which was payable from the proceeds of sale of some of its premises. The House of Lords unanimously held that the receipt was income in the hands of the payee and therefore a taxable dividend. Lord Simonds observed that:

'what may be capital in the hands of the payer may yet be income in the hands of the payee.'

and Lord Reid stated that:

'if a foreign company chooses to distribute its surplus profits as dividend, the nature and origin of those profits do not and cannot be made to affect the quality of the receipt by the shareholders.'

When commenting on that case in the Court of Appeal in the later case of *Rae (Inspector of Taxes) v Lazard Investment Co Ltd* [1963] 1 WLR 555, 41 TC 1, HL, Lord Evershed, MR stated at 19 that:

'There was no evidence whatever as to any special law governing this company and affecting its powers in South Africa, and therefore the House assumed—as it was bound to do—that, as a corporation, its powers and transactions were governed by a law similar to that which would govern an English company.'

## Rae v Lazard Investment Co Ltd

[A14.17] The case of *Rae (Inspector of Taxes) v Lazard Investment Co Ltd* [1963] 1 WLR 555, 41 TC 1, HL involved the partial liquidation of a US company (C) under the laws of Maryland, and the distribution of shares in a second US company (B), to which it had sold part of its business in exchange for an issue of shares, to Lazard Investment Co Ltd (L), the shareholder of C. Evidence was given by a Maryland lawyer that:

'[C] effected the hive-off by proceeding under the said section 70 [ie by way of a partial liquidation].[C] did not declare a dividend; under Maryland law it would not have been possible to effect this "hive-off" by way of declaration of dividend.'

The House of Lords upheld the decision that the shares received by L were received as capital and were not chargeable to income tax as the receipt of a foreign dividend. The House of Lords dismissed the argument that all distributions from a company are income unless a distribution in liquidation, a repayment of share capital or a bonus issue because this was only relevant when considering a UK company.

The relevant test is instead:

'whether "the corpus of the asset" or shares of the company or "the capital of the possession" did or did not remain intact after the [B] shares were distributed: or whether the [B] shares were merely fruit or had they in their fall taken part of the tree with them.'

This is reflected in other leading commentary on this case:

'The proper test in such circumstances is, applying the local law, whether or not the corpus of the asset is left intact after the distribution. If it is not, the receipt will be a capital receipt; if it is, the payment will be chargeable.' (Comment in Whiteman on Income Tax (Third Edition page 1107) as endorsed by HMRC at SAIM5210)'

It is therefore necessary to consider whether under the relevant foreign law the asset remains intact after the distribution. If the asset does remain intact then amounts received will be income.

## Courtaulds Investment Ltd v Fleming

[A14.18] The decision in *Rae* was reinforced by *Courtaulds Investment Ltd v Fleming (Inspector of Taxes) [1969] 3 All ER 1281* Ch D 1969, 46 TC 111. In this case a UK company received a substantial distribution from a share premium reserve of an Italian company. Under Italian company law this reserve could otherwise only be distributed on liquidation of the company, and therefore the asset (the shares) did not remain intact after the distribution. It was therefore treated as a return of capital and the High Court upheld the company's contention that this was a return of capital and not taxable income. It did not matter that the company held the same number of shares both before and after the distribution.

### First Nationwide and recent HMRC practice

**[A14.19]** In *First Nationwide v Revenue and Customs Comrs* [2012] EWCA Civ 278, HMRC argued (albeit unsuccessfully) that a dividend paid out of a share premium account by a Cayman Islands company was capital rather than income. At the same time, following the introduction of the distribution exemption from 1 July 2009, HMRC practice was to also argue that dividends paid by a UK company out of reserves created by a capital reduction were 'capital in nature', and therefore not within the exemption.

However, retrospective legislation introduced by Finance (No 3) Act 2010 confirmed that from 1 July 2009:

- the distribution exemption applies to all distributions, regardless of whether they are capital in nature;
- distributions out of reserves created by a capital reduction fall within the definition of 'dividend or other distribution' in CTA 2010, s 1000 by virtue of new CTA 2010, s 1027A.

A similar clarification applied for income tax purposes from 22 June 2010, but it is only relevant for distributions from UK companies as ITTOIA 2005, s 402 still excludes 'dividends of a capital nature'.

On 21 November 2012 HMRC also released a guidance note on the tax treatment of overseas dividends and distributions and UK dividends and distributions following a share capital reduction.

The note confirms that, following the *Nationwide* case, if a dividend is a distribution permitted in accordance with the law that governs the foreign company, then in the absence of any evidence calling into question the legal form of the payment it will be treated as a dividend for the purposes of CAT 2010, s 1000(1). Other distributions out of assets will be treated as distributions under s 1000(1)(b) other than on a winding up or to the extent it represents a repayment of capital on the shares or is equal to any new consideration received by the company.

### Bonus issue of shares

**[A14.20]** CTA 2010, s 1049 specifically excludes a bonus issue of shares by a UK resident company from being a distribution.

However it is still necessary to consider whether a bonus issue by a non-UK resident company constitutes 'income' under the principles established above. The analysis of the case law is at **A2.24**, and confirms that a bonus issue of shares is not taxable as income.

## Basic principles—'ordinary share capital'

**[A14.21]** There are a number of tax reliefs that require 'ordinary share capital' (whether issued by a UK company or not) in order for the relief to apply. The following are particularly relevant to international tax planning.

## Substantial shareholding exemption

**[A14.22]** An exemption from tax is available on gains where a company disposes of a 'substantial shareholding' in another company (see also CHAPTER A13). Certain conditions must be satisfied in order for the exemption to apply, including a requirement that the investing company must own not less than 10% of the ordinary share capital in the investee company (TCGA 1992, Sch 7AC, para 8(1)(*a*)). If the investee company has not issued ordinary share capital then the exemption will not apply.

In addition, both the investing and the investee company must (broadly) be members of a trading group. The definition of 'group' for these purposes follows the capital gains tax definition (see **A14.24**). If there is a company which has not issued ordinary share capital then it will not be a member of the group. Instead, the 'shares' which have been issued may be treated as an investment asset in the company which holds them, which may prejudice the group's status as a trading group.

In Revenue and Customs Brief 29/2011, HMRC confirmed that notwithstanding a subsidiary had not issued ordinary share capital, depending on the circumstances the 'shares' could still be treated as held for a trading purpose.

## Share for share exchanges

**[A14.23]** Share for share exchanges and certain other reorganisation provisions require ordinary share capital in order to be tax-free. For example, TCGA 1992, s 135(2) requires the new owner to hold more than 25% of the ordinary share capital of the target after the exchange of shares.

If a UK company disposes of shares in an overseas company by way of a share for share exchange, this will only be a tax-free reorganisation under Case 1 of s 135 if the overseas company had ordinary share capital. If it had not issued ordinary share capital, it would be necessary to rely on Case 2 or Case 3 of s 135 which are more onerous, as they require either a general offer made to shareholders in the overseas company, or for the acquiring company to have voting control of the target company after the reorganisation.

## Intra-group transfers

**[A14.24]** Assets may be transferred between companies which are subject to corporation tax within a 75% group without crystallising tax on any gains arising. For these purposes, a group consists of a principal company and all of its 75% subsidiaries. A company will only be a 75% subsidiary if it has issued ordinary share capital (as defined by CTA 2010, ss 1119 and 1154 by virtue of TCGA 1992, s 170). Gains may therefore arise on the transfer of an asset to a company which has not issued share capital, or which is a member of group only by linking through a parent company which has not issued share capital.

## Group relief

**[A14.25]** A company may surrender tax losses to other companies which are subject to corporation tax within the same 75% group. As with intra-group transfers, a company will only be within a 75% group if it has issued ordinary share capital (as defined by CTA 2010, ss 1119 and 1154 by virtue of CTA 2010, s 151).

## Relief for employee share acquisition

**[A14.26]** CTA 2009, Pt 12 provides a corporation tax deduction where employees acquire shares, either directly or following exercise of an option. A deduction is available where employees of a UK subsidiary acquire shares in an overseas parent company (CTA 2009, s 1008(1) Condition 3).

However, the shares must be ordinary shares (CTA 2009, s 1008(1) Condition 1). Where employees of a UK subsidiary acquire shares in an overseas parent company which are not ordinary shares, no deduction under Part 12 will be available. A deduction may be available under general principles if a cost is recognised in the subsidiary company accounts, for instance by way of a charge from the parent company.

The HMRC manuals (at ESSUM33000) give some examples of shares which will be accepted as ordinary share capital for the purposes of SAYE relief, and it is possible that the same principles would apply for the purposes of Part 12. In particular:

(a)     depository receipts will be accepted as constituting ordinary share capital, provided the holder of the depository receipt retains all the rights attaching to the ownership of the shares such as voting and dividend rights;

(b)     Swiss Bearer Participation Certificates will be accepted as constituting ordinary share capital.

## Definition of ordinary share capital

**[A14.27]** HMRC have provided guidance on what will be treated as 'ordinary share capital' in Revenue & Customs Brief 54/07. It states that there are a number of relevant factors to consider in deciding whether or not a foreign entity has 'issued share capital'. The first factor is whether the entity has a legal personality separate and distinct from that of its members, able to carry on business and own its assets in its own right, in the same way as a UK company. In other words, the entity must be 'opaque' based on the factors discussed above. If that characteristic is absent the members cannot have the type of proprietorial interest which is characteristic of holders of share capital of a company incorporated under the laws of the UK.

Assuming the entity has a separate legal personality, the Brief then lists those factors which it states:

> 'will become relevant to the question of whether a member's interest in such company is analogous to an interest in 'issued share capital' as understood in the UK.'

These factors are:

(a)   whether the member's interest is like shares (that is, a portion of the fixed capital of the corporate body) or like debt (that is, money owed by the body corporate to the members);

(b)   whether any subscription for the members' interests is payable;

(c)   whether the subscription payable for the 'shares' remains the member's property or whether it becomes the property of the company;

(d)   what proprietary rights, such as rights to participate in control by voting, rights to receive a dividend out of the company's profits and rights to share in a distribution out of the company's assets in the event of a winding up, attach to the member's interests and what responsibilities, such as a responsibility to pay up on the 'share' if called, attach to the member;

(e)   whether the member's interest can be legally evidenced in accordance with local laws; for example, by being registered in a company-held document, or with a public authority, or by a certificate or similar document;

(f)   whether the member's interest is denominated in a stated fixed value;

(g)   whether the member's interest forms a fixed and certain amount of capital, or a part of that, to which creditors can look as security;

(h)   whether the non-UK law concerned requires amounts subscribed to be allocated to capital of the company which is fixed capital, and the extent to which subscriptions are so allocated;

(i)   whether the member's interest is capable of transfer and if so whether such a transfer would be similar to a transfer of a portion of the capital of the company, with attendant proprietary rights, rather than similar to a transfer of money or a loan account; and

(j)   any other factors which point to the member's interests being 'issued' and having the character of ordinary share capital.

Background information which HMRC considers will be helpful in making a determination of whether there is an interest in share capital includes:

•   the corporate law of the relevant foreign country and any available commentaries;

•   the documents establishing and regulating the entity, especially those dealing with the subscription for capital and those governing what happens to the profits and assets of the entity; and

•   the accounts of the entity.

The brief further explains that

'it is not necessary for every factor to be present, but there should be a preponderance of indicators pointing to there being issued share capital. Different weight may need to be given to the various factors. For instance it would be of considerable importance if the member's interest had the character of debt. However restrictions on transfer of a member's interest would be of lesser importance. It is by no means uncommon for there to be restrictions on transfer of shares in a UK company.'

The brief then summarises HMRC's view on two of the most often queried entities, a Delaware LLC (DLLC) and a German GmbH.

In relation to a DLLC the brief essentially reiterates HMRC's previously stated view (as reported in *Tax Bulletin 51*) that where a member's interest in an LLC is evidenced by a certificate of limited liability company interest issued by the limited liability company, these 'shares' may be regarded as 'ordinary share capital' for the purpose of CTA 2010, s 1119. Where a DLLC does not issue such certificates the brief states that the entity may still have 'ordinary share capital' but regard must be had to the particular terms of the agreement by which the LLC has been created.

The same principles should apply to LLCs incorporated in other US states.

HMRC has stated that it will advise in particular cases in line with Code of Practice 10 (now the Clearances Service).

In relation to a German GmbH, HMRC confirms that, based upon the cases it has previously considered, the amounts of *Stammeinlage* (which is a contribution or subscription to the company) subscribed by the members may normally be regarded as issued share capital for the purposes of the Taxes Acts.

# Planning—hybrid entities

**[A14.28]** Hybrid entities may be subject to anti-arbitrage rules which are discussed at **A14.31** below. HMRC guidance on whether the rules apply to particular structures can be found at www.hmrc.gov.uk/manuals/intmanual/i ntm597000.htm. This is one of the main areas targeted by the OECD in their BEPS Action Plan issued on 19 July 2013 so it can be expected that this will be a strong area of focus for tax authorities going forward (see the preface).

However, hybrid entities also present tax planning opportunities, particularly in inbound and outbound financing structures.

### Inbound structures

**[A14.29]** The objective with hybrid financing into the UK is to:

(a)   obtain a tax deduction for financing expenses in both the UK and another jurisdiction; or

(b)   obtain a tax deduction for financing expenses in the UK, but with no corresponding income being taxed.

A finance vehicle is therefore established which is treated as a UK company for UK purposes, so that relief can be claimed for interest expenses by way of group relief or direct deduction, but is transparent for overseas purposes, so that an overseas company can also claim the deduction.

For example, in Diagram 1 the US holding company has made a loan to a UK sub-holding company. The interest on this loan can be set against the profits of the UK subsidiary by way of group relief. For US tax purposes, a check-the-box election has been made, such that the UK sub-holding company is treated as a branch of the US company. The US company is therefore treated as making a loan to itself, and does not recognise any interest income. The net result is an interest deduction in the UK with no corresponding interest receipt in the US.

Another structure is shown in Diagram 2, where the sub-holding company is incorporated in the US but is resident in the UK because central management and control is carried on in the UK. However, the company remains resident in the US as well because there is no effective tie-breaker in the UK/US DTA. The interest on the loan be set against the profits of the UK subsidiary by way of group relief, and can also be set against the profits of the US parent company by way of group relief.

Diagram 3 shows a variation on the structure in Diagram 1, where there is an external loan made to the UK sub-holding company. The interest on this loan can be set against the profits of the UK subsidiary by way of group relief, and are also treated as incurred by the US parent company because the UK sub-holding company is treated as a branch for US tax purposes.

Diagram 1

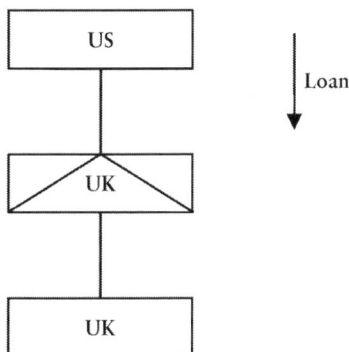

Diagram 2

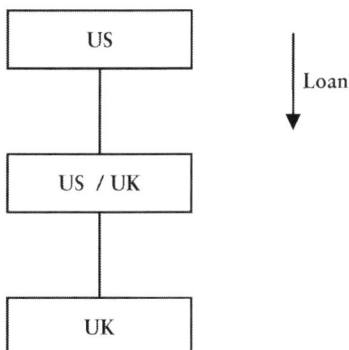

Diagram 3

```
┌─────────────────┐
│      US         │
└─────────────────┘
        │
┌─────────────────┐
│ ＼   UK   ／     │◄──────────────────────────
│  ＼     ／       │        Loan
└─────────────────┘
        │
┌─────────────────┐
│      UK         │
└─────────────────┘
```

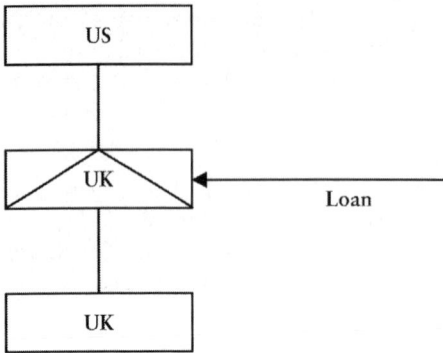

These structures may be affected by

- the anti-arbitrage rules;
- the loan relationship unallowable purpose rules;
- the group relief restriction for dual resident investing companies.

However, the anti-arbitrage rules will not apply if it can be shown that the structure was established for overseas tax reasons and not for UK tax reasons. Example 1 of the HMRC guidance covers this type of inbound structure.

There may also be rules in the overseas jurisdiction which will affect these structures. For instance, the US may disallow a deduction where it can be used against the profits of another company, under the dual consolidated loss rules.

## Outbound structures

**[A14.30]** The objective with hybrid structures out of the UK is to:

(a)   obtain a tax deduction for financing expenses in both the UK and another jurisdiction; or

(b)   obtain a tax deduction for financing expenses in the other jurisdiction, but with no corresponding income being taxed in the UK.

A finance vehicle is therefore established which is transparent for UK tax purposes, so that interest costs are treated as incurred by the UK company, but is treated as a company for overseas purposes, so that an overseas company can also claim the deduction by way of group relief or direct deduction. In some cases, the vehicle does not need to be treated as a company in order to be treated as part of a consolidated group for overseas group relief purposes.

In Diagram 4, the UK holding company has made a loan to a French SNC which is treated as a branch for UK tax purposes by HMRC (despite the decision in *Dreyfus*). The UK holding company is therefore treated as making a loan to itself, and does not recognise any interest income. For French tax purposes, the SNC is treated as a company and the interest can be set against the profits of the French subsidiary by way of group relief. The net result is an interest deduction in France with no corresponding interest receipt in the UK.

The structure shown in Diagram 5 is similar, where a loan is made to an Australian branch which is treated as transparent for UK tax purposes. For Australian tax purposes, the branch can be included within the consolidated tax group, and the interest can be set against the profits of the Australian subsidiary.

Diagram 4

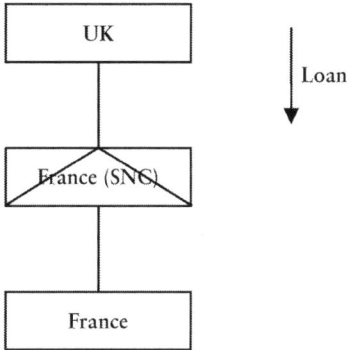

Diagram 5

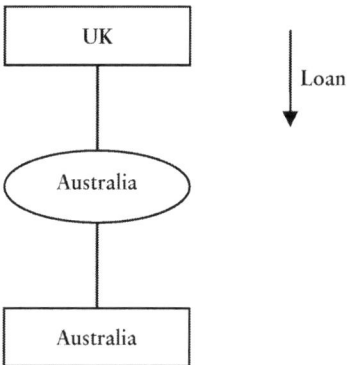

Diagram 6 shows a variation on the structure in Diagram 4, where there is an external loan made to the French SNC. The interest on this loan can be set against the profits of the French subsidiary by way of group relief, and are also treated as incurred by the UK parent company because the SNC is treated as transparent for UK tax purposes.

Diagram 6

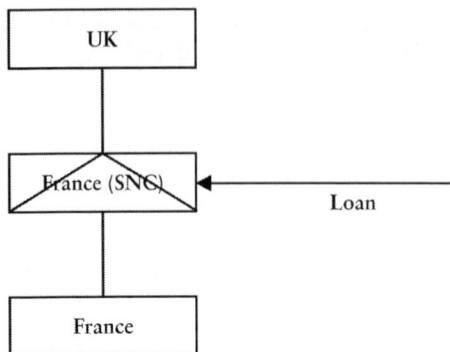

These structures may be affected by:

- the anti-arbitrage rules; and
- the loan relationship unallowable purpose rules;
- restrictions on group relief under CTA 2010, s 106 (see **A14.25**); and
- the CFC rules if the outbound financing entity is treated as a company for UK tax purposes.

However, the anti-arbitrage rules will not apply if it can be shown that the structure was established for overseas tax reasons and not for UK tax reasons. Example 2 of the HMRC guidance covers this type of outbound structure.

### Anti-avoidance provisions

**[A14.31]** The anti-arbitrage provisions (TIOPA 2010, Part 6) are designed to counteract UK tax avoidance through the use of hybrid entities and hybrid instruments. These provisions apply to 'deduction cases' and to 'receipts cases'.

### Deduction cases

**[A14.32]** 'Deduction cases' are those where a scheme involving a hybrid entity or a hybrid instrument increases a UK tax deduction or deductions to more than they would have been in the absence of the scheme.

A 'hybrid entity' is defined for purposes of the anti-arbitrage legislation as an entity which under the tax law of one jurisdiction is regarded as being a person and the entity's profits or gains are, for purposes of a relevant tax imposed under the law of any territory, treated as the profits or gains of a person or persons other than that person (TIOPA 2010, s 236).

'Hybrid instruments' are divided into four categories for the purposes of the anti-arbitrage legislation: instruments of alterable character; shares subject to conversion to debt; securities subject to conversion to shares; and debt instruments treated as equity (TIOPA 2010, ss 237–240).

Where the legislation applies its intended effect is to limit the tax deduction(s) attributable to the scheme.

The deduction rules apply if all the following conditions are met:

(a)    the transaction giving rise to the deduction forms part of a scheme involving the use of a hybrid entity or hybrid instrument;

(b)    the scheme is a 'qualifying scheme' that allows the company to claim a double deduction or a deduction which is not matched by a taxable receipt;

(c)    the main purpose, or one of the main purposes of the scheme is to achieve a UK tax advantage; and

(d)    the amount of the UK tax advantage is more than a minimal amount (ie the deductions are more than £50k).

In Diagram 4 above, no deduction would be available against the taxable profits of the UK company on the basis that:

(a)    the SNC is a hybrid entity;

(b)    a deduction for the interest is available against both French and UK taxable profits;

(c)    a loan made directly to a French company would not give rise to a tax deduction in the UK; if the SNC were used instead specifically to obtain a UK tax advantage, this would be one of the main purposes of establishing the SNC;

(d)    depending on the level of interest, the UK tax advantage may be more than a minimal amount.

If HMRC believes that the conditions are met it will issue a notice to the company. The company must then compute its profits for the specified period and for any subsequent period in accordance with two rules.

The first rule (TIOPA 2010, s 244) denies a corporation tax deduction for double deductions.

The second rule (TIOPA 2010, s 248) apples where the payee is not taxed on the receipt, or the tax charge is reduced. Specifically, this second rule applies if the tax reduction results from any of the following circumstances:

(a)    the income or gain is exempt from tax otherwise than by reason of a general exemption from tax for the payee (eg a participation exemption);

(b)    the income or gain is exempt from tax because of an exemption from income or gains that takes the form of taxing a different person in respect of the income or gain; or

(c)    the income or gain is matched by a deduction or relief for the payee that arises from transactions forming part of the scheme.

This rule does not, however, apply where:

(a)    the payee is generally exempt from tax and the payee's income or gains are not taxed as the income or gains of any other person (s 246(2)); or

(b)    the payee is liable to tax but is covered by a statutory exemption (eg a charity or pension fund is within the scope of tax but their income is typically exempt because of statutory exemptions) (TIOPA 2010, s 246(3)).

A company's return which is not amended or is not made in accordance with the notice may be regarded as being incorrect. In contrast to most provisions in the legislation, these provisions are not within the self-assessment rules in that there is no obligation on the company to self-assess an adjustment unless HMRC issues a notice.

## Receipt cases

[A14.33] 'Receipt cases' are those where a scheme involving a hybrid entity or a hybrid instrument involves a UK resident company receiving a sum that is not wholly chargeable to UK tax. Where the legislation applies its intended effect is to ensure the receipt becomes taxable.

The receipts rules apply if all the following conditions are met (TIOPA 2010, s 250):

(a)   a company has entered into a scheme under which it receives an amount which is not liable to UK tax;

(b)   that amount may be deducted from or allowed against taxable income of the person making the payment;

(c)   the mismatch in tax treatment was expected by the parties to the scheme; and

(d)   the payment constitutes a contribution to the capital of the company.

If HMRC believes that the conditions are met they will issue a notice to the company and the company must take account of the legislation in its self-assessment.

## Avoidance of tax

[A14.34] Where the avoidance of UK tax is not the purpose of a scheme involving a hybrid entity this should be clearly documented. It is possible that a hybrid entity is used for commercial reasons or to reduce non-UK tax liabilities.

HMRC will examine what alternative structures were considered, and whether a better UK tax result was achieved by using a hybrid entity. For instance if a group considered financing its UK subsidiary by way either equity or debt via a hybrid entity, this may suggest that a hybrid entity was used to avoid UK tax. All alternative structures should be clearly documented.

The anti-arbitrage rules only apply to counteract the avoidance of UK tax. If overseas tax is avoided then the rules should not apply (although similar anti-avoidance rules may apply in the overseas jurisdiction).

For example, Diagram 7 illustrates two ways in which a UK company could finance its French subsidiary. As the SNC is transparent for UK purposes, both result in taxable income in the UK but (*b*) results in a deduction in the French group for the interest paid to the UK.

Diagram 7

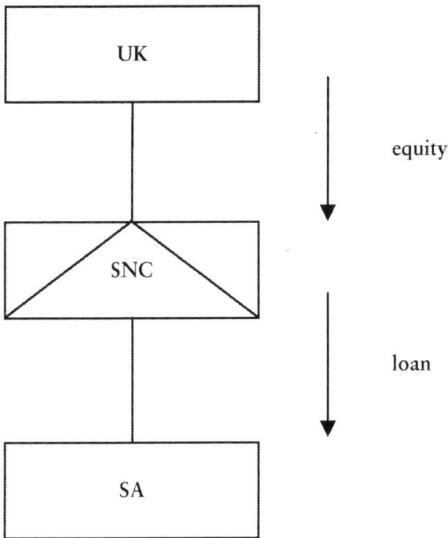

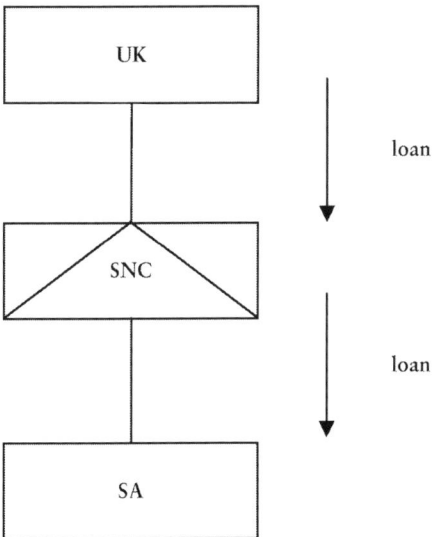

## *Group relief*

**[A14.35]** In addition to the anti-arbitrage rules in TIOPA 2010, Part 6, there are restrictions on group relief claims which can apply in some hybrid situations.

CTA 2010, s 106 provides that a UK company cannot surrender losses relating to an overseas permanent establishment where:

(a)   it carries on a trade through the overseas permanent establishment;
(b)   the losses can be relieved against the profits of another person.

For example, in Diagram 8, UK SubCo trades in Australia through the Aus Branch. Under the Australian group rules, the losses of Aus Branch are relieved against the profits of Aus SubCo. They cannot therefore be surrendered by UK SubCo to UK HoldCo.

**Diagram 8**

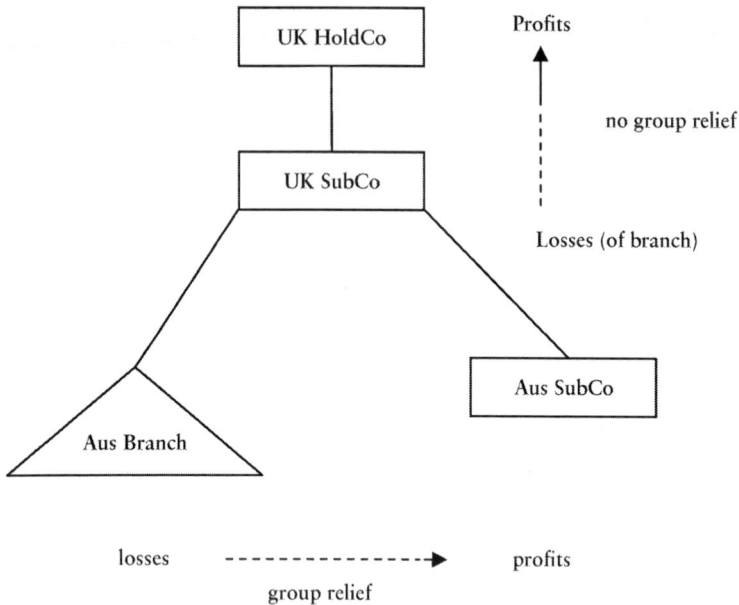

Similarly, s 107 provides that an overseas company cannot surrender losses of a UK permanent establishment to another UK group company if *any part* of those losses could be used in another jurisdiction (whether by the company owning the permanent establishment or any other company).

For example, if the losses can be carried forward against future profits of the non-UK company which owns the permanent establishment, s 107 would apply and those losses would not be available for UK group relief purposes. This restriction applies to *all* losses even if only *part* of the losses can be used in the other jurisdiction. HMRC Tax Bulletin 49 outlined some examples of overseas tax systems as a result of which a s 107 restriction could arise, but much of this article is now out of date.

Some jurisdictions (eg the US) have a similar rule such that if losses are relieved in the UK they cannot be relieved in the US. However s 107 is considered as if such a rule does not exist. In this case, the losses can be used in the overseas jurisdiction without affecting the UK tax position.

### Minimisation of withholding tax

**[A14.36]** In some jurisdictions, the distribution of a dividend via a local transparent entity can be free of withholding tax.

For instance in Diagram 9, if the German subsidiary were to pay a dividend directly to the UK company it may be subject to withholding tax because of local anti-avoidance rules which disapply the benefit of a DTA or the Parent Subsidiary Directive. Instead, the German subsidiary pays a dividend to a German KG. The KG is treated as transparent for UK tax purposes and therefore the UK company is treated as receiving a dividend directly from the German subsidiary, which may be exempt from tax (see CHAPTER **A16**).

For German tax purposes, the KG is treated as opaque, and the dividend is not subject to withholding tax because it is paid from one German entity to another. The subsequent distribution of profits by a KG is not subject to withholding tax.

Diagram 9

| Jersey |
|---|

Dividend

| UK |
|---|

Dividend

| Germany (KG) |
|---|

Dividend

| Germany |
|---|

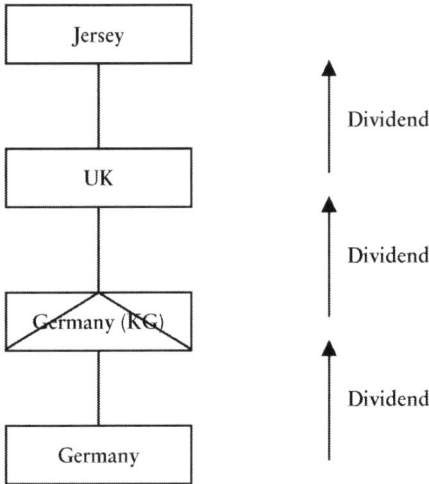

A similar treatment may apply to a co-operative in Belgium or the Netherlands.

There may be additional tax benefits of this type of structure. For instance, a capital gain arising on the disposal of shares in a German subsidiary may be subject to German tax in certain circumstances, but the transfer of an interest in a KG should not be subject to tax.

## *Hybrid investment and feeder structures*

[A14.37] Hybrid entities can also be used to provide different types of return to different investors.

In Diagram 10, a 'check-the-box' election has been made in respect of the US LLC and it is treated as a branch for US tax purposes. The US investors are therefore treated as receiving the trading income directly.

However, the LLC is still treated as a company for UK tax purposes, and the UK investors will only be taxed when income is distributed. For a UK corporate investor, this may be an exempt dividend (see CHAPTER A16), and for UK individual investors a dividend may be taxed at a lower rate than trading income.

Diagram 10

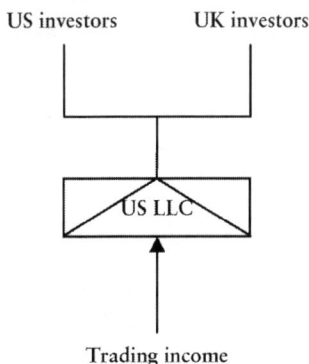

In Diagram 11, UK investors are treated as receiving the investment income and capital gains directly because the LLP is transparent for UK tax purposes. For a UK individual, capital gains will be taxed at 10%, 18%, or 28% and for a UK corporate investor they may be exempt under the substantial shareholding exemption.

Non-UK investors have invested via a Jersey company, which does not pay tax on income as it arises (although income may be subject to withholding tax). Subject to any anti-avoidance rules in their jurisdiction of residence, these investors will only pay tax when dividends are distributed by the Jersey company.

Diagram 11

Non-UK Investors

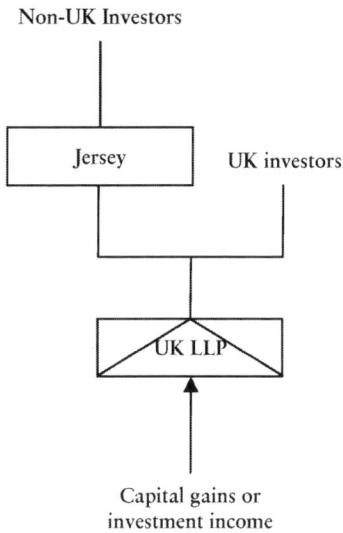

Capital gains or
investment income

## *Other financing structures*

**[A14.38]** Loans made via certain jurisdictions may have similar benefits to hybrid financing structures. Some examples are given below.

In Diagram 12, the Jersey holding company has subscribed equity to the Maltese finance company, which then makes a loan to the UK company. The UK company claims a deduction for the interest on the loan, and the Maltese company is taxable on the interest received. However, when the Maltese company pays a dividend to the Jersey holding company, most of the tax paid in Malta is refunded, which significantly reduces the effective tax rate on the interest.

Diagram 12

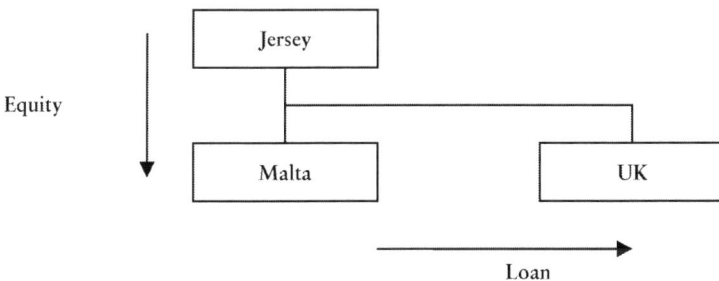

In Diagram 13, the Jersey holding company has subscribed equity to the Swiss finance company, which in turn subscribes equity to an Irish branch, which then makes a loan to the UK company. The UK company claims a deduction for the interest on the loan, but the interest is not taxable in the Irish branch because it is treated as received by the Swiss holding company. However, under the Ireland/Switzerland DTA, the interest is not taxable in Switzerland because it is received by an Irish branch.

Diagram 13

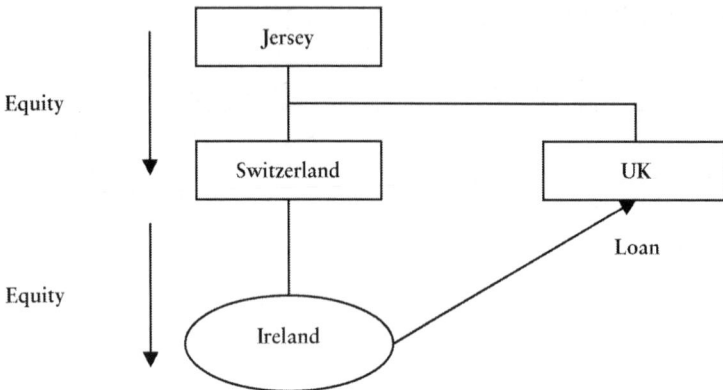

In Diagram 14, the Jersey holding company has subscribed debt, preferred equity contribution (PEC) and equity to the Luxembourg finance company, which then makes a loan to the UK company. The UK company claims a deduction for the interest on the loan, and the Luxembourg company is taxable on the interest received. However, under Luxembourg rules it is possible to claim a deduction for dividends paid on the preferred equity, which reduces the amount which is subject to Luxembourg tax. A ruling to agree the deduction can be obtained from the Luxembourg tax authorities.

Diagram 14

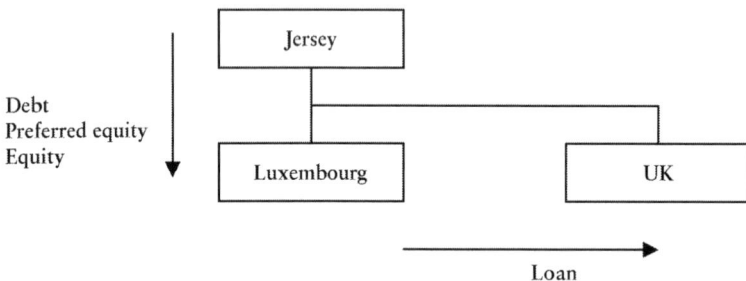

In Diagram 15, the Jersey holding company has subscribed equity to the Belgian finance company, which then makes a loan to the UK company. The UK company claims a deduction for the interest on the loan, and the Belgian company is taxable on the interest received. However, under the Belgian notional interest deduction regime, a deduction is available for deemed interest on the equity of the company. This reduces the amount which is subject to Belgian tax.

Diagram 15

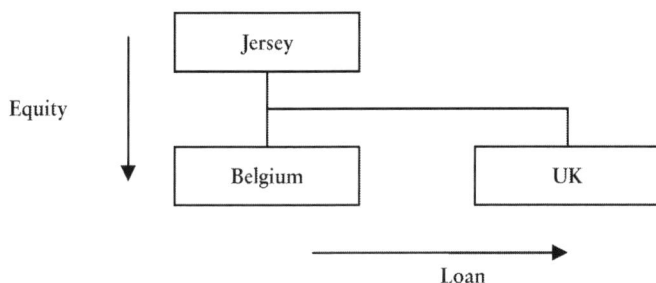

The structures shown in Diagrams 14 and 15 do not include a hybrid entity, and should not therefore be affected by the anti-arbitrage rules.

With all of these structures, it is still necessary to consider:

- the loan relationship unallowable purpose rules;
- the worldwide debt cap; and
- (if these structures are established beneath a UK holding company), the CFC rules.

Similar overseas tax rules may also be relevant, for instance CFC rules if these structures are established beneath non-UK holding companies.

It is also necessary to consider whether withholding tax will be due on any interest paid. The structures above which involve finance companies in the EU or jurisdictions with which the UK has a DTA may offer significant reductions in withholding tax

# Appendix

## List of classifications of foreign entities for UK tax purposes
## (as listed in HMRC's International manual at INTM180030)

| ANGUILLA | | Partnership | Transparent |
| --- | --- | --- | --- |
| | LLC | Limited Liability Company | Opaque |
| ARGENTINA | Srl | Sociedad de responsibilidad limitada | Opaque |
| ARMENIA | LLC | Limited Liability Company | Opaque |
| AUSTRALIA | LP | Limited Partnership | Transparent |
| | | Unit Trust | Transparent |

| | | | |
|---|---|---|---|
| AUSTRIA | KG | Kommanditgesellschaft | Trans-parent |
| | KEG | Kommand Erwerbsgesellschaft | Trans-parent |
| | GmbH & Co KG | | Trans-parent |
| | GmbH | Gesellschaft mit Beschrankter Haftung | Opaque |
| | AG | Aktiengesellschaft | Opaque |
| BELGIUM | SPRL | Societe de privee a responsabilite limi-tee | Opaque |
| | SNC | Societe en nom collectif | Trans-parent |
| | SA | Societe Anonyme | Opaque |
| | NV | Naamloze Vennootschap | Opaque |
| | SCA | Societe en commanditaire par actions | Opaque |
| | CVA | Commanditaire venootschap opaande-len | Opaque |
| BERMUDA | LP | Limited partnership with legal person-ality | Trans-parent |
| BRAZIL | Srl | Sociedad por quotas de responabili-dade limitada | Opaque |
| | FIP | Fundo de Investimento en participa-coes | Trans-parent |
| BVI | LP | Limited partnership | Trans-parent |
| CANADA | | Partnership and limited partnership | Trans-parent |
| CAYMAN IS-LANDS | LP | Limited partnership | Trans-parent |
| CHILE | SRL | Sociedad de responsibilidad limitada | Trans-parent |
| CHINA | WFOE | Wholly Foreign Owned Entity | Opaque |
| CZECH RE-PUBLIC | as | Akciova spolecnost | Opaque |
| | Sro | Spolecnost s rucenim omezenym | Opaque |
| DENMARK | | Danske Investingsforening | Opaque |
| EUROPEAN UNION | SE | Societas Europeas | Opaque |
| FINLAND | Ky | Kommandiittiyhtio | Trans-parent |
| | Oy | Osakeyhtio | Opaque |
| | Ab | Aktiebolag | Opaque |
| FRANCE | GIE | Groupement d'Interet economique | Trans-parent |
| | SNC | Societe en nom collectif | Trans-parent |

| | | | |
|---|---|---|---|
| | SCI | Societe civile immobiliere | Opaque |
| | SCEA | Societe civile exploitation agricole | Opaque |
| | SCS | Societe en commandite simple | Transparent |
| | SP | Societe en participation | Transparent |
| | SARL | Societe a responsabilite limitee | Opaque |
| | FCPR | Fonds Commun de Placement a risques | Transparent |
| | SAS | Societe par Actions Simplifiee | Opaque |
| | SA | Societe Anonyme | Opaque |
| | GFA | Groupement Foncier d'Agricole | Opaque |
| | SC | Societe Civile | Opaque |
| | SCA | Societe en Commandite par action | Opaque |
| GERMANY | | Stille Gesellschaft | Opaque |
| | KG | Kommandit Gesellschaft | Transparent |
| | OHG | Offene Handelsgesellschaft | Transparent |
| | GmbH | Gesellschaft mit Beschrankter Haftung | Opaque |
| | GmbH & Co. KG | | Transparent |
| | GmbH & Co. KGaA | | Opaque |
| | GBR | Gesellschaft des Burgerlichen Rechts | Transparent |
| | AG | Aktiengesellschaft | Opaque |
| GIBRALTAR | LP | Limited Partnership | Transparent |
| GUERNSEY | LP | Limited Partnership | Transparent |
| | PCC | Protected Cell Company | Opaque |
| | | Open Ended Investment Company with Limited Liability | Opaque |
| HUNGARY | Kft | Korlatolt felelossegu tarsasag | Opaque |
| | Rt. | Reszvenytarsasag | Opaque |
| ICELAND | | Hlutafelag | Opaque |
| IRELAND | LP | Limited Partnership | Transparent |
| | | Irish Investment Limited Partnership | Transparent |
| | CCF | Common Contractual Fund | Transparent |
| | UT | Unit Trust | Opaque |

| | | | |
|---|---|---|---|
| ISLE OF MAN | LLC | Limited Liability Company | Opaque |
| ITALY | SpA | Societa per Azioni | Opaque |
| | Srl | Societa a responsibilita Limitada | Opaque |
| JAPAN | | Goshi-Kaisha | Transparent |
| | | Gomei Kaisha | Transparent |
| | TK | Tokumei Kumiai | Transparent |
| | | Kabushiki Kaisha | Opaque |
| | | Yugen-Kaisha | Opaque |
| JERSEY | LLP | Limited Liability Partnership | Opaque |
| | LP | Limited Partnership | Transparent |
| KAZAKHAK-STAN | LLP | Limited Liability Partnership | Opaque |
| LIECHTEN-STEIN | | Anstalt | Opaque |
| LUXEM-BOURG | SCA | Societe en commandite par-actions | Opaque |
| | FCP | Fonds commun de placement | Transparent |
| | SA | Societe anonyme | Opaque |
| | SARL | Societe a responsabilite limitee | Opaque |
| | SNC | Societe en Nom Collectif | Transparent |
| | SC | Societe Civile | Opaque |
| | SICAV | Societe d'investissement a capital variable | Opaque |
| MALTA | SICAV | Societe d'investissement a capitale variable | Opaque |
| | ENC | En Nom Collectif | Transparent |
| | SC | Societe Civile | Opaque |
| NETHER-LANDS | VOF | Vennootschap Onder Firma | Transparent |
| | CV | Commanditaire Vennootschap (both 'open' and 'closed') | Transparent |
| | NV | Naamloze Vennootschap | Opaque |
| | BV | Besloten Vennootschap Met Beperkte Aansprakelijheid | Opaque |
| | | Maatschap | Transparent |
| | | Stichting | Transparent |

|  | Coop UA | Cooperatie uitsluiting Aansprakelijheid | Opaque |
|---|---|---|---|
|  | Coop BA | Cooperatie beperkte Aansprakelijheid | Transparent |
|  | Co-op WA | Cooperatie wettelijke aansprakelijkheid | Transparent |
|  | FGR | Besloten Fonds voor Gemene Rekening | Transparent |
| NEW CALEDONIA | SNC | Societe en nom collectif | Transparent |
| NORWAY | AS | Alkjeselskap | Opaque |
|  | KS | Kommandittselkap | Transparent |
| OMAN | LLC | Limited Liability Company | Opaque |
| POLAND | SP.zo.o | Spolkaz ograniczonaodpowiedzialnoscia | Opaque |
| PORTUGAL | Lda | Sociedade por quotas | Opaque |
|  | SA | Sociedade Anonima | Opaque |
| RUSSIA |  | Joint Venture under 'Decree No.49' | Opaque |
|  | LLC | Limited Liability Company | Opaque |
| SEYCHELLES | LP | Limited Partnership | Transparent |
| SLOVAK REPUBLIC | sro | Spolocnost's rucenim obmedzenim | Opaque |
| SOUTH AFRICA |  | Close Corporation | Opaque |
| SPAIN | FCR | Fondo de Capital Riesgo | Transparent |
|  | SC | Sociedad Civila | Opaque |
|  | SA | Sociedad Anonima | Opaque |
|  |  | Comunidad de bienes | Transparent |
|  | SC | Sociedad Collectiva | Opaque |
|  | SCP | Sociedad Civil Professional | Transparent |
|  | SCS | Sociedad Commanditaria Simple | Transparent |
|  | UTE | Uniones Temporales de Empresas | Transparent |
|  | Srl | Sociedad de Responsabilidad Limitada | Opaque |
| SWEDEN | AB | Aktiebolag | Opaque |
|  | KB | Kommanditbolag | Transparent |
| SWITZERLAND | SS | Societe Simple | Transparent |
|  | GmbH | Gesellschaft mit beschrankter Haftung | Opaque |

|         |         |                                                                                 |                  |
| ------- | ------- | ------------------------------------------------------------------------------- | ---------------- |
|         | KG      | Kommanditgesellschaft                                                           | Trans-parent     |
| TURKEY  | AP      | Attorney Partnership                                                            | Trans-parent     |
|         | AS      | Anonim Sirket                                                                   | Opaque           |
|         | Ltd/S   | Limited Sirket                                                                  | Opaque           |
| USA     |         | Partnership set up under the Uniform Partnership Act                            | Trans-parent     |
|         |         | Limited Partnership set up under the Uniform Limited Partnership Act            | Trans-parent     |
|         | LLC     | Limited Liability Company Including New York LLC (Mar 09)                       | Opaque           |
|         | LLP     | Limited Liability Partnership                                                   | Trans-parent     |
|         | MBT     | Massachusetts Business Trust                                                    | Trans-parent     |
|         | S. Corp | S. Corporation                                                                  | Opaque           |
|         | REIT    | Real estate Investment Trust                                                    | Opaque           |
|         | LLLP    | Limited liability limited partnership set up under the Revised Uniform Limited Partnership Act | Trans-parent     |

# A15

# Tax for shareholders and business owners

# Introduction

**[A15.1]** This Chapter focuses on the tax position of UK resident individuals who own multinational businesses. An overview of the definition of residence for individuals can be found in CHAPTER A1.

The tax objective of shareholders is generally to maximise the return on income and gains which they receive personally. The tax payable on dividends and capital gains on disposal of shares must therefore be taken into account, as well as the tax which is suffered by the company itself.

It is important therefore to ensure that:

(a)    the rate of tax paid by the shareholder on dividends and gains is reduced as far as possible by taking advantage of lower rates of tax;
(b)    if possible, the shareholder is able to obtain a credit for any taxes paid by the company or other entity carrying on the business;
(c)    anti-avoidance provisions do not apply to tax undistributed income.

Some shareholders may actively seek to roll-up (ie not distribute) income in a low-tax jurisdiction. This roll-up is often difficult to achieve because of the operation of anti-avoidance provisions relating to:

- capital gains of offshore companies (TCGA 1992, s 13);
- the transfer of assets abroad (ITA 2007, ss 720 and 731); and
- the offshore funds rules (ICTA 1988, s 756A).

There are a number of tax issues and planning techniques which are specific to non-domiciled individuals. These are outside the scope of this book, although a good discussion can be found in James Kessler's *Taxation of non-UK domiciliaries*.

# Basic principles—capital gains of overseas close companies

**[A15.2]** As detailed in CHAPTER A11, if a company which is resident outside the UK but would otherwise be a close company if it were UK resident makes a chargeable gain, part of this gain may be attributed to UK participators under TCGA 1992, s 13.

Diagram 12 in CHAPTER A11 sets out a flowchart which summarises the circumstances under which s 13 will apply. The main restrictions to its application to note are that:

(a)    it only applies to 'close' companies and groups as defined in CTA 2010, s 439, which means that in practice it applies to privately held groups rather than multinationals with many shareholders;
(b)    gains are only attributed to 'participators' (as defined in CTA 2010, s 454) with an interest of more than 25%.
(c)    Finance Act 2013 introduced an exception under s 13(5A) for economically significant activities (see **A11.30**)
(d)    FA 2013 also introduced for the first time a motive test for s 13 which should remove genuine commercial transactions from the scope.

## *Planning techniques*

**[A15.3]** In addition to the exemptions within s 13 itself, planning techniques to avoid the attribution of a gain include:

(a)     The disposal by the overseas company may qualify for the substantial shareholding exemption.

(b)     The overseas company may be resident in a jurisdiction with which the UK has a double tax agreement (DTA) which does not allow the UK to tax the gain.

(c)     Credit for any tax paid under s 13 will be given against the tax due on any distribution made within four years of the gain.

(d)     A transparent entity such as a partnership makes the gain, such that s 13 does not apply, and the shareholder obtains credit for the tax paid by the entity.

These planning techniques are also considered in CHAPTER A11.

## *Distribution of gain*

**[A15.4]** Although credit is given for any tax paid under s 13, it is not always possible to distribute the proceeds from any gain which is made.

Diagram 1

UKR individual

Loan from bank £1m

Offshore company

Sells asset for £1m

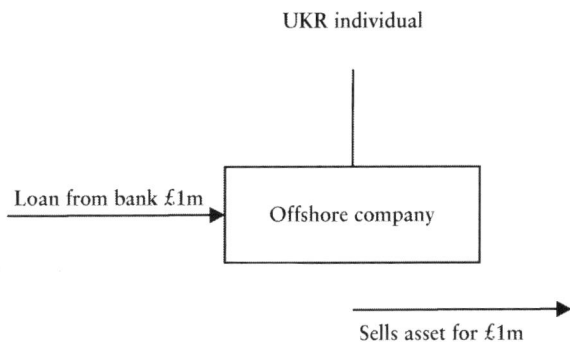

For instance, in Diagram 1, the proceeds of sale are required to repay the loan from the bank which has been used to fund other activities. No distribution can be made to the shareholder, who must fund any tax due under s 13 from other sources, which may themselves have been subject to tax.

In larger groups, reinvestment and working capital requirements may prevent proceeds from being distributed. Even if proceeds are not required in the group, banking covenants or shareholder agreements may prevent them from being distributed.

Assets on which a charge under s 13 may arise should not be held in corporate structures unless the proceeds can be distributed to shareholders to allow them to pay the tax. Instead, shareholders should hold the assets personally and then reinvest the proceeds after paying the tax.

## Basic principles—transfers of assets abroad

**[A15.5]** Complex anti-avoidance rules apply where individuals transfer assets to non-residents, including non-resident companies or trusts. These rules begin at ITA 2007, s 714 (previously ICTA 1988, s 739), and charges can arise under ss 720, 727 or 731 depending on the nature of the structure. The comments below relate to non-resident companies, and do not consider non-resident trusts or other entities.

The charge to tax arises on individuals who are resident in the UK (see CHAPTER A1) when income arises. However, there is no requirement that the individual was resident at the time the transfer was made.

As the transfer of assets abroad rules only apply to individuals who are resident in the UK, offshore structures may fall outside of the rules if an individual shareholder is only temporarily in the UK. However, care must be taken that the individual shareholder does not inadvertently become resident in the UK, under the new statutory residency test. HMRC may seek to argue that he had been resident from the day that he arrived in the UK, and therefore that the transfer of assets abroad rules applied to the structure from that date.

There are special rules for individuals who are not domiciled in the UK, which are not considered here.

The broad effect of the legislation is to charge tax on income which has been transferred to a non-resident company, and which would otherwise have been subject to tax in the UK.

Diagram 2

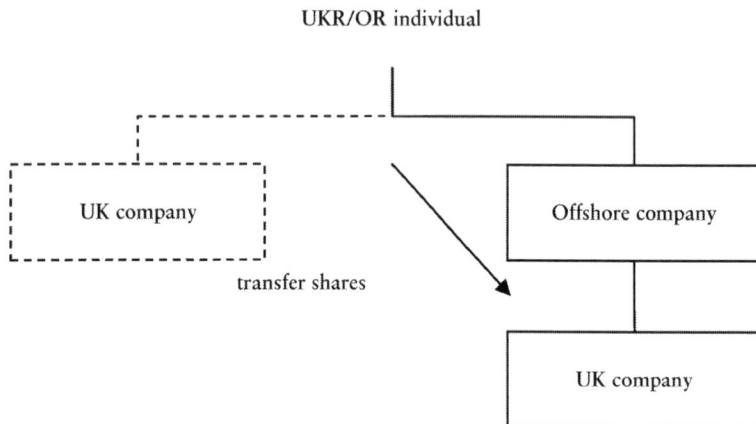

UKR/OR individual

UK company

transfer shares

Offshore company

UK company

In Diagram 2, a UK resident individual transfers shares in a UK company to a new offshore company, such that he will not receive any dividends subsequently paid by the UK company. This structure is almost certain to fall within s 720.

## Relevant transactions

**[A15.6]** A charge to tax will only arise if there is a relevant transaction. A relevant transaction is defined as (ITA 2007, ss 720(2), 728(1), 732(1)):

(a)  a relevant transfer; or
(b)  an associated operation.

### Relevant transfer

**[A15.7]** A relevant transfer is a transfer of assets as a result of which, together with any associated operations, income becomes payable to a person abroad (ITA 2007, s 716). In Diagram 2 above, the transfer of the shares in the UK company result in dividends on those shares becoming payable to the offshore company, and the transfer would therefore be a relevant transfer.

A transfer of assets includes the creation of rights (s 716(2)), so the grant of a new licence or agreement under which an offshore company receives income will constitute a relevant transfer.

It does not matter if the assets in question are already held outside the UK. Despite the heading above s 714 in the legislation ('transfer of assets abroad'), there is no requirement that the assets are transferred from the UK.

### Person abroad

**[A15.8]** A person abroad includes a company incorporated outside the UK but which is UK resident for tax purposes (ITA 2007, s 718). The income of such a company would therefore be subject to income tax under these anti-avoidance provisions, and also subject to corporation tax. Although not explicit in the legislation, the Self-Assessment Tax Return notes on the Foreign Pages provide that any corporation tax paid can be credited against the shareholder's income tax liability.

Finance Act 2013 changes this so that a UK resident company is no longer an overseas person.

### Associated operation

**[A15.9]** An associated operation is defined in ITA 2007, s 719 as one which is made in relation to the assets transferred or income arising from the assets.

In Diagram 3, an individual transfers £1m cash to a UK company, which is then transferred to an offshore company. This second transfer is made 'in relation to' the original assets transferred, and will therefore be an associated operation of the first transfer.

Diagram 3

UKR/OR individual

UK company

transfer £1m cash

transfer £1m cash

Offshore company

investment income

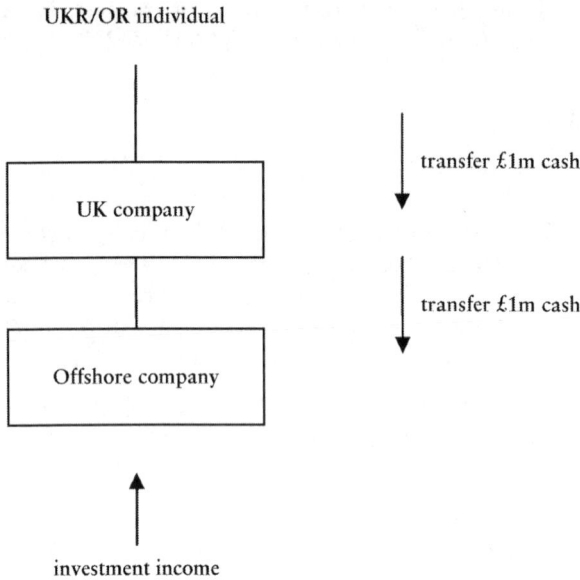

Where a company has received funds from various sources, it is important to track to where these funds are subsequently invested. Funds received from UK resident shareholders should not be invested so that income arises to an offshore company.

### *Individuals with power to enjoy income as a result of relevant transactions (ITA 2007, s 720)*

**[A15.10]** Section 720 imposes a charge to tax where an individual has the power to enjoy the income of a non-resident company as a result of a relevant transaction.

Because the power to enjoy income must arise as a direct result of the transaction, s 720 will generally only apply where the power to enjoy income arises to the individual making the transfer (or to their spouse—s 714(4)).

The power to enjoy income is defined broadly in s 723, and includes the following situations:

(a)   The individual receives or is entitled to receive at any time any benefit out of the income (s 723(1)). For example, the individual holds shares in an offshore company on which he is entitled to receive a dividend.

(b)   The value of assets held by the individual are increased in value (s 723(2)). For example, the individual holds shares in an offshore company which do not carry dividend rights, but do carry the right to receive consideration on sale.

(c)    The individual is able to control directly or indirectly the application of the income (s 723(7)). For example, the individual holds shares in an offshore company which give him the majority of voting rights over the company, and therefore how the income received by the company is applied.

A common situation which falls within s 720 is an individual who transfers cash or other assets to an offshore company in return for shares. The individual receives the power to enjoy income as a result of receiving shares in the offshore company, and these shares are received as a result of a relevant transaction which is the transfer of cash or assets.

### Individuals receiving capital sums as a result of relevant transactions (ITA 2007, s 727)

**[A15.11]** Section 727 imposes a charge to tax where an individual receives a capital sum as a result of, and in connection with, a relevant transaction, to the extent that the capital sum represents the income of the offshore company.

There is no requirement in s 727 that the individual otherwise has the power to enjoy the income of the offshore company.

Receipt of a capital sum includes (s 729(3)):

(a)    the repayment of a loan;
(b)    any sum payable otherwise than as income and not for full consideration or money's worth.

Diagram 4

UKR/OR individual

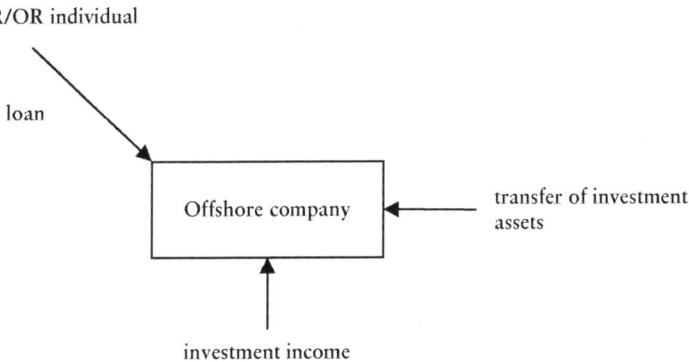

loan

Offshore company

transfer of investment assets

investment income

In Diagram 4, if the loan from the UK resident individual is repaid from the investment income received by the offshore company, then the investment income will subject to tax under s 727 if repayment of the loan was connected to the transfer of investment assets.

Where loans are repaid by offshore companies to individuals ordinarily resident in the UK, the repayment should not be made from income. If the repayment is made from capital sums transferred or held by the offshore company then no charge should arise under ITA 2007, s 727.

### Non-transferors receiving a benefit as a result of a relevant transaction (ITA 2007, s 731)

**[A15.12]** Section 731 imposes a charge to tax where an individual receives a benefit as a result of relevant transactions. There are matching rules in s 733 such that benefits are only taxed to the extent that they are matched against income received by the offshore company.

A benefit will be subject to tax if:

(a)  it is provided out of 'assets which are available for the purpose as a result of the transfer or one or more associated operations' (s 732(1)(d)); and
(b)  the individual is not otherwise liable to income tax on the benefit.

Most benefits received from an offshore company, for instance dividends or salary, will be subject to income tax and will therefore not fall within s 731.

Capital gains realised on the disposal of shares in the offshore company will not generally be a benefit provided 'out of the assets' of the offshore company. The exception may be if a purchaser is specifically using the assets of the offshore company to finance the acquisition, for instance by paying a dividend immediately following acquisition.

In practice, the only benefit which is subject to tax under s 731 in respect of an offshore company will be a distribution received on liquidation. This distribution is provided 'out of the assets' of the company, and is not subject to income tax as it is subject to capital gains tax.

Section 731 does not apply where s 720 applies (s732(1)(d)). Section 731 therefore does not usually apply where the individual in question is the transferor, as s 720 would likely apply in this case. Unlike s 720, there is no requirement in s 731 that the individual has the power to enjoy the income of the offshore company.

A charge to tax does not arise under ITA 2007, s 731 until a benefit is received by the individual. However, under s 720 a charge to tax arises even if the individual does not receive a benefit. It is sometimes therefore better that a structure is taxed under s 731 than under s 720 in order to obtain a cash flow benefit. This can be achieved if the individual who sets up a structure (the transferor) is not the same individual who subsequently holds the shares and has the power to enjoy the income arising.

### Calculation of tax

**[A15.13]** Under ITA 2007, s 720, the individual is effectively treated as receiving income directly, and is taxed on this basis. The individual is entitled to the same rates of tax (s 745), and the same reliefs and deductions as he would be if he received the income directly (s 746). For instance, if the income received by the offshore company is dividend income, then tax under these provisions would arise at an effective rate of 25% (if the company paying the dividend was UK resident) or 30.55%.

If the company receiving the income has incurred expenses which would not be deductible if incurred by the individual (for example, investment management expenses), then the income which is subject to tax may be greater than the net income of the company.

Under s 731, the individual is subject to tax at his marginal rate (20%, 40%, or 45%) on the value of any benefit received.

The tax liability under these provisions falls on the individual to whom the income is treated as arising. There are no provisions which would transfer the liability to the offshore company.

If income which has been taxed under these provisions is subsequently distributed to the individual, then s 743(4) provides that no further tax arises.

Tax under these provisions is collected through the self-assessment regime, and individuals who are liable to tax must report the liability on their self-assessment tax returns.

It is sometimes beneficial to charge income to tax under ITA 2007, s 720, in order that the subsequent distribution of the income is tax free.

For instance, in Diagram 5, if the individual received a dividend from the offshore company, it may be subject to tax at an effective rate of 32.5% (or 37.5%). If tax is paid under s 720 in respect of the dividend received by the offshore company from the UK company, tax would arise at an effective rate of 25% (or 30.55%), after taking account of the dividend tax credit on UK dividends.

No further tax would be due on the distribution from the offshore company.

The individual should therefore pay tax under s 720 at 25% rather than 32.5% (or 30.55% rather than 37.5%), albeit as it arises to the offshore company.

**Diagram 5**

UKR/OR individual

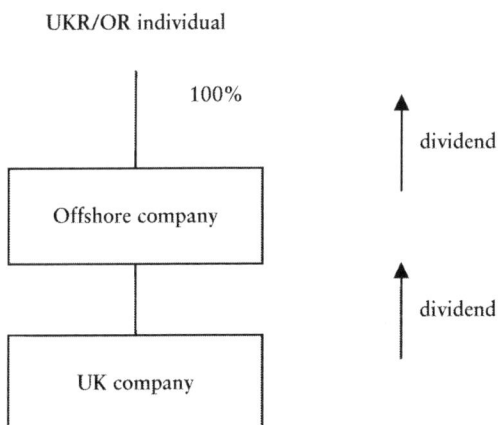

## Exemption for bona fide commercial transactions (ITA 2007, s 737)

**[A15.14]** There is an exemption from these provisions for bona fide commercial transactions.

Relevant transfers made after 5 December 2005 must satisfy either condition A or condition B which are set out in s 737.

'(1)    Condition A is that it would not be reasonable to draw the conclusion, from all the circumstances of the case, that the purpose of avoiding liability to taxation was the purpose, or one of the purposes, for which the relevant transactions or any of them were effected.

(2)    Condition B is that—

(a)    all the relevant transactions were genuine commercial transactions (see s 738), and

(b)    it would not be reasonable to draw the conclusion, from all the circumstances of the case, that any one or more of those transactions was more than incidentally designed for the purpose of avoiding liability to taxation.'

'Taxation' for these purposes means 'any revenue for whose collection and management the Commissioners for Her Majesty's Revenue and Customs are responsible' (ie all taxes). A structure established to avoid SDLT or VAT would therefore not satisfy the conditions.

Relevant transfers made prior to 5 December 2005 are subject to different conditions.

The FA 2013 has provided an additional exemption for 'genuine transactions' within the EU and EEA. The conditions are contained in ITA 2007, s 742A.

## Common structures which are subject to tax under ITA 2007, s 720

**[A15.15]** The two most common corporate structures which are subject to tax under s 720 are incorporation of a new overseas company and a share exchange with an overseas company.

### Incorporation of a new company

**[A15.16]** An individual subscribes for shares in an offshore company, and the company uses the cash subscribed to invest in trading or investment activities.

There is a relevant transfer because there is:

(a)    a transfer of assets (the subscription of cash);

(b)    as a result of which income arises (the cash is used to invest in profitable trading or investment activities);

(c)    to a person outside the UK (the offshore company receives this income).

As a result of the relevant transfer, the individual has the power to enjoy the income because he is a shareholder in the company.

Tax may therefore arise under ITA 2007, s 720.

**Share exchange**

**[A15.17]** An individual transfers shares to an offshore company in exchange for the offshore company issuing new shares to him.

There is a relevant transfer because there is:

(a)     a transfer of assets (the shares which are transferred);
(b)     as a result of which income arises (the offshore company will receive future dividends on the shares);
(c)     to a person outside the UK (the offshore company receives the dividends).

As a result of the relevant transfer, the individual has the power to enjoy the income because he is a shareholder in the company.

Tax may therefore arise under ITA 2007, s 720.

## Interaction with the Controlled Foreign Company (CFC) rules

**[A15.18]** ITA 2007, s 725 provides that income attributed under Controlled Foreign Companies (CFC) rules is not also attributed under s 720. The CFC rules therefore apply in priority to s 720.

In Diagram 3 above, if the UK company were subject to tax on the investment income by virtue of the CFC rules, it would not also be subject to tax under s 720.

**Section 720—the EU argument**

**[A15.19]** In an EU context, the UK government was served with infraction notices relating to TCGA, ss 720 and 13 on 16 February 2011 on the grounds that the rules that they stood were disproportionate and incompatible with the Treaty Freedoms of the single market. In response to this HMRC issued a consultation document aimed to make the relevant legislation EU compliant and take the opportunity to make other changes at the same time. The main thrust of this is a new exemption from s 720 which is aimed to exclude transactions which involve real economic activity and where transactions are conducted at arm's length. Final legislation was included in the Finance Act 2013 which confirmed that that the legislation would take effect from 6 April 2012.

*UK-resident but overseas registered company anomaly removed*

**[A15.20]** In s 718(2), para (a) is removed, such that a company registered overseas but UK-resident by reason of management and control is no longer treated as a person abroad

*New exemption for 'genuine transactions'*

**[A15.21]** A new, additional exemption is introduced, applying statutorily to 2012/13 and later years. This is mainly aimed at commercial arrangements but can apply to any arrangement made for personal reasons too. The new s 742A exempts 'genuine transactions' made on or after 6 April 2012 that must meet two conditions, A and B.

Condition A is that:

(a)     were, viewed objectively, the transaction to be considered to be a genuine transaction having regard to any arrangements under which it is effected and any other relevant circumstances, and

(b)     were the individual to be liable to tax under this Chapter by reference to the transaction the individual's liability to tax would, in contravention of Title II or IV of the Treaty on the Functioning of the European Union, constitute an unjustified and disproportionate restriction on a freedom protected under that Title.

Condition B is that the individual satisfies an officer of Revenue and Customs that, viewed objectively, the transaction must be considered to be a genuine transaction having regard to any arrangements under which it is effected and any other relevant circumstances.

This means that it will not be enough for the transaction to be genuine and above board (Condition A); Condition B requires an officer of Revenue & Customs to be satisfied that Condition A is met. This should not connote a subjective test of HMRC setting their own criteria but it will apply a positive requirement to give notice to HMRC of any arrangement for which the exemption is sought.

A possible area of difficulty is that Condition A requires the EU treaty to be infringed in order for the exemption to apply. The exemption for EU compliance has been added as a long stop to try to ensure that the EU will not take further infraction proceedings but this highlights the fact that the other, specific provisions may not be enough to meet EU requirements.

There is also uncertainty as to whether the exemption could apply to income arising to persons outside the EU. As outlined in **A7.14**, the free movement of capital can extend to third countries in certain circumstances. The transfer of assets abroad anti-avoidance rules existed prior to 1992, and so could be grandfathered.

### Arm's length transactions

**[A15.22]** There is a general requirement that to be considered 'genuine' a transaction must be:

*   a transaction that unconnected persons acting at arm's length would have made, or
*   on terms that would have been made between unconnected persons acting at arm's length.

Personal transactions do not need to be on arm's length terms. Subsection (5) does not apply to transfers of assets that are made:

*   for personal, not commercial reasons,
*   for the personal benefit of other individuals, and
*   no consideration is given for the transfer or for any benefit received by the other individuals.

## Business establishment outside the UK

**[A15.23]** Transfers are only exempt under the new s 742A if a person (the 'relevant person') carries on a business through a business establishment outside the UK and:

- the assets are used for the purposes of, or the income is received from that business.

The definition of a business establishment is the definition of a permanent establishment in CTA 2010, ss 1141–1143, as extended to include non-corporates as well as companies (s 742A(9)).

For a business establishment to be regarded as genuine it must provide goods or services on a commercial basis which entails:

- having staff (employed or contracted) in numbers, and of competence and authority,
- using premises and equipment, and
- adding economic value to the customer for those goods or services, commensurate with the size and nature of those activities.

This test is essentially the same as the 'economically significant activities' test applied under TCGA 1992, s 13 (see above at A15.2) but by another name.

## Other amendments

**[A15.24]** Amendments to ss 721 and 728 make it clear that the UK individual is not assessed on the income of the overseas person who receives income as a result of the ToA but on an amount equal to that income. This is a tidying-up change which eliminates the scope for confusion and double taxation or non-taxation (eg new s 728(3A)).

It is of course still open to taxpayers to lodge claims with HMRC for prior years as prima facie HMRC have accepted that they are not in accordance with EU Freedoms.

## Business profits

**[A15.25]** FA 2008 introduced a new ICTA 1988, s 815AZA (now TIOPA 2010, s 130) which affects relief from tax under ITA 2007, s 720 on business profits. Historically it has been the case that this section provides:

> 'Where arrangements having effect under section 788 make the provision mentioned in subsection (2) (however expressed) [the business profits article], that provision does not prevent income of a person resident in the United Kingdom being chargeable to income tax or corporation tax.'

However Schedule 10 of Finance Act 2013 introduces a new s 721(3A) which clarifies the position with regard to treaty relief. Using principles imported from the CFC case of *Bricom Holdings Ltd v IRC* (1997) STC 1179 it makes clear that the income being attributed to the individual is not the income of the overseas structure itself, but an amount equal to it. On that basis treaty protection now cannot be relied upon to prevent charge under s 720.

### *Planning techniques*

**[A15.26]** There are a number of planning techniques which can minimise the impact of ITA 2007, s 720:

(a)     Where the income which arises to the offshore company is dividend income (as in Diagram 5 for instance), dividends should not be paid unless they are immediately distributed to the individual shareholder. This ensures firstly that a single level of tax arises under s 720 as no further charge arises on subsequent distribution, and secondly that there is no charge until the individual actually receives the income.

(b)     Certain businesses may benefit from the s 737 exemption for bona fide commercial structures. For instance:

    (i)      certain insurance activities cannot legally be undertaken in the UK and therefore must be undertaken by an offshore company.

    (ii)     offshore funds may require an offshore fund manager under local regulatory rules, and the fund management activity therefore must be undertaken by an offshore company.

(c)     As noted above, tax does not arise under s 731 until a benefit is actually received. Where possible, a structure should be established so that it falls within s 731 rather than s 720. For example, the individual who sets up a structure (the transferor) should not be the same individual who subsequently holds the shares and has the power to enjoy the income arising.

(d)     Where an individual subscribes cash to an offshore company, this could be held separately from cash obtained from other sources. As s 720 only applies to income arising from the cash transferred, any income arising from cash which is obtained from the other sources may not be subject to tax under s 720.

(e)     Any income which is taxed under s 720 retains its character. Trading income may therefore be non-UK source, and taxed on a remittance basis for a non-domiciled individual, but only if derived through a partnership—see A15.32.

# Planning—tax on shareholder returns

### *Dividends*

**[A15.27]** Dividend income is subject to tax under ITA 2007, s 13 at a rate of either 10% (the dividend ordinary rate), 32.5% (the dividend upper rate) or 37.5% (the dividend additional rate). Section 19(2)(*b*) defines dividend income as including dividends from non-resident companies.

Special rules apply if the dividend is subject to tax on the remittance basis, which may be relevant for individuals who are not domiciled or not ordinarily resident in the UK.

In the case of dividends from a UK resident company, the individual shareholder is entitled to a dividend tax credit equal to one ninth of the dividend received by virtue of ITTOIA 2005, s 397. Section 398 provides that the dividend subject to tax is the gross amount (ie the dividend received plus the one ninth tax credit), with the result that a higher rate taxpayer will pay an effective rate of 25% on the dividend received, and additional rate taxpayer will pay an effective rate of 30.55%.

From 6 April 2008, Finance Act 2008 extended the dividend tax credit to dividends received from a non-resident company but only where the individual shareholder holds less than 10% of the ordinary share capital in the company.

Finance Act 2009 further extended the dividend tax credit to dividends received from a non-resident company where the individual shareholder holds 10% or more, but only if the company is resident in a jurisdiction with which the UK has a DTA which includes a non-discrimination article (a list of which is in the HMRC International Manual at INTM412090, current at 7 March 2012). A shareholder with at least 10% of the shares in a Jersey company would therefore not be entitled to the tax credit.

### Withholding tax and underlying tax

[A15.28] Credit is available against the UK tax liability for any withholding tax suffered on the dividend.

However, no credit is available for any underlying tax suffered by the company. This is different from the position of a UK resident company receiving a non-exempt dividend from a non-resident company, where credit can be obtained for the underlying tax (see CHAPTER A10).

### *Capital gains*

[A15.29] UK resident individuals will be subject to tax on the disposal of shares in a non-resident company at a rate of 18% or 28% (ie the same rate as applies to the disposal of shares in a UK resident company).

Furthermore, the Entrepreneurs' Relief which was introduced by Finance Act 2008 can apply to the disposal of shares in a non-resident company in the same way as it applies to the disposal of shares in a UK resident company.

As noted above, if a capital gain is realised by a non-resident company it may be subject to tax under TCGA 1992, s 13. Credit is available for the tax paid under s 13 against any tax due on a distribution of the gain within four years. However, as the rate of capital gains tax is lower than the rate of tax of dividends, if the gain is distributed by way of dividend, additional tax is likely to arise.

If the charge to tax under s 13 cannot be avoided, then the individual shareholder could consider holding the non-resident company's assets personally. This would ensure that the proceeds are received by the individual after suffering only 18% or 28% capital gains tax, rather than capital gains tax under s 13 and further tax on a subsequent dividend.

### Non-domiciled and not ordinarily resident shareholders

**[A15.30]**  Although outside the scope of this book, it is important to note that an individual who is not domiciled in the UK, or not ordinarily resident in the UK may be subject to tax on the 'remittance basis'.

From 6 April 2008, Finance Act 2008 requires payment of a £30,000 charge for certain individuals to claim the remittance basis, and for any individual claiming the remittance basis to forfeit their personal allowances. This charge increased to £50,000 per annum from 6 April 2012 for those residents that have been here for more than 12 years.

ITTOIA 2005, s 831 provides that an individual who is not domiciled in the UK, or not ordinarily resident in the UK, may elect that his 'relevant foreign income' is not subject to tax unless it is remitted to the UK.

Relevant foreign income specifically includes dividends from non-resident companies (ITTOIA 2005, s 830).

This contrasts with the remittance basis for capital gains tax (see CHAPTER A11), where gains on the disposal of shares are subject to tax on the remittance basis if the company is incorporated outside the UK.

Thus for a company which is incorporated outside the UK, but resident in the UK by virtue of its central management and control being exercised in the UK:

(a)     dividends will not be relevant foreign income, and therefore not eligible to be taxed on the remittance basis; but

(b)     capital gains will be eligible to be taxed on the remittance basis.

Income other than dividend income will be relevant foreign income if it arises from a source outside the UK and is subject to tax under one of the provisions set out in s 830, which broadly includes all trading income, property income and interest income.

### Partnerships and sole trades

#### Sole traders

**[A15.31]**  Where a sole trader carries on an overseas trade, ITTOIA 2005, s 6 provides that the trader is subject to tax in the UK:

'(1)     Profits of a trade arising to a UK resident are chargeable to tax under this Chapter wherever the trade is carried on.'

As noted below, certain individuals who are not domiciled or not ordinarily resident in the UK may be subject to tax on the remittance basis in respect of 'relevant foreign income'.

Trading income will be relevant foreign income provided it arises from 'a source outside the UK' (ITTOIA 2005, s 830(1)).

Section 7(5) provides that:

' . . . for the purposes of section 830 (meaning of "relevant foreign income"), the profits of a trade, profession or vocation arise from a source outside the United Kingdom only if the trade, profession or vocation is carried on *wholly outside the United Kingdom*.'(my emphasis)

In the context of a sole trader, it will be almost impossible to argue that a UK resident carries on the trade wholly outside the UK.

## Partnership

**[A15.32]** Where a trade is carried on in partnership, the partners are treated as carrying on the trade individually in accordance with normal UK principles.

However, unlike the provisions relating to sole trades, there is no requirement that the trade be carried on wholly outside the UK in order for the profits to be treated as relevant foreign income.

ITTOIA 2005, s 857 provides that that if:

'(1)     . . .

    (a)    a firm carries on a trade wholly or partly outside the United Kingdom,

    (b)    the control and management of the trade is outside the United Kingdom

. . .

(2)    The partner's share of the profits of the trade arising outside the United Kingdom is treated as relevant foreign income for the purposes of this Act (see Part 8).'

Therefore if a partnership is managed and controlled outside the UK, the part of the profits arising outside the UK will be treated as relevant foreign income and potentially subject to tax on the remittance basis.

## Diagram 6

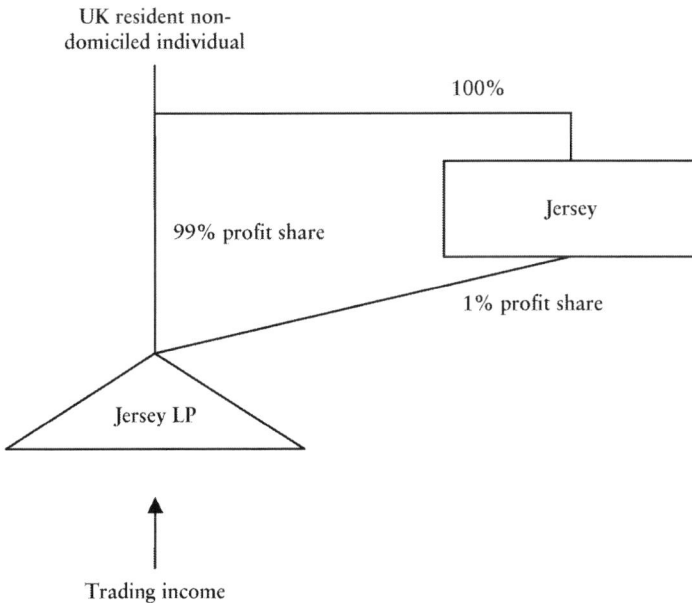

This may provide planning opportunities for a non-domiciled individual who is only taxable on relevant foreign income on a remittance basis. Rather than derive foreign income as a sole trader which would be taxable on an arising basis, a non-domiciled individual could establish a structure as shown in Diagram 6 to ensure that such income is derived through a foreign partnership and therefore relevant foreign income.

There is no definition of management and control for these purposes, but the case law relating to the management and control of companies (see CHAPTER A9) should be followed.

### Benefits of transparent structures

**[A15.33]** If a UK individual carries on an overseas business through a sole trade or partnership rather than a company this may result in certain tax benefits:

(a)    Profits are subject to UK tax as they arise, but no further UK should be due on distribution.

(b)    Credit should be available for overseas tax paid on the profits against the UK tax liability.

(c)    The UK individual will be treated as carrying on the overseas business directly, and entitled to any UK tax reliefs related to the business in question, for instance film tax credits or enhanced capital allowances. This may reduce his UK tax liability.

(d)    Any gains realised by the sole trade or partnership will be taxed as capital gains at a rate of 18% or 28%, rather than being taxed as dividends when distributed from a company.

Diagram 7

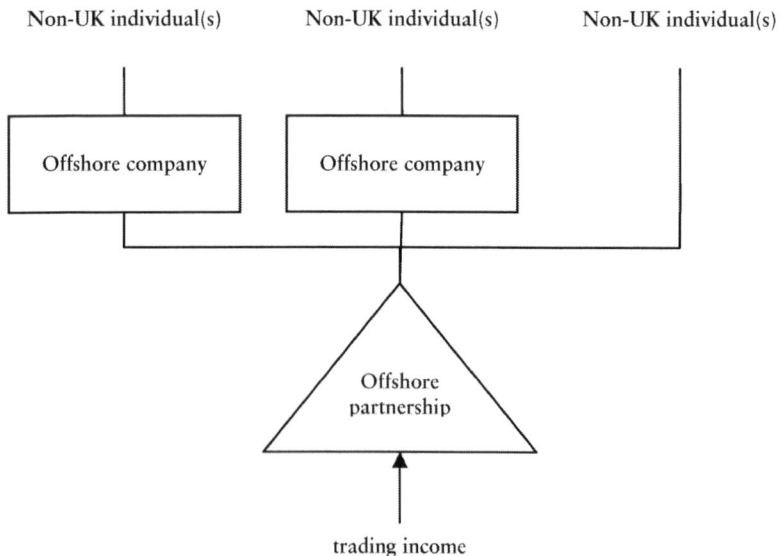

There may, of course, be commercial issues where an overseas business is not carried on through an entity which has limited liability.

Where overseas investors do not wish to invest directly into a transparent structure (for their own tax or commercial reasons), then they can establish their own separate 'feeder' structure as shown in Diagram 7. This enables investors in different jurisdictions to obtain different types of return by investing in different entities.

### Offshore funds

**[A15.34]** Certain gains on the disposal of shares in an offshore company may be subject to income tax rather than capital gains tax.

For an individual, TIOPA 2010, Part 8 and The Offshore Funds (Tax) Regulations 2009, SI 2009/3001 together provide that gains on the disposal of shareholdings in an 'offshore fund' are subject to income tax or corporation tax. This means for an individual, tax will be paid at a rate of up to 45% rather than the 28% capital gains tax rate. And for a company, tax will be paid at 28%, without the benefit of the substantial shareholding exemption which may otherwise apply to the disposal of shares. In addition, individuals who receive dividends from an offshore fund do not get a dividend tax credit, and their effective tax rates is up to 37.5% rather than 30.55%.

It is therefore very important that holding and investment structures do not inadvertently fall within the offshore funds rules.

An offshore fund may be a non-resident company, but it may also be a unit trust, partnership or any other type of arrangement governed by foreign law which creates co-ownership rights. Thus the investors' interests may be shares, units or some other form of participation.

A full discussion of the rules is outside the scope of this book, but 'Tolley's Taxation of Collective Investment Schemes' may be a useful source.

## Planning—holding companies

**[A15.35]** Based on the issues outlined above, if an individual is looking to establish an offshore company he will need to consider:

(a)    Application of TCGA 1992, s 13 to future gains realised by the offshore company. The jurisdiction in which the company is established may offer treaty protection, or the gains may be exempt under the substantial shareholding exemption.

(b)    Application of ITA 2007, s 720 to future income realised by the offshore company. The jurisdiction in which the company is established may offer treaty protection, or the structure may satisfy the bona fide commercial conditions of s 737.

(c)    Rate of tax on dividends from the offshore company. Assuming the shareholder holds more than 10% of the shares, dividends from an offshore company will be subject to tax at an effective rate of 32.5% (or

37.5%). If the shareholder holds less than 10% of the shares, they may be able to claim the dividend tax credit, resulting in an effective rate of 25% (or 30.55%).

(d)     Tax in the company. Withholding taxes may be due on any dividends paid by the offshore company, which should be creditable against the tax due on the dividend. However, credit will not be available for any underlying taxes paid by the company. This should be taken into account when calculating the overall effective tax rate for the individual shareholder.

In addition to these shareholder considerations, the tax position of the company itself will obviously be important. If it suffers withholding tax or direct tax on the income it receives, this will reduce the individual shareholder's net return.

Some of these considerations are outlined in the case study in CHAPTER B3.

## UK holding company

**[A15.36]** In some cases, a UK resident holding company may be appropriate as it will offer some advantages over a non-resident company:

(a)     TCGA 1992, s 13 will not apply to gains of a UK resident company;
(b)     ITA 2007, s 720 (or s 727 or s 731) will not apply to income received by a UK resident company;
(c)     the effective rate of tax on dividends from a UK company is 25% (or 30.55% if the dividend additional rate applies) regardless of the number of shares held by the individual shareholder.

Diagram 8 illustrates some of the issues discussed in this Chapter.

In Diagram 8(a):

(i)     The trading income received by the offshore company is subject to tax at a rate of 35%, with a deduction for any interest paid to the trust (assuming the overseas jurisdiction allows a deduction).
(ii)    If the individual set up the company, the trading income may also be subject to tax under ITA 2007, s 720, again with a deduction for any interest paid under normal UK principles for calculating trading income. This may be restricted if the transfer pricing rules apply. Credit will be available for the 35% tax paid by the offshore company.
(iii)   Assuming no dividend tax credit is available, a dividend received from the offshore company will be subject to tax at 32.5% (or 37.5% if the dividend additional rate applies), with no credit for the 35% tax paid by the company. If the trading income has been subject to tax under s 720, then no tax liability arises on the dividend.
(iv)    As the individual was not the settlor of the trust, the interest income received by the trust is not subject to tax under s 720. However, should the individual receive a capital distribution from the trust, the interest income may be subject to tax under ITA 2007, s 731.

Diagram 8

(a)

(b)

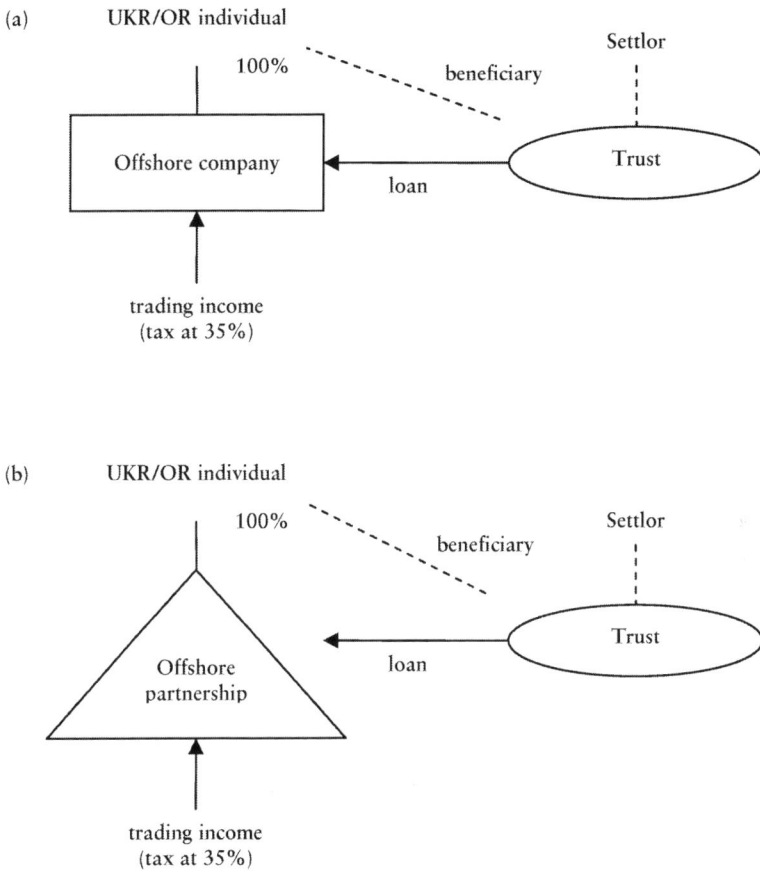

An alternative structure is shown in Diagram 8(b):

(i)     The trading income received by the offshore partnership remains subject to tax at a rate of 35%, with a deduction for any interest paid to the trust (assuming the overseas jurisdiction allows a deduction).

(ii)    However, the trading income will also be subject to UK tax as it arises to a partnership in which a UK resident is a member. There will be a deduction for any interest paid under normal UK principles for calculating trading income. This may be restricted if the transfer pricing rules apply.

Credit will be available for the 35% tax paid by the offshore company. As the trade is carried on outside the UK, the income will constitute relevant foreign income and if the individual is not domiciled in the UK, he may elect for it to be subject to tax on the remittance basis.

(iii)   No further UK tax will be due on the distribution of the income from the partnership.

(iv)    As the individual was not the settlor of the trust, the interest income received by the trust is not subject to tax under s 720. However, should the individual receive a capital distribution from the trust, the interest income may be subject to tax under ITA 2007, s 731.

The effective rate of tax (for a higher rate taxpayer) under these structures is contrasted in the table below.

|  | Company | Company (with s720) | Partnership |
|---|---|---|---|
| Profits after deduction of interest | 100 | 100 | 100 |
| Overseas tax @ 35% | (35) | (35) | (35) |
| Dividend to individual shareholder | 65 | 65 | – |
| UK tax on dividend @ 32.5% | (21) | – | – |
| UK tax on profits @ 40% | – | (40) | (40) |
| Credit for overseas tax | – | 35 | 35 |
| Net received by individual shareholder | 44 | 60 | 60 |
| Effective tax rate | 56% | 40% | 40% |

However, there may be further issues to consider, including:

(a)    this table illustrates the overall tax rate on distributing profits to shareholders; if profits are retained by the entity, it may be more tax efficient to use a company structure;

(b)    withholding tax may be due on interest paid to the trust, although it may be possible to mitigate this (see CHAPTER **A5**);

(c)    if capital gains are likely to be realised the overall tax rate may be reduced, particularly as credit will be available on the distribution of any gains for any tax paid under TCGA 1992, s 13.

# A16

# Dividend exemption

## Introduction

**[A16.1]** This Chapter outlines the conditions which must be satisfied in order for the dividend exemption to apply, and the relevant anti-avoidance provisions.

If the dividend exemption does not apply, any dividend receipt will be taxed in the company as income.

## Basic principles

**[A16.2]** Dividends received from both overseas and UK subsidiaries will be exempt if they satisfy the conditions outlined below, but will be taxable if they do not. Where they are taxable, the rules relating to double tax relief outlined at **A10.29** will apply.

### Small groups

**[A16.3]** For small groups, a dividend will be exempt if:

(a)    the payer is resident in the UK or a 'qualifying territory';
(b)    it is not a payment of interest which is treated as a dividend by CTA 2010, s 1000;
(c)    it is not tax deductible by the payer; and
(d)    it is not paid as part of a 'tax advantage scheme'.

A 'qualifying territory' is one with which the UK has a double tax agreement which includes a non-discrimination article (a list of which is in the HMRC International Manual at INTM412090). The Distributions (Excluded Companies) Regulations 2009, SI 2009/3314 provide that a dividend will not be exempt if the paying company is not entitled to all benefits under the relevant DTA. This may be the case, for instance, where the subsidiary is a special type of company to which the DTA specifically does not apply.

A 'small' group for these purposes is one which has fewer than 50 employees, and either turnover below €10m or a balance sheet total below €10m. Certain investment funds will not be treated as 'small' even if they satisfy these conditions—open ended investment companies, authorised unit trusts, insurance companies and friendly societies.

A 'tax advantage scheme' is a scheme the main purpose of which is to secure a tax advantage. There is no definition of this in the legislation, and the only guidance HMRC have given is that the payment of a dividend from a non-qualifying territory to the UK via a holding company in a qualifying territory is likely to be a tax advantage scheme. In the absence of any further guidance, the anti-avoidance rules applicable to the large group exemption (see **A16.6**) may indicate what HMRC are likely to consider as a tax advantage scheme.

UK companies which are members of small groups should as far as possible not receive dividends from subsidiaries in non-qualifying territories. Such dividends should be deferred until the group has ceased to be small, at which point the dividend may fall within one of the exempt classes.

## Large groups

**[A16.4]** For groups which are not small, a dividend will be exempt if:

(a)     it falls within an 'exempt class';
(b)     it is not a payment of interest which is treated as a dividend by CTA 2010, s 1000;
(c)     it is not tax deductible by the payer.

There are also anti-avoidance rules which prevent the exemption from being available in certain cases.

## Exempt classes

**[A16.5]** The dividend must fall within one of the following exempt classes:

(1)     Dividends from 'controlled companies'. The definition of 'control' is the same as the definition in the CFC rules, and includes 51% subsidiaries as well as joint venture companies where both joint venture partners hold at least 40% of the shares.
However, in line with the CFC rules, the definition will not be satisfied if one joint venture partner is able to acquire a shareholding of more than 55%. Problems may therefore arise if a joint venture partner holds warrants or options, or a class of shares with voting rights that may increase in future.
Most dividends from subsidiaries are likely to fall within this exempt class.

(2)     Dividends paid in respect of non-redeemable ordinary shares. The definition of ordinary shares is very narrow, and only includes shares which do not carry *any* preferential rights. The definition of non-redeemable is also very narrow, and if *either* the issuer *or* the shareholder can call for redemption, the share will be redeemable.

(3)     Portfolio dividends ie where the shareholder is entitled to less than 10% of the ordinary share capital, profits available for distribution and assets available for distribution on a winding up.

(4)     Motive test. A dividend will be exempt if it has been paid out of profits which have not been diverted from the UK, or where the diversion of profits was not one of the main purposes of the transaction which gave rise to the profits. Most dividends from UK subsidiaries should satisfy this motive test if they do not fall within one of the other exempt classes.

(5)     Shares treated as loans. Where shares are treated as loans under the loan relationship rules, the dividends will be taxed as interest, and will therefore not be taxable dividends in their own right.

All existing and new joint venture or minority shareholding arrangements should be reviewed to ensure that dividends will fall within one of the exempt classes. Dividends will only be exempt under the first exempt class if a shareholder has control of the paying company. The conditions of the other exempt classes may be more difficult to satisfy.

### Anti-avoidance rules

**[A16.6]** There are a number of anti-avoidance rules which prevent the exemption from applying in certain cases. Where an anti-avoidance rule is specific to a particular exempt class, it will not prevent the dividend from being exempt under another class.

(1)     Dividends will not be exempt under the first exempt class if:
   (a)     they are paid out of profits which arose before the recipient acquired control of the payer; and
   (b)     they are paid as part of a scheme the main purpose of which is to ensure that the dividend will fall into one of the exempt classes.

(2)     Dividends will not be exempt under the first exempt class if:
   (a)     they are a return on investment which is economically equivalent to interest; and
   (b)     they are paid as part of a scheme the main purpose of which is to secure a tax advantage.

(3)     Dividends will not be exempt under the second exempt class if:
   (a)     the shares are 'quasi-preference shares' ie the holder (or connected persons) have other rights which mean the shares are not ordinary shares or are redeemable; and
   (b)     they are paid as part of a scheme the main purpose of which is to ensure that the dividend will fall into one of the exempt classes.

(4)     When considering under the third exempt class whether a shareholder has a portfolio holding, it is necessary to also include any rights or shares held by connected persons (eg other group companies).

(5)     Dividends will not be exempt under any of the exempt classes if:

(a)     a deduction is obtained by a non-UK resident company in respect of an amount determined by reference to the dividend (eg under certain stock lending arrangements, where the lender of the stock receives a deduction for the amount of a manufactured dividend); and

(b)     they are paid as part of a scheme the main purpose of which is to secure a tax advantage.

(6)     Dividends will not be exempt under any of the exempt classes if:

(a)     a payment has been made in return for a dividend (for instance, if a company has purchased the right to receive a dividend from another company); and

(b)     they are paid as part of a scheme the main purpose of which is to secure a tax advantage.

(7)     Dividends will not be exempt under any of the exempt classes if there have been transactions between the payer and the recipient (or connected persons) on a non arm's-length basis. This would be the case where for instance a company was a shareholder in a captive insurance company but did not control it and so was not subject to either the controlled foreign company or the transfer pricing rules in respect of premiums. If premiums were overpaid, they may be tax deductible in the UK and any profit arising could be received as an exempt dividend.

(8)     Dividends will not be exempt under any of the exempt classes if:

(a)     they would otherwise be received by a company which would have been taxed on the dividend as trading income;

(b)     they are paid as part of a scheme the main purpose of which is to ensure that the dividend will fall into the dividend exemption.

### Election for exemption not to apply

**[A16.7]** It is possible to make an election for the exemption not to apply to a particular dividend.

This may be beneficial where for instance a reduced rate of withholding tax under a DTA is only available if the dividend is subject to tax in the UK. Although the dividend would then be taxable in the UK, management expenses or other deductions may be available to reduce the amount which is taxable.

# A17

# The worldwide debt cap

## Introduction

**[A17.1]** The principle of the worldwide debt cap measure is to limit relief for deductions in respect of excessive debt owed by the UK members of a group. This Chapter outlines when the worldwide debt cap applies, and planning opportunities to reduce non-deductible interest.

## Basic principles

**[A17.2]** The worldwide debt cap was introduced in Finance Act 2009 and is now found in TIOPA 2010, Part 7. In broad terms, it restricts the amount of interest which can be deducted by a UK group to the amount of third party interest which is incurred by the worldwide group.

It applies to UK groups as well as multinational groups, but will have particular relevance where a UK company has borrowed from a non-UK company in the same group. The UK company may not obtain a deduction for the interest paid, but the overseas company may still be taxed on the interest received. In this case, the group's effective tax rate will significantly increase.

The rules are very complex, and there are many areas where computational difficulties are likely to arise, such as where companies have non-coterminous accounting periods, or where they account in different currencies. Special rules exist for certain types of company, such as insurance companies and REITs, and where the parent entity of a group is not a company. This Chapter therefore only seeks to provide a discussion of the principles as they relate to international tax planning.

The debt cap only applies to groups which are large, the definition of which is the EU definition with some modifications (the same as used in the transfer pricing rules—see **A13.8**).

The rules apply to accounting periods beginning on or after 1 January 2010.

## Gateway test

**[A17.3]** The debt cap will not apply if the group meets a 'gateway' test. Meeting this test will prevent a group from undertaking the complex calculations of the debt cap itself.

Under the 'gateway' test, the debt cap will only apply if UK net debt exceeds 75% of worldwide gross debt. If both UK net debt and worldwide gross debt are nil, then the rules should not apply.

UK net debt is the sum of the average of net debt in each relevant company at the beginning and end of an accounting period. Any amounts less than £3 million are ignored. Net debt is defined as loans and amounts payable under finance leases less cash, loan receivables, amounts receivable on finance leases and government securities. Non-sterling balances are translated at the appropriate spot rate. Companies with net finance assets are ignored.

Worldwide gross debt is the average of the consolidated gross debt of the worldwide group at the end of an accounting period, and at the end of the immediately preceding accounting period. Gross debt is defined as loans and amounts payable under finance leases. Non-sterling balances are translated at the appropriate spot rate.

## Definition of group

**[A17.4]** The debt cap only applies to UK companies which are 75% subsidiaries, and these are referred to as 'relevant companies' in the rules. A company which is owned 50%:50% by two joint venture partners will not be subject to the debt cap. Such a company will not be included in the calculation of UK net debt for the purposes of the gateway test, or in the calculation of the tested amount.

However, when calculating amounts on a group basis, for instance the worldwide gross debt or the available amount, it is necessary to consider the amounts stated in the consolidated accounts prepared under IFRS or an accounting standard which is equivalent to IFRS. This may include subsidiaries in which the group holds less than 75%.

HMRC have indicated that certain accounting standards will be considered to be equivalent to IFRS, including US GAAP.

Following the FA 2014, the definition of a group in the WWDC rules has been changed with effect from 5 December 2013. The changes cover the following areas:

- It is no longer required to have ordinary share capital, so that a company that is limited by guarantee for example can be considered a relevant company for WWDC purposes.
- The definition of a 75% subsidiary has changed so that intermediaries without ordinary share capital can be 'looked through' to find the indirect ownership.

### Calculation of the debt cap

**[A17.5]** Under the debt cap, interest expense is disallowed to the extent the 'tested expense' exceeds the 'available amount'.

The tested expense is the sum of net financing expenses of relevant group companies. Net financing expenses are:

(a)     loan relationship debits excluding foreign exchange and impairment losses;

(b)     interest element of finance leases and debt factoring;

less:

(a)     loan relationship credits excluding foreign exchange and reversal of impairment losses;

(b)     interest receivable element of finance leases and debt factoring.

Any amounts less than £500,000 are ignored, and any negative amounts are treated as nil.

The available amount is the amount shown in the group's consolidated accounts in respect of:

(a)     interest on loans;
(b)     amortisation of discounts and other financing costs;
(c)     interest element of finance leases and debt factoring.

An example of the calculation of the interest disallowance is at **A17.9** below.

The debt cap applies in addition to the transfer pricing rules, but where an amount is disallowed under the transfer pricing rules, it is not included in the calculation of the tested expense.

### Relief for disallowed interest

**[A17.6]** Where interest expense is disallowed, a corresponding reduction in taxable interest income can be claimed by any relevant UK company which has net financing income. There is also an example of this below.

### Relief for disallowed EEA interest

**[A17.7]** Taxable interest income may also be reduced where interest is received from a group company which is resident in the EEA, and the payer is not entitled to a deduction in the current period, previous period or future period. There is an exception where the disallowance is due to a transfer pricing adjustment; in these circumstances, the interest would remain taxable in the UK, subject to any corresponding adjustment which is available under the relevant DTA.

### *Allocation of disallowances*

**[A17.8]** A group can choose how to allocate the disallowed interest between the relevant UK companies. A representative company can be elected to make a return which allocates the disallowance.

In the absence of a return being made, the disallowance is allocated in proportion to each relevant UK company's net financing deduction, as calculated for the purposes of the debt cap.

It is important that a group makes the return, so that the disallowance of interest is allocated in the most tax efficient way. For instance, it will usually be beneficial to allocate the disallowance to companies which have brought forward losses.

A group can also choose how to allocate the reduction in taxable interest. Again, a representative company can be elected to make a return which allocates the reduction. In the absence of a return being made, the reduction is allocated in proportion to each relevant UK company's finance income.

### *Examples of debt cap calculations*

**[A17.9]** In Diagram 1, a US parent company has borrowed from the bank, and has made a loan to its UK subsidiary. The UK subsidiary is a relevant group company because it is a 75% subsidiary of the US parent.

The tested expense is the interest paid by the UK company, which is £1.5 million. The available amount is the interest shown in the group's consolidated accounts, which is £1 million as the intercompany interest is eliminated on consolidation. £500,000 of interest is disallowed in the UK but may remain taxable in the US.

Diagram 1

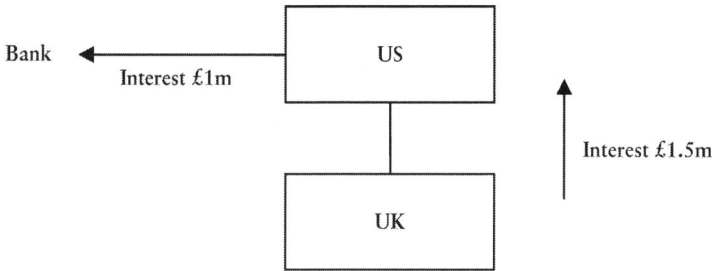

In Diagram 1, £500,000 of interest income potentially remains taxable in the US with no deduction in the UK. If part of the loan from the US to the UK were replaced with equity, there would be no requirement to recognise interest income in the US.

Where the debt cap applies, it may be necessary to replace debt with equity in order to reduce taxable income in the non-UK lending company.

In Diagram 2, the UK subsidiary has also made a loan to its own UK subsidiary. Both UK subsidiaries are relevant group companies.

Diagram 2

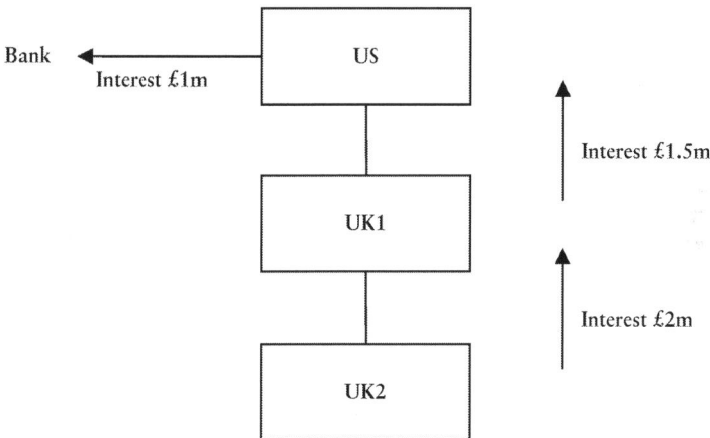

The tested expense is the sum of the net financing expense of the relevant companies (ie the UK subsidiaries). UK1 has received interest of £2 million and paid interest of £1.5 million and its net financing expense is therefore nil (amounts less than nil are treated as nil). The net financing expense of UK2 is £2 million. The tested expense is therefore £2 million.

The available amount is the interest shown in the group's consolidated accounts, which will again be £1 million. £1 million of interest is therefore disallowed in the UK. The group can choose how this disallowance is allocated between UK1 and UK2. If UK1 had brought forward tax losses, then it would be beneficial to allocate the disallowance to UK1, as the increased profits would be reduced by the brought forward tax losses.

The group's financing income can also be reduced by up to £1 million. UK1 has net finance income of £500,000, and its income will therefore be reduced by £500,000. UK2 has no net finance income and its income will not be reduced. The net disallowance for the UK group is therefore £500,000, as in the first example above.

In Diagram 3, an overseas subsidiary has made a loan to its parent company, on which interest of £1 million is paid.

**Diagram 3**

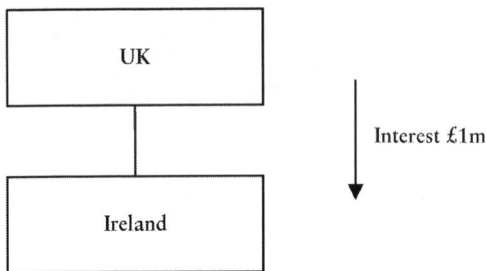

The tested expense is the interest paid by the UK company, which is £1 million. The available amount is the interest shown in the group's consolidated accounts, which is nil as the intercompany interest is eliminated on consolidation.

The entire £1 million of interest is therefore disallowed in the UK company, but may remain taxable in Ireland.

In Diagram 3, £1,000,000 of interest income potentially remains taxable in Ireland with no deduction in the UK.

## Exclusions

### Election to disregard certain loan relationships

**[A17.10]** Where a UK resident company which has brought forward non-trading loan relationship deficits or brought forward management expenses, has made a loan to another group company, the companies can jointly elect to exclude the income and expenses relating to this loan from the calculation of the tested amount. The election must be made within three years of the end of the relevant accounting period.

The benefit of this election is to reduce the amount of finance expense included in the tested amount, and the election will be most relevant where the borrower is also a UK resident company.

The purpose of this election is to ensure that brought forward management expenses and loan relationship deficits can continue to be used against inter-company interest income. If the debt cap applied, then the interest deduction for the borrower would be disallowed, and the taxable interest in the lender company would be reduced. The net income of the group would be the same, but interest and expenses would be recognised in different companies, with the result that brought forward amounts would be stranded.

## Treasury companies

**[A17.11]** If a UK company undertakes qualifying treasury activities, it can make an election to exclude its finance income and expenses from the calculation of the tested amount.

A company will undertake qualifying treasury activities on behalf of the group if it:

(a)    manages surplus deposits or overdrafts;
(b)    makes or receives deposits;
(c)    lends money;
(d)    subscribes for shares in another UK company which undertakes qualifying treasury activities;
(e)    invests in debt securities;
(f)    hedges assets, liabilities, income or expenses; and
(g)    at least 90% of its gross income is derived from these treasury activities.

The election must be made within three years of the end of the relevant accounting period.

The treasury company exclusion may simplify the calculation of the tested amount where there are a large number of transactions between the treasury company and other group companies.

## Short term loan relationships

**[A17.12]** If a loan between two group companies is repaid within twelve months, the companies can elect to exclude the income and expenses relating to this loan from the calculation of the tested amount. The election must be made within three years of the end of the relevant accounting period.

This may be useful where a non-UK parent company provides short-term financing to a subsidiary. In this case, short-term financing should be loaned separately from any longer-term financing to ensure that the twelve month condition can be met.

## *Anti-avoidance*

**[A17.13]** There are two targeted anti-avoidance provisions which may affect the operation of the debt cap.

Firstly (TIOPA 2010, s 306), the gateway test will be deemed not to be met where there is a scheme or arrangement in place the main purpose, or one of the main purposes of which, is to satisfy the gateway test, and without which the gateway test would not be met.

Secondly (TIOPA 2010, s 307), where:

(a) there is a scheme or arrangement in place the main purpose, or one of the main purposes of which is to reduce the disallowance under the debt cap; and

(b) the taxable profits of UK group companies are lower than they would be in the absence of the scheme (or the losses are greater than they would have been in the absence of the scheme);

then the tested amount and the available amount must be calculated as if the scheme or arrangement were not in place (s 309).

These anti-avoidance provisions only apply where the main purpose or one of the main purposes of the scheme is to avoid tax. Where a loan is put in place to provide financing, the main purpose is arguably to provide financing. Structuring the loan in a tax efficient way should not affect this main purpose. However, where existing loans are in place, and are restructured in order to mitigate the impact of the debt cap, the anti-avoidance rules may apply.

In addition, there are certain structures which are specifically excluded from the anti-avoidance rules—see **A17.19** below.

Further provisions were introduced in the Finance Act 2012 to combat avoidance aimed at excluding companies from the definition of 'relevant group companies'. Some groups had attempted to circumvent the definition by using guarantee companies. The provisions do contain a main purpose test so as not to catch 'innocent' companies without a share capital.

Schedule 5 FA 2012 also introduced other changes to TIOPA 2010, Part 7 which on the whole improve the operation of the worldwide debt cap where the initial legislation had been found wanting.

# Planning

## *Splitting loans*

**[A17.14]** Because balances less than £3 million are ignored for the purposes of the gateway test, it may be possible to split loans between two group companies. Similar principles apply to the £500,000 interest de minimis.

For example, in Diagram 4 the US parent company intends to lend £5 million to the UK subgroup (a). If £2.5 million is lent to each UK subsidiary then the net debt in each will be treated as nil and the debt cap will not apply (b). However, if £5 million is lent to one of the subsidiaries the gateway test will not be met.

It will not always be possible to split the debt in this way, for instance where balances are large. The anti-avoidance rules (see **A17.13**) will also need to be considered.

**Diagram 4**

(a)

(b)

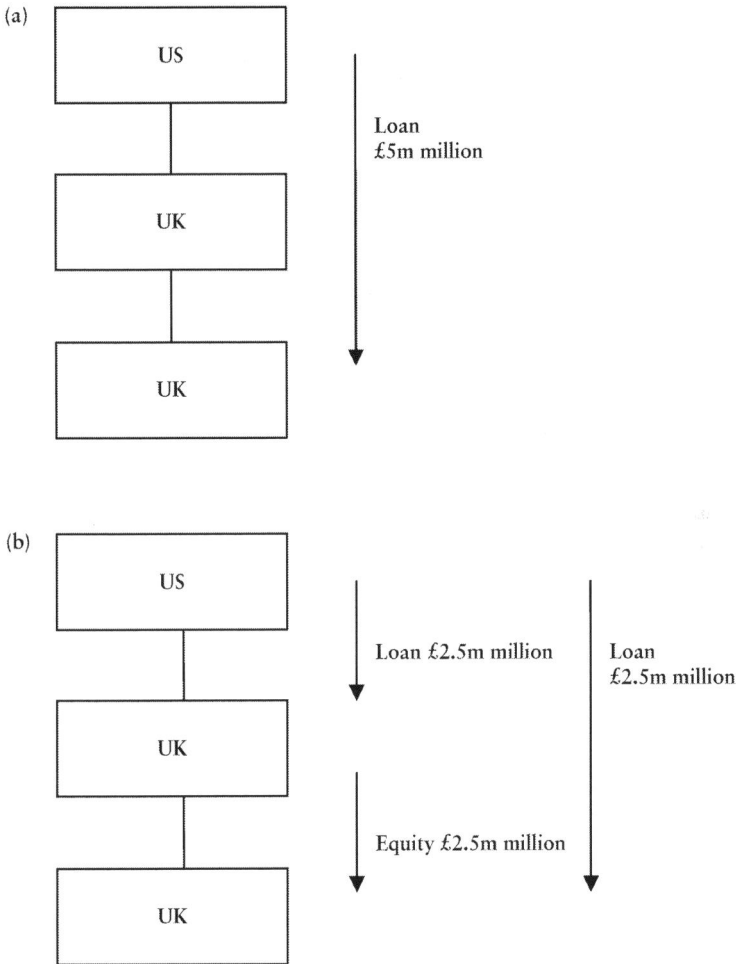

## *Eliminating loans*

**[A17.15]** Where no interest deduction is available in the UK as a result of the debt cap, the interest is likely to remain taxable in the overseas creditor company.

To remove this mismatch, the loan can be eliminated:

- an overseas subsidiary can pay an exempt dividend to repay an upstream loan;
- an overseas parent company could subscribe for further shares, the proceeds of which are used to repay a downstream loan;
- the loan could be waived, providing such a waiver would not be taxable either in the UK debtor company or the overseas creditor company.

## *Deductions which are not interest*

**[A17.16]** The debt cap only applies to interest and other finance expenses. If interest can be replaced with another expense then the debt cap rules should not apply.

In Diagram 5, the US parent company has made a loan of £10m at an interest rate of 10% to its UK subsidiary in order for it to buy a property. The group has no external debt, and therefore the available amount is nil and after applying the debt cap there is no deduction for the interest on the loan. The interest remains fully taxable in the US.

In Diagram 6, the US parent company has instead bought the property itself and charges a rent to the UK subsidiary for the use of the property. The payment of rent is not subject to the worldwide debt cap. The US company will be subject to UK income tax on the rental income (at 20%) but should be able to set this against the US tax on the same income.

The economic result in Diagrams 5 and 6 is the same, but in Diagram 6 the UK company should obtain a tax deduction.

Similar principles should apply to other assets (such as intellectual property) in respect of which rent or royalties can be paid rather than interest.

Diagram 5

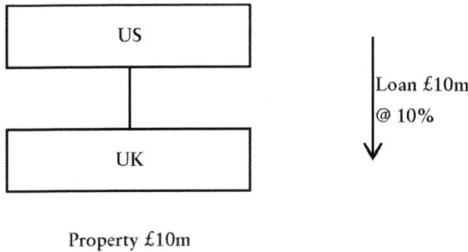

Loan £10m
@ 10%

Property £10m

Diagram 6

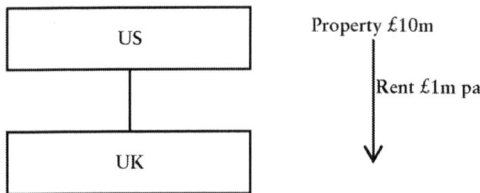

Property £10m

Rent £1m pa

## *Foreign exchange*

**[A17.17]** Foreign exchange movements are not subject to the worldwide debt, and so foreign exchange losses should be deductible in a UK company even if the interest on the corresponding loan is not.

## *Transferring assets intra-group*

**[A17.18]** In Diagram 5 above, the UK company had a disallowance under the debt cap. In Diagram 7, it has sold a subsidiary to a Canadian group company for £10 million, the consideration for which is left outstanding on intercompany loan account. Interest is charged on the inter-company account at 10% per annum.

The interest on the inter-company account should be deductible in the Canadian transferee company.

However, the UK company should not pay any additional tax on the interest because the worldwide debt cap should no longer restrict the deductibility of the interest paid to the US parent company. The available amount remains nil, but the tested amount is now also nil because the net financing expenses of the UK company is nil. There is therefore no disallowance and the interest paid to the US parent company is deductible in full, offsetting the interest income received from the Canadian company.

Diagram 7

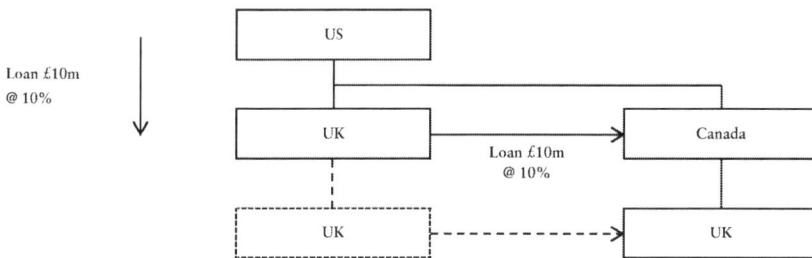

## *Anti-avoidance rules*

### Excluded schemes

**[A17.19]** The anti-avoidance provisions in TIOPA 2010, s 307 (see **A17.13**) do not apply to 'excluded schemes' specified in regulations. So far no regulations have been made, but HMRC consider (CFM92735) that the anti-avoidance rules do not apply to the following structures:

- repaying debt from surplus cash;
- a company repaying debt from the proceeds of a loan repaid to the company;
- an arm's length waiver of a loan;
- capitalisation of a debt;
- repaying an upstream loan with a dividend.

These structures will only be excluded if they do not result in a deduction for a UK company which falls outside the debt cap rules.

**Counterfactual structures**

**[A17.20]** Where the rules do apply, it is important to document both the intentions behind the loan, and any alternative structures which have been considered.

If the anti-avoidance rule in s 307 applies, any calculations for the purposes debt cap are made under the assumption that a 'counterfactual' structure has been adopted. The counterfactual structure is the structure which was most likely to have been adopted in the absence of the debt cap rules.

# A18

# Branch profits

## Introduction

**[A18.1]** Finance Act 2011 introduced a branch profits exemption. Subject to making an election, a company will be exempt in respect of profits arising in its overseas branches.

This chapter sets out when an election can be made, the profits which are exempt, and the situations where the exemption will not apply.

Where an election is not made, the profits of foreign branches remain subject to UK corporation tax, with relief for foreign tax suffered (see **A10.2** and **A10.16**).

## Basic principles

### Election

**[A18.2]** An election can be made at any time after 18 July 2011, to take effect from the day that the subsequent accounting period is expected to begin. An election can only be revoked before the day it becomes effective—after that, an election is irrevocable.

If the subsequent accounting period actually begins on a different day (for example if the accounting date is changed after the election is made), then the profits of the straddling period are apportioned on a just and reasonable basis. The profits falling after the effective date will be exempt (CTA 2009, s 18F(4)).

Once an election is made, it applies to all branches of the company (subject to deferral where a branch has previously made losses—see **A18.7**).

## Effect of election

**[A18.3]** For any period where an election applies, the profits of foreign permanent establishments are not subject to UK corporation tax (CTA 2009, s 18A). These profits are calculated in accordance with TIOPA 2010, s 43, which specifies that the profits attributable to an overseas permanent establishment are the profits which it would have made if:

- it were a distinct and separate enterprise;
- engaged in the same or similar activities;
- under the same or similar conditions;
- dealing wholly independently with the UK parent company;
- with the same credit rating as the UK parent company;
- with equity and loan capital determined under the relevant DTA (if it contains a non-discrimination article) or the OECD Model Tax Convention.

Capital allowances are deducted from the profits, based on the tax written down value of the assets of the branch at the date the election became effective (s 18C).

## Chargeable gains

**[A18.4]** The exemption also applies to chargeable gains made on assets used for the purposes of the permanent establishment, and immoveable property used for the purposes of the permanent establishment.

However, gains are not exempt to the extent that they are before the election is effective (s 18B(3)). For example, a branch of a UK company buys an asset for 100, and then an exemption election becomes effective when the asset is worth 150. The asset is subsequently sold for 250. Under s 18B, 100 of the gain is exempt, but 50 is taxable because it relates to the period before the election became effective.

## Exclusions

**[A18.5]** For small companies, the exemption does not apply to branches in countries with which the UK does not have a DTA which contains a non-discrimination article (full treaty territories). Small companies are as defined under the EU definition in 2003/361/EC (see **A13.8**).

Close companies remain subject to tax on chargeable gains (s 18P(2)), which reflects the attribution of gains from subsidiaries under TCGA 1992, s 13 (see **A15.2**).

The exemption does not apply to any profits or losses arising from transactions where a UK resident would have been obliged to withhold tax

There are also exclusions for certain plant and machinery leasing transactions (s 18C (3)) and insurance companies (s 18Q).

### Anti-diversion

**[A18.6]** The anti-diversion rule in CTA 2009, s 18G provides that the exemption will not apply to branches which are subject to a lower level of tax unless:

- the profits of the branch are less than a de minimis level of £200,000 (s18G (7)); or
- a motive test is satisfied (s18H), the conditions of which are broadly the same as the controlled foreign companies motive test—see **A6.12**.

The definition of lower level of tax is broadly the same definition as applies for CFC purposes—see **A6.10**.

A partial exemption applies where the branch only fails the transaction leg of the motive test ie:

- it was not a main reason for the existence of the branch in the accounting period to achieve a reduction in UK tax by a diversion of profits from the UK; but
- the transactions reflected in the profits for the accounting period achieved a reduction in UK tax, and it was a main purpose of the transaction(s) to achieve that reduction.

In this case, the exemption applies to the profits of the branch, except for the profits arising from the transactions which achieved the reduction in UK tax.

### Deferral where brought forward losses

**[A18.7]** The application of the exemption may be deferred where a branch has previously incurred losses. This effectively prevents double relief for losses where future profits will not be subject to UK tax, but the losses have been previously utilised against other UK profits.

The exemption does not apply where there is an 'opening negative amount' (s 18J). There will be an opening negative amount if the aggregate of the profits and losses (excluding chargeable gains) of all the company's permanent establishments from the previous six years is a loss.

In this case, the exemption will only apply once the losses have been matched against subsequent profits of the company's permanent establishments (s 18K).

CTA 2009, s 18L provides for a streaming election such that deferral can be applied on a branch by branch basis. If an election is made, the branch exemption is only deferred in respect of branches which have previously made losses, and the exemption can apply to other branches immediately,

Where a branch has been transferred between connected companies, the brought forward losses are also treated as having transferred (s 18O).

# Planning

### Relief for losses

**[A18.8]** The deferral of the election outlined at A18.7 is only relevant where losses have been incurred prior to the election. Where future losses are anticipated, planning can be undertaken. The branch exemption applies to all branches of a company, whether they are profitable or not—a company cannot therefore obtain relief for losses from loss-making branches.

If a branch is expected to have ongoing future losses, it could be held by a separate company which does not make an exemption election, as shown in the example below.

Although this structure would appear to give the most favourable result, there are two potential issues. Firstly, a company must have forecasts which allow it to have adequate visibility of losses. Secondly, if a loss-making branch is subsequently transferred to a company which has made an election, the exemption is deferred in respect of the transferred branch (CTA 2009, s 18O).

### Example—separation of branch profits and losses

**[A18.9]** In Diagram 8, Company A holds branches which are expected to make a loss, and does not make a branch exemption election. Any losses arising in the branches can be set against other profits of Company A or (subject to CTA 2010, s 106) surrendered to other group companies.

Company B holds branches which are expected to make a profit, and makes a branch exemption election. This does not affect the availability of losses in Company A.

Diagram 1

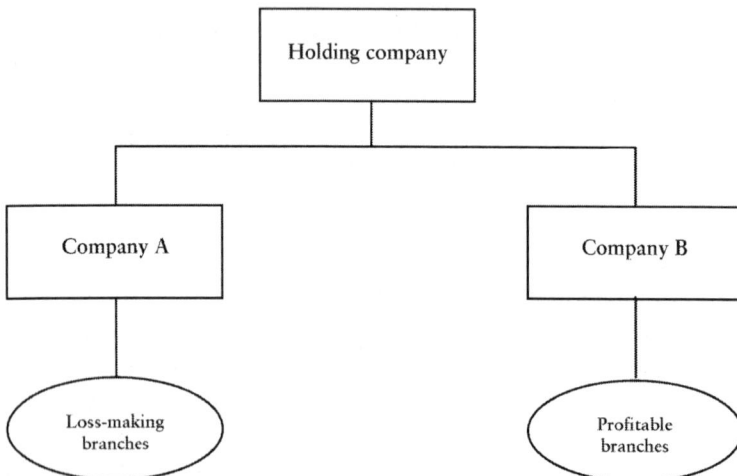

## Timing

**[A18.10]** The timing of an election is important because:

- any losses arising in an exempt branch are not available for relief;
- where a branch is subject to a low overseas tax rate, a company will want the exemption to apply as early as possible.

An election is only effective from the start of the next accounting period of the company. It may therefore be beneficial to change the accounting date prior to making the election, in order to obtain the exemption sooner. If the accounting date is changed after an election is made, the date specified in the election remains applicable, and the profits of any straddling accounting period must be split on a just and reasonable basis.

As noted above, a loss streaming election can be made under s 18L so that branches which have previously incurred losses do not defer the exemption applying to other branches. This streaming election can therefore mean that the exemption applies earlier than otherwise, but there will be a significant amount of compliance to separately record the profits and losses of the branches.

Once an exempt accounting period has begun, the election is irrevocable.

## Foreign tax credits

**[A18.11]** Any foreign tax carried forward under TIOPA 2010, s 73 is effectively lost once a branch exemption election is made. The foreign tax can only be relieved against tax on profits of the same branch (see **A10.23**), which will be exempt following an election.

In this case, a company may consider amending prior year corporation tax returns to reduce the amount of foreign tax which is carried forward. Amendments may include:

- reallocating group relief;
- claiming relief for foreign tax by way of deduction rather than credit (although if a loss is created or increased, this may defer the application of the exemption).

If the foreign tax is effectively lost, this may also reduce or eliminate any deferred tax asset recognised in the company's accounts.

## Creating a branch

**[A18.12]** The exemption only applies to profits attributable to a permanent establishment as defined under a DTA or the OECD model. It does not apply to trading profits generated from activities which are not sufficient to create a permanent establishment.

A company would therefore need to take steps to deliberately create a permanent establishment (which is of course the precise opposite of the advice normally given, where a company would seek to avoid creating a permanent establishment if possible!) Such steps could include acquiring a fixed place of business, and undertaking activities through that place of business which are more than merely preparatory and auxiliary. Where local agents are used, their authority could be extended such that they become dependent agents who conclude contracts on behalf of the UK company.

Certain DTAs may provide for a broader definition of permanent establishment which would apply for the purposes of the exemption. For example, a permanent establishment can be created under the UK/India DTA if certain types of services are performed in India. The exemption would therefore apply to profits arising from such services.

### Branch v subsidiary

**[A18.13]** One of the objectives of the exemption was to tax foreign branches in the same way as foreign subsidiaries. The foreign profits consultation document published in November 2010 stated that 'exempting foreign branch profits will ensure greater alignment between the taxation of foreign branches and foreign subsidiaries'.

However, a number of important differences remain between subsidiaries and branches, including:

- Overseas taxation, in particular on a disposal. A sale of shares in a subsidiary is unlikely to be taxed in the overseas jurisdiction, and the substantial shareholding exemption will apply in the UK. However, a disposal of assets of a permanent establishment is likely to be taxed in the overseas jurisdiction, even if it is exempt in the UK as a result of the branch exemption.
- Additional compliance burdens to calculate the taxable profit of each branch, using the method specified in the relevant DTA or the OECD Model, which may not be the same in every case.
- Application of the CFC rules. The anti-diversion rule in CTA 2009, s 18G has been amended to reflect the change in the CFC rules in 2012, as they apply to exempt branches as well as subsidiaries. However, the availability of exemptions from the CFC rules is likely to be narrower for branches than subsidiaries—in particular it is anticipated that the exemption for finance companies will not apply to branches (see **A6.20**).

Practical and commercial differences will also still be relevant (see **B4.9**). As a result of this, groups still need to consider carefully whether to establish a branch or a subsidiary.

### Compliance

**[A18.14]** The branch exemption will introduce a significant compliance burden for companies that wish to take advantage of it.

Assessing whether to make the election in the first place requires accurate profit and loss forecasts for each separate branch, which many companies may not have. Once the election is made, the profits of each branch must be calculated separately using the principles in the relevant DTA or OECD Model, and applying the adjustments required by the law.

The position is complicated still further if there are losses which defer the commencement of the exemption. Most companies do not maintain a break-down of losses between separate branches, and may not even calculate it accurately using UK tax principles. Prior to the branch exemption, there was no requirement for them to do so as branch losses are usually included within the losses carried forward in the UK trade.

# Part B

## Topics and case studies

# B1

# Overseas companies operating in the UK

**[B1.1]** For UK corporation tax purposes, an overseas company operating in the UK may have:

- a subsidiary;
- a branch (permanent establishment); or
- no presence.

This will in turn determine the UK corporation tax liability of the overseas company. A UK resident subsidiary will be subject to corporation tax on its worldwide income, whereas an overseas company with a permanent establishment in the UK will only be subject to corporation tax on the profits attributable to the permanent establishment.

If it can avoid a tax presence altogether, an overseas company will avoid a UK corporation tax liability. However, in some cases a legal entity will be preferable even where there would otherwise be no tax presence.

It is also important to consider the overseas parent company's tax position, and how the permanent establishment or subsidiary will be treated. There is no point in minimising a UK tax liability if there will be a corresponding increase in the overseas tax liability! This could be the case if the overseas tax rate is higher than the UK rate, and credit is given for UK corporation tax against the overseas tax.

There may also be overseas tax rules which can affect the tax treatment of the UK subsidiary. For example, a US parent company may decide to make a 'check-the-box' election in respect of its UK subsidiary (see **A14.13**). If this election is made, the UK subsidiary would be a 'disregarded entity' for US tax purposes, and treated as a branch of the US parent company. This election would not affect the UK tax position of the subsidiary, which would remain a UK resident company and subject to corporation tax on its worldwide income.

Other taxes (such as VAT and PAYE, which are considered later in this Chapter) may not follow the same rules, and even where there is no permanent establishment for corporation tax purposes, VAT or PAYE registrations may be required.

# Permanent establishment

### Definition of permanent establishment

**[B1.2]** CTA 2009, s 5(2) provides that a company which is not resident in the UK will only be subject to UK corporation tax if it carries on a trade in the UK through a UK permanent establishment. Where it does so, it will be subject to UK corporation tax on all profits that are attributable to the UK permanent establishment.

As the definition of permanent establishment under UK domestic law broadly follows the OECD Model Tax Convention, there are typically only small differences with the UK's double tax agreements (DTAs), for example in relation to construction sites or preparatory and auxiliary activities. One should first of all consider whether a permanent establishment exists under UK domestic law, and only if a permanent establishment does exist does one consider whether the relevant double tax agreement provides relief.

The definition of permanent establishment is outlined in CHAPTER **A4**.

A permanent establishment can exist in two ways:

(a)    a fixed place of business through which the business of the company is carried on;

(b)    an agent in the UK acting on behalf of the non-resident habitually exercising authority to do business on behalf of the company.

### Example 1—selling to UK customers

**[B1.3]** A Inc is a US manufacturer of widgets. To date, it has only traded with US customers but is now looking to sell its widgets to overseas customers.

As such, it has developed a website which is specifically targeted to UK customers, and is hosted with a UK internet service provider (ISP). It has also started delivering widgets directly from its US warehouse to customers in the UK.

A Inc will have a permanent establishment if it has a fixed place of business or if a dependent agent concludes contracts on its behalf in the UK.

Making sales to UK customers does not by itself give rise to a permanent establishment. Although the place of contract may be in the UK (for example if sales are concluded via the website), this is not a decisive factor. Applying the test in the *F L Smidth & Co v Greenwood (Surveyor of Taxes)* 8 TC 193 case requires consideration of 'where do the operations take place from which the profits in substance arise'. In A Inc's case, this is the US as all manufacturing and distribution is undertaken there.

In the UK, HMRC take the view that a server alone or together with a website does not constitute a fixed place of business for a company that is making sales through a website on a server (see *HMRC Press Release of 11 April 2000*).

A Inc should not therefore be subject to UK corporation tax as a result of its UK website or selling widgets to UK customers.

When considering scenarios with the involvement of digital business and the definition of permanent establishment, it is important to consider the OECD Action Plan on Base Erosion and Profit Shifting (BEPS) and in particular the action regarding the digital economy. This is considered in more detail in CHAPTER **A4**.

### *Example 2—business development/trade fairs*

**[B1.4]** A Inc's sales to the UK have begun to increase, and US management feel that there is potential in the UK market. They have decided to employ a business development manager in the UK who will be responsible for visiting potential customers and attending trade shows. The business development manager will be based in a home office.

US managers may also visit the UK to attend trade shows.

The business development manager's home office may be a fixed place of business if it is 'at the disposal of' A Inc as a result of the manager being entitled to use it— in which case it could constitute a permanent establishment of A Inc.

However, under CTA 2009, s 5 a corporation tax liability only arises if A Inc carries on a trade through this permanent establishment (ie if it conducts its business from the manager's home office). If the manager only ever conducts business at trade fairs or customer premises, then A Inc will not carry on a trade through the permanent establishment.

It is also possible that the trade fairs could constitute a permanent establishment if A Inc's attendance at a particular fair is:

(a)     recurrent (every year for a number years);

(b)     advertised such that customers would expect to meet with A Inc there;

(c)     for the purposes of conducting business with customers.

Even if A Inc is carrying on a trade in the UK (either through the home office or the trade fairs), a permanent establishment will not exist if the activities carried on are 'preparatory and auxiliary' to its main activities. Advertising and business development would normally fall within this category, although they are not specifically listed in the UK definition of 'preparatory and auxiliary'.

However, the UK/US DTA does specifically include a broader definition of 'preparatory and auxiliary' activities:

> '5(3)(e)  the maintenance of a fixed place of business for the purpose of advertising for the supply of information, for scientific research, or for similar activities which have a preparatory or auxiliary character, for the enterprise.'

If the activities of the business development manager are restricted to supplying information and advertising to potential customers, they should fall within this definition.

A Inc will also have a UK permanent establishment if it concludes contracts in the UK through a dependent agent. An employee will almost certainly be a dependent agent for these purposes as he is both legally and economically dependent on A Inc.

It is therefore important that the manager does not have the authority to conclude contracts. These terms should be included in his employment contract. Concluding contracts would include agreeing key terms even if he does not actually sign the contracts.

### Example 3—renting premises

**[B1.5]** A Inc's UK business is growing and it has employed additional staff, to provide customer service and administrative support.

It has also rented office premises where all staff (including the business development manager) are located. The address of these premises is shown on business cards and in local trade directories and advertising. Customers are able to phone or visit the premises.

The office premises will certainly constitute a fixed place of business through which A's trade is carried on. The breadth of activities are no longer incidental to the business of A Inc in the US and would not fall within the exclusion for 'preparatory and auxiliary' activities.

It is therefore likely that a permanent establishment will exist for A.

### Factors to determine whether a permanent establishment exists

**[B1.6]** When determining if an overseas company has a permanent establishment in the UK, the following factors should be considered:

*   Does the overseas company have premises in the UK (either owned or rented)?

- Is a UK address advertised in trade directories, on business cards or on the website of the overseas company?
- Are employees of the overseas parent company entitled to use premises?
  - do they have a desk or an office?
  - do they have permanent support (eg a secretary)?
  - do they have sign in as visitors?
  - do they have business cards showing the address or phone number of these premises (which may include a home office)?
- Will the UK activities be preparatory and auxiliary to the main trade of the overseas company? ?For example:
  - quality assurance;
  - market research;
  - storage of goods;
  - (a combination of the above may not be treated as preparatory and auxiliary).
- Do employees work for significant time in a particular location (either for a single period, or for shorter periods but frequently)? For example:
  - trade fairs;
  - client sites;
  - hotels or conference centres.

## Subsidiary v branch

**[B1.7]** If it is determined that a permanent establishment does exist, an overseas company may choose to instead form a subsidiary. There are a number of fundamental differences in the taxation of a branch compared to a subsidiary, and these are summarised in the table below.

In some cases a subsidiary will be beneficial even where there would otherwise be no tax presence. For example, if the UK tax rate is lower than the overseas tax rate, this would ensure that profits are recognised at the (lower) UK tax rate rather than the overseas tax rate (subject to any Controlled Foreign Company (CFC) rules).

| Subsidiary | Branch |
|---|---|
| Separate legal personality. | No separate legal personality. Legally part of the overseas company. |
| Required to file annual financial statements with the Registrar of Companies where they will be publicly available. Financial statements may require a UK audit. | Unless financial statements are published already, required to file financial statements of the overseas company with the Registrar of Companies where they will be publicly available. A UK audit is not required. |
| Copies must be filed with HMRC for tax purposes. | Branch financial statements of the local trade must be filed for tax purposes. |
| Subject to UK corporation tax on worldwide profits. | Subject to UK corporation tax on the activities carried on in the UK. |

| Subsidiary | Branch |
|---|---|
| Depending on overseas tax rules, profits may not be subject to tax in the hands of an overseas parent company until distributed by way of dividend. | Depending on overseas tax rules, the UK branch profits may be subject to tax in the hands of the overseas company as they arise. |
| Relief may be available to the parent company for UK tax suffered on the profits out of which the dividends are paid. | Relief may be available to the overseas company for UK tax suffered on the branch profits. |
| A UK tax deduction should be available for arm's length interest and royalty payments from the subsidiary to the overseas parent company. | No UK tax deduction for interest and royalty payments from the branch to the overseas parent company unless able to do so under the terms of a DTA. |
| Tax losses can be carried forward and set against future profits of the company or be offset against taxable profits of other UK companies within the same group. | Tax losses can be carried forward and set against future profits of the branch. |
| | Tax losses may be offset against taxable profits of other UK companies within the same group, subject to anti-avoidance rules if the losses are also available for offset against the profits of the overseas company. |
| Exit can be achieved by overseas company disposing of the shares in the subsidiary. No UK tax should arise. | Exit can only be achieved by disposing of each of the individual branch assets. UK tax would arise on the disposal of such assets. |
| Closure requires a formal winding up procedure or striking off or the appointment of a liquidator. | Closure is automatic on the cessation of trade. No formal procedure is required. |
| UK stamp duty may arise on the transfer of shares in the UK subsidiary. | No UK stamp duty is payable on the transfer of assets of a UK branch. |
| Stamp duty or land tax may arise on the sale of individual company assets. | Stamp duty or stamp duty land tax may arise on the sale of individual branch assets. |
| Transfer pricing rules will apply to all transactions with related parties unless the group is small or medium sized. | Transfer pricing rules will apply to all transactions with related parties. Profits of the branch are calculated as if it were a separate company. |
| All goods and services supplied may be subject to UK VAT, subject to the registration limit or voluntary registration, including supplies between the subsidiary and parent company. | Goods and services supplied between branch and parent are ignored for UK VAT purposes. UK VAT may apply to external sales subject to the registration limit or voluntary registration. |

The overseas parent company's short-term intentions are often the most important factor when considering the initial structure in the UK:

(a)  if the viability of the UK business is uncertain, a branch is easier to wind up than a subsidiary;

(b)  if the UK business is to be sold, it will be easier to sell the shares in a UK subsidiary than to sell the UK assets—in addition to which a UK tax liability would arise on the sale of the assets.

These intentions should be reviewed on a regular basis, as a subsidiary may be more tax efficient once the viability of the UK business has been proved.

### Example 4—using a UK DTA

[B1.8] B Inc is a Canadian company, whose UK branch has won a significant contract to provide consultancy services to a customer in Turkey. The Turkish customer will withhold tax at 20% under Turkish domestic law on any payments. Because the branch is not a treated as a resident of the UK, the UK/Turkey DTA cannot apply. There is no double tax agreement between Canada and Turkey, and the withholding tax cannot therefore be reduced.

However, if B Inc provided services from a UK subsidiary, the rate of withholding tax would be reduced to 10% under the royalties article of the UK/Turkey DTA.

# Transfer of trade from branch to subsidiary

[B1.9] If a branch is established, it can subsequently be converted to a subsidiary without any UK tax arising—and indeed a subsidiary can be converted to a branch on a similar basis.

CTA 2010, s 940A provides that where a UK trade is transferred from one company (the overseas company) to another (the UK subsidiary) without a change in ownership, there is no balancing event for capital allowances purposes. To the extent that the UK branch had trading losses, these would also be preserved.

Certain conditions must be satisfied in order for s 940A to apply, in particular:

(a)  there must be a transfer of trade or part-trade;

(b)  the transferor and transferee companies must be under 75% common ownership;

(c)  the transferor and transferee companies must be within the charge to corporation tax in respect of the trade or part-trade.

There is no requirement that both companies are UK resident companies—only that they are within the charge to corporation tax. A parent company with a UK branch transferring assets to a 100% UK subsidiary should satisfy these conditions.

Where assets are transferred between two members of a capital gains tax group, the transfer is deemed to take place at no gain/no loss (TCGA 1992, s 171).

There is no longer a requirement in s 170 or s 171 that both companies are UK resident. Section 171 will apply where both companies are within the charge to corporation tax in respect of the assets being transferred. A parent company with a UK branch is within the charge to corporation tax in respect of assets used by its permanent establishment by virtue of TCGA 1992, s 10B.

However, if within six years of the transfer, the UK subsidiary ceases to be a member of the same group as the overseas parent company a degrouping charge will arise under TCGA 1992, s 179.

A problem arises if the branch activities are not completely transferred to the subsidiary. If any assets:

(a)    are transferred outside the UK; or
(b)    remain owned by the parent company when the branch ceases trading.

A capital gain will arise calculated by reference to the current market value of the assets. (TCGA 1992, s 10B). The parent company must therefore ensure that all assets (both tangible and intangible, for example customer lists) are transferred to the branch prior to the branch activity ceasing.

The overseas tax consequences of incorporating the branch activity would also need to be considered.


# Transfer pricing

**[B1.10]** Transfer pricing can be relevant for both a UK branch and a UK subsidiary, although in practice it can be more difficult to determine arm's length transactions between a branch and its parent. For that reason a UK company is often considered to be 'cleaner' for transfer pricing purposes.


## Subsidiary

**[B1.11]** Under TIOPA 2010, Part 4, a UK subsidiary which is part of a large group is required to recognise transactions with connected parties on an arm's length basis.

For a branch, CTA 2009, ss19–32 set out how the profits of a permanent establishment in the UK are calculated. The permanent establishment should recognise profits equal to the profit it would have expected to make had it been as if it had been dealing with an independent non-resident company.

In effect, non-resident companies are required to follow the arm's length principle (using transfer pricing principles and methodologies) to calculate the profits of a UK permanent establishment. The transfer pricing rules are outlined in CHAPTER A13.

This would include all transactions between a non-resident parent company and its UK subsidiary whether explicit or implicit, for instance:

(a)    purchase price for goods;
(b)    royalty payments for the use of the group's brand names;

(c)     management charges paid to the US parent for management services provided.

## Branch

**[B1.12]** In the calculation of the taxable profits of the permanent establishment allowance will be given for expenditure incurred, including administrative expenses, as would be deductible for a UK resident company (see **A4.39**).

However, under CTA 2009, s 31, no deduction is available in respect of royalties, interest or other finance costs which are paid by the permanent establishment to its parent company.

They will only be deductible where the non-resident parent company has made actual payments and some or all of those payments relate directly to the permanent establishment. For example, the parent company may have taken out a loan which is used by the permanent establishment to purchase assets. In this case, the part of the interest relating to the permanent establishment can be attributed to the permanent establishment, and deducted for corporation tax purposes. Care must be taken that the interest does not acquire a UK source such that it is subject to UK withholding tax.

If the parent company provides significant financing or intangible assets to the UK activities, a subsidiary may therefore result in a lower UK tax liability because interest and royalties can be deducted. As an alternative, funding or licencing could be made via a sister company of the parent.

## Intangible assets

**[B1.13]** As a result of its activities in the UK market, a non-resident company may increase the value of its own intellectual property, for example a brand name. If this provides a broader benefit to the group, HMRC may argue that the UK subsidiary should receive a royalty payment from other group members.

To avoid this problem arising, inter-company agreements should clearly set out that any increase in value benefits the overseas parent company rather than the UK subsidiary, and that the UK company does not own any intellectual property or goodwill arising as a result of its activities.

## Transfer pricing strategy

**[B1.14]** The main objectives of a group's transfer pricing policy should be to:

(a)     satisfy local compliance requirements in the UK and elsewhere;
(b)     reduce the group's effective tax rate.

An overseas parent company may already have transfer pricing documentation in place, but this may not be sufficient for UK tax purposes. Both the documentation and the methodologies set out should be reviewed to confirm that they are suitable for UK purposes.

Reducing the effective tax rate would normally be achieved by increasing profits in a low tax jurisdiction and reducing profits in a high tax jurisdiction. With a US parent company, for example, this would mean increasing the profits of the UK subsidiary (which is subject to tax at 21% in the UK once its losses have been utilised) and reducing those of the parent (which is subject to tax at up to 40% in the US).

However, the US parent company may wish to reduce the amount of foreign (ie non-US) tax which is paid, for instance if it is currently unable to utilise all its foreign tax credits. To achieve this objective, the profits of the UK subsidiary would be reduced and those of the US parent increased. If the US parent has made a 'check-the-box' election such that the UK subsidiary is taxed as a branch, then US tax is paid on the profits anyway. In any case, the profits will become subject to US tax when the UK subsidiary pays a dividend.

The group should also consider other factors when determining a suitable transfer pricing policy, including:

(a)    the impact on customs duty and VAT;
(b)    the benefit of a consistent policy in all jurisdictions around the world;
(c)    the ease of implementation and maintenance by local accounting teams;
(d)    the impact on remuneration / bonus targets for local management.

### Transfer pricing methodologies

**[B1.15]** The appropriate transfer pricing methodology will depend in part on the life cycle of the business.

If the UK subsidiary is providing sales and advertising support to the US parent company, then an appropriate methodology may be for the US parent to pay it a commission which is a percentage of sales.

If the UK subsidiary is providing administrative or logistical support to the US parent, then a cost-plus methodology may be more appropriate, under which the US parent would pay a fee to the UK subsidiary equal to its cost base plus a mark up.

However, the UK subsidiary may be a full risk distributor (ie it buys them from the US parent and sells them to customers, assuming all the risks of both transactions). In this case, a fixed profit margin such as would result from a cost-plus or commission methodology would not be appropriate. The UK subsidiary should receive the full amount of income from customers, and then pay an arm's length price for goods from the US parent. This price could be set by considering the price paid by third parties for goods purchased from the US parent.

Of course, it is possible to decide how the UK subsidiary and the US parent should transact in order to achieve the desired transfer pricing strategy.

# Financing the subsidiary

**[B1.16]** Depending on the activities of the UK subsidiary, it may require funding from its parent company. A manufacturing subsidiary may require significant funding for capital investment and working capital, whereas a sales or distribution subsidiary will only require short-term funding to cover costs.

Such funding can take the form of either equity or debt.

## *Equity*

**[B1.17]** Equity is typically harder to repay than debt (even redeemable shares require reserves before they can be repaid), and dividends paid are not deductible for UK tax purposes.

Unlike interest, dividends paid by a UK subsidiary are never subject to withholding tax.

Again, it is important to consider the overseas tax consequences of any funding structure. As the rate of tax in the US is likely to be higher than the rate in the UK, in many cases the payment of interest from the UK to the US may be tax inefficient as it reduces profits taxable at the UK rate and increases profits taxable at the US rate. However, it is important to understand the US tax profile of the group, as the overseas parent company may nonetheless want to reduce its foreign tax because it cannot utilise all of its foreign tax credits.

## *Capital contribution*

**[B1.18]** Some overseas parent companies will look to make a 'capital contribution' to a UK subsidiary, a concept which is not recognised under English law. HMRC consider that capital contributions will be recognised as either a non-taxable gift or (if repayable) as a loan (HMRC Capital Gains manual CG43500). In exceptional circumstances they may be taxable in the UK subsidiary.

## *Debt*

**[B1.19]** There are a number of provisions in UK law which can restrict the deductibility of interest in a UK subsidiary:

- Transfer pricing (see **A13.62**). Interest at a rate which is more than arm's length will not be deductible. On the other hand, if interest is charged at a rate which is less than arm's length, the overseas parent may be required to recognise additional taxable income, which would only be deductible if the relevant DTA allowed the UK subsidiary to claim a compensating adjustment.
- Thin capitalisation (see **A13.62**). The transfer pricing rules will also deny a deduction for interest where the UK subsidiary is thinly capitalised (ie it has more debt than it would be able to obtain from third parties).

- Unallowable purposes. If a loan is taken out for an 'unallowable purpose', CTA 2009, s 441 provides that no deduction is available for the interest. A loan to fund UK trading activities should not fall within these rules, but if the loan is used for other transactions, particularly where they are part of a tax avoidance arrangement, they may apply.
- Anti-arbitrage rules (see **A14.31**). If a loan is treated as a loan for UK tax purposes but as equity for overseas tax purposes the interest may be disallowed under. These provisions only apply where the main purpose of the arrangements is to secure a UK tax advantage, and may not apply where it can be demonstrated that the purpose of the arrangements is to reduce overseas taxes.
- Late paid interest (see **A13.78**). Interest accrued but not paid on a loan from an overseas company may only be deductible when paid if:
  - the overseas company is connected to the UK borrower and is resident in a 'non-qualifying territory';
  - the UK borrower is a close company in which the overseas company is a participator.
- Worldwide debt cap (see CHAPTER **A17**). The worldwide debt cap broadly restricts the amount of interest which can be deducted by a UK group to the amount of third party interest which is incurred by the worldwide group. The cap applies after any other restriction such as transfer pricing or late paid interest.

# Currency

**[B1.20]** The currency of any inter-company loans is an important point which is often overlooked. Foreign exchange gains made on loan relationships are subject to tax (and foreign exchange losses are deductible), even if not realised. This accruals basis can create significant tax liabilities in subsidiaries which would not otherwise be profitable.

## Example 5—non-sterling financing

**[B1.21]** A Inc is a US parent company which has made a loan in US dollars to its UK subsidiary. The UK subsidiary has a sterling functional currency, and as sterling has strengthened against the dollar it has recognised significant foreign exchange gains, on which it has paid tax.

However, no corresponding deduction is available to A Inc because it has not recognised a corresponding foreign exchange loss. Even if it had recognised a foreign exchange loss (for instance the loan was in a third currency), this loss would not be deductible for US tax purposes until the loan was realised—a significant timing disadvantage to the group.

Careful consideration should therefore be given to the currency of loans and future currency movements, in order to avoid the problem outlined in this example.

# VAT

**[B1.22]** Any overseas company which makes VATable supplies in the UK is required to register for VAT if those supplies exceed the registration threshold, regardless of whether or not it has a UK permanent establishment.

For example, an overseas company may be required to register if it:

- sells goods from a UK warehouse;
- undertakes services from a business establishment in the UK—which is a broader definition than 'permanent establishment', and can exist even if there is no permanent establishment;
- undertakes certain types of service (such as scientific, educational or entertainment services) in the UK without a business establishment in the UK.

Overseas companies not required or able to register for VAT in the UK may still be able to recover VAT suffered by making a claim under the 8th EU VAT Directive (for overseas companies in other EU Member States) or the 13th EU VAT Directive. From 1 December 2012 the VAT turnover threshold for non-resident companies was reduced to zero.

## PAYE and NIC

**[B1.23]** An overseas company with employees in the UK may be required to account for PAYE and NIC even if there is no permanent establishment in the UK. HMRC's approach to PAYE for overseas companies is summarised in Appendix 4 of the Employment Procedures Manual (http://www.hmrc.gov.u k/manuals/pommanual/PAYE82000.htm).

In broad terms, if an overseas company has an employee in the UK for more than 183 days in a tax year, PAYE will usually be due. Even if the employee is in the UK for more than 60 days in a tax year, certain information must be provided to HMRC in order to claim exemption from a PAYE withholding obligation.

## Preparation of accounts

**[B1.24]** A UK subsidiary is required to prepare and submit accounts to Companies House, where they are on public record. Depending on the size of the subsidiary and the group, these accounts may require an audit.

There is no requirement to prepare separate accounts for the UK branch if an overseas parent company is required prepare, audit and publicly disclose accounts under the relevant overseas law. In this case, the overseas parent company accounts must be submitted to Companies House in the UK within three months of the deadline for disclosure in the overseas jurisdiction. The fact that an ultimate parent company of the group (and not the parent company of the branch itself) might publicly disclose accounts is not sufficient.

If the overseas parent company is not required to prepare, audit and disclose accounts, it must still submit accounts to Companies House. These accounts could be accounts which are prepared under overseas GAAP but they must include certain information as set out in UK law. This is set out in more detail in the Companies House guidance on Overseas Companies, which is available at www.companieshouse.gov.uk/about/gbhtml/gpo1.shtml.

From a UK tax perspective, it will be necessary to disclose to HMRC the profit or loss of the UK branch and a pro forma balance sheet separately from the overseas parent company, even if this is not shown separately in the parent company accounts. It is not necessary to prepare formal accounts for this, although the figures do need to be calculated under UK GAAP or IFRS.

# Roadmap

**[B1.25]**  The following roadmap can act as a checklist when advising overseas companies operating in the UK, and provides a cross-reference into the relevant Chapters of this book.

(1)     Is there a permanent establishment under UK law? CHAPTER **A4, B1.6**
(2)     Does the DTA provide any relief so that there is no permanent establishment? CHAPTER **A8**
(3)     Should a branch or subsidiary be formed? **B1.7, B1.9**
(4)     Are there any payments of interest and royalties from the UK which are subject to withholding tax? If possible, the overseas company should make a claim to reduce this under a DTA? CHAPTER **A5**
(5)     Transfer pricing policy for calculating profits of branch or subsidiary, including the ownership of intellectual property. CHAPTER **A13**
(6)     Should a subsidiary be financed with debt or equity?
(7)     In respect of debt, consider:
          (a)     Transfer pricing. CHAPTER **A13**
          (b)     Thin capitalization. CHAPTER **A13**
          (c)     Unallowable purposes.
          (d)     Anti-arbitrage. **A14.5**
          (e)     Late paid interest.
          (f)     Worldwide debt cap. CHAPTER **A17**
          (g)     Currency.
(8)     Is there a requirement to register for VAT? **B1.22**
(9)     Is there a requirement to register for PAYE/NIC? **B1.23**
(10)    Is there a requirement to file accounts with Companies House? **B1.24**
(11)    How will BEPS and the UK GAAR impact?

# B2

# Cross border acquisitions

**[B2.1]** There are normally two key considerations when a company makes a cross border acquisition—whether to acquire assets or shares, and whether to fund the acquisition with debt or equity. These considerations will then determine the structure, taking into account the tax position in both the jurisdiction of the target company and the jurisdiction of the acquiring company. In certain circumstances it may also be beneficial to establish a sub-holding company in a third jurisdiction to make the acquisition.

## Structure

**[B2.2]** There are a number of different structures which can be used to effect an acquisition, and these structures are often the same as if the acquiring company were establishing a new business in the target jurisdiction.

### Subsidiary

**[B2.3]** The acquiring company either buys shares in the target company, or establishes a new subsidiary to acquire assets of the target business.

This can be tax efficient if the rate of tax in the subsidiary is lower than the rate of tax in the acquiring company. Subject to Controlled Foreign Companies (CFC) rules (see CHAPTER A6), the profits of the subsidiary may never be subject to tax in the acquiring company until dividends are paid—or not at all if dividends are exempt from tax under a participation exemption.

### Branch

**[B2.4]** If the acquiring company buys assets it is likely that a taxable presence or permanent establishment will be created (see CHAPTER A4). The profits of the branch will usually be taxed in both the target jurisdiction and the acquiring company—subject to an election for branch exemption (see CHAPTER A18), this would be the position if the acquiring company were in the UK.

### Holding company in local jurisdiction

**[B2.5]** Establishing a holding company to acquire shares (or to hold shares in a local subsidiary which then acquires assets) may provide two benefits. Firstly, debt funding can be provided to the holding company in order to make the acquisition (see below). Secondly, dividends can usually be paid to this local holding company—for instance to repay loans or to reinvest in the same jurisdiction—without withholding tax arising.

The CFC rules may apply to this holding company.

### Holding company in a treaty jurisdiction

**[B2.6]** A holding company may be established in a third jurisdiction, which either makes the acquisition directly, or establishes a holding company in the local jurisdiction. This third jurisdiction should have a favourable double tax agreement (DTA) with the local jurisdiction, such that withholding tax on subsequent dividends or capital gains will be reduced.

The CFC rules may apply to this holding company.

### Partnerships/joint venture company

**[B2.7]** If an acquisition is being made jointly with another party, it will be necessary to establish a partnership or a joint venture company—which will have the characteristics of a branch or a subsidiary respectively.

## Funding

### Debt v equity

**[B2.8]** If the acquiring company establishes a sub-holding company to make an acquisition (of either assets or shares), it may fund this company with either debt or equity.

Interest on debt is typically deductible in the sub-holding company but taxable in the acquiring company—this is discussed in more detail below.

However, unlike interest paid on loans, dividends paid on equity will often be exempt from tax under a participation exemption (for example CTA 2009, Part 9A in the UK, which is outlined in Chapter **A16**). There are some participation exemptions which extend to interest but these are less common.

A certain level of equity may also be required to satisfy local thin capitalisation requirements in the sub-holding company.

## Interest deduction

**[B2.9]** As noted above, interest on debt is typically deductible in the sub-holding company but taxable in the parent company. A tax benefit may therefore be obtained if the tax rate in the target jurisdiction (where the sub-holding company is established) is higher than the rate in the parent company jurisdiction.

If a loan has been made to a holding company which makes an acquisition, a tax benefit will only be obtained if the interest on the loan can be set against the trading profits of the target company. For example:

- The trade could be transferred ('hived up') from the target company to the holding company.
- The holding company could form a tax group (or fiscal unity) with the target company, and set the losses arising from the interest against the profits of the target company (by way of consolidation or group relief).

This applies to third party funding provided to the sub-holding company in the same way as funding from the parent company. However, third party funding may be subject to less onerous transfer pricing or thin capitalisation rules. Equally some countries, eg France with its 'Charasse' rules, have targeted anti-avoidance against such planning.

## Restrictions on interest deductibility

**[B2.10]** There may be a number of restrictions on the deductibility of interest, including:

- thin capitalisation requirements as to debt/equity ratios;
- transfer pricing requirements on the rate of interest;
- earnings stripping rules which for example restrict the interest deduction to a percentage of profits.

These rules will vary from jurisdiction to jurisdiction, and may not exist at all in some—for example, Sweden does not have thin capitalisation rules although it is understood that the Swedish government are currently proposing stricter rules on interest deductibility.

### Withholding tax

**[B2.11]** In addition, withholding taxes may be due on interest paid either intra-group or to third party lenders (see CHAPTER A5). These withholding taxes may be reduced under the terms of a relevant DTA (or the Interest and Royalties Directive in the EU), but clearance may be required before the interest is paid.

Different rates of withholding tax may apply to dividends and interest, and this may also influence the funding structure.

### Hybrid financing structures

**[B2.12]** Debt may be provided by a finance company in such a way that it is not subject to tax on the interest. This may be because the finance company is not a taxable entity, or because it obtains a deduction for interest either paid or deemed to paid

Some of these hybrid financing structures are outlined in A14.30, but it should be noted that for loans made to a UK company to make an acquisition, the anti-arbitrage rules may restrict the interest deduction.

## Acquisition of a UK business

**[B2.13]** The same principles will apply when an overseas company makes an acquisition in the UK. The overseas company can establish a holding company in the UK which can obtain a loan to make the acquisition from a third party or from the parent company. The interest on the loan can be surrendered by way of group relief to the target company.

Interest deductibility may be restricted by transfer pricing, thin capitalisation (both in TIOPA 2010, Part 4 and outlined in CHAPTER A13) or the worldwide debt cap (TIOPA 2010, Part 7 and outlined in CHAPTER A17). The late paid interest rules (CTA 2009, s 373 and outlined in A13.78) will also be relevant for 'close' groups and for groups with loans from non-qualifying jurisdictions (ie those with which the UK does not have a double tax agreement which includes a non-discrimination article).

If loans are provided via a hybrid financing arrangement, the anti-arbitrage rules (TIOPA 2010, Part 6 and outlined in A14.31) will apply to restrict interest deductibility if the arrangements were designed to avoid UK tax. This structure is illustrated in Example 3 (which reflects to some extent Example 1 in the HMRC guidance 'Avoidance involving tax arbitrage').

Withholding tax of 20% is due on UK source interest (which will include most interest paid by a UK company). This may be reduced under the terms of a DTA or the EU Interest and Royalties Directive, but it is important to obtain the relevant clearance before interest is paid. It is usually best to complete this at the time of the acquisition when other financing documents are signed. The new Treaty Passport rules may also be relevant.

## Future intentions

**[B2.14]** When structuring an acquisition it is also important to determine the intentions of the acquiring company. If the target company is likely to be profitable, there may be some benefit in providing loans to a local company which makes the acquisition. A tax deduction for interest may then be available. It may also be important to establish a holding company in a third jurisdiction to reduce withholding tax on dividends.

If a capital gain is intended, the extraction of profits may be less important. However, it will be important that no tax arises on a subsequent disposal, and it may therefore be necessary to establish a holding company in a jurisdiction which has a beneficial DTA. Alternatively, a holding company may be established in a third jurisdiction, and the shares in this holding company sold, rather than the shares in the target company.

If the disposal is likely to be an asset disposal (for example the disposal of a division which is not required), then acquiring assets will provide an additional benefit, as it will establish a base cost, and reduce the subsequent gain.

The tax consequences of the capital gains which arise under these structures are outlined in CHAPTER A13.

## Asset acquisitions

**[B2.15]** An asset acquisition will typically lead to a taxable gain arising for the vendor. Although some jurisdictions do not charge capital gains tax, there may still be a claw back of allowances or tax depreciation which has previously been claimed. Brought losses may reduce this taxable gain, but there may be restrictions on the set off of trading losses against capital gains.

A participation exemption will not usually apply to a disposal of assets, although in some jurisdictions an exemption may apply to assets of an overseas branch.

These are the same principles which apply in the UK. A UK company which disposes of assets will have a chargeable gain on both tangible and intangible assets (including goodwill), as well as a balancing allowance or charge on assets in respect of which capital allowances have previously been claimed.

However, a purchaser will typically prefer an asset acquisition as it provides 'step up' in the base cost of the assets. This will increase the allowances, tax depreciation or amortisation of intangible assets which are available following the acquisition.

The only potential disadvantage to a purchaser is any transfer tax which may arise on certain assets (usually property). However, such transfer tax may in any case arise on a share acquisition. Some tax efficient property acquisition structures are outlined in CHAPTER A3.

## Share acquisitions

**[B2.16]** In the absence of specific provisions otherwise, a share acquisition will not lead to a step up in the base cost of underlying assets.

However, a vendor of shares may obtain a tax exempt gain as a result of a participation exemption (such as the substantial shareholding exemption in the UK). The conditions for such an exemption will vary by jurisdiction, and may require the vendor to have a minimum shareholding or to hold the shares for a minimum period.

Because the target company will continue in existence, any historical tax liabilities will remain due, and may have to be funded by the purchaser. It is therefore important to undertake full due diligence on the target company to determine what historical liabilities exist.

Stamp duties or transfer taxes are typically lower on shares than on assets, although some jurisdictions will tax the sale of shares in real estate companies in the same way as a sale of real estate. For example, the sale of more than 50% of the shares in a Spanish real estate company will trigger a charge to real estate transfer tax, whereas in Germany the threshold is 95%. A purchaser may seek to avoid this charge by acquiring a shareholding just below these thresholds.

If the target company was previously the member of a group or a fiscal unity, there may be degrouping charges (which may arise either to the target company or the vendor) when it leaves the group or unity. Such degrouping charges would for example arise in the UK (under TCGA 1992, s 179) or in the Netherlands (where assets and liabilities are revalued when a fiscal unity is broken).

There may be other consequences of a change in control of the target company, for example losses may be eliminated in whole or part. In the US for example, relief for losses is limited following a change in control by reference to the value of the company at the time of the change in control multiplied by the relevant interest rate which is set by the tax authorities.

## Examples

### Example 1

**[B2.17]** A UK company is looking to acquire the shares of a French company. The French tax rate is 33.33%, compared with the UK tax rate of 21%.

It will therefore be beneficial for interest to be paid from France to the UK, as the interest will be deductible at 33.33% and only taxable in the UK at 21%. In order to achieve this, the UK company will need to establish a French holding company to make the acquisition. The French holding company will be included as part of a consolidated group with the French target company, and the interest deduction set against its trading profits.

## Example 2

**[B2.18]** A UK company is looking to acquire the shares of a German company. As in Example 1, the German tax rate is higher than the UK rate, and a loan will therefore be made to a German holding company which will form a fiscal unity with the German target company.

However, there will be a restriction on the amount of interest which can be deducted, under the German earnings stripping rules. These rules restrict the interest deduction to 30% of (broadly) EBITDA (earnings before interest, tax, depreciation and amortisation), subject to a de minimis of €3 million.

The UK company will also need to consider the consequences of a change in control of the German target company. Any brought forward losses may be eliminated on the change in control, and if the German company has German real estate then a real estate transfer tax charge may arise.

The UK company should also undertake due diligence on the German target company as any historical tax liabilities will remain after the acquisition. It may be possible to obtain indemnities from the vendor against such liabilities.

## Example 3

**[B2.19]** A US company establishes a UK holding company to acquire the shares in a UK target company. The US company makes a loan to the UK holding company to fund the acquisition on which interest is charged. A third party bank also makes a loan to the UK holding company.

Losses arise to the UK holding company as a result of the interest paid which it can surrender by way of group relief to the UK target company.

Under the UK/US DTA, the withholding tax on the interest is reduced to 0%. The US company should obtain clearance from HMRC to obtain this reduced rate, in advance of receiving the interest.

For US tax purposes, the US company can make a 'check-the-box' election, as a result of which the UK company is treated as a 'disregarded entity'. The US company is then treated as having made a loan to itself, and no interest income is recognised for US tax purposes. In addition, the US company will receive a deduction for the interest on the loan from the bank.

Under the UK anti-arbitrage rules (see **A14.31**), this 'check-the-box' election may prejudice the deductibility of the interest if the acquisition would otherwise have been funded by way of equity from the US company. It will therefore be important to document the intention of the US company to provide a loan.

# Roadmap

**[B2.20]** The following roadmap can act as a checklist when advising on cross-border acquisitions, and provides a cross-reference into the relevant chapters of this book.

(1) Does any tax arise in the target company on a change in control?

(2) Undertake proper due diligence on the target company to identify historic tax issues.

(3) If the target company will undertake transactions with other group companies following the acquisition, consider a new transfer pricing policy. CHAPTER **A13**

(4) Which company in the acquiring group should make the acquisition? Consider:
    (a) Controlled foreign company rules. CHAPTER **A6**
    (b) Taxation of gains on future disposal.
    (c) Taxation of dividends. CHAPTER **A16**

(5) What acquisition structure should be used? **B2.2**:
    (a) Subsidiary.
    (b) Branch.
    (c) Holding company in local jurisdiction.
    (d) Holding company in a treaty jurisdiction.

(6) Should the assets or shares in the target company be acquired? **B2.15–B2.16**

(7) If a new company is established to make the acquisition, should it be funded by debt or equity? **B2.8**

(8) For debt, consider:
    (a) Restrictions on interest deduction. CHAPTER **A13**
    (b) Withholding tax on interest, and reducing this under a DTA. CHAPTER **A5**
    (c) Hybrid financing structures. CHAPTER **A14**

(9) How will BEPS and the UK GAAR impact?

# B3

# Establishing a holding company

**[B3.1]** There are a number of occasions when a multinational group must consider the best location for a holding company, including:

- migration or redomiciliation of an existing holding company to another jurisdiction (see CHAPTER **B8**);
- establishing a sub-holding company through which to make an acquisition or through which to expand its business into new jurisdictions;
- establishing a new holding company prior to listing on a stock exchange.

The best location from a tax perspective will be one which minimises the tax on income and gains generated by the group, and therefore the return to shareholders. This will in turn depend largely on the location of the group's subsidiaries, and the location of its shareholders.

## UK as a holding company jurisdiction

**[B3.2]** With the recent reforms to the taxation of foreign profits, the UK has become an increasingly attractive place in which to establish a holding company:

- Exemption for dividends received.
- Exemption for capital gains under the substantial shareholding exemption.
- No withholding tax on dividends paid to shareholders.

- A good network of double tax agreements (DTAs) to reduce withholding tax on dividends received from subsidiaries.

However, the controlled foreign company (CFC) rules can still be onerous despite recent and proposed reforms (see CHAPTER A6).

# Tax considerations

**[B3.3]** The desirable features for a holding company from a tax perspective are typically:

- Low or no tax on incoming dividends. Dividends may be exempt, or simply subject to a lower level of tax.
- Low or no capital gains tax on a sale of assets or shares. Gains may be exempt, or subject to a lower level of tax.
- If the holding company will also be providing financing to subsidiaries, low or no tax on interest received.
- No withholding tax on dividends and interest payments to shareholders and other investors.
- Low or no capital or stamp duties on share issues or transfers.
- Limited or no CFC legislation, so that profits of low-taxed subsidiaries are not subject to additional tax. Low-taxed subsidiaries may be used to hold the group's intellectual property or act as a group finance company.
- Availability of benefits under DTAs or the EU Parent Subsidiary Directive to reduce withholding taxes on dividends received from subsidiaries.

The relative importance of these features will depend on the nature of the group—a group which is looking to generate income rather than gains will be more concerned with the taxation of dividends (and the availability of reduced rates of withholding tax under a DTA) than the taxation of capital gains.

Table 1 sets out the features of some common holding company jurisdictions

## *Double tax agreements*

**[B3.4]** The availability of benefits under a DTA will depend on where subsidiaries are located. It is important to choose a holding company jurisdiction based on where subsidiaries are (or are likely to be) located. Certain holding company jurisdictions will work well in some cases but not others, due to the extent of their DTA networks.

This is illustrated in Example 1 at the end of this Chapter.

**[B3.5]** Care must be taken that the benefit of a DTA is actually available. Certain jurisdictions have anti-treaty shopping rules which will deny the benefit of a DTA (see A8.69). For example:

- China requires that the recipient has beneficial ownership of any income, as defined under Chinese domestic law (which is not the same as the OECD definition).

- US DTAs typically have anti-conduit and limitation on benefit articles. For example, an unlisted UK holding company which is owned by Jersey residents will not typically qualify under the limitation on benefits article in the UK/US DTA.
- Germany requires that a parent company is either listed on a stock exchange or is a trading company. Unlisted holding companies will not therefore qualify for benefits under a DTA.

The same principle applies to withholding tax on dividends paid to shareholders. Withholding tax should be reduced or eliminated under either a DTA or domestic law, and this will depend on where the shareholders are located.

Different jurisdictions may work best for different subsidiaries of a group, and it is sometimes tempting to establish a sub-holding company for each subsidiary. This can be very tax effective, but should be used cautiously. Minimising the number of holding company jurisdictions will make it easier to maintain the group, from both the perspective of tax residence and corporate law.

## Commercial factors

**[B3.6]** There will also be commercial factors to consider such as:

- Political and economic stability.
- Robustness of legal system.
- Financial reporting requirements.
- Complexity of local administration.
- Costs of company maintenance.

Finally, accessibility will be a factor. In order for the company to be treated as resident outside the UK, it will be necessary that the company is managed and controlled from its jurisdiction of incorporation. Directors based outside the jurisdiction will need to be easily able to attend board meetings.

Where dividends are taxable, relief may be available (unilaterally or under the terms of a relevant DTA) for underlying tax suffered in the subsidiary.

The rules on dividends, capital gains and capital duties/net worth taxes/stamp duties may be different where the subsidiary or holding company holds local property.

TABLE 1

| | Dividends | Capital gains | Withholding tax on dividends paid under domestic law | Treaty network / access to EU Directives | Net worth tax / capital duties / stamp duties on shares | CFC rules |
|---|---|---|---|---|---|---|
| Cyprus | Exempt | Exempt | 0% | Good treaty network and within the EU | No net worth tax or stamp duty 0.6% capital duty on issue of shares | No |
| Hong Kong | Exempt | Exempt | 0% | Limited treaty network | No net worth tax or capital duty 0.1% stamp duty | No |
| Ireland | 12.5% on dividends of trading profits from subsidiary in EU/DTA jurisdiction 25% on other dividends | Exempt where 5% trading subsidiary in EU/DTA jurisdiction 25% on other gains | 0% to shareholders in EU/DTA jurisdiction provided not controlled by Irish residents 20% in other cases | Good treaty network and within the EU | No net worth tax or capital duty 1% stamp duty | No |

| | | | | | | |
|---|---|---|---|---|---|---|
| Isle of Man Jersey Guernsey | Exempt | Exempt | 0% | Limited treaty network | No net worth tax, capital duty or stamp duty | No |
| Luxembourg | 100% exemption where<br><br>10% subsidiary or cost > €1.2m in EU/DTA jurisdiction (or similar tax to Luxembourg) held for 12 months<br><br>50% exemption on other dividends, remainder taxed at 21.84% | 100% exempt where<br><br>10% subsidiary or cost > €6m in EU/DTA jurisdiction (or similar tax to Luxembourg) held for 12 months<br><br>50% exemption on other gains, remainder taxed at 21.84% | 0% to parent company in DTA jurisdiction with similar corporate tax to Luxembourg<br><br>15% in other cases | Good treaty network and within the EU | No capital duty or stamp duty<br><br>0.5% net worth tax (subject to exemption on the same basis as dividends) | No |
| Malta | Exemption where | Exempt where | 0% | Good treaty network and within the EU | No net worth tax or capital duty | No |

| | 10% subsidiary | | | | | Limited |
|---|---|---|---|---|---|---|
| | 10% subsidiary | subsidiary in EU, subject to at least 15% tax rate or receives < 50% passive interest or royalties 35% on other dividends | (except where parent company is controlled by Maltese resident individuals) | | 2% stamp duty (usually only applies to domestic transactions) | Limited |
| Netherlands | Exempt where 5% subsidiary subsidiary holds < 50% portfolio investments or subject to at least 10% tax rate | subsidiary in EU, subject to at least 15% tax rate or receives < 50% passive interest or royalties 35% on other gains; Exempt where 5% subsidiary subsidiary holds < 50% portfolio investments or subject to tax at a rate of least 10% | 0% to parent company holding at least 5% | Good treaty network and within the EU | No net worth tax, capital duty or stamp duty | |

| | 25% on other dividends | 25% on other gains | 15% in other cases | | | |
|---|---|---|---|---|---|---|
| Singapore | Exempt where subsidiary subject to at least 15% headline tax rate; profits distributed have been subject to tax in the subsidiary; 17% on other dividends | Exempt | 0% | Good treaty network | No net worth tax or capital duty; 0.2% stamp duty | No |
| United Kingdom | Small group: exempt where subsidiary in DTA jurisdiction; Medium/large group: exempt if dividend falls within exempt class; 21% on other dividends | Exempt where; 10% trading subsidiary; trading group; 21% on other gains | 0% | Good treaty network and within the EU | No net worth tax or capital duty; 0.5% stamp duty | Yes |

Where dividends are taxable, relief may be available (unilaterally or under the terms of a relevant DTA) for underlying tax suffered in the subsidiary.

The rules on dividends, capital gains and capital duties/net worth taxes/stamp duties may be different where the subsidiary or holding company holds local property.

## Shareholder tax issues

**[B3.7]** The tax position of shareholders must also be considered when establishing a holding company. Even if taxes are minimised in the corporate structure, a shareholder will nonetheless receive a lower return if they suffer tax themselves.

For a listed company, any reduced return to shareholders because of tax may also have an impact on its share price.

A shareholder's tax position will be affected by a number of factors, including (with specific reference to UK resident shareholders):

### Shareholder anti-avoidance

**[B3.8]** The following anti-avoidance provisions are relevant to UK shareholders (companies and individuals) in overseas companies:

- A UK resident company holding at least 25% of the shares in a non-UK holding company may be subject to the controlled foreign company rules (ICTA 1988, s 747) which would attribute the income of the holding company to the shareholder (see CHAPTER **A6**).
- A UK resident individual subscribing for shares in a non-UK holding company may be subject to the transfer of assets abroad rules (ITA 2007, s 714) which would again attribute the income of the holding company to the shareholder (see **A15.5**).
- If the holding company is an 'offshore fund', gains realised on the disposal of shares may be recharacterised as dividends and subject to higher rates of tax (see **A15.34**).

Similar rules to those outlined above may exist for shareholders resident outside the UK, and it is therefore important to understand where shareholders are (or are likely to be) resident when determining the holding company jurisdiction.

### Tax rate on dividends received

**[B3.9]** The following points are relevant when determining the rate of tax paid on dividends received by UK shareholders (companies and individuals) from overseas companies:

- A small UK resident company receiving a dividend from a holding company in a 'non-qualifying territory' (ie one with which the UK does not have a DTA containing a non-discrimination article) will not satisfy the conditions for the dividend exemption (see **A16.3**).

- A UK resident individual holding at least 10% of the shares in a non-UK holding company in a 'non-qualifying territory' will not receive a tax credit and will therefore pay tax on dividends at an effective rate of 10%/32.5%/37.5% rather than 0%/25%/30.55%.

Again, similar rules to those outlined above may exist for shareholders resident outside the UK, with different tax rates on dividends received from holding companies in different jurisdictions.

### Withholding taxes

**[B3.10]** Table 1 shows that some jurisdictions levy withholding tax on dividends. Certain shareholders (for example exempt funds) may not be able to obtain credit for withholding tax on dividends paid by a holding company, and such withholding tax will therefore represent an absolute cost.

This withholding tax may be reduced if a DTA is in place between the jurisdictions in which the shareholder and the holding company are resident (see CHAPTER **A8**). However, even where a DTA is available, the withholding tax may not be eliminated entirely. There may also be considerable compliance required in order to obtain relief under this agreement such as obtaining a residence certificate or a clearance from the relevant tax authorities.

This is illustrated in Example 2.

### Refund of tax to shareholders

**[B3.11]** Certain holding company jurisdictions may refund tax to a shareholder. In Malta, for example, a shareholder receiving a dividend is entitled to a refund of part of the tax paid by the company paying the dividend (the part refunded depends on the nature of the income out of which the dividend is paid).

This can reduce the effective rate of Maltese tax to 5% but does require an application to be made by the shareholder, which may be onerous where there a large number of shareholders. It is therefore common for a second holding company to be placed above the Maltese holding company, which can then receive the refund of Maltese tax without distributing a dividend to shareholders.

### Example 1—Eastern Europe

**[B3.12]** M plc is a new company which is being funded by private shareholders in advance of an IPO. Funds are being raised to invest in property development projects in Eastern Europe. Each of these projects will be undertaken by a local special purpose vehicle (SPV), which will be funded by a mixture of debt and equity, subject to local thin capitalisation rules.

M plc should therefore be established in a jurisdiction which provides:

- DTAs with the Eastern European jurisdictions, under which the rates of withholding tax on dividends and interest are reduced;

- low or no tax on dividends or interest received

Both Cyprus and the Netherlands would provide these, as illustrated in Table 2.

|  | Moldova | Romania | Ukraine |
|---|---|---|---|
| Withholding tax rates in the absence of a DTA | | | |
| Dividends | 15% | 16% | 5% |
| Interest | 10% | 16% | 10% |
| | | | |
| Withholding tax rates under the DTA with Cyprus | | | |
| Dividends | 5% | 0% | 0% |
| Interest | 5% | 10% | 0% |
| | | | |
| Withholding tax rates under the DTA with the Netherlands (assuming less than USD300 000 invested in each SPV) | | | |
| Dividends | 5% | 0% | 5% |
| Interest | 5% | 0% | 10% |

In order to obtain the best possible tax position, it would be possible to establish a holding company in the Netherlands to hold the Romanian SPVs, and a holding company in Cyprus to hold the other SPVs. However, this would lead to additional legal complexity and it would be necessary for the directors to hold board meetings in both the Netherlands and Cyprus in order to establish residence for tax purposes.

On balance, therefore, M plc decides that a Cyprus holding company is likely to provide the better overall result. In addition, Cyprus will not tax the dividends received, and there will be no withholding tax on dividends paid to shareholders (which may include parent companies resident in offshore jurisdictions).

Interest received in the Cyprus holding company will be subject to tax, but a deduction will be available for any interest paid. There are no thin capitalisation rules in Cyprus, but the interest paid must be at an arm's-length interest. There is no withholding tax on interest paid by a Cyprus company.

The effective rate of tax on interest received can therefore be reduced by the Cyprus company paying interest to a holding company in a third jurisdiction, as shown in Diagram 1.

Diagram 1

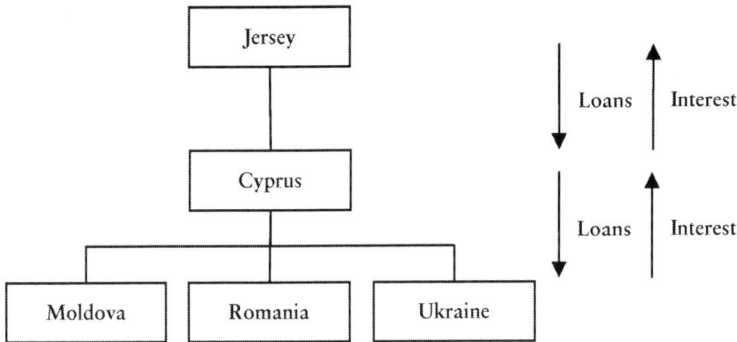

*Example 2—listed company*

**[B3.13]** D SA was established 10 years ago as a private company in Luxembourg. It originally had a small number of shareholders who were all resident in the EU and jurisdictions with which Luxembourg had a DTA. Withholding tax on dividends was therefore reduced under DTAs and the EU Parent Subsidiary Directive.

Subsequently, D SA has been listed on the UK AIM market and has a number of institutional shareholders, including funds which are resident in Jersey and other low tax jurisdictions. There are no DTAs between Luxembourg and these jurisdictions, and the domestic rate of withholding tax of 15% applies on dividends paid to these institutional shareholders. And with the increase in the number of other shareholders, there is also an increase in the paperwork required to claim a reduced rate of withholding tax even where there is a DTA in place.

D SA is therefore considering migrating or redomiciling to another jurisdiction, which offers:

• no withholding tax under domestic law so that there is no tax cost to institutional shareholders (or compliance requirement under DTAs);
• no tax on dividends or capital gains received, so that the institutional (and other) shareholders receive a return which has not been taxed in the group;
• corporate law which is easy to operate with a large number of shareholders.

The subsidiaries of D SA are located in jurisdictions which themselves have no withholding tax on dividends under domestic law (including Malta and Cyprus), and it is therefore not necessary that the holding company jurisdiction has an extensive network of DTAs.

D SA therefore decides to move to one of the UK offshore centres—Isle of Man, Jersey or Guernsey.

## Roadmap

**[B3.14]** The following roadmap can act as a checklist when advising on where to establish a holding company, and provides a cross-reference into the relevant chapters of this book (in relation to UK tax treatment of holding companies).

(1) Tax position of the holding company:
- (a) Tax on dividends received. CHAPTER **A16**
- (b) Tax on capital gains.
- (c) Capital duties and stamp duties.
- (d) Controlled Foreign Company rules. CHAPTER **A6**

(2) Double tax agreements to reduce withholding tax on dividends received from subsidiaries. CHAPTER **A8**

(3) Tax position of shareholders:
- (a) Withholding taxes on dividends paid by the holding company. CHAPTER **A5**
- (b) Tax rate on dividends received. CHAPTER **A15**
- (c) Anti-avoidance rules. CHAPTER **A15**

(4) Commercial factors.

(5) How will BEPS and the UK GAAR impact?

# B4

# UK companies setting up overseas

## Introduction

**[B4.1]** This Chapter is a case study outlining the issues faced when a UK company sets up activities overseas. A UK company is looking to expand its activities overseas, and in particular it will establish:

(a)    a factory in France;
(b)    a sales office in the US;
(c)    a sales office in Brazil.

This is shown in Diagram 1.

Diagram 1

**Taxable presence**

**[B4.2]** As a result of its activities, the UK company may have a liability to tax in these overseas jurisdictions. In particular, it may have created a permanent establishment.

### *Permanent establishment*

**[B4.3]** In order to determine whether a permanent establishment exists in France, Brazil and the US, the correct process is:

(a)     determine whether a permanent establishment exists under domestic law in the jurisdiction in question;

(b)     if a permanent establishment exists under domestic law, determine whether a permanent establishment exists under the double tax agreement (DTA) between the UK and the jurisdiction in question.

The definition of permanent establishment under UK domestic law is not relevant.

It is possible to short-cut the determination of whether a permanent establishment exists under domestic law. If no permanent establishment exists under the relevant DTA, then no permanent establishment should exist, even if one is determined to exist under domestic law, as the DTA normally has precedence over domestic law. However, this can sometimes be a high-risk approach as it does not take account of any requirements of domestic law which must be met in order to take advantage of the DTA.

### France

**[B4.4]** Article 4 of the UK/France DTA provides that:

'1.     The term "permanent establishment" shall include especially: ...

(2)     a factory;'

The DTA would therefore allow the French authorities to tax the profits arising in respect of the activities of the factory. The amount of the profits which could be subject to tax would be determined in accordance with Article 6 of the DTA:

'Where an enterprise of a Contracting State carries on business in the other Contracting State through a permanent establishment situated therein, there shall in each Contracting State be attributed to that permanent establishment the industrial or commercial profits which it might be expected to make if it were a distinct and separate enterprise engaged in the same or similar activities under the same or similar conditions and dealing at arm's length with the enterprise of which it is a permanent establishment.

. . .

Insofar as it has been customary in a Contracting State to determine according to its law the profits to be attributed to a permanent establishment on the basis of an apportionment of the total profits of the enterprise to its various parts, nothing in paragraph 2 shall preclude that Contracting State from determining the profits to be taxed by such an apportionment as may be customary; the method of apportionment adopted shall, however, be such that the result shall be in accordance with the principles contained in this Article.'

## US

**[B4.5]** Article 4(4) of the UK/US DTA provides that a permanent establishment does not include:

'(1)    the maintenance of a fixed place of business solely for the purpose of carrying on, for the enterprise, any other activity of a preparatory or auxiliary character;'

The UK company may therefore have a fixed place of business in the US (the sales office) but no permanent establishment, provided the employees are only undertaking activities which are preparatory to its main business.

The nature of the activities must be considered in relation to the activities of the parent company. If the sales office is actually owned by a company which undertakes no other activity (as in Diagram 2), then the activities of the sales office are unlikely to be considered preparatory and auxiliary, as there is no larger trade of which they are part.

In addition, Article 4(5) of the UK/USA DTA provides that:

'. . . where a person–other than an agent of an independent status to whom paragraph 6 of this Article applies–is acting on behalf of an enterprise and has and habitually exercises in a Contracting State an authority to conclude contracts that are binding on the enterprise, that enterprise shall be deemed to have a permanent establishment in that State in respect of any activities that the person undertakes for the enterprise, unless the activities of such person are limited to those mentioned in paragraph 4 of this Article that, if exercised through a fixed place of business, would not make this fixed place of business a permanent establishment under the provisions of that paragraph.'

The employees of the UK company's sales office will be 'acting on behalf of an enterprise', and will not be agents 'of an independent status' as they will be legally and economically bound to the UK company by virtue of being employees.

If these employees have and habitually exercise 'an authority to conclude contracts that are binding on the enterprise' then the UK company will have a permanent establishment in the US.

The authority of employees should therefore be limited and they should not have the authority to conclude contracts, or agree terms of contracts, which would bind the UK company.

## Advantages and disadvantages of a permanent establishment

**[B4.6]** If there is no permanent establishment, then profits of the overseas activities would only be subject to UK corporation tax.

If there is a permanent establishment, then tax may arise in the overseas jurisdiction. Where the rate of tax in that jurisdiction is higher that the corporation tax rate in the UK, additional tax may arise.

The existence of a permanent establishment will also increase compliance obligations, as the UK company would likely be required to file a tax return in the overseas jurisdiction in respect of the results of the permanent establishment.

In the case of France and the US, where the rates of tax are significantly higher than in the UK, the UK company is therefore unlikely to want to create a permanent establishment.

However, in certain cases, it may be beneficial to create a permanent establishment. Under Brazilian domestic law, for instance, if a non-resident company has Brazilian income without a permanent establishment, tax may be calculated on the basis of the gross amount of sales, or by way of withholding tax from amounts paid to the non-resident. Depending on the profitability of the activity in Brazil, this may result in more tax arising than would be the case if a permanent establishment existed.

## State and local taxes

**[B4.7]** Even if no permanent establishment exists, the UK company may be subject to other taxes in the overseas jurisdictions.

In the US, each state may charge tax if activities have a 'nexus' with the state in question. The definition of nexus varies between states, but may exist even if no permanent establishment exists for federal tax purposes. For instance, some states consider there to be a nexus if stock is stored in the state, or if a company has employees working in the state.

The UK/USA DTA does not provide relief from state taxes. Article 2 provides that the taxes relieved by the DTA are:

'(a)    in the case of the United States:
   (i)     the Federal income taxes imposed by the Internal Revenue Code (but excluding social security taxes); and
   (ii)    the Federal excise taxes imposed on insurance policies issued by foreign insurers and with respect to private foundations;'

However, the state taxes are still eligible for double tax relief (see A10.15) provided they are taxes on profit for the purposes of TIOPA 2010, s 8. Most states do charge tax by reference to profits, but a list of state taxes which are eligible for double tax relief can be found in the HMRC Double Tax Relief manual at DT19855 onwards.

### Use of UK losses

**[B4.8]** Following the principles established in *San Paulo (Brazilian) Railway Co Ltd v Carter* (1895) 3 TC 407 and subsequent cases (see Chapter **A2**), the UK company will be taxable on the profits of the overseas trades in the same way as UK trading profits.

If the UK company has trading losses, these losses will therefore be set against the profits of the overseas trades before calculating the amount of UK corporation tax against which the overseas taxes can be relieved.

To the extent that overseas taxes cannot be relieved (because the losses reduce the profits), the taxes can be carried forward and set against future profits from the same source. The taxes arising on the French profits can be carried forward and set against future French profits, and cannot be set against future US or Brazilian profits.

In order to preserve the losses, the UK company could establish a new company to carry on the overseas trades. The profits of the overseas trades would then be subject to UK corporation tax with credit for the overseas tax suffered. The brought forward losses of the UK company would not be set against these profits, and would be preserved to set against future profits.

This structure is shown in Diagram 2.

Diagram 2

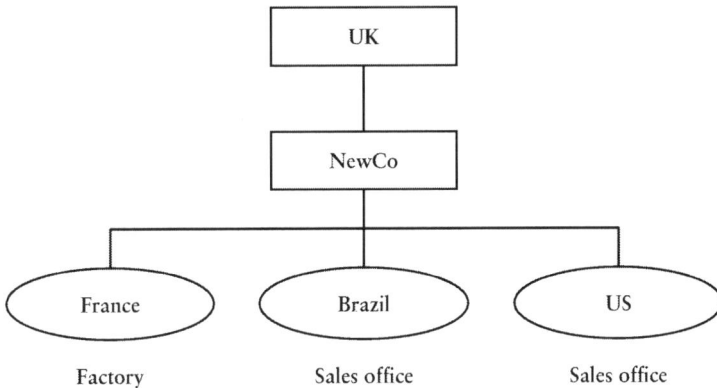

| UK |
| NewCo |
| France | Brazil | US |
| Factory | Sales office | Sales office |

# Branch versus subsidiary

**[B4.9]** Having determined that there is a taxable presence in France and the US, the group is considering whether the activities in these jurisdictions should be run as a branch of the UK company, or whether they should be run through local subsidiaries.

From 19 July 2011, it is possible for the UK company to elect that a permanent establishment is exempt from UK corporation tax—and effectively therefore subject to UK tax in the same way as a subsidiary. This exemption is outlined in more detail at **A18.1ff**.

## Rates of tax

**[B4.10]** In general, if the subsidiary would be subject to a lower level of tax in the overseas jurisdiction than in the UK, incorporating the branch can result in a tax saving, because the profits would no longer be subject to UK tax as they arise (provided no attribution is required under the Controlled Foreign Company (CFC) rules). Alternatively, a branch exemption election could be made (which would also be subject to anti-avoidance rules)/

However, in France, the US and Brazil the rate of tax is higher than in the UK. The profits would be subject to these rates if the trades were carried on through a subsidiary.

Although the headline rates of tax may remain the same, a subsidiary may be able to deduct costs which a branch is unable to. For instance, a UK branch cannot deduct interest on a loan from its parent company, but a subsidiary is able to. The availability of additional tax deductions may reduce the effective tax rate of a subsidiary.

Withholding taxes should also be taken into account, as the distribution of profits from a subsidiary may be subject to withholding tax, which would increase the tax rate on distributed profits. However, the distribution of profits from a branch can also be subject to withholding tax (in the form of branch profits tax) in some jurisdictions, including the US, although this is less common.

## Capital gains on future sale

### Sale of branch assets

**[B4.11]** A capital gain arising on the future sale of the assets of the branches will be subject to UK corporation tax, unless a branch exemption election has been made. As a UK resident company, the UK company is subject to corporation tax on gains arising on any asset wherever it is located.

A capital gain arising on the sale of the French factory may also be subject to tax in France, even if it were sold at the same time as the branch trade. The UK/France DTA not only allows France to tax gains arising on the disposal of real estate, but also to tax gains arising on the disposal of assets used in a French permanent establishment. Article 13 of the UK/France DTA provides that:

> '1.    Gains derived by a resident of a Contracting State from the alienation of immovable property, as defined in paragraph 2 of Article 5, which is situated in the other State may be taxed in that other State. For the purposes of this provision the second sentence of paragraph 2(b) of Article 5 shall not apply.
>
> 2.    Gains from the alienation of movable property forming part of the business property of a permanent establishment which an enterprise of a Contracting State has in the other Contracting State or of movable property pertaining to a fixed base available to a resident of a Contracting State in the other Contracting State for the purposes of performing professional services, including such gains from the alienation

of such a permanent establishment (alone or together with the whole enterprise) or of such a fixed base, may be taxed in the other State.'

The tax position in France would be unaffected by a branch exemption election.

### Sale of subsidiary

**[B4.12]** A capital gain arising on the sale of shares in a French subsidiary would not be subject to tax in the UK provided the conditions of the substantial shareholding exemption are satisfied. This requires that:

(a)  the investing company has held at least 10% of the ordinary shares in the subsidiary for at least twelve months;

(b)  the investing company is a member of a trading group before and after the sale;

(c)  the investee company is a trading company before and after the sale.

There is no requirement that the investee company is a UK resident company, or that the trading activities are undertaken in the UK.

The disposal of shares in a French company by a UK company should not be subject to tax in France, even where the company holds real estate. Article 5(2) of the UK/France DTA defines immovable property as including shares in companies holding immovable property:

'(a)  The term "immovable property" shall, subject to the provisions of sub-paragraphs (b), (c) and (d) below, have the meaning which it has under the law of the Contracting State in which the property in question is situated.

(b)  Shares or rights in a company or legal person, the assets of which consist mainly of immovable property situated in one of the Contracting States, shall be treated as immovable property situated in that State. For the purposes of this provision, immovable property pertaining to the industrial, commercial or agricultural operation of such a company or legal person or the performance of independent professional activities shall not be taken into account.

. . . ,'

However, for the purposes of the capital gains article, shares in companies holding immovable property are specifically excluded from falling within the definition of immovable property themselves:

'Gains derived by a resident of a Contracting State from the alienation of immovable property, as defined in paragraph 2 of Article 5, which is situated in the other State may be taxed in that other State. *For the purposes of this provision the second sentence of paragraph 2(b) of Article 5 shall not apply.*' (my emphasis)'

### Clawback of deferred gains

**[B4.13]** If gains have been deferred on the incorporation of a branch into a subsidiary (see **B4.15** below), these gains will become subject to tax if the subsidiary is sold within six years of the incorporation.

Where a disposal following incorporation is likely, the branch should be incorporated when the market value of its assets is low, such that that any deferred gains are also low.

These gains will become subject to tax even if the gain on the disposal of the subsidiary is itself exempt from tax by virtue of the substantial shareholding exemption.

### Sale of assets by subsidiary

**[B4.14]** If the French subsidiary sells its assets, including the factory, then this gain would likely be taxable in France.

Assuming that the group is 'close' as defined in CTA 2010, s 439, any gains arising in its subsidiary may also be attributed to the UK company under TCGA 1992, s 13 and subject to UK corporation tax.

However, there is an exemption from s 13 for assets used for the purposes of a trade carried on outside the UK. The gain on disposal of the factory should not therefore be subject to UK corporation tax.

A subsequent distribution of the proceeds by way of dividend is likely to be exempt under the dividend exemption rules (see CHAPTER A16).

# Incorporation of subsidiary

**[B4.15]** The UK company has decided to incorporate its French branch, and will establish a French Societe Anonyme (SA) as a subsidiary.

Diagram 3

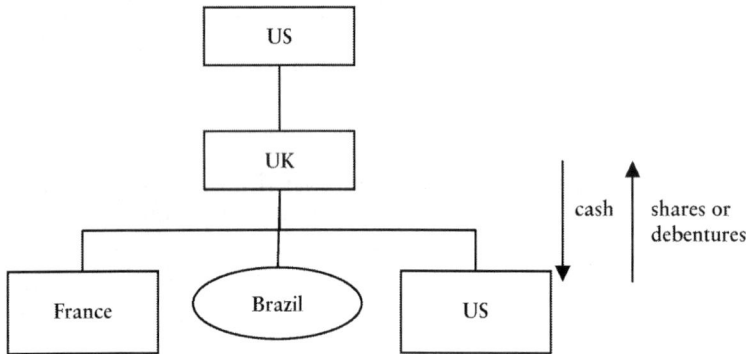

### *Transfer of branch assets to subsidiary*

**[B4.16]** In order to incorporate the branch, the UK company will transfer the assets of the branch to the French subsidiary company. This will constitute a disposal of these assets for capital gains tax purposes. To the extent that the assets are intangible assets acquired or created after 1 April 2002, income will arise under CTA 2009.

As the disposal is to a connected party, the proceeds of the disposal will be deemed to be the market value of the assets under TCGA 1992, s 17. Similar provisions exist in respect of intangible assets which fall within CTA 2009 rather than TCGA.

Under TCGA 1992, s 140 (or CTA 2009, s 827 for intangible assets), these gains may be deferred provided inter alia that the French company issues ordinary share capital in consideration for the transfer. The shares issued by French company will need to be reviewed to confirm that they constitute ordinary share capital. The definition of ordinary share capital is considered in HMRC Business Brief 54/07.

The UK company will also incorporate its US branch, and will establish a US LLC as a subsidiary. According to Business Brief 54/07, an LLC may have ordinary share capital:

> 'Unless otherwise provided in a limited liability company agreement, a member's interest in a limited liability company may be evidenced by a certificate of limited liability company interest issued by the limited liability company.
>
> If a [Delaware LLC] issues 'shares' in this way and the other factors relating to the company suggest that it has share capital then we will accept that these 'shares' may be regarded as "ordinary share capital" for the purpose of ICTA 1988, s 832.'

In order to ensure that the US LLC has ordinary share capital and therefore that TCGA 1992, s 140 applies to the incorporation of the US branch, the US LLC should issue member's interest certificates.

## Classification of French and US subsidiaries

[B4.17] According to INTM180030, HMRC consider that a French SA is treated as opaque for UK tax purposes.

Subject to the CFC rules, the income of the French company should not therefore be subject to tax until it is distributed to its UK parent.

The French company could alternatively have been incorporated as an SARL or an SAS in France. In addition to the legal differences between these entities, there may also be differences in the French tax treatment of these entities on a future disposal. For example, the transfer tax (stamp duty) payable on the disposal of an SA or an SAS will be limited to approximately €5,000, but the transfer tax payable on the disposal of an SARL will be unlimited.

For US tax purposes, the LLC will be treated as a branch of the UK company. The UK company will therefore need to file US tax returns, and will be subject to US tax in respect of the LLC's profits.

However, for UK tax purposes, INTM180030 sets out that a US LLC should be treated as a company. The US classification does not affect this. The tax which is paid by the UK company in respect of the US LLC's profits will be treated as underlying tax, and will be creditable against dividends paid by the US LLC.

## *Future disposal of French and US subsidiaries*

### Substantial shareholding exemption

**[B4.18]** If the French and US subsidiaries have issued ordinary share capital then a future disposal may be exempt from UK corporation tax by virtue of the substantial shareholding exemption. The exemption requires (inter alia) that the disposal is of ordinary share capital.

Ordinary share capital will be issued on the incorporation of the branches (see above), and so a future disposal may qualify for the substantial shareholding exemption.

### Capital contributions

**[B4.19]** It is intended that funding will be provided to the US LLC by way of a capital contribution. The case of *Fenston (F D) Will Trusts v Revenue and Customs Comrs* [2007] STC (SCD) 316, SCD confirmed that a capital contribution to an LLC will only be treated as adding to the base cost of the shares in the LLC if additional member's certificates are issued. The LLC should therefore issue member's interest certificates in respect of the capital contribution.

Increasing the base cost will be beneficial if the substantial shareholding exemption does not apply on a disposal.

### *Residence of French company*

**[B4.20]** Although the French company is required to have a board of directors, the UK company intends to manage it from the UK and will take all decisions relating to its business and strategy, in addition to taking decisions in its capacity as a shareholder.

It is very likely that the French company will be treated as a UK resident company, as central management and control will be exercised from the UK. This would be a similar position to that in *De Beers Consolidated Mines Ltd v Howe (Surveyor of Taxes)* [1905] STC198 where the parent company usurped the power of the subsidiary company's board.

Under French tax law, the company may also be considered to be resident in France by virtue of its incorporation there.

Article 4 of the UK/France DTA provides that:

> ' Where by reason of the provisions of paragraph 1 a person other than an individual is a resident of both Contracting States, then it shall be deemed to be a resident of the Contracting State in which its place of effective management is situated.'

The DTA would override the UK domestic law position by virtue of CTA 2009, s 18.

The effective management may be located where the day to day management of the company is undertaken. This may be in France if the only decisions taken in the UK relate to strategy.

If the French company were UK resident, then it would be required to file UK corporation tax returns and pay UK tax. In the first instance, it would need to notify HMRC that is was subject to UK corporation tax. If management and control were subsequently transferred to France then:

(a)     the company would be treated as disposing of all of its assets for their market value under TCGA 1992, s 185;

(b)     any gain arising on assets used for the purposes of trade carried on through a permanent establishment outside the UK could be deferred under TCGA 1992, s 187;

(c)     the deferred gain would become chargeable if the UK company sold the shares in the French company or if the French company sells the assets within six years of the incorporation.

As the trade is carried on wholly in France, it should be possible to defer the gain arising on the migration under s 187.

In addition, clearance would be required from HMRC under TMA 1970, s 109B before the migration takes place.

# Shareholding in overseas company

### Shareholding requirements

**[B4.21]** Before incorporating the subsidiaries, the group will need to confirm whether there are any requirements under local law as to the identity of the shareholders. For instance:

(a)     Some jurisdictions require that there are at least two shareholders in a company. If this is the case, a local director or another company in the group could hold shares as nominee for the UK company.

(b)     Some jurisdictions do not allow non-residents to hold more than (say) 50% of the shares in a local company, or in specified industries. A local partner would be required under these circumstances, and the UK company could possibly hold an option to acquire the partner's shares.

In this case, there may be a commercial benefit in retaining a branch rather than forming a subsidiary.

### Withholding taxes on interest, dividends and royalties

**[B4.22]** Interest and royalties paid by the French company to the UK company may be subject to withholding tax in France.

The rate of withholding tax may be reduced under either the UK/France DTA or the Interest and Royalties Directive as implemented in France. The Directive normally requires that the payer directly holds at least 25% of the shares in the recipient company, or vice versa, or that a third company directly holds at least 25% of the shares in both.

This condition should be satisfied as the UK company holds at least 25% of the shares in the French company.

Dividends may also be exempt from withholding tax under the Parent/ Subsidiary Directive as implemented in France. This may also be subject to minimum shareholding requirements. It should be noted that some jurisdictions may not regard a company as holding shares in another company if they are pledged as security to a bank.

## Roadmap

**[B4.23]** The following roadmap can act as a checklist when advising UK companies expanding overseas, and provides a cross-reference into the relevant chapters of this book.

(1)   Is there a permanent establishment under local law? CHAPTER **A4**

(2)   Does the DTA provide any relief so that there is no permanent establishment? CHAPTER **A8**

(3)   Should a branch or subsidiary be formed?

(4)   Consider in respect of a subsidiary:
    (a)   CFC rules. CHAPTER **A6**
    (b)   exemption for subsequent dividends. CHAPTER **A16**
    (c)   residence. CHAPTER **A9**
    (d)   entity classification. CHAPTER **A14**
    (e)   transfer pricing. CHAPTER **A13**
    (f)   supply chain planning. CHAPTER **A13**
    (g)   financing the subsidiary.
    (h)   withholding tax on royalties/dividends/interest/fees paid to the UK. CHAPTER **A5**

(5)   Consider in respect of a branch:
    (a)   will full credit be available in the UK for local tax suffered. CHAPTER **A10**
    (b)   election for branch exemption. CHAPTER **A18**
    (c)   transfer pricing. CHAPTER **A13**
    (d)   financing the branch.
    (e)   withholding tax on royalties/distributions/interest/fees paid to the UK. CHAPTER **A5**
    (f)   potential for subsequent incorporation. CHAPTER **A9**

(6)   If a disposal is anticipated, what tax will arise? **B4.11–B4.16**

(7)   Are any other local taxes due eg state/provincial?

(8)   Are there any indirect taxes eg VAT, import duties?

(9)   Are there any taxes due in respect of local staff eg social security, payroll withholding tax?

(10)  How will BEPS and the UK GAAR impact?

# B5

# Supply chain planning

## Introduction

**[B5.1]** This Chapter outlines a case study of a group which is undertaking supply chain planning. The supply chain describes the way in which goods and services are provided from suppliers, between group companies, and to customers.

The group illustrated in Diagram 1 has already undertaken tax planning to ensure that:

(a)    withholding taxes do not arise on payments of interest, royalties and dividends;

(b)    dividends paid to the UK company from its overseas subsidiaries are not taxable;

(c)     future disposals of subsidiaries will not be subject to tax.

However, the group still pays a significant amount of tax in overseas jurisdictions on its profits. For instance, sales are made by companies in the UK, Belgium, the Netherlands, Sweden and France, and the majority of the group's profits are recognised in those jurisdictions. The effective tax rate is therefore approximately 30%.

Without undertaking further planning to reduce the taxable profits in those jurisdictions, it will be difficult for the group to reduce its effective tax rate much further.

It has therefore commissioned a 'supply chain review' project to identify how profits could be recognised in jurisdictions (such as Jersey or Ireland) where the tax rates are lower. It should be borne in mind that going forward, this kind of tax planning is likely to be significantly impacted by the BEPS action plan (see preface). In particular under BEPS there will be a strong focus on the separation of key assets, functions and risks from the main trading operations.

## Current trading model

**[B5.2]** The current trading model of the group is complicated, and many inter-company transactions are undertaken, as shown in Diagram 2.

Each of these inter-company transactions will need to be recognised correctly for:

(a)     accounting purposes;
(b)     transfer pricing purposes;
(c)     VAT purposes.

This imposes a significant compliance burden on the UK employees who provide accounting services to other group companies.

In addition, for transfer pricing purposes, all the companies making sales act as fully fledged distributors (see Chapter **A13** which discusses characterisation of entities for transfer pricing purposes). They undertake most activities relating to the sales and assume most risks, including:

(a)     bad debt risk;
(b)     ownership of stock (even when stock is stored in warehouses owned by other group companies);
(c)     processing orders;
(d)     marketing;
(e)     invoicing and collecting payments;
(f)     pricing.

# Diagram 1

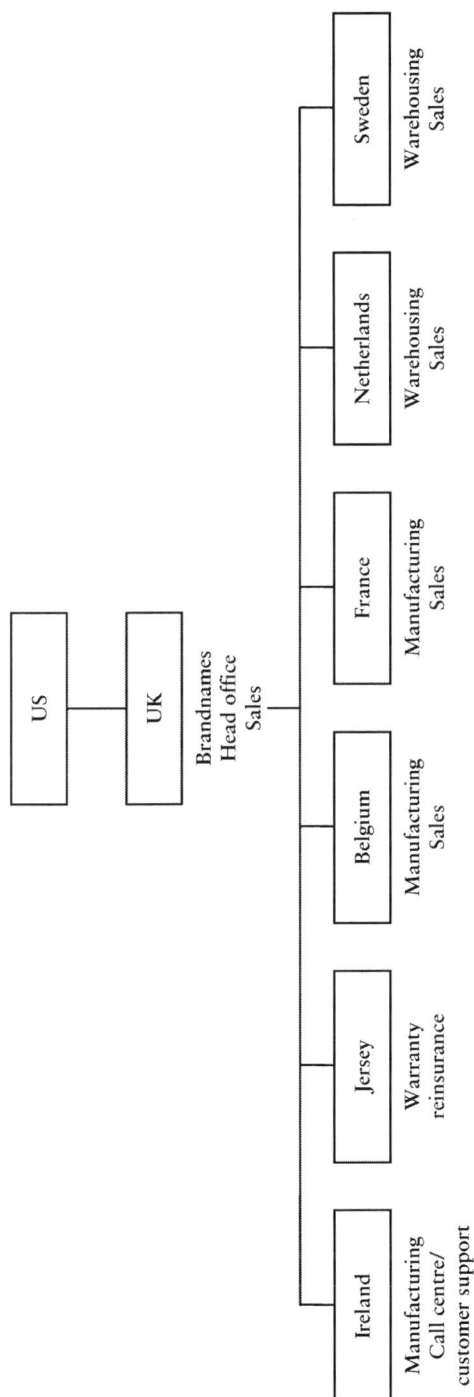

Diagram 2

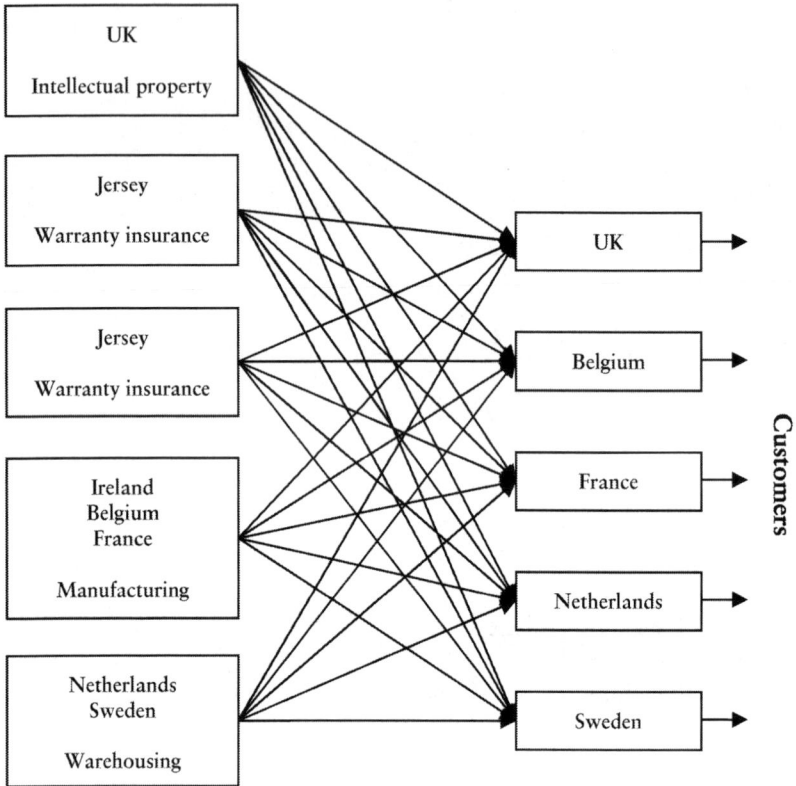

## Proposed trading model

[B5.3] Following extensive discussions with staff, the group's tax advisers have proposed a revised trading model, which is illustrated in Diagram 3.

The key changes proposed are that:

(a)    all sales will be made by the Irish company;

(b)    the companies which previously made sales in their own names will act as commissionaires for the Irish company;

(c)    the companies which previously undertook manufacturing on a full risk basis will now act as contract manufacturers;

(d)    intellectual property, including brand names, should be transferred to Jersey.

Diagram 3

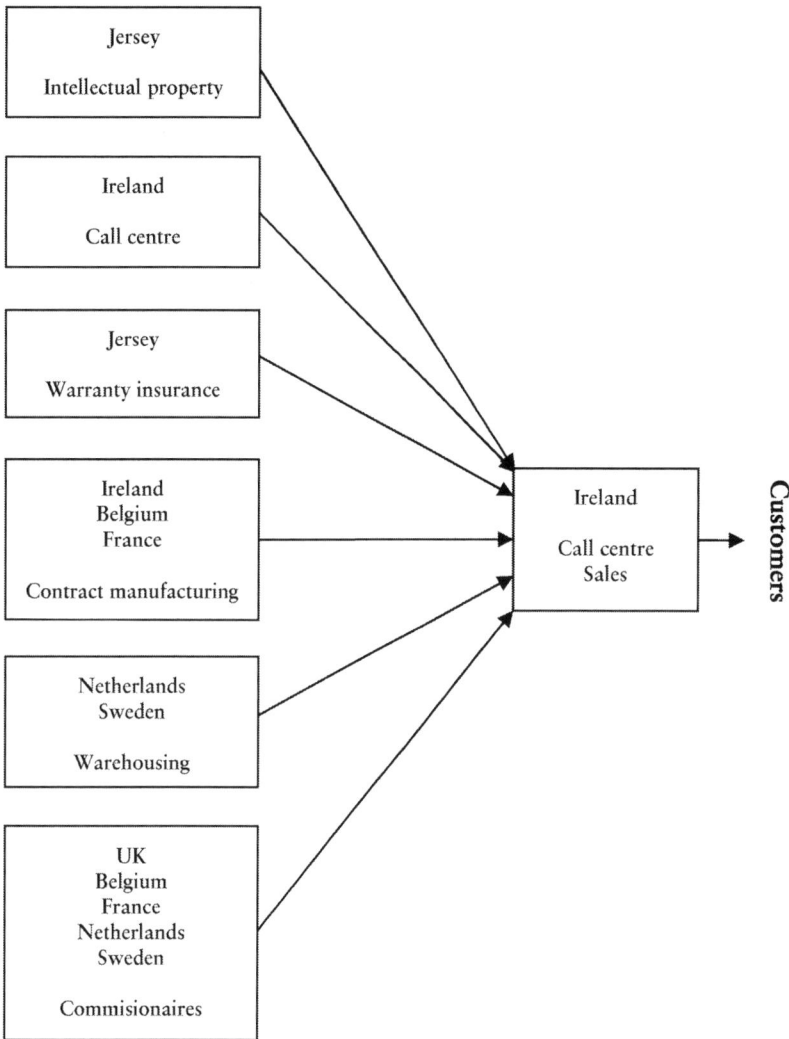

Most companies will undertake substantially the same activity as previously, but their functions will be recharacterised, and risks transferred to other companies.

The number of transactions between group companies will be significantly reduced, which in turn will reduce the accounting and book-keeping burden. It may also reduce the number of VAT returns which the group has to file.

This transaction model is sometimes referred to as a 'hub and spoke' model, where one company (the Irish company in this case) is the hub, and the other companies providing services to it are the spokes.

A more substantial change to the trading model would have involved relocating physical assets and functions in order to:

(a)    take advantage of lower labour costs;
(b)    take advantage of lower transport costs if factories were located closer to suppliers or customers.

However, the costs of implementing these changes were considered to outweigh the savings they would generate.

### Commissionaire

**[B5.4]** A commissionaire sells to customers in its own name but for the benefit and risk of an undisclosed principal, in this case the Irish company. Its risk is limited and it earns a lower return than a full distributor. It has certain advantages over the use of a commission agent, but in common law jurisdictions (such as the UK) it will be treated in the same way as a commission agent.

The commissionaire has similar functions and risks as a commission agent and remits all customer revenue to the principal and then invoices the principal for a commission on sales.

### Contract manufacturer

**[B5.5]** A contract manufacturer undertakes the operational functions required to manufacture a product on behalf of a principal, in this case the Irish company, but transfers title of the finished goods to the principal immediately.

Contract manufacturers do not carry out significant entrepreneurial activities which would result in risk-bearing or intangible asset development. Intangible assets are typically limited to customer relationships and some process technology. Production scheduling is organised by the requirements of the principal. The contract manufacturer may utilise production technology, product specifications, quality assurance and quality control procedures established by the principal or its end customer. In this case, some of the intangibles will be held by the Jersey company.

Operational functions undertaken include manufacturing and/or assembly activities and the daily administrative tasks required to maintain a viable production facility. As production is conducted solely to order for a principal, the contract manufacturer faces no market risk because its sales are guaranteed, nor does it face inventory or warranty risk.

A contract manufacturer may be remunerated on a cost plus, price per unit, or a service fee basis. The contract manufacturer faces less risk and earns, on average, lower returns than a fully-fledged manufacturer operating in the same industry and markets.

# Tax implications of new trading model

**[B5.6]** The key tax benefit of the new trading model is that more functions, assets and risks are held by the Irish company.

## Transfer pricing

**[B5.7]** Transfer pricing principles generally require that a company holding functions, assets and risks is remunerated appropriately. Many jurisdictions (including the UK) follow OECD principles when determining appropriate remuneration, and can require adjustments to taxable profits if the actual remuneration is different. Under the BEPS proposals and in particular action points 8 and 10, there will be increased focus on the movement of any intangibles within the group and alignment of risks assumed with value creation.

The Irish company will be treated as the 'entrepreneur' of the group and will earn most of the profits of the group. It will pay other group companies an arm's length rate for the limited functions which they undertake.

A full transfer pricing study should be undertaken to support these arm's length charges, but broadly:

(a)     the contract manufacturers, call centre and warehouse will be remunerated on a cost-plus basis;

(b)     the commissionaires will be remunerated based on a percentage of the sales they make;

(c)     the intellectual property holding company will receive a royalty based on a percentage of sales made by the Irish company.

## Tax calculation

**[B5.8]** The Irish profit calculation would comprise:

| | |
|---|---|
| Sales to customers | X |
| Manufacturing costs (cost-plus) | (X) |
| Sales commissions (%) | (X) |
| Royalty (%) | (X) |
| Net profit | X |
| (subject to tax at 12.5%) | |

As a result, the majority of the profit will be recognised in Ireland, and therefore subject to tax in Ireland. The Irish tax rate on trading profits is 12.5%, and therefore a significant reduction in the group's effective tax rate is expected.

## Losses

**[B5.9]** It should be noted that if even if the Irish company makes a trading loss, it will still be required to make the same payments to other group companies. These other group companies will be taxable on the profits arising from these payments, and the group will be in a position where it has net losses, but a tax liability.

### Employee incentivisation

**[B5.10]** One issue to consider is how to remunerate senior staff of the manufacturing and sales companies. Their bonuses may be based on the profitability of their companies, which will be reduced under the new trading model. Bonus targets would therefore need to be calculated on a different basis.

### Comparison of functions

**[B5.11]** Taking as an example the transformation of the sales companies into commissionaires, the functions for which the companies would be responsible would be as set out below. In some cases (eg after sales support and invoicing and administration) these functions could be undertaken by other group companies, which would receive an arm's length remuneration for doing so.

| Proposed structure | |
|---|---|
| Principal | Commissionaire (local companies) |
| Most economic risk | Little economic risk |
| Inventory risk | |
| Bad debt risk | |
| Currency risk | |
| Warranty risk | |
| | Sales and marketing |
| Distribution | |
| | Contracting with customers |
| Invoicing and administration | |
| | After sales support |

# Inter-company transactions

### Transfer pricing

**[B5.12]** As noted at B5.7, transfer pricing rules will apply to all the new transactions, and they will need to be recognised at arm's length prices.

To support the new trading model, and the tax benefits which result from it, a transfer pricing study will be undertaken by the group to determine the correct level of arm's length prices.

### Indirect taxes

**[B5.13]** VAT would need to be considered in the light of the new transactions. The nature of all inter-company transactions has changed, as have the parties to them.

For instance, rather than providing warehousing to the local companies making the sales, the Dutch and Swedish companies will provide warehousing services to the Irish company.

This may change the VAT liability of these supplies, and may require some companies to register for VAT purposes where they were not previously.

Under the commissionaire model, the commissionaires issue VAT invoices to the customers, but the Irish company would issue invoices to the commissionaires in order to 'sell' the goods to them before they are sold to the customer.

As goods would still be delivered to the same places, the customs duty liability may be unchanged. However, the names of the companies owning and importing the goods will be different, and should be notified to the relevant authorities before the new model is implemented.

### Withholding taxes

**[B5.14]** It is proposed that the group's intellectual property, including brand names will be held by the Jersey company. Any royalties paid in respect of these brand names (by the Irish company) should be tax deductible in the paying company, but not subject to tax as the recipient company is resident in Jersey.

However, these payments may be subject to withholding tax in Ireland. Together with any exit charges (see below), this may outweigh the tax benefit of the deductible royalty payment.

Under the current trading model, the intellectual property is held by a UK company. Any royalties paid by companies resident in the EU should not be subject to withholding tax by virtue of the Interest and Royalties Directive. Royalties paid by non-EU group companies should be eligible for reduced rates of withholding tax under the double tax agreement (DTA) with the UK.

# Impact on group structure

### Controlled Foreign Company

**[B5.15]** The subsidiaries of the UK sub-holding company which are subject to a lower level of tax may be treated as Controlled Foreign Companies (CFCs), and their profits subject to UK tax.

In the context of the proposed group structure, the Irish company will be subject to a 12.5% rate of tax, and the Jersey company will be subject to a 0% rate of tax. They are therefore likely to be considered to be CFCs under the new rules from 1 January 2013.

#### Ireland

**[B5.16]** On the basis that the entity based exemptions potentially allow 100% of the profits to escape tax without entering into the subjectivity of The Gateway, then one would normally consider these first.

*Entity Exemptions*

**[B5.17]** Low profits exemption

This applies normally where the accounting profits are no more than £500,000 and non-trading income is no more than £50,000 in a twelve month accounting period. 'Accounting profits' for this purpose are pre-tax profits under GAAP but excluding certain dividend income, property profits and losses and capital profits and losses. The resulting profits are then further adjusted for any transfer pricing adjustments which would be required under UK tax principles.

Alternatively, the test may be met where the taxable profits computed under UK tax rules are no more than £500,000 and non-trading income is no more than £50,000 in a twelve month accounting period. This definition thus also means that UK transfer pricing rules have to be considered. In order to benefit from this exemption the profit has to be calculated according to UK tax rules.

For both alternatives it is also important to make sure that the profits generated in Ireland stand up from a transfer pricing perspective. Due to the nature of the arrangements, this will normally need a fairly robust set of transfer pricing documentation to justify the Irish profit.

There is also the possibility of the targeted anti-avoidance rule (TAAR) which applies to the low profits exemption where an arrangement has been entered into with the main purposes of securing the low profits exemption where it would otherwise not have been due. The guidance in HMRC's Manual seems to suggest that this is focused on preventing businesses from dividing their profits up in amounts of less than £500,000 specifically to benefit from the exemption, although there are a couple of more esoteric scenarios which could fall within the TAAR which should normally be checked for the sake of completeness.

On the face of it then this would seem to be the most obvious exemption from which the Irish company (Irishco) can benefit. The next question therefore is whether Irishco may be able to generate profits of more than £500,000 without a CFC charge.

The low profits margin exemption

In broad terms this allows companies with low profit margin to fall outside of the CFC provisions. For these purposes low margin is defined as where the adjusted accounting profits before interest are no more than 10% of the relevant operating expenditure. The accounting profits of Irishco are again adjusted for excluding certain dividend income, property profits and losses and capital profits and losses, transfer pricing and interest expense.

Relevant operating expenditure includes the cost of goods purchased by the CFC under related party expenditure only where the goods are actually delivered into the CFC's territory of residence, ie in this case Irishco—as can be seen, this is in part targeted against simple reinvoicing companies.

It would not be possible to inflate relevant operating expenditure through intra-group charges, as these are excluded from its definition for the purposes of this exemption

Excluded Territories Exemption (ETE)

In the past, companies were able to rely on a 'white list' where HMRC would not in principle suggest that there was a CFC if it was on a list of otherwise high tax regimes, subject to a number of detailed conditions being met. This list is broadly replicated in the new provisions and, Ireland is not on the list. Therefore this exemption would not apply.

Finally, there is an entity exemption where profits for the CFC are at least 75% of the current UK tax rate. On the basis that the rate of tax that Irishco is paying is around 12.5%, this is not considered further.

*The Gateway tests*

**[B5.18]** If the profits of Irishco exceed the de minimis limit of £500,000 we then need to consider whether the Initial Gateway, Gateway Safe Harbour or Main Gateway test might apply to establish which profits can be exempted. Unlike the entity exemptions, the Gateway does not look at the company's results as a whole. Instead, there are different Gateway tests for different types of income, essentially non-financial (eg trading income) and financial.

Initial Gateway

Under this test the Irishco can fall outside the initial gateway as regards its non-financial profits if it meets any *one* of the following:

(a)     the non-tax purpose of the arrangement,
(b)     it has no UK managed assets or risks,
(c)     it can function without UK support,
(d)     the profits consist of non-trading finance profits or property business profits. This is because financial profits are covered under different Gateway tests and property profits are exempt from the CFC rules altogether (not considered this further on the basis that Irishco is a trading company).

We therefore need to consider whether profits have been diverted from the UK by separation of assets and risks from management activity which takes place still in the UK and the transfer pricing provisions do not deal with this sufficiently.

In other words, the sorts of scenarios which will not pass the Initial Gateway for non-financial profits are where the company's profits derive to some extent from active decision making in the UK as regards the acquisition, creation, exploitation, development of the company's assets or the taking on/bearing of risks.

In order to consider this, we could use the flowcharts in CHAPTER **A6** above in order to determine the extent to which each task might be satisfied. On the basis of the fact pattern above, this might be difficult to satisfy.

Trading Profits Safe Harbour

As an alternative, Irishco would need to have met *all* of the following five conditions in the accounting period in order to qualify for the Trading Profits Safe Harbour:

(i)     premises with a reasonable degree of permanence (hopefully this should be met)

(ii)    its UK derived income must be less than 20% of its total trading income. Clearly this depends upon the actual numbers but it is clearly designed to target any intermediary companies such as Irishco that might be reinvoicing to UK entities

(iii)   less than 20% of management expenditure must relate to UK management. This is a mechanical test which may be satisfied depending on the presence of the Group Senior Team in Ireland as measured against the total costs of the management team.

(iv)    there is no significant IP transfer from related persons in the previous six years.

(v)     less than 20% of the trading of Irishco can be generated by export of goods from the UK, unless the goods are actually delivered into Ireland. Again this is a mechanical test and Irishco would need to make sure it either fell beneath this threshold or that the goods would be actually delivered into Irishco, which may create a logistical headache.

Irishco would also need to consider the targeted anti-avoidance rule for the Trading Profits Safe Harbour test. According to HMRC guidance this only bites where:

> 'A significant part of the CFC's business has been organised or reorganised, and

> The main purpose, or one of the main purposes of that reorganisation is to ensure that one or more of the trading income exclusions is not met'

There are two possible defences to this. Firstly Irishco could argue that the establishment of the company did not have the avoidance of the CFC rules as an objective (it would clearly need to set out a commercial rationale for the office in Ireland to do this). Alternatively, given the office has existed for some time, it could argue that avoidance of new 2013 rules could not have been contemplated at the time it was set up.

*Main Gateway*

**[B5.19]** On the basis that it looks like that one of the tests in the Trading Profits Safe Harbour is failed then Irishco will fall into the Main Gateway. This then becomes a much more detailed transfer pricing exercise, but also looks at the significant people functions (SPF) and the split of where roles are performed between the UK and Ireland.

This therefore would target Irishco if it were holding an asset or a risk but did not carry out most of the key people functions and there is a lack of substantial commercial benefits in the CFC holding the asset or risk. HMRC could also argue that an independent company would not enter into such an arrangement.

Profits can only be apportioned to the UK parent under the CFC rules under the Gateway where there are UK SPFs. Even where there are UK SPFs, it does not necessarily mean that all the company's non-financial profits will be the subject of a CFC charge. The profits of Irishco subject to a CFC apportionment are reduced further where:

- the profits arise from arrangements which independent companies would have entered into; or
- where UK SPFs do not contribute more than 50% of the CFC's total income; or
- where the non-tax (ie economic) value of the arrangement is at least 20% of the total value. The difficulty here of course is valuing the non-tax element.

If the UK parent had substantive operations in the UK, then Irishco's reliance on UK people functions could mean that a good proportion of its profit would be subject to UK tax under this provision. Whilst this could mean that a detailed transfer pricing exercise could still retain some benefits of the structure, on a head count test alone this could mean a significant profit would end up in the UK.

*Conclusion*

**[B5.20]** Provided Irishco has robust documentation for transfer pricing purposes it could be entitled to the low profits exemption and therefore £500,000 profit in could escape a UK CFC charge. If Irishco had profits that were higher than this, then the other options would be either the Initial Gateway or the Trading Profits Safe Harbour. These would be mechanical tests that we would have to be performed. In practice, it seems that any group with UK connections would find it difficult for all of its CFC profits to benefit from the other exemptions mentioned.

### Jersey

**[B5.21]** It is unlikely that the Jersey company will satisfy any of the exemptions from the CFC provisions.

There may therefore be little benefit in transferring the intangible assets to Jersey as the royalty income would remain subject to UK tax under the CFC rules, and withholding tax may arise on royalty payments.

### *Residence*

**[B5.22]** Where local directors have previously taken strategic decisions relating to pricing etc, these decisions may now need to be taken by the directors of the Irish company in Ireland.

If directors of other group companies continue to take strategic decisions in relation to the Irish company (which is now the main trading company in the group), it may be considered to be resident for tax purposes in the jurisdiction where these decisions are taken (see CHAPTER A9).

### *Permanent establishment*

**[B5.23]** A non-resident company will generally have a permanent establishment in a jurisdiction if a dependent agent has the authority to, and habitually does, conclude contracts which bind the non-resident company (see further CHAPTER A4).

Under the commissionaire arrangement, the commissionaires do not contract in the name of the principal, and so should not constitute a dependent agent which can create a permanent establishment for the Irish company. The arrangements must be structured correctly in order to achieve this position (see **A4.24**).

However, in common law jurisdictions such as the UK, a commissionaire will be treated as an undisclosed agent of the principal. In the UK, therefore, the UK company will be considered to be a dependent agent of the Irish company by virtue of which there will be a permanent establishment in the UK.

Consideration should be given to implementing a different arrangement in the UK, such as a limited risk distributor, in order that the Irish company is not subject to UK corporation tax.

It should be noted that under point 7 of The BEPS action plan, it is intended to address the 'artificial' avoidance of permanent establishment risk by the use of commissionaire structures. One can also expect that if such permanent establishments are to exist, then linked work with profit attribution will also seek to raise the tax collected from the permanent establishment concerned.

# Exit charges

**[B5.24]** As part of the proposed restructuring, functions, assets and risks will be transferred between group companies. These transfers may give rise to gains on which tax will be payable.

The OECD guidance on business restructuring (see **A13.59**) will also be relevant when considering the impact of the restructuring, and the tax position of the group thereafter.

### Capital gains

**[B5.25]** In some cases, gains will clearly arise. For instance, the UK company will transfer intellectual property and other intangible assets to the Jersey company. As this is a disposal to a related party, the UK company will be treated as having disposed of these assets for their current market value.

Summarised below are other situations in which a gain could be deemed to arise.

### Contract termination

**[B5.26]** The group companies in the UK, Belgium, France, Netherlands and Sweden will terminate existing sales contracts with customers, who will then all contract with the Irish company. These contracts will be replaced with commissionaire agreements under which the companies in the UK, Belgium, France, Netherlands and Sweden will earn lower profits.

In addition, the group companies in Ireland, Belgium and France will terminate their existing contracts with other group companies under which they sell them finished goods, and instead enter into contract manufacturing agreements under which they will earn lower profits.

If these companies were dealing with third parties on arm's length terms, they would be able to claim compensation for the termination/amendment of the contracts. They should then recognise an arm's length amount of compensation under transfer pricing principles.

## Specific rules—US

**[B5.27]** Under s 482 of the Internal Revenue Code (IRC), where intangible assets are transferred by a US company, the proceeds for the disposal must be 'commensurate with the income attributable to the intangible'.

This requires consideration of the future profits which are derived from the intangible, rather than its current or historic value. Future profits must therefore be estimated at the time a US company transfers the intangible asset, and effectively subject to tax in the US at that point. If future actual profits are higher than anticipated, then it may be necessary to retrospectively adjust the price recognised on the disposal.

As a result, it is not usually possible for a US company to transfer an intangible asset so that future royalty income is not subject to tax in the US.

## Specific rules—Germany

**[B5.28]** Where a German company transfers business functions, the value of these functions must be determined. This value must take account of all aspects including the intangibles, risks and opportunities for future profit. In principle, the transferring company must recognise arm's length compensation for the reduction in its future profits. This compensation would be subject to tax.

In a similar way to the US 'commensurate with income' standard, the value of the arm's length compensation must be recalculated in future years, and further compensation recognised if the assumptions underlying the original arm's length valuation have changed such that the profits of the transferee have increased.

## Deductibility of restructuring expenses

**[B5.29]** The UK company is likely to incur all of the costs relating to the restructuring, which will mainly be represented by professional fees for the advice.

These costs will only be deductible for UK corporation tax purposes if they are incurred 'wholly and exclusively' for the purposes of the UK company's trade. As they benefit other group companies, in particular the Irish company which will see its profits increase as a result, this may not be the case.

It will be expected that the UK company would recharge a significant part of these costs to the Irish company.

## Roadmap

**[B5.30]** The following roadmap can act as a checklist when advising on supply chain restructuring, and provides a cross-reference into the relevant chapters of this book.

(1)   Identify low/high tax jurisdictions and characterise entities in high tax jurisdictions as 'low risk'. CHAPTER A13

(2)   Is there a taxable disposal on the transfer of functions/assets/risks? B5.20–B5.25

(3)   Consider transferring intellectual property to a low tax jurisdiction. CHAPTER B6

(4)   New inter-company agreements to reflect new arrangements, supported by transfer pricing study. CHAPTER A13

(5)   Review residence of all companies under new arrangements. CHAPTER A9

(6)   Ensure that new arrangements do not create permanent establishments. CHAPTER A5

(7)   Commercial implications of the new arrangements including:
(a)   Employee incentives based on profits.
(b)   Management reporting.

(8)   Customs duty and VAT liabilities and registrations under the new arrangements.

(9)   How will BEPS and the UK GAAR impact?

# B6

# Intellectual property

## Introduction

**[B6.1]** A multinational group may wish to hold intellectual property outside the UK so that:

- any gain arising on a future disposal will not be subject to UK corporation tax;
- royalties received are not subject to UK corporation tax;
- UK trading companies using the intellectual property can pay a royalty which is tax deductible for UK corporation tax purposes.

This Chapter outlines:

- tax efficient jurisdictions to which intellectual property can be transferred;
- UK tax consequences on transferring intellectual property from the UK;
- withholding tax which may arise on the payment of royalties.

Similar principles may apply to the transfer of intellectual property, and payment of royalties, from other jurisdictions.

# Tax efficient jurisdictions

## Low tax jurisdictions

**[B6.2]** If a group's intellectual property is held in a low tax jurisdiction (for example Jersey), then royalty payments would be subject to withholding tax.

As an alternative to a royalty agreement, a group could establish a cost contribution agreement as outlined in **A13.50**.

Several jurisdictions have established special regimes for taxing certain income from patents and other intellectual property. These jurisdictions are typically within the EU, or have extensive double tax agreement (DTA) networks which reduce the withholding tax on royalties.

## Netherlands

**[B6.3]** Royalties on certain intangible assets are subject to tax at a rate of approximately 5% under the innovation box regime.

Intangible assets fall within the regime if:

(a)     they are patented and have been created by the company; or
(b)     they have been created as a result of research and development activities undertaken by the company in the Netherlands, and for which a research and development certificate is obtained.

To the extent that any withholding tax is suffered on royalties received, this can be credited against the tax liability arising under the innovation box regime.

Advance rulings can be obtained which confirm the tax treatment of a particular transaction, or that the profit is being correctly recognised for transfer pricing purposes. A ruling can therefore be obtained to confirm that the innovation box applies, and to how much of the income of the Dutch company.

## Belgium

**[B6.4]** Belgian companies can claim a deduction against royalty income equal to 80% of that royalty income, provided:

(a)     the royalty income relates to patents which are licensed to other companies;
(b)     the income received is calculated at an arm's length rate.

As a result, only 20% of such patent income is taxable in Belgium, giving an effective tax rate on such income of approximately 6%.

To the extent that a company is not able to deduct the 80% (for instance if it has losses in the year), it can carry it forward against future profits.

Advance rulings can be obtained which confirm the tax treatment of a particular transaction. A ruling can therefore be obtained to confirm that the royalty regime applies, and to how much of the income of the Belgian company. However, no ruling will be granted if the relevant activity does not have economic substance in Belgium, or if the transaction involves a tax haven.

## Switzerland

**[B6.5]** A 'management company' (also known as a 'domiciliary company') can be established in Switzerland which is subject to tax on foreign-source royalties at a reduced rate of tax. This reduced rate is calculated by applying the normal rate of tax to the proportion of the income which can be directly attributed to the activities undertaken in Switzerland.

A management company is only allowed to undertake certain specified activities such as:

(a)    administration and invoicing;
(b)    licensing of intangible assets, including know-how.

A management company is not allowed to undertake any other activities, including manufacturing or the supply of goods or services in Switzerland.

In practice, advance rulings can be obtained which confirm the tax treatment of a particular transaction. For instance, a ruling could be obtained to confirm the proportion of royalty income which is directly attributable to the activities undertaken in Switzerland.

## Luxembourg

**[B6.6]** 80% of net income from qualifying intellectual property is exempt from tax in Luxembourg. This results in an effective tax rate of approximately 6%. Qualifying intellectual property includes patents, trademarks, designs, models, software and domain names provided they are acquired or created after 31 December 2007. In addition to royalty and other income, 80% of any capital gains derived from qualifying intellectual property are exempt.

Intellectual property acquired from an affiliated party is not eligible for the exemption, but this is narrowly defined and does not often apply even in the same group of companies.

## United Kingdom

### Patent box benefits

**[B6.7]** Schedule 2 of Finance Act 2012 introduced a new part 8A to CTA2010. The new Patent Box regime as it is known came into effect in the UK on 1 April 2013, giving companies that own or license patents an opportunity to substantially lower their effective tax rates.

The Patent Box is an elective regime that allows companies to benefit (ultimately) from a 10% tax rate on profits derived from qualifying intellectual property (IP). Generously, this includes the worldwide sales of any products that incorporate patented technology. Moreover, the whole product does not need to be patented. Provided a component part of a product is patented, sales of the whole product will qualify – and even sales of spare parts of that product will qualify too. Other income like royalties and licence fees also qualify, as well as income from patented processes and certain other types of IP, such as plant variety rights and medicinal and veterinary products.

As to be expected, certain conditions must be met. The company must have created the invention or significantly contributed to it (referred to as the 'development condition'). Only patents registered by the UK Intellectual Property Office, the European Patent Office or the national patent offices of specified European countries qualify. Licensed rights only qualify if they confer exclusive rights over an entire national territory (such as the right to manufacture and sell a patented product in a country).

In order to maximise the relief companies need to consider the following:

- Has the company done enough to meet the development condition, and if not, can steps be taken?
- For groups, is the IP held by the 'right' company—does that company actively manage the IP (if it didn't develop it itself)?
- How is qualifying income identified—and how can it be improved?
- Are terms of licences appropriate?

The combination of the patent box and generous reliefs for research and development combine to make the UK a very attractive jurisdiction to hold intellectual property.

# Transfer of intellectual property from the UK

**[B6.8]** The same principles apply to the transfer of intellectual property from the UK to a group company in another jurisdiction as apply to the transfer of a trade (see **A9.39** and **B4.15**). In the first instance, the UK company will be treated as having sold the intellectual property for its current market value. The gain arising is then subject to corporation tax.

Under FA 2013, Sch 49 (see **A7.49**), it may be possible for this gain to be deferred.

Alternatively, a number of structures can be used to eliminate or reduce the gain which arises, including:

- Incorporation of an overseas branch which holds the intellectual property. In order to obtain relief under TCGA 1992, s 140, it is necessary to demonstrate that the branch is actually trading rather than holding the intellectual property as an investment.
- The gain may be reduced by the use of losses or if the intellectual property has a significant base cost.
- The gain arising on the migration of a company holding the intellectual property (rather than the transfer of the intellectual property itself) may be deferred under TCGA 1992, s 187 if the company continues to have a UK parent company.

- The UK company can retain ownership of the existing intellectual property. Any new intellectual property developed is owned by the overseas company, which pays a royalty to the UK company for the use of the existing intellectual property. As the existing intellectual property is superseded by the new intellectual property, the royalty declines.
- The intellectual property can be transferred when it has low value.
- If the transferee company is in the EU (for example, Belgium, the Netherlands or Luxembourg as outlined above), group relief could be claimed under TCGA 1992, s 171. Although group relief does not apply where the transferee is not subject to UK corporation tax, this is arguably contrary to EU law.

## Controlled Foreign Company (CFC) rules

[**B6.9**] Where the overseas company holding the intellectual property is a subsidiary of the UK company it may be a Controlled Foreign Company (CFC). Although the headline tax rate in Belgium, the Netherlands or Luxembourg (for example) is high, the actual tax paid is low because of the special regimes for taxing intellectual property. A company is a CFC if the actual tax paid is less than three quarters of the tax which would have been paid in the UK—the headline tax rate is irrelevant.

Given the nature of intellectual property, it may be difficult to satisfy the exemptions from the CFC rules:

- Although Belgium, The Netherlands and Luxembourg are on the list of excluded territories, as the effective rate of tax is lower than the standard rate, this exemption is unlikely to apply.
- In addition, in the circumstances, the low profits exemption is unlikely to be in point. A company holding intellectual property (IPco) would have to prove that it could function as an independent entity without UK support to benefit from the initial gateway If the IP originated in the UK, then the trading profits safe harbour would not be met. If the exercise comes down to a consideration of the Main Gateway, then an analysis of significant people functions may push a proportion of the income back into higher tax jurisdictions.

If the CFC rules do apply, a group could establish a new holding company outside the UK to hold the company which holds the intellectual property—see CHAPTER B3.

## Withholding taxes

[**B6.10**] Royalties paid by a UK company are subject to withholding tax at 20%. This may be reduced if there is a double tax agreement (DTA) in place, and the UK company has a 'reasonable belief' that the agreement applies.

For companies outside the UK paying royalties, it may be necessary for the company holding the intellectual property (and receiving the royalties) to obtain clearance from the relevant tax authority to reduce the rate of withholding tax under a DTA.

Certain DTAs contain anti-avoidance provisions which deny the reduced rate of withholding tax. These provisions may include:

- The company receiving the royalties must have beneficial ownership of the intellectual property.
- The royalty must not be paid as part of a conduit arrangement.
- Limitation on benefits.
- General anti-avoidance provisions in the agreement, or (in respect of the Interest and Royalties Directive) under UK domestic law, that the agreement does not apply if arrangements have been put in place specifically to take advantage of the agreement.

## Deductibility of royalties by a UK company

**[B6.11]** Royalties paid by a UK company should be deductible for corporation tax purposes. Where the overseas tax rate is lower than the UK rate, this can result in an ongoing tax benefit.

However, where royalties are paid to a connected party, the transfer pricing rules may apply to restrict the amount of the royalty deductible to an arm's length amount. This arm's length amount will be determined by a number of factors, including:

- the value of the intellectual property;
- the additional activities undertaken by the company owning the intellectual property.

It is therefore important that the company owning the intellectual property has sufficient substance (ie employees undertaking genuine activity) so that it can be demonstrated that:

- the company owns the intellectual property in its own right;
- additional activities are undertaken for which a charge can be made.

This substance will also help support:

- CFC exemptions;
- entitlement to benefits under DTAs;
- that the company is resident outside the UK for tax purposes.

## Roadmap

**[B6.12]** The following roadmap can act as a checklist when advising on intellectual property planning, and provides a cross-reference into the relevant chapters of this book.

(1)   Choose jurisdiction in which to establish the company which will hold the intellectual property. CHAPTER **B6**

(2)    Calculate the gain on transfer from the UK and take steps to mitigate. CHAPTER **B6**

(3)    Withholding tax may apply on royalties from the UK and elsewhere. CHAPTER **A5**

(4)    Is there a DTA (or EU Interest and Royalties Directive) under which the withholding tax is reduced? **A5.18**

(5)    Anti-avoidance rules under domestic law or the DTA itself. **A8.46**

(6)    Clearances may be required to obtain reduced rates of withholding tax—in the UK the reduced applies if the payer has a 'reasonable belief' that a DTA applies. **A5.27**

(7)    Is the company holding the intellectual property subject to the UK CFC rules? CHAPTER **A6**

(8)    If so, does an exemption apply? CHAPTER **A6**

(9)    If no exemption is available, consider establishing a new holding company for the group. CHAPTER **B8**

(10)   Steps to ensure that company holding the intellectual property is not resident in the UK. **A9.15**

(11)   Transfer pricing rules in the UK or elsewhere under which royalties and other amounts paid to the company holding the intellectual property must be at an arm's length rate. CHAPTER **A13**

(12)   How will BEPS and the UK GAAR impact?

# B7

# Cross border financing

## Introduction

**[B7.1]** Generally speaking, companies with debt finance can obtain a deduction for interest and other finance costs. At least in the UK, this is the fundamental tax difference between debt funding and equity funding, as no deduction is available for dividends paid on equity. Where the borrower (the debtor) is subject to UK tax, but the lender (the creditor) is not, there is a further dimension as the income will only be taxable at overseas tax rates. This can create either a positive or negative arbitrage on tax rates.

In the UK, there are a number of restrictions which can limit the tax deductibility of interest, including the worldwide debt cap. This Chapter summarises these restrictions, and the roadmap at the end can be used as a 'checklist' which cross references to the detailed analysis elsewhere in this book.

Given the value of interest deductibility, it is important to identify the restrictions which are likely to apply, and where possible structure arrangements so that these restrictions do not apply.

# Factors affecting the deductibility of interest in the UK

## Transfer pricing and thin capitalisation

**[B7.2]** Loans between connected companies (ie where one of those companies controls the other, or where both are under common control) will be subject to the transfer pricing rules. The definition of 'control' is extended where loans are involved, and a creditor will be attributed the rights of all other parties acting together in relation to the finance arrangements (see **A13.77**).

Specific provision is made in the transfer pricing rules by TIOPA 2010, s 152 in relation to loans, and requires consideration of:

- the amount of the loan which would have been made if the debtor and creditor were not connected;
- the rate of interest and other terms which would have been agreed if the debtor and creditor were not connected.

Interest and other financing costs are not deductible to the extent that the interest or loan exceeds these arm's length amounts. If the creditor is subject to tax on the full amount of the interest then this can create a tax disadvantage. Some double tax agreements (DTAs) will allow the creditor to make an adjustment to reduce the amount of interest which is taxable in these circumstances. This is also possible where both the debtor and creditor are subject to UK corporation tax (TIOPA 2010, s 181 and **A13.74**).

## Late paid interest

**[B7.3]** Interest is deductible when accrued if the creditor is a company which is resident in a 'qualifying territory'. A qualifying territory is one with which the UK has a DTA which contains a non-discrimination article (a list of which is in the HMRC International Manual at INTM412090).

Where the creditor is not resident in a qualifying territory, CTA 2009, s 373 can restrict a deduction for interest which is not paid within twelve months of the end of an accounting period if:

- the creditor is connected with the debtor, or the debtor is a close company in which the creditor is a participator; and
- the creditor is not subject to the loan relationship rules in respect of the interest (for example because it is not within the charge to UK corporation tax)

The interest is then only deductible when paid.

This can cause a timing mismatch where interest is deductible in a UK debtor company on a paid basis, but taxable in an overseas creditor company on an accrued basis. Where this is likely to be the case, the debtor company should ensure that interest on all inter-company loans is paid (subject to any withholding tax considerations).

The worldwide debt cap (see below) is applied after the late paid interest rules, and this can also lead to a timing mismatch. If a significant amount of interest is recognised in the year of payment, the available amount may be insufficient to allow a full deduction—even if it would have been sufficient in the years when the interest accrued.

### Interest reclassified as a distribution

**[B7.4]** Interest on a security may be recharacterised as a dividend under CTA 2010, s 1000(1)(E)(b), where the security is a 'non-commercial security', and to the extent that the interest does not represent 'a reasonable commercial return for the use of the principal'.

These provisions can apply in similar circumstances to the transfer pricing rules, and with the same result—dividends are not tax deductible, and recharacterisation under s 1000(1)(E)(b) therefore means that the interest is not tax deductible.

### Unallowable purposes

**[B7.5]** CTA 2009, ss 441–443 provide that where a loan relationship has an 'unallowable purpose', no tax deduction is available for interest or other financing costs. An 'unallowable purpose' is one which is not amongst the business or other commercial purposes of the company, and specifically where:

* it relates to a part of the company's activities which is not chargeable to corporation tax; or
* the main, or one of the main purposes for the loan relationship is a tax avoidance purpose.

The provisions can therefore be particularly relevant to cross-border financing, where UK tax can be reduced by interest paid to a creditor who is not taxable in the UK. However, in practice, the scope of the provisions is relatively narrow. For example, HMRC confirm (www.hmrc.gov.uk/manuals/cfmmanual/CFM38160.htm) that they will not normally apply where a company borrows to acquire shares or assets, regardless of whether or not those shares or assets are in the UK.

### Anti-arbitrage

**[B7.6]** As outlined at B7.11 and A14.38, a multinational group can obtain a tax benefit if a UK debtor pays interest to a creditor which is not then taxed on the interest receipt. In some cases this can be achieved by structuring the loan as a hybrid instrument (which is treated as debt for UK purposes but equity for the purposes of the relevant overseas tax) or by structuring the creditor as a hybrid entity (which is treated as opaque for UK tax purposes but transparent for overseas tax purposes).

The anti-arbitrage provisions in TIOPA 2010, Part 6 are designed to counter-act the use of such hybrid entities and hybrid instruments. In the case of a UK debtor company, the provisions apply where:

- the transaction giving rise to the deduction forms part of a scheme involving the use of a hybrid entity or hybrid instrument;
- the scheme is a 'qualifying scheme' that allows the company to claim a double deduction or a deduction which is not matched by a taxable receipt;
- the main purpose, or one of the main purposes of the scheme is to achieve a UK tax advantage; and
- the amount of the UK tax advantage is more than a minimal amount (ie the deductions are more than £50,000).

HMRC set out their view on whether the provisions apply to particular structures at www.hmrc.gov.uk/manuals/intmanual/intm597000.htm.

### Deductibility of branch interest

**[B7.7]** UK permanent establishments of overseas companies are subject to the same restrictions on interest deduction as UK companies. In addition, no deduction is available in respect of interest or other finance costs paid by the permanent establishment to its head office (CTA 2009, s 32).

Interest will only be deductible where the head office has made actual payments and some or all of those payments relate directly to the permanent establishment. For example, the head office may have taken out a loan which is used by the permanent establishment to purchase assets. In this case, the part of the interest relating to the permanent establishment can be attributed to the permanent establishment.

### Worldwide debt cap

**[B7.8]** The worldwide debt cap was introduced in Finance Act 2009 and is now found in TIOPA 2010, Part 7. In broad terms, it restricts the amount of interest which can be deducted by a UK group to the amount of third party interest which is incurred by the worldwide group.

The worldwide debt cap (and planning opportunities arising from it) is outlined in more detail at **A17.1**.

### Withholding tax

**[B7.9]** In addition to the deductibility of interest, it is often important to also minimise withholding tax. This can sometimes be a more significant tax benefit than obtaining a deduction—for example because the creditor cannot obtain relief for the withholding tax, or if the creditor is outside the group and requires the debtor to gross up any interest payments. It can also represent a cash flow disadvantage as withholding tax must be accounted for at the time the interest is paid.

Many DTAs provide for reduced rates of withholding tax on cross-border payments of interest, and the EU Interest and Royalties Directive (implemented in the UK by ITTOIA 2005, s 757) should also apply for most payments between EU Member States. At its simplest, withholding tax planning should therefore be based on obtaining relief under a DTA or Directive. This often requires clearance applications to be made in advance—see **A12.8**. Where a beneficial DTA is not in place, it may be possible to make loans via a third jurisdiction, as shown in Example 1.

DTAs typically require the recipient to be the beneficial owner of the interest, which may not be the case where a third jurisdiction has been inserted in the financing arrangements. The definition of beneficial ownership has been considered by the UK courts in *Indofood International Finance Ltd v JP Morgan Chase Bank NA* [2006] All ER (D) 18 (May), but other jurisdictions (most notably China) have a narrower interpretation of the term—see **A8.55** and **A8.69**.

In addition, some DTAs will have specific anti-avoidance rules dealing with conduit arrangements, or an overriding limitation on benefits (for example the UK/US DTA)—see **A8.60**.

There are some specific situations in the UK, where withholding tax will not arise, including:

- Payments which are not interest. Where a loan is advanced at a discount, the payment on redemption is not treated as a payment of interest.
- Interest on a quoted Eurobond. A quoted Eurobond is defined by ITA 2007, s 987 as any security that is issued by a company, is listed on a recognised stock exchange and carries a right to interest. There is no requirement that the bond be Euro-denominated, or actively traded on the exchange.

If loans can be structured instead as deep discounted bonds or quoted Eurobonds, then no UK withholding tax should arise.

Payment in kind (PIK) loans replace a cash interest payment with a payment in kind, but may still be subject to the same withholding tax requirements (in the UK this is by virtue of the funding bond rules in ITA 2007, s 939). See **A5.5** above for changes to funding bond provisions and disguised interest.

### Example 1—DTA intermediary

The rate of withholding tax on interest paid by a Romanian company is 16%, and this rate would apply if interest were paid directly to Guernsey. However, under the Cyprus/Romania DTA, a lower rate of 10% applies. The EU Interest and Royalties Directive may alternatively apply to reduce the withholding tax to 0%.

There is no withholding tax on interest paid by a Cypriot company, and in this case the Cypriot company would be taxed on a 1% margin, with credit for the Romanian withholding tax.

Diagram 1

**[B7.10]**

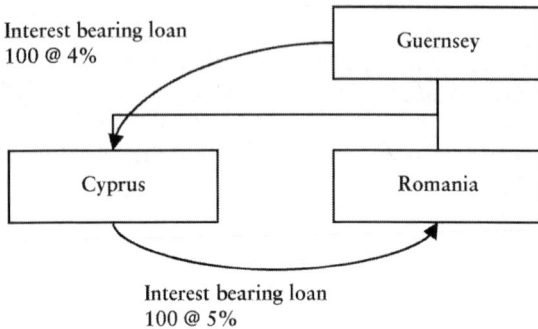

## Cross border planning

**[B7.11]** There can be differences in treatment of interest receipts and deductions in different jurisdictions. Some cross-border planning for interest exploits these differences, typically by seeking an interest deduction with no corresponding tax on the receipt. Multinational groups providing new debt funding to their UK subsidiaries will often have a choice of which (non-UK) company provides the debt, and can use this planning to minimise the overseas tax on any interest income.

Where the debtor is subject to UK corporation tax, the provisions listed in the first part of this article may restrict a tax deduction for interest in these circumstances. Particular regard must be had for the provisions relating to unallowable purposes and anti-arbitrage.

If the creditor is a subsidiary of a UK company, the Controlled Foreign Company (CFC) rules may also apply, as the creditor company will be subject to a lower level of tax. However, from 2012 the new exemption for finance companies may apply. Other CFC regimes may also need to be considered if holding companies are located outside the UK.

Examples 2, 3 and 4 illustrate structures which seek to obtain a tax deduction for a UK debtor with low or no corresponding tax on the receipt of the interest by the creditor.

**Example 2—interest free loan from Irish company**

Diagram 2

**[B7.12]**

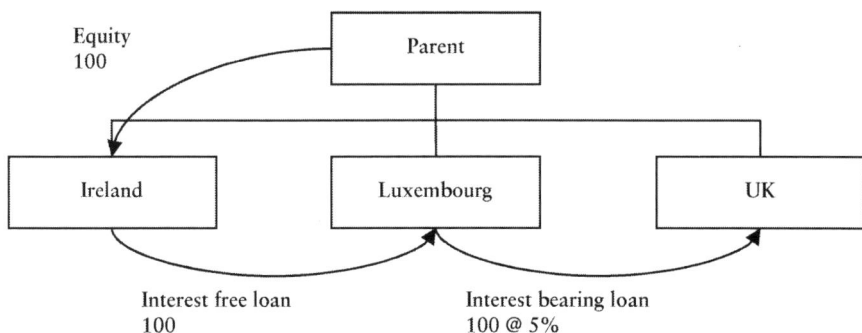

Although transfer pricing rules apply in Ireland from 2011, the rules do not apply to non-trading finance companies. There is therefore no requirement to recognise interest on the interest free loan. However, for Luxembourg tax purposes, the Luxembourg tax authorities may allow a deemed interest deduction to be claimed on the interest free loan such that a margin of say 1% is earned in Luxembourg. A ruling should always be obtained from the Luxembourg tax authorities in this situation to confirm the deemed interest deduction and the acceptable margin.

The UK company therefore obtains a deduction for interest of 5, and the Luxembourg company is only taxable on net interest income of 1.

**Example 3—exempt branch**

Under the terms of the Ireland/Luxembourg DTA, the profits of an Irish branch are not subject to tax in Luxembourg. However, the profits of a branch which is not trading in Ireland are not subject to Irish tax.

Providing the Irish branch which makes the loan is not trading, the UK company obtains an interest deduction for 5 and there is no corresponding tax on the receipt.

Diagram 3

[B7.13]

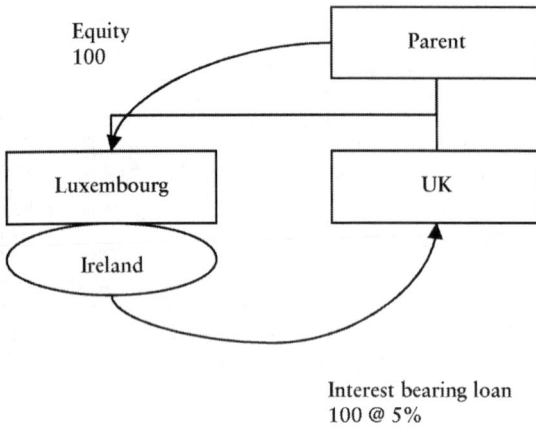

Interest bearing loan
100 @ 5%

## Example 4—notional interest deduction

A notional interest deduction regime applies in Belgium, calculated as the ten year government bond rate for the year in question (3% for 2013) multiplied by the amount of equity in the company.

In this case, the Belgian company obtains a notional interest deduction of 3%. The UK company therefore obtains a deduction for interest of 5, and the Belgian company is only taxable on net interest income of 1.2.

Diagram 4

[B7.14]

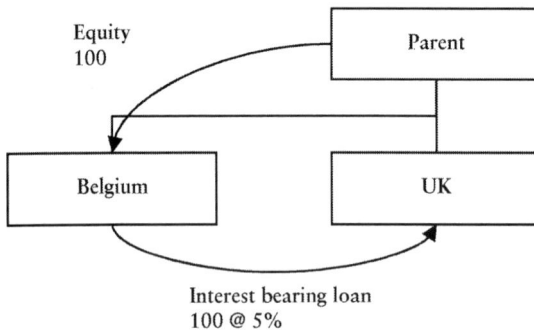

Interest bearing loan
100 @ 5%

# Roadmap

**[B7.15]** The following roadmap can act as a checklist when advising on cross border financing, and provides a cross-reference into the relevant chapters of this book.

(1)  Deductibility of interest in the UK:
  (a)  Transfer pricing. CHAPTER **A13**
  (b)  Thin capitalisation. CHAPTER **A13**
  (c)  (compensating adjustments may be available where interest is restricted as a result of a or b). CHAPTERS **A13** AND **A8**
  (d)  Late paid interest. CHAPTER **A13**
  (e)  Interest reclassified as a distribution. CHAPTER **A13**
  (f)  Unallowable purposes.
  (g)  Worldwide debt cap. CHAPTER **A17**
(2)  Withholding tax on interest. CHAPTER **A5**
(3)  Can the payment be restructured as something which is not interest—for example in the UK, a deep discounted bond (DDB) or a quoted Eurobond. CHAPTER **A5**
(4)  Ensure that relevant clearances are obtained in order to claim relief under a DTA. CHAPTER **A5**
(5)  If the lender is not a jurisdiction which has a favourable DTA, can the loan be made via a company which is? CHAPTER **A8**
(6)  Beneficial ownership and other DTA anti-avoidance provisions. CHAPTER **A8**
(7)  Consider cross-border planning under which an interest deduction is obtained with no corresponding taxable receipt, for example:
  (a)  A lender in a low tax jurisdiction.
  (b)  A lender not subject to transfer pricing rules.
  (c)  Notional interest deductions.
  (d)  Agreeing a low margin with tax authorities on back-to-back financing.
  (e)  Exempt branch.
  (f)  Double dip acquisition structures.
      (these structures may affect withholding tax and deductibility of interest expensing the UK as outlined above). CHAPTER **B7**
(8)  The use of a hybrid entity or a hybrid instrument may mean that interest is not deductible in the UK as a result of the anti-arbitrage rules. CHAPTER **A14**
(9)  How will BEPS and the UK GAAR impact?

# B8

# Migrations

## Introduction

**[B8.1]** There have been a number of high profile 'migrations' from the UK during recent years, whereby new holding companies have been established outside the UK, to which UK companies have transferred subsidiaries.

This Chapter outlines the tax objectives of a migration, how it can be effected, and the tax consequences of doing so.

## Tax objective

**[B8.2]** The tax objective and the anticipated tax benefits of a migration will depend on the existing group tax profile. In turn this objective will determine how the migration itself is effected.

## *Profits currently earned by overseas subsidiaries*

**[B8.3]** As shown in Diagram 1, profits earned by overseas subsidiaries may currently be subject to the Controlled Foreign Company (CFC) rules, or dividends paid to the UK parent company will be subject to UK tax if the dividend exemption is not available. Therefore, even if profits are subject to a low rate of tax in the overseas subsidiaries themselves, the effective rate of tax will be 21% (ie the UK tax rate).

Diagram 1

```
              ┌──────────────┐
              │     UK       │
              └──────────────┘
      ┌───────────────┼───────────────┐
┌──────────┐   ┌──────────┐   ┌──────────┐
│  Jersey  │   │  France  │   │ Ireland  │
└──────────┘   └──────────┘   └──────────┘
```

Taxed at 10%               Taxed at 33%               Taxed at 12.5%

Potential CFC attribution                             Potential CFC attribution
Additional UK tax on dividends                        Additional UK tax on dividends

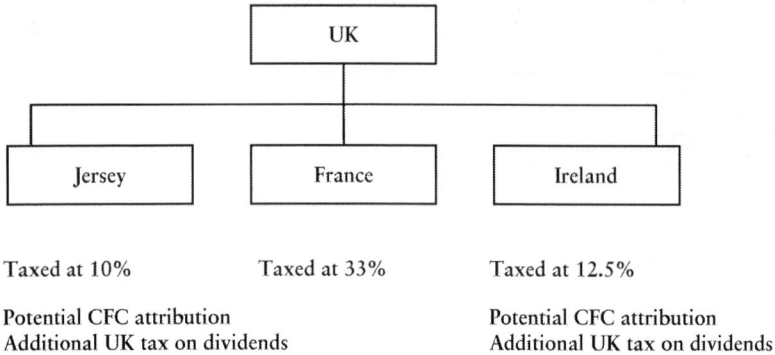

The objective of a migration in this case will be to avoid CFC and dividend taxation by establishing a holding company outside the UK to hold the shares in the subsidiaries.

Shares in a UK holding company represent a UK situs asset for the shareholders, and both dividends and capital gains will be taxed on an arising basis for non-domiciled shareholders.

If the new holding company is incorporated outside the UK, the shares will be non-situs assets for capital gains tax (and inheritance tax) purposes, such that a non-domiciled shareholder may only be subject to tax on gains which are remitted to the UK. If the company is resident outside the UK, then dividends will be relevant foreign income, such that a non-domiciled shareholder may only be subject to income tax if they are remitted to the UK.

## *Profits currently earned by UK companies/subsidiaries*

**[B8.4]** As shown in Diagram 2, profits earned by a UK company will be subject to UK corporation tax at 21%.

The objective of a migration in this case will be to move the activities which generate profits to companies which are not resident in the UK and which do not have a permanent establishment in the UK.

Diagram 2

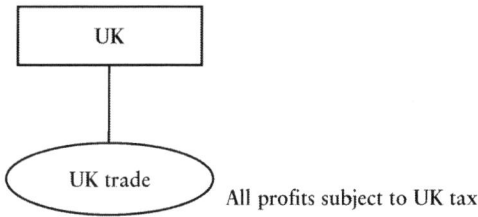

All profits subject to UK tax

This may be particularly difficult where profits are attributable to physical functions which are carried on in the UK, or assets which are held in the UK (both tangible and intangible). It may be necessary to actually move the physical functions or assets out of the UK in order to avoid the structure illustrated in Diagram 7.

It may also be necessary to create a new holding company if activities are transferred to subsidiaries in low-tax jurisdictions. If a new holding company were not created, the profits of the subsidiary could remain subject to UK tax either on the payment of a dividend (if the conditions for exemption were not satisfied) or through an attribution under the CFC rules.

## Transferring subsidiaries to a new holding company

**[B8.5]** There are broadly two methods by which a holding company outside the UK may be established:

(a)     a new holding company (above the existing UK holding company) can be established to which the subsidiaries are transferred; or

(b)     the existing UK holding company can be migrated to another juris-diction.

The tax issues will be similar in both cases:

•       the choice of jurisdiction;

•       the disposal (or deemed disposal) of assets by the existing UK holding company.

But the practicalities may be different, as establishing a new holding company may be more onerous than a migration. On the other hand, migration does not fully remove the group from the UK tax system.

It may not be necessary to transfer all subsidiaries to the new holding company—for instance:

•       where withholding taxes would be significantly increased on dividends; or

•       where the subsidiary is not within the CFC rules; or

•       where no UK corporation tax would arise on a dividend.

### Jurisdiction of new holding company

**[B8.6]** The features of a good holding company jurisdiction are outlined in CHAPTER B5. The preferred jurisdiction for the holding company will typically offer:

(a)     no CFC rules;

(b)     no tax on dividends received from subsidiaries;

(c)     no withholding tax on dividends paid to shareholders;

(d)     a good network of double tax agreements (DTAs) such that little or no withholding tax is suffered on dividends received from subsidiaries;

(e)     no tax on the disposal of subsidiaries.

Ireland is often a preferred jurisdiction because:

(a)     it is close to the UK and provides access to a qualified and English-speaking workforce;

(b)     there are no CFC rules;

(c)     dividends received from trading subsidiaries are subject to tax at 12.5% with credit for underlying tax;

(d)     dividends paid directly or indirectly to shareholders resident in the EU, or resident in a jurisdiction with which Ireland has a DTA, are exempt from withholding tax.

Switzerland, Luxembourg and the Netherlands are also used for similar reasons—an overview of holding company locations is in CHAPTER B5.

It is important that the holding company is centrally managed and controlled outside the UK as it would otherwise be treated as resident in the UK (see A9.5). The geographical location, and its proximity to the directors, will also therefore be important.

If the existing UK holding company is to be migrated to the new jurisdiction, it will also be necessary that:

(a)     residence can be established in the new jurisdiction under domestic law;

(b)     there is a DTA in place between the UK and the new jurisdiction which includes tie breaker article under which the company ceases to be resident in the UK by virtue of CTA 2009, s 18.

A number of groups have established new holding companies which are incorporated in Jersey, but resident for tax purposes in Ireland by virtue of being managed and controlled in Ireland.

This offers the benefits of the Irish tax system (which are broadly as outlined above), but also:

(a)     no stamp duty on the transfer of shares;

(b)     less onerous regulatory requirements in Jersey;

(c)     accounts are not required to be filed in Jersey;

(d)     automatic application of the Takeover Code;

(e)     company law is based on the UK Companies Act 1985.

### *Establishing a new holding company*

**[B8.7]** A new holding company can be established above the existing UK company by way of:

(a)    a share for share exchange as shown in Diagram 3; or
(b)    a scheme of arrangement under the Companies Act 2006 (which requires a lower level of shareholder approval).

Diagram 3

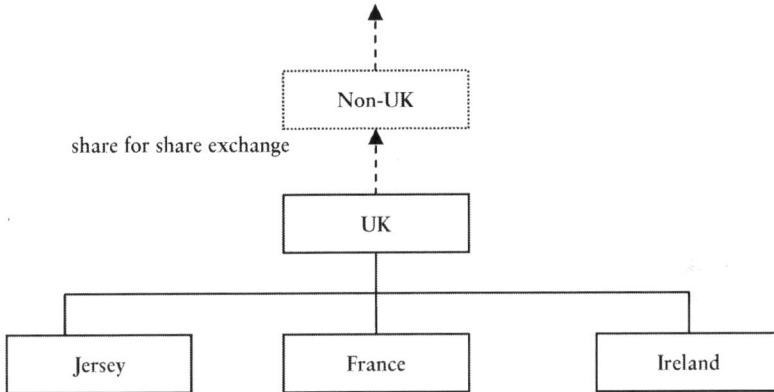

In either case, shareholders will be treated for UK tax purposes as disposing of their shares in the existing holding company, the consideration for which is the issue of shares in the new holding company.

Non-resident individual shareholders should not be subject to UK CGT unless they are subject to the temporary non-resident rules. Non-resident company shareholders should not be subject to UK tax on the disposal unless they fall within TCGA 1992, s 13 and the gain on disposal is attributed to their own UK resident shareholders.

Resident shareholders (both individual and company) will need to rely on the share exchange provisions of TCGA 1992, s 135. No gain will normally arise provided:

(a)    the shareholder holds less than 5% of the issued share capital of the existing holding company; or
(b)    the transaction is being undertaken for genuine commercial purposes (which may be difficult to support in a tax-motivated migration).

The disposal by a corporate shareholder (holding at least 10% of the shares in the existing holding company) may in addition be exempt under the substantial shareholding exemption.

### Transfer of subsidiaries

#### Chargeable gains

**[B8.8]** The transfer of the subsidiaries may crystallise a chargeable gain which is subject to UK tax. This may be exempt by virtue of the substantial shareholding exemption.

Diagram 4

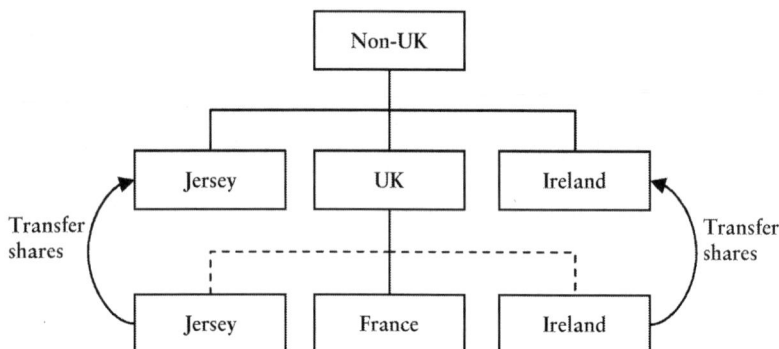

#### Consideration for the transfer

**[B8.9]** The consideration for the transfer will also need to be considered. This is discussed further below in the context of the consideration for the transfer of functions and other assets out of the UK.

#### Overseas tax considerations

**[B8.10]** The transfer of subsidiaries, even within a group, may have overseas tax consequences. For instance, if a German subsidiary has brought forward trading losses, these may be extinguished following an intra-group transfer.

### Migrate existing holding company

#### Deemed disposals and chargeable gains

**[B8.11]** A company which ceases to be resident in the UK is treated as having disposed of all of its assets for their current market value. This may crystallise a capital gain which is subject to UK tax, which may be exempt by virtue of the substantial shareholding exemption.

If the existing holding company holds assets other than shares, these could be transferred to another UK company in the group prior to the migration so that no gains arise other than in respect of the shares in the subsidiaries. As explained at **A7.49**, FA 2013, Sch 49 may in any case allow gains to be deferred.

**Clearance**

**[B8.12]** A clearance may be required under TMA 1970, s 109B for a company which ceases to be resident in the UK. This is discussed at **A9.42**.

**Controlled Foreign Company (CFC)**

**[B8.13]** The CFC rules will continue to apply to a company which is incorporated in the UK but treated as resident elsewhere under a DTA.

The profits of low-tax subsidiaries may therefore be attributed to the new holding company, and subject to UK corporation tax. This is shown in Diagram 5

The migration of an existing UK holding company may therefore only be effective in reducing the UK corporation tax on dividends received from subsidiaries.

Diagram 5

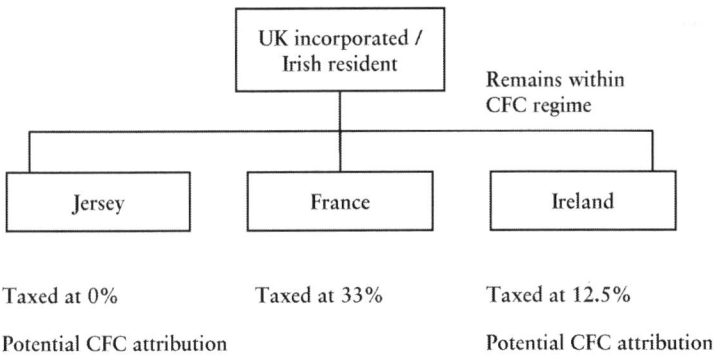

```
                    ┌──────────────────┐
                    │ UK incorporated / │
                    │  Irish resident   │     Remains within
                    └──────────────────┘     CFC regime
         ┌───────────────────┼───────────────────┐
   ┌──────────┐        ┌──────────┐        ┌──────────┐
   │  Jersey  │        │  France  │        │ Ireland  │
   └──────────┘        └──────────┘        └──────────┘
```

Taxed at 0%            Taxed at 33%          Taxed at 12.5%

Potential CFC attribution                    Potential CFC attribution

# Transferring activities from the UK

**[B8.14]** The transfer of activities from the UK is likely to crystallise a disposal for UK tax purposes, and chargeable gains may arise which will be subject to UK corporation tax.

Diagram 6

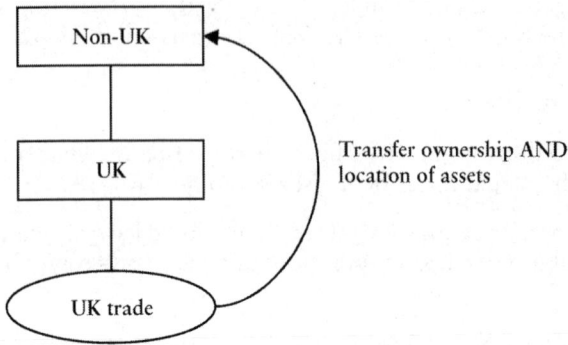

Diagram 7

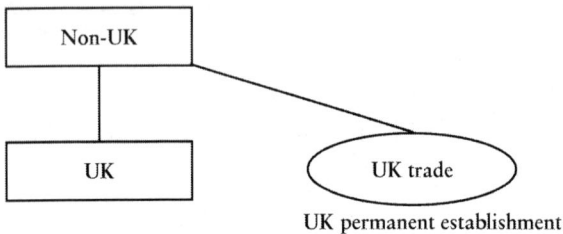

UK permanent establishment

## *Disposal of assets*

**[B8.15]** Tangible and intangible assets will be treated as disposed for their current market value (under TCGA 1992, s 17 and the equivalent provisions in CTA 2009, Part 8 for intangible assets) as they are transferred to a connected party.

The OECD Guidance on business restructuring (see **A13.59**) will apply to most migrations involving transfers of assets out of the UK. The guidance outlines ways in which tax may arise on a business restructuring, for instance:

(a)   there should be greater scrutiny of profit allocation following a restructuring;

(b)   while a business restructuring is not itself a taxable event, valuable intangibles may be transferred as part of a restructuring which may trigger a capital gain.

### Branch incorporation

**[B8.16]** The gain arising on the transfer of assets by a UK company may be deferred if the assets are used by a non-UK branch and the consideration for the transfer is an issue of shares. It may be possible to transfer assets from the UK to the branch, and then subsequently transfer them to the non-UK company.

This structure is discussed further at **A9.47**.

### Consideration for transfer

**[B8.17]** The consideration for the transfer of shares or assets from the existing UK company will usually be left outstanding on inter-company loan account, or represent a dividend in specie.

#### Loan

**[B8.18]** A loan from the UK company to the transferee may be subject to the UK transfer pricing rules. Interest will need to be recognised on this loan which will be subject to UK corporation tax. This may reduce the benefit of the migration, as the net reduction in the profit subject to UK corporation tax will be:

(reduction in UK profits)

minus

(value of subsidiaries or assets transferred) x (rate of interest)

As the value of the subsidiaries or assets may reflect their future profit, this calculation may only result in a small benefit.

If interest is actually charged on the inter-company balance, a withholding tax liability may arise.

#### Dividend in specie

**[B8.19]** If the transfer of shares or assets is effected by way of a dividend in specie, no inter-company loan balance will be created, and the tax benefit of the migration will be preserved.

In order to pay a dividend in specie, reserves will be required.

The position of the transferee company will need to be considered, as it will have received a dividend which may be subject to tax.

#### Existing cash

**[B8.20]** If the group has existing cash, this could be passed to the transferee company (by way of loan from a non-UK company, a dividend, or a capital contribution/increase in share capital), and the shares or assets purchased for cash from the UK transferor company.

The UK company may then pass the cash back to other group members, but this may also create an inter-company or a dividend, the issues associated with which are outlined above.

### Position of shareholders after migration

**[B8.21]** It is important—particularly with closely held companies—to consider the position of shareholders following the migration. If they pay significantly more tax as a result of the migration, this may outweigh benefit of the reduction in corporation tax.

### UK companies

**[B8.22]** A UK resident company shareholder may be subject to the CFC rules if it holds at least 25% of the new holding company.

As outlined in CHAPTER A16, most dividends received from subsidiaries (both UK and non-UK) are exempt from UK corporation tax, subject to certain conditions being satisfied.

### UK individuals

**[B8.23]** The income and gains of the new holding company may be attributed to a UK resident individual shareholder under ITA 2007, s 720 and TCGA 1992, s 13 respectively. Relief may be available under a DTA, and this may affect the choice of jurisdiction in which the new holding company is located.

A UK resident individual shareholder receives a notional tax credit on some dividends received from a non-resident company. The effective rate of tax on dividends will therefore be 25% in the same way as dividends from a UK resident company. However, no credit is available if the shareholder holds more than 10% of the shares and the company is resident in a non-qualifying territory (see **A15.27**).

If the new holding company is incorporated outside the UK, the shares will be non-situs assets for capital gains tax (and inheritance tax) purposes, such that a UK resident but non-domiciled shareholder may only be subject to tax on gains which are remitted to the UK. If the company is resident outside the UK, then dividends will be relevant foreign income, such that a non-domiciled shareholder may only be subject to income tax if they are remitted to the UK.

## Roadmap

**[B8.24]** The following roadmap can act as a checklist when advising overseas companies migrating a holding company, and provides a cross-reference into the relevant chapters of this book.

(1)    Identify the most appropriate jurisdiction in which to establish the new holding company. CHAPTER **B3**

(2)    If migrating the existing UK holding company:

    (a)    Consider exit charges which will arise under TCGA 1992, s 185 (which may be exempt by virtue of the substantial shareholding exemption, or deferred under TCGA 1992, s 187). Similar provisions may apply to intangible assets. **A9.35**

    (b)    Ensure that the company ceases to be resident in the UK under the terms of the relevant DTA. **A9.14**

(c)    The CFC rules will still apply to the holding company. **A6.14**

(d)    Notify HMRC prior to the migration. **A9.34**

(3)    If establishing a new holding company by way of a share exchange:

    (a)    Consider whether the reorganisation rules (TCGA 1992, s 135) will apply to UK resident (or temporary non-resident) shareholders with more than 5%.

    (b)    Issue replacement share options if necessary.

(4)    Ensure that the new holding company has ordinary share capital so that shareholders can qualify for certain tax reliefs. **A14.12**

(5)    If transferring assets from a UK company to the new holding company:

    (a)    Apply an arm's length interest rate under the transfer pricing rules to any consideration left outstanding on loan account. **A13.64**

    (b)    Disposal for market value (which may be exempt by virtue of the substantial shareholding exemption).

    (c)    Possible claim under EU law that the no gain / no loss provisions of TCGA 1992, s 171 apply to transfers to other EU Member States. **A7.16**

    (d)    Branches can be incorporated (and their assets subsequently transferred) with the gain deferred under TCGA 1992, s 140. **A9.37**

(6)    Effective tax rate on dividends for individual shareholders, and whether the dividend exemption will apply for corporate shareholders. CHAPTERS **A15** AND **A18**

(7)    Transfer of assets abroad/attribution of gains rules may apply to individual shareholders in the new holding company. CHAPTER **A15**

(8)    CFC rules may apply corporate shareholders in the new holding company CHAPTER **A6**.

(9)    How will BEPS and the UK GAAR impact?

# Part C

## Overview of some overseas tax systems

# C1

# An overview of some overseas tax systems

# Introduction

**[C1.1]** This Chapter provides an overview of some overseas tax systems, highlighting:

(a) some of the forms of business entity which can be used for undertaking business in that jurisdiction;

(b) the headline rates of tax, and the circumstances in which resident and non-resident companies are subject to tax;

(c) withholding taxes which may be due on payments made to non-residents.

This overview is not intended to be comprehensive, and is unlikely to provide any meaningful conclusions except in the most straightforward of cases.

Companies (and their tax advisers) should always seek advice on local tax obligations. Failing to obtain proper advice can result in interest and penalties. Local advice will identify compliance obligations and planning opportunities.

CHAPTERS C2, C3 and C4 provide more detail on investing into India, the US and China respectively.

# United States

**[C1.2]** Chapter C3 provides more detail on the practical issues faced by a UK company investing into the US.

## *Forms of business entity*

### Corporation

**[C1.3]** A corporation is created under state law rather than federal law. Certain states provide more flexible corporate law than others. Corporations with US resident shareholders may satisfy the conditions of Sub-Chapter S and elect to be treated as transparent entities for US tax purposes (S-Corporations). Corporations with foreign shareholders will not satisfy the conditions of Sub-Chapter S and so will only be able to create C-Corporations, which are opaque for US tax purposes. A corporation will also need to register with any state(s) where it has a place of business if this is not the same as the state of incorporation.

### Limited liability company (LLC)

**[C1.4]** An LLC offers more legal flexibility than a corporation as many issues are covered by the agreement under which it is formed rather than statute. For tax purposes, an LLC is treated as a branch (if it has a single member) or a partnership (if it has more than one member). LLCs are permitted to make an election to be treated as corporations for tax purposes. As with a corporation, an LLC must register in each state where it has a place of business if this is not the same as the state of incorporation.

### Branch

**[C1.5]** A foreign company that carries on business in the US through a branch must generally register with the state in which the branch is conducting business.

### Partnership

**[C1.6]** There are various types of partnership, the most common being the general partnership and the limited partnership. A limited partnership is one in which one or more partners, but not all, have limited liability. In a general partnership, unless specifically stated otherwise in the partnership agreement, each partner has unlimited liability for debts of the partnership.

For tax purposes, a partnership is treated as a transparent entity and each partner is taxed on the profits of the partnership. Partnerships can make an election to be treated as corporations for tax purposes.

## Rates of tax

**[C1.7]** Tax is charged in the US by both the federal government and the states. In addition, some cities (including for example New York) and counties also charge tax. Federal tax and most state taxes are creditable for UK purposes (see **A10.15**), but only federal tax is covered by the UK/US DTA (see **A8.12**).

Any state tax paid is deductible when calculating the profits chargeable to federal tax.

The profits for state tax purposes may be calculated in the same way as federal tax, but this is not the case in all states.

The current rates of US federal tax applicable to companies are:

| Taxable income (USD) | | | Rate |
|---|---|---|---|
| Up to | | 50,000 | 15 |
| 50,001 | – | 75,000 | 25 |
| 75,001 | – | 100,000 | 34 |
| 100,001 | – | 335,000 | 39 |
| 335,001 | – | 10,000,000 | 34 |
| 10,000,001 | – | 15,000,000 | 35 |
| 15,000,001 | – | 18,333,333 | 38 |
| over | | 18,333,333 | 35 |

The maximum rate of tax is 35%. The higher rates mentioned above largely operate to recapture the benefits of the lower rates.

Current rates of state tax vary from 0% to 12%.

An alternative minimum tax (AMT) may apply if this exceeds the normal tax liability. The profits subject to AMT include certain items which may not be taxable under the normal tax calculation.

### Basis of taxation for residents and non-residents

**[C1.8]** There is no concept of residence for US tax purposes. A company will either be domestic or foreign depending on its place of incorporation.

Domestic companies are subject to US tax on worldwide income.

Foreign companies are subject to US tax on income that is 'effectively connected' to the conduct of a trade or business in the US. This is not the same definition as a permanent establishment, although a double tax agreement (DTA) is likely to provide that profits can only be taxed to the extent that they relate to a permanent establishment in the US.

Foreign companies may also be subject to tax on capital gains arising on the sale of property in the US under the Foreign Investors in Real Property Tax Act (FIRPTA). Such gains are automatically treated as if they are income effectively connected to a trade or business in the US. FIRPTA also applies to disposals of shares in a US real property holding company (USRPHC), which is a company the value of whose assets are represented at least 50% by US property.

Transfer pricing rules may apply to transactions between related parties.

## Withholding taxes

[C1.9] Interest, dividends, and royalties (which are not connected with a US trade or business) paid to a non-resident are subject to 30% withholding tax.

In addition, all 'fixed or determinable, annual or periodical gains, profits and income' (abbreviated FDAP) from US sources are subject to 30% withholding tax. This includes rents, premiums, annuities, compensation, remuneration and emoluments.

If a gain is subject to tax under FIRPTA (see above), the purchaser should withhold 10% tax from the proceeds of sale, unless the vendor has reached prior agreement with the IRS to pay the tax.

The profits of a branch or partnership owned by a foreign company may be subject to a branch profits tax of 30% on any profits distributed from the branch or partnership in the same way as dividends.

# Australia

## Forms of business entity

### Company

[C1.10] There are two types of limited liability company:

(a) public companies;
(b) proprietary private companies.

More onerous legal obligations are placed on public companies than on private companies.

A proprietary company is a company that is limited by shares or an unlimited company that has a share capital. It cannot have more than 50 non-employee shareholders, and must not engage in any activity that would require the lodgement of a prospectus.

### Branch

[C1.11] To establish a branch, it is necessary to register as a foreign company in Australia with the Australian Securities and Investment Commission (ASIC).

## Partnership

[C1.12] There are two types of partnership, the general partnership and the limited partnership. A limited partnership is a partnership where at least one of the partners has limited liability. For tax purposes, a general partnership is treated as a transparent entity and each partner is taxed on the profits of the partnership. A limited partnership is treated as a company for tax purposes.

## Trust

[C1.13] It is common for trusts to carry on trading activities in Australia. A trustee manages the trust, and holds income and assets for the benefit of beneficiaries. The distribution of income from a discretionary trust is at the discretion of the trustees, but the distribution of income from a unit trust must be in proportion to the beneficiaries' unit holdings.

## *Rates of tax*

[C1.14] The current rate of Australian tax applicable to companies is 30%.

## *Basis of taxation for residents and non-residents*

[C1.15] A company is resident in Australia if:

(a)     it is incorporated in Australia; or
(b)     its central management and control is in Australia;
(c)     or it carries on a business in Australia and it has resident shareholders controlling the voting power.

Resident companies are subject to Australian tax on worldwide income. Certain income may be exempt, including:

(a)     profits from a permanent establishment which is trading outside Australia;
(b)     dividends from a foreign company provided at least 10% of the voting power is held by the Australian company.

Non-resident companies are subject to Australian tax on income with an Australian source, and on capital gains in respect of Australian property and assets used by a permanent establishment.

Common law applies to determine the source of income, although a DTA is likely to provide that profits can only be taxed to the extent that they relate to a permanent establishment in Australia.

Transfer pricing rules may apply to all transactions with non-residents, regardless of whether they are a related party.

## *Withholding taxes*

[C1.16] Dividends paid to a non-resident are subject to 30% withholding tax, unless they are fully franked dividends (broadly when they are paid out of profits which have been subject to Australian tax).

Interest paid to a non-resident is subject to 10% withholding tax.

Royalties paid to a non-resident are subject to 30% withholding tax. The domestic definition of royalties is broader than under most DTAs, and broader than the OECD definition.

# Canada

## *Forms of business entity*

### Corporation

**[C1.17]** A corporation may be established under either federal or provincial law, but incorporation under provincial law is more common as a corporation established under federal law is required to publicly file certain documents.

For tax purposes, a corporation may be defined as:

(a)  Canadian-controlled private corporation;
(b)  other private corporation;
(c)  public corporation;
(d)  corporation controlled by a public corporation;
(e)  other corporation.

The calculation of taxable income may differ depending on how the corporation is defined.

### Branch

**[C1.18]** To establish a branch, it is necessary to register as a foreign company in each province where business is undertaken.

### Partnership

**[C1.19]** There are two types of partnership, the general partnership and the limited partnership. Partners of a limited partnership have limited liability but are not allowed to take part in the management of the partnership, or act on its behalf.

A partnership is treated as a separate person when calculating taxable profits, but these profits are then subject to tax in the hands of the partners.

## *Rates of tax*

**[C1.20]** Tax is charged in Canada by both the federal government and the provinces. The provincial tax is not deductible when calculating the profits subject to federal tax.

The current rate of federal tax is 15% for certain small businesses effective 1 January 2012.

Current rates of provincial tax vary from 10% to 16% (with lower rates for certain small businesses).

### Basis of taxation for residents and non-residents

**[C1.21]** A company is resident in Canada if:

(a)    it is incorporated in Canada; or
(b)    its central management and control is in Canada.

Resident companies are subject to Canadian tax on worldwide income, and on 50% of any capital gains.

Non-resident companies are subject to Canadian tax on income derived from a business carried on in Canada. A business is considered to be carried on in Canada if the non-resident company:

(a)    produces, grows, mines, creates, manufactures, fabricates, improves, packs, preserves, or constructs anything in Canada;
(b)    solicits orders or offers anything for sale in Canada through an agent or servant.

This is broader than the definition of a permanent establishment, but a DTA is likely to provide that profits can only be taxed to the extent that they relate to a permanent establishment in Canada.

Non-resident companies are also subject to tax on capital gains in respect of:

(a)    Canadian property, including an interest in a company, trust or partnership the assets of which are at least 50% Canadian property;
(b)    assets used in a permanent establishment;
(c)    shares in a Canadian private company.

Transfer pricing rules may apply to transactions between related parties.

### Withholding taxes

**[C1.22]** Dividends paid to a non-resident are subject to 25% withholding tax.

Interest paid to a non-resident who is a related party is subject to 25% withholding tax. Interest paid to an arm's length non-resident is exempt from withholding tax effective 1 January 2008.

Royalties paid to a non-resident are subject to 25% withholding tax. This may include certain technical assistance and service fees.

Management fees which do not relate to a reasonable rate for services performed in the normal course of business are subject to 25% withholding tax. The 25% withholding tax also applies to rental payments.

The profits of a branch or partnership owned by a non-resident company may be subject to a branch profits tax of 25% on any profits distributed from the branch or partnership.

In respect to capital gains, a non-resident clearance certificate is required or the sale will be subject to withholding up to 50% of the entire purchase price.

# China

**[C1.23]** CHAPTER C4 provides more detail on the practical issues faced by a UK company investing into China.

## Forms of business entity

**[C1.24]** Non-residents are subject to restrictions on the activities which they can undertake in China. The most common forms for a non-resident establishing a business in China are:

(a)     Equity joint venture;
(b)     Co-operative joint venture;
(c)     Wholly foreign-owned enterprise (WFOE);
(d)     Representative office;
(e)     Foreign Invested Commercial Enterprise (FICE).

### Equity joint venture

**[C1.25]** An equity joint venture is formed by one or more Chinese parties and one or more foreign parties under the Sino-foreign Equity Joint Venture Enterprise Law. At least 25% of the joint venture's shareholding must be held by foreign investors.

Investors in an equity joint venture share profits and losses strictly in accordance with their respective contributions to the registered capital of the venture, and have limited liability.

An equity joint venture is subject to tax as a separate entity.

### Co-operative joint venture

**[C1.26]** A co-operative joint venture (sometimes referred to as a contractual joint venture) is formed under the Sino-Foreign Co-operative Joint Venture Enterprise Law. It may be a separate legal entity with limited liability, or similar to a partnership.

Investors in a co-operative joint venture share profits and losses in accordance with the provisions in the co-operative contract.

### Wholly foreign-owned enterprise (WOFE)

**[C1.27]** A WOFE is 100% owned by foreign investors, and is subject to tax as a separate entity.

### Representative office

**[C1.28]** A representative office can be formed to undertake preparatory services such as liaison, coordination and market research on behalf of its parent company.

### Foreign Invested Commercial Enterprise (FICE)

**[C1.29]** Foreign companies undertaking certain activities in China can form a FICE. These activities include:

(a)    Commission Agency;
(b)    Wholesaling;
(c)    Retailing;
(d)    Franchising.

### Rates of tax

**[C1.30]** The current rate of tax for both resident and non-resident enterprises is 25%.

### Basis of taxation for residents and non-residents

**[C1.31]** A company is a 'resident enterprise' if:

(a)    it is incorporated under Chinese law; or
(b)    it has its place of effective management in China.

'Effective management' will be in China if the management and control is exercised in China over production and business operations, personnel, finance and accounting, and properties (see **A9.59** for more detail).

Resident enterprises are subject to Chinese tax on worldwide income.

A non-resident enterprise is subject to Chinese tax on income that is derived from any establishment or place of business in China, and income which is 'effectively connected' to it. This is broader than the definition of a permanent establishment and includes the place of provision of services and business agents. However, a DTA may provide that profits can only be taxed to the extent that they relate to a permanent establishment in China.

Transfer pricing rules may apply to all transactions with non-residents which are related parties.

### Withholding taxes

**[C1.32]** Passive income, including dividends, interest and royalties paid to a non-resident are subject to withholding tax of 10%. It is rare that this can be reduced further by China's tax treaties with other countries.

Exchange controls may also apply to certain transactions.

# Germany

### Forms of business entity

**[C1.33]** There are a number of entities through which business can be undertaken in Germany, including:

(a)    Aktiengesellschaft (AG)—a public limited company;
(b)    Gesellschaft mit beschränkter Haftung (GmbH)—a limited liability company;

(c)    Kommanditgesellschaft (KG)—a limited partnership;

(d)    GmbH & Co KG—a limited partnership with a limited liability company as a general partner;

(e)    Gesellschaft bürgerlichen Rechts (GbR)—a civil law partnership;

(f)    Stille Gesellschaft—a silent partnership.

## Company

**[C1.34]** A GmbH is a private limited company, and is more flexible than the AG. The shareholders of a GmbH can control and instruct the management directly, whereas the shareholders of an AG cannot.

In addition to the normal board of directors, larger companies which are formed as a GmbH, and all companies formed as an AG, are required to also have a supervisory board.

## Branch

**[C1.35]** Foreign companies must register the branch at the Commercial Register where the branch is located. Information relating to the foreign company itself will need to be provided.

## Partnership

**[C1.36]** There are broadly two types of partnership, the general partnership and the limited partnership. A limited partnership is a partnership where some partners have limited liability, but must have a general partner who has unlimited liability. The general partner can itself be a limited liability company (GmbH), and such partnerships are known as GmbH & Co KG.

A 'silent partnership' may also be established, where the partnership is not disclosed to third parties. A silent partner contributes a certain amount to the business, in exchange for a participation in the profits of the partnership, but not in the property of the business. The silent partner's liability for losses can be excluded in the partnership agreement. The silent partner also does not participate in the management of the business.

Partnerships are subject to trade tax, but the partners are subject to corporate income tax on their share of the profits.

## *Rates of tax*

**[C1.37]** Companies are subject to corporate income tax, trade tax and the solidarity surcharge.

The current rate of German tax applicable to companies is 15%. This is increased by the 'solidarity surcharge' of 5.5% so that the effective rate is 15.83%. The solidarity surcharge also applies to withholding taxes (see below), but not the trade tax.

The trade tax varies depending on the municipality where the company or branch is located. The current rate varies between 7% and 17%.

## *Basis of taxation for residents and non-residents*

**[C1.38]** A company is resident in Germany if:

(a)     it is incorporated in Germany; or
(b)     its place of management is in Germany.

Resident companies are subject to German tax on worldwide income. Certain income may be exempt, including 95% of the amount of a dividend received from a foreign company. Non-resident companies are subject to German tax on profits derived through a permanent establishment in Germany. Non-resident companies are also subject to tax on:

(a)     gains on the sale of property in Germany;
(b)     gains on the sale of assets used in a German permanent establishment;
(c)     gains on the sale of shares in a German company where the non-resident company has previously owned at least 1% of the company.

Transfer pricing rules may apply to all transactions between related parties.

## *Withholding taxes*

**[C1.39]** Dividends paid to a non-resident are subject to 25% withholding tax (26.38% including the 5.5% solidarity surcharge).

Interest paid to non-residents is generally not subject to withholding tax. However, certain interest paid to a non-resident is subject to 25% withholding tax (26.38% including the 5.5% solidarity surcharge). For these purposes, interest includes the distribution of profits under a silent partnership arrangement, among others. Royalties paid to a non-resident are subject to 15% withholding tax (15.83% including the 5.5% solidarity surcharge).

Fees paid to non-residents for the use of movable property (equipment etc) are subject to 25% withholding tax (26.38% including the 5.5% solidarity surcharge).

Fees paid to non-residents for construction work are subject to 15% withholding tax (15.83% including the solidarity charge).

# India

**[C1.40]** CHAPTER C2 provides more detail on the practical issues faced by a UK company investing into India.

## *Forms of business entity*

**[C1.41]** Under foreign direct investment (FDI) rules, investment in certain sectors (for instance retail and agriculture) may be restricted, or may require prior approval from the government.

## Company

**[C1.42]** There are two types of limited liability company:

(a)     public companies;
(b)     private companies.

More onerous legal obligations are placed on public companies than on private companies.

A private company cannot have more than 50 non-employee shareholders. Both public and private companies have minimum capital requirements.

## Branch

**[C1.43]** A non-resident company can establish a liaison office or a branch office in India, with the approval of the Reserve Bank of India (RBI). A liaison office cannot undertake business activity or earn income in India. A branch office is permitted to undertake business activity which will be limited to the activity specifically agreed with the RBI. Indian branches of non-resident companies are subject to corporate income tax at the rate of 40% on Indian-source income earned by or attributed to them. There is no branch tax in addition to the normal corporate income tax.

A non-resident company can establish a project office to execute a specific project in India. No approval is required from the RBI provided certain conditions are satisfied.

## Partnership

**[C1.44]** A non-resident company can invest in a partnership subject to approval from the RBI.

A partnership is a separate taxable person. If the partnership agreement sets out the profit shares of the partners, it will be taxed at the corporate rate. Otherwise, it will be subject to tax at the tax rates applicable to the partners.

## *Rates of tax*

**[C1.45]** The current rate of Indian tax applicable to resident companies is 30%. This is increased by a 5% surcharge (if income exceeds INR10m) or a 10% surcharge (if income exceeds INR100m) and a 3% education cess, resulting in an effective rate of 30.9/32.445/33.99%.

The current rate of Indian tax applicable to non-resident companies is 40%. This is increased by a 2% surcharge (if income exceeds INR10m) or 5% surcharge (if income exceeds INR100m) and a 3% education cess, resulting in an effective rate of 41.2/42.024/43.26% The surcharge and education cess also apply to withholding taxes.

## *Basis of taxation for residents and non-residents*

**[C1.46]** A company is resident in India if:

(a)     it is incorporated in India; or

(b)    its management and control is located wholly in India.

This definition is likely to be amended by the new Direct Taxes Code (see C2.10). Resident companies are subject to Indian tax on worldwide income and capital gains.

Non-resident companies are subject to Indian tax on income arising from:

(a)    a permanent establishment in India;
(b)    a business connection with India;
(c)    income sourced in India.

This is broader than the definition of a permanent establishment, but a DTA may provide that profits can only be taxed to the extent that they relate to a permanent establishment in India. The definition of permanent establishment in many of India's DTAs includes a 'service permanent establishment' (see A4.21), which does not require a fixed place of business to exist.

Transfer pricing rules may apply to transactions between related parties.

### Withholding taxes

[C1.47] Dividends paid to a non-resident are not subject to withholding tax. However, dividends are subject to a dividend distribution tax of 15% (16.22% including the 7.5% surcharge and education cess). As the dividend distribution tax is not a withholding tax, it may not be eligible for relief under a DTA or unilateral relief in the UK.

Interest paid to a non-resident is subject to 20% withholding tax (21.02% including the surcharge and educational cess). Interest payments may also be subject to approval by the Reserve Bank of India (RBI) under exchange control provisions.

Royalties and payments for technical services paid to a non-resident are subject to 25% withholding tax.

# France

## Forms of business entity

[C1.48] There are a number of entities through which business can be undertaken in France, including:

(a)    Société anonyme (SA)—a public limited company;
(b)    Société par actions simplifiée (SAS);
(c)    Société à responsabilité limitée (SARL) — a private limited company;
(d)    Société en commandite simple (SCS) — a limited partnership;
(e)    Société en nom collectif (SNC) — a general partnership.

### Company

[C1.49] A company is generally formed as an SA, an SAS or and SARL.

The SAS is a simplified form of SA, often used for subsidiaries. Certain decisions are required to be taken by the shareholders of an SAS, and it may therefore not be appropriate for a company with a number of shareholders.

The SARL is a private limited company, and any transfers of shares must be approved by other shareholders.

## Branch

**[C1.50]** A number of registrations and approvals are required before a foreign company can operate through a branch in France, for instance application for entry to the business register, and filings with the government and commercial court.

The branch will be managed by a local manager (gérant).

## Partnership

**[C1.51]** A foreign company may become a member of a French partnership. There are various types of partnership, the most common being the general partnership (SNC) and the limited partnership (SCS).

For tax purposes, a partnership is treated as a transparent entity and each partner is taxed on the profits of the partnership. Partnerships can make an election to be treated as corporations for tax purposes.

## Rates of tax

**[C1.52]** The current rate of French tax applicable to companies is 33.33% (with a lower rate for very small companies). This is increased by the 'social surcharge' of 3.3% for companies whose income tax liability exceeds €763,000 so that the effective rate is 34.43%. For very large companies with a turnover in excess of €250m a further surcharge of 10.7% is to be employed for years ending between 31 December 2013 and 31 December 2015.

## Basis of taxation for residents and non-residents

**[C1.53]** A company is generally considered to be resident in France if:

(a)     it is incorporated in France; or
(b)     its effective management is in France.

Both resident and non-resident companies are subject to French tax on trading income generated in France.

In addition, resident companies are subject to French tax on worldwide passive income. Non-resident companies are subject to tax on rental income from French property.

Income is treated as generated in France if it is derived through:

(a)     a permanent establishment in France;
(b)     a dependent agent in France;

(c)     a 'full commercial cycle' which is undertaken in France ie the whole profit-generating process from manufacture to sale.

This is broader than the definition of a permanent establishment, A DTA may provide that profits can only be taxed to the extent that they relate to a permanent establishment in France.

Transfer pricing rules may apply to all transactions between related parties.

### Withholding taxes

**[C1.54]** Dividends paid to a non-resident are subject to 30% withholding tax (55% for distributed profits paid into uncooperative states).

Interest paid to a non-resident is subject to 18% withholding tax. Outbound interest and royalty payments are exempt from withholding tax, provided the beneficial owner of the interest/royalty is an associated company of the paying company and is resident in another EU Member State.

Royalties, and fees for technical, commercial or consulting services paid to a non-resident are subject to 33.33% withholding tax (50% for royalties paid into uncooperative states).

Capital gains are subject to withholding tax of 33.33%, which as paid at the time the transfer is registered.

The profits of a branch owned by a foreign company outside the EU may be subject to a branch profits tax of 30% on any profits distributed from the branch or partnership.

# Brazil

### Forms of business entity

#### Corporation (S/A)

**[C1.55]** Incorporating a business corporation (Sociedade Anonima or S/A) in Brazil is complex. Business corporations may be publicly held (in this case, they are supervised by the Securities and Exchange Commission – 'CVM') or closely held. The incorporation sets up with the following requisites:

(a)     subscription of all of the shares by at least two persons; and
(b)     initial payment of at least 10% of the issue price of shares subscribed in cash unless specific legislation requires a higher percentage.

No minimum capital requirements are imposed for corporations, except in specific situations. The articles of incorporation attribute responsibility for management duties solely to the board of executive officers or to the board of directors in combination with the board of executive officers. Members of the board of directors may be non-residents, as long as one resident in Brazil be elected as legal representative. An SA must publish its financial statements as well as any shareholder, board of directors, board of executive officers and audit committee resolutions.

## Limited liability company (Ltda)

[C1.56] The Limitada or Ltda is the most common form of business entity in Brazil, as well as the most flexible and easiest to manage. A Ltda must have at least two members of any nationality, being entities or individuals. Usually, no minimum capital requirements are imposed; however, some requisites may be required for specific purposes or activities. The corporate instruments of the Ltdas shall be filed with the Board of Trade for their due registration. Limitadas may increase their corporate capital any time after the subscribed capital has been fully paid-up by the members. Reduction of the corporate capital of a Limitada, on the other hand, is only permitted under certain specific circumstances. The administration of the Limitadas must be performed by a Brazilian resident (whether or not a member), who may be a foreigner with a permanent visa and work permit.

## Branch

[C1.57] Incorporating branches of foreign companies in Brazil is usually a time consuming and very bureaucratic process, since it requires prior authorisation from the Brazilian Federal Government. As a result, investors usually conduct business through subsidiaries rather than through branches in Brazil. In the event a branch is created, it will usually be subject to taxes in Brazil as if it was a subsidiary.

## Rates of tax

[C1.58] There are two corporate taxes on profits in Brazil, and their combined rate is approximately 34%. Generally, Corporate Income Tax (IRPJ) applies at a basic rate of 15%, plus a surtax of 10% on annual taxable income that exceeds R$ 240,000. The Social Contribution on Profit (CSLL) is applied at a base rate of 9%. This rate may be different for financial institutions.

There are three major options for Brazilian legal entities to calculate and pay corporate taxes on profits: the 'Actual Profit System', the 'Presumed Profit System' and the 'Simples Regime'.

The 'Actual Profit System' corresponds to applying the IRPJ and CSLL rates (34%) on the company's net book profits under Brazilian GAAP, adjusted by certain specific add-backs and deductions, such as non-deductible expenses and exempt revenues. This method is usually preferred when the profit margins are significantly lower than the predetermined profits of the 'Presumed Profit System'.

The 'Presumed Profit System' is based on a presumed net profit which is calculated by applying a predetermined presumed profit rate on the gross revenues of the company. The profit rates are determined by the Federal Government and vary according to the activity of each company. This method of calculation can be more beneficial in certain cases, such as when the actual profit of the company is higher than the presumed profit. However, this system is not available in all instances, since there are several restrictions, including a maximum turnover of R$ 78 million in the previous year.

Additionally to these two income taxes, there are more than 50 other taxes in Brazil, at a federal, state and municipal levels, including taxes on gross revenue, taxes on services, VAT-type taxes, property taxes and excise taxes.

## Basis of taxation for residents and non-residents

**[C1.59]** Generally, only companies legally incorporated in Brazil are subject to taxes as residents, since Brazilian companies must register for tax purposes. However, companies that carry out taxable activities in Brazil but are not properly registered for tax purposes are potentially subject to taxation in Brazil as well.

Brazilian tax legislation does not clearly provide for a permanent establishment concept and guidance regarding the potential tax impacts of having foreign entities carrying out business activities in Brazil. There are only a few administrative precedents in the form of tax assessments on the matter. This may be because in certain cases, the tax burden on the income of a non-resident (i.e. taxes withheld in Brazil on remittances abroad) is even higher than the eventual taxation the characterisation of a permanent establishment would create.

Domestic companies are subject to Brazil tax on worldwide income.

Foreign companies may also be subject to tax on capital gains arising on the sale of assets in Brazil.

Transfer pricing rules may apply to cross border transactions between related parties.

## Withholding taxes

**[C1.60]** Dividends are generally tax free in Brazil, provided some requirements are met and irrespective of the location of the beneficiary. Interest and interest on net equity (hybrid repatriation instrument) are subject to a 15% withholding tax (25% if the beneficiary is located in a low tax jurisdiction, which is not the case of the UK).

Cross border payments of service fees, license fees, management fees, royalties, among others, are subject to the same 15% withholding tax (25% if the beneficiary is located in a low tax jurisdiction, which is not the case of the UK), but could also be subject to up to five other taxes in Brazil, some of them borne by the Brazilian entity/individual, others borne by the recipient.

Local payments of service fees are also subject to withholding taxes, at a lower rate.

# C2

# UK companies investing in India

## Introduction

**[C2.1]** A UK company with a branch in India will typically face higher tax rates than in the UK, and therefore additional tax cost even if the Indian tax can be credited against the UK tax arising.

This Chapter also considers some of the peculiar features of doing business in India, including:

• when a taxable presence, including the 'service permanent establishment';
• restrictions on inward investment;
• the process for obtaining benefits under a double tax agreement (DTA);
• proposed changes to the Indian Direct Tax Code from 1 April 2015.

### Branch v subsidiary

**[C2.2]** A non-resident company can operate in India in various forms:

• a liaison office or representative office can undertake limited activities such as liaison or market research but cannot undertake any business activity or earn income in India;
• a branch office;
• a project office to undertake a specific project;
• establishing a local subsidiary.

Forming a liaison office, a branch office or a project office requires approval from the Reserve Bank of India (RBI).

From a tax perspective, a non-resident company will be subject to Indian income tax on income arising from:

- a permanent establishment in India; or
- a business connection with India.

A 'business connection' is broader than a permanent establishment and although it is not specifically defined in the law it has been considered by the courts in a number of cases.

Where a DTA is in place, it will typically provide that profits can only be taxed to the extent that they relate to a permanent establishment in India—this is the position under the UK/India DTA.

In addition to a fixed place of business and dependent agency, the definition of permanent establishment in many of India's double tax agreements (again, including the UK) includes a 'service permanent establishment'.

Once it is determined that a taxable presence exists, the choice between a branch and a subsidiary can be difficult. As outlined below, Indian companies are subject to a lower rate of tax than a branch, but further tax arises on the distribution of profits. The choice between a branch or subsidiary may therefore depend on whether profits will be reinvested by the Indian company.

Non-resident companies without a permanent establishment in India may suffer withholding tax on income.

### Service permanent establishment

**[C2.3]** Under the UK/India DTA, a permanent establishment will exist where a UK company carries out services in India for more than 90 days in any twelve month period. This is reduced to 30 days if services are being provided to a related party. The time spent in India by all employees must be added together when determining whether the 90 or 30 day limit is breached.

In 2010, the case of *Linklaters LLP v Income Tax Officer—International Taxation Ward 1(1)(2)*, Mumbai (2010) 13 ITLR 245 reinforced the 'force of attraction' principle in relation to a service permanent establishment. In this case, all income derived from Indian clients was deemed to arise from the permanent establishment, even if work was undertaken outside of India. However, this decision was reversed in the 2013 case of *ADIT v Clifford Chance* (ITA No 5034-5035/Mum/2004) (7095/Mum/04) (3021/Mum/05), unreported, which held that under the UK/India double tax agreement, services provided outside India could not be taxed in India.

This case also determined that the taxable income should be computed at rates actually billed by the UK partnership, rather than the rates which would have been charged for equivalent services in India.

### Tax base and rates

**[C2.4]** The rate of income tax applicable to branches and Indian companies is different, and both are increased by a surcharge (if profits are above INR10 million, approximately £140,000) and education cess. The surcharge and cess also apply to withholding taxes.

Branches are taxed at an effective rate of 42.024% (40% plus 2% surcharge plus 3% education cess). The net income of the branch which has a business connection with India is subject to tax, with a deduction for administrative expenses of the parent company limited to 5% of the income for the year.

Indian companies are taxed at an effective rate of 32.445% (30% plus 5% surcharge plus 3% education cess). However, a further tax charge arises on the distribution of profits by way of dividend. This dividend distribution tax is applied at an effective rate of 16.2225% (15% plus 5% surcharge plus 3% education cess) on any dividends paid.

The dividend distribution tax is a corporate tax rather than a withholding tax and can only be claimed as underlying tax. A UK resident individual shareholder in an Indian company cannot therefore claim credit for the dividend distribution tax.

### Example 1

An Indian company makes profits equivalent to £200,000. The Indian tax on these profits at an effective rate of 32.445% is £64,890. The remaining profits of £135,110 are distributed by way of dividend, on which the dividend distribution tax at an effective rate of 16.2225% is £21,918. A UK resident individual shareholder in the Indian company receives a net dividend of £113,192 on which tax is paid at an effective of 25% (assuming the shareholder is a higher rate taxpayer, and the notional dividend tax credit is available). After tax, the shareholder receives £84,894 having paid an overall effective rate of 58% tax.

Tax holidays are available for certain activities, but even where a holiday is claimed, a Minimum Alternative Tax (MAT) will apply. The MAT applies to book profits, the calculation of which may be slightly different to the normal tax base, as certain deductions are not allowed. The effective rate of MAT is 20.01% (18.5% plus 5% surcharge and 3% educational cess). The MAT can be carried forward for ten years and set against any income tax arising in that period. The effective rate of MAT is 19.44% for non-resident companies where total income exceeds INR 10 million (18.5% plus the applicable surcharge of 2% and the 3% education cess).

### Withholding taxes

[C2.5] Even where there is no permanent establishment, withholding taxes will apply to certain payments made by an Indian company to a non-resident. The rate of withholding tax on royalties and technical service fees is 20% unless the recipient has a Permanent Account Number (PAN), in which case it is reduced to 10%. The rate of withholding tax on interest is 20%.

The PAN is a tax registration number which all companies with a permanent establishment in India are required to have as part of their normal compliance procedures. However, since 1 April 2010 it is necessary to obtain a PAN even where the services are wholly carried on outside India. It is beneficial for a company to obtain a PAN, as this will determine the rate of withholding tax on royalties and interest. If the company does not obtain a PAN then the higher 20% withholding will automatically apply.

The only disadvantage is that a company with a PAN is also required to file tax returns in India. In most cases these would be nil returns but some companies may prefer to suffer higher rates of withholding tax rather than put themselves within the Indian tax system and the risk of a tax audit.

A PAN is also required to claim reduced rates of withholding tax under DTAs. Under the UK/India DTA, the rate of withholding tax on interest, royalties and technical service fees is 15%. In the case of royalties and technical service fees, the domestic rate of 10% (which is applicable where a company holds a PAN) would apply in priority to the higher rate under the DTA.

### Employment taxes

**[C2.6]** Under the UK/India DTA, an employee of a non-resident company is not subject to tax in India provided:

* the company does not have a permanent establishment in India;
* the employee does not spend more than 183 days in India during the fiscal year (which runs to 31 March).

If a permanent establishment does exist, employees will be liable to Indian income tax on all income earned in India, regardless of the amount of time spent in India. Tax is due on all income above INR200,000, which equates to approximately £2,000.

Credit will be available in the UK but tax compliance requirements will need to be dealt with. The employer is required to withhold tax from salaries, and employment costs will not be deductible against profits if the tax has not been correctly withheld.

### Visas

**[C2.7]** Since October 2009, all employees undertaking projects in India have been required to hold an employment visa—previously it was possible for them to just hold a business visa. Only skilled employees are able to obtain a visa.

In order to obtain an employment visa, the employee must have a PAN (see above). Where employees are being sent to India, sufficient time should be allowed—applying for PANs and employment visas is a laborious process which typically requires proof of identification being notarised.

Business visas are still available for certain activities such as purchasing or selling industrial products, and establishing new industrial and business activities in India.

### Limits on investment

**[C2.8]** In certain sectors, restrictions apply to the ownership of Indian companies by foreign investors. The level of restriction depends on the sector. For example:

* single brand retailers (maximum foreign ownership 100%);

- multi brand retailers (maximum foreign ownership 49%);
- defence (maximum foreign ownership 26%);
- agriculture (no foreign ownership allowed);
- banking (maximum foreign ownership 74%);
- gambling and betting (no foreign ownership allowed).

Even where 100% foreign ownership is permitted, approval may be required from the government before an investment is made, including where an industrial license is required, and in financial services.

Restrictions also apply to loans (referred to as External Commercial Borrowing or ECB, which includes loans from parent companies). Certain loans are treated as 'automatically' approved by the RBI if they satisfy the conditions relating to the amounts, terms and interest rates which are allowed. Other loans may require specific approval. There are also restrictions on the use of ECB, which for example cannot be used for working capital or for acquiring real estate. These must be funded by equity.

There are no thin capitalisation rules in India, but interest must be calculated at arm's length rates under the transfer pricing rules.

### Typical Indian investment structures

[C2.9] There are some general principles which can be followed when structuring investment into India:

- The dividend distribution tax is not a withholding tax, and is not therefore reduced under DTAs.
- The rate of withholding tax on interest is reduced under certain DTAs, including the India/Cyprus DTA (under which it is reduced from 20% to 10%). If permissible, financing can be provided via these jurisdictions, but in many cases there will be regulatory restrictions (as outlined above) which mean that financing must be by way of equity rather than debt.
- Where a DTA is in place, no Indian tax arises if a project can be structured so that there is no permanent establishment.

Many structures focus on avoiding Indian tax arising on the disposal of an Indian subsidiary. A typical structure is shown in Diagram 1, and the principles are also outlined in A11.13.

In the absence of any relief, a sale of the shares in IndiaCo would be subject to tax in India.

Tax would be charged at an effective rate of 21.115% (20% plus 2.5% surcharge plus 3% education cess) if the shares have been held for at least twelve months. If the shares have been held for less than twelve months, the effective rate would be 33.2175% (30% plus 7.5% surcharge plus 3% education cess).

## Diagram 1

```
┌─────────────────────┐
│        UKCo         │
└─────────────────────┘
          │
┌─────────────────────┐
│     MauritiusCo     │
└─────────────────────┘
          │
┌─────────────────────┐
│       IndiaCo       │
└─────────────────────┘
```

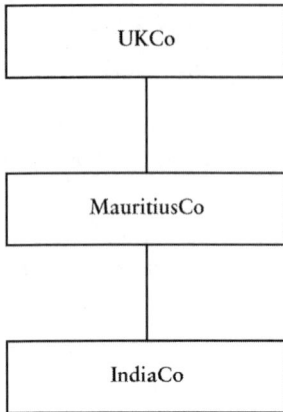

A purchaser is required to withhold this tax or he will be in default, and this should be taken into account when drafting sale and purchase agreements for Indian assets—giving the purchaser the right to recover any tax due from the vendor.

In practice, it may difficult to enforce collection of capital gains tax on the sale of an Indian company by one non-resident investor to another. In these cases the Indian tax authorities may seek the tax from the subsidiary if there is a business connection with the buyer.

However, the India/Mauritius DTA provides that the capital gain on the disposal of shares in an Indian company by a Mauritius company is not subject to Indian capital gains tax. Similar benefits are provided under the double tax agreements with Cyprus, Singapore and the Netherlands (although it is less common to see structures using Singapore or the Netherlands).

The Indian tax authorities have issued a circular to confirm that where a certificate of residence is issued by the Mauritian authorities, this certificate will be sufficient to evidence the residence status of the Mauritian company for the purpose of obtaining benefits under the DTA. However, under the proposed new tax code (see below), such a certificate will not be sufficient to prevent the general anti-avoidance rule from denying benefits under the DTA. It would then be necessary to put additional commercial substance in Mauritius to justify the structure.

No similar confirmation has been given in respect of other jurisdictions and it would therefore be necessary for residence to be determined in accordance with general principles.

The sale of shares in an intermediate holding company (for example the sales of shares in MauritiusCo by UKCo) is not the sale of an Indian asset and on general principles should not be subject to Indian tax. However, this is currently being challenged by the Indian tax authorities in a number of cases where the value of the intermediate holding company is represented by Indian assets.

The most notable of these cases is *Vodafone*, where a UK company purchased shares in a Mauritius holding company from a Cayman company in the Hutchison-Essar group. The Mauritius holding company held shares in an Indian subsidiary, and the Indian tax authorities have argued that the gain should therefore be subject to Indian capital gains tax. They have assessed the UK company which should have withheld the tax from the price paid to the vendor. Although the tax payer was ultimately successful in its arguments in the Indian Supreme Court, the Indian Government introduced legislation that applies retroactively to 1962. Therefore, tax payers need to exercise caution in this area.

### New direct tax code ('DTC')

[**C2.10**] It is proposed that a new tax code (the Direct Taxes Code or DTC) will come into effect in India from 1 April 2015. There are two key areas of the amended code which are likely to have an impact on existing inbound structures (as well as new ones).

Under current rules, a company which is not incorporated in India will only be treated as tax resident in India if management and control is located wholly in India. Under the DTC, a company will be treated as tax resident in India if its 'place of effective management' is located there. The proposed statutory definition of 'place of effective management' is:

- where the board of directors make decisions, or
- where executive directors or officers, whose commercial and strategic decisions are routinely approved by the board, perform their functions.

The DTC also introduces a general anti-avoidance rule (GAAR) which would allow the Indian tax authorities to declare any arrangement to be an 'impermissible avoidance arrangement' if:

- it results in certain tax benefits or it creates rights or obligations which would not normally be created between persons dealing at arm's length, or
- the arrangement results in abuse of the provisions of the code, or
- the arrangement lacks commercial substance, or
- the arrangement lacks bona fide business purpose.

This GAAR takes precedence over DTAs, and relief (for example against tax on capital gains as outlined above) would depend on there being sufficient commercial and business substance. The GAAR will also take effect from 1 April 2015.

The new direct tax code also aims to standardise corporate tax rates at 30% with no surcharge or excess. However, it will be supplemented by a branch profit tax and dividend withholding tax, both at a rate of 15%. The code also looks to introduce a minimum alternative tax (MAT) at a rate of 20% of adjusted book profits.

# C3

# UK companies investing in the US

**[C3.1]** This Chapter outlines the tax issues faced by a UK company undertaking activities in the US. The US tax system is sophisticated and (rightfully) considered to be complex. Tax rates are typically higher than in the UK, and withholding taxes apply to most cross border transactions. It is often important to ensure that the UK/US DTA applies. From a tax perspective, investing into the US can therefore be difficult and expensive.

## Overview of US tax system

**[C3.2]** The US federal tax rules are set out in legislation, but this is supplemented by a significant number of regulations.

Trading profits are subject to US federal tax if they are effectively connected income (ECI) ie profits connected with the conduct of a trade or business undertaken in the US. If the UK/US DTA applies, federal tax will only arise on trading profits if the UK company has a permanent establishment in the US. Table 1 shows the normal rates of federal tax.

In addition to federal tax (which is imposed by the US government), most states impose a corporate income tax on trading profits. A state will only have taxing rights if the company has a 'nexus' with that state. Each state has its own definition of nexus, but a company may have a nexus if it has premises, employees, holds stock, or delivers goods to customers in a particular state.

Profits subject to state tax are usually calculated in the same way as for federal tax, and then apportioned to a particular state based on formula—which usually takes into account property, payroll and sales in that state. Although sales only is starting to become prevalent. There is a wide disparity in state tax rates, as shown in Table 2. State tax is deductible for federal tax purposes, so the effective rate is normally lower than the headline rates.

The UK/US DTA does not apply to state taxes, and a state tax liability can therefore arise even if the DTA provides that there is no federal tax liability.

# Forms of entity

**[C3.3]** A UK company can undertake activities in the US in a number of ways.

### Corporation as a subsidiary

**[C3.4]** A corporation is created under state law rather than federal law. Certain states provide more flexible corporate law than others. Corporations with US resident shareholders may satisfy the conditions of Sub-Chapter S and elect to be treated as transparent entities for US tax purposes (S-Corporations), but corporations with foreign shareholders will not satisfy the conditions of Sub-Chapter S and so will only be able to create C-Corporations.

### Limited liability company (LLC) as a subsidiary

**[C3.5]** An LLC usually offers more legal flexibility than a corporation as many issues are covered by the agreement under which it is formed rather than statute.

For US tax purposes, an LLC is treated as a branch (if it has a single member) or a partnership (if it has more than one member). However, this does not affect the UK tax treatment and an LLC will usually be treated as a company for UK tax purposes.

An individual member of an LLC cannot therefore obtain relief for any tax paid in respect of the LLC's profits, as the tax is underlying tax—this was confirmed in the case of *Anson v Revenue and Customs Commissioners* (FTC/39/2010) (12 and 13 April 2011, unreported.

Not all LLCs issue 'ordinary share capital' for UK tax purposes, which may affect the availability of the substantial shareholding exemption or distribution exemption.

However, HMRC consider (in Revenue & Customs Brief 54/07) that where an interest in a LLC is evidenced by a 'certificate of limited liability company interest' this may be regarded as ordinary share capital. Where the LLC does not issue such certificates the brief states that the entity may still have 'ordinary share capital' but regard must be had to the particular terms of the agreement by which the LLC has been created.

An issue can arise on the sale of an LLC by a UK company. Because an LLC is a disregarded entity for US tax purposes, the UK company is broadly treated as if it were selling the US business directly. The published view of the IRS (Rev.

Rul 91–32) is that any gain arising would be subject to US tax, and although some commentators consider this view to be incorrect it must be taken into account. A UK company which is likely to sell its US subsidiary should therefore form a corporation, the gain on which would not be subject to US tax (unless it were a real property holding company).

### Branch

**[C3.6]** A foreign company that carries on business in the US through a branch must generally register with the state where the branch is conducting business.

### Partnership

**[C3.7]** There are various types of partnership, the most common being the general partnership and the limited partnership. A limited partnership is one in which one or more partners, but not all, have limited liability. In a general partnership, unless specifically stated otherwise in the partnership agreement, each partner has unlimited liability for debts of the partnership.

For both US and UK tax purposes, a partnership is treated as a transparent entity and each partner is taxed on the profits of the partnership.

## Withholding taxes

**[C3.8]** The rates of federal and state taxes are set out in Table 1 and Table 2 respectively.

A UK company may in addition be subject to US tax by way of withholding tax (s 1442), or on the sale of US property.

Withholding tax applies to Fixed, Determinable, Annual, Periodical (FDAP) income which has a US source (s 861), unless the income is ECI (see above). FDAP income includes (s 1441):

- Dividends;
- Interest;
- Rents;
- Royalties;
- Commissions.

The rate of FDAP withholding is 30%, unless reduced under the UK/US DTA (see below).

Not all distributions made by US companies will be dividends. For tax purposes, a distribution is treated as a dividend (and therefore subject to withholding tax) only to the extent that the company has earnings and profits (E&P), which is analogous to retained earnings. Distributions in excess of E&P are treated as a return of capital, which will reduce the base cost of the shares, and then crystallise a capital gain. This does not affect the treatment of distribution for UK tax purposes—if the shares remain intact following the distribution, the distribution will be income rather than capital, under the principles established in *Rae (Inspector of Taxes) v Lazard Investment Co Ltd* [1963] 1 WLR 555, 41 TC 1.

Withholding tax also applies to the disposal of US property by a non-US resident, under the Foreign Investment in Real Property Tax Act (FIRPTA). This includes the disposal of shares in US companies which hold US property (US Real Property Holding Company or USRPHC). The rate of FIRPTA withholding is 10% of the gross sale proceeds, unless the non-US resident has obtained permission from the IRS to pay a lower rate. This is not reduced under the UK/US DTA, which allows the US taxing rights over the disposal of US property, including shares in US property holding companies.

The non-US resident must then file a US tax return reporting the actual gain. The gain is taxed in the same way as ECI (see above), and a credit or refund is given for the FIRPTA withholding tax suffered.

From 1 June 2014, the Foreign Account Tax Compliance Act (FATCA) will require non-US financial institutions to report information on US account holders to the IRS. Institutions which do not comply will themselves be subject to a 30% withholding tax on all US income. HMRC has entered into an inter-governmental agreement (IGA) with the IRS under which such information will be reported by UK financial institutions. Changes will be made to certain US tax forms as a result of FATCA; for example, when completing a form W8-BEN to claim benefits under the UK/US double tax agreement, companies will be required to state if they are a financial institution.

## Other taxes

**[C3.9]** A US company (or a non-US company undertaking activities in the US) may be subject to a number of other taxes.

In addition to federal and state income taxes, a company may also be subject to income tax at the level of the city or county in which it operates. States which do not impose a state income tax may nonetheless charge a fee to undertake activities in that state or (in the case of Texas) charge a franchise tax which is broadly analogous to an income tax.

There is no federal sales tax, but most states and even some local jurisdictions levy a sales tax. This is due on sales to the final consumer of goods or services, and the rate depends on the state/locality and the type of goods or services. Where taxable goods are transferred to a state and sales tax has not been charged as in the case of some mail order, telephone or internet sales), a use tax may apply in the place of the sales tax.

Payroll taxes and social security will apply if the company has employees in the US.

## Obtaining US treaty benefits

**[C3.10]** A UK company can obtain reduced rates of withholding tax on interest, dividends and royalties under the UK/US DTA. In order to do so, it is necessary to satisfy a number of anti-avoidance provisions:

- the UK company must have beneficial ownership of the income;

- the income must not be paid as part of a conduit arrangement (ie it must not be paid by the UK company to a third party in a non-treaty country);
- the UK company must qualify for benefits under the Limitation on Benefits article (Article 23)

Other US double tax treaties contain similar provisions.

The Limitation on Benefits (LOB) article is arguably the most complex and difficult of these anti-avoidance provisions to satisfy. The UK company must satisfy conditions relating to its status, its business and/or its ownership. Some examples of companies which do satisfy the conditions are:

- A UK company which is listed, or which is a subsidiary of a UK listed company. Both HMRC and the IRS have confirmed privately that a company listed on AIM will be treated as listed for these purposes. (Article 23(2)(c)).
- A UK company which is owned at least 50% by UK residents and which satisfies a base erosion test (Article 23(2)(f)). The base erosion test requires that the UK company does not make substantial tax deductible payments to other jurisdictions.
- A UK company which is part of a group which carries on substantial business in both the UK and the US (Article 23(4)). The definition of substantial business is discussed in the US Technical Interpretation to the treaty (www.ustreas.gov/offices/tax-policy/library/teus-uk.pdf).

The limitation on benefits article is outlined in more detail at **A8.60**.

Determining the condition under which the company qualifies under the LOB article will also determine the rate of withholding tax on dividends. In most cases this will be either 0% or 5%.

The process for obtaining reduced rates of withholding tax can also be onerous. The UK company must provide the payer with a new W-8BEN-E form (previously W-8BEN), stating that it qualifies for the reduced rate under the treaty. Although this form does not need to be certified by either HMRC or the IRS, the UK company must include its US taxpayer identification number (TIN or EIN). The identification number must therefore be obtained from the IRS before the form can be provided to the payer.

For companies, form W-8BEN-E supersedes the W-8BEN as a result of the introduction of the US Foreign Account Tax Compliance Act (FATCA) (see CHAPTER **A8**) and includes substantial additional disclosures relating to the company's 'status' under FATCA.

# Typical structures for investing into the US

### *Branch v subsidiary*

**[C3.11]** Taking into account both state and federal tax, the US is a higher tax jurisdiction than the UK. It therefore makes little difference whether a branch or a subsidiary (either corporation or LLC) is formed, although a branch may be less costly to establish and allow start-up losses to be utilised in the UK.

Most planning for early stage investment into the US will focus on ensuring that no permanent establishment exists and therefore no taxable presence.

### *Pitfalls*

**[C3.12]** Once a branch or subsidiary is established, it will be necessary to comply with US transfer pricing rules. These can be more onerous than UK rules, and the US does not follow OECD transfer pricing principles. Transfer pricing should therefore always be reviewed by a US specialist.

As outlined above, the UK/US DTA will only apply if the conditions in the limitation on benefits article are satisfied. The group structure should be reviewed carefully to ensure that it does satisfy these conditions, as withholding taxes on inter-company transactions (and dividends) can be substantial.

If a US corporation is established, it will be treated as resident in the UK if it is centrally managed and controlled in the UK. Unusually, the only tie breaker in the UK/US DTA is for competent authority agreement (ie HMRC and the IRS must agree on the company's residence). Such agreement is rarely sought, and as a result a US corporation which is centrally managed and controlled in the UK will be treated as resident for tax purposes in both the UK and the US. The consequences of dual residence are outlined at **A9.18**.

### *Financing*

**[C3.13]** Interest is subject to a number of restrictions on deductibility, including:

- thin capitalisation if debt has equity characteristics;
- transfer pricing if the interest rate is above a market rate (there is currently a so-called safe harbour for interest equal to the applicable federal rate as published by the IRS on a monthly basis, which is currently 3.28% for long-term loans); and
- earnings stripping which restricts the interest deduction on loans from related parties to 50% of adjusted taxable profits.

If loans are made from a UK company to a US corporation, interest will remain subject to UK corporation tax even if no US deduction is available.

Table 1 Federal tax rates

| Taxable profits ($) | Tax is calculated as | | |
|---|---|---|---|
| 0 to 50,000 | | 15% | |
| 50,000 to 75,000 | $7,500 + | 25% | of the amount over $50,000 |
| 75,000 to 100,000 | $13,750 + | 34% | of the amount over $75,000 |
| 100,000 to 335,000 | $22,250 + | 39% | of the amount over $100,000 |
| 335,000 to 10,000,000 | $113,900 + | 34% | of the amount over $335,000 |
| 10,000,000 to 15,000,000 | $3,400,000 + | 35% | of the amount over $10,000,000 |
| 15,000,000 to 18,333,333 | $5,150,000 + | 38% | of the amount over $15,000,000 |
| 18,333,333 and up | | 35% | |

Table 2 State tax rates

| | Highest corporate tax rate |
|---|---|
| Alabama | 6.5% |
| Alaska | 9.4% |
| Arizona | 6.968% |
| Arkansas | 6.5% |
| California | 8.84% |
| Colorado | 4.63% |
| Connecticut | 7.5% |
| Delaware | 8.7% |
| Florida | 5.5% |
| Georgia | 6% |
| Hawaii | 6.4% |
| Idaho | 7.4% |
| Illinois | 7% |
| Indiana | 7.5% |
| Iowa | 12% |
| Kansas | 7% |
| Kentucky | 6% |
| Louisiana | 8% |
| Maine | 8.93% |
| Maryland | 8.25% |
| Massachusetts | 8.8% |
| Michigan | 6% |
| Minnesota | 9.8% |

| | |
|---|---|
| Mississippi | 5% |
| Missouri | 6.25% |
| Montana | 6.75% |
| Nebraska | 7.81% |
| Nevada | - |
| New Hampshire | 8.5% |
| New Jersey | 9% |
| New Mexico | 7.6% |
| New York | 7.1% |
| North Carolina | 6.9% |
| North Dakota | 4.53% |
| Ohio | 0.26% of gross receipts |
| Oklahoma | 6% |
| Oregon | 7.6% |
| Pennsylvania | 9.99% |
| Rhode Island | 9% |
| South Carolina | 5% |
| South Dakota | - |
| Tennessee | 6.5% |
| Texas | 1% of gross receipts |
| Utah | 5% |
| Vermont | 8.5% |
| Virginia | 6% |
| Washington | - |
| West Virginia | 7% |
| Wisconsin | 7.9% |
| Wyoming | - |
| District Of Columbia | 9.975% |

# C4

# UK companies investing in China

**[C4.1]** This Chapter outlines the regulatory and tax issues faced by a UK company investing into China, including:

- restrictions on inward investment;
- withholding taxes and restrictions on repatriation of profit;
- typical investment structures to reduce Chinese tax exposures.

A legal entity will be required for most activities undertaken in China, which means that a taxable presence will be created in most cases.

## Taxable presence

**[C4.2]** A UK company will only have a taxable presence in China if it has a permanent establishment as defined in the UK/China double tax agreement (DTA). This definition follows the definition of permanent establishment in the OECD Model Treaty.

In practice, however, the existence of a permanent establishment is largely irrelevant. Under Chinese law it is usually necessary to form a legal entity (as outlined below) and this legal entity will create a taxable presence. For example, if a non-resident company employs staff in China it must establish a legal entity, and will therefore be taxable.

Businesses which do not initially have a taxable presence in China (because they only undertake limited activity there) should monitor this on an ongoing basis as increased commercial activities may create a permanent establishment, or trigger a requirement to form a legal entity.

## Forms of legal entity

**[C4.3]** A non-resident company must choose the entity through which it operates in China:

- a representative office (RO);
- by establishing a local subsidiary which can be wholly foreign owned (commonly referred to as a wholly foreign owned enterprise or WFOE); or
- through a joint venture.

### Representative office (RO)

**[C4.4]** A RO is often used as a simple way of establishing a presence in China, as it allows a foreign company to engage in limited activity there. A RO cannot engage directly in profit making activities or be used as a trading vehicle. It is only allowed to undertake support activities such as:

- market research;
- supplier liaison;
- quality assurance;
- procurement;
- publicity related activities.

### Wholly foreign owned enterprise (WFOE)

**[C4.5]** A WFOE is often used by UK companies who want to carry out profit making activity in China, for example manufacturing, servicing or sales activity. It is popular because it can be owned and controlled 100% by a UK parent company.

A WFOE is subject to corporate income tax (Enterprise Income Tax or EIT) on its profits (currently at a rate of 25%) although tax incentives are available in certain industries.

Minimum capital requirements vary by location and industry although the legal minimum capital is RMB 30,000 (£2,800) rising to RMB 100,000 (£9,400) for entities with only one shareholder.

In China, companies do not issue shares or share certificates to show ownership. Company ownership is instead evidenced by the official record of owners filed with the Administration of Industry and Commerce (AIC) and Certificates for Capital Contribution issued by the company.

In most cases HMRC will accept that this constitutes ordinary share capital, although this should be reviewed when relying for example on the substantial shareholding exemption.

### *Joint ventures*

**[C4.6]** Joint ventures operated with a Chinese party may be the only option for investors who want to engage in restricted activities which require majority Chinese ownership (see below). This can be an inflexible option as arrangements between the local party and the UK company can be difficult to change.

## Tax base and rates

**[C4.7]** The rate of EIT for a company resident in China is 25%, which applies to its worldwide profits.

A non-resident company is only subject to tax on:

* income from sources within China; and
* income from sources outside of China which is effectively connected with its activities in China.

As it is a legal entity, a RO is taxable even if its activities are preparatory and auxiliary under the terms of the UK/China DTA. In the absence of full transfer pricing documentation to identify taxable income, the Chinese tax authorities will charge 15% tax on the costs of the RO to reflect tax on the assumed profits.

Rather than encouraging investment by providing tax holidays (as was historically the case), tax incentives are provided to companies engaged in industries that are encouraged by the state. For example, certain technology businesses and producers of integrated circuits are subject to a 15% corporate income tax rate.

## Limits on investment

**[C4.8]** The Foreign Enterprise Investment Projects Instruction catalogue (the Catalogue), categorises foreign investment as encouraged, restricted or prohibited. Foreign companies are not usually allowed to invest at all into prohibited sectors, and these include construction, publication (of books, magazines, newspapers etc) and arms. Foreign companies are usually allowed to invest into restricted sectors, but only if there is majority Chinese ownership. Restricted sectors include mining, telecommunications and banking.

In addition, a Chinese company is only allowed to undertake activities set out in the stated 'business scope' on its business license (which is granted by the Administration of Industry and Commerce). There is no concept in China of a company being allowed to engage in 'any commercial activity', and care should be taken that sufficient flexibility is built into the business scope to allow for additional activities to be undertaken. If not, additional activities will require further approval from the authorities.

China also has strict foreign currency controls. Opening bank accounts to process foreign currency and entering into loan agreements that require the payment of funds in foreign currency are subject to strict regulations issued by the State Administration of Foreign Exchange (SAFE).

## Employment taxes

[C4.9] The UK/China DTA stipulates that an employee of a non-resident company is not subject to tax in China provided:

- the employee's costs are not borne by a Chinese entity (either a permanent establishment or a legal entity as outlined above; and
- the employee does not spend more than 183 days in China during the calendar year.

Individuals are entitled to a fixed monthly deduction of RMB 2,000 (£180) or RMB 2,800 (£250) for foreign nationals after which they are taxed progressively at rates up to 45%. The employer must withhold tax from salaries and file annual returns.

## Repatriation of profits

[C4.10] There are two common problems when extracting profits from a Chinese company. Firstly, regulatory procedures and formalities mean that overseas remittances are subject to varying degrees of local bureaucracy. Secondly, business tax ranging from 3–20% applies to most forms of remittances. Business tax is an indirect tax similar to a sales tax and therefore is not considered creditable for double tax relief purposes.

Depending on the nature of the payment, it may also be subject to withholding tax.

Dividends are not subject to business tax, but are subject to 10% withholding tax. In addition, a dividend can only be paid if a number of regulatory conditions are satisfied:

- The registered capital of the Chinese company must be paid up;
- The company must be profit-making after accounting for accumulated tax losses;
- A dividend can only be paid to a foreign shareholder once per year;
- The statutory after-tax reserve funds must be duly provided for;
- Documents including a board resolution declaring a dividend, an audit report for the year and a tax clearance certificate are required to process the payment.

The taxes applying to different forms of remittance are summarised in Table 1.

Table 1 Taxes on remittances from China

|  | Dividend | Technical service fee | Royalty | Interest | Purchase of goods |
|---|---|---|---|---|---|
| Profit to extract | 100.00 | 100.00 | 100.00 | 100.00 | 100.00 |
| EIT (25%) | (25.00) |  |  |  |  |
|  | 75.00 |  |  |  |  |

| | Dividend | Technical service fee | Royalty | Interest | Purchase of goods |
|---|---|---|---|---|---|
| Withholding tax (10%) | (7.50) | | (10.00) | (10.00) | |
| Business tax (5%) | | (5.00) | (5.00) | (5.00) | |
| UK tax (21% less credit for withholding tax) | 0.00 | (19.95) | (9.95) | (9.95) | (21.00) |
| Net receipt | 67.50 | 75.05 | 75.05 | 75.05 | 79.00 |
| Effective tax rate | 32.50% | 24.95% | 24.95% | 24.95% | 21.00% |

One method of reducing these taxes is to structure operations so that goods are bought directly by the Chinese company from outside China. This strategy for extracting profits should be considered in preference to the alternatives such royalties or dividends.

## Financing

**[C4.11]** Debt funding is often chosen because there are fewer regulatory and administrative hurdles to overcome in order to pay interest rather than a dividend, and interest can also be more tax efficient.

However, consideration must be given to 'total investment' requirements. The total investment is the amount of funding the company needs to undertake its activities, and is determined when the company is established. Loans can only be taken out to fund the difference between the registered capital and the total investment. The total investment and registered capital should therefore be carefully considered in case further debt financing is required in the future.

In addition, China has thin capitalisation rules which disallow interest deductions on excessive related party debt financing. A debt/equity ratio can be negotiated with the Chinese tax authorities, but there is a safe harbour for trading entities of 2:1 and 5:1 for financial service enterprises.

## Typical Chinese investment structures

**[C4.12]** Most structuring focuses on the use of an intermediate holding company to avoid Chinese regulatory requirements and China State authority approvals necessary where there is a change of ownership in a Chinese entity (whether as a result of exit or a group restructuring).

An intermediate holding structure can also reduce tax on the return of funds to the UK, although the proposed new UK/China DTA offers reduced rates of withholding tax comparable to those under the Hong Kong/China DTA.

In December 2009, the Chinese tax authorities issued Circular 698 which set out that an intermediate holding company without insufficient business purpose and established for the purpose of avoiding tax would be disregarded. An intermediate holding company would need to submit evidence of its business activities to the Chinese tax authorities in order to obtain benefits under a DTA, and its commercial and economic substance will be scrutinised closely.

Hong Kong is a popular choice for an intermediate company for the following reasons:

### Reduced rates of withholding tax

**[C4.13]** The China/Hong Kong DTA reduces withholding tax on dividends (5%), interest (7%) and royalties (7%). In addition, Hong Kong does not tax dividend income or capital gains

The Singapore/China DTA offers similar benefits, and can offer benefits as a regional investment company for groups with interests in both China and India.

### Tax on Chinese capital gains

**[C4.14]** A gain on the sale of shares in a Chinese company is generally subject to a 10% withholding tax. The Hong Kong/China DTA includes an exemption to this withholding tax for shareholdings of less than 25%.

Alternatively, the shares in the Hong Kong company could be sold rather than the shares in the Chinese subsidiary. However, the Chinese tax authorities have challenged similar structures where there is insufficient substance in the intermediate holding company. They have argued that the disposal is effectively a disposal of the underlying Chinese company and is therefore subject to tax in China.

### Acting as a regional hub

**[C4.15]** As well as being used as a holding company jurisdiction, Hong Kong is a popular choice for a regional trading hub. It is close to China, English is widely spoken and business regulation is relatively straightforward. In addition, it offers a low rate of tax on trading profits (currently 16.5%).

## Transfer pricing

**[C4.16]** All cross border flows of goods, services and funds within a group of companies must be priced on an arm's length basis. The Chinese tax authorities require contemporaneous transfer pricing documentation to support the prices used.

More detailed documentation is required for companies with inter-company transactions of more than RMB 40 million (£3.75 million) or RMB 200 million (£18.75 million) for inter-company sales of goods. Failure to maintain the required documentation will give rise to penalties and unilateral transfer pricing adjustments.

Aside from the compliance requirement, reviewing a group's supply chain can present opportunities to remit funds to the UK from China which is free of withholding tax as outlined above.

# Index

Capital. *See also* Capital gains; Capital gains tax (CGT); Capital movements – *cont.*
transfer pricing A13.2
Capital gains. *See also* Capital gains tax (CGT) A11.1–A11.30
anti-avoidance A1.8, A11.21, A11.28, A11.30
Annual Tax on Enveloped Dwellings (ATED) A1.12, A3.15–A3.16, A3.18–A3.19, A11.1
attribution of gains to resident shareholders A11.20–A11.21
Australia A11.9
basic principles A11.2–A11.9, A11.20–A11.23
branches, incorporation of overseas A11.17
business establishment, test for A11.31
calculation of gain A11.22
capital contributions A11.6
China C4.14
Controlled Foreign Companies A6.2
corporation tax A11.19, A11.22, A11.27
deemed disposals A11.2
development land A3.35, A3.41
disposal of UK assets A11.2
double tax agreements A8.51, A11.10–A11.14, A11.29
India/UK DTA A11.14
intermediate holding companies A11.14
no capital gains articles A11.12
relief A11.29
typical articles in UK DTAs A11.11–A11.12
economically significant activities, definition of A11.31
entity classification A11.7
EU law A11.30–A11.31
exemptions A11.16, A11.25, A11.28, A11.30, A11.32
foreign currency A2.33
foreign exchange A11.8
France C1.54
freedom of establishment A11.30
future sales B4.11–B4.16
holding companies B3.2
intangible assets A11.19
intermediate holding companies A11.14
intra-group transfers A11.25
liquidation A11.23
Luxembourg/UK DTA A11.29
Mauritius/UK DTA A11.29
mergers A7.53, A11.18
migration B8.3, B8.7–B8.8, B8.11, B8.14–B8.15, B8.23

Capital gains. *See also* Capital gains tax (CGT) – *cont.*
motive test A11.30–A11.32
nature of assets A11.4
no avoidance purpose A11.30–A11.32
non-resident companies' liability to UK tax A1.7, A1.8, A1.12
overseas assets, disposal of A11.3–A11.9
overseas reorganisations A11.15
permanent establishment A11.3, A11.18
property income A3.18, A3.24, A3.26–A3.27, A3.31–A3.32, A3.35, A3.39, A3.47
proportionality A11.31
protected cell companies A11.20
rate of tax A11.27
real estate A11.13, A11.29
reorganisations A11.15, A11.20
residence A8.33
shareholders A11.20, A15.1–A15.4, A15.12, A15.29
substantial shareholding exemptions A11.16, A11.25
supply chain B5.25
tax havens A11.12
timing of translation of capital gains A2.33
trading profits A11.9
transactions treated as disposals A11.5
transfer pricing A13.58
trustees A11.21
UK assets, disposal of A11.2
UK company setting up overseas B4.11–B4.16
unilateral relief A11.10
value shifting A11.24
wrappers A11.31
Capital gains tax (CGT). *See also* Residential property, CGT on disposal by non-residents of
development land A3.29
double tax agreements A11.12, A11.14
India A11.14
investment property A3.32–A3.33, A3.35
Jersey A3.28
Mauritius DTA A11.14
overseas capital gains taxes A11.3
permanent establishment A11.3
share sales A3.28
wrappers A3.28
Capital movements
clearances A12.2–A12.5
debentures A12.4
EU law A7.14, A7.48–A7.50
exclusions A12.5

Visas C2.7
Visits by employees to place of business A4.9

**W**

Wagering. *See* Gaming
Websites
e-commerce A4.27–A4.30
location A4.27–A4.30
permanent establishment A4.27–A4.30
preparatory or auxiliary services A4.29
Wholly foreign–owned enterprises (WOFE) in
China C1.27, C4.5
Withholding tax. *See also* Double tax
agreements and withholding tax; Interest
and withholding tax; Royalties and
withholding tax A5.1–A5.40
acquisitions B2.11, B2.13
advance thin capitalisation agreements
(ATCAs) A12.20
anti-avoidance A8.54
Australia C1.16
basic principles A5.2–A5.25
beneficial owners B7.9
branch profit exemption A18.5
Brazil C1.60
Canada C1.22
China C1.32, C4.10, C4.13–C4.16
clearances
advance thin capitalisation agreements
(ATCAs) A12.20
double tax agreements A12.8–A12.11
Interest and Royalties Directive A12.22
Cyprus B7.10
debt finance A3.14
definition A1.16
development land A3.41
dividends A5.14–A5.15
amount of dividend subject to tax
A2.20
case law A2.22
double tax agreements A5.14
holding companies B3.10
Netherlands/UK DTA A5.14
notional UK tax credit, reclaiming the
A5.14
Parent/Subsidiary Directive A5.15
double tax agreements A5.14, A16.7
double tax relief A10.7
Eurobond exemption A3.14
exemptions A3.14
financing B7.9–B7.10
foreign entity classification A14.36

Withholding tax. *See also* Double tax
agreements and withholding tax; Interest
and withholding tax; Royalties and
withholding tax – *cont.*
France C1.54
Germany C1.37, C1.39
holding companies B3.2, B3.10
income tax A1.4
India A5.31, C1.47, C2.2, C2.5, C2.9
interest A5.2–A5.10. A5.26–A5.29
acquisitions B2.11, B2.13
debt finance A3.14
deductibility B7.3, B7.8
parent companies A4.41
quoted Eurobonds B7.9
Interest and Royalties Directive
clearances A12.8
double tax agreements B7.10
non-resident companies' liability to UK
tax A1.17
UK company setting up overseas B4.22
investment property A1.14
Malaysia/UK DTA A8.32
migration B8.5
minimisation A14.36
Netherlands/UK DTA A5.14
Non-Resident Landlords Scheme A3.4,
A3.8,
non-resident companies' liability to UK tax
A1.14, A1.16–A1.17
OECD Model Tax Convention A8.40
Parent/Subsidiary Directive A5.15, A7.51
payment in kind (PIK) loans B7.9
permanent establishment A4.40–A4.41
property A3.8, A3.14
quoted Eurobonds B7.9
rates of tax A1.16, B7.9–B7.10
rents paid A3.41
royalties A4.40, A5.11–A5.14. A5.30–A5.39
shareholders and multinational business
owners, tax for A15.28, A15.35
supply chain B5.14
thin capitalisation and transfer pricing
A13.75
transfer pricing A13.53–A13.56, A13.75
UK company setting up overseas B4.10,
B4.22
UN Model Treaty Convention A8.40
underlying tax A15.28
United States C1.9, C3.8, C3.10
Worldwide debt cap (WWDC) A17.1–A17.20
allocation of disallowances A17.8
anti-avoidance A17.13, A17.19–A17.20
basic principles A17.2–A17.5